D0218398

LL.M. Roadmap

EDITORIAL ADVISORS

Vicki Been
Elihu Root Professor of Law
New York University School of Law

Erwin Chemerinsky
Dean and Distinguished Professor of Law
University of California, Irvine, School of Law

Richard A. Epstein
Laurence A. Tisch Professor of Law
New York University School of Law
Peter and Kirsten Bedford Senior Fellow
The Hoover Institution
Senior Lecturer in Law
The University of Chicago

Ronald J. Gilson
Charles J. Meyers Professor of Law and Business
Stanford University
Marc and Eva Stern Professor of Law and Business
Columbia Law School

James E. Krier
Earl Warren DeLano Professor of Law
The University of Michigan Law School

Richard K. Neumann, Jr.
Professor of Law
Hofstra University School of Law

Robert H. Sitkoff
John L. Gray Professor of Law
Harvard Law School

David Alan Sklansky
Professor of Law
University of California at Berkeley School of Law

Kent D. Syverud
Dean and Ethan A. H. Shepley University Professor
Washington University School of Law

Elizabeth Warren
Leo Gottlieb Professor of Law
Harvard Law School

LL.M. Roadmap

An International Student's Guide to U. S. Law School Programs

George E. Edwards

The C.M. Gray Professor of Law
Indiana University Law School—Indianapolis, Indiana, U.S.A.

Wolters Kluwer
Law & Business

Copyright © 2011 CCH Incorporated.

Published by Wolters Kluwer Law & Business in New York.

Wolters Kluwer Law & Business serves customers worldwide with CCH, Aspen Publishers, and Kluwer Law International products. (www.wolterskluwerlb.com)

No part of this publication may be reproduced or transmitted in any form or by any means, electronic or mechanical, including photocopy, recording, or utilized by any information storage or retrieval system, without written permission from the publisher. For information about permissions or to request permissions online, visit us at www.wolterskluwerlb.com, or a written request may be faxed to our permissions department at 212-771-0803.

To contact Customer Service, e-mail customer.service@wolterskluwer.com, call 1-800-234-1660, fax 1-800-901-9075, or mail correspondence to:

> Wolters Kluwer Law & Business
> Attn: Order Department
> PO Box 990
> Frederick, MD 21705

Printed in the United States of America.

1 2 3 4 5 6 7 8 9 0

ISBN 978-1-4548-0239-6

Library of Congress Cataloging-in-Publication Data

Edwards, George E., date
    LL. M. roadmap : an international student's guide to U.S. law school programs / George E. Edwards.
        p. cm.
    Includes index.
    ISBN 978-1-4548-0239-6
    1. Law schools — United States. 2.   Law schools — United States — Admissions. 3.   Students, Foreign — United States — Handbooks, manuals, etc. I.   Title.
    KF272.E385 2011
    340.071'173 — dc23

                                                                        2011023129

SUSTAINABLE FORESTRY INITIATIVE

Certified Chain of Custody
Promoting Sustainable Forestry
www.sfiprogram.org
SFI-00756

About Wolters Kluwer Law & Business

Wolters Kluwer Law & Business is a leading global provider of intelligent information and digital solutions for legal and business professionals in key specialty areas, and respected educational resources for professors and law students. Wolters Kluwer Law & Business connects legal and business professionals as well as those in the education market with timely, specialized authoritative content and information-enabled solutions to support success through productivity, accuracy and mobility.

Serving customers worldwide, Wolters Kluwer Law & Business products include those under the Aspen Publishers, CCH, Kluwer Law International, Loislaw, Best Case, ftwilliam.com and MediRegs family of products.

CCH products have been a trusted resource since 1913, and are highly regarded resources for legal, securities, antitrust and trade regulation, government contracting, banking, pension, payroll, employment and labor, and healthcare reimbursement and compliance professionals.

Aspen Publishers products provide essential information to attorneys, business professionals and law students. Written by preeminent authorities, the product line offers analytical and practical information in a range of specialty practice areas from securities law and intellectual property to mergers and acquisitions and pension/benefits. Aspen's trusted legal education resources provide professors and students with high-quality, up-to-date and effective resources for successful instruction and study in all areas of the law.

Kluwer Law International products provide the global business community with reliable international legal information in English. Legal practitioners, corporate counsel and business executives around the world rely on Kluwer Law journals, looseleafs, books, and electronic products for comprehensive information in many areas of international legal practice.

Loislaw is a comprehensive online legal research product providing legal content to law firm practitioners of various specializations. Loislaw provides attorneys with the ability to quickly and efficiently find the necessary legal information they need, when and where they need it, by facilitating access to primary law as well as state-specific law, records, forms and treatises.

Best Case Solutions is the leading bankruptcy software product to the bankruptcy industry. It provides software and workflow tools to flawlessly streamline petition preparation and the electronic filing process, while timely incorporating ever-changing court requirements.

ftwilliam.com offers employee benefits professionals the highest quality plan documents (retirement, welfare and non-qualified) and government forms (5500/PBGC, 1099 and IRS) software at highly competitive prices.

MediRegs products provide integrated health care compliance content and software solutions for professionals in healthcare, higher education and life sciences, including professionals in accounting, law and consulting.

Wolters Kluwer Law & Business, a division of Wolters Kluwer, is headquartered in New York. Wolters Kluwer is a market-leading global information services company focused on professionals.

Summary of *LL.M. Roadmap* Endorsements
(See Appendix III for endorsement texts in full and endorser details)

"I regret that *LL.M. Roadmap* was not available when I was Director of Admissions of *Harvard's* LL.M. program. I would have recommended it to every recruit and admitted student who passed through *Harvard's* doors. I recommend *LL.M. Roadmap* now to anyone, anywhere in the world, thinking about undertaking the LL.M. It's a fabulously helpful text!"

— *Athena Mutua (Director of Admissions and Financial Aid, LL.M. Program of Harvard Law School (former))*

"*LL.M. Roadmap* will greatly assist students in China and neighboring East Asian countries like Japan and South Korea who want to study law in the U.S."

— *Ding Xiangshun (Assistant Dean for Foreign Affairs & Associate Professor of Law, Renmin University of China Law School, Beijing, Visiting Professor & Fellow, Waseda University Faculty of Law & Meiji University Faculty of Law, Japan*

"This book will prove an invaluable resource for students thinking of studying law in the U.S."

— *Bruce Carolan (Head, Department of Law, Dublin Institute of Technology Dublin, Ireland)*

"Practicing [legal professionals] have long recognized the potential value to their legal and business careers of intensive exposure to the U.S. legal system [and] immersion in an English-language legal learning and living environment[. *LL.M. Roadmap*] should be required reading in their due diligence on how to plan for and make the most of the LL.M. opportunity.

— *Laurence W. Bates (General Counsel, GE Japan; Director, Government Affairs and Policy, GE Asia Pacific)*

"[M]y first law degree in the U.S. was a J.D., which I followed with an LL.M. . . . *LL.M. Roadmap* provides comprehensive, valuable insights, whether you are choosing an LL.M. or a J.D. program."

— *Luz Estella Nagle Judge (Former), Medellín, Colombia)*

"*LL.M. Roadmap* is a clear, concise, and complete guidebook for anyone thinking about doing a graduate law degree in the U.S."

— *M. C. Mirow (J.D. Cornell; Ph.D., Cambridge; Ph.D. Leiden)*

"The *LL.M. Roadmap*. . . . will motivate law schools to reflect critically on the LL.M. programs they offer."

— *Meredith McQuaid (Associate Vice President and Dean, Global Programs and Strategy Alliance, University of Minnesota; President, Chair of Board of Directors, NAFSA: Association of International Educators (2011-13))*

"Bravo. The book is brilliant and long-overdue."

— *Mark Wojcik (Professor of Law, The John Marshall Law School, Chicago; University of Lucerne Faculty of Law, Lucerne, Switzerland; Permanent Guest Professor of Comparative Law and Anglo-American Law)*

"[*LL.M. Roadmap* is] the important manual for all potential international LL.M. students in the United States. LL.M. Roadmap fills a gaping hole."

— *Makau Mutua (Dean & SUNY Distinguished Professor of Law; University of Buffalo School of Law, The State University of New York; Associate Director, Harvard Human Rights Program (former))*

"Professor Edwards has demystified the process of choosing and getting admitted to a great American LL.M. program. This is how *I* would conduct my own LL.M. search."

— *Michael Peil (Executive Director, International Law Students Association (ILSA) (former))*

"Global South students earning U.S. LL.M. degrees . . . gain access to global connective networks that help in their human rights and humanitarian work. . . . *LL.M. Roadmap* [will] help international students learn which U.S. LL.M. programs are more interested in receiving tuition dollars than they are in helping LL.M. students and graduates achieve their goals, which can include returning to make a positive difference in their home countries.

— *Bruce A. Lasky (Founder, Bridges Across Borders Southeast Asia (BABSEA); Adjunct Professor of Law, Chiang Mai University, Chiang Mai, Thailand; Adjunct Professor of Law, Universiti Teknologi MARA, Selangor Darul Ehsan, Malaysia; Visiting Senior Lecturer, University of Malaya, Kuala Lumpur, Malaysia)*

"LL.M. Roadmap informs U.S. law school deans, professors, and administrators what international LL.M. students should reasonably expect from their U.S. law school experiences. LL.M. Roadmap will empower students with information needed to maximize their U.S. law school experience, and empower U.S. law schools with tools to provide high-quality student services."

— *María Pabón López (Dean & Judge Adrian G. Duplantier Distinguished Professor of Law, Loyola University New Orleans College of Law)*

Dedication

LL.M. Roadmap is dedicated to the memory of the following: my parents, Joseph L. Edwards and Emma Baker Edwards, whose love and guidance in my early years led me to where I am today; law professor Mary H. Mitchell, who reminded me not to compromise my principals or integrity — before or after tenure; and journalism professor Patrick J. McKeand, who demonstrated to me that education is about students and the greater good of society and not about tuition revenues. *LL.M. Roadmap* is also dedicated to all international students who have chosen or who may choose to attend a U.S. law school to receive their Master of Laws (LL.M.) or other law degree, and I express to you my sincere hope that U.S. law schools have fulfilled and will fulfill all their obligations to you associated with your legal education in the United States and that U.S. law schools have met and will meet all your reasonable expectations.

Professor Edwards' personal profits from publication of this edition of *LL.M. Roadmap* are being donated to the International Law Students Association (ILSA) (www.ILSA.org).

About the Author

George E. Edwards received his Juris Doctor (J.D.) degree from **Harvard Law School**, where he served as an Editor of the *Harvard Law Review*. He then served as law clerk for a federal judge in Manhattan, practiced law for a large Wall Street Law Firm, and lived for several years in Hong Kong where he worked at the **University of Hong Kong Faculty of Law** and **City University of Hong Kong Faculty of Law**. He also taught for the Law Society of Hong Kong. He received a Fulbright grant to teach in a Master of Laws (LL.M.) program in Peru, and has taught, consulted, and worked with Master of Laws (LL.M.) programs and students in many other countries. He has presented on *LL.M. Roadmap* and the topic of U.S. legal education for international students in over two dozen countries.

Professor Edwards is currently the C.M. Gray Professor of Law at Indiana University School of Law in Indianapolis. In 1997, he became Founding Director of the law school's Program in International Human Rights Law, which has recently been accredited to the United Nations by being granted *Special Consultative Status* to the *United Nations Economic and Social Council (UN-ECOSOC)*.

Professor Edwards has facilitated and supervised over 100 Indiana law student summer intern placements at the U.N. and other human rights organizations in over 50 countries on 6 continents.

Professor Edwards is an elected Executive Committee member of the Section on Graduate Programs for Foreign Lawyers of the Association of American Law Schools (AALS) and a Steering Committee Member for the creation of the NAFSA Association of International Educators Graduate Law Program SIG (Special Interest Group).

Professor Edwards was tendered as an Expert Witness in the Guantanamo Bay U.S. Military Commission case against Australian "detainee" David Hicks. He and his students provided research assistance on the cases of Mr. Hicks and Mr. Omar Khadr (who is a Canadian who was 15 when taken to Guantanamo Bay).

Professor Edwards is widely published internationally, including in domestic law journals such as at **Yale**, **Harvard**, **New England**, **Thurgood Marshall**, and **American University**, and overseas. He is an elected member of the American Law Institute (ALI) and the American Bar Foundation (ABF), and has served as a Member of the House of Representatives of the Association of American Law Schools (AALS).

He is a Life Member, **Wolfson College, University of Cambridge**, England, and has received numerous Teaching, Research and Civic Engagement Awards.

Professor Edwards became the Founding Faculty Director of his Indiana law school's Master of Laws (LL.M.) Track in International Human Rights Law, and was Executive Chair of the school's Graduate Law Programs. However, effective 2011, Professor Edwards resigned all roles within the school's LL.M. and S.J.D. programs and possesses no administrative responsibilities for those LL.M. or S.J.D. programs.

Professor Edwards has served as Faculty Advisor to many Indiana student organizations involved in international law, diplomacy, and human rights. He has also held board and advisory positions with various outside student organizations, including the International Law Students Association (ILSA) (www.ILSA.org), to which Professor Edwards is donating his personal profits from this edition of *LL.M. Roadmap*. Professor Edwards was a member of the ILSA Advisory Board.

Professor Edwards can be reached at LLMRoadMap@yahoo.com or via www.LLMRoadMap.com.

Summary of Contents

Contents

Preface

Birth of *LL.M. Roadmap*

In August 2009, I gave a presentation in Nairobi to Kenyan students departing to study at universities across the United States. U.S. officials were discussing what the students should expect at their U.S. visa interviews, what to do when passing through Immigration and Customs, and how to stay warm when encountering snow for the first time. The students had spent months under the tutelage of U.S. State Department EducationUSA advisors, who advised on choosing the right school, navigating the application process, and securing financing.

I talked about higher education in the U.S. generally, and then about studying law in the U.S. I shared a powerpoint presentation that I had prepared titled "American Legal Education — Do You Want To Study Law in the U.S.A.?" I had recently shared this presentation with international students, advisors, law professors, government officials, and others in a dozen countries on five continents. As in other countries, the Kenyan discussion revealed how much international students did *not* know about U.S. legal education, and how much they wished they had known before embarking on their overseas study quest. The discussion also revealed how much more U.S. educational advisors would like to know as they advise students about a U.S. law education.

The officials said something like, "Your powerpoint can help Kenyan students learn a great deal about studying law in the U.S. Why don't you publish it?"

Although my presentation was comprehensive, it was just a standard powerpoint presentation composed of dozens of slides containing bullet points, charts, photos, flashy graphics, and many lists. The presentation would not work as a stand-alone publication.

I was reminded of Pulitzer Prize winner Toni Morrison's remark that "If there's a book you really want to read but it hasn't been written yet, then you must write it." So I decided to convert my powerpoint presentation into a book: a guide to U.S. legal education for international students, describing and fully examining how they can reach their academic and career goals.

Below are a few words about the four most common issues international students appear to be concerned about regarding pursuing an LL.M. in the U.S.: (1) choosing the "best" LL.M. program; (2) getting admitted; (3) paying for the LL.M.; and (4) getting a great post-LL.M. job, or otherwise reaching career aspirations.

Choosing Among Over 100 U.S. LL.M. Programs and Discerning Which Is "Best" for You

About 6,000 students enroll each year in LL.M. programs at over 100 U.S. law schools. That is fewer than 50 LL.M. students per school. Larger LL.M. programs have around 200 students per year, a few schools have even more, and the smallest have five or fewer students. Not all international students can attend all schools. Not every LL.M. program is suitable for every international student. *LL.M. Roadmap* identifies and analyzes 218 criteria that you can consider as you decide what school is "best" for you. Some schools may not offer the concentration that you want, may not be in a city or region that you desire to live in, may require English language proficiency test scores higher than your scores, or may be too expensive. *LL.M. Roadmap* will help you find the right school for you.

Getting Admitted to a U.S. LL.M. Program

LL.M. Roadmap offers tips on how to make your application as strong as possible to maximize your chances of getting accepted to the "best" U.S. law school for you.

Paying for Your LL.M.

LL.M. Roadmap summarizes hundreds of LL.M. funding sources, including scholarships, fellowships, grants, loans, and temporary employment. U.S. legal education is expensive. But thousands of students from around the world receive U.S. law degrees each year, and many are paid for in the ways that *LL.M. Roadmap* describes.

Achieving Your Career Goals After You Finish Your U.S. Degree

Some international students want to work in the U.S. post-LL.M. Others want to return to their home countries or move to a third country to become law professors, judges, in-house counsel for corporations, nonprofit attorneys,

---

Top Questions by International Prospective Master of Laws (LL.M.) Students

1. Which are the "best" U.S. law schools?
2. Which schools should I apply to, and how do I choose?
3. How do I get admitted to the "best" U.S. LL.M. Program?
4. Can I get a scholarship to pay for my U.S. law degree?
5. Will I get a great job after I finish my LL.M.?

or United Nations lawyers. *LL.M. Roadmap* explains how LL.M. graduates can reach their career and personal goals.

Who Is Interested in U.S. LL.M. Programs?

LL.M. Roadmap is a helpful resource for the following international students and professionals:

1. The Next Generation of Overseas-trained Law Students in the U.S.

LL.M. Roadmap is the perfect guide for a foreign-educated lawyer, international law student, judge, law teacher, government law professional, or foreign law graduate who is considering studying for an advanced law degree, and who will consider law school in the U.S. You may be a U.S. permanent resident or citizen who received your first law degree overseas. *LL.M. Roadmap* is the complete guide from application, to admission, and beyond: the visa process, enrollment, exam-taking, graduation, and achieving your educational, personal, and professional career goals.

2. Law Firms, Corporation Counsel Offices, and Other Legal Practitioners in the U.S. and Overseas

Lawyers play a critical role in transnational deals involving U.S. and overseas law firms, corporations, governments, and entities and individuals of many nationalities. Even simple international deals require transnational lawyers. U.S. legal work is increasingly "out-sourced" to India and other countries, making it important for non-U.S. lawyers to have U.S. legal training. Small, medium, and large law firms in the U.S. can benefit from accepting international interns enrolled in U.S. LL.M. programs, particularly if the firms have clients, or want clients, in the interns' home countries. It is a great way for a U.S. law firm to establish a network among the legal elite of foreign countries, which will be helpful if the U.S. law firm ever needs the services of a non-U.S.-educated lawyer to help with deposing witnesses or otherwise gathering evidence abroad; service of process abroad; locating assets hidden abroad; or litigation in foreign courts.

3. Foreign Government Education and Scholarship Ministries and Embassies in the U.S.

Just as the U.S. government grants Fulbright and other scholarships for U.S. students to study overseas, many other countries offer their citizens scholarships to come to the U.S. to study law. Because foreign citizens ask their own governments about general law education programs in the U.S., those government officials can use *LL.M. Roadmap* as they advise their students about U.S. legal education opportunities.

4. U.S. and Overseas Law Professors

U.S. law professors teach international LL.M. students at over 100 law schools. These professors might benefit from learning about the process international students undergo in getting admitted to U.S. LL.M. programs, and from learning about the reasonable expectations that international LL.M. students have about their LL.M. programs. Overseas law professors may wish to advise their students on the study of law in the U.S., and the professors may want to come to the U.S. for an LL.M. or S.J.D. themselves, or perhaps come to the U.S. for a short-term law-related experience without enrolling in a degree program. (See Chapter 31.)

5. U.S. State Department EducationUSA Advisors

The U.S. welcomes foreign students through "public diplomacy," in which the U.S. promotes its national interests by seeking to favorably influence foreign citizens (students). The U.S. hopes foreign students will have positive experiences with her people and institutions, and return home with an understanding and openness that will further U.S. interests abroad. The U.S. promotes education through its U.S. State Department EducationUSA Advisors, at 450 embassies, consulates, and other centers around the world, who advise students on studying in the U.S.

6. U.S. Congress

Congress enacts laws regarding student visas and their terms and conditions, including visa length, student employment, and student minimum course credit

---

Who Should Read This Book?

1. You—the *new generation of international students in the U.S.*
2. U.S. law firms working overseas and U.S. in-house counsel
3. Foreign government education and scholarship ministries
4. U.S. law professors and foreign law teachers
5. U.S. State Department EducationUSA academic advisors
6. U.S. Congress
7. U.S. law school administrators, librarians, and other staff
8. University and high school academic advisors
9. Educational agents and consultants
10. Parents who want a U.S. law degree for their children

hours. Congress might examine hurdles foreign students face in achieving their U.S. law educational goals, and also come to better understand the challenges schools face in complying with U.S. immigration law.

7. U.S. Law School Administrators, Librarians, and Other Staff

The U.S. has many excellent LL.M. programs in which LL.M. administrators, faculty (including librarians) and staff understand and meet international LL.M. students' reasonable expectations. Some law schools, however, appear not to have clear ideas of LL.M. students' reasonable expectations, and problems consequently arise. *LL.M. Roadmap* helps identify what international LL.M. students typically expect (or should reasonably expect). Schools can decide which expectations it deems reasonable, and whether to meet those expectations. If schools fail to meet LL.M. students' reasonable expectations, LL.M. programs will develop poor reputations, and evaporate. *LL.M. Roadmap* discusses ways in which schools can help ensure that LL.M. student voices are heard and that students' needs and reasonable expectations are met. U.S. law school librarians, in particular, may want to read *LL.M. Roadmap* because prospective and current students, faculty, and staff turn to them for information. Indeed, *LL.M. Roadmap* is a helpful good read for *anyone* involved with international law students on any campus.

8. Academic Advisors and Teachers at Universities, Law Faculties, and Secondary Schools Around the Globe

With globalization, educators around the world are increasingly advising students on overseas law study. The U.S. is often a first choice. In *every single one* of over 24 countries I have visited in recent years, I have been asked about international students coming to the U.S. to study law. The questions came from those involved at the secondary school (high school), university, and graduate levels. *LL.M. Roadmap* addresses and answers many of those questions.

9. Education Agents and Consultants, U.S. Law Schools, and International Students

Education agents and consultants help U.S. law schools recruit international students, and help students get admitted to U.S. law schools. *LL.M. Roadmap* provides information for agents, schools, and students to help students get enrolled in the best U.S. LL.M. program for them. International LL.M. graduates may want to read *LL.M. Roadmap* to learn how to become an education agent or consultant in their home countries.

10. Parents

Parents often play a major role in determining whether their son or daughter will study for an advanced law degree, whether they will study abroad, whether they will study in the U.S., which school they will attend, and even which substantive area of LL.M. concentration they will choose. *LL.M. Roadmap* guides parents on these important U.S. legal education issues.

Key to Reading *LL.M. Roadmap*

LL.M. Roadmap is the sort of guide that you would not read cover to cover in one sitting. It is more like an encyclopedia — a resource tool that you can turn to whenever you seek guidance on a particular phase or aspect of the LL.M. process. You might read and re-read different chapters at different times, depending on whether you are choosing schools to apply to; deciding how to prepare once you are admitted; applying for a U.S. student visa or scholarship; or applying for a job in the U.S. after you graduate.

Related sections of *LL.M. Roadmap* are cross-referenced to help direct you to areas of the book that might be pertinent to issues that interest you. You may want to flip between chapters to capture all the information you need. Some repetition is inevitable, desirable, and indeed necessary in a comprehensive guide.

Visit the *LL.M. Roadmap* Website

Our website, *www.LLMRoadmap.com*, contains tables and charts with further information about U.S. law schools and LL.M. programs, and tools to help you choose the *best* law study opportunity for you in the U.S. You can also find links to U.S. government websites that provide additional information about U.S. student visas, visa regulations, and working in the U.S. Information can be found regarding international students graduating from U.S. LL.M. programs and then qualifying to practice law in the U.S., "famous" international graduates from LL.M. programs in the U.S., specializations offered at different schools, and an assortment of other interesting and helpful information.

LL.M. Roadmap Is an Information Source and Does Not Endorse, Criticize, Rank, or Assess the Reputation of LL.M. Programs or Law Schools

LL.M. Roadmap does not endorse or criticize any particular law school or LL.M. program, and does not rank or comment on schools' reputations. *LL.M. Roadmap* mentions numerous schools and programs in the context of discussing principles, policies, or practices. The absence of a mention does not constitute a non-endorsement. Nor does inclusion or mention imply endorsement. Rather, *LL.M. Roadmap* seeks to provide straightforward information based on research. It offers examples drawn from publicly available information, from communications with students, graduates, and administrators, and from personal experience. *LL.M. Roadmap* does not recommend any particular school, nor seek to dissuade anyone from attending a particular school. Each prospective student will assess his or her own criteria for choosing a U.S. law school for his or her LL.M. or other graduate law degree.

There are many excellent graduate law programs in the U.S., where you as a student will likely be able to reach your goals. *LL.M. Roadmap* provides important information. There is no good substitute for comprehensive, transparent, and accurate information gleaned directly from LL.M. program administrators and from up-to-date program websites.

Conclusion

To uproot from one's home country to study in the U.S. calls for a dramatic commitment in time and energy, and financial, physical, and emotional resources. But an overwhelming majority of international graduates of U.S. law schools I have met are immensely grateful for their U.S. law school experiences.

Many international students, including my own students, have told me they wish *LL.M. Roadmap* had been available when they were considering law study in the U.S. Many LL.M. students and graduates have reviewed this manuscript, and offered suggestions and comments, which are reflected herein. Also reflected are comments by the professors and the administrators of many different U.S. and overseas law faculties and LL.M. programs, U.S. State Department employees and affiliates, and foreign government officials.

U.S. law schools are motivated by many factors when they decide to offer LL.M. degree programs for international students. International students are motivated by many factors when they decide to pursue an LL.M. in the U.S. Foreign governments are motivated by many factors when they supply scholarships to their students to study in the U.S.; and the U.S. government is motivated by many factors when it offers scholarships to international students to study here under the Fulbright, Muskie, and other programs. All stakeholders involved can achieve their goals through transnational education—students learning in another country's educational system. Transnational education is important—it can help students reach their academic, personal, professional, and career goals.

Irrespective of motivations, cross-cultural education promotes the exchange of ideas across borders, cultivates mutual understanding among disparate peoples, and encourages recognition of the universal characteristics of members of the human family. Students studying law in other countries promote the greater goals of international peace and security and the promotion and protection of human rights and fundamental freedoms around the globe. We are all better off because of overseas education.

I dedicate *LL.M. Roadmap* to all international students and graduates for whom the study of law in the U.S. is, was, or will become a reality. Over many years I have

LL.M. Roadmap In a Nutshell

Who will be most directly affected by *LL.M. Roadmap*?	(a) Thousands of international students who want a U.S. law degree. (b) International students' advisors, professors, and scholarship providers. (c) US embassies and consulates who advise international students. (d) Wall Street and small town lawyers. (e) In-house counsel and government lawyers. (f) Many others around the globe.
What do these international students want?	To receive a U.S. law degree.
How does *LL.M. Roadmap* serve international student goals?	*LL.M. Roadmap* informs international students on how to: (a) choose the "best" U.S. law school for you; (b) get admitted to that school; (c) pay for your U.S. education; (d) succeed at a U.S. law school; (e) get a great job post-LL.M.; and (f) much more.
Why do international students want a U.S. law degree?	For many reasons including: (a) To prepare for the globalized marketplace. (b) To become a professor or judge. (c) To get a better job or earn more money. (d) To specialize. (e) To better represent foreign clients in the U.S., or U.S. clients in foreign countries. (f) To take a U.S. bar exam and practice in the U.S. (g) To be better able to promote and protect human rights and fundamental freedoms.
When do international students need information contained in *LL.M. Roadmap*?	Now. And in the foreseeable (and unforeseeable) future.

heard from so many people from so many different countries and territories around the world that studying law in the U.S. is an extremely positive and rewarding experience for international students who undergo an enriching metamorphosis as a result of their transnational legal education. I hope this is true for you and for everyone you touch in your personal and professional lives after you receive your U.S. law degree whether you remain in the U.S., return to your homeland, or move to a third country.

Any thoughts or insights our readers have on graduate law study in the U.S. are welcomed, and I invite you to share them with me so that I may pass them on to others. I look forward to including some of your apt and illuminating thoughts and insights in the next edition of *LL.M. Roadmap* or on *www.LLMRoadMap.com*. Please send comments via e-mail *LLMRoadMap@yahoo.com* or via website *www.LLMRoadMap.com*.

George E. Edwards (Harvard, J.D. — Juris Doctor)
Professor of Law
Indianapolis, Indiana, U.S.A.

Acknowledgments

General Acknowledgments

Many individuals and institutions contributed significantly in many ways to the publication of *LL.M. Roadmap*. It would be impossible to list all who assisted and nearly impossible to articulate the many specific, critical contributions each person or institution made. I had significant help at all stages, including in developing the *LL.M. Roadmap* concept, conducting research, gathering information from governmental and non-governmental sources in many countries, verifying policies and practices with professors, administrators, students and graduates, gaining insights from participants at conferences in the U.S. and overseas, and working with U.S. Embassies, U.S. Consulates, EducationUSA, and Fulbright offices around the globe. Below I acknowledge and thank in a general way many who assisted, including those who provided me inspiration and moral support. Names may be missing due to anonymity requests or to inadvertent omissions. I thank you and apologize to those whose names I missed.

I thank the first institution where I encountered international students pursuing law degrees — Harvard Law School — when I was studying there for my Juris Doctor (J.D.) degree. I became friends with Harvard LL.M. and S.J.D. students from around the globe, and am still in contact personally and professionally many years later. This is testimony of how international students in the U.S. touch the lives of U.S. students. It is reciprocated; U.S. students touch the lives of international students who come to the U.S. to study. These bonds are life-changing and life-long.

I thank the hundreds of LL.M., S.J.D., J.S.D., B.A., LL.B., J.D., Ph.D. and other students I have encountered when I was a Visiting Professor of Law, Administrator, Visiting Fellow, or Fulbright Senior Specialist at the University of Cambridge Faculty of Law (Cambridge, England, United Kingdom), University of Hong Kong Faculty of Law (Hong Kong), Queen Mary University of London Faculty of Law (London, England, United Kingdom), Universidad de San Pedro Faculty of Law (Chimbote, Peru), DePaul University College of Law (Chicago, Illinois), and Stetson University College of Law (Gulfport, Florida).

I thank the following LL.M. and S.J.D. students and graduates, and prospective students: Evelyn Aero (Uganda), Abdurrahman Abdul Aldrees (Saudi Arabia), Syed Liaquat Ali (India), Tuinese Amuzu (Ghana), Evalyn Aruasa (Kenya), Rowland Atta-Kesson (Ghana), Eman Botros (Egypt), Hein T. Bui

(Hanoi, Vietnam), Perfecto G. "Boyet" Caparas (Philippines; Program Manager of the Program in International Human Rights Law), Wele Elangwe (Cameroon), Ntsika Fakudze (Swaziland), Achim Foerster (Germany), Ibrahim Garba (Nigeria), Li Jia (China), Shang Jiang (China), Kaori Matsuo (Japan), Mohamed Abdalla Mohamedain (Darfur, Sudan), Don Nay (Hanoi, Vietnam), Koichi Nishioka (Japan), Okha Bau Okha (Cameroon), Duncan Ojwang (Kenya), Rachael Okware (Kenya), Marcela Rivera (Chile), Avril Rua (Kenya), Simeon Sungi (Tanzania), Nelson Taku (Cameroon), and Shalva "Tskhakaya" Tskhakaia (Republic of Georgia). Of course I thank the hundreds of additional graduate law students who have passed through the LL.M. programs with which I have been associated.

Thanks to Cynthia Adams, Larry Allen, Elizabeth Allington, Hon. Scott D. Bates, Karen Bravo, Robert Brookins, Jeff Cooper, Michelle Davis (Faculty Assistant to the Program in International Human Rights Law), Hon. Daniel G. Foote, Kevin Green, Therese Kamm, Andrew Klein, Tracy Knight, Aaron Krieger, Sam Ladowski, María Pabón López, Charles Maiers, Jonna MacDougall, Debby McGregor, Patrick McKeand (In Memoriam), Tamara McMillian, Steven Miller (Indiana University Law Librarian), Detra Mills, Mary Mitchell (In Memoriam), David Morton, Kevin Munoz, Fran Quigley, Jesus Rivera, Florence Roisman, Joel Schumm, Seema Shah, Chalanta Shockley, Mark Shope, Samantha Sledd, Aaron Stark, Hiroo Suzuki (Japan), Chasity Thompson, Matthew Trick, LaWanda Ward, Michelle Werner, James P. White, the Master of Laws Association (MLA), and the Program in International Human Rights Law (PIHRL), all of Indiana University School of Law. Thanks to Hamid Abbaspour (Indianapolis and Dubai, United Arab Emirates), Mike Bergin, Jim Huang (Indianapolis and Kenyon College, Ohio), Austin Lugar, Joseph McIntosh, Paul Logan, Jeff Stone, and Larry D. Sweazy of Indianapolis, Indiana.

Thanks to Jimmy Alegra (Lima, Peru), Fabiano Andreatta (Sao Paolo, Brazil), Laurence Bates (Tokyo, Japan), Abdulaziz Alhassan (Riyadh, Saudi Arabia), Sara Allaei (IUPUI Office of International Affairs), Beverly Baker-Kelly (Oakland, California; Muscat, Oman), Pat Biddinger (IUPUI Office of International Affairs), Mike Bonne (San Mateo, California), Dianne Cag (Tucson, Arizona), Federico Caprotti (University of Plymouth, United Kingdom and Shanghai, China), Stephen Carey (The British Council), Garci Carpenter (Washington, D.C.), Richard Carpenter (Washington, D.C.), Glynn D. (Doha, Qatar), Frank Folwell (McLean, Virginia), Heidi Fox (Law School Admission Council — LSAC), Hon. Miriam Goldman Cedarbaum (New York City), Soraya Eftekhari (Washington, D.C.), Adrian Peter Gonzalez-Maltes (Paris, France), Marina Hadjioannou Waters (Indianapolis Interpreters, Inc.), Martha Huaman (Lima, Peru), Nancy Keteku (Accra, Ghana), Bruce Lasky (Bridges Across Borders Southeast Asia — BABSEA, Chiang Mai, Thailand), Paul Lemerise (Geneva, Switzerland), Erica Lutes (Brussels, Belgium), Ma Bo and Ma Lun (Tianjin, China & Tokyo, Japan), Patricia Marks (Law School Admission Council — LSAC), Meredith M. McQuaid (President, NAFSA Association of International Educators; Associate

Vice President & Dean, Global Programs and Strategy Alliance, University of Minnesota, Minneapolis), Beryl Meiron (IELTS International), Lorna Middlebrough (Baghdad, Iraq), Jonathan Miller (Pearson PTE), Stephanie Y. Moore (Washington, D.C.), Lt. Col. Michael "Dan" Mori (Oahu, Hawaii), Wendy Morrish (Bridges Across Borders Southeast Asia — BABSEA, Chiang Mai, Thailand), Connie Mutazindwa (Kampala, Uganda), Danielle Mwakaba (Nairobi, Kenya), Mari Nelson (Nairobi, Kenya), Sherry Ricchiardi (IUPUI and McLean, Virginia), Judy Schilling (Washington, D.C.), Sennane Riungu (Nairobi, Kenya), K. Sathinathan (Singapore), Mary Catherine Scarborough (British Council, British Embassy, Washington, D.C.), Elyssa Skaff (Doha, Qatar & Beirut, Lebanon), Susan Sygall (Mobility International USA/NCDE), Jim Vaseleck (Law School Admission Council — LSAC), Coll Thrush (Vancouver, British Columbia, Canada), Michael N. Wade (Ft. Lauderdale, Florida), Greg Wagoner (Indianapolis, Indiana), Meg Wenger (Educational Credential Evaluators, Inc.), Dustin White (Jeffersonville, Indiana), and the December 2006 participants of the NYC Pitch and Shop Algonkian Conference. Thanks to William J. Kurtz (who was with the project from its inception and who was, along with Donna Bussey, in Rome, Italy when I gave my first *LL.M. Roadmap* presentation at Fulbright).

Thanks to the following professors, LL.M. program directors, and staff at various law schools (including law schools I visited while researching *LL.M. Roadmap* and law schools I did not, but *not including* representatives of all law schools I visited): Raymond Atuguba (University of Ghana Faculty of Law), Dorothea Beane (Stetson University College of Law, Gulfport, Florida), Leslie Burton (Golden Gate University School of Law, San Francisco), James Busuttil (Queen Mary University of London Faculty of Law), Andrew Byrnes (University of New South Wales, Sydney, Australia), William H. Byrnes, IV (Thomas Jefferson School of Law, San Diego, California), Bruce Carolan (Department of Law, Dublin Institute of Technology, Ireland), John Cerone (New England School of Law, Boston, Massachusetts), Carolyn Coolidge (University of Arizona, Tucson), John Cooper (Stetson University College of Law, Gulfport, Florida), Marcella David (University of Iowa College of Law), Stephanie M. Deckter (George Washington University Law School, Washington, D.C.), Brian Dennison (Uganda Christian University, Mukono, Uganda), Ding Xiangshun (Renmin University of China Law School, Beijing, China; Waseda University Faculty of Law & Meiji University Faculty of Law, Japan), Jeffrey Dodge (Hofstra Law School, Hempstead, New York), Rosie Edmond (American University Washington College of Law; EducationUSA, Tokyo, Japan), Toni Fine (Fordham Law School, New York), Martin "Marty" Geer (University of Nevada School of Law, Las Vegas), Antonio Gidi (University of Houston Law Center, Houston, Texas & Bahia, Brazil), Linda S. Greene (University of Wisconsin Law School, Madison, Wisconsin), Craig Hoffman (Georgetown University Law Center, Washington, D.C.), Skip Horne (University of San Diego School of Law, San Diego, California), Khary D. Hornsby (University of Minnesota School of Law, Minneapolis, Minnesota),

Craig L. Jackson (Thurgood Marshall School of Law, Houston, Texas), Robert Lancaster (Louisiana State University "LSU" School of Law, Baton Rouge, Louisiana), Lyonette Louis-Jacques (University of Chicago Law School, Chicago, Illinois), Jeremy Levitt (Florida A & M University College of Law, Tallahassee, Florida), Gregory Marsden (IE Business School, Madrid, Spain), Vincent Mutai (Moi University School of Law, Eldoret, Kenya), Athena Mutua (University of Buffalo Law School), Makau Mutua (University of Buffalo Law School), Luz Estella Nagle (Stetson University College of Law, Gulfport, Florida), Leslye Obiora (University of Arizona College of Law), Michael Peil (Washington University School of Law, St. Louis); James Wilets (Nova Southeastern School of Law, Ft. Lauderdale, Florida), John Pluebell (Golden Gate University School of Law, San Francisco), Ellen Podgor (Stetson University College of Law, Gulfport, Florida), John N. Riccardi (Boston University School of Law, Boston, Massachusetts), Charlie Rose (Stetson University College of Law, Gulfport, Florida), Mary Rose Strubbe (Chicago Kent College of Law, Chicago, Illinois), Jane E. Schukoske (University of Baltimore School of Law, Baltimore, Maryland; S.M. Sehgal Foundation & Institute of Rural Research & Development (IRRAD) in Gurgaon, Haryana, India), Jane E. Scott (St. John's University School of Law, Queens, New York City, New York), Mark Shulman (Pace Law School, White Plains, New York), John Smagula (Temple Law School, Philadelphia, Pennsylvania), Celia Strino (Fordham Law School, New York), Susan C. Wawrose (University of Dayton School of Law, Dayton, Ohio), Mark Wojcik (John Marshall Law School, Chicago, Illinois), and Simon Young (University of Hong Kong Faculty of Law, Hong Kong, China).

I acknowledge and thank Kurt J. Ihrig for his illustrations, Greg Wagoner for his lettering (http://tcdriver.smugmug.com), and photographer Douglas Mola (for his photograph of Hon. Scott Bates) and photographer Sam Scott. I thank George Minot (Rome, Italy) for his extensive general editing, his wordsmithing, and his encouragement. Thanks to FedEx Office® (Kinkos) Broad Ripple (Indianapolis, Indiana) personnel who over an extended period of time expertly (and patiently) prepared multiple spiral-bound *LL.M. Roadmap* manuscript iterations, and *LL.M. Roadmap* flyers and posters that have been hand-carried to or otherwise disseminated within dozens of countries around the globe. Thanks to Joe Yeager (joeyeager@att.net) whose travel agency services helped facilitate journeys for *LL.M. Roadmap* research and presentations on six continents.

Thanks also to Aspen / Wolters Kluwer editors Christine Hannan, Christie Rears and Dana Wilson, Publisher Carol McGeehan, and all others from the publishing house who are to be credited with any *LL.M. Roadmap* success, including members of the design, production, sales, marketing and other teams. Thanks also to the over a dozen outside anonymous manuscript reviewers retained by Aspen, who reviewed the *LL.M. Roadmap* manuscript multiple times over an extended period, and whose comments and suggestions were tremendously helpful.

Special thanks to the International Law Students Association (ILSA) (www.ILSA.org), to whom my personal profits from this edition of *LL.M. Roadmap* are being donated. Thanks also to the ILSA staff, Board, and Jessup Moot Court competitors from dozens of countries, for all they do to promote international education for law students around the globe.

I thank EducationUSA Advising Centers and Advisors I have encountered in dozens of cities and countries, in particular those in Nairobi, Kenya where *LL.M. Roadmap* was born, and in Italy where I shared *LL.M. Roadmap's* first draft. I have had the privilege of visiting, giving Powerpoint presentations at, or sharing about U.S. LL.M. programs at EducationUSA offices and affiliates in Argentina (Buenos Aires), Austria (Vienna), Bahrain (Manama), Botswana (Gaborone), Cameroon (Yaoundé), China (Beijing), Ghana (Accra), Japan (Tokyo), Kenya (Nairobi), Kuwait (Kuwait City), Laos (Vientiane), Peru (Lima), Philippines (Manila), Saudi Arabia (Riyadh), Singapore, Taiwan (Taipei), Thailand (Bangkok & Chiang Mai), Uganda (Kampala), the United Kingdom (London) and Vietnam (Hanoi). As this book is going to press, I have agreed to tape an *LL.M. Roadmap* video at the U.S. Embassy in Beijing, China and soon after to participate in an LL.M. Workshop at the Franco-American Commission for Educational Exchange (Fulbright Association) in Paris, France — both at the invitation of EducationUSA U.S. Department of State affiliates. Thanks also to the organizers and participants in the *EducationUSA Middle East and North Africa (MENA) Triennial Conference 2011 "Opening Doors Through Education"* held in Doha, Qatar 11 – 15 April 2011, at which EducationUSA Advisors shared international education experiences from MENA Region countries and territories, including Algeria, Bahrain, Gaza, Egypt, Iran, Iraq, Israel, Jordan, Kuwait, Lebanon, Libya, Morocco, Oman, Palestinian Territories, Qatar, Saudi Arabia, Syria, Tunisia, United Arab Emirates (UAE), West Bank and Yemen. Thanks to the EducationUSA and the Brazilian Embassy in Washington, D.C. for organizing the *2nd Annual EducationUSA Forum* held in Washington, DC 22 – 24 June 2011, attended by close to 100 EducationUSA advisors from around the globe. EducationUSA has helped shrink the world for budding legal professionals seeking a transborder education.

I thank the following personnel from the Institute of International Education (IIE) for their various contributions, including their work in organizing and sponsoring conferences and seminars, supporting and providing information about countless funding opportunities for international students, serving as technical and logistical experts, and generally supporting international education for many individuals and entities around the globe: Martin "Marty" Bennett, Shannon Harrison, Brandon Howe, Nichole Johnson, Mark Lazar, and Daniel Obst.

Thanks to the Chatham House / Royal Society of International Law (London, United Kingdom) and the Atlantic Council that co-sponsored the *Transatlantic Dialogues on International Law: Human Rights and International Law* in November 2010. Thanks also to the organizers and participants in the

Association of American Law Schools (AALS) annual meeting held in San Francisco in January 2011, the Global Legal Skills Conference VI held at The John Marshall Law School held in Chicago in May 2011, and the *NAFSA Association of International Educators Annual Conference and Expo* held in Vancouver, British Columbia, Canada in May and June 2011. My participation in these conferences furthered *LL.M. Roadmap*.

I have visited dozens of LL.M. programs at law schools in the U.S. (and overseas) and talked with countless LL.M. administrators, law faculty personnel, law professors, government officials, educational agents, academic advisors, students and graduates. Again, I mention that it would be impossible to list everyone who helped on this journey.

Comments and Suggestions; Anticipatory Thanks

No one mentioned above is responsible for any errors in *LL.M. Roadmap*. This falls on me. If you spot any errors, or if you have comments or suggestions that could be incorporated into the next *LL.M. Roadmap* edition or our website (www.LLMRoadMap.com), will you please let me know? Your insights will certainly prove useful for prospective, current and former LL.M. students. You may write to *LLMRoadMap@yahoo.com* or visit www.LLMRoadMap.com. Also feel free to follow us on Twitter @llmroadmap, and join us on Facebook at LLM Roadmap.

Conclusion

I look forward to meeting more of you as I continue my work in the field of graduate law programs in the U.S. for international students. In the meantime, I would like to again thank everyone who contributed to the success of *LL.M. Roadmap*, and I wish success to all who use *LL.M. Roadmap*.

George E. Edwards (Harvard, J.D. — Juris Doctor)
Professor of Law
Indianapolis, Indiana, U.S.A.
LLMRoadMap@yahoo.com & www.LLMRoadMap.com

Twitter: @llmroadmap
Facebook: LLM Roadmap

Abbreviations

AA	Alcoholics Anonymous
AAA	American Automobile Association
AALS	Association of American Law Schools
AARP	American Association of Retired People (formerly)
ABA	American Bar Association
ALMA	Italian LL.M. Association
AT	Academic Training
B.A.	Bachelor of Arts
BLS	Bureau of Labor Statistics (U.S.)
B.S.	Bachelor of Science
CASIN	Council for American Students in International Negotiations
COA	Cost of Attendance
CPT	Curricular Practical Training
CV	Curriculum Vitae
DS-2019	Certificate of Eligibility for Exchange Visitor (J-1) Status
DSO	Designated School Official
EAD	Employment Authorization Document
e.g.	*exempli gratia* (for example)
EH	Economic Hardship
ELSA	European Law Students Association
ESL	English as a Second Language
ETS	Educational Testing Service
FAFSA	Free Application for Federal Student Aid
FINAID	Financial Aid
GAPSFAS	Graduate and Professional School Financial Aid Service
GATT	General Agreement on Tariffs and Trade
GLBT	Gay, Lesbian, Bisexual, Transgendered
GMAT	Graduate Management Admission Test
GPA	Grade Point Average
GRE	Graduate Record Examination
I-20	Certificate of Eligibility for Nonimmigrant Student Status
I-94	Arrival/Departure record/card
ICC	International Criminal Court
ICE	Immigration and Customs Enforcement (U.S.); or In Case of Emergency

ICTR	United Nations International Criminal Tribunal for Rwanda
ICTY	United Nations International Criminal Tribunal for the former Yugoslavia
ID	Identification
i.e.	*id est* (that is)
IELTS	International English Language Testing System
IGO	Intergovernmental Organization
ILEC	Cambridge International Legal English Certificate
ILSA	International Law Students Association
IP	Intellectual Property
IRS	Internal Revenue Service
J.D.	Juris Doctor
J.M.	Juris Master
J.S.D.	Doctor of Juridical Sciences/Doctor of the Science of Law (also S.J.D.)
LGBT	Lesbian, Gay, Bisexual, Transgendered
LL.B.	Bachelor of Laws
LL.M.	Master of Laws
LPR	Lawful Permanent Resident (U.S.)
LSAC	Law School Admission Council
LSAT	Law School Admission Test
LSDAS	Law School Data Assembly Service
M.B.A.	Master of Business Administration
MBE	Multistate Bar Exam
M.C.J.	Master of Comparative Jurisprudence
M.C.L.	Master of Comparative Law
M.J.	Master of Jurisprudence
M.L.I.	Master of Arts in Legal Institutions
MPRE	Multistate Professional Responsibility Exam
MRP	Machine Readable Passport
NA	Narcotics Anonymous
NAFSA	National Association of Foreign Student Advisors
NAGAP	National Association of Graduate Admissions Professionals
NALP	National Association for Legal Career Professionals
N.B.	*nota bene* (note well)
NBA	National Bar Association (U.S.)
NCBEX	National Conference of Bar Examiners
NGO	Non-governmental Organization
NSEERS	National Security Entry and Exit Registration System
OPT	Optional Practical Training
PDF	Portable Document Format
Ph.D.	Doctor of Philosophy
RA	Research Assistant
ROLI	Rule of Law Initiative (ABA)

SBA	Student Bar Association
SEVIS	Student and Exchange Visitor Information System
SEVP	Student and Exchange Visitor Program
S.J.D.	Doctor of Juridical Sciences/Doctor of the Science of Law (also J.S.D.)
SSN	Social Security number
TESOL	Teachers of English to Speakers of Other Languages
TIN	Tax Identification number
TOEFL	Test of English as a Foreign Language
UN	United Nations
UNDP	United National Development Program
USCIS	U.S. Citizenship and Immigration Service
VCCR	Vienna Convention on Consular Relations
WTO	World Trade Organization

LL.M. Roadmap

Part I

International Students Earning U.S. Law Degrees:

What Is So Special About U.S. Legal Education?

PART I U.S. Law Schools

PART II "Best" Schools	PART III Admissions	PART IV Schools Respond	PART V Student Visas	PART VI Finances	PART VII Employment	PART VIII Other Degrees	PART IX Miscellaneous	PART X Conclusion

Chapter 1

Globalization and the Need for Transnational Lawyers

CHAPTER HIGHLIGHTS

- Globalization is permanent.
- Globalization creates the need for transnational legal practice.
- Although law is typically "local," lawyers need to learn the law of other countries.
- The U.S. is a great choice for your LL.M. degree, but it is not your only choice.
- *LL.M. Roadmap* will help you decide if the U.S. is the "best" choice for you.
- *LL.M. Roadmap* will help you find the "best" U.S. law school for you.

A. Transnational Lawyers[1] in a Globalized Environment

Whether you view globalization as a positive or a negative, it is a permanent phenomenon. National economies and communities around the globe will become increasingly interconnected and interdependent. Private individuals and entities are inextricably linked by communication, trade, investments, culture, and mutual inquisitiveness. Everyone on earth is affected by decisions or actions taken outside their own country. Globalization affects us all, whether we like it or not.

Despite globalization's far reach, the practice of law is essentially local. Domestic laws are unique to each country, and countries generally limit foreign lawyers' practice rights. Lawyers must adapt to transnational realities so they can better satisfy client needs. They must learn laws and practices of countries other than their own.

---

1. *LL.M. Roadmap* uses the terms "lawyer" and "attorney" interchangeably. Distinctions between the two are not widely known outside the U.S. legal profession and are not strictly adhered to even within the profession.

U.S. Law Schools

Lawyers trained in Africa, South America, or Europe might represent govern-mental interests at a World Trade Organization (WTO) proceeding in Geneva. Lawyers from Asia, North America, or Australia could investigate and prosecute human trafficking involving multiple jurisdictions. Lawyers from anywhere might represent defendants charged in an international criminal tribunal — such as the International Criminal Court (ICC) or the United Nations International Criminal Tribunal for Rwanda (ICTR) — for genocide, crimes against humanity, or war crimes. They may work in domestic courts with defen-dants charged with international crimes such as drug smuggling or terrorism, or they may work on refugee or asylum cases in domestic administrative proceedings.

Lawyers from dozens of countries may work on deals involving multi-national corporations. They could work for, or on behalf of, a wide range of entities, including General Electric, IBM, Toyota, Microsoft, the International Committee of the Red Cross, Greenpeace, the European Union, Amnesty International, or government ministries of most countries.

Lawyers from different countries have different reference points, based on their legal traditions and models (common versus continental or civil, adversar-ial versus inquisitorial, religious versus secular). But it is not clear that all law schools train their students for transnational legal practice.

B. Lawyers Studying Outside Their Home Countries — Exporting Legal Education

Law schools in virtually all 200 nations of the world do a fine job of preparing students to practice law, with instruction focused primarily on the home coun-try's legal system, be it based on a civil code, the common law, or religion, or be it a mixed or other legal system. But today's lawyers require that schools prepare them to work in the transnational marketplace, either domestically or abroad, and thus they demand training in laws and practices other than their own.

Law schools "export" legal education when they teach students from other countries; law degrees are in effect commodities that students travel abroad to acquire.[2] This legal education opens doors to international clients, legal trans-actions, and other career and work opportunities as transnational lawyers.

---

2. Professor Ronald Brand, who directs the Center for International Legal Education at **Pittsburgh School of Law**, notes that educating foreign lawyers "clearly fits" within "services trade" of the General Agreement on Trade in Services (GATS) but that "few efforts have been made to catalogue the extent and impact of this component of services trade." (*The Export of Legal Education: Its Promise and Impact in Transition Countries*, University of Pittsburgh). The American Bar Association (ABA) Section of Legal Education and Admissions to the Bar, *Report of the Special Committee on International Issues* (15 July 2009), p. 7, notes that in 2007 the U.S. exported $6.4 billion in legal services. But it is not clear how much the U.S. exported in legal education.

U.S. Law Schools

A French law school, for instance, may train Brazilian students who may remain in France postdegree and represent Brazilian companies operating in France. They may return to Brazil and represent French companies doing business in Brazil. Both the French and Brazilian lawyers benefit greatly from learning the language of the law in their own jurisdictions, and from learning the law in the opposite, host jurisdiction.

This scenario repeats globally. It applies to corporate lawyers and lawyers in criminal law, environmental law, international trade law, and even human rights law. Clients include governments, nongovernmental organizations, intergovernmental bodies (such as the United Nations [UN]), and individuals.

C. Should an International Student[3] Choose the U.S. — or Another Country — for an LL.M. Degree?[4]

Chapter 2 discusses good reasons why a U.S. law school is a great place, and in many instances the best place, for an international student to receive an LL.M. degree — depending in large part on the student's goals. But there can be economic advantages to earning a law degree outside the U.S., as well as other substantive reasons, such as curricula and professorial resources. LL.M. programs in the U.S. face stiff competition from overseas programs in many regions and countries, including:[5]

(a) **Europe.** Europe has many highly regarded LL.M. programs where the language of instruction is English, including in non-English-speaking countries. If you want an LL.M. in European law, why not get it from a European university? Your school would be in the jurisdiction you are studying, and your teachers would know and live European law. Tuition may be less in Europe, which has a lower cost of living.

---

3. *LL.M. Roadmap* focuses on "foreign-educated law graduates" with overseas degrees, or "foreign lawyers" licensed to practice outside the U.S. Most are not U.S. citizens. Some are U.S. permanent residents (green card holders). No term tidily includes the range of people eligible for a U.S. LL.M. They could be called "foreign students" (though some U.S. citizens hold overseas degrees), or "foreign-trained" or "foreign-educated" law graduates or lawyers (though some U.S. LL.M. programs accept overseas students with no law degree or who are not admitted to practice overseas). *LL.M. Roadmap* uses the imperfect term "international student" to encompass those educated outside the U.S. who endeavor to participate in a globalized world by crossing borders to pursue an education and possibly a career. *LL.M. Roadmap* also uses the term "foreign-educated" when referring to international students who earned law degrees outside the U.S. and who are, for example, required to take special LL.M. courses to introduce them to U.S. legal practice, which lawyers educated in the U.S. are not required to take. The term "LL.M." is defined below.

4. "LL.M." stands for the Latin *Legum Magister*. In English it is called "Master of Laws." "*Legum*" is the genitive plural form of "*Lex*" (meaning "law"). Double "LL" represents "laws" or "*Legum*," and reflects the Latin rule that plurals are formed by repeating the letter. It is neither "Masters of Law" nor "Master's of Law" because the "s" should be attached to "Laws" and not to "Master."

5. The *LL.M. Roadmap* website — *www.LLMRoadmap.com* — lists links to overseas law schools. The ABA has compiled statistics on law student enrollment, graduation, attrition, and other categories, and posted it at www.americanbar.org/groups/legal_education/resources/statistics.html.

(b) **Africa and the Middle East.** Significant LL.M. programs in English exist in different African countries, including in Egypt, Kenya, Lesotho, Namibia, Nigeria, South Africa, Tanzania, Uganda, and Zambia.

(c) **The Americas.** There are great LL.M. programs in Canada and Mexico, and elsewhere in North, South, and Central America. They are taught in Spanish, French, Portuguese, and, of course, English.

(d) **Australia and New Zealand.** Many international students join English-language Australian and New Zealand LL.M. programs that are less expensive than in other parts of the world and that may provide significant scholarships.

(e) **Asia.** English-language LL.M. programs exist in Japan, Korea, China, Singapore, and elsewhere in the region. Some are offered through U.S. law schools. Some are offered through local schools. Some are hybrids. Many are new. Other programs, such as the LL.M. program at the **University of Hong Kong** Faculty of Law, have been in place for many years. Many East African and other international students receive LL.M. degrees in India, an English-speaking jurisdiction where educational costs are significantly lower than in western countries. Other schools in Asia that offer LL.M. degrees and/or U.S.-style J.D. degrees, in English, include **Peking University School of Transnational Law (STL)** in Shenzhen, China and **Singapore Management University (SMU)** in Singapore.

D. Do U.S. Graduate Law Students Learn to Be "Transnational Lawyers"?

The ABA reported that in 2008 over 6,000 students were enrolled in U.S. non-J.D. (Juris Doctor) law programs,[6] with over 4,000 LL.M. degrees awarded. Most recipients, representing close to 200 nationalities, were not U.S. citizens.

Many U.S. law schools have broad and deep curricula that promote trans-national legal practice. Some offer LL.M. degrees that specialize in different legal areas (see Chapter 4), and some offer similar concentrations or certificate programs in their J.D. curricula. All offer general U.S. law courses, useful for foreign lawyers who would want to represent U.S. companies in the lawyers' home countries, or represent companies from their home countries doing business in the U.S. Many have study abroad programs, and overseas exchange and internship programs. U.S. law schools do not and should not exist in a vacuum, shielded from transnational realities.

---

6. In the United States, the J.D. is the first professional law degree offered. (See Chapters 5 and 30.) The J.D. is available to U.S. students after they have received a B.A., B.S., or other undergraduate level degree. The B.A. or B.S. would be in a field other than law because law is not offered as an undergraduate degree in the U.S.

U.S. Law Schools

E. Globalized Legal Education — Can Lawyers Practice in *Any* Country? (See Chapter 28)

Much has been written about globalization in legal education and legal practice.[7] The American Bar Association (ABA) recently discussed, debated, participated in initiatives related to, and published reports on globalization of legal practice; foreign lawyers sitting for U.S. bar exams and getting admitted to U.S. law practice; international student LL.M. study at U.S. law schools; ABA certification of U.S. LL.M. programs; and ABA accreditation of non-U.S. law schools.[8] Notably, the ABA's Section of Legal Education and Admissions to the Bar has participated in ABA initiatives, such as:

- Developing model practice rules for Foreign Legal Consultants in the U.S.;
- Representation on the ABA Task Force on International Trade in Legal Services;
- Advising and assisting foreign law schools on courses of study and accreditation;
- Sponsoring and participating in conferences and meetings regarding international legal practice and bar admission; and
- Assisting with the ABA Rule of Law Initiative (ROLI) on matters regarding legal education in foreign jurisdictions.[9]

The *ABA 2009 Report on International Issues* recognized that U.S. clients want foreign-educated lawyers, who are currently permitted to practice in over 25 U.S. states. It noted that an ABA Commission recommended that states permit "foreign legal consultants" to practice without taking a U.S. bar exam, and permit foreign-educated lawyers to practice temporarily ("fly-in, fly-out"). It noted that in 2007 the Conference of Chief Justices (CCJ) adopted a resolution urging permission for Australian-trained and admitted lawyers to be admitted to U.S. jurisdictions, and a resolution calling on the ABA to develop a scheme to certify the quality of the legal education offered in other common law countries.

In July 2010, an ABA Commission recommended continued consideration of accrediting law schools outside U.S. borders.[10] But in December 2010 it was

---

7. Professor Carole Silver has written extensively on the topic, in particular regarding U.S. LL.M. program students and graduates. *See, e.g., The Variable Value of U.S. Legal Education in the Global Legal Services Market,* 24 Georgetown Journal of Legal Ethics 1 (2011); *Educating Lawyers for the Global Economy: National Challenges* (Kyung Hee University Law Review (2009/2010)). *See also* Harry W. Arthurs, *Law and Learning in an Era of Globalization,* 10 German L. J. 629, 630 (2009) (www.germanlawjournal.com/article.php?id=1111).

8. The ABA is a voluntary organization open to anyone licensed to practice law in the U.S. Associate status is available to lawyers licensed outside the U.S., and to legal educators, paralegals, legal assistants, law-office administrators, law librarians, consultants, and others interested in law. Students (including LL.M.) may join (www.americanbar.org).

9. ABA Section of Legal Education and Admissions to the Bar, *Report of the Special Committee on International Issues* (15 July 2009) (*See* Introduction).

10. *Report of Special Committee on Foreign Law Schools Seeking Approval Under ABA Standards* (19 July 2010).

U.S. Law Schools

decided that for now there would be no attempts to accredit foreign law programs.[11] In the spring of 2011, the ABA circulated for discussion the "Proposed Model Rule on Admission of Foreign Educated Lawyers." (See Chapter 28.)

F. Conclusion

LL.M. Roadmap will help you—as an international prospective student— make well-informed decisions about whether to seek an LL.M. degree, whether to pursue your LL.M. outside your home country, and whether to come to the U.S. for your LL.M. If you choose the U.S. for your LL.M. degree, *LL.M. Roadmap* will help you choose the "best" school for you to be best poised to meet your educational, personal, and career goals. These decisions are not easy; this guide is designed to assist you in making sound decisions. You should not and need not decide in a vacuum.

Thousands of students enroll in U.S. LL.M. programs each year, and are spread out at over 100 law schools. Whether you decide to seek a U.S. LL.M. degree now, later, or never, you will be better positioned to make an informed decision after you read *LL.M. Roadmap*.

Good luck as you enter this next important stage of your career! And a warm welcome to all of you who decide to journey to the U.S. to supplement your legal education!

CHAPTER SUMMARY

- Globalization is permanent and requires lawyers to engage in transnational legal practice.
- Lawyers must learn foreign law (the law of other jurisdictions) *and* international law.
- Why choose the U.S. for your LL.M. degree? There are many good reasons. However, keep in mind that the U.S. is not your only choice. Excellent LL.M. programs taught in English exist in many countries.
- *LL.M. Roadmap* will help you decide if the U.S. is the "best" choice for you.
- *LL.M. Roadmap* will help you find the "best" U.S. law school for you.

---

11. Edward A. Adams, *ABA Puts Off Decision on Accreditation of Foreign Law Schools* (www.abajournal.com/news/article/aba_puts_off_decision_on_accreditation_of_foreign_law_schools). Professor James P. White, Emeritus Consultant on Legal Education to the American Bar Association, contends that the ABA should not accredit overseas law schools. *ABA Approval of Foreign Law Schools: My Response* (http://apps.americanbar.org/legaled/accreditation/Comments%20on%20Foreign%20Program%20Accreditation/JamesWhite.pdf). He noted that the ABA has accredited U.S. programs "to give assurance to the State's highest courts that graduates of ABA approved law schools meet minimum qualifications for law admission." He continued "I do not believe that an approval process for foreign law schools can give that assurance" (*Id.* at 5-6).

Chapter 2

Seventeen Reasons to Earn an LL.M. Degree in the U.S.

CHAPTER HIGHLIGHTS

- This chapter focuses on 17 reasons why you might choose a U.S. law school for your LL.M. degree.
- It is important to determine what professional and/or personal reasons you have for obtaining an LL.M. in the U.S. Different people have different reasons.
- You must discern whether your professional and/or personal objectives are reasonable. *LL.M. Roadmap* provides advice in this area.
- Although U.S. degrees have many advantages, it may be "best" for you to earn your LL.M. in a country other than the U.S.
- If you conclude that the U.S. is the best jurisdiction in which to earn your LL.M., you have many options. Over 100 U.S. law schools offer LL.M. programs for international students.

A. Why Earn a U.S. Graduate Law Degree?

There are many reasons why the LL.M. is an excellent choice for an advanced law degree, and why the U.S. is a great place for earning your LL.M. This chapter highlights 17 of these reasons.

Each year thousands of international students choose U.S. law schools for their LL.M. degrees. Not all students make this choice for the same reason or reasons. But the principal reason undoubtedly is that they believe an LL.M. from a U.S. law school will help them achieve their personal and professional goals, whatever those goals may be. The rapid, sustained growth of international students in U.S. LL.M. programs is testimony to the faith international students have in U.S. law programs, and to the willingness of U.S. law schools to attempt to satisfy international student demand. It is also testimony that U.S. LL.M. degrees are well respected around the world; that they are widely accepted globally in academia, business, and the international public arena; and that they help create significant opportunities for LL.M. degree holders and can open up further options for them in the future.

Some of the reasons listed may not apply to you, and some reasons that apply to you may not be listed. You may not consciously recognize a reason as applying to you, when indeed it does. Some of the many rewards of a U.S. LL.M. may not materialize until after you graduate, much later in your career. So, be patient and keep an open mind.

B. Seventeen Reasons Foreign-Educated Lawyers Want U.S. LL.M. Degrees

1. To Improve Your Marketability to U.S. Clients in Your Country, and to Clients from Your Country in the U.S.

Around the globe, law firms, governments, and others place a high value on locally trained lawyers who also hold U.S. law degrees. In their home countries they are equipped to offer legal services that local lawyers without U.S. degrees cannot. For example, a Korean-trained lawyer who goes to the U.S. for an LL.M. will gain knowledge about U.S. law, practice, and customs, which may benefit Korean clients that do business in the U.S., or Korean clients that do business with U.S. companies in Korea. Korean lawyers with U.S. law degrees may also be attractive to U.S. clients that want to do business in Korea, or that want to do business with Korean companies in the U.S.

You may choose a U.S. LL.M. program if you want to work with U.S. clients who do business in your home country; with clients from your home country who do business with the U.S. government or U.S. companies; or with intergovernmental organizations in which the U.S. is a key player or for which many other U.S.-trained lawyers work. Studying law in the U.S. gives you credibility with all clients who have any dealings with U.S. actors or U.S. law.

2. To Learn U.S. Law and to Prepare You to Practice Law in the U.S.

Many foreign-educated lawyers who earn an LL.M. in the U.S. sit for and pass the New York bar exam or the bar exam of another U.S. state.[1] Some take a bar so they may stay in the U.S. and practice law, whereas some take a bar and return to

---

1. Some U.S. law schools advertise that their LL.M. program is not designed to prepare LL.M. graduates to practice law in the U.S., but other U.S. schools expressly state the contrary — that international students will gain knowledge that will aid them should they seek to take a U.S. bar exam. Some schools offer special bar review training courses for international students seeking to sit for a U.S. bar exam.

In some states a foreign-educated lawyer may sit for a U.S. bar exam *without* having received an LL.M. from a U.S. law school. (See Chapter 28.)

Seventeen Reasons to Earn an LL.M. Degree in the U.S.

1. Enhance your marketability to U.S. and foreign clients
2. Learn substantive U.S. law and prepare to practice in the U.S.
3. Bolster your credentials to prepare for the globalized legal marketplace
4. Specialize in an area of law and become an expert
5. Become a law teacher and scholar
6. Broaden your professional and personal network
7. Qualify to become a judge
8. Retool, recast, or reframe yourself for prestige, to get a better job, or for personal satisfaction
9. Gain or enhance your intercultural professional competence
10. Gain an advantage in a non-law career
11. Rejuvenate with a well-needed break from law practice
12. Improve your legal English
13. Prepare for outsourcing
14. Learn to be a better lawyer
15. Seize economic efficiencies
16. Increase your competitiveness if you are a U.S. green card holder
17. Further public diplomacy, and promote peace, security, fundamental freedoms, and human rights

their home countries and work for local companies that do business with U.S. companies, or for U.S. companies doing business there. Some take the bar not to practice in the U.S., but to acquire an important credential that distinguishes them from other international students who graduate from U.S. LL.M. programs.

In addition to being a practical accomplishment, passing a U.S. bar exam is prestigious. It is a major feat to sit for and pass any U.S. bar exam, especially for international students whose native language is not English, whose first degree was from a civil or continental law country, and who only have one year of law training in the U.S.

LL.M. graduates must, and do, overcome hurdles in acquiring employment in the U.S. If you want to work in the U.S., begin planning early. Think about steps to take before, during, and after your LL.M. program. Consider your post-LL.M. plans *before* you choose which U.S. law school to attend and which courses or bar exam to take. (See Chapters 26–28.)

3. To Upgrade Your Credentials — Whatever Your Field of Law

In the legal profession, paper credentials often appear to be more important than expertise or practical experience. Some prospective employers might be more inclined to accept a candidate who has a particular diploma with particular grades or marks, rather than a candidate who has demonstrated experience in the area of law or practice in question. An LL.M. degree is no substitute for competence, but holding an LL.M. degree may open doors for you with employers. After the door is open, you still must prove your abilities in order to sustain your employment.

Acquiring an LL.M. degree is an excellent way to upgrade your credentials, to help prepare you for the globalized legal marketplace, particularly if your LL.M. is in a specialized law area that greatly interests you and in which you want to work.[2] An extra credential may give you an advantage over lawyers who do not have an LL.M. degree, and may also give you an advantage over a lawyer who has an LL.M. *without* the specialization that you have. If one job candidate has a general LL.M. without a specialization, and another job candidate has an LL.M. that specializes in international law, if the job in question relates to international law, chances are the LL.M. candidate with that specialization will be the favored candidate. (General and specialized LL.M. programs are discussed in Chapter 4.)

Once you receive your LL.M. degree in the U.S., you will be able to list that degree on your business cards, your office stationery, and in legal directories in your home country and abroad. You may accrue many tangible and intangible benefits from an LL.M. degree from a U.S. law school.

4. To Become an Expert in a Specialized Area of Law

You may want to become an expert in an area of law in which you will practice, teach, or become a specialized judge or arbitrator. For example, you may focus on securities law so that you can advise foreign clients on financial market regulation in the U.S., or so that you may specialize in international taxation to represent multinational corporations subject to taxes in multiple jurisdictions. You may want to gain specific expertise required to teach intellectual property law, international environmental law, information technology, telecommunications, or another esoteric area. If you strive to become an international criminal tribunal judge, you may want to specialize in international criminal law, international human rights law, or international humanitarian law. Many practitioners, teachers, and others working in these

---

2. *LL.M. Roadmap* cautions against a student joining a specialized LL.M. track that the student does not have a strong, compelling interest in. This happens when, for example: (a) a domestic J.D. graduate is prohibited from joining a general LL.M. track reserved for international students so instead the J.D. graduate joins a specialized track; or (b) a domestic or international student wants to join a particular specialized LL.M. track (e.g., trade law) but is unwilling to commit to its requirements (e.g., writing a thesis), or is denied admission, so she joins another track (e.g., international law). In those cases, the student seeks to reap benefits of the first track, even though she is not enrolled in it. When a track is a poor fit for the student, problems ensue for all concerned, including for students in the track who would prefer classmates with similar enthusiasm, interests, and goals.

and other specialized areas of law hold LL.M. and other graduate law degrees. You will be more competitive if you also hold an LL.M. degree, particularly from a U.S. law school.

You may want to learn skills to practice in new legal areas. Maybe you want to apply old skills to a new area, develop new legal skills entirely, or learn more about your current field of law.

5. To Become a Law Teacher (Lecturer, Professor), Legal Scholar, Law Faculty Administrator, or Law Dean

In many countries to become a full professor on a law faculty a teacher must hold not only a B.A., LL.B. or other first law degree, but also a higher degree in law, such as (a) an LL.M.; (b) an LL.M. *and* an S.J.D. (also called a "J.S.D."); or (c) an LL.M. and a Ph.D. Some of these law faculties will accept higher degrees from local law faculties in the country where the school is; other law faculties require higher degrees from overseas law faculties. For example, if you check the **National University of Singapore** Law Faculty biography web page (http:// law.nus.edu.sg/about_us/faculty/staff/staffdiv.asp), you will find that virtually all teaching staff have an LL.M., S.J.D., or Ph.D. from a law school in the U.S. or the U.K.

Foreign law teachers who wish to go overseas for an LL.M., S.J.D., or Ph.D. must, of course, choose a country and a school. The U.S. is popular because of the high quality of legal education it offers. U.S. law schools have extremely positive reputations among most overseas law faculties. Many overseas law professors possess U.S. law degrees.

United Kingdom law schools are popular for foreign law teachers from around the globe, as are Canadian, Australian, Italian, Swiss, and French schools. Law teachers from the Middle East have a history of gravitating to

---

Deans and Associate Deans of U.S. Law Schools Who Were International Students Who Earned Their LL.M. and/or S.J.D. Degrees in the U.S.

- Camille Nelson (Dean, **Suffolk University School of Law**)
- Makau W. Mutua (Dean, **University at Buffalo Law School**)
- Symeon C. Symeonides (Dean, **Willamette University College of Law**)
- Penelope (Penny) Andrews (Associate Dean for Academic Affairs, **CUNY Law School, New York**)
- James Thuo Gathii (Associate Dean for Research and Scholarship, **Albany Law School**)

Please let us know at *www.LLMRoadmap.com* or *LLMRoadMap@yahoo.com* if you know of others we can add to this list!

Egyptian and French law faculties with excellent reputations. However, the U.S. remains extremely popular and has many advantages. To consider teaching in the U.S., consult the Association of American Law Schools (AALS) website (www.aals.org). Many professors currently tenured at U.S. law schools came to the U.S. to receive their LL.M. and/or S.J.D. degrees and then stayed to join U.S. law faculties. Read the faculty biography web pages of U.S. law schools that interest you. Also, consult the AALS *Directory of Law Teachers* at www.aals.org/services_directory.php.

6. To Broaden Your Professional Network to Include LL.M. Graduates Around the World Who Work as Lawyers, Judges, Professors, Corporate Executives, Human Rights Workers, and Government Officials

Whether your U.S. law school has a small LL.M. program of 10–15 students or a large program of 200 students or more, you will broaden your professional network during your LL.M. year in the U.S. You will meet graduate law students from around the world and domestic U.S. J.D. students, many of whom have professional and personal interests similar to your own. You will encounter students from graduate programs in other disciplines at your U.S. university — perhaps from the physics, languages, business, medicine, biology, education, or public health departments — and you will likely form lifelong bonds. You will meet lawyers and judges from the school's local community, many of whom will be graduates of your school. You will connect with law faculty, staff, and alumni at many levels. And you will meet the future legal leaders of tomorrow — your J.D., LL.M., and S.J.D. classmates from around the world, who may return to their home countries and serve as part of your extended professional and personal network. Many of these people will be, or will become, judges, law firm partners, elected or appointed public officials, or corporate counsel in your home country or in countries where you do business or who have business with intergovernmental organizations such as the United Nations (UN).

Your professional and personal databases will grow exponentially, facilitating your ability to draw upon these friends and business contacts for years to come, even after you have returned to your home country. When you are deciding which law school to attend, you might ask the law school administrators about the social and other networking activities taking place among students, prospective students, and alumni. This may give you an idea of how your professional (and personal) network may expand if you choose to attend one law school over another.

You will be enriched — and this enrichment works both ways: You may have a positive, long-lasting impact on many people you meet in your LL.M. program and elsewhere in the U.S., just as they may have such an impact on you.

U.S. Law Schools

Famous and Influential Public Figures Who Hold LL.M. Degrees from U.S. Law Schools

- Mary Robinson (former President of Ireland; former UN High Commissioner for Human Rights)
- Navanethem "Navi" Pillay (Judge, International Criminal Court (ICC) and ICTR; UN High Commissioner for Human Rights)
- Mikheil Saak'ashvili (President of the Republic of Georgia)
- Surakiart Sathirathai (former Foreign Minister, Thailand)
- Guiliano Amato (former President, Italy)
- Rubén Blades (Grammy award–winning singer and Minister of Tourism, Panama)

Please let us know at *www.LLMRoadmap.com* or *LLMRoadMap@yahoo.com* if you know of others we can add to this list!

7. To Help Prepare You to Become a Domestic or International Judge, or a Governmental Official

Judges on domestic courts in many countries and on international tribunals hold LL.M. degrees from U.S. law schools. For example, judges with U.S. LL.M. degrees sit on the UN International Criminal Tribunal for the former Yugoslavia (ICTY), the UN International Criminal Tribunal for Rwanda (ICTR), the Tribunal for the Law of the Sea, and the High Courts of Canada, Australia, the Philippines, Kenya, France, and Thailand.

Elected and appointed officials of many countries hold LL.M. degrees from U.S. law schools. These include current or former presidents of Ireland, the Republic of Georgia, and India. They have also included Prime Ministers, Foreign Ministers, and other high-ranking cabinet members.

If a Thai lawyer wants to become eligible to become a judge in Thailand based in part on legal education in the U.S., she may be required to earn a degree that has a curriculum, or a combined curriculum, of at least two years. A typical LL.M. degree in the U.S. has a curriculum of only one year, so increasingly Thais who want to become judges seek to earn two LL.M. degrees. In many cases, the degrees must be earned at two different U.S. law schools, because law schools may offer only one LL.M. degree, even if the school has different "tracks," "concentrations," or "specializations." That is, at some schools, all "tracks," "concentrations," or "specializations" are offered under the umbrella of *one* LL.M. degree, and are

If you seek to become a judge in Thailand based in part on U.S. legal education and you need two years of a law curriculum in the U.S., check to see if you can earn two separate LL.M. degrees at the same U.S. law school, or whether your U.S. law school will only permit you to earn one LL.M. degree. You may have to study for one year at the first U.S. school, and the second year at another (see www.thailawforum.com/articles/charununlegal5.html).

not separate degrees. Be certain to ask the law school before you enroll whether you can earn more than one *LL.M. degree* at the same school by enrolling in separate tracks or concentrations.

8. To Help You Get a Better Job or Do Your Current Job Better; to Earn a Higher Salary for Work Either in Law or Another Field

A U.S. LL.M. degree may permit you to retool, recast, or reframe yourself professionally and advance your career. In an LL.M. program, you can acquire skills and experience that may help you be promoted by your current employer, facilitate a switch to another department, receive a raise in salary, or change employers. A U.S. LL.M. may also help boost your self-image because getting a U.S. LL.M. degree is prestigious and generally highly regarded in most countries. It is a degree that will build your self-confidence and, as a result, make you more attractive as a job candidate.

A U.S. LL.M. may be a way to further your current career (which may or may not be in law) or it may allow you to change careers. Students earn LL.M. degrees for many different reasons and they end up working in many different fields.

You may have practiced for several years in your home country and are bored with your work life. You might have decided you want a change but you do not know what you want next, or how to get it. Maybe many lawyers in your home country are also stagnant, for instance due to a slow economy.

Though a U.S. LL.M. as a highly regarded credential may help open up opportunities in your home country, in the U.S., or in a third country, be aware that not all law firms or institutions in all countries consider the LL.M. to be a necessary degree;[3] and in some cases, the LL.M. degree may in effect be "devalued," due to the high number of LL.M. graduates in that country.

---

3. *Freshfields* (a U.K. law firm with 27 offices in 15 countries) answered the question "Would an LL.M. help my application?" with the response: "No. If you want to do an LL.M., then do so, but the degree gives you no advantage in securing an offer from us. You create the advantage through your personality and by demonstrating to us how you think, reason and analyse things" (http://careers.freshfields.com/global-careers/en/uk/trainees/faqs.aspx#5).

However, *Linklaters* (a law firm with offices in 26 cities worldwide) noted that "We offer LL.M. students a range of positions in a number of offices throughout the world" (www.linklaters.com/JoinUs/LLM/Pages/index.aspx).

9. To Gain or Enhance Your Intercultural Professional Competence

While in a U.S. LL.M. program, you will necessarily learn about U.S. culture and the cultures of other countries your classmates come from. You will be exposed to the food, attire, holidays, and traditions of many different lands.

You will also gain intercultural professional and legal competency. You will learn about the laws of the U.S. and the practice of U.S. law, and you will learn about the law and practice of the law of other countries, through both in-class and out-of-class exchanges. For example, an LL.M. class assignment might require you to conduct legal research, write a legal brief, and present a case in a "moot court" along with students from the U.S. and other countries. Your fellow students may come from common law traditions where advocates actively participate in courtroom proceedings, and civil or continental law countries where judges conduct the inquiries. Some students may be from countries where lawyers' written legal submissions are lengthy legal "briefs," whereas others are used to short "skeletal" outlines.

Intercultural professional and legal competency will help you flourish post-LL.M. in any law (or non-law) field and in any country you choose to plant yourself.

10. To Give You an Advantage in a Non-Law Career, Particularly If a Degree in Your Specific Area of Interest Is More Difficult to Acquire Than an LL.M.

It is easier for a foreign lawyer to join an LL.M. program in the U.S. than it is for a foreign student to join a program for a U.S. graduate degree in virtually all other fields, including business, medicine, and engineering. The LL.M. requires only a minimum of a law degree (or law license) from your home country, an acceptable English language proficiency test score, and several other academic requirements (see Chapter 12). *You do not need to take an LSAT, GRE, GMAT, or other substantive exam to get admitted to a U.S. LL.M. program.* For other U.S. degrees you need to take (and presumably perform at least passably well on) certain exams, such as the GRE or GMAT.

An instructive anecdote: In Lima, Peru, a recent law graduate told me he wanted an *international relations graduate degree* from a U.S. school. He said he wanted to work for the United Nations Development Program (UNDP) at UN Headquarters in New York, and he was interested in natural resources and development in the Americas. By the end of our discussion, he had decided to explore U.S. specialized LL.M. programs, particularly in the fields of development law, natural resources law, international law, and environmental law. In an LL.M. program, he could take international relations courses from non-law departments at his U.S. university and write a thesis in his areas of interest. With an LL.M., he would not be confined to working as a lawyer, but could pursue the UN development work that interests him. Indeed, with an LL.M. he might have an advantage over colleagues with graduate degrees in other disciplines, including in international relations. Perhaps a relative ease of access is what really convinced him to explore an LL.M.; the fact that international students *are not required* to take the GRE, LSAT, or any other substantive test to enter a U.S. LL.M. program. An international relations degree requires the GRE. (The Juris Doctor degree in the U.S.—J.D.—generally requires an LSAT. See Chapter 30.)

11. To Give You a Break, a Sabbatical, or a Leave of Absence from Your Current Job

Many of us wish for an opportunity to take a break from our current job. Maybe we would like to sit on a beach for a while, climb Mount Everest, write our first novel, or sail around the world. Such experiences might be good for our psychological, physical, even spiritual health—but they may not be great for career advancement.

Why not take a break doing something you will enjoy, gain valuable experience from, and be able to use to help your career? Taking a 9-month leave from your current law job to return to school can be an efficient, fun, and productive way to take a break from your career, while at the same time boosting your career prospects.

While earning an LL.M., you will have an opportunity to rejuvenate, and at the same time learn a new area of law, brush up on areas of law with which you already have familiarity, and expand your contacts, as well as your intellectual capacity and professional capability.

After you return to your home country from the U.S., you will be refreshed, and ready to tackle all manner of challenges that face you.

12. To Improve Your "Legal English" and Your English Language Skills

During your LL.M. program in the U.S., your "legal English" will automatically improve. You will learn the peculiarities of the English language that facilitate nuanced negotiations. Virtually all classes taught in all U.S. LL.M. programs are in English, with large quantities of reading, writing papers and exams, and class discussions also in English.[4]

---

4. You can study for an LL.M. with courses taught in English at schools in many other countries. (See Chapter 1.) However, all the benefits described herein are good reasons to choose to study in English in the U.S. This applies even if the LL.M. is offered "off-site" of the U.S. school, with content delivered online, or through U.S. law school LL.M. degree programs physically taught on campuses in countries such as China, Japan, and Singapore. One need not travel to the U.S. to acquire a U.S. LL.M. degree with instruction in English. (See Chapter 3.)

U.S. Law Schools

If you practice in a transnational legal environment, you must use legal English well, orally and in writing. You need English when you represent clients of different nationalities in transactions, when you negotiate, when you litigate before international tribunals, or when you approach foreign governments. English is by far the most prevalent common language used for transnational legal dealings in the public and private sectors. English is the global language of law, particularly when that law transcends national borders.

Though many languages are helpful for negotiating contracts and treaties involving representatives of many countries, if there is no other common language, quite typically English is the language of choice. English is the first or second language for lawyers in many countries. If you are negotiating with a dozen lawyers from as many countries and you each have a different first language — for example, German, Russian, Arabic, Lithuanian, Swahili, Chinese, French, Japanese, Portuguese, Norwegian, Italian, and Dutch — which language will you use to negotiate? Chances are high that the common language spoken by the 12 negotiators will be English. And it won't be colloquial street English. *It will be legal English.*

13. To Prepare You for "Outsourcing," Where U.S. Law Firms and Businesses Hire Lower-Priced Lawyers Outside the U.S.

U.S. lawyers charge clients — particularly corporate clients — substantial fees for services. U.S. corporate clients would naturally prefer to pay lower fees. U.S. law firms and corporations are increasingly "outsourcing" their legal work, hiring overseas lawyers who can perform the legal work for a lower fee.

An example of a major company involved in outsourcing is Thomson Reuters, which on November 18, 2010, announced that it had acquired an Indian legal process outsourcing company named Pangea3 in a deal likely worth almost U.S. $40 million.[5] Pangea3 operates what it refers to as "Legal Process Outsourcing (LPO) Services by Lawyers for Lawyers" and provides services in various areas, including: (a) contracting and licensing services (drafting, reviewing, and revising contracts); (b) reviewing documents and providing litigation support services (identify data pertinent to litigation or corporate due diligence, populate databases and prepare reports, compile expert and lay witness background reports); (c) drafting patent applications and supporting clients' patent application and prosecution processes (prior art searches, patent landscapes, invalidity and infringement studies, patent illustrations); and (d) conducting and analyzing research including federal, state, and international case law and federal, state, and municipal regulatory codes and legislative history using industry-standard databases.

---

5. Press Release, *Thomson Reuters Acquires Pangea3: Gives Thomson Reuters a leadership position in fast-growing legal process outsourcing market* (18 November 2010) http://thomsonreuters.com/content/press_room/legal/318316.

With outsourcing, a U.S. or foreign corporate client may request assistance from a U.S. law firm; the U.S. law firm would then retain a U.S.-trained foreign lawyer in a foreign country with lower costs (such as India); the foreign lawyer conducts the research and sends it back to the U.S. law firm; and finally, the U.S. law firm reviews the work and presents it to the corporate client in the U.S. (or elsewhere). Because the bulk of the work was performed by a foreign lawyer overseas for a lower fee, the U.S. law firm can charge the client less than if all the work had been done in the U.S. (Or, alternatively, they can charge more and make more money in the process!)

India recently passed a rule disallowing U.S. law firms from opening satellite offices in India, which may well increase the need for Indian lawyers with U.S. graduate law training to work in the outsourcing of legal services industry. Law firms of the U.K. routinely engage Indian lawyers to perform legal services involving U.K. law, because Indian lawyer fees are less than U.K. lawyer fees. Many countries other than India are becoming known for outsourcing.

14. To Help You Become a Better Lawyer, Learning from U.S. Law Professors, and from J.D. and LL.M. Classmates

International LL.M. students stand to learn a great deal during their one-year LL.M. programs in the U.S., which by all accounts have positive impacts on lawyering or other professional activities engaged in post-LL.M.

International students supplement their education and experience with insights gained from theoretical, practical, and experiential courses taught at U.S. law schools. International LL.M. students take classes with some of the best and brightest J.D. students at U.S. law schools, who are being trained as lawyers. Professors who teach LL.M. students are generally dedicated and open to working with international LL.M. students, to help ensure that the students absorb the knowledge sought to be transferred.

These advantages and other insights gained by international LL.M. students necessarily result in their getting an edge on other lawyers in their home countries who have not been able to benefit from an advanced U.S. law degree. International LL.M. students learn a great deal from students, faculty, staff, and the general U.S. legal community, and that knowledge will stay with the LL.M. students long after they graduate. All told, international LL.M. graduates from U.S. law schools generally benefit greatly from their experiences.

15. As a Sound Economic Investment, Especially if Your Home Currency Is Strong Compared to the U.S. Dollar

Though a U.S. LL.M. degree is expensive, the value of the U.S. dollar may be low vis-à-vis the currency of your homeland, making a U.S. LL.M. degree a bargain. The global economy, as it has affected your country and the U.S., may render your U.S. degree a good deal. Earning a U.S. LL.M. is a lifelong, permanent investment.

The U.S. remains a leader in educating international law students, and will likely remain so, despite difficulties faced by international students seeking visas, regardless of the state the U.S. economy may be in, and in spite of the high costs of these U.S. degrees. The U.S. is an economic and political power-house, and has a rich presence in transnational transactions involving lawyers and the law.

On any given day, U.S.-trained lawyers act on behalf of private clients or the government in multinational corporation board rooms, at UN and other diplomatic conferences, at educational institutions around the world, in civil and criminal proceedings globally, and in many other arenas. The U.S. has always maintained a numerical advantage in such proceedings and a substantive advantage in public and private sectors. Foreigners with U.S. law degrees would be well-equipped to do battle with other U.S.-trained lawyers in these contexts.

16. To Increase Your Competitiveness if You Are a U.S. Permanent Resident (Green Card Holder) or U.S. Citizen Who Earned Your First Law Degree Overseas

To be admitted to a U.S. LL.M. program, generally you must hold a J.D. from the U.S., a law degree from another country, or a license to practice law in another country. It is common for U.S. citizens or permanent residents to hold a foreign law degree or law license, but not hold a U.S. J.D. degree. U.S. citizens or permanent residents without a J.D. are motivated by many of the same factors as international students to earn an LL.M., such as to increase their competitiveness, to prepare themselves to work outside the U.S., to gain a credential they think will help them become a law professor, or to permit them to take a U.S. bar exam and practice law in the U.S.

17. To Promote Global Peace and Security, and Fundamental Freedoms and Human Rights

In 1956, U.S. President Dwight D. Eisenhower spoke about intercultural exchanges and noted that "If people get together, so eventually will nations." His ideas, and ideas of many who preceded and followed, suggested that study-ing abroad and other citizen exchanges help facilitate "understanding and mutual respect between individuals" that "peaceful relations between nations requires." Senator Fulbright (after whom the Fulbright Scholarships are named — see Appendix II) noted that through educational and other exchanges across borders we bring "more knowledge . . . reason [and] compassion into world affairs and thereby increase the chance that nations will learn at last to live in peace and friendship."

U.S. Law Schools

Studying overseas *does* help promote global peace and security, and fundamental rights and freedoms.[6] This is a good reason to come to the U.S. for an LL.M. — to do your share to help make the world a better place for current and future generations.

Whether you remain in the U.S., return to your home country, or venture to a third country post-LL.M., your year in an LL.M. program will have helped open the eyes of your classmates about your homeland's cultures and traditions, and exposed you to U.S. culture and traditions and those of your LL.M. classmates. And you will naturally carry what you learn back to your family and friends at home or elsewhere. Your U.S. study will *necessarily* result in intercultural exchange, dialogue, and mutual understanding, and these will serve, either directly or indirectly, to help further peace and human rights — even if your LL.M. focuses on esoteric and seemingly unrelated topics of securities, taxation, or entertainment law. With your LL.M. experience in the U.S., you will touch and have a positive impact on countless people you encounter throughout your personal and professional life for years to come, and they will touch and have a positive impact on you.

C. Further Thoughts on Choosing the U.S. for Your LL.M. Degree

1. Make Certain That Your Goals and Expectations Are Reasonable!

Each international student who comes to the U.S. for an LL.M. degree does so for a different reason. You may have *multiple* reasons for studying law in the U.S. It is likely that no two students will have exactly the same reasons for pursuing this endeavor.

It is critical that you be sure that your goals are *reasonable*. If your goals are reasonable, your expectations will likewise be reasonable. Indeed, it is likely that only *reasonable expectations* will be met. Conversely, it is likely that *unreasonable* or *unrealistic expectations* will not be met.

Unfortunately, some U.S. law schools choose not to meet reasonable needs of international LL.M. students. Such schools are disappointments, which at times leads to decreased enrollments (because negative word about schools travels widely and swiftly), and causes faculty and staff to either leave the schools or

---

6. These notions harken to Kant's Enlightenment Era assertion that the "commercial spirit cannot co-exist with war," which I believe supports the notion that war is averted and peace is promoted through transnational exchanges of the sort occasioned by international LL.M. students at U.S. law schools. *See* Immanuel Kant, *Perpetual Peace: A Philosophical Essay,* trans. and ed. Mary Campbell Smith (Swan Sonnenschein and Co Lim, 1903) (1795) (quoted in Mark R. Shulman, *Making Progress — How Eric Bergsten and the Vis Moot Advance the Enterprise of Universal Peace* in S. Kröll, L.A. Mistelis, V. Rogers, and P. Perales Viscasillas (eds.), *Liber Amicorum Eric Bergsten. International Arbitration and International Commercial Law: Synergy, Convergence and Evolution* 2011) (manuscript on file with author).

resign from their LL.M. program responsibilities. But even if your U.S. school experience disappointed you, you may nevertheless use school, and non-school resources (including *LL.M. Roadmap*), to achieve reasonable and lofty aspirations. You may have post-LL.M. expectations of working as a lawyer for the UN, or becoming a judge or minister in your home country. Your goal may be to improve your legal English so you can better perform your current job, or to develop expertise in an area that you were not able to study in your first law course. Your goal may be to network with U.S. lawyers and law students, to find clients, to become a law professor, or to practice law on Wall Street.

All those goals *could* be reasonable. Any *could* be attainable. But each goal's attainment might require a different, distinct path. You must ensure you take the path that is most likely to lead to your goals. You must make many decisions, including which school to attend, which courses to take, which extra-curricular activities to join, or whether to write a thesis or take a U.S. bar exam. If you do not make prudent, realistic decisions, your perfectly reasonable expectations may not be met.

LL.M. Roadmap seeks to help you assess which of your goals are reasonable, and to advise on how to achieve those goals in and through a U.S. LL.M. program. If you follow steps in *LL.M. Roadmap*, including ensuring that your goals and expectations are reasonable, you may stand a better chance of meeting those goals. If you have unreasonable expectations, your expectations stand a good chance of being unmet.

2. Changing Your Mind *After* You Arrive in the U.S.

Your goals may change before you arrive in the U.S. or after you have been in classes for a while. You may change your mind about your LL.M. specialization, whether to write a thesis, whether you want to return home immediately post-LL.M. or work in the U.S. for a year or more, or whether to finish your LL.M. at your original U.S. school or try to transfer to another school. You may decide that you want to take a different path than what you had originally decided.

That is okay. Given your best-laid plan, prudence and experience counsel flexibility and imagination. You may change your mind about the best path to take.

It is not uncommon to arrive at a U.S. law school thinking you want to stay for the 9-month LL.M. program, get rejuvenated and refreshed, and return to your home country. Then your LL.M. classmates might share their plans with you, which might include applying for an S.J.D., working in the U.S. for a year, or sitting for the New York or California bar exam. U.S. professors might expose you to different opportunities — grants, fellowships, internships, employment prospects, and further graduate degree possibilities you hadn't thought of before. You might like these possibilities for yourself!

You will likely encounter these and a further wealth of ideas and opportunities waiting for you in the U.S. that you could not have known about before you arrived and immersed yourself in this new world. Good. Now you have a new set of prospects to consider and pursue. Be sure you adapt to this new path with the same deliberate, prudent, imaginative, yet realistic approach you learned from *LL.M. Roadmap* and other sound sources of advice and support.

LL.M. Roadmap explains ways to adapt to your new realities and new ideas. Though you may never have considered these opportunities before you arrived in the U.S., you might decide to explore them once you are here.

Keep an open mind!

Audace! Toujours audace!

CHAPTER SUMMARY

- You can choose from many countries for your LL.M. degree.

- There are many advantages to earning a U.S. LL.M. degree.

- Thousands of international students have received LL.M. degrees from more than 100 U.S. law schools.

- LL.M. graduates are presidents of countries, high-ranking UN officials, star athletes, and even a Grammy Award winning musician.

- Examine your personal and professional motivations before you apply.

- Are your goals reasonable? Unreasonable expectations will disappoint you.

- After arriving in the U.S., you may change your mind about your specialization, or whether to stay in the U.S. post-LL.M. to work, sit for a U.S. bar exam, or pursue an S.J.D.

- Keep an open mind! You have many options.

Chapter 3

Seven Types of LL.M. Programs

CHAPTER HIGHLIGHTS

- U.S. LL.M. programs do not fall into discrete categories; some of the categories overlap.
- Traditionally, international students traveled to a U.S. law school campus, enrolled in classes, took exams, perhaps wrote a thesis, remained on campus for one academic year, and received their degrees.
- Today LL.M. programs have multiple methods of delivering educational content, involving teaching and learning physically in the U.S., abroad, and through the Internet.
- Although you should get all of the sound advice and support you can, only you, ultimately, can decide which "type" of LL.M. degree program will work for you.
- If you wish to sit for the bar in a U.S. state, be careful to choose a type of LL.M. program that will satisfy any bar examination eligibility requirement that state may have.

A. Introduction

When U.S. law school LL.M. programs first admitted foreign-educated students decades ago, there were few distinctions among the types of programs. Some early LL.M. programs were *general*, some were *specialized*. (See Chapter 4.) Some were *course-based*, some were *research-based*. (See Chapter 15.) But generally, international students traveled to the U.S. law school campus, enrolled in traditional classroom courses, remained on campus for one academic year, wrote theses or other papers, and received their LL.M. degrees.

Today there are many differences among "types" of LL.M. programs, aside from whether they are general or specialized, course-based or research-based. This chapter describes and examines some of these differences, focusing on how LL.M. programs are structured, particularly where and how educational content is delivered.

There is no universal agreement as to how systematically to categorize today's LL.M. programs. Developing a comprehensive typology would prove necessarily elusive, in light of the depth and breadth of programs available; modern technology (which increases the range and flexibility of possible instruction models); schools' creativity in developing new ways to export U.S. legal education; and the increase in fiscal incentives to attract students.

LL.M. Roadmap seeks to share a variety of options available to international students interested in receiving an LL.M. degree from a U.S. law school. Inexact groupings of such LL.M. programs include traditional programs that require international students to travel to the U.S. and study on a U.S. law school campus, as well as programs that permit (or require) students to study on a campus overseas, or that permit (or require) students to study wholly or partially online.

There are many reasons why a prospective student might wish to choose one type of LL.M. program versus another. One very important point to consider is whether completion of the LL.M. program will render you eligible to sit for the bar examination in one of the U.S. states or territories. This topic is discussed more fully in Chapter 28.

Generally, one might divide LL.M. programs into the following overlapping categories:

(a) **Regular LL.M. programs** offered on law school campuses in the U.S.

(b) **Executive LL.M. programs** offered on law school campuses in the U.S.

(c) **Regular or Executive LL.M. programs** offered on law school campuses in the U.S., but with components of the program offered outside the U.S. (either on an overseas U.S. or overseas non-U.S. school campus)

(d) **Regular or Executive LL.M. programs** offered exclusively outside the U.S. (either on an overseas U.S. or overseas non-U.S. school campus)

(e) **Wholly online or wholly virtual LL.M. programs** (in which the student is not required to appear on campus for any purpose)

(f) **Partial online or partial virtual LL.M. programs** (in which the student may be required to appear on campus for some purposes)

(g) **LL.M. programs so creative that they do not fit any category above.**[1]

---

1. Some jest that each week it seems that U.S. law schools announce new LL.M. program types, or twists on old types, involving on- or off-campus creative course delivery options. Administrators involved in U.S. LL.M. programs routinely share information about new types of LL.M. programs and new ways to deliver content. Venues for these discussions include professional conferences, such as those held by the Association of American Law Schools (AALS). *Please check each U.S. law school for its most current LL.M. offerings!*

All U.S. law schools discussed in *LL.M. Roadmap* with LL.M. programs for international students are AALS members. On January 7, 2011, the AALS Section on Graduate Programs for Foreign Lawyers sponsored an AALS Annual Meeting panel titled *Exploring Alternative LL.M. Programs: Executive, Mixed Delivery and Dual/Multi-Degrees (Non-US and Cross-Discipline)*. Speakers included John Cooper, **Stetson University College of Law** (Dual US LL.M.-European Degrees and leveraging the Erasmus program/Bologna process); Cara Cunningham, **University of Detroit Mercy School of Law** (Tri-Degrees—NAFTA: USA-Canada-Mexico); Marc Mihaly, **Vermont Law School** (Joint Degrees of Institutional LL.M.-M.A. via online); Michael Perlin, **New York Law School** (Joint Degrees via mixed delivery); Dorsey D. Ellis, **Washington University in St Louis School of Law** (Dual US-European degrees); William Byrnes, **Thomas Jefferson School of Law** (Video-Conference and Mixed Programs; Global Foreign Degree Partnerships with multilanguage programming); Marshall Tracht, **New York Law School** (Moderator). Panelists explained how their institutions create and run "innovative" or "alternative" LL.M. programs.

U.S. Law Schools

B. Seven LL.M. Program Categories

1. Traditional, Residential LL.M. Programs Offered on Law School Campuses in the U.S.

In a traditional LL.M. program, the international student travels to the U.S. with a student visa and enrolls in classes taught on a law school campus. The program typically takes two semesters (9-10 months). Most international LL.M. students are enrolled in these residential programs. Students may have recently received their first law degrees in their home countries, they may have graduated a few years earlier, or they may be seasoned practitioners who are returning to school many years after receiving their first law degrees. The traditional program gives students maximum interaction with professors, other LL.M. students, and J.D. students. It also permits international LL.M. students to be exposed to U.S. culture, to network and develop personal bonds, and to gain a lifetime of memories of their year living and studying in the U.S.

2. Executive LL.M. Programs Offered on Law School Campuses in the U.S.

Executive LL.M. program students tend to be mid-career professionals with well-established jobs. These programs may require the same number of academic credits as a traditional, residential program, but the classes may be spread out (more than 9-10 months), or squeezed into concentrated, shorter periods.

For example, an executive program may require students to take "regular" classes only in the U.S. summer (June–August) and may require them to complete their degree in three years rather than one year. Students can work at their regular jobs (for 9-10 months) each year and be at school only for short periods. Or a program may require students to take "concentrated" classes squeezed into shorter periods (less than 9 months). This, too, would permit them to work full-time jobs with minimal absence.

While Executive students may have maximum exposure to professors and other LL.M. students in their program, they may have less exposure to LL.M. students not in the Executive program or J.D. students who may not be on campus during Executive LL.M. class session periods.

3. Regular or Executive LL.M. Programs Offered on Law School Campuses in the U.S., but with Program Components Outside the U.S. (Either on an Overseas U.S. Campus or at an Overseas Non-U.S. School Campus)

Some U.S. law schools have campuses overseas, or partnerships or other collaborations with overseas law faculties at which a U.S. and/or international

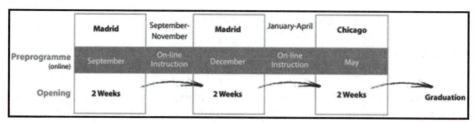

Source: Executive LL.M. program offered by IE Law School and Northwestern University School of Law.

student may earn credits toward a U.S. LL.M. degree. These students might primarily take courses on the campus in the U.S., and then take a few courses outside the U.S., or might take a considerable number of courses outside the U.S. Schools with such programs include **New York University School of Law** (Singapore), **Temple University Beasley School of Law** (Japan and China), **Loyola Law School Los Angeles** (Bologna, Italy), and **Northwestern University School of Law/IE Law School** (Madrid, Spain). Figure 3-1 illustrates the structure of the Executive LL.M. Program offered by **Northwestern** and **IE Law School**. Students may earn internship or externship credit overseas, or participate in summer study abroad programs affiliated with their own U.S. law school or another school.

4. Regular or Executive LL.M. Programs Offered Wholly Outside the U.S. (Either on Overseas U.S. Campus or Overseas Non-U.S. School Campus)

U.S. law schools are increasingly permitting students to receive U.S. LL.M. degrees without ever appearing on a law school campus in the U.S. Some of these programs permit students to take courses in the U.S., whereas other schools offer the degree program exclusively outside the U.S. The student would receive a U.S. LL.M. degree. Some schools offer this option for only international students, but other schools offer this option for U.S. students also.

In 2007 **New York University (NYU) School of Law** created a dual-degree program that permits students from the **National University of Singapore (NUS)** and NYU to complete two LL.M. degrees—one from each institution. Students take courses from NYU and NUS professors—in Singapore. Graduates may opt for a 10-week program at NYU in New York City on U.S. law practice. "[I]n September 2009, the New York State Court of Appeals granted NYU Law's petition to allow graduates of the program beginning with the class entering in May 2010, who complete the NYU LL.M. outside the U.S. and fulfill certain other requirements, to sit the New York Bar Exam." (Please check the websites of **NYU** and similar programs and the New York Board of Law Examiners for information about New York Bar Rules that took effect in May 2011. See also Chapter 28.) **Temple University, Washington University in St. Louis, Northwestern**, and other U.S. schools also permit international students to take LL.M. courses on campuses outside the U.S.

U.S. Law Schools

NYU's Executive LL.M. Part-Time Distance Education Program

1. Staff videotapes a class session and then posts the recording onto the course Blackboard site.
2. Professors make class videos available to students in traditional "live" sections and online sections.
3. The following semester, if the Professor does not teach the same course, the Blackboard site and videos are made available again. The Professor inspects the materials to ensure they reflect current law and are pedagogically sound.
4. Students in live sections and online sections take the same final exam and are graded on the same curve.

Source: www.law.nyu.edu/llmjsd/executivellmtax/curricularrequirements/index.htm

5. Wholly Online or Virtual LL.M. Programs (in Which the Student Is Not Required to Appear on Campus for Any Purpose)

For wholly online or virtual LL.M. programs, students do not need to physically appear on the U.S. campus to take classes, to take exams, or to graduate.[2] Classes are presented online, and students may "attend" the classes wherever in the world they have access to a computer with a high-speed Internet connection, microphone and speakers, and possibly a video camera connected to their computer and other technical configurations.

In some instances, lectures are in real time, with all students expected to be at their computers for presentations, irrespective of the country where the students are or their time zones. In other instances, lectures are recorded and made available for students to review at times convenient to them. Students may be required to communicate with the professor and classmates in online interactive discussion groups or in online postings, which some professors require even in regular classes where students physically appear on campus.

Such courses would be supported by a website similar to ones established for regular classroom courses. Professors can post assignments, handouts, and announcements, and students can upload papers and assignments. Students and faculty can communicate via message boards or blogs, and they can share documents created in Microsoft PowerPoint, Microsoft Word, WordPerfect, and other software.

---

2. I refer to online LL.M. programs, *not* online J.D. programs. According to the ABA, "no law schools that provide a J.D. degree completely via distance education are approved by the ABA" (www.abanet.org/legaled/distanceeducation/distance.html) (*citing* ABA Standard 206 on Distance Education).

Wholly online or virtual LL.M. programs[3] give students maximum flexibility. Students may attend classes from their homes, offices, or Internet cafes. On the other hand, students lose the benefit of in-person contact with professors and J.D. and LL.M. students. But they would still have face-to-face experience — virtual, anyway — at least for those programs where students are expected to be online at the same time.

6. Partial Online or Virtual LL.M. Programs (in Which the Student May Be Required to Appear on Campus for Some Purposes)

For partially online or virtual programs, students may take some courses or exams via the Internet but may be required to be on campus for some purposes, such as final exams or mini-courses.

7. LL.M. Programs That Do Not Fit into Any of the Above Categories

U.S. law schools constantly develop new types of LL.M. programs that defy easy categorization in any typology. Schools desire to accommodate and integrate many factors, including the often changing needs of international students seeking U.S. degrees; advancing technology permitting easy and effective content delivery; evolving legal community views on acceptability of degrees earned outside the traditional on-site, residential classroom setting; and the willingness of U.S. legal education and practice regulators to consider expanding the scope of study possibilities and innovative forms.

For additional information about new LL.M. program types for international students to earn U.S. LL.M. degrees, please check — or send new information to — *www.LLMRoadMap.com.* We will be happy to learn about any new LL.M. programs, or changes in existing programs, so please let us know.

---

3. **Thomas Jefferson**'s Associate Dean for Distance Education Programs William H. Byrnes IV pioneered online legal education in creating the first U.S. Internet-delivered LL.M. offered by an ABA-approved law school (www.tjsl.edu/directory/william-h-byrnes-iv).

CHAPTER SUMMARY

- It is not easy to categorize the types of LL.M. programs that exist.
- U.S. law schools continually find creative ways to deliver LL.M. content.
- Today, prospective students must ask many questions, including:
  - Am I required (or permitted) to spend time on the U.S. law school campus (and if so, how much time and when)?
  - Are courses offered on campuses outside the U.S.?
  - Can courses be taken online without leaving my home country?
  - Does the academic work lead to one or multiple LL.M. or other degrees?
- Technology will lead to even more interesting and effective ways for international students to earn U.S. LL.M. degrees.
- Online degrees may save money, but they are not the same as immersion on a real U.S. campus, with students and faculty for you to learn from and share with.
- Many different styles and profiles of LL.M. programs exist, and you must choose the best style and profile for yourself.
- If you want to sit for a U.S. bar exam, find out if bar authorities require completion of an LL.M. degree from a particular type of LL.M. program.

Chapter 4

General and Specialized LL.M. Degrees

CHAPTER HIGHLIGHTS

- You can choose a *general* LL.M. degree or a *specialized* LL.M. degree.
- Which degree you choose depends on what you seek to accomplish.
- When you choose a school that has a specialization, check to make sure that the specialized courses are being offered *during your semesters* at the school.
- Make certain that the school offers a sufficient number of specialized courses for you to satisfy specialization requirements.
- Make certain that the professors whose classes you want to take will be teaching those classes and will not be on sabbatical during your LL.M. program.
- In a general LL.M. program, you may be able to take enough "specialized" courses in a subject area to gain sufficient specialized knowledge and expertise.

A. Introduction — General and Specialized LL.M. Degrees

In the U.S., LL.M. degrees typically are either general or specialized, as follows:[1]

- A *general LL.M. degree* offers students a wide range of courses in many different areas of law, with *no* area of "specialization" or "concentration" noted on the diploma or transcript; or
- A *specialized LL.M. degree* focuses on a particular area of law, with the area of legal "specialization" or "concentration" typically noted on the diploma or transcript.

---

1. Some schools offer a "certificate" in a subject area to complement a student's LL.M. degree.

U.S. Law Schools

1. General LL.M. Degree

Many U.S. LL.M. programs that accept international students offer a general LL.M. degree, where students design their own curricula by choosing from a wide variety of courses in many areas, based on specific interests or career goals. The school may offer one or two mandatory courses for international LL.M. students, but otherwise you may select courses you want. Some schools permit you to take first year J.D. courses (such as torts, civil procedure, or contracts), whereas other schools permit you to take only advanced elective courses. A general LL.M. offers a cross-section, spanning the substantive spectrum, to help train you as generalists. You will not formally declare a "specialization," and no subject area specialization is indicated on your diploma or transcript.

In a general LL.M. program, you may choose courses primarily in a particular area, and gain deep insights into that area. For example, **Yale Law School**, **University of Hawaii School of Law**, **University of Miami School of Law**, and other schools offer general LL.M. degrees. But if you are particularly interested in an area, such as international law, you can take many international law courses, perhaps as many or more than international law courses offered in a typical specialized program. If you take a large number of the courses offered in a specific area you will gain substantive benefits similar to those you would gain with a "specialized" LL.M. degree, in this case, in international law. But your diploma or transcript will not list a specialization. You will have a general degree, despite the number of specialized courses taken. As explained below, a specialized LL.M. diploma will typically list the specialization as an "LL.M. Degree in International Law" (or in whatever the specialization is), and you would be able to list the specialization on your curriculum vitae (CV). If you want a specialization listed on your diploma or transcript, choose a specialized program. If you just want the knowledge and are not concerned about having a specialization listed on your diploma, you can choose a general degree and take specialized courses. On your CV you may list the specialized classes you took, which will give employers a sense of your exposure to those topics.

In **Hawaii**'s general LL.M. program students "are free to design their own course of study in consultation with the LL.M. Director. You may develop specialized expertise in one area of law or choose a more general course of study to give you a broad knowledge of fundamental U.S. and international legal principles" (p. 5 of brochure).

Miami notes that "[e]ach of our LL.M. students creates a course of study that matches his or her career goals" (p. 3 of brochure).

Yale notes that its "completely elective program has no formal specializations, but students are encouraged to create a course of study that reflects their particular background and interests. Advisers are available to assist in designing individual academic programs and exploring course options" (p. 1 of brochure).

If you are interested in a specialized area of law, *do not ignore schools that do not list that area as a specialization.* Check each school's catalogue for courses,

How Flexible Is a General LL.M.?

"*Flexibility* is the best word to describe **Temple Law School's** general studies LL.M. program. International lawyers have the freedom to design a course of study tailored to their interest and aspirations. With the exception of two required research and writing courses, students select from more than 180 courses offered annually in American and international law" (p. 2 of brochure) (italics in original).

professors, extracurricular activities, and campus and community events in that area. You may be able to take a wealth of specialized courses and gain in-depth knowledge at schools that offer no formal specializations.

2. Specialized LL.M. Degree

A specialized LL.M. degree focuses on a particular area of law in which you take a series of required courses. Specialized degrees permit you to gain expertise in a focused area, and to be exposed to and interact with interested professors and students. U.S. law schools on the whole offer dozens of LL.M. specializations, though many individual schools offer only one or two of them. Popular specializations include international law, intellectual property, international human rights law, and business law.

B. Are There Enough Specialized Courses to Fulfill the Degree Requirements?

Some schools do not offer enough specialized courses for you to satisfy course requirements. So, for example, if you choose an intellectual property (IP) law specialization, make certain the school offers enough IP law courses. Check before you enroll. Do not risk having to graduate with a general LL.M. rather than a specialized LL.M. If a school does not offer sufficient courses for you to complete your LL.M. specialization, it could be because the school is a cash cow and has not invested sufficient funds into the specialized area.

I learned of a European student enrolled in an LL.M. program with an IP specialization and the school had insufficient IP courses for him to satisfy the specialization. From the student's perspective, there was a bait and switch (i.e., false advertising). How disappointed would you be if you enrolled in a specialized LL.M. program and learned in your first semester that the school did not offer enough specialized courses and you could not complete the degree in the specialization?

For descriptions of LL.M. specializations offered at U.S. law schools, see Appendix I.

C. Are Courses Offered When You Are Enrolled?

Before you choose a school, be certain that professors will teach courses you want *during* your LL.M. year. Law schools warn that not all courses are offered every semester. A course you want — or need — may be offered only once every second year, or the professor who teaches it may be on sabbatical (or on leave) during your study year. This risk may be higher if your area is "highly specialized"; maybe only one faculty member teaches a given course. At schools with very large faculties, you should generally not have problems, as there should be enough professors to substitute for absent professors. Some schools with faculties that are not as large as others may offer sufficient specialized courses, for example **Vermont Law School**, which states on its website that it offers over 50 environmental law courses. Find out who the primary faculty members are in your area(s) of interest. If those professors are not available, you still might be able to have an excellent LL.M. experience taking other courses from other professors. But check — and check early.

For example, the **University of Houston Law Center** LL.M. Handbook (p. 8) warns that "Not all classes are offered every year, and offerings are subject to change. Please check the Law Center website for current course offering."

University of California, Davis, School of Law offers a Summer International Commercial Law LL.M. program. Their website indicates which of the "intensive courses with an international perspective" are offered in 2011, 2012, and 2013. Students can plan better because they know well in advance which courses are offered in which academic period.

D. LL.M. Specializations at U.S. Law Schools

Following is a list of LL.M. specializations[2] reported to be offered at one or more U.S. law schools that permit international law students to enroll and that list the name of the specialization on the student's diploma or transcript upon graduation. Descriptions of each of the specializations can be found in Appendix I, along with a list of job descriptions and the types of organizations in which LL.M. graduates with these specializations work.

---

2. Some schools use slightly different names for essentially the same specialization. For example, "International Law" at one school may be labeled "International Legal Studies" at another school. In those instances, I selected one name or I combined names for efficiency. In some instances where schools adopted significantly different names for essentially the same concentration, I included both names (e.g., "employment law" at one school may be "labor law" at another school, so I listed "employment law/labor law").

Concentration Course Availability

If a school offers a specialization, make sure the school offers enough specialized courses that interest you and that those courses will be offered during the 9-month period in which you will be enrolled. You do not want to be disappointed because the courses or professors you want or need are unavailable during your 9 months on campus.

This chapter was originally to have two additional lists: (a) a list of LL.M. specializations (or concentrations) in alphabetical order, and next to each specialization the name(s) of the U.S. law school(s) that offer that specialization; (b) a list of each U.S. law school in alphabetical order, and next to each school the name(s) of the specialization(s) offered by that school.

However, it proved difficult to compile an accurate, comprehensive, authoritative list for many reasons, including: schools occasionally add and remove specializations; some specializations "offered" by the schools and listed on school websites are dormant, with no students currently enrolled; some specializations are listed in school's promotional material, though the specializations are "suspended" with no determination as to when or if they will be reactivated; and some specializations "offered" by schools were created to bolster the school's image, with no committed intention to admit students to those specializations. Further, some schools informed me that they were in the process of developing an LL.M. program with specializations, but had not yet done so.

Please visit *www.LLMRoadmap.com* to find lists of schools and concentrations, and links to other lists. The websites of each specific school that interests you should be consulted. Again, before you enroll, ensure that the school has enough courses to permit you to satisfy course requirements for your specialization, and that the relevant professors will teach the courses when you are on campus.

Specializations That U.S. Law Schools List on Their Website or Otherwise Advertise as Offering

1. Administrative Law (Public Policy; Government Law)
2. Admiralty Law (Maritime Law, Coastal Law; Ocean Law)
3. Advanced Legal Studies (General LL.M.; As Approved)
4. Agriculture Law (Food Law)
5. American Business Law (Business Law; International Business Law; International Economic Law; International Trade Law; Trade Regulation)
6. American Law for Foreign Lawyers (Foreign Scholars Program; U.S. Law for Foreign Lawyers; U.S. Legal Studies)
7. As Approved (Advanced Legal Studies; General LL.M.)
8. Asian and Comparative Law (Comparative Law; Comparative Legal Thought)
9. Asylum Law (Immigration Law)
10. Banking Law
11. Bankruptcy Law
12. Biotechnology Law (Genetics Law; Genomics Law)
13. Business Law (American Business Law; Global Business; International Business Law; International Economic Law; International Trade Law; Trade Regulation)
14. Child Law (Family Law; Juvenile Law)
15. Civil Rights Law (Human Rights Law; International Human Rights Law)
16. Climate Change (Environmental Law; International Environmental Law; Oil & Gas Law; Natural Resources Law; Sustainable Development)
17. Coastal Law (Admiralty Law; Maritime Law; Ocean Law)
18. Communications Law (Telecommunications Law)
19. Comparative Law (Comparative Legal Thought; Asian and Comparative Law; International Law)
20. Comparative Legal Thought (Comparative Law; Asian and Comparative Law; International Law)
21. Corporate Finance Law (Corporate Law; Finance & Financial Services Law)
22. Corporate Law (Corporate Finance Law; Finance & Financial Services Law)
23. Criminal Law (Prosecutorial Science; International Criminal Law)
24. Democratic Governance Law (Rule of Law)
25. Development Law (Environmental Law; International Development Law; Land Development Law; Sustainable Development Law)
26. Dispute Resolution
27. Economics (Law and)
28. Education Law
29. Elder Law
30. Employee Benefits (Employment Law; Labor Law)
31. Employment Law (Employee Benefits; Labor Law)
32. Energy Law (Development Law; Environmental Law; Environmental Sustainability; Land Development Law; Natural Resources Law; Oil & Gas Law; Sustainable Development)
33. Entertainment (Media Law)
34. Entrepreneurship (Law and)
35. Environmental Law (Climate Change; Development Law; Environmental Sustainability; International Environmental Law; Land Development Law; Natural Resources Law; Oil & Gas Law; Sustainable Development)

U.S. Law Schools

36. Environmental Sustainability (Climate Change; Development Law; Environmental Law; International Environmental Law; Land Development Law; Natural Resources Law; Oil & Gas Law; Sustainable Development)
37. Estate Planning
38. Experiential Law Teaching (Teaching, Experiential Law)
39. Family Law (Child Law; Juvenile Law)
40. Finance & Financial Services Law (Corporate Finance Law; Corporate Law)
41. Food Law (Agricultural Law)
42. Foreign Relations Law of U.S. (Comparative Law; International Law; International Legal Studies)
43. Foreign Scholars Program (Advanced Legal Studies; American Law for Foreign Lawyers; As Approved; General LL.M.; U.S. Law for Foreign Lawyers; U.S. Legal Studies)
44. General LL.M. (Advanced Legal Studies; As Approved)
45. Genetics Law (Biotechnology Law; Genomics Law)
46. Genomics Law (Biotechnology Law; Genetics Law)
47. Global Business Law (American Business Law; Business Law; International Business Law; International Economic Law; International Trade Law; Trade Regulation)
48. Government Law (Administrative Law; Public Policy)
49. Health Care Law (Health Law)
50. Health Law (Health Care Law)
51. Human Rights Law (Civil Rights Law; International Human Rights Law)
52. Immigration Law (Asylum Law)
53. Indian Law (Indigenous Law; Tribal Policy, Law & Government)
54. Indigenous Law (Civil Rights Law; Human Rights Law; Indian Law; International Human Rights Law; Tribal Policy, Law & Government)
55. Information Technology Law
56. Insurance Law
57. Intellectual Property Law (IP Law)
58. Inter-American Law (Latin American Law)
59. International Business Law (American Business Law; Business Law; Global Law; International Economic Law; International Trade Law; Trade Regulation)
60. International Criminal Law (Criminal Law; Prosecutorial Science)
61. International Economic Law (American Business Law; Business Law, Global Law; International Business Law, International Economic Law; International Trade; Trade Regulation)
62. International Environmental Law (Climate Change; Environmental Law; Natural Resources Law; Sustainable Development)
63. International Human Rights Law (Civil Rights Law; Human Rights Law; Indigenous Law; Indian Law; International Law; Tribal Policy, Law & Government)
64. International Law (Comparative Law; International Human Rights Law; International Legal Studies; U.S. Foreign Relations Law)
65. International Legal Studies (Comparative Law; International Law; U.S. Foreign Relations Law)
66. International Tax Law (Tax Law)
67. International Trade Law (American Business Law; Business Law; Global Business Law; International Business Law; International Economic Law; Trade Regulation)

U.S. Law Schools

68. IP Law (Intellectual Property Law)
69. Judicial Process (Juridical Studies)
70. Juridical Studies (Judicial Process)
71. Jurisprudence (Legal Theory)
72. Juvenile Law (Child Law; Family Law)
73. Labor Law (Employee Benefits; Employment Law)
74. Land Development Law (Development Law; Environmental Law; Oil & Gas Law; Natural Resources Law)
75. Latin American Studies (Inter-American Law)
76. Legal Theory (Jurisprudence)
77. Litigation (Trial Advocacy)
78. Maritime Law (Admiralty Law, Ocean Law; Coastal Law)
79. Media Law (Entertainment Law)
80. Military Justice System (Military Law)
81. Military Law (Military Justice System)
82. National Security Law
83. Natural Resources Law (Climate Change; Energy Law; Environmental Law; International Environmental Law; Land Development Law; Oil and Gas Law; Sustainable Development Law)
84. Ocean Law (Admiralty Law, Coastal Law; Maritime Law)
85. Oil and Gas Law (Energy Law; Environmental Law; Natural Resources Law; Sustainable Development Law)
86. Prosecutorial Science (Criminal Law; International Criminal Law)
87. Public Policy (Administrative Law; Government Law)
88. Real Estate Law
89. Religion (Law and)
90. Research
91. Rule of Law (Democratic Governance)
92. Science / Technology (Law and)
93. Securities & Financial Regulation
94. Space Law
95. Sports Law
96. Sustainable Development Law (Climate Change; Development Law; Environmental Law; International Environmental Law; Land Development Law; Natural Resources Law; Oil and Gas Law)
97. Tax Law (International Tax Law)
98. Teaching, Experiential Law
99. Technology / Science (Law and)
100. Telecommunications Law (Communications Law)
101. Trade Regulation (American Business Law; Business Law; Global Business Law; International Business Law; International Economic Law; International Trade Law)
102. Trial Advocacy (Litigation)
103. Tribal Policy, Law & Government (Indian Law; Indigenous Law)
104. U.S. Foreign Relations Law (Comparative Law; International Law; International Legal Studies)
105. U.S. Law for Foreign Lawyers (American Law for Foreign Lawyers; Foreign Scholars Program; U.S. Legal Studies)
106. U.S. Legal Studies (American Law for Foreign Lawyers; Foreign Scholars Program U.S.; Law for Foreign Lawyers)
107. Urban Affairs Law (Urban Studies Law)
108. Urban Studies Law (Urban Affairs Law)

CHAPTER SUMMARY

- You can choose a general LL.M. degree or a specialized LL.M. degree.
- You may be able to accomplish your goals with either type of degree.
- Make sure specialized courses are offered while you are enrolled.
- Make certain the professors you want to take courses from will be on campus and will not be on sabbatical.
- In a general LL.M. program, you may be able to take enough specialized courses to give you expertise, but your degree will not list the specialization. You can list those specialized courses on your CV.
- Just because a school lists a particular specialization does not mean that the school is accepting students in that specialized track, that the school offers sufficient specialized courses, or that the school ever really intended to offer a legitimate track with that specialization. Research a school's track before you accept an offer to attend, and before you enroll.

U.S. Law Schools

Chapter 5

U.S. and Foreign Legal and Legal Education Systems

CHAPTER HIGHLIGHTS

- The U.S. legal system is complex but thousands of international students learn the system during their LL.M. year.
- You must learn about the U.S. legal system if you want to practice law in the U.S. or represent U.S. clients in your home country.
- The U.S. legal education system may be quite different from the legal education system in your home country.
- Although most international students in U.S. law schools study for the LL.M. degree only, some earn the J.D. (before or after their LL.M.), the S.J.D. (after their LL.M.), or one of various other law-related degrees.

A. Introduction

No matter which type of general or specialized LL.M. program you join in the U.S., you will be exposed to the structure of the U.S. government that serves as the backdrop to and foundation of the *U.S. legal system*, and you will be immersed in the *U.S. legal education system*. You should learn more than a little about these systems before you arrive. Compare and contrast them with the legal and education systems in your home country. In this small but necessary and meaningful way you will have gotten a head start on your LL.M. program in the U.S.

This chapter introduces (a) the U.S. governmental structure and the U.S. legal system (including incorporation of international law into U.S. law); (b) other legal systems of the world; (c) U.S. legal education; (d) legal education outside the U.S.; and (e) paths that international and U.S. students take to receive LL.M., S.J.D., J.D. and other law or law-related degrees.

U.S. Law Schools

B. The U.S. Governmental Structure and the U.S. Legal System

The U.S. is a constitutional democracy, with a legal system based on the U.S. Constitution. The Constitution created the three coequal branches of the U.S. government, and is the basis for the following relationships: (a) between the federal government and the people of the U.S.; (b) between U.S. states; (c) between the federal government and the states; and (d) between the U.S. and other countries. Every action by the U.S. government and its agents must comply with the U.S. Constitution.

The three U.S. government branches are: (1) the executive branch; (2) the legislative branch; and (3) the judicial branch. The three branches deal primarily with federal law that applies in every U.S. state and territory.

Executive branch. The executive branch includes the president, the vice president, the presidential cabinet (heads of federal departments), the military, and other nonjudicial, nonlegislative offices. The president appoints federal judges (who are part of the judicial branch), negotiates treaties (which are the "supreme law of the land"), and issues executive orders (which have the force of law).

Legislative branch. Article 1, Section 1 of the U.S. Constitution creates the two houses of Congress of the legislative branch: (a) the U.S. Senate; and (b) the U.S. House of Representatives. Congress enacts statutes that bind all individuals and entities subject to the jurisdiction of the U.S.

Judicial branch. The judicial branch is led by the U.S. Supreme Court, and includes appellate and district courts around the country. They interpret the U.S. Constitution and deal with rights guaranteed to citizens and others under U.S. law. The president appoints federal judges, who are in turn "confirmed" by the U.S. Senate.

Checks and balances. The three branches act as "checks and balances" over one another. Each branch can "check" each of the others. For example, the executive branch (the president) can "check" the legislative branch (Congress) by vetoing congressional legislation. Congress can impeach the president or federal judges. The judicial branch (federal judges) can declare federal statutes or executive orders unconstitutional.

State government versus federal government. Parallel to the federal branches are state branches: (a) the state executive branch; (b) the state legislative branch; and (c) the state judicial branch. The U.S. government is based on the system of federalism, where the national (federal) government imposes laws that govern across the country, and individual states impose laws that govern in those states but are not valid if they contradict federal law. Federal branches and state branches strike a balance between umbrella federal rules and localized state rules. These jurisdictions share some powers, and have some separate and exclusive powers.

The U.S. Constitution "trumps" federal statutory law, and all federal laws "trump" state law (including state constitutional law).

C. International Law Is Part of U.S. Law

International law governs relations between and among different nations, and between and among other international actors, including nongovernmental organizations, intergovernmental organizations (such as the UN), territories not recognized as nations, and individuals. It includes the law related to many different areas, including creating and enforcing UN treaties, armed conflict between countries, international human rights, international environment, space, the sea, international trade in goods and services, and many other areas. Though an international student may study international law when he or she is in the U.S., most international LL.M. students study more U.S. law than international law.

International law is part of U.S. law, and LL.M. students enrolled in U.S. law programs will likely be exposed to some aspects of international law. The U.S. Constitution provides that international treaties "shall be the supreme Law of the Land," and the U.S. Supreme Court has ruled that international law "is part of our law" and must be recognized by U.S. courts.[1] Furthermore, U.S. law should be interpreted to avoid violations of U.S. international law obligations arising under a treaty, customary international law, or other international law source.[2]

The U.S. strongly incorporates international law and international principles into the fabric of its legal tradition. Thus, international LL.M. students should know a good deal about the relationship between U.S. law and international law.

D. Legal Systems of the World

Though the legal systems of many countries are rooted in the common law, as is the legal system of the U.S., the U.S. legal system is marked by

---

1. The U.S. Constitution provides: "[A]ll Treaties made, or which shall be made, under the Authority of the United States, shall be the supreme Law of the Land; and the Judges in every state shall be bound thereby". (Article VI, cl. 2). The U.S. Supreme Court ruled: "International law, is part of our law, and must be ascertained and administered by the courts of justice of appropriate jurisdictions, as often as questions of right depending upon it are duly presented for their determination." (*The Paquete Habana*, 175 U.S. 677, 700 (1900)). The *American Law Institute, Restatement (Third) of the Foreign Relations Law of the United States* notes: "International law . . . of the United States [is] law of the United States and supreme over the law of the several States." (§111(1)).

2. *See, e.g., American Law Institute, Restatement (Third) of the Foreign Relations Law of the United States*, §§114-115. The "Charming Betsy Rule" was articulated in 1804. *See Murray v. The Schooner Charming Betsy*, 6 U.S. 64, 118 (1804) ("[A]n act of Congress ought never to be construed to violate the law of nations if any other possible construction remains.").

idiosyncrasies that lead U.S. LL.M. programs to require international LL.M. students to take one or more courses on the law of the U.S. These courses carry titles such as "American Legal System" or "Introduction to American Law."

This section of the chapter introduces you to the common law system, and to some of the other leading legal systems of the world, including the legal system that may operate in your country. You may learn more about these various legal systems in a comparative law course in your LL.M. program, or through discussion with your LL.M. classmates hailing from countries with different legal systems.

1. Common Law Systems[3]

Common law originated in England and spread through its colonies, including the 13 colonies that became the U.S. in 1776. The common law is a system for deciding judicial cases based on precedent; that is, based on rules or law and principles either enunciated in or interpreted and applied in cases that come before courts. When a court decides a case applying a particular principle in a particular way, inferior courts must follow that precedent. Much common law in the U.S. has been converted to statutory form, and can be found at both the state and federal levels. All U.S. states operate exclusively in the common law tradition, except for the state of Louisiana, which also incorporates civil or continental law, which is described below.

2. Continental or Civil Law Systems[4]

Continental law is based on codes promulgated by lawmakers. Judges interpret and apply the code, without being bound to follow the manner in which any previous judge interpreted and applied the code. There is no system of precedent, where courts are bound by previously decided cases, as exists in common law systems.

Continental law is also known as "code law," "Napoleonic Law," "Roman Law," or "in the French Tradition." Continental law is the most common type of legal system in the world.

Continental law systems are principally inquisitorial in nature, where judges participate in investigations and pose questions directly to witnesses at trial, unlike common law trials that are adversarial, where lawyers for the parties seek to prove the "truth" by examining and cross-examining witnesses and

---

3. Information about different legal systems was gathered from various sources, including JuriGlobe (University of Ottawa Faculty of Law) (www.juriglobe.ca/index.php).

4. Some refer to these law systems as "civil law systems." However, in the U.S., "civil law" refers principally to private law, as opposed to criminal law.

presenting evidence. In adversarial proceedings, the judge is meant to be impartial, and to act as an umpire as lawyers oppose each other, fighting for their clients.

3. Religious Law Systems

In countries that operate under religious law, religious rules and principles govern behavior of all persons and institutions within the country. Most countries with a type of religious law also incorporate aspects of civil, common, or customary law.

Rather than being based on membership in a church, temple, mosque, sect, or denomination, religious law generally governs based on territoriality — on affiliation or citizenship of the country concerned, or on the basis of a person living in or visiting that country.

4. Customary Law Systems

Customary law is based on long-term beliefs, policies, and practices in place that are recognized as controlling behavior within populations, particularly indigenous populations. These policies and practices are considered as law within the community or populations concerned.

5. Mixed Law Systems

The legal systems of many jurisdictions are mixed, in that they incorporate elements of two or more types of legal systems. For example, some states may incorporate aspects of both civil and common law, while others may incorporate a mix of common, civil, and customary law.

E. U.S. Legal Education and Law Degrees (LL.M., J.D., S.J.D., and others)

U.S. law schools are broad-based, and tend to teach students how to think like lawyers, rather than merely serve as trade schools. In addition to traditional doctrinal, theoretical courses, however, law schools are increasingly instructing students through clinical or experiential modes, where students get hands-on exposure to lawyering.

(1) *J.D. (Juris Doctor or Juris Doctorate).*   Unlike in many other countries, the U.S. offers no undergraduate law degree. The first available U.S. law degree is the Juris Doctor (or Juris Doctorate), which is a three-year degree considered as a "graduate degree." To enter a J.D. program, U.S. students ordinarily are required to hold an undergraduate B.A. or B.S. degree. (See Chapter 30.)

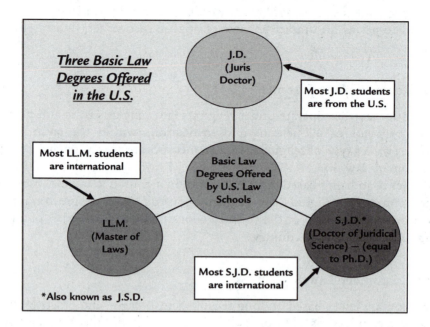

(2) *LL.M. (Master of Laws).*   A U.S. student would ordinarily complete a three-year J.D. before entering a one-year Master of Laws (LL.M.) program. The overwhelming majority of J.D. graduates do not proceed to the LL.M. or the S.J.D. (described below). One can practice law in any state with a J.D. (and by passing a bar examination). One can also be a judge or law professor with a J.D. Fewer than 1 percent of all J.D. holders in the U.S. proceed to the LL.M. Even fewer proceed to the S.J.D. Law jobs in the U.S. typically do not require more than a J.D.

(3) *S.J.D. or J.S.D. (Doctor of Juridical Science or Doctor of the Science of the Law).*   The Doctor of Juridical Science (S.J.D. or J.S.D.) is the terminal degree in law offered at U.S. law schools. It is considered by some to be equivalent to the Ph.D. offered at schools outside the U.S., and tends to be sought by students interested in pursuing careers in law teaching, research, or another scholarly endeavor. (See Chapter 29.)

(4) *Other U.S. law or law-related degrees.*   Some law schools, and other faculties, offer law or law-related degrees other than the J.D., LL.M., and S.J.D. These include a Ph.D. in law, and various other master's degrees (such as the Master in Comparative Law). (See Chapter 30.)

F. Legal Education Outside the U.S. — Generally

Non-U.S. legal education receives little attention in *LL.M. Roadmap*. You are likely familiar with legal education in your own country. It is worth noting, however, that legal education differs in different legal systems — and even within a single legal system. For example, in some common law countries law is an undergraduate or first degree (B.A. or LL.B.), whereas in other common law countries it is a graduate or second degree (as in the U.S.). Some jurisdictions require five years of study for a law degree, and others require only three or four years.

U.S. law schools *will not* accept every overseas law degree. For example, some U.S. LL.M. programs will not accept a Sharia law degree or certain three-year overseas law degrees.

G. Legal Education Outside the U.S. — The Legal Education Reform Index (22 Factors in 6 Categories)

The American Bar Association (ABA) and others concluded that a high-quality legal education is critical in producing legal professionals capable of fostering the rule of law in "emerging democracies" and "transitioning states." The ABA Rule of Law Initiative (ABA-ROLI) found that the rule of law suffers in countries where law faculties do not rise to high levels and do not produce lawyers capable of effectively establishing or sustaining the rule of law. It is difficult for poorly functioning law schools to produce highly qualified legal practitioners.

The ABA-ROLI developed the *Legal Education Reform Index (LERI)* to gauge whether legal education in selected transition countries reflects internationally established principles.[5] The *LERI* consists of 22 factors to analyze legal education-related laws and practices in select countries, and is drawn from legal education standards developed by many entities, including the ABA, the Commonwealth of Independent States, the Council of the Bars and Law Societies of Europe, the Council of Europe, the EU, the Organization for Security and Cooperation in Europe, and the UN.

If your country's legal education lacks a significant number of the internationally recognized 22 factors listed below, you may find a compelling need to supplement your law degree earned in your home country with an LL.M. from a U.S. law school. You can instructively use these 22 factors to question and gauge the level of legal education in your home country.

These 22 factors (summarized and in 6 categories) are:

(1) *Licensing and accreditation.* Are your country's law faculties authorized by a governmental body or professional association of lawyers; sanctioned using clearly defined, acceptable, and rigorous standards

---

5. www.abanet.org/rol/publications/legal_education_reform_index_factors.shtml

with external evaluations; transparent, uniform, and internationally accepted quality-wise; and periodically reviewed using fair standards?

(2) *Admission policies and requirements.*   Do law schools in your country have admission by fair, rigorous, and transparent exams and uniform standards employed in a nondiscriminatory fashion, with measures to increase representation of disadvantaged or underrepresented groups?

(3) *Institutional holdings and capacities.*   In your country's law schools, do students and faculty have adequate and appropriate legal materials, physical facilities, and technological capacities with reasonable class sizes and appropriate administration and staff support?

(4) *Faculty qualifications, promotion and tenure, compensation, and academic freedom.*   Do your country's law schools have competent and qualified law teachers, with rigorous, fair, uniform, and transparent criteria for hiring, review, promotion and tenure, compensation, and academic freedom?

(5) *Curriculum and teaching methodology.*   Do law schools in your country have clearly articulated educational goals; comprehensive curricula; instruction in ethics and codes of conduct; instruction in professional skills, including problem solving, legal research and writing, advocacy skills, and client relations; and teaching methods that develop and encourage critical thinking, problem solving, and analytical reasoning?

(6) *Student evaluation/examination, awarding of degrees, and recognition of qualifications.*   Do law schools in your country have student performance and achievement assessed by fair, uniform, and stringent examinations or other objective and reliable assessment techniques; award appropriate degrees; and participate in national, regional, and international quality assurance and recognition networks?

H. Paths to Three Basic U.S. Law Degrees — J.D., LL.M., and S.J.D.

The following schematic illustrates different paths to U.S. law degrees by students with a U.S. or overseas legal education. The categories are: (a) wholly educated in the U.S.; (b) wholly educated outside the U.S.; (c) educated outside the U.S., with an LL.M. and possibly a S.J.D. or J.D. in the U.S.; and (d) educated outside the U.S. with a J.D. in the U.S. and then possibly an LL.M. and a S.J.D. in the U.S. (See also Chapters 29 and 30.)

U.S. Law Schools

(1) Path for students educated wholly in the U.S.

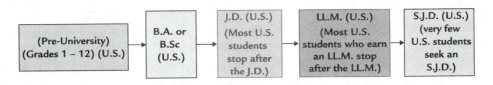

(2) Path for students educated wholly outside U.S.

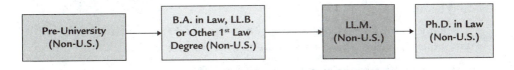

(3) Path for international students who come to the U.S. to receive an LL.M.—They can choose a J.D. or an S.J.D. in the U.S. after they receive an LL.M. in the U.S. They can also choose a Ph.D. in Law in their home country or a third country after their U.S. LL.M.

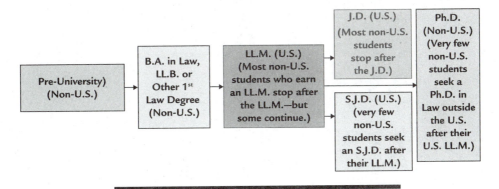

(4) Path for international students who come to the U.S. to receive a J.D.—They can choose an LL.M. in the U.S. and stop, or choose an LL.M. in the U.S. followed by an S.J.D. in the U.S. After their U.S. LL.M., they could also choose a Ph.D. outside the U.S., either in their own country or a third country.

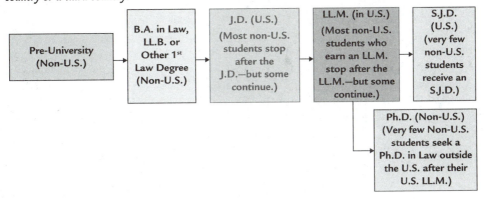

CHAPTER SUMMARY

- Although the U.S. legal system may at first appear to be complicated, it is not so different from many legal systems around the world.

- Learning how U.S. law schools operate is critical for international LL.M. students — you must know who the actors are and their responsibilities.

- Before you arrive in the U.S., learn as much as possible about the U.S. legal system and U.S. legal education. It will help you adjust to the U.S. and to your U.S. law school. It will also help you succeed in your U.S. law degree program and beyond.

- There are many different paths through the legal education systems in the U.S. and other countries. Choose the route that works best for you.

Part II

Ranking, Reputation, and Reality

218 Criteria for Choosing the "Best" U.S. LL.M. Program for You

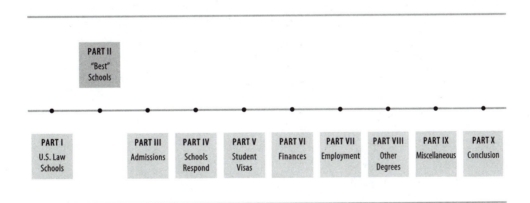

Chapter 6

Law School Ranking and Reputation

Choosing the "Best" U.S. Law School for You (and Avoiding Cash Cows and Diploma Mills)

CHAPTER HIGHLIGHTS

- Despite warnings of the hazards associated with ranking and reputation, prospective LL.M. students often consider ranking and reputation in choosing the law school and LL.M. program that they deem to be "best" for them.

- There are many factors to consider when you think about rank and reputation — and whether you should even consider them as you decide about schools.

- The rank and reputation of the program *are not important if that program will not help you reach your goals*.

- If you think rank and reputation are important — which many students, graduates, and employers do — make sure you understand how those terms are defined, and how they are measured by different players.

A. Choosing the "Best" U.S. Law School — Ranking and Reputation

International students seeking an LL.M. often say they want to attend the "best U.S. law school." Some want to go to the "highest ranked" school that accepts them, the school with the "best reputation," or a "top 10" or "top 50" school.

But what is the "best U.S. law school," the "highest ranked" school, or the school with the "best reputation"? Even if you easily identify the best, highest ranked, or best reputed school, is that school really the "best" choice *for you*? Should you be considering factors other than rank or reputation?

In short, I think it is better *not* to focus on the *"best law school,"* but to focus on the "best law school *for you."*

The "best" law school *for you* may not be the "best" law school for another student. The "best" law school *for you* may not be the highest ranked with the best reputation. It may not be the most prestigious, the most popular, or the most famous. The best school *for you* may not be in your favorite city or even favorite U.S. geographical region. The best school *for you* may not have the fanciest advertising campaign, the flashiest website, the most professors or graduates who recruit prospective students in your home country, or the largest LL.M. scholarships.

Among the over 100 U.S. law schools with LL.M. programs, there is likely *a perfect law school for you*. You must identify that school, apply, get accepted, and enroll!

B. What School Suits Your Academic, Career, Personal, and Financial Needs?

You have educational, personal, professional, geographical, and other needs. What factors about a law school (and its LL.M. program) are most important to you? Are you concerned about the law school's name; whether it is attached to a prestigious university; whether it has famous alumni; whether it has a career office to help LL.M. students find legal jobs; whether it has good sports teams or fraternities; whether it has excellent professors and students; whether it permits LL.M. students to work on law journals; whether it offers your chosen specialization; whether it has a diverse student body; whether it permits LL.M. students to do pro bono legal work for poor clients; or whether it offers overseas internships for LL.M. students? Not all U.S. law schools, and their LL.M. programs, are equal. In Chapter 7 you can learn about factors you might want to consider in choosing where you will receive your LL.M. degree. In that chapter I identified 218 criteria, in 26 different categories, for you to think about before you pick a school.

Many of these factors may be important to you, but one factor may not be as important to you as another. They may all have different levels of importance to different students. When choosing a school, you must set priorities, assess, make decisions, and then take action to begin your quest for a solid U.S. legal education.

C. What Is the Best LL.M. Program in Mountain Law? Or Agricultural Law? Or Energy Law?

Have you ever heard of *mountain law*? If so, and you wanted to receive a graduate degree in that esoteric legal area, which school would you choose? Which LL.M. program in mountain law is "best" for you?

I did not find a U.S. law school that offers a mountain law LL.M. But I found schools that offer courses in natural resources, human rights law, and law and development — all of which relate to mountain law. Will one of those schools fit your needs? Or would you need to find a school in another country that offers a mountain law LL.M. degree? There are many factors you will need to consider as you choose the "best" LL.M. for you, and the program that is "best" for you may or may not possess the name that you might expect it to be called.

What if you want an LL.M. in *food and agricultural law*? There is a U.S. school that offers such a degree — the **University of Arkansas**.[1] Is that school the "best" school for you because it is the only school with your explicit specialization — food and agricultural law? Or would you choose another school that has no food and agricultural law specialization but offers a few or many related courses, in another bigger or smaller city or state, with different sized classes, with higher or lower tuition, with more or fewer international students from your country? *How do you decide?*

D. Law School Rankings and Reputation — The "Best"

No objective measures exist to rank LL.M. programs, or to measure their relative competitiveness or academic rigor.[2] No comprehensive U.S. LL.M. exam tests how competently graduates practice law, and no statistics are compiled of the merit or academic achievements of LL.M. applicants at U.S. schools. Any existing ranking information is at best imprecise, and any reputation (positive or negative) enjoyed by LL.M. programs is anecdotal.

Nevertheless, applicants, students, graduates, employers, and others want to know which LL.M. programs are the "best" or the "highest ranked."

Does "best" mean that the school is ranked #1 in the U.S., or that the school has the best reputation? What does it mean to be ranked #1 or to have the best reputation? What does it mean to be in the "top 10" or "top 50"?

Should ranking or reputation matter? If so, should it be the ranking or reputation of the law school itself, of the specific LL.M. program, or of the university of which the law school and LL.M. program are part? Should you choose a school that has a high ranking over a school where you will thrive — where you

---

1. "The University of Arkansas School of Law offers the only advanced legal degree program in agricultural and food law in the United States, with a curriculum specializing in the law of food and agriculture" (http://law.uark.edu/prospective/llm-program.html).

2. Professors Carole Silver and Mayer Freed note that "[a]s a result of the difficulty of assessing LL.M. students based on their educational program alone, both LL.M. graduates and prospective employers rely on bar passage to provide an evaluative assessment of the LL.M. experience." Silver & Freed, *Translating the U.S. LL.M. Experience: The Need for a Comprehensive Examination*, 101 Nw. U. L. Rev. Colloquy 23 (2006) (www.law.northwestern.edu/lawreview/colloquy/2006/3). Professors Silver and Freed propose "the creation of a new examination for LL.M. graduates, an alternative comprehensive exam of U.S. law ('CEUSL'). Substantively, the CEUSL will address areas of U.S. law relevant to foreign lawyers." *Id.*

Ranking versus Reputation — Definitions

Can a highly ranked school have a bad reputation and a lower ranked school have a good reputation?

RANKING.   The hierarchical ordering or rating of schools in comparison to each other based on performance or some other rating system. If all LL.M. programs were ranked, each program would have a number corresponding to its position on the list, with the highest ranked at the top (or first) and the lowest ranked at the bottom (or last) on the list. *There are no official ranking systems for U.S. law schools or LL.M. programs.*

REPUTATION.   The level of regard with which a program is viewed. Programs with a favorable or positive reputation are viewed with high regard, and programs with an unfavorable or negative reputation are viewed with low regard. Schools may have a general "bad," "good," or "excellent" reputation, and so on. Or they may have a good reputation in one area (e.g., for having high-quality professors) but a poor reputation in another area (e.g., for not adequately helping students and graduates find jobs).

can *best* achieve your academic, personal, professional, and career goals? Again, you must decide what is "best" for you. What is "best" for you may not be "best" for another student. This applies to rank and reputation.

Is it reasonable to want the "best" (ranking-wise and reputation-wise) when choosing a cell phone, TV, or another high-priced item to purchase? What enters into our mind when we are making such purchases? What influences our decisions? In addition to our most obvious and immediately evident desires, do we also look at our own personal needs and resources before we buy? There are many criteria to consider when choosing a car, laptop, or LL.M. program. Ranking or reputation should be only part of the equation.

Are My Expectations About U.S. Law Schools Reasonable?

(1) Choose the school that suits *you.*
(2) Make certain *you have reasonable expectations* about the school you choose to apply to and strive to attend.
(3) Determine if you believe the school is able and willing to meet your *reasonable expectations.*
(4) You may have a bad law school experience if you do not have *reasonable expectations.*
(5) You may have a bad law school experience if your school is unable or unwilling to meet your *reasonable expectations.*

1. Ranking Versus Reputation

Although ranking and reputation, when spoken of, often go hand in hand as if they are similar and related, in fact they are quite separate and distinct.

Ranking, in theory at least, is based on systematic, methodical surveys that use objective criteria to determine how schools or programs fit into a quantifiable numerical hierarchy. The concept of ranking may be criticized for many reasons, including disagreement as to the criteria used to rank, the selection of the categories chosen to rank, methods used for measuring quality, and the opportunities to manipulate data surveyed in the ranking process.

Reputation, on the other hand, is more of a sense of how good or bad a school is perceived to be, how desirable or undesirable, or generally what people think about either the school itself or about the school as compared to one or more other schools.

A school may be ranked #1 (at the top) but may have a negative reputation. Likewise, it may be ranked near the bottom, but have an excellent reputation.

2. ABA Accreditation of U.S. Law Programs

The Juris Doctor (J.D.) degree is the first professional law degree in the U.S., and is the only degree the ABA accredits.[3] Currently 200 "ABA-approved" J.D. programs exist.

Neither the ABA nor any governmental or professional agency in the U.S. accredits LL.M., S.J.D., or any other "post-J.D." or "graduate" law degree program. The ABA notes that LL.M. and similar programs are created by the law schools themselves and do not reflect any ABA judgment regarding the quality of the programs. The ABA does not evaluate LL.M. admission requirements, particularly for international students, and particularly because admission requirements vary from school to school.[4]

The ABA notes that it "reviews post-JD degree programs [like the LL.M. or S.J.D.] only to determine whether the offering of such post-JD program would have an adverse impact on the law school's ability to maintain its accreditation for the JD program. If no adverse impact is indicated, the ABA 'acquiesces' in the law school's decision to offer the non-JD program and degree."[5]

---

3. Since 1952, J.D. programs in the U.S. have been subject to accreditation by the ABA Council of the Section of Legal Education and Admissions to the Bar. Although "the Council" and not "the ABA" regulates J.D. programs, the term "ABA" is often used in accreditation discussions. ABA-approved J.D. programs must pass a rigorous process that may take years to complete, and after approval are inspected every seven years (www.americanbar.org/groups/legal_education/resources/accreditation.html). However, Chapter 28 discusses a 2011 ABA proposal that considers the possibility of L.L.M. program certification by the ABA. J.D. programs in the U.S. are offered at law schools, and law schools that offer Council/ABA accredited J.D. programs are often referred to as "ABA-approved" or "ABA-accredited" schools, again, even though it is the J.D. program, *and not the school*, that is accredited. To re-emphasize, the ABA does not accredit LL.M. programs and does not even accredit schools; *only J.D. programs are accredited.*

4. www.americanbar.org/groups/legal_education

5. www.americanbar.org/groups/legal_education/resources/post_j_d_non_j_d.html

"Best" Schools

All the U.S. LL.M. and S.J.D. programs examined in *LL.M. Roadmap* are offered at one of the 200 law schools with ABA-approved J.D. programs.[6] *LL.M. Roadmap* does not pass judgment on degrees offered by or at law schools that offer the J.D. but whose J.D. programs are not ABA-approved.

3. No Official Law School Rankings

The ABA does not rank law schools, and neither does the Association of American Law Schools (AALS), nor does any other bar or official law organization in the U.S. None of these groups ranks J.D. programs, LL.M. programs, or any other programs at U.S. law schools.

Schools do not rank themselves officially (although some schools implicitly tout their subjective superiority). Indeed, there are no official rankings of any U.S. law school or any U.S. law degree program.

Websites and other sources that purport to "rank" law schools, choose a certain number of characteristics about schools and assign scores to each ranked characteristic, identify people to query about those characteristics, solicit responses from those queried, tally the scores, and then compile results in a "rank" order. Characteristics reviewed include faculty–student ratio, entering class GPA and LSAT score, amount of money spent per student, law school diversity, and breadth of classes. People chosen to be surveyed may include current students or graduates of law schools, but not necessarily of the law schools about which those students and graduates are being questioned.

U.S. News and World Report "ranks" law schools and their J.D. programs generally, but not LL.M. programs. Even if these law school rankings were valid, which many people, within and outside the field dispute, there is no guarantee that a highly ranked law school would have an LL.M. program that was as highly ranked. Indeed, some would argue that there is not necessarily a correlation between the quality of a law school (and its J.D. program) and the quality of its LL.M. program and of its specialized tracks.[7] Although J.D. programs and LL.M. programs are linked, they are distinct degree programs that the ABA demands be to some extent treated separately. Schools with relatively low rankings tend to denounce the results, whereas schools that rate more favorably tend to trumpet their rank.

---

6. The LL.M. is offered by at least one U.S. non-law school—The Fletcher School of Law and Diplomacy at Tufts University. It has no ABA-accredited J.D. program.

7. U.S. News and World Report does "rank" some specializations within J.D. programs. Some argue that if a specialization within a school's J.D. program is highly ranked, chances are that the LL.M. at that school in the same field is or should be highly ranked as well. They argue that even if you discredit rankings, you can draw an inference about a specialized LL.M. from information about the J.D. in that same area.

American Bar Association (ABA) Statement on Law School Ranking. In a press release dated March 9, 2011, the ABA reiterated its policy on not recognizing law school rankings.

> Neither the American Bar Association nor its Section of Legal Education and Admissions to the Bar endorses, cooperates with, or provides data to any law school ranking system. Several organizations rank or rate law schools; however, the ABA provides only a statement of accreditation status. No ranking or rating system of law schools is attempted or advocated by the ABA.[8]

Association for American Law School (AALS) Statement on Law School Ranking. The AALS adopted the following statement in 1990, but in 2011 noted that "it remains relevant today."

> Although we have not had the opportunity to review the U.S. News and World Report article, we believe that any ranking or rating of law schools, based upon the data the magazine has asked deans to provide, must be meaningless or grossly misleading. The survey does not, and could not, measure many important factors involved in evaluating the quality of law schools. Statistics cannot reflect such factors as the quality of faculty, curricular offerings, adequacy of library resources, and quality of life. Most importantly, the U.S. News and World Report ranking or rating is, in significant part, based on responses of legal educators, judges, practicing lawyers, and others who could not possibly know enough about each of the 175 ABA accredited law schools to rank or rate the law schools by quality quartiles. This survey is designed more to sell magazines than to inform the public about the relative merit of law schools.[9]

4. Law School Reputation

"Reputation" is not a ranking or rating scheme, and is based on impressions or feelings. What impressions do practitioners in your field have about your school or LL.M. degree program? Do they think highly of it? Do they think it is sufficiently rigorous and challenging? Do they think it produces good lawyers?

If you want to consider a school's reputation, you may want to consider opinions of many individuals and groups, based on your goals. If you are interested only in acquiring knowledge in an LL.M., then perhaps only your own personal opinion of the school is important. If you want to try to impress a particular prospective employer, you might want to choose a school that the employer holds in high regard. If you want to work in a particular field or city, look for a school that is highly regarded by prospective employers in that field or city.

---

8. www.abanow.org/2011/03/aba-statement-on-law-school-rankings. It continued: "Prospective law students should consider a variety of factors in making their choice among schools." *Id.*

9. www.aals.org/about_handbook_sgp_ran.php. This statement was adopted by the AALS, the ABA Section of Legal Education and Admissions to the Bar, the Law School Admission Council, and the National Association of Law Placement. *Id.*

"Best" Schools

Ranking Websites and Related Information (in alphabetical order)

- *100 Most Popular Law Schools 2010 in the U.S.A.* — LLM-Guide (www. llm-guide.com/most-popular/usa)
- *Go To Schools, The* — National Law Journal (NLJ) list of law schools with the highest percentages of J.D. graduates hired by NLJ 250 firms (www.law.com/jsp/ nlj/PubArticleNLJ.jsp?id=1202443758843&slreturn=1&hbxlogin=1)
- *Interplay between Law School Rankings, Reputations, and Resource Allocation: Ways Rankings Mislead, The,* by Jeffrey Evan Stake — Indiana Law Journal, Symposium on the Next Generation of Law School Rankings, Vol. 81, p. 229 (2006) (http:// papers.ssrn.com/sol3/papers.cfm?abstract_id=700862##)
- *Judging the Law Schools,* by Thomas E. Brennan — Internet Legal Research Group (ILRG) rankings by such factors as faculty, library, diversity, salary, value, tuition, employment, and student services (www.ilrg.com/rankings/index.html)
- *Leiter's Law School Rankings,* by Brian Leiter (U. of Chicago) — Rankings by such factors as "quality" of faculty and students, scholarly impact, U.S. Supreme Court clerkships, and where law faculty went to school (www.leiterrankings.com)
- *Princeton Review's "The Best 172 Law Schools"* — Eleven ranking lists based on a survey of more than 18,000 students at 172 law schools, and data collected from school administrators (www.princetonreview.com/law-school-rankings.aspx)
- *Ranking Game, The,* by Jeffrey E. Stake and Indiana University School of Law– Bloomington (http://monoborg.law.indiana.edu/LawRank/index.html)
- *US News and World Report* — "Best Graduate Schools: Law Specialties" — Rankings in the following areas: clinical training; dispute resolution; environmental law; healthcare law; intellectual property law; international law; legal writing; part-time law; tax law; and trial advocacy (http://grad-schools.us-news.rankingsandreviews.com/best-graduate-schools/top-law-schools)
- *US News and World Report* — "Best Law Schools Ranked in 2011" — Ranking "top" law schools, based on a survey of 184 accredited programs (http://grad-schools.usnews.rankingsandreviews.com/best-graduate-schools/top-law-schools/law-rankings) (For links to websites of the "top" 100 in this survey and other ranking information see http://www.llminsider.com/BeforeTheLLM/ LLMRankingsLawSchoolsRankings)
- *Vault Top 25 Law Schools* — Ranking based on interviews of 400 law firm employers, hiring personnel, and others on topics such as law graduate research and writing skills; knowledge of legal doctrine; and possession of other relevant knowledge (www.vault.com/wps/portal/usa/education/law-ranking)

5. Reputation Considerations

Choosing a school or LL.M. program based *only* on its "reputation" would be contrary to the considered depth and nuance *LL.M. Roadmap* offers as

American Bar Association Statement on Law School Rating or Ranking

No rating of law schools beyond the simple statement of their accreditation status is attempted or advocated by the official organizations in legal education. Qualities that make one kind of school good for one student may not be as important to another. The American Bar Association and its Section of Legal Education and Admissions to the Bar have issued disclaimers of any law school rating system. Prospective law students should consider a variety of factors in making their choice among schools.

Source: "ABA Standards and Rules of Procedure of Approval for Law Schools 2010-2011," Council Statement 5, at 145, www.americanbar.org/content/dam/aba/migrated/ legaled/accreditation/Council_Statements.authcheckdam.pdf.

a guide for comprehensive inquiry. But on the other hand, reputation matters — it is a valuable, recognized currency in the real world; ignoring reputation altogether may not be advisable. That said, you might want to consider "reputation" according to the following categories, depending on your goals.

a. Reputation of the LL.M. Program in the U.S.

Some schools are well known (and well regarded) in the U.S., but not well known outside the U.S. If you plan to remain in the U.S., you might consider choosing such a school, even if the school is not well known internationally.

b. Reputation of the LL.M. Program in the School's City, State, and/or Region.

Many U.S. schools have great reputations in their states and home cities, but are not known well nationally or internationally. Should you join an LL.M. program at such a regional school? It depends. Does the school offer the concentration you want, in the academic or geographical environment that suits you, for a price you can afford? Do LL.M. graduates of that school have the sort of job that you want? Do you plan to stay in that city or state, take the bar exam in that state, and try to practice law there?

c. Reputation of the LL.M. Program in Your Home Country.

If the U.S. school has a good reputation in your home country, and you plan to return to your home country to work — great. Before you enroll in an LL.M. program, find out which lawyers in your country have U.S. degrees, and which schools they attended. If many graduated from a particular U.S. law school, why not apply? You can check listings in *Martindale-Hubbell*, *Lexis*, or *Westlaw* (and find out names of lawyers in your country you might want to meet, seek LL.M. program advice and assistance from, network with, and seek a job from).

d. Reputation of the LL.M. Program in the Subject Area Where You Will Work.

Some schools are well known for some fields, but less known for others. For example, say several schools have good reputations in their international trade law concentration, but only marginal reputations, or no reputations, in some other area of law. Should you be concerned about the other tracks if your international trade reputational demands are met? Maybe. Maybe not. No one can decide for you. But posing and answering questions such as this yourself could make all the difference between an ill-chosen and a well-chosen education and career path.

e. Reputation of the LL.M. Program Among Its Graduates.

Does your school help you contact graduates to ask their opinions? Do graduates post messages on LL.M. student or LL.M. graduate blogs? If graduates generally have negative feelings about your school, *beware*. Of course, you must assess the credibility of the person making the comments. Just as a person who had a negative experience may write negative things about the school, a person who had a positive experience may have very positive things to say. But, what if the "negative experience" was that the person perhaps received a low exam grade or the person's thesis was rejected because the person did not work hard? What if the "positive experience" was that the person received excellent grades in a school that gives virtually all LL.M. students excellent grades? Try to glean and grasp the context in which graduates make positive or negative comments about an LL.M. program, and understand that their reactions are opinions: They are necessarily subjective and, given the context, limited. You can't possibly know, from where you sit and imagine, their whole story, the full experience and implications, claimed and omitted.

f. Reputation of the LL.M. Program Throughout the World.

Some schools have a positive global reputation. If reputation is important to you and you want to attend one of these schools, that is great — so long as the school offers the concentration you want, you can afford that school, and that school accepts you. If a school has a great global reputation, but will not meet your concentration or other academic or career needs, would that be the "best" school for you?

g. Reputation of the LL.M. Program in Your Mind.

What thoughts come to mind when you think of the school? Did you know anything about the school before you started researching LL.M. programs in the U.S.? Do you have positive feelings about the school based on

"Best" Schools

what you have heard from people you trust? Ultimately, you are the one who will choose a school, attend it, graduate from it, and live as part of that school's family forever. Will you likely have positive feelings about the school many years later?

h. Reputation, Ranking, and LL.M. Student Recruiting.

Some U.S. LL.M. programs devote significant financial and other resources to extensive, elaborate advertising campaigns to attract international students. Their websites, brochures, and other promotional materials may be flashy, with dozens of bright photos of smiling international LL.M. students having wonderful experiences. Other U.S. LL.M. programs expend virtually no resources for such advertising, and have stark websites without flashy graphics. Should you choose a school that has extensive advertising versus a school that has virtually no advertising? Is extensive advertising a sign that the school has more interest in students than other schools, or a sign that the school is desperate for more students? Does a law school's "ranking" or "reputation" determine how much the school needs to advertise? In short, some extremely good LL.M. programs advertise a great deal, and some extremely good LL.M. programs advertise very little or not at all. Do not judge based on the quantity or quality of its advertising. Choose the best school for you based on the merits of each school. At which school will you be able to meet your academic, personal, and professional goals?

E. Cash Cows and Diploma Mills

Unfortunately, some U.S. LL.M. programs possess negative characteristics of "cash cows" and/or "diploma mills." This section of the chapter describes and discusses "cash cows" and "diploma mills," and discusses how you can avoid them.

1. Cash Cows

Some law school LL.M. programs in the U.S. have been criticized as being "cash cows" that deny international LL.M. students reasonably expected services because in part the LL.M. tuition revenue is diverted away from the LL.M. programs.[10]

A "cash cow" is a business model where a certain undertaking generates significantly more revenue than the expenses associated with that undertaking, and

---

10. For a discussion of these issues, *see* Karen Sloan, "'Cash cow' or valuable credential?: Law schools add LL.M. programs, but their value may be limited." *The National Law Journal* (20 September 2010, www.law.com/jsp/nlj/PubArticleNLJ.jsp?id=1202472170557&Cash_cow_or_valuable_credential).

"Best" Schools

An LL.M. program does not become a "cash cow" simply because it charges a high tuition rate. An LL.M. program is a "cash cow" if it fails to reinvest the LL.M. tuition revenue into the LL.M. program, and the LL.M. program lacks resources it needs to meet the reasonable expectations of LL.M. students.

the excess revenue (profit) is used for other purposes within the organization. If an LL.M. program generates significant tuition and fees and diverts that income away from the LL.M. program, leaving the LL.M. program lacking resources needed to ensure that the school meets LL.M. students' reasonable expectations, then the "cash cow" label would apply. If the school fails to provide its LL.M. students with the services they reasonably need and want, then the students suffer. Eventually the school will suffer when it develops the reputation for treating its LL.M. program, and LL.M. students themselves, like "cash cows."

An LL.M. program *is not* a cash cow if LL.M. revenues (or other funds) are used to build and sustain a high-quality LL.M. program in which the school sets out to meet *and does meet* LL.M. students' academic, career, and other reasonable expectations. Everyone expects LL.M. programs to provide appropriate resources to help LL.M. students achieve their ambitious and reasonable goals, and it should be no surprise that many schools do an exceptionally good job at helping their LL.M. students, going over and beyond. These are the types of schools that prospective students should choose — schools that have excellent track records fulfilling their goals. Unfortunately, however, some schools *are* cash cows and do not fulfill basic responsibilities vis-à-vis LL.M. students. Serious prospective LL.M. students should *identify* and *avoid* cash cows.

I emphasize that the "cash cow" moniker itself is not so much about the school's motivation as it is about how the school uses its LL.M. tuition, fee revenue, and other resources. It is about whether or not the LL.M. program fulfills its pledges to LL.M. students.

Just because an LL.M. charges high tuition and fees or has revenues greater than expenses does not make that LL.M. program a cash cow. Schools are businesses, generally speaking are run like businesses, and like any other businesses would prefer to be profitable rather than in debt. An LL.M. program does not become a cash cow simply because high LL.M. tuition proceeds are used to help cover costs of other programs, such as the school's J.D. program. But there should be equity and fairness.

Some schools charge international and domestic LL.M. students the same rate, which is the same rate they charge J.D. students. Other schools charge LL.M. students a higher tuition rate. If LL.M. and J.D. students are charged identical tuition, service should be either identical (which may not be appropriate, given the different needs and expectations of the different categories of students), or at least comparable and equitable.

Some schools do not hide the fact that a principal reason, if not *the* principal reason, they created an LL.M. program was because such programs generate substantial tuition revenues with minimal expenses, and the LL.M. tuition

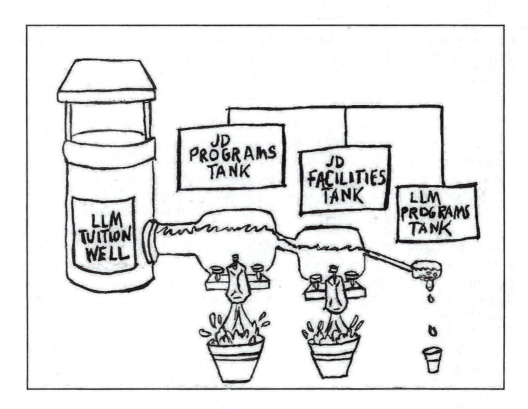

"Best" Schools

revenue could be used to supplement the J.D. and other non-LL.M. law school programs and activities. Before creating an LL.M. program, law school administrators must convince the faculty, and possibly university officials, that the prospective LL.M. is a viable, feasible undertaking that will benefit the law school (and the university) more than the LL.M. program will cost the law school (and the university).

Law schools are not charities, and do not routinely create major programs such as an LL.M. program because of the greater good it will do, or out of a sense of altruism. As mentioned, law schools are motivated in great part by the revenues that an LL.M. program for international students will generate. Also, the revenues generated by an LL.M. program for international students can be plenty, outpacing costs to the school.

Because LL.M. students and J.D. students take classes together, schools need not hire additional professors because most courses are offered already. Incremental costs associated with each new LL.M. student are *de minimis*. Each LL.M. student may add $20,000, $30,000, or $40,000 or more to the law school's (or university's) bank account but may cost the school a small fraction of that in expenses. How is that money used? *Again, it is not the tuition level difference that creates the cash cow, it is the failure to reinvest the LL.M. tuition into the LL.M. program*, or to adequately meet the needs and reasonable expectations of the LL.M. students who paid substantial tuition.

2. Diploma Mills

The concepts of "cash cow" and "diploma mill" are related to each other. I do not suggest that "cash cow" LL.M. programs are all "diploma mills" that crank out worthless degrees.[11] They are not. The U.S. has many excellent LL.M. programs that have been meeting international students' reasonable expectations for many decades. *Likewise, unfortunately, some LL.M. programs in the U.S. exist in which students' reasonable expectations are not met. LL.M. Roadmap* can seek to clarify many issues, questions, and hidden corners and shadows of issues and questions, but ultimately leaves it to your judgment to determine which schools and programs you believe can offer you what you need in a U.S. graduate law program. That is, you must ask yourself, and answer for yourself, the question of at which school and in which program you will likely have your reasonable expectations met.

---

11. A "diploma mill" is defined as "a usually unregulated institution of higher education granting degrees with few or no academic requirements" (Merriam Webster Dictionary, www.merriam-webster.com/dictionary/diploma%20mill). An LL.M. diploma mill would have low standards for admission and would bestow LL.M. degrees at a high price but with little worth, or would fail to recognize the special needs of international LL.M. students and fail to meet LL.M. students' reasonable expectations.

3. How to Identify, and Avoid, Cash Cows and Diploma Mills

You can now identify a cash cow LL.M. program — one that devotes insufficient resources to assist LL.M. students with academic, professional, career, personal, professional, or other assistance needed before the LL.M. students arrive on campus, during their LL.M. year, and after they graduate. Chapter 7 discusses criteria LL.M. students should consider when choosing an LL.M. program. A major factor is whether you believe that the LL.M. program will be able to help you satisfy your goals, including whether the school devotes appropriate and adequate resources to LL.M. administration, career, academic assistance, alumni, and other services you believe you need.

It is *not* the school's *intention* that is most critical; it is the school's *actions*, and the school's *record of success* at satisfying needs of its LL.M. students. Many if not most schools do decently or very well. Some do not. Sadly, some LL.M. students enroll in "cash cow" LL.M. programs without realizing it until they hear from friends at other schools, or through the LL.M. listservs or websites, how much better resourced other LL.M. programs are. By then it is too late. *LL.M. Roadmap* aims to help you choose wisely to avoid cash cows and diploma mills.

"Best" Schools

CHAPTER SUMMARY

- If you consider "rank" and "reputation" when choosing a school, how do you define "rank" or "reputation"? Whose measuring tools do you use?

- These terms mean different things to different students, graduates, and, perhaps most important, to prospective employers.

- Do not forget to think about your own needs — your personal and professional goals. How can you best achieve them?

- If you believe you need a highly "ranked" or "reputed" school or program to achieve your goals, by all means go for it — after you determine clearly what tools you will use to determine "rank" or "reputation."

- What do you believe a school's LL.M. program must possess for you to reach your professional and personal goals?

- Can the particular school(s) you are considering offer you all that you need to reach your professional and personal goals?

- Examine the factors discussed in Chapter 7. Do the features the school offers match your substantive interests — mode of instruction, faculty and student body composition, school and class size, even the weather in the school's city — whatever factors you consider important. Just be certain that you make an *informed* decision!

- Learn how to identify "cash cows" and "diploma mills." Avoid them!

Frequently Asked Questions (FAQ)
218 Criteria For Choosing the "Best" U.S. LL.M. Program For You

---

CHAPTER HIGHLIGHTS

- This chapter discusses 218 criteria you can use to assess over 100 U.S. law schools you can choose from for your LL.M. degree. These criteria are listed in 26 categories, from A to Z.

- As you review the criteria, remember your reasons for pursuing an LL.M. (Chapter 2), and ask yourself which of the 218 criteria are most important to you as you seek to satisfy your goals.

- All schools will not possess all 218 criteria. No student will consider *all* 218 criteria as critically important. You must decide what is important for you.

- You will want to give the most weight to those characteristics of law schools that will help you meet your professional and personal objectives.

- The school that is the best fit for another student may not be the school that is the best fit for you.

- You will want to choose the law school that will meet your own professional, financial, and personal needs.

- You will want a law school that will meet your reasonable expectations.

Introduction

A young girl or boy does not wake up one day and say, "I want to be an Olympic athlete," and then the next day win an Olympic gold medal. They must convert "I want to be an Olympic athlete" into action. They must research, train, set goals, and adopt and follow a roadmap. They may be suited for one sport but not another. Maybe they prefer skiing (Winter Olympics) or swimming (Summer Olympics). They must decide what is best for them. What is best for one athlete may not be best for another.

"Best" Schools

Likewise, a non-U.S. lawyer who thinks, "I want a U.S. LL.M." must take action. She must follow a roadmap that will lead to the best U.S. law school for her.

Just as an Olympian assesses numerous criteria in developing her roadmap, you will assess criteria to help you decide which U.S. law school's LL.M. program will best help you achieve your personal and professional goals.

Approximately 6,000 students enroll in LL.M. programs in the U.S. each year. Not all those students can go to **Harvard Law School**, which enrolls only around 200. The other 5,800 students enroll at one of over 100 other LL.M. programs spread across the U.S.

Finding the Best U.S. Law School for You

Because all students cannot go to any one particular law school, how do you find the best school for you? Each school is different. Students' goals, strengths, and needs differ.

In a November 2010 *National Jurist* article, Rosie Edmond, who was then assistant director of admissions for legal studies at **American University Washington College of Law**, spoke on what applicants should consider when choosing a U.S. LL.M. program: "Look at the programs, the faculty, the student population; talk to alumni from your country" (*The American International LL.M. Degree, A World of Choices*). Ms. Edmond is currently the EducationUSA Advising Coordinator (REAC) for Northeast Asia and the Pacific. Mark Shulman, **Pace Law School**'s assistant dean for graduate programs notes, "Students should also look for a teaching culture and environment in which they'll thrive."

"Best" Schools

Criteria for choosing the Best LL.M. Program for you (A to Z)

A. Type of LL.M. Degree Program
B. Specialized or General LL.M.
C. Law School Faculty
D. LL.M. Degree Coursework and Academic Credit Requirements
E. School and LL.M. Program Size
F. Non-Classroom Activities (Internships, Clinics)
G. Other Degrees and Certificates Offered
H. Nature of School; School's Philosophy
I. LL.M. and J.D. Student Integration
J. Thesis or Substantial Writing
K. Grading Schemes
L. Academic Support on Campus
M. Law Journals, Law Reviews, Other Groups
N. Career Development
O. Jobs (On Campus, Summer, OPT, CPT, AT)
P. LL.M. Student Handbook
Q. J.D., LL.M., and S.J.D. Student Body
R. Law School Alumni
S. Law School Administration and Staff
T. Law Library
U. Bar Exam Preparation
V. Finances (Expenses, Scholarships)
W. Location, Location, Location
X. Campus Facilities
Y. Ranking and Reputation
Z. Finding the Best Law School for You (Applicant Self-Assessment)

Those LL.M. administrators raise important points.

This chapter identifies 26 groups (A–Z) of considerations to help you choose the best law school for you, or at least, the best law school(s) for you to apply to. Remember — the best school for you may not be the best school for another international student, and certainly cannot be the best school for all 6,000 international students who enroll in U.S. LL.M. programs each year!

Gathering Information About U.S. Law Schools and U.S. LL.M. Programs

LL.M. Roadmap is not the only source for LL.M. program information! Check student and graduate blogs and commercial websites, some of which are listed elsewhere in *LL.M. Roadmap* or on *www.LLMRoadmap.com*. School websites provide good information about LL.M. policies, procedures, and personnel. Contact students, graduates, and prospective students. These people may help you, but

"Best" Schools

many are very busy. Save personal contacts to get critical information you cannot find elsewhere. Do not abuse your communication privileges.

Should You Ignore a School That Does Not Possess All the Characteristics or Traits Listed Below?

No law school in the U.S. possesses all the characteristics listed in this chapter. Some schools possess more than other schools, and some possess fewer.

I *do not suggest* that you should ignore a school if it does not possess particular criteria mentioned in this chapter, or that you should necessarily consider all of the criteria in choosing which school to apply to or to attend.

I *do suggest* that you consider which criteria are important to you, and consider their presence or absence thereof in your decision. If you possess the requisite background and credentials, can sort out finances, and have sufficient will and determination, you will likely get admitted to a U.S. LL.M. program and you can succeed in that program. This is particularly so because some U.S. LL.M. programs admit *all* international students who meet bare minimum admission standards.

You might apply, get accepted, and enroll without getting answers to some issues in this chapter. Some LL.M. administrators will not divulge certain information, sometimes due to confidentiality requirements. Ideally you can make informed choices with credible information. I encourage you to tap as many credible sources as possible for information about schools and programs.

Beware a school that lacks criteria from the Chapter 7 list you consider basic or important. It may have other unappealing traits. In all cases **beware** (and avoid):

(a) a **cash cow** LL.M. program where the law school disproportionately diverts LL.M. tuition and fees revenue to other programs, leaving the LL.M. program lacking in critical services and other resources, and is unwilling or unable to recognize LL.M. students' special needs and meet LL.M. students' reasonable expectations; or

(b) a **diploma mill** LL.M. program that has low standards for admission and bestows LL.M. degrees at a high price but of little worth.

Criteria International Students Should Consider When Deciding Which LL.M. Programs to Apply To or Enroll In — *The Treasure Hunt Is On!*

When choosing an LL.M. program, there are many things to consider. Below are 218 questions you might think about in evaluating schools and

LL.M. programs that interest you. More details about these topics can be found elsewhere in *LL.M. Roadmap*.

A. Type or Category of LL.M. Degree Program (See Chapter 3)

International students can choose from various types of U.S. LL.M. programs, full-time or part-time, with classes taught in the U.S. or overseas, or online. Choose a school that suits your needs, interests, resources, and personal and career goals. If you want maximum contact with professors and classmates, immersion in the U.S. legal system and culture and the Socratic method, then you would likely prefer an LL.M. program that demands your physical presence on a U.S. campus. If you cannot leave a job or family for a year, you might choose an executive LL.M. offering flexible scheduling. To save U.S. living costs and visa issues you might choose an online LL.M.

1. Are You Selecting the Type or Category of LL.M. Program You Want?

(a) *Regular LL.M. programs* — Offered on law school campuses in the U.S.

(b) *Executive LL.M. programs* — Offered on law school campuses in the U.S.

(c) *Regular or executive LL.M. programs* — offered on law school campuses in the U.S., but with components of the program offered outside the U.S. (either on an overseas U.S. or overseas non-U.S. school campus)

(d) *Regular or executive LL.M. programs* — Offered exclusively outside the U.S. (either on an overseas U.S. or overseas non-U.S. school campus)

(e) *Wholly online or wholly virtual LL.M. programs* — In which the student is not required to appear on campus for any purpose.

(f) *Partial online or partial virtual LL.M. programs* — In which the student may be required to appear on campus for some purposes.

(g) *LL.M. programs so creative that they do not fit any category above.*

B. Academics — A General or a Specialized LL.M.? (See Chapter 4)

Some LL.M. programs offer "specializations" or "concentrations" that permit you to focus on specific areas of law with the name of that specialized area embossed on your diploma or transcript. Other programs offer general degrees with no specializations. You may be able to take narrowly focused courses in a general LL.M. program. When choosing an LL.M. program, make sure the school offers courses you need and that the courses will be offered while you are on campus.

2. Does the Law School Offer an LL.M. That Specializes in the Specific Area(s) of Law That You Want?

Chapter 4 and Appendix I discuss approximately 100 specializations offered by U.S. LL.M. programs that offer expertise by intensive study in specific areas with that specialization's name appearing on your diploma, transcript, or official law school records. If a specific area of law interests you, or you wish to work in that area post-LL.M., you might choose a program that offers that specialization. If a school offers only a general LL.M. with no specializations, you may still gain expertise in a particular area of law by taking a number of courses in that area. For example, **Hawaii**, **Miami**, **Yale**, and other schools offer a general LL.M., but students at these schools may gain expertise in a specific subject by taking numerous courses in those areas. The students' diplomas will not list a specialization. A specialized program's diploma may read "Master of Laws in International Law" or "Master of Laws in Health Law." A general program's diploma would read "Master of Laws" with no specialization noted, despite the number of focused or specialized courses you take.

3. If a School Offers No Specialization in an Area That Interests You, Should You Still Enroll?

If you want to gain expertise in a particular area, consider schools that offer a specialization in that area. However, you can gain expertise without joining a specialized program. Many schools offer a number of specific, narrowly focused courses in different fields of law without offering a specialization. However, if a general LL.M. is not available and you are choosing among available specialized tracks, *do not* choose a specialized track unless you have a strong interest in and commitment to that track. Other students in that specialized track will be dedicated, and you may disappoint them, and yourself, if you do not share their commitment. It can be painful for all involved if you are in the wrong track.

4. Does the School Offer Sufficient Courses for You to Satisfy All Academic Requirements for Your Specialization?

Before you enroll ensure that the school offers *sufficient* courses in your specialization area. Examine the depth and breadth of course offerings. Make sure you will have a wide selection of specialized courses to choose from. A school may offer a specialization but fail to offer enough courses to satisfy student needs. I witnessed a case in which an international student entered a U.S. law school's LL.M. track in intellectual property, and while he was enrolled the school failed to offer enough courses on the subject for him to satisfy his basic specialized degree requirements. *Beware!*

5. Does the School Offer Courses in Your Concentration *When You Will Be Enrolled*?

Law schools rotate courses. Every course is not offered every semester or year. Thus a course you want to take may not be offered during your LL.M. year. Usually in March or April schools will confirm which courses they will offer in the following fall semester. *Before you enroll* ask the LL.M. office if specific courses you want will be offered, and if favored professors will be available during your time on campus. Professors are entitled to go on sabbatical, meaning they can spend every 7th year away from campus; their courses may not be offered then, and they will likely not supervise theses while they are gone. Schools may know over a year in advance if a professor is scheduled for sabbatical. If your favored professor is on sabbatical, you may still have an excellent experience with other professors, including visiting or adjunct professors.

Warning! — LL.M. Course Rotation and Course Availability

Several current LL.M. students expressly asked me to emphasize the following:

- Each school lists many law courses as part of its LL.M. curriculum. Every course is not offered every semester, or even every year.
- Before you enroll, ask the LL.M. office *if the courses you particularly want to take will be offered during your LL.M. year.*
- Also, make certain that the school offers *a sufficient number of specialized courses* so you can satisfy Track or Concentration requirements.
- If you want to study under a particular professor, make sure that professor is teaching and not on sabbatical.

---

6. If the Specialized Track Requires a Thesis and You Do Not Want to Write a Thesis, Should You Choose Another Track? If You Are Denied Admission to a Specialized Track, but Admitted to a Different Track, Should You Enroll Anyway in That Track That You Do Not Really Want to Specialize In, Hoping to Somehow Enjoy the Benefits of the Track That Rejected You? Will LL.M. Administrators Steer Students Away From Specialized Tracks with Thesis or Other Challenging Demands, but Permit Them to Enjoy Benefits of the Specialized Tracks, Such as Internships?

It is wise to enroll *only* in an LL.M. track in which you have sincere, compelling interests, and not to enter one track, hoping to slip into the back door of a different track. Administrative, academic, and interpersonal problems are caused when students enroll in tracks that do not suit them. Students

"Best" Schools

in the wrong track have a worse chance of having their LL.M. academic goals met. Beware schools at which LL.M. administrators steer students to less demanding tracks while permitting those students to take advantage of some of the benefits of the more demanding track. Each student should enroll in a track that is designed to meet that student's academic interests and needs.

7. Does the School Admit U.S. J.D. Graduates into Specialized LL.M. Programs Even If They Have No Particular Interest in That Specialized Track?

Most LL.M. programs are designed for international students who want general degrees in U.S. law or specialized degrees in specific areas. But some U.S. citizen graduates from J.D. programs do pursue LL.M. degrees for many reasons — for example, to bolster their credentials to help them get a job. Many general LL.M. programs that focus on U.S. law do not routinely accept domestic U.S. J.D. graduates. But specialized LL.M. programs often do. A problem is created when U.S. J.D. graduates want to bolster their degree, and the only LL.M. program they are eligible for is in a specialized area that does not interest them. Some schools permit these J.D. graduates to join the specialized program even if they have no significant interest in that area. The students get frustrated because they are forced to take specialized courses and delve into minutiae in an area of no real interest to them. Fellow LL.M. students in the specialized track wonder why the U.S. student is there, given the student's lack of commitment to the track. A specialized track should have like-minded fellow students. You can learn from them: If your heart lies elsewhere — go there.

8. Is the School Accepting Applications for Admission into Your Specialized Area for the Year You Want to Attend?

Schools with LL.M. specializations or tracks may suspend such tracks. If a specialization is suspended, the school may encourage you to join another track, saying you may still take courses in the suspended track's area of law and write a thesis in the suspended area. The school would be offering you expertise in your first-choice area, but not notate your diploma in that area because your preferred track has been suspended. **Beware!** If a school promises that you can gain expertise even when a track is suspended, red flags are raised. Why was the track suspended? How can a student gain as much expertise in the area of a suspended track as they could if the track were operational? Try to learn why the track was suspended. Was it because of deficiencies or perceived deficiencies in the LL.M. program? Those deficiencies may not be cured by the time you enroll, and may not be cured even by the time you graduate. If you want that particular expertise, you can wait until the concentration is re-opened — or choose another school.

Ensure that the track you want will be *fully operational* when you are enrolled, and that any LL.M. program deficiencies are *fully remedied*.

9. If the LL.M. Track You Want Is Suspended and the LL.M. Program Administrators Steer You Toward Another Track, Should You Accept the Other Track?

If you are committed to a track, choose it. If your first-choice track is not available, be cautious about shifting to another track at the same school. Do you have as strong a commitment to the substitute track as you do to your first-choice track? If you accept the substitute track because you think you might still avail yourself of offerings in the suspended track (e.g., thesis supervision by the original track faculty, internships, or pro bono opportunities in the original track), you may be sorely disappointed. LL.M. administrators should be frank in directing you to the curriculum that is best for you, not a curriculum that is best for the school's enrollment figures or income stream. *Beware of schools with cash cow mentalities!*

C. LL.M. and Other Law School Faculty

Law school websites reveal faculty members' backgrounds, courses taught, research interests, and even personal information such as hobbies. Ask if enough professors teach and research in areas that interest you, if they have relevant non-teaching experience, if they have ties to your country or speak your language, and if they will be on campus (or away on sabbatical) while you are enrolled. Ask administrators, students, and graduates if professors you want to work with are personable, approachable, and willing to work with international LL.M. students — or if they are too busy.

10. What Is the Student-to-Faculty Ratio?

If school *A* has ten students for each full-time professor, and school *B* has only five students per professor, the students at school *B* can have more of the professors' personal attention. The American Bar Association (ABA) currently requires a reasonable student–faculty ratio. Although the ABA may modify its rule, it has determined that a ratio of 20 to 1 is presumptively reasonable (and constitutes compliance with the ABA rule) and a 30 to 1 ratio is presumptively unreasonable (and would amount to noncompliance).[1] This ratio applies to the entire school (J.D. and LL.M. and any other programs). If LL.M. student numbers dramatically increase with no faculty increase, the student-to-faculty ratio will worsen. Ask the LL.M.

---

1. www.americanbar.org/groups/legal_education/resources/standards.html.

"Best" Schools

administrators what the student-to-faculty ratio is at the school generally, and in particular in the LL.M. program or programs.

11. How Many Full-Time, Regular Law Professors Are Part of the Faculty? Are There Enough Faculty Members to Handle the Students in the J.D. and LL.M. Programs?

The more students a law school has, the more professors the school should have. Professors have heavy administrative burdens (sitting on faculty committees), scholarly burdens (publishing books and articles), service burdens (working with outside organizations, doing pro bono work), and teaching burdens (classroom or virtual teaching, paper and exam grading). The more LL.M. students a school has, the less time professors will have to meet with students outside of class, supervise papers and theses, and grade theses and exams. Some schools argue that they cannot afford to hire new professors to handle an increased LL.M. student body, despite the high tuition revenues generated by LL.M. students. *Beware!*

12. Does the School Have Expert Professors in Your Specialization Area?

Law professors gain expertise through scholarly research and practical field experience. LL.M. students can learn a great deal from law professors who are legal experts, rather than from law professors who may lack experience or may teach a subject with which they are not very familiar. *Before you accept a school's LL.M. offer to attend/matriculate/enroll, check the online biographies of the school's law professors—and in particular of professors scheduled to teach courses you're interested in.* Having scrutinized their profiles, are you confident they possess the right kind of knowledge, experience, and insights to suit your needs, and that they will share these and more with you, or can and will otherwise help you reach your career goals?

13. What Are the Faculty's Credentials in Teaching, Publishing, Service, and Practice? Are They Practicing Lawyers? Bar Members? Public Service Volunteers? Judges or U.N. Officials? Do They Have Extensive Contacts in Areas in Which You Would Like to Make Your Career?

Faculty websites describe faculty members' backgrounds, interests, and experiences. Similar information is available from Internet news searches, scholarly work searches, sources such as the *AALS Directory of Law Teachers* (www.aals.org), and current students and alumni.

14. Is the Faculty Personable, Approachable, and Available?

Ask the LL.M. office whether you can contact a professor directly before you enroll. You can learn about professors from correspondence with them.[2] To find out about professors, ask current students, graduates, or school administrators. If you want to take a particular professor's course or have him or her supervise your thesis, send an e-mail message to the LL.M. office and ask for guidance. Ask about the professor's accessibility and approachability. Mark Adams, **Valparaiso University School of Law**'s associate dean for academic affairs, said that at his school you will find the entire faculty, not just him, to be extraordinarily accessible ("The American and International LL.M. Degree, A World of Choices," *National Jurist*, November 2010, p. 38). Ideally, all law schools can make similar faculty accessibility claims and live up to that ideal. Unfortunately, reality is not ideal.

15. Are Faculty Members Willing and Able to Advise and Mentor You?

Ask current students and alumni about their experiences with faculty. Professors in your area of interest should be prepared to advise and mentor you during your course of study and after you graduate. Once you commit to joining a particular school, professors should be willing and able to work with you, even before you arrive on campus.

16. Will the Relevant Professors Be on Sabbatical?

Every seven years, professors are entitled to go on sabbatical. During this period they are relieved of teaching and advising responsibilities, and may be absent from campus to pursue research, writing, or other activities. If the professor you want to serve as your thesis advisor, or to teach you a course, is on sabbatical during your LL.M. year, you are out of luck. Check before you enroll!

17. Is the Faculty Diverse? Does the School Pride Itself on the Diverse Backgrounds and Experiences of Its Faculty?

When you skim the biographies of faculty, do you note a range of races, genders, ethnicities, backgrounds, and experiences? When you dig deeper, do you find a rich variety?

---

2. Professors are extremely busy and are not expected to reply substantively to all e-mail messages from hundreds of prospective students each year, and may forward your note to the LL.M. office for reply. Also, remember that e-mail messages or phone calls to administrators, current students, or graduates should be reserved for critical information you cannot easily get elsewhere. Respect their time. They try to be as helpful as possible.

"Best" Schools

"Famous" or "Star" Law Professors

Would you want to attend a law school whose faculty includes "famous" full-time or adjunct professors, perhaps politicians, judges, legal commentators, or renowned authors? Some professors are media personalities, and may even host their own shows.

These professors have a wealth of insight and experience to offer foreign LL.M. students. But will they devote time to students outside of class, given their other commitments? If you want to work with such professors or ask them to be an academic advisor, you might ask current students or alumni whether the professors were available and accessible to LL.M. students or whether they were too busy.

18. Can You Work with a Professor as a Research Assistant?

There are not enough research assistant positions for all students who want to work with professors. If you want to work for a particular professor, contact the LL.M. office for guidance in pursuing that aim.

19. Are Famous Professors on Your Faculty?

Many U.S. law schools have famous or star professors, politicians, judges, legal commentators, or celebrated authors among their faculty. Some professors are media personalities who regularly comment on local, national, or global events, and some may even host their own television or radio shows. Former U.S. Senators Russ Feingold and Arlen Specter became law professors in 2011 at **Marquette University Law School** and **University of Pennsylvania School of Law**, respectively. All of these types of professors have a wealth of insights and experience to offer international LL.M. students. But will they be available to work with you, or will they be too busy?

20. Does the School Have Many Adjunct Professors?

Adjunct professors tend to be legal professionals who hold full-time jobs in the local community and teach one or more classes at a law school part time. They may hail from any area of law and from any type of law work, including private law firm practice, the judiciary, the military, international organizations, or the criminal justice system (prosecutors or defense counsel). The ABA recognizes that adjunct professors add to the quality of a school's curriculum. The ABA requires, however, that the majority of courses at law schools be taught by full-time professors employed by the school, not by adjuncts. The majority of LL.M. courses should *not* be taught by adjuncts if J.D. students are being taught by regular, full-time faculty members, unless there is a particular substantive need for adjuncts to instruct LL.M. students. For example, **St. Thomas School of Law**'s LL.M. in Intercultural Human Rights offers courses taught by a series of eminent scholars, judges, UN and foreign government officials and professors, each of whom travels to the **St. Thomas** campus for short periods over the course of one or two semesters to provide high-level course instruction to LL.M. students. These esteemed lecturers are brought in for sound pedagogical reasons. Compare programs that retain adjuncts to teach LL.M. students because it is less expensive than having LL.M. students taught by full-time professors. Indeed, some schools have an official policy of retaining less expensive adjunct professors for LL.M. courses whenever possible, reserving full-time professors for J.D. courses. *Avoid schools with a cash cow mentality.*

21. Does the School Have Many Visiting Professors?

A visiting professor may be a full-time professor at another law school who teaches at your school temporarily to fill a need. The visiting professor may want to join your school's faculty, or may have another motive. The school may want to provide their students with a particularly skilled professor for a limited period, or replace a professor on sabbatical. A visiting professor may also be a well-known expert in a field of law or a high-ranking government or UN official.

22. Do Faculty Live in the Same City as the School, or Do They Commute There? Are They Absent from Campus? Often?

Generally, U.S. law professors are not obligated to live in the same city as their school, or even in the same metropolitan area. Some live hundreds of miles away and commute. For example, a professor's home may be in California, the law school in Chicago, and the professor travels once a week between the two places. Maybe he spends Monday to Wednesday at school in Chicago, flies home Wednesday night and stays there through Sunday, and then begins the cycle again the next and each working week. This schedule and arrangement can be problematic for students if, due to his regular absence, the professor cannot fulfill mentoring or administrative responsibilities vis-à-vis students. Students can end up sorely disappointed. Commuting professors may not have the time to devote to you. Professors living in the same city as the school could be equally unavailable and absent from campus. Ask if your school has **commuting or absent professors**, and if so, ask how much time they are available for consultations, advising, or counseling. Note that Associate Deans and other LL.M. administrators have a greater responsibility to be on campus than regular professors. *Be particularly wary of a school if the Associate Dean for the LL.M. program commutes or is otherwise absent.*

D. LL.M. Degree Coursework Academic Credit Requirements; S.J.D. Preparation (See Chapters 15, 16, and 28)

Although the ABA is considering a proposed scheme to "certify" LL.M. programs, neither the ABA nor any other agency directly regulates LL.M. programs in the U.S. Each school determines its LL.M. program's curriculum, coursework, and academic requirements, which differ at each school. LL.M. degrees may be course-based or research-based, may require as few as 20, or as many as over 30 credit hours, or require on-campus residency for a certain period. Programs have different rules regarding independent study, courses for LL.M. students only, and/or limits on courses LL.M. students may take. Check the school's LL.M. Student Handbook before you enroll to determine if you are able and willing to comply with the school's rules. Recently amended New York Bar eligibility rules may impact academic requirements of some LL.M. programs. See Chapter 28 for a discussion of the ABA proposal and the amended New York rules.

23. Is the LL.M. Degree Program Course-Based or Research-Based?

A **course-based** LL.M. program requires you to earn most or all your academic credits taking traditional classroom courses. A **research-based** LL.M. requires you to earn a substantial number of credits researching and writing a thesis. Some schools have both course-based and research-based tracks. Choose a school that offers the type of track you want. (See Chapters 15 and 16.)

24. How Many Credit Hours Are Required to Complete an LL.M. Program?

For a course-based or research-based LL.M., students must complete between approximately 20 and 30 or more credit hours, with different schools requiring different numbers. Most schools require between 24 and 26 hours. Students earn credits by taking traditional or experiential courses, by independent study, or through theses or other writing projects. Each school has its own rules regarding credit hours and course load requirements. Find out what these rules are, and be sure you understand them. (See Chapter 16.)

25. Can LL.M. Students Enroll Part-Time?

U.S. law requires students on visas to study full-time, meaning they must be enrolled for at least 8 credit hours each semester. You could in theory take 8 credit hours during each of three semesters to finish a 24-credit-hour degree. An exception to the visa law's 8 credit per semester minimum permits students in their final semester to drop below 8 credits. Thus, if you take 10 credit hours in the fall and 10 credit hours in the spring, you would still be "in status" visa-wise if you enrolled in 4 credits in the final semester. Another exception is that you may take zero credits during the summer if you are enrolled the previous spring and the following fall. These restrictions do not apply to U.S. citizens or permanent residents who do not need a student visa.

26. What Is the Maximum Course Load for International LL.M. Students Per Semester?

It does not appear that most LL.M. programs expressly limit the number of courses a student may take in any particular semester. However, if the program requires enrollment for at least two semesters, it would likely be advisable to split the credits somewhat evenly between the two semesters. Or you might take a heavier course load during the first semester, to give you more time to write a thesis, to work, or to do an internship in the second semester.

27. What Is the Time Limit to Complete Your LL.M.?

Schools appear to permit you at least one calendar year, with some permitting five or more years to complete an LL.M. If you are on an F-1 or J-1 visa, U.S. immigration law will govern the amount of time you will be permitted to remain in the U.S. to complete your degree. Some students complete most coursework in the U.S., and complete their thesis overseas and send it to the school via e-mail or post.

28. What If You Cannot Finish Your LL.M. Degree in the Time Period the School Requires?

Some LL.M. programs strictly enforce a fixed number of years or semesters in which an LL.M. must be completed, lest you forfeit all work completed to date. Other schools are more flexible and may waive their maximum. Schools may require that all LL.M. work be completed within one or two years, or even up to five years. If you think you may need to take longer than anticipated to complete your degree (e.g., family emergency, illness), ensure that your school permits it.

29. Can You Take a Leave of Absence from the LL.M. Program?

Sometimes students must return home for short periods because of family issues, a work project with their employer, or a medical emergency. Your school's *LL.M. Handbook* should, and likely does, detail the leave of absence rules. Inform yourself. You do not want to be surprised if an emergency arises and you certainly do not want to learn, too late, that leaves are prohibited. You must also learn the U.S. visa rules regarding leaving the U.S. and returning before you graduate.

"Best" Schools

30. Can You Take Summer Classes?

You may wish to extend your 9-month (September–May) LL.M. program to 12 months (including June–August), which you can easily do if your school offers summer courses that would satisfy your LL.M. requirements. *Before you enroll*, ask if it permits LL.M. students to take summer courses. Otherwise, if you do not earn your 24 credits by May, you might not receive your degree until the following December — over a year after you entered.

31. Do the Classes You Want to Take Conflict with Each Other?

A school may offer classes with professors you prefer, but you cannot take those classes because they are scheduled at times that conflict with each other. You cannot be in two classrooms at once. Some schools deliberately schedule popular classes or professors in conflicting time slots to force students to choose one course or the other. *Before you enroll*, check the class schedules for the current year to get a sense of whether you might be able to take classes you want. Schedules may change each year. Ask the LL.M. Office for guidance.

32. Will Classes Satisfy Requirements for the New York, California, Washington, D.C., or Other Bar Exams?

F-1 and J-1 LL.M. graduates may sit for some state bar exams under some circumstances. (See Chapter 28.) State bars may require LL.M. students to have taken certain courses. If you want to take a bar, find out if that bar requires you to take certain LL.M. courses. Make sure — in advance — that your school offers those courses, and permits you to take them.

33. Can You Earn Two or More LL.M. Degrees at the Same School?

Although U.S. LL.M. programs have tracks or concentrations, schools *tend* to offer only one actual LL.M. degree. The tracks may have different requirements for theses, internships, or classroom credits. All tracks *may* be part of a sole LL.M. degree. If you wish to earn a second LL.M. degree, you *may* have to earn it at another school. *Find out from the school if you are allowed to receive two separate LL.M. degrees from the same school.*

34. Can You Take First-Year J.D. Law Courses (or Only Second- and Third-Year Courses)?

First-year J.D. students across the U.S. enroll in foundation law courses such as criminal law, torts, civil procedure, and legal research and writing. Not all law schools permit LL.M. students to take these first-year courses; some allow only upper-level courses. (See Chapter 30.)

35. Can You Audit Courses? Must You Pay Audit Tuition?

Most LL.M. programs require students to earn 24 credits, and most courses are between 2 and 4 credits. You will likely take (and pay for) 7 to 10 courses during your LL.M. year of study. If you are interested in certain courses that you do not want or need academic credit for, your school may permit you to audit those courses. You would attend class, participate in discussions and do class readings, but be prohibited from taking the exam. Schools may permit free audits, but others require you to pay full or partial tuition to audit. If your school charges a fixed amount of tuition per semester, you will not be charged for auditing. However, your school may have rules related to how many classes you may sit in on. Ask.

36. Does the School Offer Trendy Courses in New, Exciting, Cutting-Edge Areas, Such as Climate Change or Oil Law Hazards?

These courses help students keep abreast of legal trends. For example, as climate change and global warming issues become increasingly popular, so do law school courses on these topics. After the U.S. election in 2000, election law courses increased, as did national security law courses after 9/11. The 2010 Gulf of Mexico oil spill spurred a surge of interest in courses on oil and gas law. Schools with cutting-edge courses in developing areas may be demonstrating their desire to satisfy intellectual and pragmatic needs of students about to enter the law marketplace. Take note.

37. Can You Receive Credit for Independent Study?

When you add up your three- and four-credit-hour courses to reach the total required to graduate, you may discover that you need only one additional credit, but the school does not offer one-credit-hour courses. A school may permit you to earn one or more independent study credits by writing a paper or engaging in pro bono work. You may need to ask a professor to supervise you. You might also be able to earn independent credit if you want to do extra research in areas that particularly interest you, or to help a student group or outside initiative. Independent credit is a great way to gain valuable experience outside the classroom.

38. Can You Join a Study Abroad Program Outside the U.S.?

Students on visas in the U.S. may be able to join a U.S. school's short-term study program outside the U.S. However, this prospect could be complicated because of your U.S. visa terms (F-1 or J-1), and because you may need a visa for the country where the courses are offered. Also, it may counter your goals of

U.S. culture immersion if you leave the U.S. during your LL.M. year. And summer or semester study abroad credits might not count toward educational equivalency requirements for the New York or other bars. If you leave the U.S. during your LL.M., be sure you have appropriate documentation to return to the U.S. (See Chapters 15 and 16.)

39. Can You Get Credit for Courses Taken Before You Enter the LL.M. Program (e.g., for Work in Another School's J.D. or LL.M. Program; an Exchange Program; or an Overseas Program Conducted by a U.S. Law School)?

Some LL.M. programs permit transfer of credits earned in a J.D. or LL.M. program at other schools. If you are enrolled in a B.A. or LL.M. program abroad, and you participate in an exchange program and take classes at a U.S. law school, you may be able to transfer those credits into the U.S. LL.M. program. Similarly, if you are an international LL.B. or B.A. student in a U.S. law school's study abroad program, some schools will permit you to transfer credits earned in the summer program to the LL.M. program, permitting you to enter the LL.M. program with "advanced standing," meaning you will have already satisfied some course credit requirements.

40. Can You Get Credit for Courses Taken at a U.S. or Overseas Law School?

An LL.M. program may not offer a particular specialized course you want when you are enrolled. Your program may permit you to take that course at another U.S. or overseas law school and transfer credit to your program. If you take a course at another law school, your own law school will not receive your tuition for that course. Thus, your program may charge you a transfer fee, which could be a percentage of what you would have paid for the course at your own school. For example, if you pay $1,000 for a course at a different law school, your law school may charge you a 50 percent transfer fee of $500, meaning the course would end up costing you $1,500, in total, rather than only $1,000. Schools want you to spend tuition dollars at their school, and they want to discourage you from taking classes at other institutions.

41. Can You Get Academic Credit for Courses Taken at a *Non-Law School*?

If a university or college offers a course that is related to your LL.M. specialization, you might ask your LL.M. program to permit you to receive academic credit for that course. If the non-law school is in a different city, you might take the course over the summer.

"Best" Schools

42. Does the School Have Special Courses for LL.M. Students from Continental Law and Other Non-Common Law Jurisdictions?

Many LL.M. students hail from countries with continental law or other legal systems, and are not familiar with U.S. common law. Some schools offer special courses for students who need extra guidance in common law.

43. Does the School Require a Legal Writing Course? A Skills Course? A Legal Communications Course? Are These Courses Taught by Professors with Substantial Experience Researching, Publishing, and Teaching Legal Writing and Skills for International Students?

If your school does not require these courses, **take them anyway**. These courses are invaluable. They will help you learn an extremely important lawyer's skill — *legal analysis and communication*. **Ask if your school's legal writing professors have broad experience with legal writing for foreign lawyers.** This is a specialized area, and not every professor or lawyer who speaks English is proficient at teaching legal writing to international students. Ask if your professors have written books and articles on teaching legal writing to international students, and have broad experience in the U.S. and overseas. Do the professors participate in professional activities in the field, such as the Global Legal Skills Conference? (See Chapter 17.)

44. What Courses Are Required for International LL.M. Students?

Some schools permit international LL.M. students to satisfy their 24 credits by taking any courses they wish, with no required courses. The more courses that are required, the fewer elective courses you can take. Chances are you will benefit greatly from the courses that the LL.M. program requires (such as Legal Writing or U.S. Law for Foreign Lawyers). If you feel you have a sufficient background in the subject of a required course, you may petition the LL.M. program for a waiver to permit you to take another elective course instead. (See Chapter 16.)

45. Does the School Offer Pre-LL.M. Summer Courses to Help You Prepare for the LL.M. Rigor?

Many schools offer a several week or longer pre-LL.M. program consisting of courses such as U.S. law, legal reasoning, common law traditions, or legal writing. Some schools restrict their courses to their own incoming LL.M. students; some require incoming LL.M. students to take the course. If your school does not offer or require such a course, you might consider joining a pre-LL.M. course offered elsewhere in the U.S. or online. (See Chapter 14 for a list of such courses.)

46. How Will You Know Which Courses Will Help You Reach Your Career Goals?

You will likely be able to take only three to five courses each semester, yet your school may offer dozens of courses related to your chosen area of law or that are well suited for students with your career goals. How do you choose which courses to take? If your post-LL.M. goal is to work on corporate issues, should you take Securities Regulation or Mergers and Acquisitions (M&A)? Corporate Finance or Financial Reporting for Lawyers? Private Equity or Mutual Funds? What will law firms, corporations, or government employers want to see? *Academic advisors, who are members of your law school faculty, should advise you on the courses that will likely help you reach your goals.*

47. Is It Better to Take More Courses and Risk Lower Grades, or Fewer Courses with Possibly Higher Grades?

You want to learn as much as you can in your given area of interest or specialization. You will want to impress potential employers with your broad or deep expertise and diligence. You will also want high grades. If you take additional courses, you will have less time to study, and you may have lower grades. You will need to choose carefully your course of study, school, and LL.M. track. You must decide which program and track will afford you the best opportunities for your career. Check with your faculty academic advisor.

E. School and LL.M. Program Size (See Chapter 16)

Law schools, and their LL.M. programs, are differently sized. They all offer courses with a mix of sizes — large, medium, or small numbers of students.

48. Is the School Big, Medium, or Small in Terms of Students, Faculty, Classes Offered, or Campus?

Larger schools tend to have more faculty, wider course offerings, and more student organizations and extracurricular activities. They tend to have more tuition revenue, which *may* translate into more law school resources. Smaller law schools may have fewer students, and may have a better faculty-to-student ratio, offering students more personalized classroom and out-of-class exposure to faculty.

"Best" Schools

49. How Many LL.M. Students Does the School Have?

Some LL.M. programs have well over 200 students, whereas others have 5 or fewer. If you prefer to network with dozens of international LL.M. students in a larger program, you will likely not have as much personalized faculty or staff attention, but you may have a greater global experience, meeting and interacting with students from many different countries, cultures, and legal systems. Smaller LL.M. programs can be very attractive for different reasons. For example, **Florida State University College of Law** notes that its small LL.M. program in American Law for Foreign Lawyers enrolls no more than seven students each year, and assures that every student will receive personal attention and counseling (www.law.fsu.edu/academic_programs/llm_program/index.html).

50. Has a Given School's LL.M. Enrollment Increased in Recent Years? Decreased? Why? Is the Increase or Decrease Related to the School's Positive or Negative Reputation? Is It Related to the School's Cash Cow Mentality?

A dramatic *increase* can result from the school's improved commitment to meeting LL.M. students' reasonable expectations. *Positive reputations of LL.M. programs spread swiftly*. But the *increase* may be because the school hired a marketing firm to attract students, offered more tuition discounts, assigned a fancy name or title to their "tuition discount scholarships," or decreased student services to reduce costs. If LL.M. enrollment has *decreased* dramatically, it could be because the school believes limited enrollment permits more personalized service to LL.M. students. But *decreased enrollment* can also result from the school's or the program's failure to satisfy LL.M. students' reasonable expectations, and students and graduates consequently informed friends, families, overseas faculty advisors, embassy officials from their home countries, scholarship sponsors, and others about their negative LL.M. experiences. *Negative reputations of LL.M. programs spread swiftly*. Be careful about gossip and rumors. If there has been a recent marked increase or decrease, *ask the LL.M. program administrators why*. Even better, also ask current students and former students why. Make sure that enrollment did not increase because the school became a **cash cow**. Or that the enrollment did not decrease because students were madly fleeing from a flagrant **cash cow**.

51. What Is the Average Size of a School's Elective (or Specialized) Classes?

Are they small enough that you might receive individualized attention from the professors? At some schools, elective, specialized courses might have 50, 75, or even over 100 students. In a class that big, it is not possible for a professor to provide each student in the class with individualized attention, inside or outside the classroom. At some schools, many electives have fewer students — 30, 20, or even fewer. In smaller classes, professors and students can interact on a more personal level, and can more readily exchange ideas and engage in productive, instructive exchanges. *Before you enroll,* check the school's course calendar; preliminarily choose courses that interest you; and ask the LL.M. administrator how many students will likely be in each class. Whether you want large or small classes, you can make an informed decision.

F. Non-Classroom Activities (for Academic Credit or Not) — Internships or Externships, Clinics, Pro Bono, and Other Experiential Opportunities; Field Trips, Lectures, Exposure to Law Practitioners (See Chapters 15 and 16)

Different law schools have different rules regarding whether LL.M. students can participate in particular non-classroom activities at the same level as J.D. students (if at all), and whether LL.M. students can earn academic credit for such activities. If you want to participate in particular non-classroom activities, please check with the school before you enroll.

52. Can LL.M. Students Do Internships (Domestic or Overseas) for Academic Credit?

Most LL.M. programs require LL.M. students to earn about 24 credits for their degrees, which translates into about 3 to 5 courses per semester. Most credits are earned in traditional classroom courses or through thesis writing. Many schools permit LL.M. students to earn credits through domestic or overseas internships. If you think you may want to earn internship credits, ask about it *before you enroll.* Some schools prohibit LL.M. students from earning internship credits. Some internships take place during the academic year (between September and May), and others take place in the summer following your first two semesters of school. If you do a summer internship, you might not graduate until August — 12 months after you enter the LL.M. program. It would be unusual, but perhaps you can arrange to do an internship the summer *before* the LL.M. academic year, so that you graduate and receive your LL.M. degree upon satisfactory completion of the coursework in May.

53. Can LL.M. Students Do Pro Bono Work for Academic Credit?

Law schools permit students to provide pro bono (or free) legal services to people and groups who may not otherwise have access to lawyers. You may be able to receive academic credit for such work. A professor involved in outside work may permit you to volunteer, and may supervise your activities for pro

"Best" Schools

"Best" Schools

bono academic credit. You will gain valuable legal experience, help poor and otherwise underprivileged people, and help satisfy your course requirements.

54. Can LL.M. Students Participate in Live-Client Clinics? For Academic Credit?

Most law schools have live-client clinics where students under law professor supervision may provide legal services to poor clients, even representing them in court. Schools and courts require students to take preparatory courses or gain certification before beginning clinic work. Because LL.M. students are enrolled for only two semesters, there may be no chance for them to take the preparatory courses. Thus, LL.M. students may be denied clinical experiences. *Ask before you enroll. Plan ahead.*

55. Does the School Provide Law-Related LL.M. Field Trips, Seminars, and Other Events?

Law schools are not obliged to entertain LL.M. students. But schools should ensure that LL.M. students are offered maximum exposure to U.S. culture, law, and legal institutions. LL.M. programs typically host field trips to federal and state executive branch, legislative branch, and judicial branch offices. Trips could be to the state capital, the nation's capital (Washington, D.C.), state and federal courts, state bar associations, local city councils, and county commissions. Ideally, international LL.M. students would have opportunities to observe hearings and meetings, and to talk with officials and others about them.

56. Does the School Support LL.M. Attendance at Academic Conferences and Colloquia?

Each year hundreds of conferences are held in the U.S. and overseas focusing on different law areas. These conferences may be sponsored by law schools, governments, or intergovernmental organizations like the UN. Some law schools fund LL.M. students to attend and participate in such conferences. LL.M. students can present papers, sit on panels, learn about a specialized area of law, and network with prospective employers and clients.

57. Does the School Have a Travel Budget for Conferences?

If the school has no conference budget for LL.M. students, you still might be able to convince the school to fund you. You could prepare a conference funding proposal that states the conference name and subject matter, sponsors, location, likely attendees, and how participation will assist your academic work and career goals. Describe contributions you will make at the conference (e.g., you might present a paper, sit on a panel, or participate in a roundtable discussion). Discuss how your law school might benefit (e.g., you might write a follow-up article and publish it in a law school journal, or you might generate a news item for the law school website or make a presentation to the student body or in one of your classes). Include a budget of estimated conference costs, including airfare, hotel, food, registration, and local transportation. Indicate how much of your own personal funds you can contribute. Demonstrate that you are prepared to make sacrifices to attend, and maybe that you have also gone outside the law school to seek support.

58. Does the School Host LL.M. Seminars?

Ohio Northern University's LL.M. in Democratic Governance and Rule of Law offers four weekend seminars during which prominent scholars and practitioners participate in intensive two-day seminars with LL.M. students. Students interact informally with experts. Recent topics included transition from one-party rule, women's rights, post conflict reconciliation, and international criminal law (http://llm.onu.edu/curriculumnew.html).

59. Does the School Fund Special Projects?

Some schools fund special projects undertaken by LL.M. students on an ad hoc basis, such as participation in UN Shadow Reporting (where advocates submit reports to the UN about human rights violations in different countries), teaching opportunities outside the U.S., human rights investigations and reporting missions, and pro bono work for prisoners at Guantanamo Bay, or the ICTR and ICTY. At one school, such opportunities were once readily available for LL.M. students, but have since been limited to J.D. students. That LL.M. students participated in prior years does not guarantee that LL.M. students will be able to participate in subsequent years. *Find out before you enroll.*

G. Other Degrees Offered – J.D.; S.J.D.; Dual Degrees; Joint Degrees? (See Chapters 29, 30, and 31)

All schools highlighted in LL.M. Roadmap offer the J.D. degree and the LL.M. degree. Some of these schools offer joint degrees (including joint J.D./LL.M. degrees), and other degrees such as the Master in Comparative Law (M.C.L.) and the S.J.D.

60. Is the LL.M. the Only Non-J.D. Law Degree Offered?

All U.S. law schools discussed in *LL.M. Roadmap* that enroll international LL.M. students also have J.D. programs. Most do not offer law degrees beyond the LL.M. Fewer offer the S.J.D. Some schools offer one or more of several other

"Best" Schools

degrees that are geared toward people with legal training, and also for those with no legal training. (See Chapters 29, 30, and 31.)

61. Does the School You Are Considering Offer an S.J.D.?

If you want to pursue an S.J.D., you might want to do your LL.M. at a school that also offers the S.J.D. If you join such an LL.M. program, try to cultivate relationships early with professors who may be prospective S.J.D. dissertation advisors. Graduating from a school's LL.M. program will not guarantee admission to its S.J.D. program. Some schools accept S.J.D. candidates only from among their own LL.M. program graduates. (See Chapter 29.)

62. Will Your LL.M. Program Help Prepare You for an S.J.D.?

If you want to earn an S.J.D. after your LL.M., choose an LL.M. program that will help you reach that goal. Your LL.M. program should have high thesis standards, with published thesis guidelines, and strict thesis review and assessment by faculty or a committee. Write a high-quality thesis and ask the LL.M. program to help you publish it. If your thesis is of poor quality, suffering from inadequate supervision, your S.J.D. admission chances diminish. If the S.J.D. program you want generally selects candidates from its own LL.M. program, try to join their LL.M. program. Before you enroll in an LL.M. program, ask how many of its S.J.D. students received LL.M. degrees from that school. Also ask how many LL.M. graduates have enrolled in S.J.D. programs at other law schools.

63. Can You Earn a Joint J.D./LL.M. Degree?

Some schools combine the LL.M. with other degrees. *If you are interested in a joint degree, understand the requirements before you enroll in the LL.M. program.* You may need to take an additional entrance exam (e.g., GRE, GMAT). You may need to declare your dual-degree interest before you begin classes because, for example, you may need to take courses in a certain order. It may be to your advantage to begin the LL.M. first, and then later add the other degree before you complete the LL.M. (e.g., to create the possibility of an LSAT waiver). Ask! (See Chapter 30.)

64. Should You Go for a J.D. or an LL.M.?

Many reasons exist for an international student to pursue: (a) a J.D. and not an LL.M.; (b) an LL.M. and not a J.D.; or (c) an LL.M. and then a J.D. later. With a J.D. from an ABA-accredited law school's program, you may sit for a bar in any U.S. state, whereas with an LL.M. you may sit only in some states.

To enroll in the J.D. first, you must take the LSAT; but if you enroll first in an LL.M., your school may waive the LSAT if you begin the J.D. later. (See Chapters 3, 5, and 30.)

65. Can You Switch from the LL.M. to the J.D. Program, or Join the J.D. Program Post-LL.M.? Will the J.D. Program Waive Your LSAT, or Admit You if Your LSAT Is Very Low?

Some schools are flexible in the relationship between the J.D. and LL.M. programs for international students, permitting international students to do joint J.D./LL.M. degrees, or letting LL.M. students or graduates join the J.D. program with or without taking the LSAT. J.D. applicants ordinarily must take the LSAT, and international J.D. applicants compete against all J.D. applicants. This may disadvantage international students because they may not have significant experience sitting for standardized tests like the LSAT; though it also could be to their advantage—if, for instance, they already have a law degree. If you join an LL.M. program, and then decide to join that school's J.D. program, your school may waive the LSAT (particularly if you performed well as an LL.M. student). Also, you may be able to earn a combined J.D./LL.M. degree in less time than it would take to do the two degrees separately. (See Chapter 30.)

66. If You Join a J.D. Program Post-LL.M., or While Enrolled as an LL.M. Candidate, Can You Transfer LL.M. Credits Toward Your J.D. Degree and Gain Advanced J.D. Status?

Some schools have more fluid relationships than others between their LL.M. and J.D. programs, for example, in permitting students to apply LL.M. credits toward a J.D. degree. Other schools are more rigid, and allow students to apply credits accumulated in a program *only for that specific program*. If you are considering switching from one program to the other, or seeking to have credits applied in some nontraditional manner, *ask the LL.M. program administration about it as soon as possible*—preferably before you are stuck with credits you do not need or want.

67. Do International LL.M. Students Who Transfer to the J.D. Program Tend to Successfully Complete the J.D.? Or Is Permissive LL.M. Transfer to the J.D. Program Another Indication That the School Is a Cash Cow—Offering Another Opportunity for the School to Earn International Student Tuition Dollars?

Some schools make it incredibly easy for international LL.M. students to join the J.D. program without taking the LSAT, without achieving particularly high LL.M. grades (or receiving inflated LL.M. grades), and without even mastering the English language at a level suitable for communicating in *any* U.S. law program. Schools first extract one year's LL.M. tuition from an international student, and then extract two or more years' J.D. tuition from that student, and that student may not be able to compete in a J.D. class with U.S. classmates. These international J.D. students who were former international LL.M. students suffer low J.D. grades, risk expulsion due to low grades, and risk high levels of frustration with and resentment at the school for granting them entry into the J.D. program when the odds were highly weighted against them. *Cash cows show no mercy on such students.* I am reminded of the financial crisis in the U.S. in the 1990s and 2000s, where banks gave mortgages to countless home purchasers without high regard as to the purchaser's ability to repay the loans. Some schools offer J.D. admission to international LL.M. students or graduates without high regard as to whether the LL.M. transfers or graduates can success-fully complete the J.D. program.

68. Does the School Permit You to Cross-Register for Courses in Other Parts of the University?

Some schools, such as **The University of Pennsylvania** believe that exposure to multiple disciplines enhances LL.M. students' critical thinking, and enables them to more skillfully navigate and perform as leaders and influential decision makers. At **Penn** and other schools, LL.M. students may take courses at non–law-school graduate and professional schools at the university level.

H. The Nature of the School; The School's Philosophy; The School's Goals; The Program's Competitiveness

The more than 100 law schools that accept international LL.M. students are located in many U.S. states and territories, and have many distinct features and characteristics. Some schools are private, some are public. Some are stand-alone, some are associated with a parent university. Some have a regional focus, and some have a national or global focus. Some are associated with religious traditions. You have many to choose from!

69. Is the Law School Part of a University, or Is It a Stand-Alone?

If your law school has a parent university, you may have greater access to multidisciplinary faculty, staff, and students, and opportunities to take courses in other departments. If it is stand-alone, there may be less bureaucracy.

70. Is the School Independent; and Is It a Member of a Consortium of Law Schools?

For example, the following four independent ABA- and AALS-accredited U.S. law schools have formed the Consortium for Innovative Legal Education

"Best" Schools

(CILE) — **California Western School of Law; New England School of Law; South Texas College of Law;** and **William Mitchell College of Law**. They seek to offer a cooperative model for legal education (www.cile.edu/voyage.htm# mission). It is possible that schools in such consortia may cooperate with each other, which may further your networking and other opportunities while enrolled and after you graduate.

71. Is the School Associated with a Religious Tradition That Interests You?

John Garvey, former AALS president, noted "religiously affiliated law schools whose missions are defined or influenced by particular faiths" (www.aals.org/ events_am2009.php). In 2006 the Association of Religiously Affiliated Law Schools was formalized as an organization (www.baylor.edu/pr/news.php? action=story&story=40002). You may wish to attend such a school.

72. Is the Law School Part of a Historically Black College or University (HBCU)?

These schools may have substantial numbers of J.D. students of African descent and other minorities. LL.M. (and J.D.) students at these schools can hail from any country and can be of any race or ethnicity. *All are welcome!*

73. Is the School a Public (State) School or a Private School?

Public schools rely in part on funding from state governments, and must be responsive to the state on budgetary issues. Private schools do not have those constraints.

74. Is the Law School Global, National, Regional, or Local? Does It Advertise Regionally, Nationally, or Internationally?

Does the law school and LL.M. program website contain information about only regional events, or does it mention national or international events? Does it feature international LL.M. students, the LL.M. program for international students, or other information that would lead you to think the school is internationalized, or will cater significantly or at all to the needs of international students?

75. Does the *Law School* Have a Mission Statement or Strategic Plan?

If the law school does not have a *Mission Statement* or *Strategic Plan*, **beware.** The ABA requires law schools to have such plans, and to identify means to achieve established goals. The school *must* assess its success in realizing goals, and periodically re-examine and appropriately revise its goals. Each school should clearly articulate its purpose, promise, and performance. The school should display this Mission Statement or Strategic Plan plainly and openly, in full view for prospective and current LL.M. students and graduates and anyone interested. **Avoid schools that do not present a coherent picture of who they are, of what they hope to accomplish in legal education, and their promises for LL.M. students and graduates.**

76. Does the *LL.M. Program* Have a Mission Statement or Strategic Plan? Does This Document Express the Law School's Goals and Aspirations for Its LL.M. Program?

The LL.M. program should have its own *Mission Statement* or *Strategic Plan*, separate from the law school's, and the plan should be announced clearly on the school's website. **Avoid an LL.M. program that has no such plan, or that does not post it on its website.** That LL.M. program may not have a clear idea of what it is and what it hopes to accomplish. It may be a cash cow.

77. Is the LL.M. Program's Mission Statement or Strategic Plan Narrowly Focused, with Specific, Articulated, Measurable, and Quantifiable Goals, That Are Credible and Attainable?

Goals might include enrolling a specific number of LL.M. students from certain countries interested in studying in certain substantive areas; training students to return to their home countries for non-profit work; preparing students for entry into S.J.D. programs; or preparing students for careers teaching law. Ask the LL.M. administrator about its goals and mission. Ask for a copy of the LL.M. program's *Mission Statement* or *Strategic Plan* if you do not find it on the school's website. If the program has none, *beware.*

78. If the LL.M. Program Goals Are Firm, Can You Determine Whether They Have Been Met? (For Example, Can You Count How Many Graduates Have Become Law Professors, Returned to Public Service in Their Home Countries, or Otherwise Carried Out the Mission the LL.M. Program Promised?)

If you learn that a school's goals have not been met, *ask* whether the shortfall will be met — and *when*, and *how*. If, for example, the school's *Strategic Plan* calls for an increase in LL.M. students, and you learn that the LL.M. population has not risen, ask the school why. If the plan calls for hiring an LL.M. career officer and that person has not been hired — ask why. Ask students and recent graduates what is going on.

"Best" Schools

79. What Are the LL.M. Program's *Quantity*, *Quality*, *Mix* Enrollment Goals? (See Chapter 8)

Each U.S. LL.M. program should be able to clearly articulate — and consistently achieve — its enrollment goals — the *Quantity*, *Quality* and *Mix* of students it wants to admit on yearly and other periodic bases. Some LL.M. programs will want to admit as many students as possible, so long as the students meet bare minimum academic standards and have sufficient money for tuition and fees. **Beware — such programs may be cash cows.** Other LL.M. programs have carefully crafted enrollment goals that aim to cater to students with certain narrowly focused, substantive interests, with specific career objectives (such as teaching law), or who share a common bond (such as those associated with LL.M. programs at faith-associated schools). Determine whether each school's enrollment goals match your goals.

80. Do the School's Goals Match Yours? How *High* or *Low* Are Your Goals?

If your goal is to get admitted to whatever school you can, to receive a degree doing as little work as possible, and to have an easy time in your LL.M. program, then you may be happy with a cash cow or diploma mill. If you want to study, learn, achieve high academic goals, fulfill serious personal and career goals, and contribute to global society during and after your LL.M. program, then you will want to go to a school with noble goals that match yours. There are many such schools and LL.M. programs in the U.S. for you to choose from.

81. Is the LL.M. Program Competitively Selective and Difficult to Get Accepted Into? Or Does the School Accept 100 Percent of All International LL.M. Students Who Apply Who Meet the Bare Minimum Application Standards? Or Something in Between?

The competitiveness of a law school or its LL.M. program can be measured in many ways. Some argue that a competitive school or LL.M. program is one in which the number of applicants far exceeds the number of students admitted, while a non-competitive school accepts all or most applicants who meet the bare minimum admission requirements. This may or may not be the case.

Highly competitive schools. Some highly competitive U.S. LL.M. programs may accept fewer than one in every ten applicants. Their selectivity and entry competitiveness may reflect the high quality of applications and of the programs themselves, and the programs' reputations and ranks. These schools do not have enough seats to accommodate all applicants with impeccable records, and many extremely highly qualified applicants with outstanding records will not get admitted to these schools. U.S. LL.M. programs admit about 6,000 students each year, but schools with larger entering LL.M. classes may have only around 200 students or more. Many of the 6,000 students will enroll in competitive schools. Find out the acceptance rate of the school or schools that interest you. Even more important, find out *why* the acceptance rates are at their levels.

Non-competitive schools. Some U.S. LL.M. programs accept almost all applicants who satisfy the basic application requirements, which include: submission of transcripts, a minimum English language proficieny test score, recommendation letters, a personal statement, other required documents, and the application fee. If the school admits close to 100 percent of all applicants, what are the school's standards?[3] Is the school admitting students with very low English language proficieny test scores or low transcript marks? Some LL.M. programs may attract very few applications because of their reputations as cash cows or diploma mills.

82. Will You Choose a Competitive or Non-Competitive School?

You must decide your personal requirements — your own standards. If your goal is to join *any* LL.M. program that admits you, you may be in luck. Some schools, as stated, accept up to 100% of international applicants who meet minimum requirements. If you want an LL.M. from a competitive school with high standards, your choices — and concomitant requirements — are different.

83. What Is the History of the LL.M. Program You Are Leaning Toward? How Long Has It Been in Operation? Does It Have a Rich Tradition of Success? Does the LL.M. Program Have a Reputation for Being Dysfunctional, With Disgruntled Students and Graduates?

An LL.M. program need not be very old to be successful. Young programs may be well constructed, replete with skilled and dedicated professors and administrators, well focused, with fresh, strong energy, and altogether excellent at fulfilling most LL.M. students' reasonable expectations. Older, well-established programs may be equally excellent. However, young programs, and older programs, may be stale or dysfunctional, and calculated to spoil your desire for a high-quality education. Will your reasonable personal, educational, and career expectations be met? Learn a school's promises before choosing a school. Do you believe those promises will be kept?

---

3. Highly competitive schools may have high acceptance rates if, for example, the school attracts a narrow set of candidates who meet the school's needs. For example, if the school offers an LL.M. in an esoteric area of law, perhaps only a few candidates will apply. The school may admit all of those highly qualified applicants because of the low number of applicants. This is different from a school that admits all applicants who meet the bare minimum admission requirements.

84. Does the LL.M. Program Rely on One or Two Faculty Members Only? Or Is the Program Supported by the Faculty and Administration as a Whole?

Some LL.M. programs were established by one or two professors or administrators who also currently run the programs, and whose names and reputations are inextricably tied to the programs. They will work with you during your LL.M. year and be in touch after you graduate. You will gravitate toward them, and they will gravitate toward you. This type of person places significant importance on the LL.M. program and its students, and is highly dedicated. He or she will help you at every turn. Problems can arise, however, if a school has one or two dedicated professors or administrators of the type described above, but other faculty and staff (for instance, the dean) are apathetic and uninterested in the LL.M. program or LL.M. students. Good plans and intentions may be blocked or lie stagnant; the dedicated professor or administrator may retire, or move to another school, or resign from their LL.M. duties. Will the LL.M. program (or LL.M. track) fail because the key individual is gone, and the rest of the faculty or administration do not have the ability, desire, or commitment to the LL.M. program, or, by extension, to its students? Inquire; investigate! Also, ask students if they have relationships with *non-LL.M. faculty* and administrators. Are these "outside" professors (and staff) invested in the LL.M. program, or at least open to supporting it or its students and their needs and initiatives?

85. Does the School Have an Evening Division? Can LL.M. Students Take Day and Also Evening Classes?

Schools with evening classes offer flexibility. You can meet and study with part-time students who work during the day and go to school at night. They

---

Howard University Law School's History and Mission

Howard University School of Law "opened its doors in 1869 during a time of dramatic change in the United States. There was a great need to train lawyers who would have a strong commitment to helping black Americans secure and protect their newly established rights. In those days, the law school did not have classrooms. . . . [The six students in the first class] met at night in the homes and offices of the faculty. . . . The school grew not only in size, but also in the depth of its curriculum and in the outreach of its programs. In the 20th century, it became not only a school, but also the embodiment of legal activism. It emerged as a "clinic" on justice and injustice in America [and] a clearinghouse for information on the civil rights struggle. Our law school and its alumni have fulfilled their mission as agents for social change continuously for more than 133 years" (www.law.howard.edu/19).

"Best" Schools

tend to be older and more experienced than day students, and tend to have career and family obligations they juggle with law school obligations. You can learn a great deal from them.

86. Does the School Appear to Embrace Diversity, Non-Discrimination, and Human Rights?

Your school should have and enforce policies that protect against discrimination based on sex, age, race, color, national original, religion, creed, disability, citizenship, marital status, domestic partnership status, family status, sexual orientation, gender identity, genetic predisposition or carrier status, veteran status, or any other characteristic protected by law. If the school is not up front, not clear, or otherwise deficient in these important policies — **beware!** Are there any red flags, shady reputations, or unsavory rumors? They may be unfounded — but check them out!

87. Does the School Issue Conditional Admission to Students with Low English Language Proficiency Scores?

A conditional admission permits an LL.M. applicant to come to the U.S.; but before the applicant is fully admitted into the LL.M. program, the applicant must satisfy certain conditions. This often involves an applicant who has low English language proficiency test scores (Cambridge ILEC, IELTS, PTE Academic or TOEFL), but the LL.M. program still wants to admit the student. The school will require the applicant to enter an English language course and attain a certain test score or indication of English proficiency. The English classes could be taken at the university where the LL.M. program is, or maybe elsewhere in the U.S. **If you receive a conditional admission, you must satisfy the English language proficiency condition (or other stated condition)** *before you can take LL.M. classes.* Some LL.M. programs advertise that they *do not* offer conditional admits, when in fact they do *have other ways to facilitate entry* of students who have low English test scores. If your English proficiency scores are below a school's required level, and you have a particular interest in that school, you might consider applying anyway. *Do not give up; but do not be unrealistic.* Do your best to cut a clear path to full acceptance to the LL.M. program and credited entry to the classes. (See Chapter 12.)

A law school should not grant conditional admission if it does not believe you can reach the required level of English proficiency in a reasonable amount of time. A school may be tempted to offer conditional admission to applicants with very low English scores, and invite the students to the U.S. campus to spend many thousands of dollars on English language training, even though the school does not believe the students can reach the LL.M. program's required level of English proficiency. Maybe a school believes it is helping the student by giving them a chance. But the school may be motivated by revenue, particularly if the student is sponsored by a government that will pay tuition and living

"Best" Schools

expenses for their students to learn English. The students pay English language tuition, but the school has no obligation to admit them to the LL.M. program. The longer the student is studying English, the more tuition the school earns. If your goal is to study English in the U.S., choose an English language program. If your goal is an LL.M., choose an LL.M. program. (See Chapter 12.)

88. What Is the School's Primary Focus? Advocacy? Research? Training Practitioners to Work in the State? Skills Training? Does the School's Emphasis Match Your Goals?

For example, if you are interested in advocacy, you might want to choose a school that has a particularly strong advocacy program. You could choose as a foundation the ordinary LL.M. course offerings, which might include advocacy courses, and also participate in the many advocacy experiential opportunities that are likely offered at schools that emphasize advocacy.

89. Is the School's LL.M. Program a Cash Cow?

Review Chapter 6 for information to help you decide if a school's LL.M. program is a cash cow. If your goal is only to receive a U.S. law degree, and you are not concerned about the quality of services received at the law school, you might be satisfied with an LL.M. experience in a cash cow program. *LL.M. Roadmap* expressly and emphatically **does not** recommend cash cow LL.M. programs. (See Chapter 6.)

90. Is the School's LL.M. Program a Diploma Mill?

Review Chapter 6 for information to help you decide if a school's LL.M. program is a diploma mill. If your goal is merely to receive a U.S. law degree, and you are not concerned about the quality of your LL.M. education, how little work you may need to do to earn your degree, or how little you may learn while in school (or later learn as a result of being in school), or how your LL.M. degree from that program is perceived in the legal marketplace, you might find a diploma mill LL.M. program (and degree) to be satisfactory to you. *LL.M. Roadmap* expressly and emphatically **does not** recommend diploma mill LL.M. programs. (See Chapter 6.)

I. Equal Treatment for LL.M. and J.D. Students; LL.M. Students Integrated into the J.D. Student Body (See Chapters 15 and 16)

U.S. law schools should treat LL.M. and J.D. students equitably, and not unfairly elevate J.D. or other students at the expense of the LL.M. students or program. LL.M. and J.D. students learn a great deal from each other, and they can develop lifelong,

"Best" Schools

deep friendships with each other. LL.M. programs integrate the two groups in many ways, but should recognize and respect differences. International LL.M. students may need extra academic support, counseling for adjustment issues, or extra financial assistance. There should be an LL.M. office with full-time LL.M. personnel—separate from the J.D. program—dedicated to LL.M. students and LL.M. issues. J.D. and LL.M. students have different needs. Good programs meet LL.M. students' reasonable expectations. J.D. students need not suffer. On the contrary, the best U.S. law schools meet the needs of J.D. and LL.M. students (and graduates) equitably.

91. Are LL.M. and J.D. Students Treated Equitably? Do LL.M. *and* J.D. Students Have Access to Campus Recruiting, Assigned Career Coaches, Tutoring, Academic Assistance, Student Organizations, and Clinics?

J.D. students and LL.M. students are different and need not be treated *equally*, but they must be treated *equitably*—fairly vis-à-vis J.D. students. LL.M. students should *not* be afforded disproportionately fewer resources and opportunities than J.D. students.

92. Is There a Comprehensive Orientation Session for LL.M. Students? Do Non-LL.M. Faculty Participate?

Some schools have separate LL.M. orientations with no J.D. student attendance or participation. Others combine orientations but carve out special sessions for J.D. or LL.M. matters. Some schools invite *all* professors to participate in LL.M. orientation, not just professors involved with the LL.M. program. Open sessions with full participation demonstrate a desire to welcome and integrate LL.M. students into the law school family: to help the new LL.M. students realize the school is there to help meet the students' needs, that the faculty and staff salaries are paid by student tuition and fees, and that the LL.M. students are not present merely to fatten the law school's coffers.

93. Does the School Give LL.M. Students Priority in Oversubscribed Courses?

LL.M. students are enrolled for only a year, so they should have priority in taking popular courses. J.D. students will have more than a year to take those courses.

"Best" Schools

94. Do LL.M. and J.D. Students Take Courses Together? Do They Have an Opportunity to Become Friends?

Many schools create only one or two courses solely for LL.M. students, to introduce them to concepts and skills they did not learn in their home countries and that J.D. students likely have already covered. The remaining LL.M. student credits are generally earned in courses sitting side-by-side with J.D. students. LL.M. and J.D. students learn from each other. They spend time together in class and outside of class, perhaps studying, and possibly becoming friends. At some schools, LL.M. and J.D. students generally stay in their own circles outside of class, despite LL.M. program efforts to mix the groups. Each group has its own interests and concerns, and no one has much time in their busy schedules. If you want to get to know J.D. students better, you may need to take some initiative. *Do not be shy about reaching out to J.D. students!*

95. Does the School Sponsor LL.M. Dinners, Lunches, or Other Events?

Law schools are not responsible for the social or entertainment calendars of LL.M. students (or J.D. students). However, the nature of LL.M. programs for foreign lawyers demands that LL.M. students interact with J.D. students and faculty, and have access to other opportunities for enrichment and networking, informally and formally, outside the classroom. It is reasonable to expect LL.M. programs to host dinners, lunches, and other events generally; as well as for holidays and other social occasions such as Thanksgiving, Halloween, New Year's, and the end of the semester and school year. **Such events are not bonuses; they are expected.** LL.M. programs collect enough LL.M. tuition revenue to pay for these helpful and necessary networking opportunities.

96. Does the School Promote Interaction Between LL.M. Students and Non-LL.M. Faculty?

The school could host lunches or other events with small groups of international LL.M. students and non-LL.M. faculty who you would not otherwise meet. Students may form nonstressful ties with professors who are not their teachers. Professors may naturally interact more freely with students not in their classes. These interactions and ensuing bonds help non-LL.M. professors become and remain invested in the LL.M. program and its students and graduates. And they further bond the LL.M. students to the school and a many-faceted faculty, fostering relationships that may last for many years after the LL.M. students graduate.

"Best" Schools

97. Do LL.M. Students Sit on the Student Bar Association (SBA) or Other Organizations That Represent Students?

LL.M. students should hold seats on student governance bodies, as J.D. students do. LL.M. students can join the Student Bar Association (SBA), which serves as a student "legislature" for the school's student body, or join its leadership. If LL.M. students are denied an effective voice in student governance, this is a red flag: You might want to choose a different law school where student voices are heard.

98. Do LL.M. Students Sit on Faculty Committees (For Example, Faculty Hiring Committee, Disciplinary Committee, Dean's Advisory Committee)?

Some schools permit J.D. students to sit on different faculty committees that deal with, for example, law faculty hiring (interviews and hiring professors); academic affairs (sets the school curriculum); graduate affairs (deals with LL.M. and S.J.D. matters); and admissions (sets and implements admission policy, reviews incoming applicants, and decides which specific students to admit). Although LL.M. students may be present at a law school for only two semesters, they have a vested interest in the school's operation and future, and should be permitted to participate in decision making on topics such as curriculum, faculty hiring, and administration of the LL.M. program. If J.D. students can participate, why not LL.M. students? If the school cannot give a compelling reason for denying LL.M. students a voice in law school governance and operation, you might consider choosing a different school's LL.M. program.

J. Thesis or Substantial Writing Opportunities — Optional, Required, or Prohibited (See Chapter 17)

Thesis rules vary among LL.M. programs. Some LL.M. programs require theses. Some prohibit theses. Some permit a student to opt for a thesis. Make sure the program you choose matches your desire regarding a thesis.

99. Does the School or Program Require a Thesis? Is a Thesis Optional? Are Theses Prohibited?

If you want to earn an S.J.D. or Ph.D. after your LL.M., you definitely want to write an LL.M. thesis that might become the subject of your S.J.D. dissertation proposal. International students may need an LL.M. thesis (published) and an S.J.D. to compete against J.D. graduates for a U.S. law professor position, and an S.J.D. to teach in your home country. You likely do not need to write a thesis to work for a law firm, corporation, nongovernmental organization, or even the UN.

"Best" Schools

100. How Many Thesis Credits Are Earned?

Schools may award as few as 2 credit hours for a thesis, or as many as 12 (or more) credit hours. Realize and consider that, as a practical matter, the more attention you devote to research, the fewer credits you can earn in classroom courses.

101. Does the School Require Thesis-Track Students to Have a Faculty Thesis Advisor? Does Each Thesis-Track Student Have a Thesis Committee?

A faculty thesis advisor will help you choose a thesis topic, guide your thesis research and writing, review your drafts, afford support, and see the project through to the end. Choose a school with active, informed, helpful, and available faculty thesis advisors. A Thesis Committee — in addition to the faculty thesis advisor — may generally guide you in researching, writing, presenting, and defending your thesis.

102. Did the School Recently Eliminate a Thesis Requirement for One or More Thesis Tracks? If So, Why? If the School Permits or Requires Theses, Is the School Willing and Able to Provide Resources to Support the Research and Writing Needed for High-Quality Theses?

Researching and writing an LL.M. thesis is very hard work for students. Requiring theses requires LL.M. administrators, professors, librarians, and tutors to work hard as well, to support thesis-writing students. A school may have sound pedagogical reasons for *not* requiring or permitting LL.M. students to write a thesis. For example, there may be other ways for students to demonstrate their expertise and command of the subject matter. However, a school may prohibit thesis writing because of the burden it poses on faculty and staff, and the school's general costs associated with theses. If an LL.M. program permits or requires students to write theses, the school must provide faculty members to supervise the theses, legal communication professors to instruct on writing, librarians to instruct on research, and possibly tutors, particularly for students whose native language is not English. The school may need to create Thesis Committees, conduct thesis defense sessions, and collect submitted theses for housing in the law library or other repository. A school may decide that the costs associated with thesis writing are too high for the school, and accordingly drop the thesis requirement. If you want to write a thesis, choose a school that will permit you to do so, and make certain that the school is willing and able to support your thesis writing at the level you need for you to reach your thesis goals.

103. Does the School Permit You to Defend Your Thesis?

At some schools, LL.M. students submit their theses to their faculty advisors, who then assign a grade. That is it. The advisor might not even offer feedback to the student, nor assist with publication. Other schools require LL.M. students to have a thesis committee of three or more faculty members, to whom the students present their thesis in writing, and also defend orally, and a grade is awarded if the thesis committee approves. If you want to publish your thesis or use it as the basis of an S.J.D. proposal, you might choose an LL.M. program that has a rigorous, academically challenging thesis curriculum, and that will actively assist you throughout the process. If you plan to return to your home country, ask if your country's academic authorities will recognize a U.S. thesis for which you did not have to mount a defense.

104. Will the School Help You Publish Your Thesis?

If you want to become a law teacher, you should definitely publish your thesis. Ask the school if and how it will help you publish your thesis. Your faculty thesis advisor and school should facilitate your access to paid subscription services to access law journal publishing guidelines, and help you submit your articles to journals.

105. Are LL.M. Theses Filed in the Law School's Library?

Before you write your thesis, read theses tendered by the school's LL.M. graduates. Are they of good quality? Have they been published? Are they in an online database? Look for signs that the schools have a strong interest in assisting LL.M. students in their research and writing, and in promoting student written work even after they graduate.

106. Are Theses Posted on the School's Website?

Some schools are proud of their graduates' research and writing and post the work on their LL.M. program's website. Some schools list only the titles and areas of research of the theses, whereas others post the entire thesis. In short, some schools are more committed than others to their students' writing.

107. Does the School Publish *Thesis Guidelines*?

Acquire the school's Thesis Guidelines *before you enroll.* Be certain the school can meet your thesis research, writing, and publication expectations. If you do not find

"Best" Schools

Thesis Guidelines online, ask an LL.M. administrator to send them to you via e-mail. She should. Unfortunately, some schools have no *Thesis Guidelines,* and LL.M. students must fend for themselves, working ad hoc with a professor. If the school does not have *Thesis Guidelines,* do not enroll.

K. Grading Schemes; Minimum Grade Point Average (GPA) Required to Stay Enrolled and Graduate; Graduating with Honors (See Chapter 15)

LL.M. programs assign grades to students for their academic work. Each school's grading scheme differs from the next. The National Jurist *recently reported that U.S. law schools have a new wave of grade inflation, spurred in part by the job woes of their recent graduates.*[4] *Grades are important!*

108. Are LL.M. Grades Inflated?

Some schools grade international LL.M. students more generously than other schools do, resulting in inflated high grades for those students. Schools that hand out inflated high grades develop reputations as being "easy," and prospective employers discount the grades. This implicit devaluation penalizes students at those schools who legitimately earned high grades. Artificially high grades can also harm graduates whose grades are inflated because prospective employers might have higher expectations of them than will bear out. If the graduates do not perform at the high level that their high grades might predict or promise, the school's program loses credibility, and other graduates will not be taken seriously.

109. Is It Too Easy for LL.M. Students to Graduate with Honors?

Some LL.M. programs almost automatically bestow honors on the overwhelming majority of their LL.M. graduates. If you want to graduate with honors, attend one of these schools. (See Chapter 15.) But do not attend one of these schools if you want these "honors" to be taken seriously.

---

4. Karen Dybis, "Why Law Schools Are Inflating Grades," *The National Jurist,* September 2010, at 18. Law schools mentioned as having "changed their grading system over the past few years" include NYU; Georgetown University Law Center; Tulane University Law School; Golden Gate University School of Law; Loyola Law School Los Angeles; University of Southern California (USC) School of Law; University of California, Los Angeles (UCLA), School of Law; and University of California, Hastings College of Law.

110. Is a Professor Required to Grade LL.M. and J.D. Students in the Same Class Using the Same Criteria, or Required to Grade the Two Groups Separately?

Some schools require separate grading to protect J.D. students, in case LL.M. students who already have law degrees may fare better than J.D. students who are in their first degree program. Separate grading might also protect LL.M. students, who may receive lower grades than J.D. students who are used to the Socratic method, and taking and typing U.S. law school exams. Some schools let individual professors decide how to grade J.D. and LL.M. students. Some schools grade all J.D. and LL.M. students on the same scale.

111. Does the School Grant Accommodations for LL.M. Students, Such as Extra Time to Take Exams, or Permitted Use of a Foreign Language Dictionary?

Some LL.M. programs permit LL.M. students to have more time than J.D. students to take exams. For example, if J.D. students must take a two-hour exam in two hours, an LL.M. student might have more time — for example, three hours for the same exam. Some schools permit LL.M. students to use a foreign language dictionary during their exams. Other similar accommodations are not uncommon.

112. What Are the LL.M. Retention and Graduation Rates?

Some schools permit international LL.M. students to pass their courses and graduate almost irrespective of how poorly they perform academically. This is not an exaggeration. Some schools, however, require LL.M. students to maintain a certain grade point average (GPA) or be dismissed from the program, with no tuition or fee refund, and little prospect of being able to transfer to another LL.M. program.

113. At What GPA Will an LL.M. Student Be Suspended?

Some schools require J.D. students to maintain a higher GPA than LL.M. students. For example, some schools require J.D. students to maintain a 2.3 GPA to be in good standing and graduate, and require an LL.M. student to maintain only a 2.0 to be in good standing and graduate. Some schools have different GPA requirements for students in different LL.M. tracks. Less competitive schools tend to be less demanding, allowing LL.M. students to continue with a low GPA. More competitive schools may insist on a higher GPA for their LL.M. students.

114. **Does the School Offer Accommodations for Disabled Students? Does the School Have a Disability Services Office? Are There Any Disabled Current Students or Graduates You Can Communicate with About Their Experiences at the Law School? Is the School Connected with the National Clearinghouse on Disability and Exchange or Other Groups That Promote Educational Opportunities for Disabled Persons?**

You should know the answers to these questions whether or not you are disabled. You can learn a great deal about a school based on how willing it is to accommodate people with special needs, and whether the school merely meets or goes beyond its legal obligations regarding disabled persons. Under U.S. law, U.S. schools are obligated to provide equal access through "reasonable accommodations" to persons with disabilities. U.S. LL.M. programs should not discriminate against disabled applicants, and should not discriminate against disabled students who enroll. You should ask whether the school has a disability services office, and ask if that office will provide the services that you need. Different schools may have different abilities, and willingness, to provide different accommodations. You can get further information about the law related to disabled students from the *National Clearinghouse on Disability and Exchange,* which is funded by the U.S. State Department and administered by Mobility International U.S.A., which is a cross-disability organization serving those with cognitive, hearing, learning, mental health, physical, systemic, vision and other disabilities. Mobility International U.S.A. seeks to empower people with disabilities to achieve their human rights through international exchange and international development. Scholarship information for disabled LL.M. students can be found on its website at www.miusa.org. (See Chapter 24 and Appendix II.)

L. Academic Support Services

International LL.M. students have academic needs that differ from the academic needs of domestic J.D. students (and from the academic needs of domestic LL.M. students). Many international LL.M. students are unfamiliar with the Socratic method of law school teaching, with taking notes in class on a laptop during Socratic dialogue, and with law school essay exams. International LL.M. students may need extra academic support, for example, in the form of tutoring, briefing cases, or preparing for exams. Good LL.M. programs will have academic support services in place specifically to assist LL.M. students who need extra help adjusting to graduate law study at a U.S. law school.

115. Will You Have a Faculty Member as an Academic Advisor?

Schools may provide LL.M. students with different types of advisors (e.g., English language, or law school adjustment advisors), who may or may not be faculty members trained in law. Your faculty academic advisor should be able to help you choose law courses, help sort out thesis advising issues, help you focus your career aspirations, advise on internships, and be available to discuss and advise on any academic issue arising during your LL.M. year of study. Current students and graduates can inform you whether their academic advising needs were met by the staff assigned these roles. Academic advisors with "lofty" credentials may not be as effective as those without.

116. Does the School Have an Academic Support Team to Assist If a Student Is on Academic Probation?

For example, **Temple**'s academic support team teaches LL.M. students studying techniques, provides them with exam preparation strategies, and affords them the opportunity to review their coursework with their professors throughout the semester.

117. Does the School Have Tutors for LL.M. Students?

At **California Western** J.D. students tutor LL.M. students. **The University of Baltimore School of Law** assigns a J.D. student to serve as a Law Achievement Workshop (LAW) Scholar for each class to assist LL.M. students with approaches to study for classes, and with general questions about classroom procedures. **Baltimore** also has academic counselors and an academic resource center, and explicitly notes that each LL.M. student will be given the opportunity to work with a mentor to further the student's interests and educational goals. The Career Office there will assist the student in identifying a mentor from among the faculty or law alumni network.

The school might also assign you to a tutor who will assist with English communication issues or with substantive law issues. Schools may have an "Achievement and Learning Center," or similar office, where students and tutors or other staff may discuss weekly law school classes, assignments, legal writing, or other issues or areas.

118. Is Each International LL.M. Student Assigned a J.D. Student Mentor Who Will Assist the LL.M. Student?

These students are called different names at different schools. For example, **American** has "diplomats," **University of Minnesota Law School** has "mentors," **Boston College Law School** and **Stanford Law School** have "buddies," **USC** has "J.D.-LL.M. partners," and **Ohio Northern** has "International Peer Advisors" or "IPAs." They help familiarize LL.M. students with the school, U.S. culture, and the city in which the school is located. They help students adjust to a new environment, answer questions, and point students in the right direction for needed assistance.

"Best" Schools

"Best" Schools

119. Are Practice Exams and Exam Review Sessions Offered for LL.M. Students?

The school should begin preparing you for exams *before* the first semester begins! You may need significant guidance on how to study for and take U.S. law school exams, which are no doubt very different from what you experienced in your first law degree. If you want to do well in exams, choose a school that begins training you for exam-taking during the summer before your classes begin, and that has exam review sessions where you take practice exams in the first semester. Your U.S. professors expect you to perform in substance and style at the same level as domestic J.D. students. Your school should help prepare you to accomplish this.

120. Does the School Have Counseling Services Available for LL.M. Students Who Need Assistance with Stress, Adjustment, or Other Issues?

Do not be alarmed! It is well known that some LL.M. students have adjustment difficulties when they arrive in the U.S., during exams or other periods of great stress, when they receive a grade lower than expected, during holidays when they are away from home, or when incidents happen in their homelands or with their families far away. **It is not uncommon for law students to be stressed.** Every law school should have in-house counseling services or referrals to counselors on the law school or university campus, or in the local community. It is a good idea to try to prevent stress, and to tackle any stressful issues that may arise. Stress and anxiety arise nevertheless, despite our precautions. Before you arrive at school, find out what services will be available to you to help you to deal with adjustment and other personal issues. Just knowing that counseling is available may be enough to help you avoid stress, and it will let you know where to go and how to deal with any stress that does arise. **LL.M. students should be aware that there is no shame in seeking counseling at any time during their LL.M. program.** Indeed, stress management is an important personal skill to learn — to be an effective student and lawyer and person — and to have and enjoy a reasonably happy life! Some cultures may spurn or stigmatize any applied psychology or emotional therapy treatment. U.S. domestic students, professors, staff, and many others in the U.S. routinely utilize these services when issues arise. You should, too. In many cases, these services are covered by your health insurance so you will either have to pay nothing or only a small amount.

121. Is the School Internationalized?

An internationalized school's culture caters to international students, and to integrating U.S. and foreign schools and other institutions. It values U.S. professors and students who teach and study abroad and who have strong interests in transnational education. It integrates U.S. J.D. and international LL.M. students, but recognizes the differences between the two groups, which both rightly demand that their needs be accommodated. The school's website should indicate the school's commitment to internationalization, and should reveal if the school *is* internationalized. International LL.M. students may suffer at a non-internationalized school.

M. Law Journals, Law Reviews, or Other Prestigious Groups in Which LL.M. Students Might Participate?

International LL.M. students can learn a great deal and gain valuable research and writing experience working on a U.S. law school law review or law journal or other prestigious student publication.

122. Can LL.M. Students Work on Law Journals or Law Reviews?

LL.M. students can gain valuable research, writing, and editing experience working for a law journal or law review during their LL.M. year. Traditionally, J.D. students at the end of their first year of law school participate in a school's law journal competition, and they may earn a place on a journal. Competition winners begin journal work at the beginning of their second year of law school, and work until they graduate. If you enter an LL.M. program in August or September, you will have missed the law journal competition in May of that year. The next competition is the following May, the month you graduate! LL.M. students may be denied this excellent experience. If you want to do journal work, ask your school if you qualify. Some schools permit it. For example, **Duke University Law School** selects up to five international LL.M. students per year as editors of its *Journal of Comparative and International Law*; **Harvard** permits international students to be editors of the *Harvard Human Rights Journal* and the *Harvard International Law Journal*; and **Columbia Law School** invites LL.M. students to be editors of the *Columbia Journal of Transnational Law*. **St. Thomas** requires its *Intercultural Human Rights Law Review* to have an LL.M. co-editor and executive editor.

123. Can LL.M. Students Write and Publish Articles in Law School Journals Even if LL.M. Students Cannot Be Journal Editors?

Even if the school's law journal or review will not accept LL.M. students as editors or other workers, you still might be able to publish an article, book review, comment, or other work in a school's publications. You might even publish your thesis or an essay or other piece you write for a law school class, or publish something you wrote before you arrived to work on your LL.M. degree. *Ask the faculty member responsible for advising the law review or journal of interest to you, and ask the student law review or journal editorial board(s).*

"Best" Schools

124. Can LL.M. Students Write and Publish Articles on Nonjournal Publications, Including Web or Electronic Publications?

Law schools may publish working papers series, other substantive law essays or bulletins, alumni magazines, or pamphlets on degree programs. LL.M. students might write and publish articles or essays therein. LL.M. students themselves can be suitable subjects of features in these law school publications. LL.M. students have a wealth of experience, accomplishments, and talents that schools may like to highlight in distributions to alumni, current students, law school friends, and prospective students. Review law school websites and publications. Look for evidence that the school values LL.M. students and graduates.

125. Subscribe to a Law School's News Listserv; Join Their Social Network.

Contact law schools whose LL.M. programs interest you. Request to be subscribed to the law school listserv so the school will send you e-mail messages about law school, LL.M. program events, or other information. You can learn a great deal about a school, a program, and what that program values by reading what is included in the e-mail listserv messages and communicating with schools through social networking.

N. Career Development (See Chapter 26)

The career development office should assist you in finding part-time work during school, work in the U.S. for a year post-LL.M., work in a third country, or work in your home country. The office's job is not to find you a job, but to assist you in developing and reaching your career aspirations. Depending on your needs, make certain that the school you choose has career development personnel and resources to assist you as an LL.M. student and LL.M. graduate. If you plan to return to your pre-LL.M. home country to work, the career office can also assist you, perhaps by introducing you to cross-cultural work exercises, mock interviews (so you can learn about interviewing from both candidate and employer perspectives), or even business etiquette seminars.

126. Does the School Have an Excellent Career Development Office That Serves the Needs of International LL.M. Students?

The Law School Admissions Council (LSAC) notes that "One of the tests of a good law school is the effort the institution makes to help its students and graduates understand their career options and find satisfying employment."[5]

---

5. www.lsac.org/JD/Choose/law-school-features.asp#. Although this statement was made in the context of law schools as a whole, it applies to LL.M. programs. LL.M. programs breach their promises if they do not help students and graduates reach their career aspirations. Unfortunately, *many* LL.M. students at *many* schools complain that their LL.M. programs do not adequately help them find satisfying employment.

A significant complaint I have heard is that LL.M. programs do not provide adequate guidance and assistance to LL.M. students who want to work in the U.S. post-LL.M. They are not complaining that the school does not find jobs for the students. *The complaint is that the LL.M. program does not provide adequate and appropriate assistance.* How much is adequate? A good starting point is the amount of job search and other career development the school provides to J.D. students. LL.M. students should be provided with proportionate, equitable assistance. Some schools provide LL.M. students *far less* career assistance, proportionately, than they provide J.D. students. Some schools do not have career officers devoted to, or trained to, work with international LL.M. students, and do not even permit LL.M. students to use career office services reserved for J.D. students. This second-class student citizenship status is unacceptable! Do not accept it: meaning, do not *choose* a program or situation that will automatically, structurally, or subsequently place you in a secondary or lower status position.

However, if the school expressly informs you, before you enroll, that it will not provide you with career assistance, you cannot reasonably complain after you enroll. If the school informed you beforehand of this deficit, you were free to choose another school that provided the career services you desired. A problem arises in part because international LL.M. students might reasonably expect to receive career assistance at a level equitable as compared to J.D. students, but the school is unwilling to provide LL.M. students with this basic service and fails to inform the LL.M. students until it is too late, after they are already on campus.

Some LL.M. programs, both large and small, have an office, or at least personnel, to serve the specific career needs of international LL.M. students. For example, at Loyola-New Orleans College of Law, "LL.M. students . . . have full access to the services" of the Office of Career Services, which "assists students and alumni with career counseling and professional development needs" (http://law.loyno.edu/career-services-program). No two LL.M. program career offices are the same. Some are excellent. Some are not. An excellent LL.M. career office is critical for LL.M. students and graduates, even if they are not currently looking for jobs. *Before you accept a school's offer to attend, find out what career services it offers.* In all cases, the law school should serve LL.M. students who want internships, or temporary or permanent U.S. or overseas work at law firms, corporations, intergovernmental organizations, or nongovernmental organizations.

127. Does the School's Career Office Serve Both LL.M. and J.D. Students? Does the School Have Personnel Whose Job Description Specifically Requires Them to Provide Career Services to International LL.M. Students?

Schools with small LL.M. programs may not need a separate LL.M. career office, but they need career personnel who can adequately assist international

"Best" Schools

LL.M. students. Larger LL.M. programs should have a separate LL.M. career office with dedicated staff specifically trained and qualified to address LL.M. student career needs. Working with domestic J.D. students differs markedly from working with international LL.M. students. The groups have different backgrounds, different visa and other eligibility issues, different credentials, different levels of exposure to career development in a U.S. context, and perhaps different aspirations. Career counselors need different sets of skills and knowledge bases to competently serve domestic versus international students. If career counselors are not trained or do not possess the highly specialized tools needed to work with international LL.M. students, the career office cannot satisfy LL.M. students' needs. International LL.M. students should reasonably expect an LL.M. program to provide appropriate career services. A program that does not do this expressly, fully, and well fails to fulfill LL.M. students' reasonable expectations. This causes tension and results in disgruntled LL.M. students.

128. Should You Enroll If the School Does Not Have a Separate LL.M. Career Office and Does Not Have Dedicated LL.M. Career Personnel?

Maybe. Maybe not. If you have a job waiting for you in your home country, or if you plan to do an S.J.D., you may not care about LL.M. career personnel, at least not now (though you may need their services later). On the other hand, if you want a new job now, you will want immediate and abiding career assistance. If the school has inadequate career assistance now, it will likely have inadequate assistance later. Also, if the school suffers from inadequate career assistance, it may well prove inadequate in other as yet unknown but significant ways. Take it as a bad sign! Even though some professors or LL.M. instructors may be able to help you in an ad hoc manner, you might be out of luck. You cannot and should not expose your job security and future career prospects to the whims of such an operation. *Avoid such programs if you need career services. Before you accept a school's offer to attend, make sure they have in place the career services you need.*

129. Are the LL.M. Career Counselors J.D. or LL.M. Graduates?

Effective career counselors *need not* be J.D. or LL.M. graduates, but they must have substantial insight into the layered fields of law and the complex web of domestic and international markets and networks for LL.M. students and graduates. Career counselors with other educational backgrounds — with experience, for example, as a law firm recruiter — may have rich knowledge and experience to assist international LL.M. students seeking employment, and may have extensive contacts in the layered fields of law.

130. Has the Career Office Successfully Facilitated LL.M. Student Career Placement?

LL.M. career offices should tell you how successful they have been in facilitating placements. Ask for data. Ask whether graduates work, and whether they work in the types of jobs in cities or countries you find desirable. The career office can provide contact information for graduates whose placements interest you. Build a strong network through graduates. Some LL.M. graduates may not find jobs for many reasons, including poor grades, lack of prior suitable or impressive work experience or performance, few job openings in their areas of interest, or a poor economy. If you do not find the job of your dreams, it may not be the fault of your career office or school! The career officer's job is to assist you, not to find a job for you. You must fulfill your part of the bargain—you have to get good grades, prepare an acceptable CV, and hold reasonable expectations given your background, experience, and the job market and economy.

131. Does the School Support LL.M. Career Development with the Same Level of Commitment That It Affords J.D. Career Development?

The school should devote proportionate resources to all law programs, and not disproportionately favor the J.D. over the LL.M. program (or vice versa). Schools may argue that their career offices are not equipped to deal with international LL.M. students whose backgrounds and career goals differ so much from domestic J.D. students', and who are viewed differently by employers, and who have employment limitations associated with their F-1 or J-1 visas. Resumes and CVs of international LL.M. students *do* differ, in form and substance, from those of domestic J.D. students. Furthermore, J.D. employment levels, and not LL.M. levels, factor into commercial rankings by U.S. News & World Report for ranking purposes, and are considered by the ABA. Also, the ABA requires that J.D. programs not be harmed. But these are excuses—not good reasons to neglect LL.M. students' vital and legitimate needs. **If you want assistance with post-LL.M. employment, the school's career office should be able to assist you, as they assist J.D. students.** If they cannot or simply will not help you in this crucial matter of career, *do not go to that school,* if post-LL.M. job placement and subsequent career are important to you. The school need not have a listing of every lawyer and law firm thousands of miles away in a foreign country (though U.S. law schools do, indeed, have access to such information through *Lexis, Westlaw,* or *Martindale Hubbell*), nor can they possibly host events on campus for foreign prospective employers at the same level as they host events on campus for prospective employers from the city and region where the school is. But U.S. law schools must effectively assist international LL.M. students in achieving their career objectives. **If a school**

"Best" Schools

is not prepared to meet reasonable career assistance expectations of LL.M. students, perhaps the school should not have an LL.M. program. Or at least maybe you should not go there. Chapter 26 contains more information about LL.M. job hunting.

132. Have LL.M. Graduates from the School Worked in Your Country, in the Country Where You Want to Work, and in the Field of Law That Most Interests You? If So, Has Your Career Office Helped Facilitate Your Communication with Those Graduates of Your School?

Before you choose a school, check whether it has graduated anyone from your country, or whether any graduates work in your country or in the city or country where you want to work, or in fields of law that interest you. Contact them. Remember to be respectful of their time, and the possibility that dozens, if not hundreds, of other prospective students may contact them as well. Ask them about their experiences with the U.S. law school and the LL.M. program. Do they recommend that you join that LL.M. program? Do they discourage it? Did the program help them achieve their goals? You might find that those graduates may also prove to be important networking contacts for you when you begin a job search. Chapter 26 discusses networking and other ways to help you reach your career goals.

133. Where Do the School's Alumni Work?

LL.M. alumni can provide you with good information before you apply, while you are enrolled, and after you graduate. They can also be excellent networking resources. You can find LL.M. alumni on *Lexis, Martindale-Hubbel, Westlaw,* and other websites. You can search for LL.M. graduates from your country; from your home university; from your U.S. LL.M. program; who work in specific industries or for particular law firms or private companies; or who fall into a number of other pertinent categories. You can ask the U.S. Embassy in your country (and also your country's embassy in the U.S.) for a list of people from your country who have studied at different U.S. law schools, faculty members of your home university who may have studied in the U.S., and lecturers and staff from other parts of your university. Ask the LL.M. office of the schools that interest you for alumni contact details, and recognize that though the schools will have some privacy rules that prevent your acquiring all the contacts you might want, they will provide contact information for alumni who have volunteered to be contacted. Check to see if alumni are listed on the school's website. **Wake Forest University School of Law**, for instance, posts alumni photographs, names, countries, and current employment or school or other information — of all LL.M. graduates from the inception of their LL.M. program in 1998 through the current graduating class. Again, alumni contacts may answer your questions and assist as you select a school to attend, or may help you land a job after graduation. **Do not be shy!** But of course be mindful that alumni are very busy people with full lives, and they may not have as much time to devote to you as you might like. You might contact them only after you have tried to get information from other sources.

134. Does the School's Career Office Have Reciprocity with Other Law Schools' Career Offices?

Many U.S. law schools have arrangements with other law schools in other U.S. cities that permit students from either school to use the career offices of both schools. Thus if your Los Angeles school has a relationship with a school in Chicago, and you want to work in Chicago, you can fly to Chicago and use the career services of the Chicago school, which will surely have more listing for jobs in Chicago than the Los Angeles school's office will have. Conversely — reciprocally — students at the Chicago school can likewise use the career services office at your Los Angeles school. In this way, even if your school is not in the city where you want to work, you may still get good access to job opportunities in other U.S. cities.

"Best" Schools

"Best" Schools

135. Does the School Publish an *LL.M. Legal Employment Guidebook?*

Many LL.M. program websites do not post an *LL.M. Legal Employment Guidebook* online. However, some schools do have excellent guides for students seeking employment in the U.S., their home countries, or third countries. If you do not find an *LL.M. Legal Employment Guidebook* on your school's website, request one via e-mail. Also check the **Yale** website for its employment guide (which is cited as a great resource for employment or guidance by more than one other LL.M. program).

136. Does the School Sponsor an LL.M. Job Fair Where Employers Interview Students from Your School and Other Schools? Does Your School Participate in LL.M. Job Fairs Held at Other Schools?

LL.M. job fairs are important venues — not only are they where LL.M. students might meet their next employer, but also where they might gain valuable interviewing experience, learn about the legal markets where they might eventually work, and learn a great deal about their own aspirations and abilities. An LL.M. student necessarily engages in self-assessment as she prepares for the interviews at a job fair, and during and after the interviews as well. And at LL.M. job fairs, LL.M. students might meet LL.M. students from other schools who are from your same country or who speak your language. More important, you may meet LL.M. students who are interviewing at the same firms or similar firms, who are interested in the same subject matters, or who have similar — or contrasting, and illuminating — experiences and ambitions. Altogether, LL.M. job fairs are an excellent opportunity to network and learn. However, some job fairs are only available for LL.M. students from certain law schools. *Ask the LL.M. program administration whether it participates in any of the major job fairs held in different parts of the U.S.*

137. What Other Career Development Strategies Does the School Deploy to Benefit and Advance of Its LL.M. Students?

LL.M. career offices must be creative in how they assist international LL.M. students. For example, **Minnesota** founded a *Judicial Observation Program* where LL.M. students spend time in chambers and in court working with local judges. Other LL.M. programs have since copied this program, which not only provides LL.M. students with an opportunity to gain insight into U.S. law and the U.S. judicial system, but also adds to the substantive experience base they can include on their CV — and introduces them to judicial officers and lawyers who may be able to offer them guidance or assistance.

O. Jobs: On Campus, Off Campus, Summer, Optional Practical Training (OPT), Curricular Practical Training (CPT), or Academic Training (AT) (See Chapters 21, 22, and 27)

Many international LL.M. students want to gain practical legal work experience in the U.S. during their LL.M. program and after. Some may be willing to volunteer, while others need to earn money. F-1 or J-1 students may work on campus up to 20 hours per week while school is in session and up to 40 hours per week during breaks and holidays. Law schools should reserve on-campus slots for international students who are unable, by law, to work off campus (unlike U.S. citizens or permanent residents, who may work off campus). LL.M. graduates may work full time for 12 to 18 months post-LL.M., depending on whether they are an F-1 or J-1 student.

138. Does the School Reserve On-Campus Jobs for LL.M. Students?

LL.M. students on F-1 (or J-1) visas may work only on campus for up to 20 hours per week when classes are in session, and up to 40 hours per week during school breaks. U.S. citizens or permanent resident students may work on or off campus. LL.M. programs can reserve on-campus jobs for international students, some of whom may need to work to help cover unexpected living or other expenses, and some who want to gain U.S. work experience. Because international students generally arrive in the U.S. and on campus immediately before classes begin, domestic students who live in the city or who arrive earlier might get the jobs first. An LL.M. program could reserve slots for international students in the law library, law school computer labs, or, if necessary, in law school food services. Ask about reserving a job before you arrive on campus in the fall.

139. Does the School Have Summer Clinics, Research Institutes, or Programs That Might Either Qualify for Practical Training (OPT, CPT, or AT) — or That Otherwise Might Be Available Under Your Visa Status?

The rules for OPT, CPT, and AT are discussed in Chapter 21, and will not be covered in detail in this chapter. In brief, F-1 students may work for 12 months post-LL.M. in jobs in the U.S. that are related to law. **Optional Practical Training (OPT)** is designed to give students an opportunity, as a continuation of the LL.M. academic experience, to gain practical, hands-on experience working in the law. It may not be easy to find OPT work due to the lack of paid jobs offered by many U.S. law employers. Although OPT is available for volunteers, few LL.M. students can live for a year in the U.S. and work without pay. Some schools facilitate the OPT work of F-1 students in law school clinics, research institutes, or other campus law programs. Pay may be minimum wage, but at least you will

"Best" Schools

gain legal experience during the OPT period. **Curricular Practical Training (CPT)** for the F-1 student is available while an LL.M. is enrolled (pre-gradua-tion). **Academic Training (AT)** is available for J-1 students pre- or postgradua-tion. *Before you enroll at the school,* ask an LL.M. administrator about possible OPT, CPT, or AT work. During your LL.M. year, consider working part time at a law campus institute, do an excellent job, and make it easier for that or a similar institute to hire or recommend you for a job after you graduate.

140. Can LL.M. Students Give Occasional Lectures, Talks, or Otherwise Present Themselves — Informally, Formally, or Professionally — Outside the Classroom to Faculty, Students, and the Outside Community?

Yes. On campus, you can give lectures, speak at faculty or student seminars, or participate in working groups in subject areas of interest to you or in which you have expertise. If you are offered an honorarium, ask your LL.M. administrators before accepting it to ensure you comply with relevant U.S. government regulations. If you lecture or participate in activities off campus, you might, through networking or happenstance, be able to land a paid opportunity, either through part-time work while in school or full-time work after you graduate.

141. Can LL.M. Students Teach Courses on Campus Outside the Law School?

If you have teaching experience, or work experience or expertise in a specialized area, you might want to — and you would be allowed to — teach a course in a non-law undergraduate or graduate department on your campus. You could teach a course in your native language, in economics or geography, criminal justice or international relations — in some area in which you have the requisite compe-tence. You will gain a teaching credential for your CV, and extra money.

142. Can LL.M. Students Teach Courses at the Law School?

Some schools permit LL.M. students to teach courses or seminars or give lectures in their areas of pre-LL.M. practice or expertise, or teach courses in the students' native languages. Many LL.M. students already have rich careers as judges, legislators, practitioners, and even professors, and have a wealth of knowledge and experience to share.

P. LL.M. Student Handbook (See Chapter 15)

Law schools should make available to LL.M. applicants the set of rules the applicant must comply with while a student. That is only fair. Some law schools post their LL.M. Student Handbook online for any member of the public to download and read. Some make the LL.M. Student Handbook *available only upon matriculation. Other schools have no* LL.M. Student Handbook *at all, and on many matters expect the* J.D. Student Handbook *to be adequate.*

143. Does the School Have an *LL.M. Student Handbook?* Is It Comprehensive, Separate, and Distinct from the *J.D. Student Handbook?* Is It Available Before You Apply? Before You Enroll?

LL.M. Student Handbooks should offer clear, comprehensive guidance on LL.M. students' rights and obligations before and during the course of their programs. Some programs offer ad hoc rules, or rules mixed in with a J.D. student guide, that do not speak directly to LL.M. students, or are incoherent. **You should request the** *LL.M. Student Handbook* **before you enroll.** To avoid unpleasant surprises, read it, think about it, and decide whether you believe the rules are reasonable and fair and whether you believe you can and will comply with them.

144. Can You Abide by the School's Academic Requirements Contained in the *LL.M. Student Handbook?*

You must agree to comply with general rules in the *LL.M. Student Handbook*, and with the academic requirements contained therein. For example, the school may require that LL.M. students maintain a certain grade point average, be resident for at least two full semesters, write a thesis, or take and pay for certain courses even if you already took and passed similar courses in another degree program. You will only know if you are prepared to meet the guidelines if you read the *LL.M. Student Handbook*. And you cannot know what you are in for if you do not.

Q. Student Body Diversity and Breadth; Nature of Fellow Students

International LL.M. students benefit greatly from U.S. law schools with diverse student bodies — different races, ethnicities, socio-economic backgrounds, sexual orientations, political perspectives, and law and non-law hobbies and interests. Diversity is important within the J.D. student body, as well as in the LL.M. student body. LL.M. students can benefit most if the school helps ensure that J.D. and LL.M. students are integrated in classes and extracurricular activities.

145. Does the School Regularly Have LL.M. Students from Your Country? From Your School?

If a school has students from your country, and you learn who those students are, and their backgrounds, you can maybe ascertain with a fair degree of accuracy whether you and your background fit the "profile" of students usually admitted at

"Best" Schools

that school from your country. Having a shared national background, you will have a common ground for comparison, maybe a good grasp of who they are, to help gauge your own eligibility for admission, as well as the likelihood of your being able to attain your own goals through a particular LL.M. program. Also, you will have a ready-made database of contacts you can consult about applying to that school, about life as an LL.M. student there, and about post-LL.M. prospects. Each school should be able and willing to provide you with a list of LL.M. students and graduates from your country, or from any other country of interest to you, and to give you contact details for graduates. They should also be able to provide details about students and graduates from countries where you want to work, from organizations you want to join, or who work in areas of law that interest you. You might, upon inspection, decide that there are too many LL.M. students from your country for your internationalist aspirations, and you would prefer to go to a school with more student diversity in the classroom and on campus.

146. Are Most Students in the LL.M. Program from the Same Country or School?

If most students in a program are from a particular country or school in that country, it may reflect the program's substantive focus; serendipity; or an arrangement between the program and a foreign law faculty, or between an LL.M. faculty member and an overseas school. Large concentrations of students with little diversity are fine. But you should know, in advance, the likely ethnic or national breakdown. If the school caters to large numbers of Asian, African, or European students, if you are not from those regions you may feel disappointed, or disadvantaged for networking and for other purposes or needs. On the other hand, you would have a great opportunity, in that setting, to interact with students from different backgrounds, and expand your networking horizons.

147. Are the LL.M. Students from Widely Diverse Work or Professional Backgrounds?

If most of the students in an LL.M. program are prosecutors in their home countries, or military lawyers, or law faculty members, and you are not a prosecutor, military lawyer, or law faculty member, you may feel you do not fit in, or that the school does not cater to your needs. Or you may see that variety or particular mix as a positive: The more diverse the class is, the greater the opportunity for you to develop relations with students with different backgrounds and interests. It increases your range of experience, and widens and deepens your networking pool.

148. Will Other Students Share Career and Other Goals?

If an LL.M. program focuses on preparing graduates for S.J.D. degrees and to become law teachers, would you want to join that program if you do not want an

S.J.D. or to teach law? It would be better to join an LL.M. program with students who share your goals.

149. Does the School's Website Have Student or Graduate Testimonials?

Testimonials posted on an LL.M. program website are likely to be positive. Dig deeper for feedback from current students and graduates who may have negative or critical comments about a program. Assess the credibility of those who have positive and negative comments. Testimonials can also be found in books. Stuart Loh, a 2009 Australian graduate of **Stanford**, chronicled his experience in *LL.M. Experience: A Year at Stanford Law School.*

150. What Are the Schools' Advertising Materials Like? Warm? Focused on Students? Or Photos of Deans and Professors, Only?

Scrutinize each LL.M. program's advertising. Advertising is designed to convince you to apply and enroll. You will not find advertising that highlights a program's flaws and faults. Ask yourself if each LL.M. program you might be interested in possesses attributes or flaws among the 218 considerations in this chapter that might convince or deter you.

151. Does the School Send Professors, Administrators, Current Students, or Graduates to Recruit Prospective LL.M. Students in Your City or Country?

If recruiters come from different schools to the city or country where you live, try hard to attend their information sessions. These are great opportunities to hear firsthand about particular schools. Recruiters will want to know that you have researched their schools (which you can do on the Internet). Their visits are excellent opportunities to ask follow-up questions, particularly questions you might not want or think to ask in an e-mail message. You might consider making a list of the school characteristics that are important to you, and ask the recruiter to provide you with more information along those lines. You can use the 218 criteria here in Chapter 7 as a guide or checklist for your questions!

R. The School's Alumni

Alumni can describe what the LL.M. program was like when they were students, such as relations between faculty and students, and other details of student life. They can tell you whether the school helped them reach their personal and professional goals, and whether their program expectations were met. Contact alumni and ask about aspects of the LL.M. program that are important to you. If finding a post-LL.M. job is important to you, ask alumni about their experiences with the career office. Ask whether the LL.M. office helped them publish their theses, find housing, or sort out financial matters. Were faculty genuinely interested in LL.M. students? Every school should provide you with alumni contact details. Also track down alumni from different U.S. law schools through independent sources such as Martindale-Hubbell, Lexis *or* Westlaw, *the Internet, or the U.S. Embassy in your country. Ask them their honest opinions.*

152. Does the School You Prefer Have an Active Alumni Association? In Your Country?

Before you apply find out if the school has an alumni association in the city or country where you live or where you are from. Ask for alumni contacts. Contact them. They may offer valuable assistance as you apply, while you are enrolled, and after you graduate. Ask about alumni associations from all U.S. schools that interest you. *You may contact alumni from one school, and end up enrolling at a different school. That's fine. Do not be shy!*

153. Does the Law School Alumni Association Have LL.M. Graduate Members?

Some law schools do little to recognize that LL.M. graduates, like J.D. graduates, are valued members of the law school's family. Law school alumni associations should welcome LL.M. graduates, send them copies of alumni bulletins and newsletters, and report news about them on their websites. At some schools, alas, LL.M. alumni are ignored. **Beware of these schools!**

154. Does the Alumni Board Have LL.M. Graduate Members?

A school's alumni association may have an Alumni Board that governs it. If your school's Alumni Board has no LL.M. graduate members, how can the board readily identify and address LL.M. needs? Ask the LL.M. office why there are no LL.M. graduates on the Alumni Board. Better yet, ask the Alumni Board directly.

155. Does the Law School's Board of Visitors Have LL.M. Graduate Members?

A law school's Board of Visitors, which usually consists of noted graduates or others with a bond to the school, advise the dean and senior law school administration on the school's policies and practices. If a Board of Visitors has no LL.M. graduates, will it readily identify and cater to the needs of LL.M. students, who are an important part of any U.S. law school?

156. Does the Law School or University Alumni Directory List LL.M. Graduates?

Many schools' alumni directories list graduates' names, employers, and contact details. If LL.M. graduates are not listed, this not only disrespects them, it also disserves those who may want to contact each other. It deprives J.D. graduates from learning identities, locations, and employment status of the international LL.M. graduates, who could help with networking. J.D. graduates working at U.S. firms should be able to consult the directory to find LL.M. alumni who work in foreign countries who could be hired as local counsel or could advise on transnational issues. Students or graduates going on holiday may want to learn if there are alumni in the countries they plan to visit.

157. Does the School Maintain a Database of LL.M. Graduates' Contact Information?

A law school's database should contain names, employers, work and home addresses, and other contact information for international LL.M. graduates, The school needs to send graduates transcripts, diplomas, and certificates, and the school should send graduates alumni association details and bulletins. If the school has such databases, it should easily be able to connect current and prospective students with graduates (for general networking, for business, or for holiday contacts). (If the school can track down LL.M. graduates to collect owed tuition or other debts, it should certainly be able to track you down to provide information about joining the Alumni Association and about enjoying privileges of being a graduate of the law school!)

158. Do LL.M. Graduates Contribute Financially to the Law School?

U.S. schools rely on alumni financial contributions to help cover general expenses. This may seem bizarre, given high tuition costs, but it is a tradition. Alumni with fond law school memories and loyalty may contribute handsomely. Ask how many LL.M. graduates contribute. Schools publish glossy magazines listing alumni contributors, with amounts. Are any LL.M. alumni listed? The quantity of LL.M. alumni contributors speaks louder than their dollar contributions. Many LL.M. graduates donating small amounts is more impressive than a few LL.M. large money donors. I know one school with a sizeable LL.M. class that requested each LL.M. student to contribute $10 to the school. *The response was miniscule, and not because students did not have $10 — the cost of a hamburger and fries. The LL.M. students did not contribute because they were not happy with the school.*

"Best" Schools

S. Law School Administration, Staff, and Other Resources

Better LL.M. programs have superb administrators and staff who satisfy LL.M. students' reasonable expectations. The best personnel exceed LL.M. student expectations. An excellent administrator will not compensate for an LL.M. program that lacks curricular basics, critical services, or other fundamentals. That program will fail no matter how nice, efficient, and helpful its personnel are. Current students and graduates may candidly assess administrators and staff. Ask them. Would an inept, unhelpful administrator tell you directly that he is inept or unhelpful? (Though he may tell you indirectly, through inept and unhelpful actions, such as failure to reply to e-mails, or being absent from campus for half of each work week.) Whomever you ask, you can assign whatever weight you deem appropriate in deciding whether to rely on the person's comments.

159. Is the Dean Vested (or Invested) in the LL.M. Program?

The law school dean is the highest ranking law school employee, with authority over all academic, administrative, and other school matters. The dean is responsible for all degree programs, including the J.D., LL.M., and S.J.D., and for all personnel (including the LL.M. associate dean, other associate deans, professors, and staff). Deans are busy, but should devote sufficient time and energy to LL.M. students.[6] Successful LL.M. programs have deans who are invested in those programs. Such deans take a strong, personal and active interest in the LL.M. program's smooth operation and efficacy, and a personal interest in LL.M. students. A vested dean is dedicated to the LL.M. program, and takes all measures to ensure that the program meets LL.M. students' reasonable expectations and needs, and supports the LL.M. program with all the resources necessary to be successful. Vested deans ensure that the school facilitates LL.M. students' abilities to reach their academic, personal, professional, and career goals. If the dean is not vested in the LL.M. program, the LL.M. program will likely not succeed.

How can you know if the dean is vested?

Ask current students if they have ever met the dean, or if the dean ever or often appears at LL.M. functions. Has the dean reached out to LL.M. students, for example, by holding a town hall to find out how the LL.M. year is going, if LL.M. students are encountering any difficulties, and if LL.M. student expectations are being met? Do current students know the dean's name, or what the dean looks like? At some schools LL.M. students meet the dean, or see the dean

---

6. The dean does not need to hike with LL.M. students (as one dean apparently did with LL.M. students at Diamond Head in Honolulu, Hawaii). But, the dean should be present and available, and should demonstrate a solid commitment to the LL.M. program.

face-to-face for the first time, when the dean presents them with their diplomas on stage at graduation. If an LL.M. program has over 200 students, one would expect a different level of attention than if the LL.M. program has only 5 or 7 students, or even 30 or 40 students. A vested dean ensures that the LL.M. program is not secondary; and is not dysfunctional; that any dysfunction is not blamed on employees; and that any problems are cured. **The buck stops with the dean. Or should.**

If the dean does not consider the LL.M. program to be a priority, then the dean, the administration, the faculty, or other decision maker might consider terminating the LL.M. program. It may be better to have *no* LL.M. program than to have an LL.M. program that is poorly run, with an apathetic dean, in which LL.M. students, graduates, and other stakeholders are dissatisfied. Or, as one reviewer of the *LL.M. Roadmap* suggested, "perhaps the apathetic Dean should be terminated."

160. Is the LL.M. Associate Dean, LL.M. Faculty Director, or Other Head of the LL.M. Program Vested (or Invested) in the LL.M. Program?

An LL.M. associate dean or LL.M. faculty director is responsible for academic and administrative matters in the LL.M. program. For ease, I refer to this person as the "associate dean." The associate dean must be "vested" or "invested" in the LL.M. program, perhaps in some ways even more than the law school dean. The dean is responsible for the entire law school, but the associate dean is directly responsible for the LL.M. program itself, and reports to the law school dean. More important, the associate dean is the custodian of LL.M. interests, and is particularly responsible for ensuring that the reasonable expectations of LL.M. students are met. The associate dean must advocate to the dean on behalf of the LL.M. program, to help ensure that the LL.M. program is not a cash cow, that the program has all the resources it needs to be effective, and that LL.M. and non-LL.M faculty members are supportive of the LL.M program. The associate dean should regularly canvass the LL.M. students to assess smooth running of the program, and should rectify any problems. If the associate dean is absent from the school or absent from the program, the needs of the LL.M. students will likely not be met. Ask current students and graduates about their relationships with the associate dean. I have encountered international LL.M. students who on the very last day of classes at the end of a fall semester told me that **they did not know that their LL.M. program even had an associate dean**, when in fact there was an associate dean responsible for LL.M. academic and administrative affairs. This circumstance was unfortunate, but might be expected with absent administrators. Associate deans fulfill critical roles that cannot be delegated to lower level staff members, and are not appropriately handled by e-mail or phone.

"Best" Schools

161. Do the Principal Administrators (e.g., Associate Dean) of the LL.M. Program Live in the Same City or State as the School, or Do They Commute Long Distances? Are They Present and Visible on Campus? Are They Absent? Are They Available to Deal with Problems That Arise in the Evenings or on Weekends?

It is important that associate deans and other LL.M. principal program administrators live near the school, and be present, so they can handle administrative, academic, and personal matters that arise with international LL.M. students. The chief administrator (who may be an "associate dean") oversees all LL.M. academic and administrative issues and should be present to deal with LL.M. issues, particularly related to health (physical or mental), security, and safety. International LL.M. students are adults and can handle many issues on their own, but they are entitled to the full service they pay for. Residential LL.M. students have a reasonable expectation that the person with direct responsibility (associate dean) will be on hand in person, whereas an

"Best" Schools

LL.M. student in an online program would not. Some associate dean responsibilities are not appropriately delegated to other staff. Is it possible for an LL.M. program to function properly if the associate dean lives far away, commutes to school, and is physically present in the school's city only two to three days per week? *Be particularly wary if the associate dean for the LL.M. program commutes or is otherwise absent. Take caution if the associate dean for the LL.M. program will be a Visiting Professor at an out-of-state law school and will not be present during your semesters on campus. You are entitled to a full-time, present academic leader of your LL.M. program while you are enrolled.*

162. Do LL.M. Administrators or Academic Advisors at Your School Possess J.D., LL.M., or Other Law Degrees from the U.S. or Overseas?

Not all LL.M. administrators have or need law degrees. It is ordinarily advisable, however, that the administrator expressly charged with advising on academic matters possesses a law degree — bearing in mind, when scrutinizing their credentials, that administrators without law degrees can be as helpful and even more helpful. The vast majority of law professors in the U.S. hold J.D. degrees, but not LL.M. or S.J.D. degrees. (See Chapter 5.)

163. Does the School Have an LL.M. Office for LL.M. Administrators? Are Administrators Dedicated to the LL.M. Program?

If a school has only five or so LL.M. students, there may be no need for a large team of administrators dedicated exclusively to those few, or any need for a large dedicated physical space. In such cases, LL.M. administrative, academic, and personal (student) matters may be ably handled by existing personnel working out of their current offices, who might receive additional salaries for their added work. But a sizeable LL.M. program needs a dedicated physical office space with personnel expressly dedicated to the program. The J.D. program is separate from the LL.M. program, and each program should have dedicated resources.

164. Does the Law School Employ Current Students in Positions of Authority over Other Current Students?

Current J.D. students should not serve as LL.M. student admissions officers, or in any other positions of LL.M. program authority. J.D. students and LL.M. students are essentially peers and take classes together. If a current J.D. student has official authority over LL.M. classmates, equity among students is shot, and conflicts may arise.

"Best" Schools

> ### *Get Answers to "Sensitive" LL.M. Program Questions*
>
> • If you get admitted to more than one U.S. law school, how will you choose which is best for you? How do you get information to compare the schools?
> • How do you learn if the LL.M. career office provides excellent service? Do you ask the career office "Do you provide excellent service"?
> • How do you learn if the LL.M. administration is responsive to student complaints? Do you ask the LL.M. administration?
> • Are school officials the most reliable sources for such sensitive information?
>
> **You need *other* sources of reliable information. Asking the administration is not enough.**
>
> • Consult current LL.M. students and recent graduates.
> • Read news articles about the school. Read blogs.
> • Conduct your own, in-depth research into different schools.
> • Find out if the school that interests you is indeed the best for you.

165. When You Phone the LL.M. Office, Are You Put on Hold? Does It Take More Than 24 to 48 Hours to Receive Replies to E-mail Messages That You Send to the LL.M. Office? Do You Repeatedly Receive Out-of-Office Auto-Replies?

LL.M. offices are busy during many periods, including at the beginning of the first semester when LL.M. students are arriving, and at the end of the academic year when plans are being made for the commencement ceremony. But even during busy periods, an LL.M. office should not be *too busy* at least to communicate. If the LL.M. office appears to be understaffed or too busy when you contact it for information before you enroll, the situation may well be the same, or worse, after you enroll. Choose a school that is demonstrably well equipped to deal with students. Be mindful that your expectations about reply time must be reasonable. You cannot expect a school to reply in 30 minutes to every e-mail message that you send. Be courteous and professional when you communicate with the school. Some schools keep notes in application files of applicants' rudeness or disrespect, or of applicants' courtesy and professionalism, and can be expected to take these behaviors into account when deciding whether to admit or reject an applicant. For surely your behavior as an applicant may be as good an indication as any of what your behavior would likely be as a student.

166. Does the LL.M. Administration Have an "Open Door" Policy?

A good LL.M. office is open to current LL.M. students, prospective LL.M. students, and LL.M. graduates alike. You should feel welcome to stop by to browse materials and to inquire about any issue that may interest you.

Administrators have many responsibilities and you may need to make an appointment to discuss matters that may take some time to resolve. But the LL.M. office should be eminently "open door": where you feel invited and welcome to stop in.

167. Do LL.M. Administrators Have Business Cards?

All administrators and personnel associated with LL.M. programs should have business cards. When you meet LL.M. personnel or visit their offices, ask for their business cards. They will help you to remember their names, give you a clearer picture of their job responsibilities (based on the job title), and remind you whom to contact with questions or problems. An LL.M. administrator at one school reported that their school *did not* provide LL.M. staff with cards because of costs. A school cannot afford to deny business cards to staff. A school that cannot afford business cards is in trouble, and should be considered seriously suspect. The program is purportedly preparing LL.M. students to thrive in the professional world, where business cards are universally valued and required.

168. Are LL.M. Administrators Members and Leaders of Professional Organizations Dealing with Graduate Programs?

Various professional organizations are devoted to, or have divisions related to, U.S. graduate programs. Check to find out if administrators and professors of your school are members, leaders, or active participants in groups such as the AALS Section on Graduate Programs or Graduate Legal Exchange; the NAFSA: Association of International Eduactors; the National Association of Graduate Admissions Professionals (NAGAP); the ABA; or other organizations. Ask if they participate in conferences such as the *Global Legal Skills Conference.*[7] Participation in these organizations exposes administrators to the latest trends in graduate education, and helps to keep their schools on the cutting edge of LL.M. program operation and content delivery.

---

7. The 2011 Global Legal Skills Conference was held at the John Marshall Chicago School of Law, and featured several panels that focused on LL.M. programs. Topics included: empowering international LL.M. students to participate actively in law school classes; team teaching international LL.M. students — pairing a linguist with a lawyer; helping international LL.M. students find a job; and preparing international LL.M. students for the New York Bar Examination.

A roundtable titled "Meeting the Needs of International LL.M. Students" had as participants the following law professors: Jane E. Scott (**St. John's University School of Law**), Mary Rose Strubbe (**Chicago Kent School of Law**), Susan C. Wawrose (**University of Dayton School of Law**), and George E. Edwards (**Indiana University School of Law, Indianapolis**).

The 2012 Global Legal Skills Conference will be held in San Jose, Costa Rica, in March.

"Best" Schools

169. Are LL.M. Principal Administrators Available to LL.M. Students Monday Through Friday?

LL.M. administrators should be available during regular business hours, and reasonably available evenings and weekends for emergencies. LL.M. administrators are not babysitters, and LL.M. students are not children. However, LL.M. programs do — or at least should — provide a full range of agreed services to LL.M. students. Administrators should — and usually do — work to satisfy reasonable LL.M. student needs. Many, if not most, LL.M. programs succeed on this score.

170. Ask Current Students and Graduates About the Administration's Competence and Effectiveness.

Be sure to get accurate information about the school's administration *before you enroll.* Current students and graduates can no doubt tell you a lot. *Ask them.*

171. Does Your School Participate in LL.M. Recruiting Fairs, Where Prospective LL.M. Students Can Meet Administrators from Different U.S. LL.M. Programs?

If you happen to be in the U.S., you might be able to participate in a fair for prospective LL.M. students, such as the one held at **DePaul University College of Law** each fall. Representatives from different LL.M. programs are present at these fairs, and they provide information about their programs, students, and graduates. The fairs are a great way to learn about a school that interests you, and any number of others while you are at it.

172. Does the LL.M. Program Publish Newsletters? Does It Have a Facebook or Other Page for Students and Graduates?

Quality, frequency, degree, and depth of involvement or engagement with newsletters or social networking may indicate the level of a school's commitment to its students and graduates, in whose welfare the school should be interested long after the LL.M. year. Schools also want their students and graduates to have a long-lasting, vested interest in the LL.M. program and the school. You want to join a school that takes pride in its programs, its students, and its graduates. You will also want to join a school that communicates with its stakeholders.

173. What Technology or Social Network Does the Law School Administration Use to Interact with Prospective Students, Current Students, and Alumni?

Some administrators interact with applicants via Facebook, Skype, or e-mail to address queries and concerns. Schools may conduct information sessions online with participants around the world. Current LL.M. students can address issues related to them, and graduates can share their experiences. Some schools have LL.M. alumni networking sites on their websites, or maintain Facebook or similar pages. This helps graduates stay in touch and helps prospective and current LL.M. and J.D. students network.

174. Is There a Student Organization Specifically for LL.M. Students?

All law schools have a Student Bar Association (or similar group) that governs the student body. Schools should have an LL.M. Association (perhaps titled Master of Laws Association — MLA) to address LL.M. student concerns (which differ markedly, as we have seen, from J.D. student concerns). If this type of organization does not exist at your school, start one! Or do not go to that school! An LL.M. student organization could, for example, raise LL.M. concerns with the administration; organize panels at which members give presentations about the legal systems of their respective countries; organize international cultural events; and promote interaction among J.D., LL.M., and S.J.D. students. It could remind the administration in pointed and potentially helpful ways that LL.M. students have reasonable expectations and needs that differ from those of J.D. or S.J.D. students.

175. Does the LL.M. Admissions Committee Consist of More Than One Person? More Than Two?

It will not be easy for you to get answers to these questions. But the answers are germane: The fewer the members on the admissions committee, the fewer the number of applications the school likely receives — and the more likely the school will be less competitive or selective in whom it admits. You might ask the LL.M. office.

176. Are LL.M. Students or Graduates on the Admissions Committee?

J.D. students routinely sit on J.D. admissions committees, review applications, and vote on admitting J.D. students. LL.M. students (and graduates), likewise, could sit on LL.M. admissions committees. At the very least, LL.M. students and graduates should be permitted to have a voice in the direction of the school regarding LL.M. admissions, just as J.D. students have a voice regarding J.D. admissions. LL.M. students and graduates have an interest in determining the incoming class's quantity, quality, and mix. (See Chapter 8.)

177. Does the Dean or Associate Dean Convene Regular LL.M. Town Hall Meetings?

At town hall meetings the dean and associate dean can address LL.M. student concerns. Few or no such meetings could mean the deans are not very or not at

"Best" Schools

all conversant in the needs and concerns of the LL.M. students under their purported tutelage and professional stewardship and care. Even if the administration does not actively seek your input, the administration *needs* your input. If the administration does not convene town halls, does not have an LL.M. Advisory Board that meets with the dean regularly, or does not have any other mechanism for hearing LL.M. student complaints and concerns, *you* must figure out an appropriate manner of conveying complaints and concerns to the administration. Unfortunately, at some schools, the administration does not take the lead and initiate such discussions with the students. The burden shifts to students, who want and need to be heard.

T. Law Library

You will surely become very familiar with the law library during your LL.M. year, and law librarians may become some of your best friends. When choosing law schools, inquire about library facilities (number of books; UN Depository status; number of seats; level and types of technology). Ask whether LL.M. students are assigned to a particular law librarian who will train them in legal research and assist with research assignments.

178. Is the Law Library a UN Depository?

Of the 450 UN Depository Libraries, 45 are in U.S. universities. About 24 of those U.S. schools have LL.M. programs. This access may be helpful or crucial if you are doing international law research.

179. Does the School Have International Librarians?

Many LL.M. students conduct research in foreign or international law. If your thesis or specialization lies in these areas, ask if the school has librarians with relevant expertise. They can help you with any research project you have, and become your best friends — academic and personal.

180. Do the Law Librarians Have Law Degrees, Library Degrees, Both or Neither? Do They Have Critical Skills Needed to Assist LL.M. Students?

Librarians assist LL.M. students in many ways. They are helpful to students writing theses, who have research exercises associated with classes, who need information about prospective employers or about advanced law degrees, or who need other information not readily available in an Internet search. Librarians can become the best friends of LL.M. students, who can and often may consult their law school's librarians even after they graduate.

181. Are LL.M. Students Assigned to Law Librarians (or Are Librarians Assigned to LL.M. Students)?

Librarians can assist with thesis, class, homework, or other research assignments. International LL.M. students can learn a great deal from law librarians, and law librarians can learn a great deal from international LL.M. students.

182. Does the School Have a Substantial Foreign Law Collection in English? A Substantial Foreign-Language Law Collection?

Many international LL.M. students write theses related to the law of their home countries or regions. Their primary materials may not be in English. Some schools have stronger foreign-language collections than others. If you need a special database, ask the school's library to subscribe to it, or purchase relevant volumes for you. Or the library might borrow the materials from another school's library.

183. Does the Law Library Have Up-to-Date Technology? Are Its Hours Reasonable?

Law libraries tend to be fully wired, but some have inadequate electrical outlet access and arrangements, and lack other basic or advanced technology to satisfy typical student demand. Libraries should be open in the mornings before classes, on nights, and on weekends — times that LL.M. students may want to study. Law libraries should have extended hours during exam and other busy seasons.

184. Does the Law Library Contain Adequate Student Seating, Particularly During Exam Periods?

Many LL.M. students prefer to study in the library and may spend long days, nights, and weekends there. Law libraries should have sufficient space for LL.M. students to work comfortably. Often LL.M. students are assigned their own reserved library carrels.

U. Bar Exams — Practicing Law in the U.S. (See Chapter 28)

If you want to sit for a U.S. bar exam, carefully choose your LL.M. school. Some bars require foreign degree holders to have a certain number of U.S. law course credits of a particular type. Ensure that the U.S. bar you plan to take will accept credits from your LL.M. program. Check the bar pass rate for LL.M. students from your school and from your home country. Ask bar passers from your school and country what steps they took to pass. Some states will permit you to sit for the bar without an LL.M. from a U.S. school. As this edition of LL.M. Roadmap *is going to press, an ABA proposal is circulating that could*

"Best" Schools

impact bar eligibility for international students. In the spring of 2011, New York amended rules took effect that govern the eligibility of international LL.M. graduates to sit for the New York Bar. Furthermore, proposals have been circulated by the ABA on possible LL.M. program certification and other bar-related issues. It is imperative that you seek updated, current information from the websites of the ABA, the New York Bar, and the relevant organizations for the bars of other states that interest you.

185. Your School Should Maintain Records on International Student Bar Passage. Did Anyone From Your Country Who Graduated From the School Take and Pass a U.S. Bar Exam?

Your school can provide you with information about LL.M. graduates from your country who passed a U.S. bar exam, in the state where you want to take the bar. Inquire. Contact those graduates. Ask them how they prepared.

186. What Is the School's Bar Pass Rate for International LL.M. Students?

LL.M. graduates from some schools routinely have high U.S. bar pass rates, which does not guarantee you will pass a bar if you attend that school, any more than attending a school with a low rate means you will fail the bar. But it is helpful to know a school's pass rate. The school may provide tutorials to help students prepare for the bar, or may focus on skills needed for bar success — such as legal analysis, memorization, and English language skills. Although knowing a school's bar passage rate is helpful, it should not be construed as the best measure of "quality" legal education or training.

187. Is a "Bar Review Course" Offered in the City Where Your School Is? Which Bar(s) Do LL.M. Graduates from the School Typically Take?

Most graduates who take a U.S. bar exam enroll in an expensive multiweek bar review course offered by a private company. You would take such a course designed specifically for the state where you plan to take the bar. If you live in that state, the company may offer the course in your own city; maybe even in your law school's classrooms. If your school is not in the state where you want to take the bar, you might have to travel to take the course, or access lectures via podcast. Find out which bar exams graduates of your law school typically take and find out how they have routinely prepared for those exams.

188. Can LL.M. Students Take "Bar Courses" During Their LL.M. Period?

The difference between a "bar review course" (see above) and a "bar course" is explained in Chapter 28. In brief, a "bar course" is a regular law school class on a topic that is routinely covered on bar exams. Some schools deny LL.M. students the opportunity to take certain "bar courses" offered as part of the law school's curriculum. Thus, an LL.M. student may be deprived of a subject area she feels she needs or wants to be adequately prepared for the bar. Some schools schedule bar-related courses during periods that conflict with mandatory LL.M. courses. *If you want to take a bar and want to take bar-related courses during your LL.M. year, be certain to ask before you enroll. Find out the rules. Check the scheduling.*

189. Does the School Provide LL.M. Students with Adequate Information About State Bar Examinations and Examiners?

Some LL.M. programs provide students little bar exam information. Others provide considerable information and assistance. Schools can assist by compiling information for the more popular bars. Students ultimately must contact the individual bars themselves, but the support and advice from their LL.M. program is invaluable. In the spring of 2011, New York revised the requirements for international lawyers with U.S. LL.M. degrees to be eligible to sit for the New York Bar examination, and other states are considering similar revisions to their local rules. Also in the spring of 2011, the ABA circulated for discussion the "Proposed Model Rule on Admission of Foreign Educated Lawyers." It is extremely important that LL.M. programs provide you with accurate, up-to-date information, and that you also seek information from the bar agencies for the states that interest you. (See Chapter 28.)

190. Will the LL.M. Program Help Prepare You for the Bar Exam of a Particular State?

Many LL.M. programs state that they do not intend specifically to prepare international LL.M. students to sit for any state's bar, but others state the opposite — that their LL.M. program is intended to prepare international graduates for a U.S. bar. Some programs provide information to LL.M. students about bar admission, advise them on LL.M. courses that might prove useful, or offer special courses that will help satisfy bar exam eligibility requirements. Chapter 28 discusses some of these facts about schools and some bar requirements. If you want to sit for a U.S. bar exam, make certain that your LL.M. program meets the relevant requirements.

V. Finances (See Chapters 23, 24, and 25)

Chapter 23 focuses on costs associated with an LL.M. degree, including LL.M. application (and pre-application costs); travel to and from the U.S. (including visa fees); tuition and fees (including books and laptops); U.S. living expenses; employment costs (during and postdegree); and ways to save money. Chapter 24 focuses on scholarships and grants. Chapter 25 focuses on loans.

"Best" Schools

191. Does the School Offer Endowed Scholarships for LL.M. Students?

Endowed scholarships are typically awarded based on criteria established by a school benefactor who donated money to be used for certain categories of LL.M. students (e.g., from certain countries, studying certain subjects). Not many LL.M. programs offer substantial amounts of funding through endowed scholarships. (See Chapter 24.)

192. Does the School Offer LL.M. *Tuition Discounts* (or "Tuition Discount Scholarships")?

Although many schools advertise that they do not provide tuition discounts to LL.M. students, many schools do provide them. If a school gives you a tuition discount, you will pay a discounted tuition rate, that is, you will pay less than full tuition, in the same way that an airline passenger would pay less for an airline ticket if the ticket is discounted. The school does not give you any scholarship money, just as an airline will not give any money to the passenger who bought the discounted ticket.

For example, if tuition is $40,000 per year, the school may grant you a scholarship of $10,000 (or 25%), meaning you must pay only $30,000 (or 75%) for the year. Schools may tell you the scholarship is based on merit or on your financial need. The school may see a value in your enrolling, and will want to entice you. At some schools, **most** LL.M. students are offered tuition discount, irrespective of merit or need. These schools offer discounts to help bolster their enrollment, and to compete with more attractive schools.

Some schools may assign fancy names or titles to their tuition discounts, to bolster enrollment by suggesting that the routine tuition discounts are based on merit and are worthy of a level of recognition that would justify students listing the titled scholarship on their CVs. So, for example, a school may award a student a discount called a "George Washington Scholarship" or an "Abraham Lincoln Scholarship," with the hopes that if the tuition discount with that name is mentioned in the student's admission letter, the student might be more inclined to accept the offer and enroll, with the benefit being: (a) the tuition discount (which the school would have offered anyway); and (b) the opportunity to list "George Washington Scholarship Recipient" on their resume. Offering tuition discounts is as much of a commercial transaction as offering discounts on loaves of bread at the market, or offering discount air tickets. The discount is an inducement to enter into a relationship. It is business.

193. Bargaining for a Higher Tuition Discount or Scholarship.

If you are offered a tuition discount or an endowed scholarship, you might use that school's offer to try to attract the attention of another school that interests you more. For example, say that tuition at school *A* and school *B* is the same — $40,000 per year. School *A* offers you a $10,000 discount and school *B* offers you $20,000. You could send an e-mail message to school *A* (which you would rather attend), inform *A* about school *B*'s higher scholarship offer, and ask *A* if it will match *B*'s $20,000 scholarship. *A* may meet the offer.

194. Does the School Offer Full Tuition Awards Requiring You to Pay Zero Tuition?

Few schools offer *full* scholarships that cover housing, books, food, and other expenses above tuition. Most schools will waive only a portion of the tuition. The student must still pay for housing, books, food, transportation, or other expenses. Other funds will be needed.

195. Can You Afford the Tuition?

LL.M. programs in the U.S. are expensive. (See Chapter 23.) Not everyone can afford an LL.M., or afford it presently. Some students will work, save money, and then apply. Others may wait until they earn an outside fellowship. Consider how you will meet your short- and long-term costs. Keep an open mind and explore *every* funding opportunity.

196. Does the School and Its LL.M. Program Appear to Be Worth the Money?

Only you can determine whether you believe the school and its LL.M. program will meet your reasonable expectations at a cost agreeable to you. After reading the Chapter 7 selection criteria, you can better make that determination.

197. Are Application Fees Reasonable?

Chapter 23 discusses LL.M. degree costs, including tuition, fees, and other early expenses. There are fees associated with English language proficiency tests; Internet access to LL.M. program information; other resources (library fees, and books such as *LL.M. Roadmap*); LL.M. application fees (including postage); fees for translating (transcripts and letters of recommendation); air fare to the U.S.; and other expenses. At least one school had an unreasonably high application fee ($105) — the highest I have seen, and such fees must be paid to apply.

198. Is the Cost of Living in the City the School Is in High or Low?

Some U.S. cities have high costs of living, whereas other cities have low costs of living. Make an informed, prudent choice based on your budget, taking into account tuition, fees, and other financial and nonfinancial variables that may cause you to lean toward one school over another.

> For tips on how to save money while going to an expensive U.S. law school, see Chapter 23.

"Best" Schools

199. Does the School Permit Tuition Payments on an Installment Plan?

Some schools permit you to spread tuition payment over the course of an academic year. Otherwise you must pay in full early each semester. If you pay late, you may be denied access to campus e-mail, the library, and other facilities, and you may be charged penalties or fines. Until you pay, you may be banned from attending classes, taking exams, or receiving campus notices.

200. Will the School Assist LL.M. Students Who Suffer Financial Difficulties? Does the School Offer LL.M. Students Emergency Loan Funds? Will It Offer You a Short-Term Loan, or Increase Your Tuition Discount Scholarship Amount? Will the School Force You to Drop Out of School and Face Deportation?

For example, at one school — this is true — an LL.M. student's second-semester tuition was transferred from his home country and arrived late because of his family's drought-induced financial hardships. The tuition was short by U.S. $800 (for tuition of about $30,000 for the year). The school almost suspended the student from classes for not paying the $800, which would have led to the student's deportation for being out of status. He was to be sent home without a degree. The school showed no mercy. It would not offer the student an increase of $800 in scholarship or tuition remission, and would not provide the student with a loan. A professor loaned the student money from his personal funds. (In similar cases, I have known students to sponsor bake sales, charity collection drives, and other means to raise tuition and living expenses for fellow international LL.M. students who encountered short-term financial difficulty.)

W. Location, Location, Location — and Other Fixed Characteristics

All schools have characteristics that will not change, like physical location. Regarding such immutable characteristics, you must decide which you want your U.S. law school to possess. If you want mountains versus flatland, beaches versus landlocked, big city versus small city — your choices are limited. Be certain to rely on accurate information when considering these characteristics.

201. Is the School in a Large City or a Small Town?

Big-city life differs significantly from small-town life. LL.M. programs exist in both, and in medium-sized cities as well. In big cities you may live in a high-rise apartment, travel by subway, and encounter dozens or hundreds of strangers each day. In a small town you may walk, bike, or drive, live in a house with a yard and trees, and encounter few strangers daily. Schools may be comparable, but non-school atmospheres can differ radically. Where do you think you will feel comfortable?

202.   Is There a Community That Matches Your Ethnicity or Nationality?

You may enjoy a city with many people whose ethnicity, language, or cultural background match or resemble yours. But you may prefer to live where local people may have had little exposure to people with your background. If few familiar faces are near, you will be forced to adjust to life in the U.S. more quickly, which could help you inside and outside of the classroom.

203.   Is the School in a City or State Where You Want to Work or in a State That Would Permit You to Sit for the Bar Exam?

If so, you could get a head start on future employment by learning about the local legal market and making contacts there.

204.   Do You Have Family or Friends in the City or State Where the School Is?

You might want to be close to familiar faces for support. Or you might want to branch out on your own, and choose a city or state where you have minimal contacts.

205.   What Is the Weather Like in the City the School Is In? The Topography?

If you want snow, you might choose a school in the Midwest or Northeast. If you want sunny beaches, you might choose Hawaii, Southern California, or Florida. Many schools are in regions that enjoy four full seasons: fall, winter, spring, and summer. Choose wisely!

206.   Does the City or Town the School Is In Have a Low Crime Level in the Area Where Your School Is Located or Where You Might Live?

Crime exists in all types of towns and cities. Police maintain statistics on crimes in cities, and universities maintain statistics on campus crime. Before you apply and enroll, you might inquire about crime rates in the area where your school is, and where you might live. The rate may be high in the city overall, but low in the area where your school is or where most LL.M. students live.

207. Will Your School Provide You With Details About Crime on Its Campus? Is the Crime Level Low?

Per the *Jeanne Clery Disclosure of Campus Security Policy and Campus Crime Statistics Act* (2 USC 1092(f)), your school *must* publish and distribute annual security reports containing safety and security policies and procedures and campus crime statistics. Some schools openly inform applicants about the availability of such information. For example, **Hofstra Law School**'s LL.M. application provides: "You may obtain a copy of this report by contacting the Department of Public Safety."

X. Campus Facilities

Campus facilities are important. You will likely spend significant time in classes, the library, or the LL.M. student lounge. You will want to be comfortable. Decide which aspects of campus life are important to you, and seek schools accordingly. Only you can decide how important it is for you to have access to a space on campus where LL.M. students can meet and hang out, to have parking for your car, to have lockers so you do not have to carry your books and heavy coats around all day, or to have an accessible gym.

208. Is the School Technologically Up-to-Date (Classrooms, Lobbies, Study Areas, Library)?

Check the level of technology available at the school. Technology changes rapidly, and schools at the forefront today may be behind the curve tomorrow. Do not presume. Be sure.

209. Does the School Have Health and Recreational Facilities?

Schools with student health and recreational facilities are more likely to recognize that students need balance in their lives. Being an LL.M. is about studying, but it is also about a healthy mind, spirit, and body. Healthy bodies lead to healthy minds. Take a break. Exercise. All work and no play makes for a weary, bleary-eyed, unfocused LL.M. student — an unhappy person.

210. Is There Adequate Student Parking? If It Is Not Free, Is It Reasonably Priced?

In medium-sized cities and smaller cities, many LL.M. students drive. Their apartments or houses may be miles away from campus. Student parking is always a problem. Although some schools such as **Pace** and **University of the**

Pacific, McGeorge School of Law provide free parking for LL.M. students, that is rare. If you want to purchase a car, be certain your budget includes car-related expenses such as gasoline, oil, car washes, unexpected repairs, appropriate licenses and registration, insurance, and parking. (See Chapter 23.)

211. Do LL.M. Students Have Study Carrels or Storage Space (e.g., Lockers)?

LL.M. students study hard, and many are in the library all the hours it is open. At many schools, LL.M. students are assigned carrels in the law library, reserved specifically for them, where they can research, read, and write (and maybe even have a sleep). LL.M. students should also be assigned locker space where they can store books, winter coats, and other belongings.

212. Is There a Dedicated LL.M. Lounge or Other Space?

LL.M. students need a place on campus to call their own, where they can congregate, hold meetings, or relax. Some schools have LL.M. lounges, which could be a small room, a converted classroom, or even a section of a bigger room. But it should be expressly for LL.M. students.

213. Is LL.M. On-Campus Housing Available?

Before you leave your home, your school should send you information about on- and off-campus housing, including costs, availability, type, amenities, distance from campus, prospective landlords or leasing offices, and transportation. The school should help you secure housing suitable to you. You should not be forced to scramble on your own. They should send you sufficient information so you can make informed, timely decisions about where and how you will live.

Y. Ranking and Reputation of the Law School's Parent University? Of the Law School? Of the LL.M. Program? Of the LL.M. Specialization or Track That Interests You? Of the School's Specific Programs — For Instance, the Legal Writing, or the Tax Program? (See Chapter 6)

If you consider ranking or reputation in choosing a school, scrutinize the ranking systems and information sources. (See Chapter 6.) No foolproof method exists for choosing a school. The best school for you may not be the best for your neighbor or friend. Decide which factors are most important to you and choose the school you believe is the best match for you.

"Best" Schools

"Best" Schools

214. What Is the Unofficial Commercial Ranking of the Parent University of the Law School? Of the Law School? Of the LL.M. Program? Of the LL.M. Specialization or Track That Interests You? Of the School's Specific Programs — For Instance, the Legal Writing, or the Tax Program?

Despite hazards of relying on commercial rankings when choosing an LL.M. program, students do at times rely on them. If you consider rankings, be sure to distinguish between rankings of a school and rankings of an LL.M. specialization. A school may be ranked 100th overall, but the LL.M. specialization (say of international law) may be ranked in the top 10. Which is more important to you, the ranking of the school, or of the specialization?

215. Is the LL.M. Program Discussed on Blogs? What Are People Saying? Can You Assess Blog Posters' Credibility? Are Negative Comments in Revenge or Anger? Are School Employees Posting Positive Messages, Trying to Bolster the School's Reputation? Are Educational Agents Posting, Trying to Boost Reputations of Schools That Pay High Agent Commissions?

Posters and postings may be anonymous. Some postings are inaccurate, at times deliberately. Ingest with a grain of salt.

216. If You Are Considering Reputation, Whose Opinion Will You Consider Important?

Is the school's reputation in your country important? It might be if, for instance, you plan to return to your home country to work. If you want to work in a third country, will you ask about your school's reputation there? Does your school enjoy a good reputation in the city and state where it is located; in Washington or New York or other big cities in the U.S.? What about the law school's reputation among its own alumni? Some LL.M. graduates do not view their LL.M. experiences very favorably, and may have a poor view of the reputation of their school and their school's LL.M. program. (See Chapter 6.)

Z. Finding the "Best" Law School For You: To Meet Your Needs and Meet Your Reasonable Expectations

Only you can decide which school will best help you satisfy your personal and professional goals. Not all schools can meet your expectations. Not all schools will deem your expectations reasonable; some may not attempt to meet your expectations. The best law school for you will consider your expectations reasonable, will try to meet them, and will actually meet them. You must find that school. If you are admitted to more than one school that suits you, that is great. You are ahead of many who may have been denied admission to any LL.M. program. If you consider the criteria here in Chapter 7 and in LL.M. Roadmap as a whole, you will be well positioned to make an excellent decision about which school you will attend. Good luck! Go forth and prosper!

217. Have You Engaged in Serious Self-Assessment and Reflection in Choosing to Pursue an LL.M., and in Choosing to Pursue the LL.M. at a U.S. School?

If you have read this far, you have probably carefully considered whether you want to pursue an LL.M., and whether you want to study in the U.S. versus studying in another country. Congratulations on that decision.

LL.M. Roadmap focuses on helping you choose the best school for you. This calls on you to reflect on characteristics of U.S. law schools and, in particular, LL.M. programs important to you. **Only you know what you want, and why you want it.** Only you know whether what you want, and why you want it, justify your choice of LL.M. programs. And you may not even know yourself the real underlying reasons for your desires and predilections!

By the time you apply to an LL.M. program, I hope you will have a good sense of what you hope to accomplish with the degree. By the time you arrive on campus, I hope you will have an understanding of how the degree from that school will best further your goals. If you do not have good answers to these questions before you enroll — wait; reconsider; reconfigure — or you may end up *not* choosing the "best" LL.M. program for yourself.

You will likely be better off if you honor choices you truly feel, after careful consideration, are best for you. I sincerely hope your choices lead you to an enjoyable and rewarding LL.M. experience, and to a fruitful career and life, wherever you end up post-LL.M.

218. What Is Your "Gut Feeling" About the LL.M. Program?

Sometimes you will *just know* when you have been admitted to the school that is the best for you. You will just feel like it is the right school, for the right reasons, at the right time. This feeling is hard to describe; but it can be strong, unyielding, illuminating: a moment of clarity.

Ask current LL.M. students the following question: "How did you know that this school was the right school for you?" Ask LL.M. graduates that same question. And imagine how you would answer if someone were to ask you, "Why did you choose *this* school for your LL.M.?"

Would you be able to articulate the reason(s) that you believe that the school and the LL.M. program you chose are indeed the *"best U.S. law school and the best U.S. LL.M. program for you"*? I hope so, and I wish you well as you make this decision, which I am *certain* will be an informed decision. Good luck!

CHAPTER SUMMARY

- This chapter lists 218 criteria you might consider as you choose the *best* law school and best LL.M. program *for you.*

- No school possesses all 218 of these characteristics. Do you need them all?

- Which criteria are most important to you? Specialization? Size? Famous faculty? Career services? Geographical location? Library resources? Cost? Scholarships or tuition remissions? Other Criteria?

- Focus on what is most important to you. Your needs? Your resources?

- Which school will meet your reasonable expectations?

- Which school, and which LL.M. program, do you believe are "best" for you? Only you can decide.

- You will have much to think about as you make these important decisions.

- Again, good luck!

Part III

How Do I Get Admitted to the U.S. Law School I Choose?

Admissions

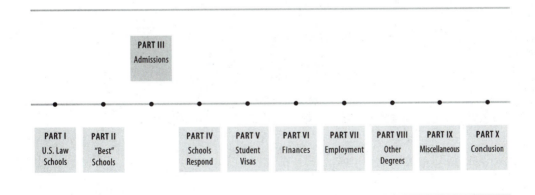

Getting Admitted — U.S. Law School Admission Policies and Practices; Mission Statements; Educational Agents; and Admission Consultants

---

CHAPTER HIGHLIGHTS

- Schools want to admit students who have a high likelihood of success.
- Schools want students with great intellect, ability, commitment, and motivation.
- The basic components of LL.M. applications are roughly the same at all U.S. LL.M. programs. However, some schools have higher standards than others, and are more competitive.
- You must follow application guidelines, and present yourself in your application in a manner that will convince the school to admit you.
- Some students use educational agents and admission consultants to facilitate their LL.M. applications.
- Some schools use educational agents to recruit international LL.M. students.
- Beware of law schools reputed to be diploma mills that consider their LL.M. programs to be cash cows.

A. Introduction

U.S. law schools may create LL.M. programs with the genuine intention to provide international LL.M. students with a first-class education. The schools may seek to improve global society by sending these students back to their home

Admissions

countries after their respective LL.M. enlightenments, and by helping the students achieve their academic, personal, professional, and career goals.

Maybe so. But law schools may have more immediate motivations than the best interests of their students and graduates and of the international community.

U.S. law schools are businesses. They have revenues (tuition) and expenses (faculty and staff salaries, program costs, heat, and air conditioning). If a school's revenues are greater than its expenses, it operates "in the black" — with profit — with money left in the bank. If expenses are greater than revenues, it operates "in the red" — at a loss. U.S. law schools — like all businesses — want to operate in the black. They want revenues to be greater than expenses so they do not go bankrupt and become forced to lay off staff, cut back services, or even close down.

Unfortunately, some schools appear to consider student welfare to be important only insofar as it is consistent with the school's goal for financial viability or success. Students and graduates are increasingly alleging that some law schools make false promises to applicants, who are induced to pay high tuition, whereupon schools fail to provide career or other promised services.[1]

On the other hand, we must remember that schools have practical limits. Most U.S. law schools do not have the capacity to admit all applicants — even if the applicants have tuition money in hand. Schools have limited classrooms, professors, and other resources. Though some smaller, less popular schools may admit close to 100 percent of LL.M. applicants, many law schools are more selective and admit only a small portion of applicants.

Consider which type of school is more likely to cater to the needs of international students — one that makes false promises, or one that honors respectable admission limits?

This chapter explores law schools' perceived motivations as they admit students to their LL.M. programs, and policies and practices law schools employ in this regard. This chapter also discusses educational agents, who may work for the school, the student applicant, or both the school and the student applicant, in the areas of LL.M. program recruiting and admissions. It also discusses LL.M. admissions consultants who work exclusively for prospective LL.M. students.

B. What Do LL.M. Programs Look for in Their LL.M. Student Applicants?

LL.M. admission committees may review hundreds or thousands of applications each year. How does the admission committee choose among the highly

---

1. *See, e.g.,* Debra Cassens Weiss, *Angry Law Grads, Beef, Blog and Move On; Tuition Makes $15K Total in 80s Seem Paltry*, August 16, 2010, www.abajournal.com/weekly/article/angry_law_grads_beef_blog_and_move_on_big_tuition_pales_next_to_15k_total_i; Leslie Kwoh, *Irate law school grads say they were misled about job prospects*, N.J. Star-Ledger, August 15, 2010, www.nj.com/business/index.ssf/2010/08/irate_law_school_grads_say_the.html. Criticisms of J.D. programs in the U.S. could also apply to LL.M. programs.

qualified applicants when it cannot possibly admit everyone who applies, irrespective of how strong the applications might be?

The answer is simple.

All LL.M. programs have (or should have) goals as to the "ideal" LL.M. incoming class. These goals relate to:

1) the *quantity* of LL.M. students the school wants to admit each year;
2) the *quality* of LL.M. students the school wants to admit each year; and
3) the *mix* of LL.M. students the school wants to admit each year.

1. Quantity of LL.M. Students a School Wants to Admit

Each school has an "ideal" number of students it wants in each LL.M. class. Schools with larger programs, such as **Harvard** or **Columbia** may have ideals of 150 or 200 or more LL.M. students per year. Schools with an ideal of 200 students may be happy with 180 or 190, but may not want over 200.

Small programs may have an ideal class size of 5–7 students per year (for example, **Louisiana State University Law Center; University of Iowa College of Law; Florida State University College of Law; Brigham Young University Law School**). They do not receive as many applications as schools with 200 or more LL.M. students.

A school determines ideal class size based on many factors, including the revenue stream, expenses, and available resources to provide a high-quality education. A school needs faculty to teach and advise on academics and theses. Staff is needed to reply to inquiries, and for administrative matters including course registration, immigration, and LL.M. career needs. Schools need lockers, study carrels, lounges, and other LL.M. student facilities. The school must comply with local fire department rules that limit how many students each classroom can safely accommodate.

LL.M. students pay high tuition (revenue). For example, say a school charges $30,000 tuition for a 9-month LL.M. program. If the average student receives a 10 percent discount ("scholarship" or "tuition remission"), then the average student pays $27,000. For 25 students, revenues are $27,000 × 25, which equals $675,000.

On what will the law school (or the university) spend the $675,000? Should LL.M. students care?

According to this scenario, there may be substantial profit for the school. Law schools, like other businesses in our capitalist system, are entitled to earn "profit." But if the profit is gained at the expense of an under-resourced LL.M. program, the program will be weak, its students will suffer, and the anemic program will lose credibility in the marketplace of prospective students and employers.

When choosing a school, ask if its LL.M. program's "profit" is reinvested into the LL.M. program. Are LL.M. revenues used to reduce LL.M. tuition? Are LL.M. revenues used for LL.M. scholarships, career services, English language writing and speaking tutorials, trained linguists, field trips, or other LL.M. activities? Are

LL.M. revenues used to pay for dedicated LL.M. administrators (who do not also have to work for the J.D. or other programs), higher LL.M. staff salaries, LL.M. staff professional organization dues, conferences, or staff or professorial stipends (for contributions above their regular work)?

If not, perhaps the law school's LL.M. program is a *cash cow* (see Chapter 6), in which LL.M. proceeds are not reinvested into the LL.M. program. It is fine for LL.M. profits to be used to supplement the J.D., S.J.D., or other programs. But if that profit is substantially diverted away from the LL.M. program, there is a good chance that the LL.M. program is not given the attention that it needs and is not meeting LL.M. students' reasonable expectations. **Beware.**

The Stetson Philosophy

"Stetson is committed to teaching excellence, legal scholarship, law reform and service to the public and the legal profession. Our goal is to educate men and women who not only will serve ethically and competently in the practice of law and related professions, but who will contribute to making a better world.

"Personal attention to the needs of students is one of the hallmarks of Stetson's educational philosophy. Because our faculty and staff are committed to a caring environment for personal and professional growth, students quickly find themselves woven into the fabric of this close-knit community. An active and welcoming student body provides social and moral support, while tutors and mentors offer academic and professional guidance. Our students in the Juris Doctor (J.D.) program come from diverse backgrounds, including a growing number from foreign countries. *The Master of Laws (LL.M.) class will be kept small to ensure that each student can maximize his or her potential.*" (emphasis added)

Source: www.law.stetson.edu/tmpl/academics/inlaw/LLM/internal-1-sub.aspx?id=664

---

2. Quality of LL.M. Students a School Wants to Admit Each Year

The concept of student "quality" is subjective. In general, schools seek to enroll highly qualified, talented, accomplished, dedicated, and determined students with solid academic ability, with a high likelihood of finishing the program and performing well — and who can afford tuition and living expenses.

Schools that are more motivated by profit may reach a compromise, and focus more on who can afford tuition, and less on academic abilities. Evidence of this is that *some U.S. LL.M. programs admit more than 90 percent of applicants, and some as much as 100 percent of applicants,* so long as the applicants meet bare minimum admission requirements. Thus if you have passable academic credentials and can afford tuition, some U.S. LL.M. program will likely accept you. These programs are not competitive, and *may* be cash cows or diploma mills. They may even admit unqualified applicants who will perform poorly and drag down other students, but from the school's perspective those applicants contribute handsomely through tuition revenue, which is important for cash cows and diploma mills.

Each year each U.S. law school will decide its LL.M. enrollment goals taking the following into account:

- The *quantity* of LL.M. students it will admit;
- The *quality* of LL.M. students it will admit; and
- The *mix* of LL.M. students it will admit

Most international applicants to U.S. LL.M. programs may be interested in receiving a rigorous, high-quality degree, studying with highly accomplished and competent classmates in a stimulating atmosphere. Students want competitive LL.M. programs, with highly selective admissions standards, that admit only the "best of the best" applicants. LL.M. students in such programs can learn from their classmates, who can become lifelong friends and professional contacts.

Choose a school that admits the sorts of students you want as classmates. If you want quality, choose a school that can offer that. If you learn how a school assesses "quality," you can better decide whether to choose that school or another one.

a. Applicants' Profiles

Each school likely determines ideal characteristics it wants its students to possess — that is, a profile, or an average measure of the students. This measure, which can be vague and amorphous, can take into account the level of the students' marks or grades in their first law degree, their English language proficiency scores (Cambridge ILEC, IELTS, PTE Academic, or TOEFL), the merits of their personal statement, the strength of personal references, or even the tidiness of their actual physical applications. Schools may not tell you what their precise preferred profile is, but you might glean this from the profiles of their students, faculty, or graduates.

Emory University School of Law notes that "the key to admission into Emory's Foreign LL.M. program is an excellent academic record and a serious interest in experiencing additional legal education in a superior American educational environment."[2] At **Duke University School of Law** "[a]ll applications will receive very careful scrutiny"; criteria for admission include "the applicant's

---

2. Sources for quotes in this paragraph are from the following LL.M. program websites: www.law.emory.edu/admission/how-to-apply/llm-program.html; www.law.duke.edu/internat/graduatedegrees; www.chapman.edu/law/programs/LLM/Int_Comp.asp#Admissions; and www.law.harvard.edu/prospective/gradprogram/llm/index.html.

academic promise as revealed by previous academic performance." **Chapman University School of Law** notes "An applicant will only be admitted if the applicant's record, viewed as a whole, indicates that the applicant is likely to complete the Program successfully. The applicant's academic record (at the undergraduate, graduate, and law level) and relevant experience are the primary factors considered." **Harvard** notes that it "is interested in attracting intellectually curious and thoughtful candidates from a variety of legal systems and backgrounds and with various career plans." Some schools seek students interested in working in the area of social justice, whereas others cater to students who want to become law teachers. Profiles differ at different schools.

b. Specializations

Another component of student "quality" relates to the program's subject area. If a program specializes in international criminal law (such as one of the tracks at **Case Western Reserve University School of Law**), then the school will seek students with demonstrated interests in international criminal law. The "quality" characteristic is a shared interest in that subject, which will spur students to thrive in that track — which at **Case Western** consists of international criminal law courses, internships at international criminal tribunals, guest speakers from the diplomatic and practitioner ranks, and scholarly publications.

Regrettably, however, some U.S. schools' specialized LL.M. programs admit students with no demonstrated interest in those particular specializations, which inherently compromises the programs' "quality" for other students with strong specialized academic and professional interests. In such cases the school prioritizes quantity over quality. They increase student enrollment and revenues, while degrading and diluting the LL.M. student experience.

c. Personal and Professional Motivations of the Students

Some LL.M. programs seek students who wish to return to their home countries upon completing their degree, or to remain in the U.S. temporarily to work. Such schools discourage international LL.M. students from staying in the U.S. For example, **Hastings School of Law** notes that: "The LL.M. degree is primarily intended for students who plan to return to their home country to practice law or plan on working in the United States only for limited periods of time. . . . Prospective students who definitely plan on practicing law permanently in the United States should consider applying to the J.D. program instead" (www.uchastings.edu/prospective-students/llm/apply.html).

d. Ability of Students to Pay

From a business perspective, many schools would prefer students who have their own personal or family funds to pay the tuition and fees, or who have received lucrative sponsorships from the U.S. government, foreign governments, student employers, or other sources. Such students would not normally be plagued with the financial problems that often befall students from poorer backgrounds who have no outside sponsors. One would hope that more schools would help ensure that all students who fit the "quality" criterion be offered a seat, irrespective of ability to pay, and that efforts be made to help the student secure funding. (See Chapters 23, 24, and 25.)

Ohio State University College of Law Discusses LL.M. Applications and the "Mix" of the LL.M. Student Body

Since we are carefully looking for the right mix of individuals to accomplish [our] goals, it is important that you present your strengths; profile your practical experiences, accomplishments and academic excellence; and give us insight into your goals for the future. We will carefully examine all the elements of your application package in an attempt to get to know you better.

Source: http://moritzlaw.osu.edu/programs/llm/

---

3. Mix of LL.M. Students a School Wants to Admit Each Year

After a school determines the ideal "quantity" of students in its entering class, and the ideal "quality" (profile) of the students, it will seek to reach an ideal "mix" of students.

A school with multiple tracks may want a certain number of "quality" students in all the tracks, rather than too many students in one track. Schools may seek diversity of nationality or occupation. Some schools may seek a balance of students who are able to pay full tuition and students who require scholarship assistance. Some strive for substantive diversity, seeking, for example, a mix of students with backgrounds in corporate law, human rights, law practice, or government work. **Harvard** notes that each year when about 1,500 applicants apply for 150 LL.M. student spots, its "LL.M. students include lawyers working in firms, government officials, law professors, judges, diplomats, human rights activists, doctoral students, business men and women, and others. The diversity of the participants in the LL.M. program contributes significantly to the educational experience of all students at the School." (www.law.harvard.edu/prospective/gradprogram/llm/index.html). **Stanford** considers a geographical mix in its LL.M. class.

4. Nondiscrimination Policies

U.S. law prohibits schools from discriminating against applicants based on various established criteria. Some schools have broader nondiscrimination policies, and prohibit discrimination on a longer list of criteria. Many law schools, by law and/or policy, do not discriminate on the basis of sex, disability, race, color, religion, creed, age, national origin, ancestry, marital status, sexual orientation, gender identity, status as a veteran, or family status. Discrimination laws are enforced under various federal laws, including Title IX of the Educational Amendments of 1972, Title VI of the Civil Rights Act of 1964, Section 504 of the Rehabilitation Act of 1973, and the Americans with Disabilities Act of 1990. Accommodations for disabled students are mentioned below.

5. Disabled Students

Under U.S. law, U.S. schools are required to provide equal access through "reasonable accommodations" to persons with disabilities. U.S. LL.M. programs should not discriminate against disabled applicants, and should not discriminate against disabled students who enroll. When choosing a law school, ask whether it has a disability services office, and ask whether that office will provide the services that you need. The school may offer you contact details of other students with the same disability, who can share their experiences with you. A great source of information is the *National Clearinghouse on Disability and Exchange*, which is a project funded by the U.S. State Department and administered by Mobility International U.S.A. (www.miusa.org).

C. General LL.M. Admission "Policies"

In conjunction with the *quality, quantity,* and *mix* calculations, some U.S. law schools specifically inform applicants what the school is looking for in individual students, and for the program as a whole. Check schools' websites for "admissions policies" — what the schools consider to be strong points in applications; what schools desire or require of students; and the different backgrounds and experiences they want students to possess.

If you know what a school wants, you will know whether you meet the school's criteria. If you feel you don't fit the profile, you can choose to apply to a different school, or try to modify yourself or tailor your application toward the "ideal" student from the school's perspective. **But do not include false or misleading information in your application to try to impress an admission committee. Do not plagiarize — that is, do not steal someone else's personal statement or otherwise copy another person's application.** It is highly recommended that you tailor each application to the specific school to which you are sending it. You can adapt each application to try to demonstrate how you meet the criteria established by that particular school. It is imperative that you narrowly craft each application to each school, speaking directly to that particular school's admission committee.

University of Missouri Law School's LL.M. Admission Policy

The LL.M. Admissions Committee reviews the total application package and selects qualified applicants who would best benefit from and contribute to the LL.M. program. These are complex judgments based on factors including but not limited to the following:

- The Committee is especially interested in how applicants plan to combine their prior experiences with our LL.M. education to advance a career in dispute resolution. Applicants' statements of purpose should address this as specifically as possible.
- The Committee looks for indications that applicants have the ability to do the rigorous academic work in the program. The LL.M. program is not primarily a training program. Although the program includes practical skills courses, a majority of the work is theoretical and involves a substantial amount of reading, research, and writing. The Committee reviews applicants' transcripts from law school and other educational programs but applicants may demonstrate academic ability in other ways, especially if a significant period has elapsed since the applicants were in school.
- The Committee prefers applicants with significant prior legal experience. Applicants without significant prior legal experience are considered more favorably if they have other relevant full-time work experience or accomplishments and/or a demonstrated interest in dispute resolution.
- Applicants whose native language is not English must be able to read, write, understand, and speak English sufficiently well to participate in and contribute well to the class experience.
- The Committee tries to select a group of students with a combination of experiences that provides some relevant diversity as well as shared experiences to make for a rich class experience.

Source: http://law.missouri.edu/csdr/llm/admissions.html#

D. Law School *Mission Statement* or *Strategic Plan* — Your Law School's Goals and Aspirations for Its LL.M. Program

Each law school in the U.S. has (or should have) a "master plan" that outlines the school's mission, philosophy, strategic plans, goals, and aspirations for the school and all its programs, including LL.M. programs. These documents might be called a "Mission Statement," "Law School Philosophy," "Strategic Plan," "Law School Vision," or another similar name.

Each school should also have a "master plan" *exclusively* for its LL.M. program, that will outline the school's LL.M. aspirations, and outline promises to LL.M. students about what the school hopes to accomplish for itself and for you — its LL.M. students and graduates. The LL.M. Mission Statement should be more focused than the general Mission Statement of the law school, and should narrowly outline specific goals of the LL.M. program itself. These documents should offer insight to prospective students about what they can expect of the school when they enroll, during their course of study, and after graduation.

LL.M. Student Admissions Process from a Law School's Perspective

1. School develops internal LL.M. strategy (decides on the quantity, quality, and mix of students it wants).
2. School receives applications from prospective students.
3. School reviews the applications and evaluates applicant credentials.
4. School assesses applicants using its quantity, quality, and mix criteria.
5. School admission committee decides which students to admit.
6. School admits, does not admit, puts applicants on hold, or waitlists applicants.
7. School notifies admitted students (including you!).
8. Students accept the school's admission offer.
9. School prepares for students' arrival (e.g., helps with visa, course selection).
10. School welcomes arriving students, who officially join the law school family.
11. School teaches students.
12. School helps students meet their reasonable academic and career goals.
13. School holds graduation/commencement ceremony!
14. School continues to serve alumni after graduation.
15. School wants graduates to tell other prospective students to apply.

These documents may be used to inform outsiders what the school considers to be important about itself, or to offer insights into the overall direction in which the school is going or wants to go. The documents may be shared with donors, who may be trying to decide whether to donate money to the school (hence the content may be designed to please the donors and prospective donors).

If you do not find these master plan documents on the LL.M. program website, send an e-mail message to the school requesting a copy, which they can send to you in an e-mail message. **If the law school does not have a master plan that specifically addresses the LL.M., think twice about attending that school.** If the LL.M. program is not specifically included in the master plan, this *may* be a sign that the school is a cash cow, and that LL.M. students may be treated like second-class citizens, subordinate to other law school stakeholders. (See Chapter 6.) It may signify a lack of commitment to the full nurturing and development of the LL.M. program.

The Mission Statement for **Ohio Northern**'s LL.M. in Democratic Governance and Rule of Law states what it seeks to provide for its students — "training and tools to implement law reforms that support stable democratic institutions and the rule of law in a free-market economy." Its Mission Statement announces steps it will take to help ensure that these goals are met: small classes; seminars and field trips; intensive education; fully funded scholarships; and a student commitment to two years of public service upon return to their home countries. **Ohio Northern** also notes:

> While our focus is on lawyers from transitional democracies, we also welcome lawyers from developed democracies who share the commitment to the rule of law and would like to advance their understanding and qualifications for international democracy and governance reform.
> *Source:* www.llm.onu.edu/qualificationsnew.html

E. Who Sits on LL.M. Admission Committees?

Each school decides how many people will sit on its LL.M. admission committee, the identity of those people, and the level of responsibility the committees will have for making firm or conditional offers of admission, rejecting applications, requesting that applicants supplement their applications, placing applicants on hold or on waitlists, admitting applicants from hold or from waitlists, and making decisions about scholarships or other financial assistance.

Some schools have an admission committee that consists of only one member, who is empowered to make admissions decisions unilaterally. Other schools have only two members on the admission committee, and some schools have significantly larger committees. Chances are that if an admission committee has only one or two members, that school does not receive a significant number of applications.

Primary Goal of LL.M. at Southern Methodist University (SMU) School of Law

[T]o enhance the international student's legal skills so that he or she may become a more effective lawyer and member of society. In this respect the program seeks to develop:

(i) an appreciation of the role of law in national and international development;
(ii) the ability to identify, through comparative and international studies, policy considerations of various legal rules;
(iii) an appreciation of the role of the lawyer in social and economic change;
(iv) legal analysis and problem solving abilities to enable the student to meet the complex needs of our modern world;
(v) a basic understanding of the U.S. legal system, as studied from a comparative perspective; and
(vi) a frame of reference for dealing with business and legal interests in a transnational setting.

Source: www.law.smu.edu/Prospective-Students/LL-M — S-J-D–Programs/
Master-of-Laws-for-Foreign-Law-School-Graduates.aspx

Admissions

Admissions

As a prospective student, or even as an actual student, you may never learn the identities of admission committee members, who could be the dean, associate dean, assistant dean, track director, an actual admissions officer, or career officer, or possibly LL.M. students, LL.M. graduates, or professors. Some committee members may have full voting rights, whereas other members do not. For some schools, you may be able to identify likely members, based on which professors teach in areas of LL.M. track specializations, which professors have administrative responsibilities related to LL.M. students, or which professors' names and photos appear on the school's LL.M. program website. Of course applicants can always ask the LL.M. administration who sits on the admission committee, or they can ask current LL.M. students or recent graduates.

LL.M. students and graduates should be represented on LL.M. admission committees, just as J.D. students are represented on J.D. admission committees.

F. Educational Agents Help Schools Recruit Students and Help Applicants Get Admitted

1. Educational (Recruiting) Agents

Real estate agents or real estate brokers serve as intermediaries in home purchase and sales. On the one hand you have the seller (the homeowner), on the other hand you have the purchaser (the consumer), and in between you have the broker or agent.

In LL.M. school admission and enrollment, the seller is the LL.M. school and the purchaser is the applicant. One type of broker is known as an "educational agent."

The educational agent can play one of three roles:

(a) Work for the school's LL.M. program by helping the school recruit international LL.M. students (the school pays the agent a fee or commission);

(b) Work for the international student applicant, to try to get them admitted to LL.M. programs (the student applicant pays the agent a fee);

(c) Work for *both* the school *and* the student applicant (the school pays the agent a fee or commission *and* the applicant pays the agent a fee).

Before you work with an educational agent, find out if the agent is working for a school ("school agent"), working for you ("student agent"), or working for both you and a school ("dual agent" or "double agent").

2. What Services Do Educational Agents Provide?

Educational agents may provide a wide range of services depending on whether the agent works for the school, the applicant, or both.

a. Agent Working for the School (a "School Agent")

Agents who work for a school may solicit applications from students in targeted countries, represent the school at recruiting events, operate a website in foreign countries advertising for the U.S. school, conduct preliminary interviews of applicants, distribute school information and applications materials, collect applications and send them to the school, and receive tuition from admitted students and forward the tuition (minus commission and fees) to the U.S. school. The school may pay a fixed fee to the agent per month or per year, and pay a commission for each student recommended by, or processed through the agent, after that student enrolls (or after the student successfully completes the first semester of the LL.M. program).

A school agent owes their principal loyalty to the school, and will try to steer as many students as possible to that school. If the agent works for more than one school, then the agent might be motivated to steer students to the school that pays the highest fees or commission.

b. Agent Working for the Student (a "Student Agent")

An agent who works for a student may meet with the applicant (and his or her parents or family) to find out the student's academic and professional needs; research the student's background to assess his or her academic achievements and potential; and examine information about all U.S. LL.M. programs and make recommendations about which LL.M. program might be best for the applicant. The agent may help the applicant gather application materials, negotiate scholarships, and advise on the visa interview. The agent may check with the applicant after they enroll to ensure that all is going well in the placement. The applicant will pay a fee to the agent, who will not receive a fee or commission from the school.

A student agent owes their principal loyalty to the student applicant, and will try to get the best deal for the student in the LL.M. program that is "best" for the student. Because the agent receives no fee or commission from the school, the agent can more easily keep the student's best interests in mind.

c. Agent Working for the School and the Student Applicant ("Dual Agent" or "Double Agent")

When the agent works for *both* the school *and* the student applicant, matters become more complicated. There is an inherent conflict of interest in this "dual agent" or "double agent" arrangement. Each of the agent's decisions and actions could be construed as "pro-school" or "pro-student applicant." At each turn the agent's loyalty is tested. Does the agent recommend a school because the school pays the highest commission, or because it is the best school for the student? This becomes more troublesome if the student applicant does not know the agent is receiving money from *both* the student *and* the school. **An agent who works for the school *and* an applicant has a built-in conflict of interest.**

Admissions

Good Agency Practices

1. The agent should make the students' best interest paramount.
2. The agent should follow a clear and applicable Code of Conduct.
3. The agent should ensure the student strives for the "best" school suited for the student, and not for the school that pays the agent the highest commission.
4. The agent must be transparent to the student and to the schools.
5. The agent must have sufficient knowledge about the U.S. legal education system, and LL.M. programs in particular, to help direct the student to the proper law school.
6. The agent should be registered in the countries in which it operates.

---

3. Educational Agents — Codes of Conduct

Despite conflicts, the number of educational agents servicing law schools and LL.M. applicants around the globe has increased dramatically in recent years. Agents are responsible for many thousands of people studying outside their home countries, in the U.S., and elsewhere.

To reduce conflicts and perceived conflicts, efforts have been made to increase transparency in agent transactions, to help ensure that law school and student needs are not compromised. For example, the British Council formulated a "Code of Conduct" for educational agents, and EducationUSA has addressed the issue. Some of the discussion below draws on those and similar assessments.

4. Student Applicant Responsibilities in Dealing with Educational Agents

If you are considering working with an educational agent to help get admitted to a U.S. LL.M. program, you should ask the following questions:

(a) Do the schools you want to apply to deal with educational agents? Some law schools, such as **Columbia**, discourage it and state it might hinder the process or worse. (See text box, p.167.)

(b) Is the agent licensed in your country?

(c) Does the agent receive a fee or commission from more than one law school?

(d) Does the agent charge you, as a student applicant, a fee? If so, how much?

(e) Will you be required to pay the agent if you are not admitted to a U.S. LL.M. program? What if you are not admitted to your first-choice school?

(f) Will the agent give you the names of other students from your country they have placed at U.S. law schools? What do those people say?

(g) Has the agent worked with the school before?

(h) Does a U.S. law school refer you to a particular agent?

(i) Does the agent have any students currently placed at a U.S. law school?

(j) How will the school ensure that your private information is maintained if passed through an agent? (e.g., U.S. schools must maintain privacy over information provided by applicants and students pursuant to the Family Educational Rights and Privacy Act of 1974 (FERPA)).

5. Law School Responsibilities in Dealing with Educational Agents

(a) The law school is responsible for supervising the professional behavior of everyone the school involves in admission, promotional, and recruitment activities (including educational agents, graduates, students, and faculty).

(b) Law schools must educate agents about relevant laws, accreditation standards, and school policies.

(c) Law schools must not abdicate responsibilities to agents.

(d) Law schools must not shift blame to third parties.

6. Educational Agents' Responsibilities in Dealing with Schools and Student Applicants

(a) Agents should be candid about financial and loyalty information regarding schools and applicants, and inform all stakeholders (schools and applicants) about all relationships the agent has with them.

Columbia's Position on Educational Consultants

Q. Are applications submitted on my behalf by educational consultants or third-party advisors accepted?

A. Applications submitted by third-party advisors or educational consultants are strongly discouraged, with the exception of applications from Fulbright or other scholarship organizations. Such applications do not in any way enhance the applicant's chances for admission to [Columbia]; in fact, unless submitted through Fulbright or another scholarship organization, they may hinder an applicant's chances or render the application incomplete, as we have no way of verifying that the application is indeed the work of the applicant. [Columbia] requests that all application materials be submitted by the applicant directly, and requires that all inquiries regarding the status of an applicant's file be communicated by the applicant. We will not report on an applicant's status to a third-party advisor.

Source: www.law.columbia.edu/LLM_jsd/LLM/faq

(b) Agents should know relevant details about the law school's LL.M. programs, including details about the school's academic requirements (including transcript, class rank, required English language proficiency scores) and financial requirements (including tuition and fees).

(c) Agents should be honest, accurate, and comprehensive, and conduct themselves with integrity.

(d) Agents should not engage in puffery, and pass on false information about the school, or improperly compare the school or its programs to others.

G. LL.M. Admission Consultants

Admission consultants may provide a range of services on behalf of the LL.M. applicant, to help you make as strong a case as possible so that you may get admitted to the LL.M. program of your choice. Unlike educational agents who may work for and be paid by a school, admission consultants work exclusively for applicants, who pay the consultants for services rendered.

Overall, admission consultants endeavor to help you emphasize your strengths, mitigate your weakness, and help you present your case as forcefully and persuasively as possible. Their analysis may begin by communicating with you about your goals and ambitions, and about your educational, employment, and personal background. The consultant may advise on which LL.M. programs at which schools might best help you reach your academic and personal goals (and could in theory recommend that you choose an LL.M. program outside the U.S.), and also might advise as to which school (in which country, state, or city) may likely admit you.

Admission consultants may help you develop ideas for your personal statements or essays, help you determine from whom you might request letters of recommendation, advise how many schools to apply to and when to submit each application, and advise on requests for admission interviews. They might further advise on whether you should reach out to professors at different law schools, and if so, what topics to cover in your correspondence; and advise on whether you might reach out to alumni of the schools that interest you, with an eye toward learning something that may help your application.

Admission consultants may be former members of J.D., LL.M., or S.J.D. admission committees, with experience reviewing applications. They may have insights into the inner workings of LL.M. admission committees. Some may also have little or no experience with LL.M. program admissions, but feel or want you to believe they have other qualities that will render them effective.

Admission consultants may charge on a per-hour basis for services rendered. Thus, you may be charged for the amount of time the consultant spends

Admissions

communicating with you about your background and interests, reviewing your draft essay, or reviewing your completed application before you submit it. Admission consultants might also charge a fixed fee (e.g., per application).

H. Gather Information from All Available Sources — Do Your Homework!

1. Gathering Information, Generally

When you decide to explore the possibility of applying to an LL.M. program, it is best to gather as much information as possible, from as many sources as possible, to give you a solid factual basis for making decisions. Your task is to find out as much credible information as possible, analyze that information, and decide how you want to use that information.

Gail J. Hupper, **Boston College**'s director of LL.M. and international programs, summarizes nicely what you might do as you engage in the application process:

> [Y]ou should do some homework before applying. Consider the kind of educational experience you want to have, and look for schools that seem to offer that experience. Then, when you apply, make clear on your application that you've done your homework. That makes your application stand out among the many each school receives, and helps convince its admissions officers that you would be a good "fit" for the school.
> *Source:* "LL.M. study in the U.S.: Why, what and how?" http://graduateschool.-topuniversities.com/articles/law/llm-study-us-why-what-and-how

2. Sources of Information About LL.M. Programs

There are many sources of LL.M. information available to you.

(a) *Law school websites* provide basic information about different schools and their LL.M. programs. (See links at www.LLMRoadMap.com.)

(b) *Current LL.M. students and graduates* can be very helpful.

(c) *Prospective students* who are considering applying or who are currently in the application process can be helpful. You can connect with them through various LL.M.-focused websites.

(d) *School visits* are very helpful, but not practical for many international LL.M. applicants.

(e) *LL.M. program fairs held in the U.S.*, at which LL.M. program admissions officials gather and present their schools and programs to prospective students. For example, **DePaul** hosts an LL.M. Recruitment Fair and Program Panel in Chicago in the fall, at which different LL.M. programs share information about their respective programs to prospective LL.M.

Admissions

Admissions

students. These fairs are not to be confused with *LL.M. Job Fairs* (see Chapter 28), at which law companies interview LL.M. students and LL.M. graduates for jobs.

(f) *LL.M. Program Fairs held overseas*, at which U.S. LL.M. program representatives recruit international students. Information about several of these fairs held in Germany is found at:

· e-fellows.net (www.e-fellows.net/show/detail.php/12489)
· German-American Lawyers' Association (www.dajv.de/llm-fair-222.html)
· JurStart and University of Muenster (www.jurstart.de/node/19)

(g) *LL.M. Roadmap*—An incredibly excellent source of credible, accurate information!

3. Websites, Books, and Organizations

Below are a few of the many websites that provide information about LL.M. programs and about matters relevant to LL.M. students.

(a) *LL.M. Roadmap*—www.LLMRoadMap.com
(b) *Law School Admissions Council*—*(LSAC)* www.lsac.org/LLM/Degree/LLM-intro.asp (A nonprofit corporation that administers the LSAT and provides services for international LL.M. applicants.)
(c) *Italian LL.M. Association (ALMA)*—www.llm.it
(d) *LL.M. Guide*—www.llm-guide.com/usa
(e) *LL.M. Study*—www.llmstudy.com
(f) *LL.M. Insider*—www.llminsider.com
(g) *International Graduate*—www.internationalgraduate.net/llm.htm
(h) *American Bar Association (ABA)*—www.abanet.org/legaled/postjd programs/postjd.html
(i) *Der LL.M: Das Expertenbuch zum Master of Laws* (by Steffi Balzerkiewicz, Martin Heckelmann, Daniel Voigt, and Tanja Lau). A German-language guide to LL.M. programs, discussing applications, funding, employment and other important practical information from LL.M. graduates and others.
(j) *LL.M.-Programme weltweit* (by Thomas Lundmark). A German-language guide to LL.M. programs, discussing the application, funding, employment, and other important practical information from LL.M. graduates and others.
(k) *USA Masterstudium für Juristen (LL.M, M.C.L., M.C.J.)* (by Hans P Ackmann, Anja Mengel, Daniel Biene, Ina M von Raven, and Arne von Freeden). A German-language guide to U.S. law programs; German-American Lawyers Association / Deutsch-Amerikanischen Juristen-Vereinigung).

(l) *National Jurist* — www.nationaljurist.com (A magazine widely distributed on law school campuses. Publishes an LL.M. issue each November. The November 2010 issue can be found at www.nxtbook.com/nxtbooks/cypress/nationaljurist1110/)

(m) *International Law Students Association (ILSA)* — www.ilsa.org (A nonprofit association of students and lawyers dedicated to the promotion of international law, through academic conferences, publications, student chapters, the Philip C. Jessup International Law Moot Court Competition, and by publishing a list of LL.M. programs.) (The author is a former member of the ILSA Board of Directors, and is donating his profits from this edition of *LL.M. Roadmap* to ILSA.)

(n) *Council for American Students in International Negotiations (CASIN)* — www.americanstudents.us (Educational nonprofit NGO that organizes student delegations to meetings of various UN bodies, the Assembly of States Parties (ASP) of the International Criminal Court (ICC), the Pan-American Health Organization, and the Biennial Meeting of States on Small Arms. Also publishes student-edited scholarly journals.) (The author has served as Member and Chair of the CASIN Advisory Board.)

(o) *European Law Students Association (ELSA)* — www.elsa.org (World's largest law student organization. Independent, nonpolitical, nonprofit. Run by and for law students and recent graduates. Offers trainee programs, publications, and a WTO moot court competition.)

CHAPTER SUMMARY

- Schools admit students they think will succeed in school and post-LL.M.
- Ask for the LL.M. program's *Mission Statement* or *Strategic Plan*.
- Follow all application procedures.
- Complete your own application. Do not ask someone else to do it for you.
- Choose a school that you believe has the application requirements (quantity, quality, and mix) that suit your needs.
- Avoid cash cows and diploma mills. They primarily want LL.M. tuition revenue.
- Check numerous sources for credible information.

Chapter 9

Your LL.M. Program Application
How to Convince a U.S. Law School to Admit You

CHAPTER HIGHLIGHTS

- Your application is your attempt to convince the LL.M. admission committee to accept you.
- You must demonstrate that you are the best applicant for them and you must "market" yourself.
- Your application will have a *formal component* composed of transcripts, diplomas, certificates, honors, and other documents.
- Your application will have an *informal component* composed of what impressions the admission committee will glean from you and your application — whether documents are neat or sloppy, whether submissions were late or timely, whether directions were followed, and so on.
- It is unethical to hire someone or ask a friend, agent, or consultant to complete your application. You must complete the application yourself.

A. Convincing an LL.M. Program to Admit You

Your LL.M. application must offer persuasive evidence of your achievements and your potential to succeed in a rigorous academic program. In the application process you must effectively self-assess and inventory your background, abilities, and motivations and present these aspects convincingly. Preparing your application may be one of the more difficult parts of your LL.M. But you can meet this challenge, with commitment, positive energy, and determination, and with the clarity that comes with self-examination.

Your application will have many components, both **formal** and **informal**.

1. Formal Components of Application

Your LL.M. application must be submitted by a certain deadline, and will **formally** contain proof of your academic success such as transcripts, diplomas, certificates, list of honors, class ranking (if available), record of work experience and extracurricular activities, recommendation letters, personal statements and essays, CV, English language proficiency test scores, and possibly a phone or in-person interview.

2. Informal Components of Application

Your application will **informally** consist of impressions that the admission committee may gather from the courteous or noncourteous manner in which you communicate with them; your application's tidiness or sloppiness; your perceived ability or inability to follow directions; your responsiveness or non-responsiveness to follow-up questions or concerns; and your general attitude, as perceived by the admission committee and others at the law school with whom you come into contact during the application process.[1]

Components of an LL.M. Application

1. Evidence of solid academic achievement and potential
2. Law training or bar membership
   a. Foreign law degree
   b. Admitted to overseas law practice
   c. Substitute for overseas law degree or practice
3. Personal statements, essays, CV, personal interviews
4. Recommendation letters
5. English language competency (Cambridge ILEC, IELTS, TOEFL, or PTE Academic) (Remember—*No LSAT, GRE or GMAT is required!*)
6. Financial resources proof
7. Transcript, diploma, bar certificate, and class rank (verified or authenticated)
8. Evidence of honesty and integrity
9. For specialized LL.M., demonstrated interest in the specialization, and for a research-based LL.M. demonstrated interest in research and writing a scholarly paper
10. Application fee
11. Application submitted and received by deadline
12. Convincing appeal to the school to admit you!

---

1. **Helpful Hint:** Do not bombard the LL.M. administration with petty questions via e-mail or phone. More than one administrator has noted that their school marks these "unimpressive inquiries" in its database and takes them into account when deciding whether to admit.

Applying for admission to LL.M. programs is a major undertaking involving more than meets the eye. This chapter identifies the overarching criterion that LL.M. programs consider in admitting students—evidence of solid academic achievement and potential. Furthermore, it identifies all the formal and informal elements of your LL.M. application and the application process— your appeal to the law school to admit you as an LL.M. student.

Your goal as the applicant is to persuade the law school that you have what it takes to succeed as a student—that you possess the requisite intellectual, emotional (and financial) resources.

B. LL.M. Program General Application Requirements

1. Solid Academic Achievement and Potential

a. Formal Submissions and Informal Impressions

Law schools in the U.S. seek LL.M. students who have demonstrated solid academic achievement and the potential to perform well in the LL.M. program. Applicants present evidence of achievement and potential through *formal* submissions and through *informal* impressions. Formal evidence includes transcripts, diplomas, class rank, and language proficiency test scores. Informal evidence includes indicating that you can follow directions (such as honoring page limits in essays), application tidiness or sloppiness, and adherence to deadlines. The burden is wholly on you—the applicant—to prove that your application and all it contains meet the selection criteria established by the law school. There are no fixed grades or marks, or awards or honors that applicants must possess to get admitted to a U.S. LL.M. program. But the more outstanding your academic record is, the greater the likelihood you will get admitted. LL.M. programs want to examine your entire record, not just your awards.

b. Standardized Tests *Are Not Required*

U.S. LL.M. programs do not require the Law School Admission Test (LSAT), the Graduate Record Exam (GRE), or the Graduate Management Aptitude Test (GMAT). You may need a GRE or GMAT for a joint LL.M.-M.B.A., or for other joint degrees. The LSAT is required for J.D. programs, but some schools waive the LSAT for international LL.M. graduates. Some schools advertise that current LL.M. students at their law schools *need not* take the LSAT to transfer into the J.D. program. If your goal is to earn a J.D. but you did not perform well on the LSAT or you do not want to take the LSAT, you might avoid the LSAT and enter the J.D. via the LL.M.

c. For Thesis-Based LL.M. Programs

For thesis-based LL.M. programs, you must produce evidence of your ability to carry out complex research and writing projects. Not all lawyers or law students are well suited to conduct research resulting in a substantial publishable work, and not all lawyers or law students want to engage in such exercises.[2] So there is no shame in choosing an LL.M. that does not involve a thesis. If you choose a thesis track, schools generally want to be as certain as possible that you are capable of, and willing to do, the work.

2. Foreign Law Degree, Admitted to Overseas Law Practice, or Substitute[3]

a. Foreign Law Degree

Typically, the first law degree earned by overseas students is a three-, four-, or sometimes five-year undergraduate degree, depending on the country. Foreign law graduates generally must have completed at least the first basic course of university law studies (roughly the equivalent of the U.S. J.D.) that qualifies the candidate to sit for the bar examination or that meets other criteria. **The University of Virginia School of Law,** for example, requires the French *Matrise en Droit* or the *Magistere de Juriste,* or the German "First State Exam in Law." **Virginia** requires for recipients of a European Bologna degree both the bachelor and master degrees or their equivalents. For the UK, **Virginia** notes "we will consider an application where the bachelor degree is in a non-law subject if the applicant has also completed the two-year program at a college of law required to qualify as a solicitor if the applicant does not have a first degree in law."

If the home country bar exam does not require a specific degree, applicants should either be experienced members of the bar or have completed at least the first university degree in law. At some schools in the U.S., a Sharia law degree may not be considered adequate for LL.M. admission.

Missouri's LL.M. Program May Admit Students Without a Law Degree

"The LL.M. program requires students to have completed and received the first degree in law (J.D. degree or equivalent) required for practice or law teaching in the country in which law studies were pursued. In exceptional cases, applicants may be admitted without a law degree if they have a bachelor's degree and substantial experience in dispute resolution."

Source: http://law.missouri.edu/csdr/llm/llmfaq.html

---

2. Some schools' prohibition of LL.M. theses is consistent with their LL.M. program's status as a cash cow or diploma mill. Thesis research and writing classes and thesis faculty supervision require faculty, library, and administrative resources that some schools are not willing to expend. Such schools may use LL.M. tuition for J.D. and other programs and projects, and not use LL.M. tuition substantially for the LL.M. program.

3. Only one of the following three conditions must be met: (a) possession of a foreign law degree; *or* (b) admission to overseas law practice; *or* (c) possession of a substitute for foreign law degree or law practice admission. Some LL.M. programs do not permit U.S. citizens or U.S. permanent residents to enroll, even if their first degree was earned overseas or they are licensed to practice outside the U.S. For example, **Wake Forest** provides that to "qualify for admission to the program, LL.M. applicants . . . [m]ust not be a permanent resident of the U.S." (http://llm.law.wfu.edu/about/admissions).

Admissions

Admissions

Columbia notes that "applicants must hold a *first degree in law*" and that "A degree in a field other than law, even if followed by a master's degree in law, generally does not suffice for admission. . . . Applicants who have earned a law degree by correspondence course work or distance learning are not eligible for admission" (p. 2 of application). It is interesting that some LL.M. programs, such as **Columbia**'s, render "not eligible for admission" persons who are "[g]raduates of foreign law schools who have already had a year of residence in an American law school."

b. Possess a Law License to Practice Law Overseas

Some countries do not require a law degree to be admitted to practice law in that country. If you have a law license in your country but have no law degree, you may still be eligible for a U.S. LL.M. program.

c. Have a Substitute for a Law License *and* Bar Admission

Some LL.M. programs in the U.S. do not require a law degree or law license before you enroll. **Missouri**, for example, does not require that applicants to its LL.M. in Dispute Resolution possess a law degree or law license. **Penn** in "exceptional circumstances" will admit students with no law degree but such students typically "hold a Ph.D. or M.D. or an equivalent graduate degree, will have already embarked on an academic or professional career, and will be able to show how legal training is important to the advancement of this career and/or their scholarly work" (www.law.upenn.edu/prospective/grad/apply).

Southern Illinois University Warns That Applications Should Contain Only What Is Requested

"Any supplementary information that is not required nor requested (videotapes, pictures, writing samples) will be destroyed and not returned. Applications should not be bound, laminated, or put in a folder."

Source: www.law.siu.edu/admission/pdf/MLS%20Application%20Instructions.pdf

---

3. Personal Statements, Essays, CV, and/or Personal Interviews

Admission committees want to know more about you than can be found on your transcripts, diplomas, or certificates. You have a chance to tell the committee who you are as a person, your goals, and your motivations. (See Chapter 10.)

Begin Your LL.M. Study in the U.S. in August/September 2013 — Sample 12-Month Timeline to Getting Admitted and Enrolling

Month	Activity to Accomplish
As soon as possible—Now!	• Read *LL.M. Roadmap.* • Collect information about U.S. law schools and LL.M. programs. • Think about financing issues (how will you pay for your LL.M.?).
August-December 2012	• Register for the Cambridge ILEC, IELTS, PTE Academic, TOEFL, or similar English proficiency test. • Ask referees for letters of recommendation. • Request transcripts and other documents. • Register with LSAC (if required or if you choose).
September 2012-March/April 2013	• Send in first LL.M. application(s)—early—before deadlines! • The earliest deadlines are in November or December, but some schools have deadlines as late as April or May. • Some schools may send admission letters as early as October or November!
January-February 2013	• Wait to hear from schools . . . (Submit more applications?) • Receive admission, non-admission, hold, or waitlist letters.
March-April 2013	• All your applications should be submitted! • Receive more admission, non-admission, hold, or waitlist letters.
April-June 2013	• Receive more admission, non-admission, hold, or waitlist letters. • Negotiate holds and waitlists. • Accept an admission offer. • Receive I-20 (or DS-2019) from school. Complete SEVIS form. • Make sure financing is in order for your year in the U.S. • Prepare materials for U.S. visa. Apply for visa. • Receive U.S. visa; paste into your passport. • *If you have not been admitted yet, send more applications!*
May-June 2013	• Confirm travel to the U.S. • Organize housing (your law school will send you housing information). • Contact school about a part-time job on campus.

Admissions

Month	Activity to Accomplish
June 2013	• Prepare academically for your LL.M. program. (Read U.S. law textbooks. Practice writing memoranda. Become familiar with U.S. law research tools, available through your law school's website.) • Ask your school to connect you electronically with your new LL.M. classmates. Start a Facebook page for your incoming class! Read LL.M. websites frequented by international LL.M. applicants, students, and graduates. • Practice your English.
July 2013	• Fly to the U.S. and arrive in your new city. • Take an on-campus English Language Placement Test. • Enroll in a pre-LL.M. study program. (See Chapter 14.)
August-September 2013	• Welcome to your U.S. law school! • Attend orientation for LL.M. and J.D. students. • Begin classes.

4. Letters of Recommendation

Most LL.M. programs require you to submit at least two letters of recommendation from professors, work supervisors, or others who can speak with personal knowledge about you and your accomplishments, work, and other attributes. The referees should attest to your professional academic background and proficiency. (See Chapter 11.)

5. Evidence of English Language Competency

You may need to supply results of your Cambridge International Legal English Certificate (ILEC), International English Language Testing System (IELTS), PTE Academic (Pearson Test of English Academic), Test of English as a Foreign Language (TOEFL), or similar test. LL.M. students must be able to communicate effectively in English — reading, writing, speaking, and comprehending. (See Chapter 12.)

6. Financial Resources and Scholarships or Grants

You must convince the school and the U.S. embassy that you have sufficient funds to pay for your LL.M. (See Chapter 20.) *But you can still request a law school scholarship!*

Admissions

7. Verified or Authenticated Transcripts, Diplomas, Bar Certificates, and Class Ranks

Some LL.M. programs require international applicants to submit supporting materials through a credential verification service that collects, assembles, authenticates, and processes transcripts, English language proficiency test scores, and other documents. Applicants might open an online account with the service, pay a fee, and submit original documents. The service then authenticates or verifies the documents and transfers reports on the documents to the school(s) you designate. Such services include the LSAC Credential Assembly Service. (See Chapter 13.)

8. Evidence of Honesty and Integrity; Diligence and Thoroughness

Lawyers and law students have particularly high ethical standards in the profession. Your application is meant to be honest, comprehensive, and not misleading, deceptive, or incomplete. If the law school learns that your application is deficient in these or similar ways, it will not admit you. If it learns of such deficiencies after you enroll, it can expel you, and can even revoke your degree if it learns of them only after your graduation. Many law schools include "Full Disclosure Requirements" on the face of their application materials. Some schools remind you of ethical rules. For example, **Boston College**'s Application Materials for 2011 provide: "Your application and all attachments (other than letters of recommendation and official documents) must be solely the product of your own efforts. [**Boston College**] reserves the right to deny admission to any applicant, and dismiss any student, who has received external assistance with his or her application" (www.bc.edu/content/dam/files/schools/law/pdf/LLM/Application%20201112.pdf).

9. Demonstrated Interest in an LL.M. Specialization, Program Type, or Post degree Career Aspiration (Varies from School to School)

If you seek admission to a specialized LL.M. program, you must demonstrate a clear interest in that particular specialization, and if you seek to enter a program that requires a thesis, you must demonstrate interest in researching and writing such a scholarly paper. You must show the school that you are willing to meet specialized demands of the program. The University of Arizona College of Law suggests that you present "evidence of commitment after graduation to teaching at the law school level, performing government service, or practicing international law" (www.law.arizona.edu/Tradelaw/admission.cfm). **Ohio Northern** notes that "[a]dmission is open to lawyers with two to five years experience in the public or non-profit (NGO) sectors, working on governance and rule of law issues" (www.llm.onu.edu/qualificationsnew.html).

10. Application Fee

Most schools charge an application fee. Some schools do not. Do not forget to ask the school to waive the application fee! (See Chapters 13 and 23.)

11. Application Submitted by the Deadline

a. Application Deadlines, Generally

For schools with highly competitive admissions, fixed deadlines permit the admission committee to have all applications in hand at the same time to make easy comparisons. An early, fixed deadline permits early admission decisions, allowing more time for admitted students to prepare to attend. If you apply early and the committee asks you follow-up questions, you may have time to answer. Applying by deadlines demonstrates that you can follow directions, reinforcing your competence, interest, commitment, and potential.

b. Apply Early

After you finish preparing your applications, set them down for a few days. Reflect on your answers to the questions. Review for errors. Beat deadlines.

c. Rolling Admissions

Many schools admit on a "rolling basis" or "until the class is filled." They decide to admit or not admit each application as that particular application is complete. If you submit your applications early, you *may* have a better chance of being admitted and you will certainly have more time to decide which school is "best" for you. **Loyola-Los Angeles** provides that applications "will continue on a rolling basis until the program is full" (www.lls.edu/programs/italy/admissions.html). But when is the program "full"? **You may fare better if you apply as early as possible.**

d. Flexible Deadlines

If the deadline has passed, should you still apply anyway? Yes. Apply even if the official deadline has passed. Schools may publish a "fixed" deadline and not advertise deadline "flexibility." Some may accept applications postdeadline and admit late-applying students close to the beginning of classes. If a school has empty seats in its class, it will admit students who fit the school's criteria, even if the application is "late." It is similar to airline travel — airlines would rather have the flexibility to be able to fill the plane on the travel day rather than let the plane leave with empty seats. So go ahead and apply after deadlines if you have to. If you have financial resources available and can get your visa and other documents processed before the semester begins, the school *may* admit you after the deadline. Indeed, I have witnessed students admitted late who arrived at the school in the U.S. *after* classes began for the semester. **But if there is a deadline, you should endeavor to meet it. Some schools — particularly very competitive schools with hundreds or thousands of applications — will not even**

Flexible Deadlines?

Two anecdotes:

(1) On a Wednesday in August 2009, a U.S. permanent resident applied to a U.S. LL.M. program, was admitted on Thursday, accepted the admission offer that day, and started classes the following Monday.

(2) In December 2009, an overseas prospective LL.M. student contacted a school about admission for January 2010. The administrator accepted the late application in December and admitted her, but her visa could not be acquired in time.

**It is recommended that you meet deadlines.
But apply anyway if you are late!**

open an application that arrives after the deadline, no matter how compelling the application. For example, **Columbia** notes that applications postmarked after the deadline "will not be processed," even though "[a]dmission decisions are made on a rolling basis" (p. 3 of application).

Marquette LL.M. in Sports Law Requirements

Admission to the LL.M. program in Sports Law is selective and will be based primarily on previous performance in legal studies, although professional accomplishments, publications, and other factors will be given significant weight. No rigid requirements for grades or class rankings will be used, but the Admissions Committee expects that successful candidates will have strong academic records and substantial professional and/or scholarly achievements, especially in the area of Sports Law and related fields.

e. Deadline Schedule

U.S. law schools generally admit students to begin study either in August (for the fall term) or in January (for the spring term). Application deadlines are tied to these enrollment dates, as schools need adequate time to process applications and admit students. Also, students need time to accept an offer, acquire visas, and make financial and travel arrangements.

- *Fall admission deadlines.* For fall entry (August), applications from international students may be due ten months in advance — as early as October or November of the previous year for competitive schools. But for

> ## University of Chicago LL.M. Program Cautions
> ## You To Keep Your Application Simple
>
> "Candidates occasionally put lots of effort into preparing elaborate booklets or bound documents describing in extensive detail their work or background. Photographs are often included. Please do not do this! One of the ways an application will be evaluated is how well the candidate can effectively and efficiently present the important aspects of his or her background to us. We will be impressed by what you tell us about yourself—not the elaborate way you do it. Plain white paper will be fine.
>
> Do not put any of your materials in a binder or enclose them in clear plastic covers. Our application file folders will not hold these items so we have to remove them when the application is received."
>
> *Source:* www.law.uchicago.edu/prospective/llm/apply

other schools, international student applicants are typically due no later than April or May—only four or five months before classes begin. It is important to meet each school's deadline. But if you miss the deadline, you should apply anyway. Some schools may accept your late application, and if you have a suitable application, may admit you.

- *Spring admission deadlines.* Some schools do not permit LL.M. students to begin their program in the spring semester (January). For schools that permit January enrollment, deadlines for international students would be no later than October.

f. Deadlines for U.S. Citizens or Permanent Residents

Deadlines for U.S. citizens or permanent residents can be later because they do not need visas. They might apply as late as July for August classes, and November for January classes.

12. A Convincing Appeal to the School to Admit You

Ultimately, you—the applicant—must convince the admission committee that it should select *you* to join their LL.M. class; that *you* possess all the attributes the school seeks in its prospective students; that *you* have an excellent record of academic achievement and great potential; that *you* will gain a great deal from your LL.M. experience at that school; and that *you* will also contribute to the school not only during your LL.M. year, but also long after you graduate. LL.M. programs seek to admit ambassadors—students who matriculate for a year of study, graduate, and then tell the world about how wonderful the school is. When a school admits you, it is admitting a new member of its family. You will be part of that family forever.

Admissions

Final Thoughts and Tips Before You Submit Your LL.M. Applications

1. The entire application process is about marketing yourself to the admissions committee.
2. Applications contain information about what you have accomplished and your potential. What have you done? What will you do?
3. Get involved in extracurricular activities now — *before you apply*.
4. Contact EducationUSA for guidance and advice.
5. Find alumni of schools — ask about their experiences.
6. Be realistic about your goals, attributes, and finances.
7. What are your research interests?
8. Clearly state who you are — advocate on your own behalf.
9. Meet, or beat, deadlines. Begin early — months in advance.
10. Follow directions.
11. Did you choose the "best" schools for you to apply to?
12. Did you "self-assess," judging your own academic background and accomplishments, test scores, and experience to determine which schools might admit you?
13. Did you apply to a range of schools — some that have higher entry requirements and are more competitive than others?
14. Be persuasive. Inform the school about your career and personal goals.
15. Demonstrate to the school that you are mature, professional, collegial, and hardworking.
16. If your academic scores are not great now, improve those scores before you apply.
17. Write and publish even short articles in law journals or newsletters. This will help demonstrate your aptitude, writing skills, and commitment. Write and publish in English, if possible.
18. Remember that each contact you have with the school is part of the application process. Schools keep track of contacts.
19. Spell-check your application carefully. Be certain it contains no errors.
20. Ask a classmate, professor, or academic advisor to review your documents to help ensure they are complete. But be certain to *do your own work. Prepare your own application*. Be mindful that your personal statements should be written by you and about you (or about whatever questions or issues the school may pose).
21. After you "complete" your applications, set them down overnight or for a couple of days. Then look at them again with a fresh eye to make sure there are no errors.
22. Make sure you are consistent and accurate — check spelling, font, punctuation, grammar, and for unclear abbreviations or slang.

CHAPTER SUMMARY

- There are many things you can do now, even before you apply, to help prepare you for the application process. It is never too early to start!
- Application requirements for all U.S. LL.M. programs are *roughly* the same.
- Follow all application guidelines.
- You must convince the school to admit you. You must market yourself.
- Schools want to learn more than your test scores. They want to get a sense of who you are.
- Each contact you have with the admissions office is noted. Your e-mail messages and phone calls may become part of your file.
- Do not e-mail the LL.M. Office a question that shows that you did not read the school's website. Check the website first for information.
- Are there food or coffee stains on your application? Late, sloppy, illegible, and otherwise messy applications are noted.
- Complete your own application. It is unethical for someone else to do it.

Admissions

Chapter 10

Personal Statements, Essays, CVs, Writing Samples, and Interviews

---

CHAPTER HIGHLIGHTS

- Law school admission committees want to know who you are beyond what they can gather from your transcripts, CV, class rank (if available), or diplomas.

- Schools can learn a great deal about you when you "speak" to the school directly through your personal statements or essays.

- Most international LL.M. applicants will not be able to have personal interviews with school admission committees, so personal statements and essays are in some way a substitute for the personal interview.

- Each school has different requirements for personal statements, essays, CVs, writing samples, and personal interviews, so be certain to follow directions.

A. Introduction

LL.M. program admission committees want to get to know you — your personality — who you really are, what drives you, what makes you tick. Committees cannot easily do that based on objective components of your application.

Your diplomas, course certificates, GPA, recommendations, English language proficiency test scores, or CV do not present a full picture of you. Committees see many similar objective documents from most applicants. Indeed many applicants have very similar credentials and similar applications.

Can you distinguish yourself from the thousands of other highly qualified LL.M. applicants? Yes, by carefully thinking through, drafting, and presenting in the finest form possible your personal statement, essays, writing sample, and CV. You must try to convince the LL.M. program to accept you because you are one of the best candidates for that school, and because that LL.M. program and school are the best choice for you. In-person interviews are rare for LL.M. applicants, so generally you — and the admission committee — must rely on these other items.

Based on your objective application, the admission committee already knows that you are bright and accomplished enough to succeed. But they need to know that you are appropriately motivated, with insights, commitment, and aspirations that render you eminently suitable to join the school's ranks. You must convince the committee that it will make the right decision by admitting you, that you outshine other candidates — that you can offer the school a great deal. They want to know more than that you take examinations well.

This chapter discusses the following subjective components of your application: personal statements, application essays, writing samples, CVs, and personal interviews. If you paint a solid picture of yourself with these subjective components, you can distinguish yourself from other applicants, and will stand a better chance of being admitted. You want the committee to choose **you**.

B. Personal Statements and Application Essays

U.S. LL.M. applications generally require students to submit a personal statement or answers to essay questions. Schools pose different issues that they want you to address, and some even provide a word limit (e.g., 500, 1,000, or 1,500 words); a page limit (e.g., no more than 1–3 typed pages); or a space limit (e.g., your statement must fit into a space built into the application). Take great care to address particular issues that the applications request, and to follow all directions related to word, page, or space limits.

Some schools ask you to address broad, open-ended issues or questions — and they do not provide word, page, or space limits. How do you respond? With discretion. Show your competence and good judgment.

Below are a few guidelines to consider when writing your personal statements.

1. Follow Instructions

As mentioned above, LL.M. applications will have instructions regarding personal statements. Follow those instructions. If the instructions call for 500 words, do not submit 501 words. If there is a page limit, stick to it. Be certain to answer the specific questions asked, or address the specific issues presented.

The **University of Miami School of Law** LL.M. application requires students to:

> Submit a statement of purpose of approximately 500 words in English, addressing your academic and professional background, your professional goals, specific areas of interest, and other matters which you think are of

Admissions

importance. This statement is to be prepared by you without any outside help or evaluation whatsoever, and is to contain a statement to that effect. We encourage you to summarize your background in a resume or curriculum vitae (p. 13 of brochure).

Miami's request is clear. They do not want a 1,000-word essay about a pressing, topical legal issue. **Miami** wants to know about you — your background, goals, interests, and what you consider important. Tell them that. Then stop.

Fordham University School of Law provides: "Submit a typewritten 500 word personal statement describing your reasons for pursuing this graduate degree, where you plan to practice in five years, and the contributions you hope to make to the legal profession upon completion of the course of study" (http://law.fordham.edu/llm-program/2052.htm). Thus, do not submit a 501-word personal statement to **Fordham**.

2. Purpose of Personal Statements

Remember that admission committees want to learn more about you as a person, in your own voice, and to learn about other qualities you have that are not reflected well in other parts of the application.

Different LL.M. Tracks or Concentrations at the Same School May Have Different Personal Statement Requirements

Stetson's personal statement requirement for the LL.M. in International Law is as follows:

"Please prepare a separate Personal Statement of your reasons for pursuing LL.M. studies in International Law. Describe any personal, professional or academic achievements that relate to your aptitude for this program. A concise, typewritten format of no more than five (5) pages is preferred. Please put your name on your Personal Statement."

Stetson's personal statement requirement for the LL.M. in Elder Law is as follows:

"Please prepare a separate Personal Statement of up to five pages single-spaced addressing your reasons for wishing to pursue the LL.M. in Elder Law. The admissions committee is particularly interested in reading about your special accomplishments; personal, professional or academic achievements; or any other information that may help us evaluate your application and understand your interest in earning this degree. The personal statement may also be used to bring to our attention any information you believe necessary to evaluate your candidacy but not otherwise reflected in your application. Beyond your transcripts and recommendations, the personal statement is a way for us to get to know you; please take advantage of it! Please be sure to include your name on your personal statement."

The quote from the **Miami** LL.M. application above illustrates what many schools want to know, and why. Schools want to know if you will fit in with their vision of their school, their student body, and their graduates.

The **Pepperdine University School of Law** requires students to answer a specific question in their personal statements.

> The Pepperdine University School of Law provides academic excellence in an environment that recognizes Christian values and encourages adherence to the highest moral and ethical standards. How would you expect to contribute to this environment?
>
> *Source:* http://law.pepperdine.edu/straus/content/straus-application.pdf

3. Emphasize the "Personal" (Be Honest but Do Not Be *Too* Personal)

A personal statement is an opportunity for the admission committee to learn more about you as a person. Of course they do not want to know the most intimate details about you or your life, but it would benefit you if you paint a picture of yourself that illustrates your strengths, particularly what you can bring to the school and what you will do with your education post-LL.M.

Your statement must be "personal" — written by you, about you. You must write in your own voice, and tell your own story. *Do not* ask friends or family to write your personal statement, and certainly do not hire anyone, including an educational agent or LL.M. consultant, to write your personal statement for you. *Never* plagiarize anything, and certainly never plagiarize a personal statement. Use your own ideas and express them in your own way. It is an outright **ethical violation** to have someone else write your personal statement.

4. I Am Human. And I Can Communicate in English!

You are not a collection of documents, or a robot. You are a free-thinking human who would like to join a school filled with students from around the world, with professors and staff — all involved in an education mission. Your personal statement should reflect your humanity.

It *is not* a legal research piece in which you demonstrate your legal reasoning aptitude. It *does not summarize your CV or diplomas.* In fact, some schools, such as **Columbia**, explicitly state that they "will not consider your application without a Personal Statement, and will not accept a resume or curriculum vitae in place of the statement." Treat your personal statement like an in-person interview, and let the school learn about the real you. **University of Florida Fredric G. Levin College of Law** notes that you might "[c]onsider your written personal statement to be 'an interview on paper'" (www.law.ufl.edu/programs/comparative/admission.shtml).

Things to Avoid in a Personal Statement

- *Do not* be boring.
- *Do not* be incoherent; do not wander.
- *Do not* send a handwritten personal statement.
- *Do not* write something unless you believe it.
- *Do not* lie or be phony.
- *Do not* mention the name of the wrong school!

Your personal statement is also an excellent opportunity for you to show the admission committee that you have a solid command of written English, which is critical as you interact in the classroom, and as you interact in the hallways, offices of professors, with staff, and with members of the general community off campus.

5. What Would an Interviewer Want to Know About You?

Not many LL.M. programs in the U.S. conduct in-person interviews with LL.M. applicants. Some schools, however, do interview candidates by telephone. Interviews offer candidates an opportunity to "sell themselves" in ways that they cannot possibly do on paper (in a personal statement or otherwise). An LL.M. administrator at one school that conducts telephone interviews wrote recently that the telephone interviews of viable candidates were the *"most"* important part of the application process. During the interview, the school can get a sense of the candidate's open-mindedness, maturity, resourcefulness, and expectations. Many applicants have excellent test scores and first-class credentials and recommendation letters. How do schools distinguish these highly qualified candidates from one another? An interview can tip the scales and work to your advantage, whether you have solid paper credentials or not.

If you *do not have an interview*, then what? Your personal statement will have to convey intangibles — the real you.

Ask yourself:

- What would the Admissions Committee want to know about me that they do not know already?
- What about my background can I expound on briefly, to highlight my strengths?
- What I can bring to the school if admitted?
- How can I distinguish myself from the other highly qualified applicants from around the globe?
- How can I demonstrate my open-mindedness, maturity, resourcefulness, and expectations?

6. Be Certain to Write Your Own Personal Statement (Not Written by an Educational Agent, Consultant, Friend, or Family Member)

Some LL.M. applications expressly remind that you should prepare your personal statement on your own. For example, **Duquesne University School of Law**'s application provides: "Please sign your name and the date at the end of this statement to certify that the statement is true and is the product of your own work" (www.duq.edu/law/academics/_pdf/LLM-application.doc). Schools want to know about you, in a statement created only by you. You are obligated to provide schools with your own thoughts, as you are best able to express them, in English, in writing. They want to have a sense of how well you write, and they may and certainly will use the personal statement as a writing sample. Some schools will deem it a violation of its honor code or code of ethics if it requires you to prepare the statement yourself, and you nevertheless receive assistance from others. Other schools recognize that applicants may ask a native-English speaker to review their personal statements, and will not penalize the applicants for this. **If you sign your name and the work is not yours, you will have committed an ethical violation, and will have breached the honor code of the law school even before being admitted to the school! Do not start your LL.M. career off on the wrong foot.**

> **What Kind of Personal Statement Would *You* Write for Ohio Northern's LL.M. in Democratic Governance and Rule of Law, Based on Their Mission Statement Below?**
>
> "The LL.M. in Democratic Governance and Rule of Law provides young lawyers with the training and tools to implement law reforms that support stable democratic institutions and the rule of law in a free-market economy. The core of the LL.M. is a fully-funded, one-year program of study designed for lawyers practicing in the public sector whose first law degree was earned from a law school outside the U.S. Students are required to commit to 2 years further public service upon return to their home countries. A small number of lawyers from the United States and other developed democracies may be considered for admission as well. Through small classes with outstanding faculty, close interaction among the students and with the faculty, and numerous short seminars and field observations, students will receive an intensive education in practical democracy and law."

7. Possible Personal Statement Discussion Points

Below are some sample discussion points that you might consider raising in your personal statement or essay response (depending on what the school asks you to write about).

1. Why do you want an LL.M. degree?
2. Why have you chosen to study law?
3. How will the LL.M. degree help you reach your career goals in your home country, in a third country, or wherever you want to work?
4. What do you hope to accomplish at this particular U.S. law school?
5. What does the school or LL.M. program have to offer you?
6. What do you have to offer the LL.M. program or the school?
7. Why did you choose this particular school and LL.M. program instead of another (e.g., faculty, specialization, weather, family friends, reputation)?
8. What is your specific interest in this particular LL.M. program or school?
9. What are your career ambitions? Your long-term and short-term goals?
10. What do you hope to accomplish after you complete your degree?
11. Do you want to pursue an S.J.D. after you complete your LL.M.?
12. Name your best qualities (e.g., honesty, organization, decision-making ability). (Do not be reticent; but don't engage in puffery. Give examples.)
13. What incidents affected your major life decisions?
14. What would you say about yourself if you had a personal interview?
15. What are your academic interests? How have you nurtured those interests?
16. Have you demonstrated intellectual curiosity and practical achievements? How?
17. Have you encountered and overcome any significant obstacles (e.g., disability, addiction, discrimination)?
18. Are you mature? Do you exude confidence?
19. Did you participate in any extracurricular activities when you were in school? Were you a leader? What did you learn? What did you contribute?
20. Did you do any volunteer or pro bono work?
21. Do you have any work experience? Is it related to the area of law you want to study in your LL.M.?
22. What else? What else should they know to understand the real you? Perhaps something completely unrelated to study or law or work? Only you know "the real you."

Admissions

An LL.M. administrator at a well-known U.S. law school emphasized in comments to *LL.M. Roadmap* that it would be a great service to applicants and schools to remind you, the applicant, to write your own personal statement. The administrator notes that when a personal statement is written with a level of English proficiency that exceeds the applicant's reported TOEFL score, the administrator tends "to give very little weight to obviously contrived statements." It hurts your application if your personal statement appears to be written by someone else.

8. Do Personal Statements Carry Much Weight?

Different schools put different weight on the personal statements in applications. But statements and essay responses are certainly *very helpful* to committees.

As mentioned, admission committees can learn a great deal about you by your personal statements and replies to essay questions, such as whether you can follow directions, whether you are neat or sloppy, whether you appear to take great care or hold pride in your work efforts (as evidenced by, for example, whether you proofread your statement before submitting your application, or whether it had many or any typographical or other errors). Also, they want to learn more about you than is revealed in the rest of the application — your motivation, and your ability to follow directions and comport yourself impressively. Do not underestimate the value that admission committees place on personal statements.

C. Writing Samples, Plagiarism, and Honor Code Violations

Not many U.S. law schools require that LL.M. applicants submit writing samples. But if they do, you might submit the best piece of legal writing you have done. Chances are that you wrote legal essays while studying for your first degree. You may have memos that you wrote while working as an intern or as a practicing lawyer. Choose a sample that you believe accurately reflects the strengths of your legal writing, and your ability to analyze legal issues. If you feel that the only samples you have do not accurately reflect the quality of your writing or analysis skills, you might explain that briefly in a cover note. If you wrote the memorandum for work, be certain that you obtain appropriate permissions and redact any confidential or protected information before you submit the memo.

Be certain that the writing samples you submit *were written by you*. This cannot be stressed enough. **Do not submit writing samples that were written by someone else. Do not submit writing samples that copy the work of others.** Your writing samples should convey your own original thoughts, in English, expressed in the best way possible *by you*.

Tips on a Good Personal Statement

- If you have trouble talking about yourself or bragging, practice!
- Set aside cultural inclinations that might prevent you from talking about yourself. Talk with others from your country or culture who have written their own personal statements. Get their advice.
- Talk about yourself. Tell your own story. Use your own voice. Highlight your strong points.
- Discuss your work and school experience.
- Discuss items not discussed fully elsewhere in your application.
- Distinguish yourself from other applicants.
- Be specific, concrete, and factual.
- Be honest and sincere. Do not embellish.
- Write your own personal statement. Do not have someone else write it for you.
- Ask a former student — an LL.M. graduate — for guidance or advice.
- Think of yourself as a living, breathing, feeling person — not just a bunch of numbers (grade point averages, English language proficiency test scores).
- Write a draft, set it aside, and then finish it later.
- Follow directions (length, format, and subject matter).
- Check your grammar and spelling. Proofread it. Use a dictionary and thesaurus.
- Discuss challenges you have overcome, if any.
- Type your personal statement.
- Focus on the specific school and LL.M. program.
- Do not copy someone else's statement. Again, *write your own personal statement!*

If you copy someone else's work and submit it with the representation that it is your own writing sample, you will have committed plagiarism — which is defined in various dictionaries as stealing or appropriating someone else's ideas or words and passing them off as your own. (See Chapter 17.) **Do not begin your LL.M. career with an ethically wrong and illegal act: appropriating someone else's ideas or words and presenting them as your own. Submit your own writing sample. Write your own personal statement.**

D. CVs (Resumes)

Not many U.S. law schools expressly require LL.M. applicants to submit CVs, but some do. If the school does not request a CV, and you have a CV available, you might consider submitting it because a properly constructed CV should paint a concise, strong picture of you for the committee to see at a glance. CVs are excellent marketing tools, if prepared well. **If a school requests that you *not* include a CV, then *do not include one.*** Follow directions!

E. Personal Admission Interviews

Most schools do not require personal interviews. Indeed, some schools expressly prohibit personal interviews on the grounds that banning interviews for everyone levels the playing field for all. It is quite expensive for international students to travel to the U.S. for a personal interview, and quite challenging given visa and other concerns. Only students with the greatest resources (including access to appropriate U.S. visas) would be able to visit the campus for an interview. This exclusive access for the applicants who interview could lead to a distinct advantage over those who cannot interview. So, no personal interviews are conducted.

On the other hand, a personal interview may be required. For example, **Ohio Northern** notes that "A personal interview, either in person with one of our faculty and staff, or by telephone, is also required." Similarly, **St. Thomas** requires an interview "in person or conference call."

Interviewers ask specific questions for reasons—they want to learn more about you than is disclosed in the written application. They want to understand your motivation, or they want to know if you are prepared to abide by certain rules. But the admission committee can learn other things as well. They want to observe how you "think on your feet" (how you spontaneously respond, compose, and present yourself and your thoughts or feelings); whether you look them in the eye; whether you carry in your demeanor, comportment, and expression the conviction of your words; and whether you radiate integrity or evince shadiness, uncertainty, or other positive or negative characteristics.

CHAPTER SUMMARY

- You probably will not have a personal interview. Your personal statements and essays are a substitute for the interview. You can—indeed, you must—"speak" directly to the admission committee in your personal statements.

- Each school has different requirements for personal statements, essays, CVs and resumes, writing samples, and personal interviews. Be certain to follow directions.

- Do not send the committee more, or less, than they request.

Chapter 11

Recommendation Letters

CHAPTER HIGHLIGHTS

- Virtually all U.S. law schools will require you to submit recommendation (or referee) letters along with your LL.M. applications.
- Your recommendation letters should be from professors, employers, or others who can speak about your academic, work, or extracurricular contributions.
- Admission committees tend to rely heavily on the recommendations.
- Be careful to ask people to write your recommendation letters only if you believe those people will provide positive and reaffirming information, rather than negative information.
- There are things you can and should do now to help ensure that you get good recommendations when it is time for you to apply to an LL.M. program.

A. Introduction to Recommendation Letters

LL.M. admission committees typically require applicants to submit letters from professors, employers, colleagues, and others to inform the committee of the applicant's qualities that may not be fully captured elsewhere in the application. **Admission committees rely heavily on these letters**. The letters help cement an image of the applicant, with whom the committee will usually not have had the opportunity to meet. Most LL.M. programs require applicants to submit at least two recommendation letters.

This chapter covers topics such as

(a) identifying the sort of people to write recommendation letters for you;
(b) avoiding people who will write "bad" recommendation letters for you;
(c) deciding on people to ask to write a letter, and how to cultivate relationships with those people; and
(d) helping to ensure that people who write your letters include all the wonderful attributes you (and the admission committees) think are important.

This chapter will also cover the traits and characteristics that LL.M. programs like to see in their applicants, that can also be developed in recommendation letters and in standardized forms (which some schools provide for referees in lieu of letters). The chapter provides a sample recommendation letter (that worked for a student who was admitted to a competitive Ivy League LL.M. program) and examples of information that may be specifically requested to be included in recommendation letters.

B. Who Should Write Recommendation Letters, and Why

The best recommendation letters are written by people who personally know you, and who are familiar with your intellectual abilities, your work and other accomplishments, and your actual personality. Your referees should be able to inform the LL.M. admission committee, with relative specificity, that you will likely succeed in the U.S. graduate law program, and indeed that you will likely do very well.

Matthew Parker, the LL.M. assistant dean at the **University of Pennsylvania**, offered this advice: "Try to get those who write your recommendations to talk about why you would do well and how you would fit in." (*The American and International LL.M. Degree: A World of Choices*, National Jurist, November 2010, at 42)

I agree with Dean Parker.

Good referees can be former professors, employers, work colleagues, or even clients. These people are in good positions to know you and your work well, and can easily attest to your professional and academic background and proficiency. Referees should be able to address specific points about you and your background that would make you a great candidate for the LL.M. program.

A referee should agree to write a recommendation only if he or she can write a positive one. So when you approach a professor, ideally you would ask the professor if they will write a "good" or "strong" letter of recommendation. But that can be a very awkward question to ask your professor! Even so, you should try to find a way to learn if the professor will indeed write a good recommendation. Maybe you could ask the professor whether she thinks you would be a good

---

Recommender's Overall Assessment (Pittsburgh Application)

_____ I recommend without qualification that the applicant be admitted.
_____ I recommend that the applicant be admitted.
_____ I recommend with some reservation that the applicant be admitted.
_____ I do not recommend that the applicant be admitted.

LL.M. student, or what she thinks your strong and weak points are. The professor's answer should give you a fairly clear idea about whether she will write a "good" or "strong" recommendation letter. If she tells you that you should consider an option other than an LL.M. program, or that you have more weaknesses than strengths, then you should choose another person to write your recommendation. There is nothing worse for an application — and for the applicant — than a "bad" recommendation letter, or a letter that is not very supportive. *It is better not to have a recommendation than to have a bad recommendation.*

C. Bad Recommendation Letters

Law faculty deans, judges, prominent lawyers, legislators, or other public figures are great people to have write recommendation letters for you, *but only if they have sufficient personal knowledge of you and your work, substantive accomplishments, and the characteristics that would make you an excellent LL.M. candidate.*

A dean's recommendation letter does not help much if it can only state that you have good marks and you never got into trouble, or if it does not address any personal exposure to your work or accomplishments.

If you get a recommendation from a person of "high status" (for example, a governor, judge, or legislator), make sure that you are not relying on the person's status to help you get admitted. You should rely more on what the person says about you specifically, and the basis for what that person says, rather than rely on who that person is, or his or her status.

To reiterate: A bad recommendation is worse than no recommendation.

D. Who Will Write Your Recommendation Letters? How Do You Cultivate Relationships with and Approach That Person?

1. Someone with Whom You Have a Good Relationship Who Knows Your Work

Be smart when you decide whom you ask to write on your behalf. Ideally, you will choose persons with whom you have a good relationship — a previous or current employer, or a professor. It is probably easy to develop a relationship with an employer — your boss — because you work with that person, perhaps on a daily basis. That person would have an opportunity to observe your skills and your performance, and to get to know you as a person as well. Presuming that you performed well, that boss would likely be a good candidate to be a referee, as you would have a well-established relationship with that person, and that person thinks highly of you and your work.

2. How to Cultivate Relationships with Professors and Others

Getting to know a professor well, and getting that professor to know you well, may not be as straightforward as it is when you get to know your boss. However, it is imperative that you forge relationships with professors, not only so that you can learn from them, but also so that they can get to know you in ways that will make it easy for them to say yes when you ask them for a recommendation letter later on.

Of course a professor can get to "know" you if you participate in class discussions, ask questions after class, or stop by the professor's office. A professor can get to know you and your work better if you work as the professor's paid research assistant, volunteer to do pro bono work under the professor's direction, write your thesis under the professor's supervision, or engage the professor and other students in discussions (in class and outside of class) on a wide range of topics.

You might think about prospective referees long before you apply to a U.S. school. You might cultivate relationships with prospective referees sooner rather than later, giving them ample opportunity to gain positive impressions. It may be very difficult, in your culture, to cultivate the kind of relationship that will yield the sort of recommendation you need. But, if you want to do an LL.M. in the U.S., you must try, and be successful. Remember, thousands of students from around the world study law in the U.S., and they all had to get reference letters from teachers. You can do it too!

3. What If Your Referee Does Not Speak or Write in English?

If your referee does not speak or write in English, the letter can be written in their language of choice, and you or another person can translate the letter into English. You should submit the original letter and the English translation to the schools as part of your LL.M. application.

4. What If Your Referee Asks You to Draft the Letter? Is That Okay?

Professors or other referees around the globe are in high demand to produce recommendation letters for current students to get admitted to graduate programs, or to move on to new jobs. Former students may request letters five or ten years after they graduate, long enough for the referee to not remember all of the details about the students' performance. It takes considerable time and effort and recall to write good recommendation letters.

For these reasons, some referees may request that you provide them with a summary of traits you want the referee to discuss in the letter, or a list of accomplishments that may not be on your resume. You might be asked to provide a "draft" or "skeleton" letter. The referee might appreciate being reminded of the personal interaction you had with him or her, which could have been years earlier. It is appropriate to provide the referee with as much information as requested to help make the letter as comprehensive and compelling as possible.

If a referee requests you to provide a draft, the referee may adopt relevant portions of your draft, or not. The letter will ultimately be signed by the referee, and will be the referee's letter on your behalf. Providing a draft is appropriate. However, ethical issues would arise if, for example, your draft is provided in English and the referee does not speak or read English, and essentially signs a document without reading it.

5. What Do Professors Think About Writing Recommendation Letters?

Law professors around the world accept that writing recommendation letters is part of our job. We have a duty to provide this service for our current and former students. However, we are not obligated to write positive letters if we do not believe they are merited. We should be honest, in part so that employers and admission committees will continue to rely on our letters. You should determine which professors you believe have favorable impressions of you and your work, whom you trust, and on whom you can rely to write and submit a solid, thoughtful, positive, and timely letter.

Instructions to Referees of Stanford LL.M. Program Applicants

"Applicants to Stanford Law School's LL.M. program are required to submit at least two letters of recommendation.

Each candidate is asked to describe his or her experience in legal practice; especially as it relates to the specialization to which the candidate is applying. An applicant may provide you with a copy of his or her application with these instructions.

Please make your letter as detailed and frank as possible. In writing your reference, it would be helpful to the Committee on Graduate Admissions if you were to consider the following selection criteria:

1. The applicant's experience in legal practice.
2. How an LL.M. degree might be useful to the applicant's ongoing work, professional development, and career goals as a lawyer.
3. The applicant's intellectual ability, maturity, and aptitude for legal scholarship.
4. The applicant's reliability, character, and ability to engage in collaborative intellectual interaction.
5. The applicant's English language proficiency."

Source: www.law.stanford.edu/program/degrees/advanced/admissions/
pdf/LLMRefereeForm2007.pdf

I write dozens of recommendation letters each year, for students seeking graduate degrees, law firm and government jobs, UN and corporate positions, and many other opportunities. Rarely does anyone ask me to write a reference letter if I do not know them fairly well. If necessary, I call the person in to meet with me. I typically ask for a copy of any personal statement they plan to submit with the school or job application, what motivates them for the opportunity they seek, and how they think their background prepares them for it. I want to find out what I can tell the employer or admission committee about traits I believe the candidate possesses that will make the candidate an excellent fit for the position.[1]

I begin my letters by stating my background and then telling how I know the candidate. I share insights about my exposure to the candidate's work. I summarize how and why I believe the person is well suited for the position or program. Below is a modified version of a letter I wrote for a student who was admitted to an Ivy League LL.M. program. The names, activities, and other details were changed, but the format was not.

Sample Recommendation Letter

Below is a modified *excerpt* from a letter by *LL.M. Roadmap* author on behalf of a successful candidate for an Ivy League LL.M. Program. Names and facts have been changed from the original.

Dear Admission Committee:

It is with pleasure that I recommend *Ms. Mary Smith* to your LL.M. program. I believe that with her drive, determination, and commitment to academics and public service, she will contribute greatly to your program and perform well academically.

I am a law professor and I have taught at XYZ University for many years.

My knowledge of Ms. Smith's abilities
I have known Ms. Smith in several capacities, as follows:

a. as my student in three classes, who earned top scores in all these courses;
b. as a student who received many awards during her law program;
c. as a student leader, who was well regarded by her classmates and other faculty;
d. as a student who has demonstrated an ability to achieve academically, as evidenced by her class rank;
e. as a student with solid analytical skills and scholastic abilities, and with determination and drive to accomplish goals; and
f. as a person who will become a fine addition to your school, who will learn a great deal, contribute a great deal, and perform well.

(letter continued on next page)

---

1. Each referee handles recommendations differently. After you join your LL.M. program, ask your LL.M. office how to approach professors for references, or ask the professors directly.

Other information

I was Ms. Smith's Faculty Supervisor during her human rights work in Antarctica, where she worked for penguins' rights. On her own initiative, she developed a special monitoring project that identified penguins harmed by climate change, and researched and drafted a proposal that she submitted to the United Nations on that topic. She endured difficult circumstances to achieve her goals. She utilized research skills that she had acquired when she worked for a federal judge, and she polished her leadership skills she had gained as a corporate intern. With these skills and experience she was able to convince the UN to act favorably toward the penguins. She also created the Save Antarctica's Penguins Association (SAPA), which is a law student group that conducts penguin research.

Ms. Smith pays attention to detail. Her grades reflect her ability to grasp complicated concepts, analyze them, and arrive at reasonable conclusions.

Conclusion

In addition to the above qualifications, Ms. Smith is bright, talented, and seized with enthusiasm. She will join your school advantaged by her intercultural experiences and accomplishments. Furthermore, she has a fine personality that will ensure she will get along well with everyone she encounters on your campus — students, faculty, and staff.

If you have further questions of me, please do not hesitate to contact me. I can be easily reached by e-mail — professorXYZ@lawschoolXYZ.edu.

Best regards,
(signature)

Professor XYZ

E. What Should a Good Recommendation Letter Contain?

There are many topics that are suitable for inclusion in a recommendation letter, including:

1) The referee's job title or description.
2) How long the referee has known the applicant, and in what capacity (as the student's professor, advisor, work supervisor, and/or colleague).
3) The student's intellectual capacity, motivation, habits, work ethic, knowledge, expertise, and adaptability.
4) The student's academic performance and academic promise.

Admissions

5) The student's quantifications, if possible. (Is the student in the top 5% of his or her class? Top 10%, 25%, or 50%?)

6) Whether the student's goals are reasonable, and how the student's personality and academic performance relate to that goal.

7) The student's temperament, and ability to interact with others.

8) The student's accomplishments (including awards and extracurricular activities).

9) The student's contributions to school, family, and/or society.

10) How the student will benefit and how the student will contribute to the school.

11) Any other positive qualities about the student, the student's background, the student's abilities, and the student's potential.

12) Specific topics the U.S. law school asks for.

A recommendation letter should be an honest assessment of the student. It does not need to be long. Specific examples are better than vague generalities. Quality comments are important, perhaps more than the quantity of the comments.

F. How Many Recommendation Letters Does Each LL.M. Program Require? Are There Guidelines?

Most schools require two recommendation letters. Some require at least one letter from a professor in your most recent law program, whereas other schools permit you to choose referees more freely. Some require referees to use particular forms submitted in certain ways (e.g., e-mail attachment, online), whereas other schools permit referees to use their own letterhead and submit the letter by e-mail, fax, or post. Some present the referee with an evaluation form or chart that the referee is asked to complete by filling in rankings regarding the applicant's ability, accomplishments, and other traits. Sometimes schools require referees to use this form, and in other cases the referee may submit a letter in lieu of such a form.

The following chart reflects categories that some U.S. LL.M. programs request referees use in evaluating applicants.

How Do You Evaluate the LL.M. Applicant Regarding the Following Qualities?

Please check the appropriate boxes below.*

(A recommendation letter might discuss attributes mentioned in this chart and can be submitted in addition to, or in lieu of, the chart.)

	Below Average (Bottom 1/3)	Average (Middle 1/3)	Good (Top 1/3)	Very Good (Top 15%)	Excellent/ Superior (Top 5%)	Exceptional/ Outstanding (Top 2%)	Inadequate Chance to Observe
Intellectual Qualifications							
Ability to Analyze Problems							
Ability to Conduct Research							
Motivation							
Maturity and Judgment							
Potential for the Study of Law							
English Language Writing Skills							
English Language Oral Skills							
Flexibility							
Interpersonal Relationships							
Leadership Ability							
Quantitative Skills							
Ability to Work Independently							

(continued on next page)

Admissions

	Below Average (Bottom 1/3)	Average (Middle 1/3)	Good (Top 1/3)	Very Good (Top 15%)	Excellent/ Superior (Top 5%)	Exceptional/ Outstanding (Top 2%)	Inadequate Chance to Observe
Independence of Thought							
Creativity							
Breadth of Knowledge							
Adaptability							

Compilation of evaluation categories from various LL.M. program websites.

CHAPTER SUMMARY

- Most LL.M. programs require applicants to submit recommendation letters.
- Schools want to learn more about you than test scores and exam grades.
- You should ask for letters from professors, employers, and others who can write positive things about your academic, occupational, or extracurricular contributions.
- Admission committees tend to rely heavily on recommendations.
- Ask people you feel confident will write positive things about your academic and professional abilities.
- Identify recommenders now, long before your LL.M. applications are due. Form bonds with professors and employers who you want to recommend you later.

Chapter 12

Parlez-Vous English?
English Language Proficiency
Requirements

CHAPTER HIGHLIGHTS

- Without exception, you must be able to understand, read, write, and speak English to succeed in your LL.M. program.
- Schools require you to submit proof of English language competency.
- It is better to improve your English before you apply.
- If you already earned a degree where instruction was in English, or if you are from a country where English is an official language, you may be able to get a "waiver" from English language proficiency tests.
- Different schools require different English language test scores.
- If your English language scores are not high enough to meet the school's ordinary admission standard, that school may grant you "conditional admission."

A. Introduction

All U.S. law schools require all law students — J.D., LL.M., S.J.D., or other — to be "proficient" in the English language. This is hardly unreasonable, given that almost every course in U.S. law schools is taught in English, with English language materials and English-speaking professors and students. And the U.S. law system is conducted in English. Furthermore, English is the *lingua franca* of the international law and business realms.

This chapter deals with various issues that arise, including:

1) Defining and measuring "English language proficiency"
2) English language proficiency test scores required by LL.M. programs
3) Waiving English language proficiency tests
4) Bonuses of English as a second or third language
5) Hazards of English as a second or third language

6) Conditionally admitting students with low English scores
7) Pre-LL.M. academic and English courses

B. Defining and Measuring "English Language Proficiency"

LL.M. students at U.S. law schools are expected to read and understand copious amounts of legal material, write essays and exams, and communicate orally in and out of class — *all in English.* These tasks will be impossible if you are not proficient in English. But what does it mean to be proficient in English?

No universal definition of "English language proficiency" exists for purposes of gaining admission to a U.S. LL.M. program or for purposes of performing well. But all U.S. LL.M. programs would likely agree with **Missouri**, which notes that

> [a]pplicants whose native language is not English must be able to read, write, understand, and speak English sufficiently well to participate in and contribute well to the class experience.[1]

All LL.M. programs place the burden on you — the applicant — to prove that you possess English language proficiency. You must show that:

1) *You are a "native" English speaker.* Programs define "native" differently with some schools excluding persons from certain Anglophone countries where English is widely spoken;

2) *Or — You studied in an English-language law program within a certain period before your application.* Some LL.M. programs distinguish between persons who studied in English in some specified countries versus in other countries. For example, at **Chicago**[2]

> The TOEFL and IELTS will not be necessary if the applicant studied in full-time status for at least one academic year prior to the date of application, within five years of the date of application, **in the United States, the United Kingdom, Ireland, Australia, New Zealand, or English medium universities in Canada or South Africa. Students who have studied in English in other countries** — for example, India, Pakistan, the Philippines, Hong Kong, Singapore, African countries, etc. — are **not exempt** from this requirement and must provide either TOEFL or

---

1. UCLA notes that its S.J.D. students "must be able to read and discuss in class difficult technical material" and that the "work of daily class preparation is very demanding. Students with serious English language limitations will have difficulties coping with a new cultural, social, and academic environment, especially if they are enrolled in a discipline like law, which requires a very high level of English reading and writing proficiency" (www.law.ucla.edu/home/index.asp?page=1666). This would certainly apply to LL.M. programs as well. **University of California, Berkeley, Boalt Hall School of Law** notes that "Although we do not expect all students who are not native English speakers to be perfectly fluent in English, it is clear that a student with serious language limitations will have great difficulty coping with a new cultural, social and academic environment" (www.law.berkeley.edu/5673.htm). **Berkeley** may consider applications even if the English language proficiency test score is below the minimum.

2. Compare the **Missouri** English language competency waiver rule (below, Part D).

IELTS scores with their applications — this requirement will be waived if all the candidate's university law courses were conducted entirely in English. (emphasis added)

Source: www.law.uchicago.edu/node/121

3) *Or — You received a certain English language proficiency test score, verified by a recognized agency* (such as Cambridge ILEC, IELTS, PTE Academic, or TOEFL).

- **Cambridge ILEC (International Legal English Certificate).** This test consists of four separate papers testing listening, writing, reading, and speaking, and lasts about three and a half hours. The speaking test is conducted face-to-face. Cambridge ILEC is based on realistic tasks and topics that legal practitioners might expect to encounter in their daily working lives.
- *IELTS (International English Language Testing System).* This test is jointly managed by the University of Cambridge Local Examination Syndicate (UCLES), the British Council, and IELTS Australia, and contains four sections: listening, writing, reading, and speaking.
- *PTE Academic (Pearson Test of English Academic).* This test contains three parts: speaking, reading and listening.
- *TOEFL (Test of English as a Foreign Language).* This test is provided by Educational Testing Service (ETS) and has four sections: listening, writing, reading, and speaking.

4) *Remember — A great Cambridge ILEC, IELTS, or PTE Academic, or TOEFL score is not enough.* The question is "can you communicate effectively with classmates and professors in your LL.M. program?" Sometimes students with great scores have difficulty communicating with others generally, and so they will have the same difficulties in their LL.M. program.

C. English Test Scores Required for LL.M. Admission

Each school decides what English proficiency scores applicants must achieve. Generally, more competitive, highly sought after schools require higher scores.

Many schools accept a paper-based TOEFL score of 550–575, though some schools demand higher, perhaps 600 or 625. It is not unusual for schools to require a score to be at or higher than: a computer-based TOEFL of 230; an Internet-based TOEFL of 89; or an IELTS of 6.5. For comparison of the various tests and test scores of different testing companies, you may wish to contact Cambridge ILEC, IELTS, PTE Academic, or TOEFL.

Some U.S. law schools accept "First Grade" on the national Japanese English Proficiency Society for Testing English Proficiency (STEP) Exam. Some schools accept Intensive English/Masters Prep at English as a Second Language (ESL) Centers to satisfy the English requirement.

Admissions

D. Waiver: Getting Excused from Taking, Cambridge ILEC, IELTS, PTE Academic, TOEFL or Other English Language Proficiency Tests

Generally, as mentioned above, U.S. law schools will not require English language proficiency test scores if the applicant received a degree where the language of instruction was English, or if English is the applicant's native language. For example, **Missouri**[3] provides that international applicants and non-native English speaking applicants must show evidence of English-language ability by providing acceptable TOEFL or IELTS scores. **Missouri** waives English proficiency scores from applicants from various territories, including **Australia, New Zealand, the British Caribbean Islands, Canada (except French-speaking areas), Ireland, the UK,** and **Kenya.** They also waive scores for applicants who have successfully completed at least 24 credit hours of college-level work in the past two years at a school in the U.S. or another country where English is the native language (http://gradschool.missouri.edu/admission/degree-seeking/international/).

E. English Language Testing on Arrival at Your Law School

Some schools require international LL.M. students to take an English language "placement" test when they arrive on campus to begin their LL.M. program, even though those students already submitted English language proficiency test scores acceptable for admission to the LL.M. program. Despite student complaints about the repeat testing, schools persist. Some schools argue that the test on arrival is conducted because sometimes applicants submit fraudulent English test scores, and schools need to verify proficiency before LL.M. classes begin. Whether this double testing is justified is an issue, but the reality is that you might prepare yourself to sit for an English language test on arrival, even though your school may not inform you of this requirement before you accept their offer of admission. You may have to pay for this test.

F. Conditional Admission — You Must Improve Your English Before You Can Enroll in the LL.M. Program

If you meet all requirements to enter an LL.M. program except that your English proficiency scores are too low for a school, it may admit you on a conditional basis: To be fully admitted, you must satisfy the condition that

---

3. Compare the **Chicago** English language competency waiver rule (above, Part B(2)).

you improve your English to the school's required level. You cannot enroll in LL.M. classes *until you fulfill the English language proficiency requirement.*

You may be permitted to come to the U.S. to study the English language at the university attached to your law school or elsewhere. The LL.M. program determines its requirements. This sort of admission is truly *conditional — if you do not satisfy the condition, you cannot join the LL.M. program.* You may be forced to return to your home country without a U.S. LL.M. degree. If you are admitted conditionally, be sure to fulfill the condition by reaching English language proficiency.

An ethical question is raised when a law school is deciding whether to conditionally admit an international LL.M. student with low English test scores, and the school is not convinced at that time that she will be able to achieve the required scores in a reasonable amount of time. The school may believe that it is better for her to come to the U.S., and at least try to improve her English scores. The law school may benefit from having her join an English-language study course at the law school or on the university campus, at which she will pay tuition, and even if she does not reach the English language scores in a reasonable time, at least the school or university will have received tuition money. Perhaps she will have a favorable experience studying English in the U.S., particularly if her tuition is paid not by her or her family, but by the government of her country. Is it a disservice to everyone involved if a U.S. law school conditionally admits a student who is not likely to raise his or her English test scores in a reasonable period?

1. Law Schools That Offer Conditional Admissions to Their LL.M. Programs

No two schools have identical standards regarding the level of English required at the time of conditional admission; the level of English students must achieve before being admitted fully into the LL.M. program; and modalities available to help students reach the English language proficiency required for the LL.M.

Schools may conditionally admit students if they have not achieved the required English language proficiency scores, but have a "strong overall record" (**American**), "are otherwise well-qualified for the program" (**Lewis & Clark Law School**), or whose scores fall within a particular overall band score, or who undergo an "evaluation process that includes an extensive interview" (**The University of San Francisco School of Law**).[4] Other schools that conditionally admit include **Wake Forest, Missouri-Kansas City,** and **University of Dayton School of Law.**

---

4. These quotes are from www.wcl.american.edu/ilsp/llmadmissions.cfm; www.lclark.edu/law/programs/environmental_and_natural_resources_law/llm/international_students; and www.usfca.edu/law/llm/apply/, respectively.

2. Law Schools with Policies of Not Granting Conditional Admissions

Some schools have policies of not offering conditional admissions. **Georgetown** notes that students "must meet the prerequisites for admission" before admission (www.law.georgetown.edu/admissions/faq_llm.html). **NYU** concurs that "[t]here is no conditional admission status" for applicants who do not meet the minimum (www.law.nyu.edu/llmjsd/graduateadmissions/faqs/allgraduatellmjsdandadvancedcertificateapplicants/index.htm).

Some law schools state that they do not offer conditional admissions, but in practice *may* permit (or they have permitted) an otherwise highly qualified applicant to be conditionally admitted, subject to satisfaction of one or more agreed but not officially stated condition.

In all cases in which conditional admissions are granted, if the student *does not* satisfy the condition, then the student *will not* be able to enroll in the LL.M. program.

G. Should I Apply Even If I Have Low English Language Proficiency Test Scores?

Yes. Some U.S. LL.M. programs will routinely admit international students with low English language proficiency test scores, even though the school may state on its website that it will not accept scores below a certain minimum.

Some schools will admit these students on a conditional basis, as described above, where the student may study English in the U.S. and begin LL.M. classes only after the student satisfies the condition of reaching a particular level of English proficiency. Some schools will admit the students in the normal fashion, but permit the student to take English language courses *while* the student takes regular LL.M. law courses. Some schools will not advertise that they offer conditional admits, or that they waive the English language proficiency requirement, when, in fact, they will offer these options. Because the cost of applying for an LL.M. degree is low, why not apply to many different schools, even if you do not possess scores as high as the schools list as requirements?

Of course, if your English is not at a stage at which you can read, converse, and understand at the level needed to succeed in an LL.M. program, it would be frustrating to you, and deeply disadvantageous for you, to enter into the course of study without first improving your English significantly, because you will not be able to reap the full benefits of the legal training offered in the LL.M. program. Your comprehension level would be low. You would likely not be able to perform well on exams, homework assignments, or theses. You would fall behind and/or lose your way. You could hold your classmates and professors back during discussions of complex legal thought because you would be stuck

Admissions

just trying to figure out what they were talking about. Additionally, they might feel pressed, unfairly, to spend an inordinate amount of time and effort communicating with you inside and outside the classroom. You do not want your progress to be problematic or stymied. You do not want to be a burden to others. You do not want language ability to contribute to your having a negative LL.M. experience.

H. Pre-LL.M. Academic and English Courses Offered in the U.S.

English language skills, particularly legal English, are taught in pre-LL.M. programs held in different parts of the U.S. in the summer before the fall semester, or during the fall or spring semesters. Some of these programs are at law schools, and some are restricted to students enrolling in an LL.M. program. Other English language courses are open to LL.M. students enrolling at any U.S. law school. I mention here just a couple of these. Several similar programs are mentioned in Chapter 8.

1. Pace's *Legal Academic and English Skills Course for International Law Students and Lawyers*

This program runs for 14 weeks from January–May. It is intended to provide overseas students "with the language and academic skills needed to succeed in an American law school as well as the English necessary for legal purposes and understanding of American laws." **Pace** notes that it takes a "legal academic and English skills-based approach with legal content" to introduce students "to legal writing, reading, listening and speaking skills required for graduate law school" in the U.S. and that the course "builds on and reinforces skills acquired in the summer '*English for Lawyers Program*,' introducing new legal knowledge, vocabulary, and concepts, and, through a workshop approach, assists current international graduate law students in mastering challenging legal academic and language skills as they come up in the course of the academic year" (www.pace.edu/page.cfm?doc_id=28914).

2. Temple's *Four-Week Intensive Pre-LL.M. English Language Program in Beijing*

To enhance LL.M. students' English language proficiency in a U.S. legal context, **Temple** offers its students this program in August before the LL.M. program begins. It includes four courses: American Legal System; Case Briefing; Law School Skills; and Legal English: Listening and Speaking (www.law.temple.edu/Pages/International/Graduate_Masters_Law_Beijing_Additional_Courses.aspx).

3. Programs at Other Law Schools

Other LL.M. programs also offer pre-LL.M. programs with a mix of preparatory substantive law and English language courses. Some of these programs are restricted to students from a particular school's LL.M. program, whereas other programs accept students from different LL.M. programs. This plentiful list includes **Stanford** and **Georgetown**. (See Chapter 8.)

I. Bonuses of English as a Second Language

LL.M. students whose first language is not English may enjoy various "bonuses." These bonuses are intended to help level the playing field between native English speakers and non-native English speakers, but some argue that they are unfair, in part because of how it is determined which students from which countries and backgrounds can enjoy these bonuses, and which cannot.

1. Extra Time to Take Exams

Some LL.M. programs grant non-native English speakers extra time to take each law school exam, perhaps one and a half times the amount allotted for native speakers. If the normal exam period is three hours, the student would be permitted four and a half hours. Controversy arises when some international LL.M. students are considered native English speakers for some purposes, but not native English speakers for other purposes. For example, some schools require applicants from certain Anglophone African countries to submit English language proficiency test scores, even though those countries are English-speaking and the applicants studied in English. Then, when the students enroll and sit for exams, they are denied the extra time allotted to non-native English speakers. They are considered native speakers for exam purposes, but non-native speakers for LL.M. admission purposes. **NYU** apparently does not have this issue because **NYU** allots the same amount of exam time for *all* LL.M. students.

2. English/Foreign Language Dictionary Use During Exams

Some schools permit non-native English speakers to bring a foreign language dictionary to exams. If an Anglophone African student who was required to submit English language proficiency test scores is permitted to bring a dictionary to the exam (though she may be denied extra time), what sort of dictionary would she bring? Her native language is English. If she brings an English language dictionary, then shouldn't everyone be allowed to take a dictionary into the exam?

3. Extra Tutoring or Exam-Taking Sessions

At some schools professors, law students, or qualified English as a Second Language (ESL) instructors tutor LL.M. students on exam-taking. One would hope all LL.M. programs would have pre-exam tutorials for all LL.M. students for whom the LL.M. exams will be their first experience taking U.S. law school exams. The better LL.M. programs do have these, and they also have tutorials for students whose first language is not English, which might be conducted by ESL instructors.

4. Lenient Exam and Paper Grading

When grading exams, some professors do not hold non-native English speakers to the same standard of grammar, syntax, or spelling facility that they demand of native English speakers. Though exams are meant to be graded anonymously, international students' exam papers, whether handwritten or typed, are often easily distinguishable from those of native speakers. Some non-native speakers may benefit grade-wise, as the professor may not deduct for all mistakes.

J. Hazard of English as a Second Language: What Happens If You Do Not Practice Your English?

Many of you speak English just fine, have spoken it for years, and perhaps use English daily in your country. English may be second nature to you, and you will do very well in your LL.M. program. You will not slip into any bad habits.

But some of you may encounter hazards in the U.S. — particularly if you do not use English frequently in your country. You will be forced to use English constantly in the U.S. — not only in school, but in all you do. It may be challenging to suddenly have to use English for everything. Reading English language law books is one thing. But now you will have to use English with grocery clerks, bus and taxi drivers, apartment landlords, barbers and hairdressers, and medical doctors — all of whom might use English words or expressions you have never heard, or they may speak so quickly, or pronounce words or whole monologues so strangely that it seems like another foreign language altogether. It can be bewildering, frustrating, and exhausting.

Your school may have many students who speak your native language, or your city may have many linguistically similar people. It may become incredibly tempting for you to gravitate toward them. You can speak with them easily and freely. They are familiar to you, and may make you feel comfortable. They understand your accent and your body language. Their barbers know your home country hairstyle, and their restaurants cook food like you eat with your family back at home!

But your English may grow stale. You may find it difficult to keep up with your LL.M. work. Spending too much time with your country-mates and speaking too much in your home language may defeat what you had hoped to accomplish in the U.S. — to gain a solid education inside and outside the classroom. Professors can tell when international LL.M. students do not speak English outside the classroom, because their English does not improve throughout the course of the year.

Take full advantage of your LL.M. period to communicate in English! Get roommates who do not speak your native language, so you will be forced to speak English at home. Join student organizations with students who will speak English with you. (See Chapter 19.) Read English newspapers and listen to English radio. Volunteer at a homeless shelter, or at an orphanage. Join civic organizations in your town. Spend your "free" afternoons at the local courthouse, listening to cases tried in English (pick up some English *and* legal pointers as well). There are many things you can do to help ensure that your English improves during the course of your LL.M. year.

CHAPTER SUMMARY

- You will not succeed in your LL.M. program if you have not reached an acceptable level of English language proficiency.
- You must be able to read, write, and speak English to do well.
- Your English language proficiency test scores will prove to the school your English language competency.
- You may be excused from the English proficiency tests if your first degree was taught in English, or if you are from an English-speaking country.
- If your scores are below a school's stated minimum, the school may grant you "conditional admission." You can come to the U.S. and study English. When your scores improve enough, you can join the school's LL.M. program.

Chapter 13

Other Components of an LL.M. Application

(Document Authentication and Verification; Financial Resources Proof; and Scholarship Requests)

CHAPTER HIGHLIGHTS

- In addition to what was discussed in earlier chapters, schools' applications have other requirements.
- Be certain to provide everything the school requests, in the format and manner requested.
- If you do not follow a school's directions, the school may reject your application and deny you admission.

A. Introduction

Chapter 9 lists the various formal and informal components of an LL.M. application. Chapters 10-12 discuss personal statements and essays, CVs, personal interviews, letters of recommendation, and proof of English language proficiency.

This chapter discusses other components of a successful LL.M. application, including

1) Authenticated or verified transcripts, diplomas, and certificates;
2) Proof of financial resources; and
3) Scholarship requests.

Overall, you must convince the admission committee that you have attained solid academic achievement, that you have great potential to succeed in the LL.M. program, and that you will contribute solidly to the school, both while enrolled and after you graduate. Just as you invest in the school, the school invests in you.

B. Authentication and Verification of Your Application Documents

U.S. LL.M. programs generally require applicants to submit evidence of solid academic achievement. The primary documents required in this regard are transcripts from schools you have attended, and diplomas and certificates you have received. Schools also require bar admission records and other similar professional documents.

1. Difficulties Schools Encounter with Documents

Schools have encountered difficulties with these documents for at least three reasons:

a) Some of the documents may not be in English.
b) Foreign transcripts may use grading scales with which U.S. schools may not be familiar or for which U.S. schools cannot readily ascertain grade equivalencies.
c) U.S. schools may not be certain that those documents are authentic, and not false or fraudulent.

2. Schools Require Independent Agencies to Help Resolve Difficulties

Many schools require international applicants to submit documents to an independent agency that provides one or more of the following services:

a) *Translate documents.*   The agency will translate an applicant's documents into English, or if the applicant already translated them or has had them translated, the agency will verify that the translation is correct and valid.
b) *Prepare course list with grades or marks.*   The agency will list all courses the applicant has taken, the U.S. unit/hour equivalent, the U.S. grade equivalent (and information regarding any grading scales), the U.S. degree equivalent, and other relevant standards and nuances.
c) *Verify foreign documents.*   The agency will verify that the original documents are genuine, and are not forged (requiring that the applicant's foreign schools send transcripts, diplomas, and certificates directly to the agency).

d) *Collect, assemble, and transmit foreign documents.*   The agency may also serve a "collection, assembly, and transmittal" function for other materials that the applicant sends them, or that referees, schools, or others send on the applicant's behalf. The agency will collect, assemble, and transmit all gathered relevant material to the U.S. school.

e) *Evaluate international student credentials.*   The agency prepares a "credential evaluation report" that contains all materials it collected, assembled, authenticated, and evaluated on the applicant's behalf. The applicant requests that the agency transmit a credential evaluation report to one or more U.S. LL.M. programs to which the applicant applies.

Such agencies help resolve difficulties schools encounter with foreign documents and credentials, and provide a convenient and efficient means that can benefit schools and applicants. Applicants should receive a copy of the credential evaluation report, and should be able to monitor the agency's delivery of the reports to the respective U.S. law schools. The applicant should verify that the agencies have translated or verified accurately, and should challenge any discrepancies.

Listed in the text box here and on the next page are some of the many credential evaluation agencies used by U.S. graduate programs. Each law school decides whether it: (a) requires the use of a credential evaluation agency for students with overseas credentials; or (b) accepts credential evaluation reports only from specific agencies (which may or may not be listed below). **Please check with each U.S. law school to find out what it requires.**

Some Authentication, Verification, and Assembly Companies

Ask your school which company it prefers, recommends, or requires, if any. Or, check the *National Association of Credential Evaluation Services.* (www.naces.org)

1) *Center for Applied Research Evaluation & Education, Inc.,* International Evaluation Service, P.O. Box 18358, Anaheim, CA 92817-8358, eval_caree@yahoo.com

2) *Educational Credential Evaluators, Inc.,* P.O. Box 514070, Milwaukee, WI 53202-3470, eval@ece.org

3) *Educational Records Evaluation Service, Inc.,* 601 University Ave., Suite 127, Sacramento, CA 95825-6738, edu@eres.com

4) *Foreign Educational Document Service,* P.O. Box 4091, Stockton, CA 95204, www.documentservice.org

5) *Foundation for International Services, Inc.,* 14926 35th Ave., West, Suite 210, Lynnwood, WA 98087, info@fis-web.com

6) *Global Services Associates,* 409 North Pacific Coast Highway, # 393, Redondo Beach, CA 90277, info@globaleval.org

(list continued on next page)

7) *International Consultants of Delaware, Inc.,* P.O. Box 8629, Philadelphia, PA 19101-8629, 3528, icd@icdel.com

8) *International Education Research Foundation, Inc.,* P.O. Box 3665, Culver City, CA 90231, www.ierf.org

9) *Josef Silny & Associates, Inc.,* International Education Consultants, 7101 SW 102 Avenue, Miami, FL 33173, www.jsilny.com

10) *LLM Credential Assembly Service for International Applicants,* 662 Penn St., Box 8511, Newtown, PA 18940-8511, **http://LLM.LSAC.org**; https://llm.lsac.org/llm/logon/splash.aspx

11) *World Education Services, Inc. (WES),* P.O. Box 5087, Bowling Green Station, New York, NY 10274-5087, www.wes.org

C. Proof of Financial Resources (See Chapters 20 and 21)

For at least two reasons, U.S. law schools require international LL.M. applicants to prove that they have financial resources sufficient to pay for their tuition and living expenses in the U.S.

First, schools do not want to invest resources in an applicant who cannot afford to attend and for whom the school is not able to provide adequate financial assistance. It would be impractical and surely frustrating for the applicant and for the school.

Second, the U.S. government requires all international applicants to prove they have adequate financial resources before the school is permitted to issue an admitted student an I-20 or DS-2019 form, either of which is required for a student to receive a U.S. student visa. These forms and visa regulations are discussed in Chapters 20-22. Here it will suffice to discuss the types and amount of financial resources the student must prove, and the sources of those resources, which will convince the school to issue the admitted students an I-20 or DS-2019, and which in turn will allow the U.S. consular officials to confidently issue the student visa.

1. Cost of Attendance

Each school prepares a Cost of Attendance (COA) figure that estimates a student's expenses for the academic year, including tuition, fees, insurance, housing, and books. U.S. government guidelines permit the COA to include school charges and costs for the student to live. The COA is a figure applicable to all students, though actual costs may vary from student to student depending on, for example, whether the student lives in a shared apartment or has a big appetite. More information about COA can be found in Chapter 23.

2. Types of Documents (See Chapters 20 and 21)

a. School Documents for LL.M. Program Application

Before the school issues you an I-20 or DS-2019, you must provide the school with documents showing that you can cover your COA for the academic year. Schools will accept a wide range of evidence of financial resources, but the most common documents submitted are bank statements (if the student is self-funded — that is, funded by personal or family funds) or letters from governments or foundations (if the student has been awarded a non-law school scholarship or grant for the LL.M.).

Bank statements can be for current accounts (checking accounts), savings accounts, money market accounts, or other types. They can be accounts of the applicants, parents, relatives, or outside sponsors. In addition to statements, schools request a signature from the person(s) guaranteeing or taking responsibility for ensuring the funds will be available — the student's financial sponsor.

Generally, schools will issue an I-20 or DS-2019 based on the apparent soundness of financial documents received by, or on behalf of, the student. I do not know that U.S. law schools make in-depth inquiries into whether the accounts represented by the financial statements actually contain the funds, whether there are any other inaccuracies, or that the individual who signed the financial sponsor form is in fact interested in, or committed to, supplying the funds for the student's education as promised. I-20 and DS-2019 forms may be routinely granted.

b. Embassy or Consulate Documents for Student Visa Application

A person who wants a student visa must be interviewed by a U.S. consular official, usually at a U.S. embassy or consulate in the person's home country. The person must present the I-20 or the DS-2019 to the official, along with financial resource documentation. At that point, the person has a heavy burden of proving the existence of sufficient funds available to cover the COA, and that those funds will be used for that purpose.

Scholarship or grant letters tend to be nonproblematic, and easily relied on by U.S. consular officials when deciding whether to issue a student visa. The issuers of such scholarships and grants tend to be well known to consular officials.

Problems can arise, however, with visa requests from self-funded applicants, who must show that there are private funds available to pay for their LL.M. COA.

Chapter 20 provides information about visa interviews.

3. How Much Money Must Be in the Account or Source of Funding?

Before you provide bank statements to the school or consulate, you will want to know how much money should be in the account. The answer to that

Admissions

question is not so simple, because even a balance larger than your COA may not satisfy the consular official.

The consulate official may want to know when the money was deposited and the money's source. For example, the official may request several months of statements, and look for patterns of deposits into the account. If all the money was deposited recently, then the official may want to see other documentation for the money's source. The consular official will want to know that the money was not deposited only for appearances, for visa application purposes. They want to avoid a situation in which your visa is granted, you travel to the U.S. and start school, and when it comes time to pay your second semester tuition, the money that was in the account is no longer there. Your "financial sponsor" used the money for other purposes; maybe that money was never intended to be used for your tuition and fees. Maybe the money was deposited only for visa purposes.

4. Filing False Financial Documents

As suggested above, applicants (and their sponsors) have been known to shuffle money into an account shortly before the visa interview, hoping that the consular official will see the balance of the account, observe that the balance is greater than the COA, and grant the visa.

University of Southern California Discusses Financial Support Documentation

Types of financial support normally accepted:

- Savings deposits, checking accounts, or deposit certificates
- "Approved" educational loans
- General bank letters or solvency certificates from a bank
- Time/fixed/term deposits or government bonds if document states that funds mature by or near the beginning of your first term or can be withdrawn at any time
- Employer and government sponsorships/scholarships
- Provident funds if document states that the funds can be withdrawn at any time

Types of financial support not accepted:

- Mutual funds, investments or stocks, securities
- Retirement funds, pensions, life insurance policies
- Tax returns
- Salary/payroll statements
- Statements of assets or property, mortgages, jewelry, residences, automobiles
- "Pending" educational loans
- Accountant portfolio

Source: http://lawweb.usc.edu/how/gip/llm/appinfo.cfm

If the school learns that an applicant has submitted false or spurious financial documents, the applicant will not be admitted. If the student has already been admitted, the admission will be withdrawn. If the student has already arrived in the U.S. and has begun taking classes, the school may subject the student to Honor Code violations, dismiss the student, and notify U.S. government officials. The U.S. government may revoke the student's U.S. visa and deport the student to his home country. The student would not be entitled to any refund for tuition, visa, or other expenses, and could be barred from returning to the U.S. The student would not receive an LL.M. degree. You do not want your funding to dry up when you are in the U.S. trying to study, prepare for exams, or write a thesis. It is a serious distraction — or worse — that has caused many LL.M. students great distress. This unfortunate outcome can be a very unpleasant scenario for all involved, and should be avoided at all costs.

D. Scholarship — Do Not Forget to Request a Scholarship!

1. Three Types of "Scholarships"

U.S. law schools might offer one of three types of "scholarships"[1] to LL.M. students:

a) *Merit-based scholarships*   (to try to attract highly qualified students who may have options to attend other schools);
b) *Need-based scholarships*   (for applicants who could not afford to attend unless they received a scholarship);
c) *LL.M. program scholarships to bolster enrollment*   (well-established LL.M. programs that satisfy their students' reasonable expectations do not need to offer significant scholarships to bolster enrollment because the programs attract enough or more than enough strong applicants to meet their enrollment goals).

2. Schools Offering Scholarships — Additional Information

Some schools offer merit-based or need-based scholarships, or both, or neither. Schools might provide space on their applications for you to indicate whether you would like to be considered for an LL.M. scholarship. Other schools indicate that all applicants will automatically be considered for LL.M. scholarships. Other schools are silent on the issue.

---

1. Many law schools offer LL.M. students "tuition discounts" or "tuition remissions" (which they may refer to as "scholarships"), permitting students to pay less than the full tuition.

Admissions

If the school requests that you indicate your interest in a scholarship, and if you are interested, I encourage you to submit a statement of your interest along with your application.[2] I believe that schools will generally make admission decisions based on your solid academic achievement and potential, and *not* on your scholarship request or needs. I doubt that schools will deny admission to a highly qualified applicant because the student requests a scholarship. Proof of your having sufficient funds for your LL.M. degree is critical during the visa acquisition process, but is not as important during your LL.M. application process. If you are highly qualified for admission, schools should permit you to raise funding *after* you are admitted, and perhaps assist you in identifying funding sources.

Indeed, schools may provide you with a scholarship to help pay for your LL.M. Further information about LL.M. scholarships, grants, and fellowships can be found in Chapter 24, and Chapter 25 has more information on loans. Also see Appendix II.

Some schools attach prestigious-sounding names to the tuition discount scholarships they offer to LL.M. students to try to convince them to join. In fact, these scholarships may differ from the school's regular scholarships or discounts only by the name. **Take caution.** Schools might better attract you by offering high-quality educational resources to help you achieve your personal and professional goals. Attaching a fancy name to a tuition scholarship is not likely to help you substantially after you graduate. A school may offer an "International Law Scholarship" (for a student enrolled in an international law track), a "Distinguished LL.M. Scholarship" (for an international LL.M. student), a "Grotius LL.M. Scholarship" (for an LL.M. student studying international law, named after Hugo Grotius, the "founder" of modern day international law), or a similarly named scholarship. Are these discounts evidence that a school is a cash cow, where they seek to attract students by offering them prestigious-sounding "scholarships" that in fact provide the same amount of tuition discount offered without the prestigious-sounding scholarship name? What international student wouldn't be attracted by a scholarship with a fancy name attached to it? It would be better, however, to be attracted to a high-quality LL.M. program, that will offer you the high-quality legal education you seek.

---

2. If a school requests that you *do not* mention finances or scholarships in your *personal statement*, you may still raise the issues in a separate letter to the school's admission committee.

CHAPTER SUMMARY

- Every school's application requires different things. Many schools require the following:
  - Authentication/verification of documents, including transcripts
  - Proof of financial resources
  - Scholarship requests
- Be prepared to supply everything the school requests.
- Be certain to follow directions regarding format and manner of submission.
- Some schools may not admit you. But, if they do not admit you, it should not be because you did not follow application instructions.
- Do not submit false financial or other information in your applications.
- Do not forget to request scholarship or other funding from the school, particularly if you learn that the school is seeking to boost the number of LL.M. students in its program.

Admissions

Part IV

School Replies to Your Application:

What to Expect Next

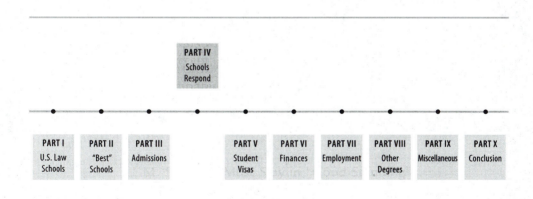

| PART IV |
| Schools |
| Respond |

PART I	PART II	PART III		PART V	PART VI	PART VII	PART VIII	PART IX	PART X
U.S. Law	"Best"	Admissions		Student	Finances	Employment	Other	Miscellaneous	Conclusion
Schools	Schools			Visas			Degrees		

Chapter 14

Receiving the School's Letter or E-Mail Message

You Are Admitted (Firm or Conditional), Not Admitted, Put on Hold, or Waitlisted

---

CHAPTER HIGHLIGHTS

- Law schools can admit you, not admit you, or put your application on hold or on a waitlist.
- If you are admitted to one or more U.S. LL.M. programs (Congratulations!), you must decide which school to attend.
- You may decide to defer enrollment for a year or more if the school(s) will allow it.
- After you accept an offer, you must prepare for your journey to the U.S., which involves many steps.
- You may decide to attend a special pre-LL.M. preparatory course in the U.S. in the months before your LL.M. commences.

A. Introduction

1. Four Possible LL.M. Program Responses After You Submit Your Application

Weeks or months after you submit your applications, a law school may send you an e-mail message or letter that may contain one of four messages:

(a) Admitted (Firm or Conditional);
(b) Not Admitted;

(c) Put on Hold; or

(d) Waitlisted.

2. What Happens If a School Does Not Admit You?

Even if you are not admitted to any school, or not admitted to the school you believe is "best" for you, there still may be possibilities for you to gain admission to a U.S. law school. Do not despair. Do not give up.

In all cases, whether you are admitted, not admitted,[1] or are some place in between, there are actions you may want to take to follow up. This chapter discusses these actions.

B. Not Admitted

If a school does not admit you, it may inform you that it received many applications from very highly qualified candidates, and that it was extremely difficult for the admission committee to make admission decisions, and that it regrets that it will not be able to offer you a seat in their class. This may be true. Many law schools receive far more applications than they have seats to offer in their LL.M. class. However, if your goal is to receive an LL.M. from a U.S. law school, and you have done your research well, you might find that there may be another law school that would be more likely to admit a person with your background, experience, and credentials. Some schools admit a higher percentage of applicants than other schools, or seek candidates of a different mix. (Chapter 8 explores some rationales used by schools in their LL.M. admission decisions.)

If a school initially does not admit you, it may be difficult for you to convince that school to overrule itself and admit you, at least in *that same year*. But if you contact the school and ask why they did not admit you, the school *may* review your application and decide they overlooked components of your application, or that the school's circumstances have changed, and then admit you. Though unlikely, this outcome is possible, at least at schools that do not have a flat policy of refusing to review applications it has assessed once. Again, you might consider reapplying to a school the next year, or the year after that, if the school does not admit you the first time. **There is no shame in applying more than once.** You should try to ascertain what your first application lacked (experience, adequate grades or marks, strong recommendation letters) and try

---

1. The opposite of "admitted" is "not admitted." The term "rejected" is negative and does not wholly reflect reality. If a school does "not admit" you one year you can apply to that same school again the next year. The school has "not admitted" you *this year*, not *next year*. "Reject" seems more permanent. Your scores may improve, you may have additional accomplishments, or the school may have different admission criteria and goals the next year.

to remedy those shortcomings. Ask the school's LL.M. office if it will tell you why you were not admitted. Or ask a professor from your own school, or a current LL.M. student or graduate, to review your application and advise you on how you might improve it for next time.

Decide whether you want to gain additional legal experience or otherwise improve your credentials and apply next year. Decide if you want to apply to different LL.M. programs, even for the current year.[2] Assess your motives for wanting to study for an LL.M. in the U.S., and then decide whether and how to reach your goal. If your goal remains to receive a U.S. law degree, you may still figure out a way to do that.

C. Put on Hold

Being put "on hold" generally means the school has *not decided* to admit you, but has also *not decided* to deny you. It will make its decision later.

The school may be waiting to determine whether other candidates will apply who are a better fit with the school's quantity, quality, or mix goals. (See Chapter 8.) The school may be reassessing its own curricular priorities, and cannot yet decide how you as an LL.M. student would fit into their program.

Being "on hold" is not as bad as receiving a "not admit" but may not be as good as being waitlisted. If you have received an offer from one school and are on hold at another school, you might inform the hold school of your offer. But, if you press the matter with the hold school, the hold school may change your status from "hold" to "not admit" — so be careful, and be patient.

D. Put on the Waitlist

For some schools, the waitlist serves the same function as a hold. At other schools, if you are on a waitlist, the school may have offered seats to many applicants, and if one or more of those applicants do not enroll, you *may* be admitted.

It is similar to airplane travel where the airline confirms more seats than are available on the plane because it believes that some of the passengers will not turn up, and the seats of those passengers can be filled from the waitlist. A waitlisted passenger does not get seated unless someone with a confirmed seat does not show up at the airport. Similarly, there is no guarantee you will

---

2. Less competitive U.S. schools accept LL.M. applications as late as July or even later, with admitted students enrolling in August or September if their visas can be issued that quickly. Otherwise those students may enroll the following semester, in January.

clear a school's waitlist and be admitted. It is not easy for waitlisted applicants to know how long an LL.M. program's waitlist is, how many seats the LL.M. program wants to fill, how many applicants the school has already admitted, or how many admitted LL.M. students will accept and enroll.

LL.M. websites, chat rooms, and listserves circulate anecdotal information about LL.M. waitlists. If you are on a waitlist, you might send an e-mail message to the school and ask for clarification about your prospects. *Be cautious when corresponding with the law school about the waitlist — you do not want to create negative impressions!*

E. Conditional Admission (Admit If Conditions Are Satisfied)

It is not bad to receive a conditional admission. But understand that a "conditional admission" is different from a regular, firm admission. With a firm admission, you do not need to fulfill any special requirements before you can enroll.

Conditional admissions may be granted, for instance, to applicants who meet the school's academic requirements but have not reached the school's required English language proficiency level. (See Chapter 12.) Before you can enroll, you must satisfy the *condition* that you raise your English language proficiency score to a certain level. If you raise your score within a certain time, you may enroll in the LL.M. program.

Schools may issue you documents permitting you to travel to the U.S. to study English for a certain period, either at the school or elsewhere. While in the U.S., you must work hard to improve your scores. If you do not reach the required level, you will be required to depart the U.S. and return to your home country *without* entering the LL.M. program.

If you have solid credentials and are enrolled in the final semester of your first degree, a U.S. LL.M. program may admit you on the condition that you finish your final semester and receive your degree. If you have law-related test results pending, or pending admission to the bar of your home country, the U.S. school may grant you admission on the condition that you pass the test or get admitted to your bar.

F. Firm Admission — Admitted!

Congratulations! With a firm admission in hand, you should begin preparing for the day you board the plane for the U.S. to begin your LL.M. program. I suggest that you make a list of steps, draw up a timeline, and get started. You may finally be on your way to the U.S.!

Schools Respond

G. Admission to One LL.M. Program, or More Than One ... What Do I Do?

If you have been admitted to only one school, you have options. You also have options if you are accepted to more than one school. Some of these options are obvious. But maybe some of them are not. (See Section H below.)

1. Admitted to One School Only

If you were admitted to one school only, your choices include:

(a) *accept the offer* (and *enroll*);
(b) *reject the offer* (and *not enroll*);
(c) *put the school on hold* (and not enroll until you have had an opportunity to exhaust any waitlist or hold you might still be on at another school; or negotiate a higher scholarship)[3]
(d) *request a deferral* (accept the offer but do not plan to attend right away — if the school grants the deferral, enroll the following spring or summer semester, or, at an agreed deferred point you might reject the offer and not do an LL.M. after all, or enroll in an LL.M. program at another school).

Before you take any action, make a fresh decision about whether the school that admitted you is the "best" school for you in general terms, and whether it is the "best" school for you at this particular time in your life and career. Now would be a great time to review the 218 criteria on how to choose an LL.M. program outlined in **Chapter 7** so that you can be as certain as possible that your long- and short-term goals can be met through this particular law school's LL.M. program.

You may decide to wait a year and apply to different schools that may be better for you. You may decide to stay home and earn more money for a year before attending school (and meanwhile apply to other schools). You may decide to attend the school that admitted you, enroll, and have a wonderfully enriching experience. If you review Chapter 7's criteria before you accept, you can make a more informed decision.

---

3. If a school makes an admission offer to you, it will reserve a seat for you, and it may give you a deadline to accept. It may put other applicants on hold or waitlist, waiting to learn if you accept. If you inform that school that you have not yet decided, then the school will keep other applicants on hold or on a waitlist — until you let the school know if you will attend. In this way, students with offers can and do cause other applicants to remain on hold or on waitlists. But this is their right — and yours, if accepted — and it is the way the system is set up, and it does not mean they or you should feel pressured to rush your decision on behalf of the imagined eager others on the waitlist or on hold.

Schools Respond

2. Admitted to Two or More Schools

If you are admitted to two or more law schools, you might review the **Chapter 7** criteria to try to sort out which of them is indeed the "best" school for you. This can be tricky, as the schools may appear to be quite similar. But you can be discerning in your study by peeling off the layers and inquiring more deeply into those areas that are most important to you. Your principal concerns might be the availability of courses in your specialization area, the experiential courses available at the school, the nature of the student body, the number of credits needed to graduate, whether a thesis is required, optional, or prohibited — all things you may not have thought about until you read *LL.M. Roadmap*.

Just because you were admitted to more than one LL.M. program does not mean you must enroll, or that you must enroll immediately. You can defer until the next spring or fall (if the school permits). You can decide that none of the schools that admitted you is the "best" for you, and you could then decide to apply to other schools. You might even enroll at one of the schools, and after the first semester *try* to transfer to the other school (although this is not recommended).

3. Deferring Enrollment for a Year

Many schools, but not all, will permit you to defer enrollment for one year or more. This may give you time to earn additional money for your expenses, improve your English skills, study substantive law materials to give you an edge when you enroll, or give you an opportunity to decide if, in the end, you really want to join a U.S. LL.M. program. It also provides you with an opportunity to further study or feel out the school(s) that admitted you, and make an informed decision as to which, if any, of the schools will allow and help you to fulfill your personal, educational, professional, and career objectives. You can decide if the schools of most interest to you will likely satisfy your reasonable expectations.

4. Negotiating a Higher Scholarship

It never hurts (and it may help!) to ask for a higher tuition remission or scholarship, no matter how much of a favor you think the school has done to admit you! The school will not retract your admission offer or decrease your scholarship if you request more money. If you receive offers from two or more schools and each school offers you a different amount of scholarship, you might ask the school that you want to attend to match the highest scholarship offer.

5. Bargaining Your Way Off a Waitlist or Off the Hold Pile

If you are waitlisted or on hold at a school that you believe is the "best" school for you, or that is "better" for you than the one that admitted you, inform the holding or waitlisting school about your acceptance elsewhere and ask whether it can update you on its likelihood of admitting you. If you are admitted to a noncompetitive school that receives few applicants and you are waitlisted or on hold at a competitive school with thousands of applications, you will not have much leverage.

6. Are You Going to Do the LL.M. or Not?

The following section of *LL.M. Roadmap* is important once you decide to accept an offer to join an LL.M. program.

H. Items on Your List — To Prepare After You Choose Your New School

1. Regular Admission or Conditional Admission?

Determine whether your offer is for "firm admission" or "conditional admission." (See above and **Chapter 12**.)

2. Thank You Note

Send an e-mail message to thank all schools that made you an offer of admission, whether it was a conditional admission or firm admission. You want to acknowledge to the school that you received their letter or e-mail message. (By the way, in the U.S., generally, "thank you notes" are an important social tradition, and are written, for example, after someone gives you a gift, takes you to lunch or dinner, or does a special favor for you.)

3. If You Were Conditionally Admitted, Ask Questions About the Conditions

Make certain you understand what conditions you must satisfy to receive a firm admission to the LL.M. program; the standard for determining when the condition is satisfied; the length of time you have to fulfill the condition; and any other questions you have about the conditions. If the condition is that you must raise your English proficiency level, be certain that you understand exactly what score demarcates that level; when you will be tested to determine if you meet the level: whether you must pay for the test; whether the school will accept an alternative method to meet the condition; and **what happens if you do not fulfill the condition in the allotted time.** If you do not satisfy the condition, you *may not* be permitted to enroll in the LL.M. program or take LL.M. courses. It is also possible you will not be able to remain in the U.S., even to take additional English classes.

4. Ask Follow-up Questions to Schools That Admitted You

Now is a good time to ask questions about the offer or about the school — *before you accept the offer.*

a. Scholarship Questions

The admission letter may inform you that you are receiving a "scholarship" of a certain amount, and that the amount will be deducted from your tuition. The scholarship may actually be a tuition remission or discount. (See Chapter 24.) If you want a greater tuition remission (scholarship), now is the best time to ask for one. Once you accept the offered amount, you will have significantly less bargaining power.

b. LL.M. Program Selection Criteria (See Chapter 7)

After you are admitted you should seek to verify or clarify promises the LL.M. program made on its website or other material. Try to make sure that the school is not a cash cow or diploma mill. Ask questions such as:

- Will the courses I want to take be available?
- Will the school have sufficient courses for my specialization?
- Will professors I want to study with indeed be there and teaching, or will they be on sabbatical?
- Will the school have a career officer dedicated to LL.M. students?
- Will the associate dean live in the same city or state as the law school where the LL.M. program is located, or commute from another city or state and not be available to handle LL.M. student issues that arise in the school's LL.M. program?
- Will the associate dean be working full time at an out-of-state law school and not be available to handle LL.M. student issues that arise in the school's LL.M. program?
- Will there be a physical office at the law school dedicated to the LL.M. administration and LL.M. employees?
- Will faculty centers associated with LL.M. tracks have physical space at the law school, or will such centers exist in name only (this could be another sign of a cash cow)?

Schools Respond

- Will the school provide LL.M. exam review sessions and academic tutoring?
- Will the school and its LL.M. program satisfy your reasonable personal, academic, and career expectations?

Again, you will want to check that the LL.M. program is not a cash cow or diploma mill, and will likely adequately help you reach your academic, personal, and career goals.

5. Contact Current and Former Law School People

Your school will provide contact information for students, graduates, faculty, staff, administrators, and faculty advisors. Contact them. Ask students and graduates if the school meets students' expectations.

6. Contact Schools That Did Not Admit You or Where You Are on Hold or on the Waitlist

If you have a firm offer but you think another school you applied to is "best" for you, why not contact that other school to find out under what circumstances they might admit you? If it "rejected" you, it will probably not change its mind. But what do you have to lose by asking them to review your application? Now would be the time to try to negotiate your way off a hold pile or waitlist.

7. Make Your Final Decision About Schools![4]

If you believe that a particular school will best help you reach your academic, personal, and professional goals — and that school admits you — then perhaps that is the "best" school and LL.M. program for you! Choose that school!

8. Accept an Offer!

After you decide on the school that will adequately help you achieve your academic, professional, career, and personal goals — accept that law school's offer! Send that school an acceptance e-mail message. Congratulations!

9. Reject Other Offers

Send a note of thanks to schools that made an offer, or put you on hold or on a waitlist. They appreciate your telling them which offer you accepted.

---

4. Be sure to review *LL.M. Roadmap* and www.LLMRoadMap.com again *before* you make your final decision choosing the LL.M. program in the U.S. that is **best for you**.

Schools Respond

10. Tuition Deposit

Send a tuition deposit to the school you plan to attend. This will reserve your seat in the LL.M. class.

11. Receive an I-20 or DS-2019 from the Law School

The school will determine which form to send to you: **Form I-20** (if you or your family will pay your tuition and living expenses **(for an F-1 student visa))**; or **Form DS-2019** (if a non-school scholarship or U.S. or foreign government is paying *(for a J-1 student visa))*. (See Chapter 20.)

12. EducationUSA

EducationUSA Advisers are U.S. State Department officials or affiliates who advise international students on study in the U.S. They have over 450 offices in 200 countries and territories, located at U.S. embassies and consulates, universities, Fulbright offices, and other centers. Ideally you should have contacted EducationUSA *before* you applied to U.S. law schools. If not, you can still get advice on your U.S. student visa, travel to the U.S., and other matters (www.educationusa.info).

13. Your U.S. Visa Application Process

Prepare to apply for your visa (gather financial statements from your family or sponsor; gather other documents for your visa interview; pay SEVIS fee; follow U.S. visa steps outlined in **Chapter 20**; apply for your visa).

14. Travel Plans

Make your plans to travel to the U.S. and make your booking.

15. Medical Issues

Take care of medical issues (for example, prescriptions written in English; refills that may be less expensive at home; a physical exam; spare eyeglasses or contacts; vaccinations).

16. Vaccinations

Your school will inform you of state laws or campus rules that require students to be vaccinated against certain diseases, such as diphtheria, measles, mumps, rubella, pertussis, polio, and tetanus. **You may not be permitted to enroll unless you provide proof of vaccinations.**

17. Substantive Preparation

Ask if there is an LL.M. reading list (perhaps books on U.S. law). The school should send you a "welcome packet" containing information about orientation, campus arrival, housing, course schedule, and other matters. Conduct research in the areas of law that most interest to you and that you will likely study. Get a head start. Join a summer course offered by law schools or other institutions that help prepare foreign lawyers for their LL.M. year at U.S. law schools (see item 24, below).

18. Read in Your Area of Specialization

Ask the LL.M. office for reading lists for courses you will take in your specialization area. Contact professors who teach in that area and ask if there are books or articles you can or should read before you arrive on campus. Ask current students or graduates for copies of their course syllabi. Begin thinking about a thesis topic. You can get a head start on your specialization area.

19. Student Visa

Receive your student visa from the U.S. embassy or consulate in your country. It will be pasted into your passport.

20. Airline Ticket

It is getting close to departure time! Reconfirm your booking. Pick up your airline ticket. Pack your suitcases.

21. Finances

Sort out outstanding financial matters. How will you pay tuition (i.e., by credit card or bank draft)? How will spending money reach you (by money transfer from your parent to you)?

22. Practice English

Soon you will be reading, writing, and speaking English every day, all day long! Practice English. Read. Watch movies in English. Relax. Many LL.M. administrators suggest that working to improve your English in the weeks and months before you arrive in the U.S. is critically important, perhaps even more important than reading law books. There will be plenty of law books to read once you arrive in the U.S., but scarce or no time to study English.

23. U.S. Touchdown

Arrive in the U.S. Your student visa permits you to arrive no more than 30 days before your course of study begins. But under some circumstances you may be able to arrive earlier. (See Chapters 21 and 22.)

24. Pre-LL.M. Study Program in the U.S.?

Some institutions in the U.S. offer pre-LL.M. training programs during July or August, immediately before LL.M. classes begin. These programs introduce you to the study of U.S. law, to legal research and writing, and to other topics that will help you get a head start on your LL.M. There are many such programs, at different costs and with different substantive emphasis and lengths. Some programs are available only to LL.M. students who will enroll at particular law schools, or who are sponsored by particular programs, such as Fulbright. Check www.LLMRoadMap.com and course websites. The course providers may provide visa documentation for your travel to the U.S. pre-LL.M.

(a) *International Law Institute.* Washington, D.C. (July and August classes: Legal English and Writing, U.S. Legal System) (www.ili.org/orientation/orientation.htm)

(b) *Institute for U.S. Law.* Washington, D.C. (Classes: English, U.S. Legal Methods, U.S. Law) (www.iuslaw.org)

(c) *Orientation in U.S.A. Law.* Davis, California, and Berkley, California (http://extension.ucdavis.edu/unit/international_law)

(d) *Pre-LL.M. "Boot Camp."* Lansing, Michigan (www.law.msu.edu/llm/als/program-benefits.html)

(e) *Overview of U.S. Law Project: An Online Course Providing an Overview of U.S. Law.* Gulfport, Florida (Classes: Contracts, Torts, Criminal Law, Civil Procedure, Evidence, Family Law) (www.law.stetson.edu/tmpl/academics/internal-1.aspx?id=7064)

25. Begin your LL.M. at the U.S. law school that is best for you! How exciting!

CHAPTER SUMMARY

- After you are admitted, there are many things for you to do.
- First, you might review the 218 criteria in Chapter 7 for choosing an LL.M. program. Decide if the school that admitted you is the "best" for you.
- After you accept an offer, you must get a visa, organize funding, and make travel arrangements. Make a "to do" checklist, and follow it. You will be busy!
- You may attend a pre-LL.M. summer course in the U.S. focusing on "Legal English," American law, or both.

Schools Respond

Chapter 15

Degree Requirements for LL.M. Programs

Tips on How to Do Your Best and How to Succeed in Your LL.M. Program

---

CHAPTER HIGHLIGHTS

- Each school has academic requirements you must fulfill to graduate with your LL.M. degree.
- Make sure you understand these requirements and follow them.
- Some schools will have checklists, progress reporting procedures, and other mechanisms to help students follow procedures. But ultimately students are responsible for making sure they themselves satisfy the degree requirements.
- It is the school's duty to inform you of its degree requirements; this is usually done in the *LL.M. Student Handbook*.
- Ask for a copy of the law school's *LL.M. Student Handbook* before you accept a school's offer. Read it. Make *certain* you are able (and willing) to satisfy all the requirements of the LL.M. program.

A. Introduction

All LL.M. programs have academic requirements that students must fulfill to earn their degrees. This chapter covers general degree requirements in LL.M. programs across the U.S. It discusses:

- the *LL.M. Student Handbook*;
- course-based versus research-based LL.M. program requirements;
- general versus specialized LL.M. program requirements;

- courses to fulfill academic requirements (including number of credits and mandatory versus elective courses);
- academic credit earned without taking traditional courses (earning credits creatively, including through independent research, clinical courses, internships/externships, judicial observation courses, non-law school electives, courses at other schools including correspondence and outside the U.S., transfer credits, and civil law courses);
- auditing courses;
- grading schemes (including LL.M. students receiving extra time to take exams);
- receiving an honors LL.M.;
- waivers of academic requirements;
- maintaining academic, legal, and financial standing and status;
- honor code, plagiarism, or other academic responsibility violations; and
- length of study; maximum time to complete an LL.M.; and the academic calendar.

B. LL.M. Student Handbook

A good information source for degree requirements is your school's *LL.M. Student Handbook*, which you might find — preferably before you enroll — online[1] or receive via e-mail from the LL.M. administration. You might also get information from your school's website or course catalogue, your academic advisor, and the LL.M. office. The school will give you additional information at LL.M. Orientation. Each school has different rules that its LL.M. students must follow. You should become familiar with the most significant of these rules *before you enroll* so you can decide whether you are willing and able to comply with them.

> Ask for the school's *LL.M. Student Handbooks* before you apply, and definitely before you agree to enroll. You should know in advance the most important rules and regulations that will govern your course of study.

The *LL.M. Student Handbook* will inform you of what the program and school expect from you, and what you as a student should reasonably expect from the program and the school. A good *LL.M. Student Handbook* contains course requirements, the school's honor code (if it has such a code), and information about attendance policies, student services, school activities, faculty and

---

1. Houston, Lewis & Clark, Baltimore, Pace, and other schools post their *LL.M. Student Handbook* online for anyone to review and download. Other schools distribute *LL.M. Student Handbooks* only to accepted students. If a school has no *LL.M. Student Handbook*, and relies on a J.D. handbook or no student handbook at all, beware. You may want to consider choosing another school.

Schools Respond

staff, LL.M. concentrations, visa compliance rules (including course load minimums and employment restrictions), good standing rules, leaves of absence, LL.M. graduation requirements, theses, holidays, computers, exams and exam accommodations, academic support, housing, campus offices, and security. Request an *LL.M. Student Handbook* early, preferably *before* you apply. If a school will not send you a set of the rules that will bind you when you enroll, reconsider whether you want to attend that school.

C. Course-Based or Research-Based LL.M. Program

Your U.S. LL.M. program will either be *course-based* or *research-based* (or a combination of the two).

Most LL.M. programs are substantially **course-based**, where students earn most credits in traditional classroom courses, with a professor teaching in front of a room full of students. These can be lecture or seminar style classes, large or small, in different law areas, with an exam at the end. A course-based program may require students to write a thesis, though such theses would likely be for fewer academic credits than theses in a research-based program.

In **research-based** LL.M. programs students earn substantial academic credit by undertaking significant scholarly research and writing. These programs still require at least some traditional coursework, but not as much as in a course-based program.

Iowa, Yale and other programs are course-based but emphasize research. **University of Tulsa College of Law**'s LL.M. in American Indian and Indigenous Law program requires students to choose either the "academic track" (course-based) or the "research track" (research-based) upon enrollment, though they may switch tracks with written permission later. **Berkeley** offers both course-based and research-based tracks, and students may apply to one or the other or, once enrolled, choose between the two.

D. Course Requirements — General Versus Specialized LL.M.

LL.M. programs can be *general* (where students take a wide range of courses in different subject areas, based on interest or whim), or *specialized* (in which students take numerous courses in a particular subject area). In both program types, students must satisfy academic requirements. (Chapter 4 is devoted to general versus specialized LL.M. programs, which are also discussed in Chapter 7.)

Schools Respond

> ### Minnesota's LL.M. for Foreign Lawyer Program Provides:
>
> "The 2011-2012 LL.M. Program for Foreign Lawyers begins on August 11, 2011, and continues through May 12, 2011. In the first three weeks of the program, all LL.M. students complete the mandatory *Introduction to American Law* course, which prepares students for the demands of the academic year. Topics introduced in the course include U.S. history, legal history, civil procedure, constitutional law, legal English, and legal research and writing. Students will learn how to brief cases, analyze judicial opinions, interact in the classroom, and prepare for the full-time study of law at the University of Minnesota." (p. 1, Application)

E. Courses to Fulfill Academic Requirements

1. Number of Credit Hours to Complete LL.M. Degree

Most LL.M. programs require students to complete about 24 academic credits to receive their degrees (though some require as few as 20 and others require more than 34). Most courses are worth 3 credit hours and a few courses are worth 2 or 4 credit hours, so most LL.M. students take 8 to 10 courses to satisfy their requirements. This works out to 3 to 5 courses per semester.

Different schools require (or permit) students to take a mix of different types of courses, including traditional classroom courses; seminars; thesis or other writing courses; independent research; or experiential courses (such as clinics, internships, or externships).

2. Mandatory Courses for International LL.M. Students

Most programs have mandatory classes exclusively for LL.M. students educated outside the U.S. These include topics such as Introduction to American Law, American Law for Foreign Lawyers, or American Legal System — designed to introduce foreign-educated lawyers to U.S. law and practice. Schools may also require these students to take legal writing, research, and advocacy courses to introduce and develop U.S.-style skills training.

3. Mandatory Courses for a Specialized LL.M. Track

All specialized LL.M. programs require students to take a certain number of courses in the specialization area. For example, a health law LL.M. would require a certain number of health law courses, and an international law LL.M. would require a certain number of international law courses. This is not a surprise. What is surprising is what the school may count as a "health law course" or an "international law course." Some schools with purported specialized

Schools Respond

Sample Course Selection — General LL.M. (Without Thesis)

Fall Semester	Credit Hours for Fall	Spring Semester	Credit Hours for Spring
Course(s) required for International LL.M. Students (Intro to U.S. Law; Legal Research and Writing?)	3–4	Course(s) required for International LL.M. Students (Intro to U.S. Law; Legal Research and Writing?)	3–4
Elective Courses	6–8	Elective Courses	6–8
Total Credits Per Semester	10–12	Total Credits Per Semester	10–12
Total for Degree	Law Schools Average 24 Academic Credits for an LL.M. Degree		

Sample Course Selection — Specialized LL.M. (With or Without Thesis)

Fall Semester	Credit Hours for Fall	Spring Semester	Credit Hours for Spring
Course(s) required for International LL.M. Students (Intro to U.S. Law; Legal Research and Writing?)	2–4	Course(s) required for International LL.M. Students (Intro to U.S. Law; Legal Research and Writing?)	2–4
Required Specialization Courses	4–6	Required Specialization Courses	4–6
Elective Courses	3	Elective Courses	3
Thesis	1–2	Thesis	1–2
Total Credits Per Semester	10–12	Total Credits Per Semester	10–12
Total for Degree	Law Schools Average 24 Academic Credits for an LL.M. Degree		

programs *do not* offer sufficient bona fide courses for students in the given specialization. If you want a specialized degree, make sure the school has appropriate and sufficient courses on offer. Also make certain you understand the degree requirements and that you can meet those requirements.

Schools Respond

> Find a professor at your law school who will supervise your creative work so you can earn independent credit!

4. Elective Courses (Taught at the Law School)

Any course you take that is not a required course is an *elective course*. If your LL.M. requires you to take a total of 24 credit hours, and requires you to take 6 hours of mandatory courses, you will be left with 18 hours to complete your degree. Those 18 hours will be your *elective course* hours. Ordinarily, you would fulfill your elective hours with courses at the law school. Those courses can be traditional classroom courses, or they can be nontraditional courses, as described below. At some schools and under some circumstances you may be able to take courses at other schools and transfer credits back to your school, or earn elective credits through study abroad courses.

5. Credit Without Taking Traditional Courses: Creative Credits

a. Independent Research Credit (at the Law School)

Some schools allow LL.M. students to earn academic credit for independent research they conduct under the supervision of a law professor. This permits students to deeply research substantive areas of law of special interest to them, especially when the subject is not covered in a traditional lecture or seminar course. To work on an independent research project, the student will need to have an advance appreciation of the subject area, possess the requisite research and writing skills, appreciate the need for original thinking that is required for any law school research paper (for a course or seminar, or for a thesis or dissertation), and identify a willing professor to supervise the research. Independent research is particularly helpful if an LL.M. student needs only one or two additional credits to complete his degree, and if there are not any one- or two-credit hour classroom courses of interest. The student can conduct independent research without the workload and other requirements of a regular course. Also, if the student needs only one credit hour, the student can pay for only one credit of independent research without paying for the extra credits associated with a two- or three-credit hour course. If your school charges a fixed dollar amount for tuition each semester, then you would not need to pay extra for one or two additional hours to satisfy your credit requirements.

American permits LL.M. students to receive up to six credit hours of independent research credit for researching and writing on an international legal topic under a faculty member's supervision. Each credit hour equates to approximately 25 double-spaced typed pages of text.

Tulsa students in the American Indian and Indigenous Law program "may earn Independent Study credit for non-traditional projects such as drafting a tribal code on a particular topic or writing a manual for handling certain types of cases" (p. 6 of Handbook).

LL.M. students have received academic credit for conducting research and drafting memoranda and motion papers on behalf of Guantanamo Bay, Cuba "detainees" (for the U.S. Military Commissions in Cuba), on behalf of Slobodan Milosevic (who was on trial before the ICTY), and on behalf of victims of human rights violations (before various UN treaty bodies). LL.M. students can be very creative in working on — and receiving academic credit for — projects of interest to them.

Beware of schools that rely on independent credits to make up for insufficient specialized courses. LL.M. students should not have to depend on ad hoc, independent projects to fulfill LL.M. course requirements.

b. Clinical Courses (Offered by Your Law School)

Most schools permit students to work in clinics where they represent actual clients to gain practical, real-life legal experience. This "experiential" opportunity lets students learn by doing rather than *learn by reading, by lecture,* or *by discussing*. Students engage in real lawyering, and gain valuable, concrete, hands-on legal experience. Students are also challenged to reflect on that experience, and to understand rules of professional responsibility with which lawyers must comply, and to understand the moral, ethical, and legal challenges associated with law practice.

Students may conduct legal research, interview clients and witnesses, draft court pleadings, take depositions, appear in court, and even examine and cross-examine witnesses. They work in many legal areas including criminal defense, civil practice, disability, immigration, international human rights, tax, and elder law. They help clients who may not be able to pay for legal services.

Clinics are an excellent opportunity for students to "get their feet wet" (or "have real experience with" — for those of you who haven't yet mastered the many colloquialisms of the English language) in U.S. legal practice, without having to take a bar exam. Check with the school to make sure that international LL.M. students are eligible. Some clinics require students to satisfy certain

---

Three Types of Clinical Experiential Learning

INTERNAL CLINICS. Real clients from the outside, non-law school community come to the law school for free legal assistance. Supervised by professors, students advise and represent the clients.

EXTERNAL CLINICS. A legal aid office or a law firm permits law students to come to their office to help provide advice and legal services to clients. The clinic is not housed at the law school, though professors supervise the students. Students may conduct research at the law school and send memoranda or draft documents to the outside lawyers.

SIMULATION CLINICS. The "clients" are not real. Students engage in mock interviews, trials, negotiations, and other legal processes. Simulations ordinarily take place at the law school.

Schools Respond

requirements *before* they begin clinic work. LL.M. students in a two-semester degree program may not have enough time to complete prerequisites.

c. Academic Credit for Internship or Externship Courses

Many law schools permit LL.M. students to earn academic credit for work performed during internships (also called "externships"), during which students engage in law-related work performed for and with non-law school entities such as law firms, corporations, government offices, or intergovernmental agencies. Interns (or externs) engage in whatever sort of law-related work is engaged in by their lawyer supervisors at the host organizations.

American states that it encourages students to consider internships in the Washington, D.C., metro area and that it "has an internship coordinator who works one-on-one with our students to help them find internship opportunities" (www.wcl.american.edu/ilsp/faq.cfm).

Missouri provides fellowship funding and academic credit for LL.M. students to work in dispute resolution organizations in New York.

University of Pittsburgh School of Law notes that its LL.M. students "can intern at a law firm or other organization associated with his or her field of interest. Because our program is small, we work to match our LL.M. students with the best possible internships for their legal careers." (www.law.pitt.edu/academics/international-lawyers-programs/llm/requirements).

Georgetown offers LL.M. students two credits for unpaid externships (internships) at nonprofit and for-profit organizations during the spring semester. The LL.M. student must secure an internship position under the direct supervision of an attorney at an appropriate organization. **Georgetown** maintains a list of "pre-approved organizations," or students can seek approval for internships at other organizations (www.law.georgetown.edu/graduate/documents/Externshipinformation.pdf).

- Law clinics offer students an opportunity to gain "real-life" legal experience representing "real-life" clients.
- Be certain to inquire about LL.M. eligibility for clinics before you begin the fall semester.
- Make certain that your school permits LL.M. students (and not only J.D. students) to receive academic credit for clinical work.

d. Judicial Observation Courses for Academic Credit

Several schools offer Judicial Observation programs where international LL.M. students receive academic credit for working with federal judges, observing appellate and trial proceedings, and memorializing and recording observations in journals or portfolios.

e. Elective Courses Taught Outside the Law School (in Undergraduate and Graduate Programs on Campus, or at Nearby Law Schools)

Many law schools permit LL.M. students to "cross-register," which means to take courses in

Schools Respond

non-law graduate or undergraduate courses in other university departments and earn credits from these courses toward the LL.M. degree. For example, **Hawai'i** permits LL.M. students to earn up to six credits from taking courses offered by many of its university schools and departments, including the Schidler College of Business, Matsunaga Institute for Peace, School of Ocean and Earth Sciences and Technology, and East-West Center. The **Cardozo School of Law** permits students to earn LL.M. degree credits for one law-related, approved course through the Graduate Faculty or the Milano School of Management and Urban Policy of the New School for Social Research (p. 9-10 of Bulletin).

f. Courses Taught at Other Law Schools

Some LL.M. programs permit you to take courses at other law schools, and transfer those credits toward your LL.M. degree. Another school may offer a course that your school does not, or you may want to take a course in another city, to experience another region or another type of LL.M. program. **Houston** permits LL.M. students to take up to six credit hours at another ABA-approved law school *outside of the city of Houston*, and to take courses at another law school *in the city of Houston* if they are not offered at **Houston** (p. 13 of Handbook).

g. Elective Courses Taught by Correspondence

It seems rare for an LL.M. program to accept transfer credits earned through a correspondence course. It does not appear to be an impossibility. **Ask.**

h. Academic Credit for Courses Taken Outside the U.S.

Some U.S. law schools permit LL.M. students to receive academic credit for study outside of the U.S. in J.D. "study abroad" programs sponsored by the U.S. law schools. For example, **Stetson** permits LL.M. students to earn credit for studying in **Stetson**'s overseas study abroad programs in The Netherlands (The Hague), Germany (Freiburg), China (Tianjin), Spain (Granada), and Argentina (Buenos Aires). If an international student studies overseas in a **Temple** study abroad program, that student may apply for "Advanced LL.M. Degree Standing for Visiting Students," which, if granted, would count toward their **Temple** LL.M. degree.

If you are interested in studying in a U.S. law school's overseas program, you should check with your LL.M. program to find out if your school will count those credits for your LL.M. degree. Also consider that once you are in the U.S., you might have difficulty acquiring a visa to travel to a third country to study, and you might have difficulty returning to the U.S. due to U.S. visa issues. Please check *in advance*. And remember that one reason to come to the U.S. for an LL.M. is to become immersed in U.S. culture, and this opportunity is diminished if you spend substantial time in another country during your LL.M. year.

> Ask your academic advisor any questions you have about your curriculum. The faculty member responsible for the LL.M. program, and other administrators, may have creative suggestions to help you reach your academic and professional goals.

i. Transfer Credits for Courses Taken Before Joining a U.S. LL.M. Program

Some schools permit students to receive credit toward their LL.M. degree for some pre-*LL.M.* courses. For example, **Chapman University School of Law** permits students to petition to receive up to six credits toward an LL.M. for "certain LL.M. level courses or advanced J.D. level courses taken at any ABA-accredited law school during the three academic years preceding matriculation into the" **Chapman** LL.M. program. **Iowa, Tulane,** and **Penn State** *do not* permit J.D. credits to transfer to a subsequent LL.M. program. **Ohio Northern** counts nine hours of J.D. elective credit toward the 24 credit hours needed for their concurrent J.D./LL.M. program.

j. Special Courses for International Students from Civil Law Jurisdictions

Cardozo's General Studies LL.M. program permits students to choose from all first year and upper level courses and has a "special requirement for students from civil law countries" requiring such students to enroll in at least one of the following courses: Contracts (full-year course); Torts (fall semester course); or Property (spring semester course) (p. 18 of Handbook). **Loyola-New Orleans** permits LL.M. students to earn a certificate in civil law.

k. Some Required or Elective Courses *May Not Be Taught* During the Period That You Are Enrolled

Not all courses at all law schools are taught every semester. Schools rotate course offerings, and offer courses based on availability of professors, student demand, and other factors. Most law professors will teach a maximum of four courses each year (two per semester). Professors who teach specialized courses may be on sabbatical during your entire LL.M. period, and the specialized course you want may not be taught that year. **UCLA** cautions that LL.M. applicants "should bear in mind that, due to curriculum scheduling and faculty availability, not every class listed is taught each year" and that this "is most often true in the case of specialized seminars." **UCLA** further notes that its "final schedule of law classes will be available shortly before the enrollment process begins in July."

> As you choose which LL.M. program to join, make certain that the general and specialized courses you want to take will be offered during your *LL.M. study period.*

l. Some Courses May Not Count for the New York or Other State Bars

If you want to take the New York or another bar exam, make sure the LL.M. specific classes you take qualify as ones that the New York and other bars may require. Be certain to check the amended New York Bar eligibility rules (effective May 18,

2011) and the ABA Proposed Model Rule on the Admission of Foreign Educated Lawyers. (See Chapter 28.)

F. Auditing Courses

Most law schools permit LL.M. students to "audit" courses, that is, to attend classes and participate in classroom learning alongside other students, but be excused from exams. The auditor would receive no grade or academic credit, and may not be permitted to "retake" the course for credit. Some schools permit LL.M. or S.J.D. students to audit at no cost, whereas other schools may charge one-half or one-third tuition. Some professors require full classroom participation from auditing students, and they also have to do all reading and homework exercises — even though the student will receive no course grade. Full participation would likely be required for auditors if the class is small and demands small group work among students, where it would be disruptive to have one student excused from participating. If your school's tuition is charged per semester and not per credit, you may be able to audit more courses. Ask.

G. Grading Schemes

1. Who Cares About Grades?

Most LL.M. students are concerned about grades. You might want high grades because you think they will help you get hired by a Wall Street law firm or multinational company.[2] You may want high LL.M. grades because you want to work for your home government, become a judge, or apply for an S.J.D. You might want to earn certain grades because your scholarship sponsor insists (or perhaps your parents insist) that you earn certain grades. You might want certain grades because the school requires them to stay "in status," and ultimately to graduate.

Grading schemes differ at different LL.M. programs, and it is important to understand those grading rules if you have specific grading goals. In all cases, you will want to know whether grading policies at different schools are liberal, whether grades are based on a curve, and whether J.D. and LL.M. students are graded together on the same curve or graded separately.

---

2. If you begin your LL.M. program in August, and you want a new job after you graduate in May, interviews for that job might begin in October, several months before your first semester grades are released (January). Thus, your LL.M. grades will play *no role* in the interviews you have in the first semester. If you have interviews after your first semester grades are released, your LL.M. grades will be more important.

Schools Respond

Some LL.M. programs have developed a reputation for being "easy," meaning that it is very easy for international LL.M. students to receive high grades. Others have developed reputations for being "hard," meaning it is not easy to receive high grades. I believe that a student should choose the sort of school where his or her personal, career, and professional goals can best be met.

2. Choosing a Professor Who Gives High Grades

Some professors have reputations for giving high grades — to all categories of students, or perhaps to LL.M. students only. Some LL.M. (and J.D.) students seek to take courses from these professors, even if the students do not really have a strong interest in those courses. I would like to be able to convince you to take courses only in the areas that are most interesting to you, or that you think will be most helpful to you in your career after you graduate. But you would need to be convinced that learning the subject matter of a course is more important than the grade for the course. This may not be an easy choice for you, particularly if you are struggling with English, have low LL.M. grades, and LL.M. administrators and others direct you to take courses in which they believe you may be able to receive a high grade — whether you are interested in those courses' subject matter or not. You must decide what is most important for you.

3. Do You Want a School Where Virtually All LL.M. Students Receive High Grades?

Some LL.M. programs have reputations for giving high LL.M. grades (for having so-called **liberal grading policies**) with a disproportionate number of students graduating with honors. Some schools permit students to earn many credits that are graded pass or fail (satisfactory or unsatisfactory), where competition for high grades is diminished, and pass or fail grades are not included in GPA calculations. Some schools have a very low minimum GPA requirement for LL.M. students, so a student would have to be failing almost all her courses before she is suspended for academic reasons.

To the contrary, schools with so-called **non-liberal grading policies** have higher grading standards; graduate fewer LL.M. students with honors; and require students to achieve and maintain a higher GPA in order to remain in good standing and to graduate. These more competitive schools do not permit as many credits to be graded pass or fail.

High grades look brilliant on CVs and diplomas, improve students' self-confidence, and help satisfy LL.M. alumni, who will think highly of their alma mater. A student who is suspended or expelled from school because of low grades will cause the school to lose tuition money. Law schools have short-term incentives to have a nonrigorous curriculum with low standards: appeasing students who are concerned about high grades but not interested in working for them. Though this may improve the image of the school in some circles, in the long term the school's reputation will suffer because the legal community will recognize the devalued credentials, and students will stop enrolling.

> If you have strong feelings about how LL.M. and J.D. students are graded, check the *LL.M. Student Handbook before* you enroll.

4. The Grading Curve

Professors generally have full academic freedom and may design and implement any grading scheme they wish. However, some schools impose grading requirements that may take the form of a "curve," wherein a professor is obligated to assign (or is strongly urged to assign) grades along a bell curve.

For example, material from the **NYU** website informs LL.M. students that the **NYU** "curve is not mandatory for upper level courses, but it is strongly recommended." Furthermore, it notes that "Most people will get Bs. The target is for less than 20% of the class to get As" (www.law.nyu.edu/ecm_dlv1/groups/public/@nyu_law_website__llm_jsd__graduate_affairs/documents/documents/ecm_dlv_007176.pdf). At **Florida Coastal School of Law**, the mean for courses must be 3.00, with an acceptable deviation of no more than 0.10. If grades deviate from the curve, the professor "will provide an academic dean with a written notation and rationale for the departure" (p. 9 of Handbook).

Should J.D. and LL.M. students sitting next to each other in the same class be graded on the same scale, when they have had the same professor, the same material, and the same examination — and the J.D. and LL.M. students are competing for high grades? Or, should LL.M. students be graded separately from J.D. students?

Most J.D. students who take classes with LL.M. students are native English speakers, have had at least a year of U.S. legal education, and may be used to taking (and typing) law school exams. Most LL.M. students are foreign-educated, have a non-English native language, have little U.S. legal education or exam-taking experience, and have probably never typed an exam. But most LL.M. students already possess law degrees, may have already taken several courses on the subject matter of some of the courses taken with J.D. students, and may have years of practical law experience.

Some schools require all students — LL.M. and J.D., international or not — who take the same course from the same professor at the same time to be graded together on the same scale or grading curve.

Some LL.M. students consider this unfair because LL.M. students must then compete with J.D. students for the highest grades in the class, and they argue that J.D. students have an advantage because of their backgrounds and experience. Those LL.M. students would prefer that LL.M. students and J.D. students be graded separately, with each group ranked within itself. J.D. students would then compete with J.D. students for grades, and LL.M. students would compete with LL.M. students. With separate grading, LL.M. students

Schools Respond

LL.M. exam rules generate significant discussion and debate each year. If this concerns you, check the *LL.M. Student Handbook*. One perennially contested issue is whether international LL.M. students can bring a foreign language dictionary into exams. Check the *LL.M. Student Handbook* or ask — before you enroll!

would compete only with other LL.M. students for the limited number of high grades that are given in any particular class.

International LL.M. students with prior degrees in international law or international human rights law and UN experience can enjoy a *significant substantive advantage* over the J.D. students with whom they take an international law class. An international LL.M. student taking a U.S. domestic law class, such as criminal procedure or constitutional law, might have a significant *substantive disadvantage*, because they do not possess a domestic U.S. law foundation like J.D. students do. Check the *LL.M. Student Handbook* or ask your LL.M. administrator about this matter *before you enroll.*

5. Do LL.M. Students Receive Extra Time to Take Exams?

Many schools recognize that international students, particularly those whose native language is not English, may be disadvantaged if they are given the same amount of time to take an exam as students who are native English speakers. LL.M. programs have therefore adopted a range of rules, generally summarized as follows:

a. Permit All LL.M. Students Whose Native Language Is Not English Extra Exam Time[3]

Students may receive extra time if they were required to take an English language competency exam. They receive no extra time if they are from Australia, Canada, Jamaica, or certain other countries in which English is spoken.

b. Permit *All International LL.M. Students* Extra Exam Time, Irrespective of Their Native Language

LL.M. students would qualify for extra time whether they come from Australia, the UK, China, Brazil, or any other country.

c. Permit *No LL.M. Students* Extra Time

For example, at NYU all LL.M. students and J.D. students are allotted the same amount of time to take an exam.

---

3. A common rule allots one and a half times more than the regular exam time. If the ordinary exam is two hours, a person allotted extra time would receive one and a half multiplied by two hours, or a total of three hours for the exam.

d. Require Any International Student Seeking Extra Exam Time to Petition the School

For example, **Baltimore** provides that: "In courses which have both J.D. and LL.M. students, LL.M. . . . students for whom English is not a first language may petition the Associate Dean for Academic Affairs for up to one additional hour to complete the examination and for permission to use an English-foreign language dictionary" (p. 16 of Handbook).

H. Receiving an Honors LL.M.

Law schools may award honors using Latin or English terms. Latin honors may be *summa cum laude* (with highest honor), or *magna cum laude* (with great honor), or *cum laude* (with honor). In English, they may be *highest honors*, *high honors*, and *honors*. In both schemes a degree with no honors is listed as "LL.M." rather than, for example, "LL.M. *summa cum laude*" or "LL.M. with honors."

As mentioned, some U.S. law schools generously award high grades generally, and award honors to many graduating LL.M. students. This "grade inflation" or "honors inflation" may entice applicants, who might have reasonable assurances that they will be able to receive an honors degree.

In the spring of 2010, an unofficial survey was conducted of selected U.S. law schools' policies in awarding honors.[4] The range was remarkable: Some law schools granted lowest honors (*cum laude*) to as much as 48 percent of the J.D. graduating class (**Georgia**); and some schools awarded lowest honors to as few as 10 percent (**Penn State**). According to the survey, schools that award lowest honors to 30–35 percent of their graduating class included **Cincinnati**, **Connecticut**, **Cornell**, **Duke**, **Georgetown**, **Harvard**, **Hastings**, **Maryland**, **Northwestern**, **UNC**, and **Washington**. Some offered lowest honors to only 25 percent of graduates (**Alabama**, **Arizona**, **Fordham**, **Mercer**, and **NYU**). It is unclear how these statistics translate into, or reflect on, the substantive legal educational experience offered and received at LL.M. programs that may be at these or other surveyed schools.

I. Waivers of Academic Requirements

LL.M. program administrators may sometimes "waive" certain admission or graduation requirements, and thus excuse international LL.M. applicants or students from having to satisfy those particular requirements.

---

4. Joshua Auriemma, *A Comparison of Law School Graduation Honors Requirements* (9 April 2010) (http://legalgeekery.com/2010/04/09/a-comparison-of-law-school-graduation-honors-requirements/).

For example, at **Missouri** the "Director of the LL.M. Program may waive graduate requirements of taking LL.M. courses ... for individual students based on their prior course work, training, and/or experience." If a required course is waived, the student would receive no credit for it, but would take another course instead of the waived course (http://law.missouri.edu/csdr/llm/handbook.html).

Some schools will not waive admission or graduation requirements. For example, some require *all* foreign-trained LL.M. students to take a course on American law, even if the student has a significant background in U.S. law through education or experience. Though the student might better spend her money, time, and effort on courses in areas in which she has little or no experience, a school may refuse to waive the requirement.

J. Maintaining Academic, Legal, and Financial Standing and Status

1. Good Academic Standing

Students must maintain "good academic standing" while enrolled in the LL.M. program. You must maintain a certain GPA. A low GPA may lead to academic suspension, where you are banned from classes. Good academic standing requires you to attend and participate in classes, turn in assignments, and sit for exams. If you fail to participate in classes as required, the professor may drop you from the class and you may fall below the minimum number of credit hours required, which could lead to visa problems and other complications. You must not drop below the minimum credit hours the U.S. government requires each semester, which is typically eight credit hours, though certain exceptions exist whereby you may drop below eight hours.

2. Good Legal Standing

LL.M. students must maintain legal immigration status. (See Chapters 20, 21, and 22.) If you commit certain crimes in the U.S., you may be rendered ineligible to continue on F-1 student status, and you may be required to leave the U.S. It is not only imperative that you comply with federal immigration law, you must also comply with *all* U.S., state, and locals laws.

3. Good Financial Standing

If you fail to pay tuition or other fees, you may be prohibited from continuing your LL.M. coursework. You may be suspended from school, and you would not be in good academic standing (see above). You could voluntarily

Schools Respond

depart the U.S. and return to your home country—without being able to earn your degree. If you do not depart voluntarily, you may be deported.

K. Honor Code, Plagiarism, or Other Academic Responsibility Violations

Although international LL.M. students are typically not yet licensed to practice law in the U.S., it is reasonable that as law students they be required to understand the rules of ethics applicable in the legal profession and to abide by them. LL.M. students are also bound by any Honor Code or Code of Ethics applicable at their school, and if none exists they are expected to abide by reasonable rules of academic integrity.

Students must not plagiarize. (See Chapter 17.) This is a serious academic offense, whether or not there is an Honor Code. Plagiarism is defined differently at different schools, but most definitions are in concurrence with that in place at **Stanford**: "For purposes of the Stanford University Honor Code, plagiarism is defined as the use, without giving reasonable and appropriate credit to or acknowledging the author or source, of another person's original work, whether such work is made up of code, formulas, ideas, language, research, strategies, writing or other form(s)" (www.stanford.edu/dept/vpsa/judicialaffairs/students/plagiarism.sources.htm). In your LL.M. legal research and writing classes, you will learn more about how to give "credit" to original authors and sources you use in your research and writings. Punishment for committing plagiarism might include receiving a failing grade for the course or research paper, suspension from school, or expulsion.

L. Length of Study

Residential U.S. LL.M. programs generally require one academic year of full-time courses. An academic year is typically nine to ten months (from August or September through May or June) divided into two semesters. Most LL.M. programs operate on a semester basis, with a fall semester (August–December) and a spring semester (January–May). Two semesters, or nine to ten months, is ordinarily enough time to finish your degree with full course loads each semester.

Students with F-1 and J-1 visas are permitted to take as few as eight credits per semester. Schools may permit you to stay for the summer or an extra fall to complete a thesis or spread out your coursework. You might finish your degree after 15 months (fall, spring, summer, fall). Or, you might finish in 12 months (fall, spring, summer).

During the summer, you may earn credits for your thesis, internships, study abroad programs, or regular classroom courses. **Check before you enroll. Not**

Schools Respond

all summer credit-granting opportunities may be available to international LL.M. students.

M. What Is the Maximum Time to Complete Your LL.M. Degree?

Some schools require students to complete all degree requirements within one, two, three, or even as many as five calendar years after commencing study. Though the ABA requires all J.D. students to complete their degrees within five years, neither the ABA nor any other regulatory agency governs the maximum period of time permitted for LL.M. degree completion.

Limited Situations in Which an LL.M. Student
May Be Able to Drop *Below* 8 Credit Hours
(SEVIS usually requires international LL.M. students
to be enrolled *full time*—8 credit hours.)

Reason for Reduced Enrollment Below 8 Credit Hours	Documents Required	Restrictions or Limitations
Academic Difficulties	Academic Advisor certification	• Permitted *once* in LL.M. period • Must take at least 4 credit hours
Medical Reason	Letter from doctor or psychologist	• Aggregate of 12 months • No minimum credit hours required
Final Semester of LL.M. Study (for example, only one course or thesis left to complete)	Academic Advisor certification that remaining credits will satisfy degree requirements	• Permitted *once* during LL.M. period
Student Requests Complete Course Withdrawal (for personal or other reasons)	Student written request	• Must depart U.S. within 15 days • May return to U.S. 30 days before next semester (visa must be up-to-date to return to the U.S.)

Note: Check with your school's administrators for the *current* rules and regulations that apply to *your specific circumstances*.

Schools Respond

N. In Which Semester Can You Begin Your Study?

All U.S. law schools permit LL.M. candidates to commence study in the fall semester, which typically begins in August. Some also permit students to begin in the spring (January). A few permit students to begin in the summer.

1. Commencing LL.M. Study Program in the Fall Semester

Schools may require you to arrive on campus two to four weeks early for orientation, for English language instruction, or for English language proficiency verification tests. Ordinarily, your student visa becomes valid 30 days before your LL.M. program begins. For example, if your school requires you to attend orientation or take tests on August 1, your F-1 visa would permit you to arrive in the U.S. no earlier than 30 days before August 1, although classes may not begin until September.

2. Commencing LL.M. Study Program in the Spring Semester

Some schools permit LL.M. students to begin study in the spring semester. They would arrive in the U.S. in late December or early January. *Spring admits have a distinct advantage over fall admits.* They may easily take a break from studies in the summer months (June–August), during which period they can work in the U.S. or in their home country, relax and travel in the U.S., or take summer classes. These students would return to classes in the fall and could complete their degrees in December.

3. Commencing LL.M. Study Program in the Summer

Summers in most LL.M. programs are reserved for international students to travel to the U.S., get situated, take English language courses (if necessary), or participate in pre-LL.M. courses (including those mentioned in Chapter 14).

LL.M. Students Must Stay in "Good Standing"

GOOD ACADEMIC STANDING.   LL.M. students must maintain a certain grade point average and comply with all university regulations.
GOOD LEGAL STANDING.   LL.M. students must comply with all immigration requirements.
GOOD FINANCIAL STANDING.   LL.M. students must pay all tuition and other fees.

O. Academic Calendar

U.S. law schools post their *LL.M. Academic Calendar* on their websites. The *LL.M. Academic Calendar* identifies the starting and ending dates of classes each semester, exam periods, holidays, and other breaks, and other significant information related to the academic year. It might highlight critical information for LL.M. students, such as LL.M. orientation dates, dates for pre-LL.M. English Language courses or placement testing, and LL.M. pre-exam academic review sessions.

Sample LL.M. Academic Calendar
(Each U.S. law school has a different academic calendar!
Check at each school.)

Fall Semester	2011–2012	2012–2013	2013–2014
Pre-LL.M. Courses; English Language Training and Placement Test; Introduction to U.S. Law	July/August	July/August	July/August
LL.M. and J.D. Student Orientation (may be combined with special sessions for LL.M. students only)	Late August	Late August	Late August
LL.M. and J.D. Classes Begin	Aug. 22	Aug. 20	Aug. 18
Labor Day (no classes)	Sept. 5	Sept. 3	Sept. 1
Fall Recess Begins (Fall Break)	Oct. 10	Oct. 8	Oct. 6
Classes Resume	Oct. 17	Oct. 15	Oct. 13
Thanksgiving Recess Begins	Nov. 22	Nov. 20	Nov. 26
Classes Resume Postbreak	Nov. 28	Nov. 26	Dec. 1
Classes End for Semester	Dec. 3	Dec. 1	Dec. 3
Final Exams Begin	Dec. 5	Dec. 3	Dec. 5
Final Exams End	Dec. 19	Dec. 17	Dec. 19
Spring Semester	2012	2013	2014
Classes Begin	Jan. 9	Jan. 7	Jan. 8
Martin Luther King Jr. Holiday	Jan. 16	Jan. 21	Jan. 20
Spring Recess Begins (Spring Break)	Mar. 12	Mar. 10	Mar. 8
Classes Resume Postbreak	Mar. 19	Mar. 17	Mar. 15

Schools Respond

Fall Semester	2011–2012	2012–2013	2013–2014
Classes End for Semester	Apr. 16	Apr. 14	Apr. 12
Spring Exams Begin	Apr. 19	Apr. 17	Apr. 15
Spring Exams End	May 4	May 2	May 1
Commencement	May 5	May 4	May 6

CHAPTER SUMMARY

- To receive your LL.M. degree, you must satisfy many academic requirements. Be sure you understand these requirements and follow them!

- Acquire a copy of the school's *LL.M. Student Handbook* from their website. Or they will send it to you as a PDF file. The *Handbook* will tell you what is expected of you and when. There should be no surprises.

- You should get the *Handbook* before you apply, and certainly before you enroll.

- Some of the requirements are:
  - You must take mandatory courses and choose electives.
  - You must maintain an acceptable GPA.
  - You must submit certain forms before graduation.
  - You must remain in "good" academic, legal, and financial status at all times.

Schools Respond

Chapter 16

How Do They Teach Law at U.S. Law Schools?

CHAPTER HIGHLIGHTS

- U.S. law schools employ many modes of instruction, both inside and outside the classroom.
- Many professors in the U.S. conduct classes using the "Socratic method," a method of teaching in which the professor asks pointed questions, and students are required to "think on their feet" and reply.
- Teaching at U.S. law schools occurs both inside and outside of "traditional" classrooms, and involves professors, LL.M. and J.D. students, staff, and others, including, sometimes, outside "clients" for whom students may provide legal services.
- The range of educational experiences you might have depends in part on the school you attend and its resources, but it also depends on the manner(s) of instruction that suit you — and on your own initiative.

A. Introduction to Law School Teaching — Inside and Outside the Classroom

This chapter covers different ways U.S. law professors teach and students learn, inside and outside the classroom. At most schools LL.M. and J.D. courses sit side-by-side in the same room, with the same professor and course material. (Thus, Chapter 30, which discusses the J.D. program, is closely related to Chapter 16.)

B. Why Do U.S. Law Schools Teach the Way They Do?

Before discussing *how* U.S. law schools teach, which constitutes the bulk of this chapter, some background is in order regarding *why* U.S. law schools teach the way they do.

Law schools mix classroom and out-of-classroom teaching techniques to help students develop a keen knowledge of the law, the sources of law, and how law is interpreted and applied in a wide range of scenarios and circumstances — in courts, parliaments, treaty negotiations, corporate boardrooms, refugee camps, family dispute resolution centers, and in any other venue where law is spoken and applied. U.S. law schools teach students how to "think like lawyers," so they will be prepared to grapple with new laws applied to new factual situations that may arise in whatever area or specialization the graduate goes on to work in. U.S. law training is dynamic, interactive, and intense. It can also be very enjoyable, as you acquire the training and skills you seek to help you satisfy your personal and professional predilections and objectives.

C. The Socratic Method

In your mandatory and elective LL.M. classes, *do not* expect the professor to stand in front of the class and read from notes; and do not expect a lecture where only the professor speaks. Most professors require students to participate in a process called the "Socratic method" in which the professor and students engage in a dialogue structured around questions and answers.

To prepare for each Socratic class, you must read, synthesize, and absorb assigned materials. But there is more than that. To develop critical analytical skills needed to function as a lawyer, you will read cases — mostly decisions of U.S. courts on the subject matter of your course — and the professor may ask questions that refer to the cases, to determine if you understand what you read and can recall it. Professors ask about the facts of the cases, the laws applied, the court procedure, and other issues. In response, you must "recite" (but you do not need to stand when speaking anymore; this used to be a tradition in law schools).

The professor may then ask more probing questions triggered by student replies. The Socratic dialogue is a quest for the truth about issues and belief systems, and it exposes fallacies in rationale or assumptions. It helps you learn how to pierce through fallacies to reach reasonable, sound conclusions.

The professor wants you to think on your feet, to readily discern elusive rules, and to nimbly apply them to new and different facts. The professor may require you to articulate the rule of law a judge announced in the case under discussion; identify facts the judge relied on in the ruling; explain how the judge applied the law to the facts; assess the judge's conclusions; and explain how the court reached the conclusion despite earlier cases in which similar rules and similar facts were present.[1] The professor might then add a twist, and ask you to apply a *new* rule of law to the original facts, or apply the original rule to *new* facts. You must analyze the "new" case — with a new rule or with new facts — and solve it.

---

1. This method of teaching is called the "case method" and it was made popular by former **Harvard** Dean Christopher Columbus Langdell (1826–1926).

1. Be Prepared to Talk in Class

Learning at U.S. law schools requires students to participate in class. You learn as you sit anxiously while your classmate is reciting, knowing you may be called on next. If the professor calls on your classmate, you should answer the question silently in your head, or write or type a reply. The professor may ask you to continue the dialogue where your classmate leaves off. Pay attention!

Many professors — particularly in small, upper level courses — award points for students who speak in class. These points will enhance your final course grade. If you do not participate in class, you may receive a lower grade for the course than you think you deserve or than your exam grades or grades on papers might indicate.

2. Ask Questions — Raise Your Hand!

Professors expect you to raise your hand in class, ask or answer questions, or make comments. If you have a question or concern, another student in the class

likely has that same question or concern. The point you raise may trigger another student to ask a different question. This exchange benefits everyone, including your classmates. Do not ask the student sitting next to you questions, as that will distract them, other classmates, and the professor. Raise your hand and ask the professor. Ask the professor after class, before the next class, or during the professor's office hours. Your professor may even reply to an e-mail message.

3. Do Not Be Shy

You will invest significant time, effort, and money on your LL.M. degree. Take advantage of all available resources. The classroom is a valuable venue for exchanging ideas. Get to know your classmates (LL.M. and J.D.) and your professors. Engage them!

4. Do Not Expect the Teacher or Students to Slow Down for You

You will be expected to communicate freely in class, to speak, and to understand the professor and other students. You will receive no special accommodations because you speak with a different "accent" than they do. *This is a key reason to practice English before you arrive.*

5. Caution — Socratic Method May Not Be Easy for You!

Do not be alarmed if you encounter difficulties with Socratic teaching. It differs significantly from the lecture style that you may be more familiar with, and disfavors those with little experience with direct teacher–student interaction.

The Socratic method rehearses you for law practice in the adversarial legal tradition in which the U.S. is steeped, where lawyers routinely combat one another on behalf of their clients. If your country's tradition is not adversarial, you might be surprised at the nature of the exchange between and among the professors and students. It may seem strange, aggressive, or even confrontational. *It is!* You may feel ill-equipped to handle the back and forth. But this is the adversarial system you must get used to. Indeed, you must become adept in this particular skill of oral intellectual sparring.

Socratic teaching has been criticized as disadvantaging students from different educational legal systems, and also for discriminating against women, minorities, and others who may not be "socialized" for such combat.[2] But the method is well adapted to teaching the U.S. adversarial system of legal argument. Indeed, as a traditional approach to legal education, it is an inherent part of the system.

---

2. Professor D.A. Jeremy Telman discusses pioneering research on the impact of Socratic teaching on men versus women, on people of different races, and on people in minority or other groups. Carol Gilligan, *In a Different Voice: Psychological Theory and Women's Development* (6th ed. Harvard Univ. Press 1993); Lani Guinier, et al., *Becoming Gentlemen: Women's Experiences at One Ivy League Law School*, 143 U. Pa. L. Rev. 1, 62 (1994); Taunya Lovell Banks, *Gender Bias in the Classroom (2)*, 14 South. Ill. U. LJ. 527, 531-533 (1990).

D. The Academic Life of an LL.M. Student: How Do You Manage Your Studies as an LL.M. Student?

To prepare for a class session in which the Socratic method is used, an LL.M. student must read the assigned material in advance, comprehend the material, think about how the material relates to topics covered in earlier class sessions, and try to anticipate how the professor might expect the student to apply the material to new facts and issues presented in the next class session.

But what tools does an LL.M. student use to do this?

Do you read the material the evening before class, take notes, prepare an outline, discuss the material with other students, consult outside cases and other sources related to the assigned readings, or prepare sample answers to possible questions that the professor may ask in class the next day? Do you rush to the school bookstore and purchase a commercial outline that covers the subject matter of the course? Do you ask students who took the class the previous year for a copy of their notes?

During the class session the next day, if the professor calls on another student, do you open your laptop and type the questions the professor asks, and the answers given by the other student? Do you type the answer *you* would have given if the professor had called on you? Do you type up a list of the issues that you do not understand? Do you listen, and type nothing?

After the class, do you review your class notes? Do you compile your class notes into an outline that you might use to study for your exams? Do you review your notes before the next class session? When do you begin preparing for end-of-the-semester exams? How do you prepare for exams? Do you prepare for exams *at the same time* that you are going to classes? Do you wait until the end of the semester to begin preparing for exams?

These are some of the many questions that LL.M. students face. Indeed, J.D. students face precisely these same challenging questions during their first year of law school. By the time they are second-year students, they have grown accustomed. *But you have only two semesters as an LL.M. student, which does not give you much time!*

Don't worry—you'll figure it out. The answer might be a mix of all of the above possible approaches. Trust your judgment, be open to new methods, and work hard. Many resources exist to help J.D. students cope with challenges faced when they enter law school. Some of those materials will be helpful to you. Your school's LL.M. program *should* provide you with tutorials and resources on adjusting to the academic side of your U.S. law school program. Other resources are on *www.LLMRoadMap.com*,[3] including more specific ideas and suggestions expressly for international LL.M. students who have a limited amount of time during their year in the U.S. to adopt an effective plan of study.

---

3. *www.LLMRoadMap.com* lists many resources that will be helpful for international LL.M. students. For example, the list includes *The African American Law School Survival Guide* (by Evangeline M. Mitchell, Foreword by Derrick Bell) (Hope's Promise Publishing 2006). This book provides information, advice, and

E. Earning LL.M. Academic Credit in and Outside the Classroom

This section of the chapter discusses general characteristics of classes at U.S. law schools: types of classes, what professors expect from students, what students can expect of professors, and aspects of U.S. law classes that might surprise international students who may have encountered such classroom experiences only through movies or books.

1. Classes — Generally

You *must* attend classes. Listen carefully, take notes, and concentrate. Ask the professor to speak more slowly, if necessary (and sometimes the professors will actually slow down, though they are not obligated to!). Read all assignments and do all homework. You may earn extra course points for participation, and you may perform better on exams. Participating in classes will help you and your classmates to learn.

2. Class Size and Style

You may have classes with as few as 3 or 4 students, or as many as 150 students, depending on school policies, the nature of the course, the professor's popularity, and the time of day (or evening) the class is held.

3. Large Lecture Classes

If the school requires or recommends that J.D. students take a particular course, that course would tend to have large enrollments, maybe over 150 students. You may wish to take large J.D.-required courses such as professional responsibility, criminal law, U.S. constitutional law, or evidence.

Courses with over 150 students tend to be primarily lecture courses with little Socratic interaction. However, some professors may assign students to "panels" before a class session, and during class will engage in Socratic dialogue with students on the panel. Other professors call on students randomly, regardless of how many students are in the class.

Large classes may have one exam at the end of the semester, and may exclude class participation as part of the final grade. Some professors will reduce a student's grade for non-attendance, and raise the grade for speaking in class.

---

strategies that can be used by *any* J.D. or LL.M. student at *any* U.S. law school, but particularly helpful for students in the minority at U.S. law schools. Many issues related to African Americans as a minority are presented for international students, who are in a minority at all U.S. law schools. Resources also include nontraditional resources, such as *Aspen Law Studydesk* (www.AspenLaw.com/Studydesk), which is productivity software that helps students take control of their law school studies by organizing case briefs, class notes, and statutes.

Schools Respond

4. Smaller Classes

Smaller classes can have as few as 3-4 students, or up to 15-20 students, or perhaps 30. These classes would tend to be upper-level elective courses, typically not required in either the J.D. or LL.M. curricula. These classes tend to be graded based on in-class exercises, papers written outside of class, or perhaps an exam. Students will be expected to speak in class more frequently when classes are small. "Extra credit" is more readily given in small classes where the professor and the students interact more, and professors get to know students better. It is said — anecdotally — that professors tend to give higher grades in smaller classes.

5. Other Factors Affecting Class Size

Classes taught by "popular" professors tend to have higher enrollments. Courses taught late on Fridays tend to have lower enrollments. Classes on esoteric topics that will not be tested on bar exams may have lower enrollments. Classes may have increased enrollment if the topics concern "sexy" and "cutting edge" areas of law that become popular due to significant or highly reported trends or "global" events, such as cyberspace law (post-Internet), natural disaster law (post-Hurricane Katrina), the law of war (after the 2001 World Trade Center terrorist attacks and "detainees" taken to Guantanamo Bay), piracy law (after pirate attacks off the Somalia coast), or oil and energy law (post-Gulf Oil spill of 2010 and post-Japan earthquake and tsunami of 2011). Students find these elective courses intriguing, even if the subjects are not tested on bar exams.

6. Experiential Hands-On Courses Including Law Clinics, Internships and Externships, and Independent Research or Pro Bono Projects

Some schools teach outside the traditional classrooms in "experiential" courses. This breaks the traditional Socratic mold and adds a new dimension of fun and experience to learning. It permits students, for example, to render legal services on a pro bono basis to individuals and groups in the community who would otherwise not have access to such services. Students earn credit from different experiential activities. *Before you enroll, ask the school if international LL.M. students are eligible to earn credit for such activities.*

7. Legal Clinics (Domestic and International)

Some schools have live-client clinics in which legal services are provided at no charge to indigent clients. Clinics work in many different areas of law, including

Schools Respond

criminal law, elder law, international human rights law, tax law, immigration law, and corporate law. Students may be permitted to represent real clients in certain civil and criminal proceedings in court. *Before you enroll, ask the school if international LL.M. students are eligible to engage in these kinds of projects, clinics, or services for credit.*

8. Internships (Called "Externships" at Some Schools in the U.S. and Abroad)

Students may intern at law firms, government offices, intergovernmental offices, NGOs, and other types of entities. Students gain legal experience, learn about law practice in different areas, and earn academic credit. Some students intern in the same city where their LL.M. law school is, while others work in different cities, different U.S. states, or overseas. If you want to intern during a semester while you are taking classroom courses, then you should join an LL.M. program in a city with internship opportunities. Otherwise, you may intern during a summer or other term when you are not in the classroom. Large cities such as Washington, D.C., and New York have many internship opportunities, given the many public and private organizations located there.[4] Many LL.M. (and J.D.) students compete for those positions, however. Internships are also available in smaller cities where LL.M. programs are located. *Before you enroll, ask the school if international LL.M. students are eligible for internships, in particular internships for which they receive academic credit!*

9. Independent Research or Pro Bono Projects

You may decide to research an area in which you have a particular interest, and for which there is no formal course offered. You might ask a professor to supervise your independent research in that area. Or a professor might be writing an article or a book, or working on a pro bono litigation project, and you might join in the task. In either case, you could be awarded academic credit for independent research work on the project.

10. Moot Court and Moot Court Competitions

In "moot court" you learn trial or appellate courtroom advocacy by playing the roles of judge, witness, defendant and defense lawyer, prosecutor, plaintiff

---

4. For example, **Catholic University of America Columbus School of Law** notes that "LL.M. students may complete externships for credit. Students may avail themselves of all the opportunities that Washington, D.C. has to offer due to our convenient location" (http://llm.cua.edu/faq.cfm).

and plaintiff lawyer or bailiff. You research law related to civil and criminal issues, make oral and written submissions, and present cases in a trial or appellate court setting. Some schools hold intramural moot competitions, usually for J.D. students. Some schools participate in regional, national, and international moot competitions, and in competitions involving arbitration, negotiation, client counseling, and other areas of law or practice. If you want to participate in moot court, approach the faculty member or administrator in charge.

Some competitions are very attractive to international LL.M. students. Examples include the **Philip C. Jessup International Law Moot Court Competition**,[5] the **Willem C. Vis International Commercial Arbitration Moot (in Vienna or Hong Kong)**, the **International Environmental Moot Court Competition**, the **Inter-American Human Rights Moot Court Competition**, the **International ADR (Alternative Dispute Resolution) Mooting Competition** and the **International Criminal Court (ICC) Trial Competition**. Perhaps you can convince your school to participate in a new competition, such as the **World Human Rights Moot Court Competition**.

11. Judicial Observation Programs

Judicial observation programs for international LL.M. students offer academic credit for working with federal trial and appellate judges. These programs offer you hands-on exposure to the U.S. judicial system.

12. Law Reviews, Law Journals, and Newspapers

You can gain valuable experience researching, writing, and editing for law school journals. Entry is typically reserved as an honor to J.D. students who compete via grades or in writing competitions. LL.M. students would not ordinarily be enrolled at the school long enough to qualify for journal or review membership through grades or a competition. But some schools reserve journal positions for LL.M. students. U.S. employers value the journal credential. **Harvard, Duke, Colombia**, and other schools permit LL.M. students to participate on some journals. **St. Thomas'** *Intercultural Human Rights Law Review* has Co-Editors-in-Chief (one LL.M. and one J.D.), and Co-Executive Editors (two LL.M. and two J.D.).

---

5. Every law school in the U.S. that has an international law program or center should field a team in the **Jessup Moot Court Competition**, which is the most prestigious international law competition in the world, and the largest, with participants from 500 law schools in 80 countries (www.ilsa.org/jessup). If you are interested in international law, you should be cautious about joining an LL.M. program at a U.S. law school that does not actively participate in **Jessup**. (NB: The author, who is a former member of the ILSA Advisory Board and a former Faculty Director for Jessup, drafted this footnote many months before the thought occurred to him to donate his profits from this edition of *LL.M. Roadmap* to ILSA!)

You can also acquire valuable experience working for an online or hard copy law school newspaper; for student blogs; or for student organization newsletters. You can write a short article about a law topic of interest to you, or that you already know something about, such as recent legal developments in your home country. You may submit the article to your LL.M. program's website for publication, or to the alumni magazine of your LL.M. program or law school.

Stuart Loh, a **Stanford** LL.M. graduate from Australia, recently published a "coffee table" glossy picture book titled *The LLM Experience: A Year at Stanford Law School.* You can write a similar book based on drawings from diaries that you keep, e-mail messages that you send and receive, or social networking pages that you maintain. Your writings may be interesting to current LL.M. students, fun and reminiscent to LL.M. graduates, and inspiring for prospective LL.M. students—and maybe even interesting to other humans! You can write in English or in your mother tongue for submission to publishers in your home country or a third country, or for publication in a journal or newspaper in the foreign language department of your law school's university. And you can add the publication to your CV.

13. Writing Competitions; Calls for Papers

Many LL.M. students write theses that are of the subject matter, length, and quality suitable for entry into law school, regional, national, or international writing competitions. Information about these competitions can be found on various websites, and the information should also be available through the LL.M. office. (See www.LLMRoadMap.com for a list of writing competitions.)

Each year, **Cornell Law School** hosts the **Cornell Inter-University Graduate Student Conference** at which 20 to 25 LL.M. and S.J.D. students from around the U.S. (and from overseas) present their research (often theses or dissertation drafts). Participants are chosen through a highly competitive process, and may have their papers published in a **Cornell** journal. If you are interested, check the **Cornell** website at www.lawschool.cornell.edu.

14. Student Organization Pro Bono and Assistance Projects

Student organizations create opportunities such as Teen Court or the Street Law Program of Equal Justice Works. Students may also work for the Volunteer Income Tax Assistance Program (VITA), which, through the U.S. Internal Revenue Service (IRS), offers free tax preparation help to low- to moderate-income people. Be certain to check whether there are any prerequisites for participation, and whether international LL.M. students are eligible to participate.

15. Independent Research with Professors

Working as a professor's research assistant provides excellent academic and work experience. Try to work for a professor who specializes in an area that interests you. In this way you can spend quality time with an expert in your field outside of class, explore interesting issues in-depth, *and* earn money (about $12 or more per hour at some schools).

Research assistants engage in a wide range of work, including helping to research legal issues, draft articles or book chapters, or design teaching materials. They may also tediously proofread documents, photocopy and assemble teaching packages, or prepare tables of contents or indices. Whatever your assignment, you can favorably impress the professor, which may help later when you ask the professor to write a letter of recommendation.

F. Law School Exams

Law school exams in the U.S. are difficult for both J.D. and LL.M. students. International LL.M. students find exams particularly challenging. These exams are significantly different from exams in many countries. Despite challenges, you can succeed if you prepare, taking into account several points.

First, unlike law exams in many countries, U.S. exams require you to identify relevant rules of law and apply the law to facts, and to resolve a dispute. You must write "essays" that demonstrate that you can perform like practicing lawyers who must resolve all sorts of legal conundrums presented and faced by clients. Exams in some countries may focus on how much law you know or can recall, rather than on how you apply that law.

Second, LL.M. students at U.S. law schools have many resources available to assist with exams:

- LL.M. programs should have exam preparation training, beginning as early as orientation — it is never too early to start preparing for exams.
- Professors will meet with you outside of class to answer exam-taking questions.
- J.D. "mentors" or "ambassadors" may teach you about exam taking.[6]
- An overabundance of books, videos, and online resources instruct on exam-taking, offering tips and strategies that LL.M. students can follow.

Third, you may benefit from studies comparing law exams in different legal education systems. An example is *Examinations in Civil Law Countries*, prepared

---

6. For example, your J.D. colleagues may teach you that "take home" exams do not permit you to take the exam back to your home country to complete it!

by Professors Julie Campagna (**John Marshall Law School**, Chicago) and Radka Chlebcová (**Masaryk University**, Brno, Czech Republic).[7]

Fourth, gain confidence knowing that thousands of international LL.M. students take and pass U.S. law school exams each semester. *You can, too!*

G. Law Teachers in the U.S.

Law professors need not be law graduates, but most hold J.D. degrees. A small minority hold LL.M. or S.J.D. degrees, and some hold Ph.D. degrees in other disciplines. Law professors need not take a bar exam, and many are not active bar members.

Most teachers at U.S. law schools are addressed as "Professor" with the title of Assistant Professor of Law, Associate Professor of Law, or Professor of Law.[8] There are also Clinical Professors of Law, as well as lecturer ranks (typically "Lecturer in Law" or "Instructor"), and visiting professors.

Professors can be full-time tenured, or full-time tenure-track. These professors are the highest paid teachers at U.S. law schools, and have security in their jobs. Thus they are freer to exercise academic freedom without fear of being terminated.

Law teachers can also be visiting professors or adjunct professors who have temporary teaching appointments. Visiting professors tend to be full-time teachers at a different law school, and are "on loan" for a short period. Adjunct professors tend to be full-time lawyers or judges in the community who teach part time at the law school.

Adjunct professors tend to be the lowest paid teachers at U.S. law schools but can be a great addition to faculties, as they often bring with them years of

---

7. Paper delivered at the **Global Legal Skills Conference IV**, held on June 4–6, 2009, at **Georgetown** (on file with author).

8. The proper form of address for U.S. law school professors may not be obvious to or of great interest to students, but it is keenly obvious to and important to some professors! Titles designate rank within the faculty, and professors are entitled to be referred to by their ranks, whether being addressed in person, or as identified on their business cards, stationery, or e-mail signature. Students should be interested because a professor's rank sometimes has a bearing on the level of security, authority, and freedom the professor has vis-à-vis other professors and the school itself.

The following illustration may not become clear until you arrive on campus and encounter professors of various ranks. But it is instructive to provide this example now.

An assistant professor of law is appropriately referred to as "John Doe, Assistant Professor of Law" or "Assistant Professor of Law John Doe." An associate professor would be "John Doe, Associate Professor of Law" or "Associate Professor of Law John Doe." A professor who has reached the highest rank would be "John Doe, Professor of Law" or "Professor of Law John Doe."

Some adjunct professors may refer to themselves on their business cards or in e-mail signature lines or elsewhere as "Professor Jane Doe," when in fact their correct title would be "Adjunct Professor Jane Doe" or "Jane Doe, Adjunct Professor of Law." Some academics believe dropping the word "Adjunct" from the title causes confusion between a temporary non-faculty member (adjunct) and a person who has achieved the highest rank of "Professor" (see above).

If you have any doubt on how to address a law teacher or staff member, *ask!*

experience and insights. Too many adjuncts teaching LL.M. courses, however, may be a sign that the LL.M. program is a cash cow or diploma mill. Some schools have an express policy of diverting adjunct, temporary resources to LL.M. student courses and activities whenever possible, because adjuncts earn considerably less salary than full-time professors. Such schools reserve full-time, more highly paid faculty to teach J.D. courses. For example, a school may have full-time legal writing professors who have significant experience teaching international LL.M. students, lecturing around the globe, and publishing books in the field. The school may require those highly qualified professors to teach J.D. students, and have less qualified, less experienced adjunct teachers teach international LL.M. students. In this case, the school would be diverting critical resources from the LL.M. to the J.D. program, perhaps offering LL.M. students disproportionately less than it offers J.D. students. **Beware.**

Lieutenant Colonel Michael Dan Mori (U.S. Marine Corps) has been a Visiting Professor, Visiting and Guest Lecturer, and Fellow at U.S. law schools (e.g., **Duke**, **Stetson**, and **Hawaii**); at overseas law schools (e.g., **Melbourne** and **Tasmania**); and at other prestigious institutions such as **West Point**. Lt. Col. Mori represented David Hicks, an Australian "detainee" convicted at the U.S. Guantanamo Bay Military Commission at Guantanamo Bay, Cuba.

H. Guest Professors and Lecturers

All law schools have guest professors and lecturers who share their expertise in specific areas of law. Guests hail from local, state, national, or international government (legislators, judges, or executive branch officials); law firms; corporate in-house counsel offices; intergovernmental organizations (such as the UN); think tanks; and other law faculties. Their wisdom and experience enhance students' education.

I. Contact with Professors Outside of Class

In some non-U.S. countries and legal education systems, students have little contact with professors outside of class. The principal "contact" is when the professor lectures in front of the class. These professors are inaccessible to students generally.

It is common in the U.S. for law professors to talk with students in the classroom or hallways, to have lengthy discussions with them in the professor's office, or even to have a coffee or lunch with them in the school cafeteria. These conversations are generally about the legal issues covered in the courses. They can also include career advice. These are good opportunities for a student to

Professor Scott Bates has been a Visiting Professor, Visiting and Guest Lecturer, and Fellow at U.S. law schools (e.g., **Indiana**), in schools in other countries and territories (e.g., **Afghanistan, Iraq, Kosovo**), and at other prestigious institutions. Professor Bates is the former Secretary of State of the Commonwealth of Virginia and counsel of the U.S. House of Representatives Select Committee on Homeland Security.

develop a personal relationship with a professor, so you will be better positioned to ask the professor for a recommendation letter when you apply for an S.J.D. or for a job.

Meeting with professors outside of class helps to humanize the teacher, which might make it easier for you to raise and discuss legal, career, and other issues. You may learn that your professor has hobbies similar to yours — stamp collecting, for example, or marathon running, piano playing, opera, horse riding, or cricket. Many law professors in the U.S. are extremely approachable. They will talk with students, work on projects with students, and may even co-author articles with students.

Jealousies and tensions may develop if some students perceive that others have a close relationship with a particular professor. Professors must treat all students equally and must not develop intimate or otherwise inappropriate, nonprofessional (or unprofessional) relationships with students. Professors also are obligated to ensure that their behavior does not create an "air or impropriety," such that it *appears* that they have an improper relationship with a student, or it *appears* that some students have a special advantage because of a relationship with a student.

Get to know your professors as well as you can. We enjoy our students. We learn a great deal from you.

Law School and Lawyer Skills

The U.S. Bureau of Labor Statistics (BLS), law schools, and other resources highlight skills lawyers need that law schools develop and test. Indeed, law schools require that you possess some of these skills, or demonstrate the ability to acquire them, before they admit you. Some of these skills appear below, borrowed from and built upon the BLS listing (http://online.onetcenter.org/link/summary/23-1011.00).

1. **Oral Communication.** You must speak clearly, concisely, cogently, confidently, and convincingly. People you seek to influence or persuade — clients, judges, opposing counsel — must be able to understand you. You must be able to understand them. You must disseminate and acquire information effectively.

2. **Written Communication.** You may have to write legal briefs and memoranda, court pleadings, demand letters, contracts, memos to your files, and notes to clients. You must be able to communicate effectively in writing, which means

Schools Respond

writing appropriately for your intended audience. (Join a campus law review or law journal and publish a student article! Write for a blog or listserv.)

3. **Critical Thinking.** You must think clearly and logically, when you write, read, or speak, or whether you are just thinking. You must use sound logic and reasoning to assess situations that arise in law, and distinguish cogent, persuasive points from ill-conceived ones.

4. **Complex Analytical and Problem-Solving Skills.** You must be able to identify the existence of problems, assess their complexity, and analyze and solve those problems. You must be able to identify strengths and weaknesses in arguments, balance them against each other, apply law to facts, and reach reasonable solutions. You must be able to identify and propose alternatives, and assess and implement options.

5. **Listening Skills.** Listening can be more important than talking. You must engage in "active listening," paying complete attention to what others say, understanding them, questioning them when you do not understand, and acknowledging your comprehension.

6. **Legal Research.** You must have excellent research skills, whether you use Google, Lexis, Westlaw, or hardcover books in a library.

7. **Reading Comprehension.** U.S. law students are expected to read a great deal, sometimes 400 to 500 pages per week. You must read quickly and critically. You need not memorize the materials, but you must understand it and be conversant in it. U.S. legal education trains students how to think like lawyers. The law constantly changes, as do the facts presented by client matters. Lawyers must learn to read and understand the law, and to effectively apply it to whatever facts are presented.

8. **Exercise Judgment.** At times there are not clear right or wrong answers. You must exercise judgment. You must assess risks and rewards of alternative actions and decisions, and make informed, logical, and fair judgments.

9. **Persuasion.** You will often be charged with persuading others to adopt your position, or that of your client. You can persuade in written or oral communication, or by merely taking or refraining from certain actions.

10. **Negotiation.** Lawyers can play the role of peacemakers. To resolve legal disputes, you may need to negotiate — to compromise. You must weigh the costs of different alternatives, and decide on the best course of action for your client. Your client may not always get everything he wants. Negotiations may help him get everything he needs.

11. **Active Learning.** You will be presented with new information daily or hourly. You must understand how that information affects your clients. Never close your eyes and ears to new information, which you must absorb and use to your client's benefit.

12. **Organization and Management.** Lawyers work with complex matters requiring juggling multiple issues, tasks, and competences. Lawyers must be strong organizers and managers.

13. **Oriented Toward Service and Justice.** Law is a service industry in which lawyers cater to the needs of clients. The goal of lawyering is justice.

Sample Calendar for a Foreign LLM Student's Semester

(1) U.S. Law for Foreign Lawyers (3 credit hours; meets 3 hours each week)
(2) Legal Writing, Research and Communication for Foreign Lawyers (3 credit hours; meets 3 hours each week)
(3) Elective Course (2 credit hours; meets 2 hours each week)
(4) Elective Course (3 credit hours; meets 3 hours each week)
(5) Thesis and Thesis Preparation Course (2 credit hours)

Study Period = Time preparing for class; doing homework; research for thesis; preparing for exams

	MONDAY	TUESDAY	WEDNESDAY	THURSDAY	FRIDAY	SATURDAY	SUNDAY
8:00–9:00	Study Period	Study Period	Study Period	Study Period	Study Period	Relax	Relax
9:00–10:00	(1) U.S. Law for Foreign Lawyers (9:00–10:00)		(1) U.S. Law for Foreign Lawyers (9:00–10:00)		(1) U.S. Law for Foreign Lawyers (9:00–10:00)		
10:00–11:00	Study Period	(2) Legal Writing, Research and Communication for Foreign Lawyers (10:00–1:00) (3 credit hour course)	Study Period	(3) Elective Course (10:00–12:00) (2 credit hour course)	Study Period		
11:00–Noon							
Noon–12:30	Lunch and Relax		Lunch and Relax	Lunch and Relax	Lunch and Relax		
12:30–1:00	Study Period		Study Period	12:30–2:30– Schools may reserve time for extracurricular activities	Study Period	Study Period	Study Period
1:00–2:30		Lunch and Relax					
2:30–3:00		Study Period	2:30–3:30 (4) Elective Course (3 credit hours)	Study Period	2:30–4:30 (4) Elective Course (3 credit hours)		
3:00–3:30	(5) Thesis Seminar (3:00–5:00) (2 credit hours) (may not meet every week)						
3:30–4:30			Study Period				
4:30–5:00		4:30–6:00. Schools may reserve time for extracurricular activities			Study Period		
5:00–6:00	Study Period						
6:00–7:00	Exercise	Exercise	Exercise	Exercise	Exercise	Relax	
7:00–8:00	Dinner and Relax	Dinner and Relax	Dinner and Relax	Dinner and Relax	Dinner and Relax		
8:00–9:00	Study Period	Study Period	Study Period	Study Period	Relax		
9:00–10:00	Relax	Relax			Relax		

CHAPTER SUMMARY

- There are many ways for you to learn at a U.S. law school.
- Most LL.M. students take classes with J.D. students, learning side-by-side.
- Chapter 30, which focuses on the J.D. program, offers further insights into teaching and learning at U.S. law schools.
- Learning via the Socratic method can be challenging for international LL.M. students, but you may come to enjoy it once you get used to it!
- You will have an opportunity to learn in many different ways at U.S. law schools. Much happens outside the traditional classroom.
- At many non-U.S. law schools, teachers lecture in front of the class, and the students have very little direct interaction with the professor, in class or outside of class. This is not so in a U.S. law school, where you will likely have substantial interaction with your professors.
- You might find some of the informality of the law school environment uncomfortable at first, but that feeling will likely pass.
- Be certain to take advantage of as many different modes of teaching as possible. Do not take only classroom courses. Do some experiential work with real clients in internships or pro bono projects.

Schools Respond

Chapter 17

Legal Communication
Legal Analysis, Research, and Writing

CHAPTER HIGHLIGHTS

- Everyone communicates, but the world expects lawyers to communicate better than other professionals.
- Legal analysis, research, and writing classes during your LL.M. program are critical to further developing your communication skills.
- Most schools have mandatory courses in these areas for international LL.M. students — but if you have the option take as many as you can.
- Legal analysis, research, and writing classes will help you in your course work, exams, papers (including theses), S.J.D. proposals, and beyond the academic environment.

A. Legal Communication

An important reason to study in the U.S. for your LL.M. degree is so that you can take courses that improve your ability to communicate effectively as a legal professional, in English. This will help you reach your career goals and personal goals.

Effective legal communication involves more than understanding, speaking, and writing in English, and more than having a large vocabulary or a good command of English grammar. When you join your LL.M. program, you will be expected to be proficient in those areas already. You need more than mere proficiency. You will need expertise in legal communication skills — that is, in legal analysis, research, and writing.

This chapter briefly discusses how LL.M. programs in the U.S. can help you fine-tune the legal communication skills that you need to excel in your LL.M. program and to succeed in your career after you graduate.

Many, if not most, international LL.M. students arrive on campus with experience in using the Internet. But perhaps you may not be so familiar with online legal research software, databases, tools, and strategies. In your LL.M. program, you should receive instruction on how to use technology to help prepare you for the globalized law environment many will work in post-LL.M.

B. What You Will Learn in Your Legal Communication Courses

Your legal communication courses will help you to improve your analytical and problem-solving skills, to think more critically, and to improve your legal argumentation and counter-argumentation skills. You will learn to communicate in "legal English," meaning that you will learn "plain English" and not "legalese." You will cast aside long, complicated sentences and archaic vocabulary and instead adopt simple, straightforward words and phrases.

You will learn library research and online research skills, and citation styles. Your knowledge of substantive law will increase, as will your familiarity with common law. Your legal vocabulary will improve, and so will your editing skills.

In LL.M. programs, legal communication courses require students to research hard copy and online resources, to work in small groups or alone on oral presentations, and to engage in moots (practice arguments). You may draft legal documents such as memoranda of law, briefs, contracts, court pleadings (complaints, motions, and other filings), client letters, and demand letters (and replies). Your LL.M. program may employ simulations, in which you learn by playing the role of lawyer, client, or judge handling simulated legal problems or moots. You may also be given instruction on taking U.S. law exams, which may be substantially different from law exams in your home countries.

You will conduct research, analysis, and writing exercises in the classroom and at home. Your professors will review your work and mark it, then engage you in one-on-one review sessions for private instruction and directed revision.

C. How Your Legal Communication Courses Will Help You

What you learn in your legal communication courses will benefit you in your other LL.M. classes. For example, you will be able to use these skills in your homework and classroom assignments, in-class discussions, and exams—which may help you earn higher LL.M. grades. You can use these skills to research and write an LL.M. thesis, to prepare an S.J.D. dissertation proposal, or to write an article for a law review, a bar journal, or some other student, faculty, or outside law publication.

You will also be able to use your legal communication skills to help enhance your competitiveness in the employment market after you graduate, to help you acquire a job, and to help you perform that job more effectively. During your interviews for post-LL.M. Optional Practical Training (Chapter 27) or Academic Training (also Chapter 27), you will be able to express yourself more clearly, using communication skills that you learned — identifying critical points, and advocating those points about yourself, your background, and your future that you believe portray you positively to the prospective employer. At your new workplace, you will be able to communicate concisely, comprehensively, and cogently — not in "legalese" but in plain English. You will be deemed articulate and competent because you use a logical framework for expressing yourself orally and in writing. You will be deemed articulate and competent because you *will be* articulate and competent.

What you learn in your LL.M. legal communication classes will definitely help prepare you for any bar examination you decide to take after you complete your LL.M. (See Chapter 28.)

D. Legal Communication Teachers

1. Background and Experience of Professors Who Teach Legal Communication to International Students

Many professors teach legal communication — legal analysis, research, and writing. Not all these professors have the training, experience, and cultural sensitivity needed to successfully teach these subjects to international LL.M. students. Special talents are needed when the students come from many different legal systems, traditions, and cultures, and when the students may have studied and practiced law in languages other than English. Some LL.M. programs have professors who, in addition to holding law degrees, hold Ph.D. degrees and other higher degrees in subjects related to communication, such as linguistics. Some LL.M. programs employ certified teachers of English as a Second Language ("ESL," "TESL," or "TESOL").

2. Teachers Who Research, Publish, and Lecture *About* Legal Communication, and Bring Their Expertise into the Classroom to Teach International Students

Some programs have full- and part-time professors who hold law degrees and who have developed a *niche* expertise by researching the topic of teaching legal communication to international law students, publishing books and articles on the topic, and actually gaining extensive experience teaching international students in the U.S. and abroad. These professors also tend to be actively involved in professional organizations that hold conferences and workshops on teaching legal communication to international law students, and they may give presentations, exchange ideas with professors in the field around the world, publish teaching manuals that are used by other professors at different schools, and

Schools Respond

Schools Respond

promote best practices to help ensure that LL.M. students at U.S. law schools are provided the legal communication training they need.

If you are attracted to a school that has such highly trained and accomplished legal communication professors, with significant experience working with international LL.M. students, you might seriously considering enrolling at that law school so you can reap the benefit of the expertise of those professors. However, before you enroll, make certain that those professors will be teaching legal communications to LL.M. students. At least one school has a policy of not permitting such highly qualified professors to teach LL.M. students, but assigns temporary, lower-paid adjunct professors to the LL.M. students. At that school, the full-time professors, as a matter of school policy, are assigned to teach J.D. students and not to teach LL.M. students. **Just because a school may have a solid reputation for legal writing, research, and communication courses does not mean that LL.M. students will have the benefit of professors who research, publish, teach, and lecture in the field. Ask the LL.M. administrators whether your legal communication classes will be taught by full-time professors, or by adjuncts.**

3. Acquiring Information About Schools' Legal Communication Programs and Professors

You can find out from school websites which legal communication teachers are actively involved in research, writing, and teaching *about* legal communication. You will benefit greatly if you choose an LL.M. program where your legal analysis, research, and writing courses are taught by highly qualified professors who are artful in the classroom and generous in the time they spend with you, one-on-one in their offices, paying personal attention to you and your skill development. Choose an LL.M. program that has such professors.

E. Full-Time Professors Experienced in Working with International Students Outside of Classes

All LL.M. programs for international students should have law professors who teach legal communication classes to LL.M. students. However, some schools take extra steps — for example, by adding academic staff who are devoted to assisting these students outside of class to help them achieve their legal communication needs. These staff members may not teach the courses, but may work with the students in the evenings or weekends, one-on-one, or in small groups. They may assist LL.M. students with their classwork, essays, theses, and other writing assignments. Successful LL.M. programs for international students employ such staff who are experienced, skilled, and dedicated to LL.M. students.

F. Legal Writing and Academic Integrity — Plagiarism

Many LL.M. program administrators and professors agree that a major problem in LL.M. programs in the U.S. is that many international LL.M. students come to the U.S. with a different understanding of how to properly use source materials and the work of other writers. Administrators complain that some international students liberally use ideas and writings of others, without giving others credit for their work. That is, they copy the work of others and pass it off as their own, without giving the original author due credit. In the U.S., this is known as plagiarism. It is cheating. It is a blatant violation of the honor codes or rules of *every law school in the U.S., and every U.S. LL.M. program.*

LL.M. programs in the U.S. ought to provide LL.M. students with full training on how to avoid plagiarism problems. Professors in LL.M. programs should examine the written work of international students closely, to make certain it fully complies with the rules of attribution. The idea is not to try to punish students, but to train them to understand the views and practices in this area that the U.S. legal and legal education communities consider to be so important.

So please pay close attention to your LL.M. program's warnings about plagiarism — which extend not only to copying text from library books or materials found on the Internet, but also includes copying from your classmates' or colleagues' papers without proper attribution. Copying is plagiarism. Plagiarism is cheating. It will get you into trouble. Learn exactly what constitutes plagiarism, and what does not — and *never plagiarize!* Your legal communication instructors will offer you **many** examples of what constitutes plagiarism, and what does not. Pay attention!

G. Selected Books and Other Resources Related to Legal Communication — Legal Analysis, Research, and Writing

Many high-quality books have been written on legal communication. The ones listed here are a mere cross-section of the vast literature on the topic. Please check www.LLMRoadmap.com for a lengthier list.

1. Veda R. Charrow, Myra K. Erhardt & Robert P. Charrow, *Clear and Effective Legal Writing* (3d ed., Aspen Publishers 2001).
2. Elizabeth Fajans & Mary A. Falk, *Scholarly Writing for Law Students: Seminar Papers, Law Review Notes, and Law Review Competition Papers* (4th ed., West 2011).
3. Bryan A. Garner, *Legal Writing in Plain English: A Text with Exercises* (U. Chi. Press 2001).
4. George Gopen, *The Sense of Structure: Writing from the Reader's Perspective* (Longman 2004).

Schools Respond

5. Craig Hoffman & Andrea E. Tyler, *United State Legal Discourse: Legal English for Foreign LLMs* (Thomson/West 2008).

6. Legal Writing Institute, *Teaching International Students* (http://lwionline. org/teaching_international_students.html).

7. Deborah B. McGregor & Cynthia M. Adams, *The International Lawyer's Guide to Legal Analysis and Communication in the United States* (Aspen Publishers 2008).

8. Nadia E. Nedzel, *Legal Reasoning, Research, and Writing for International Graduate Students* (2d ed., Aspen Publishers 2008).

9. Laurel Currie Oates & Anne Enquist, *The Legal Writing Handbook: Analysis, Research, and Writing* (4th ed., Aspen Publishers 2006).

10. Theresa J. Reid Rambo & Leanne J. Pflaum, *Legal Writing by Design: A Guide to Great Briefs and Memos* (Carolina Academic Press 2001).

11. Jill J. Ramsfield, *Culture to Culture: A Guide to U.S. Legal Writing* (Carolina Academic Press 2005).

12. Wayne Schiess, *Better Legal Writing: 15 Topics for Advanced Legal Writers* (William S. Hein & Co., Inc. 2005).

13. Eugene Volokh, *Academic Legal Writing: Law Review Articles, Student Notes, Notes, Seminar Papers, and Getting on Law Review* (3d. ed., Found. Press 2007).

14. Mark E. Wojcik, *Getting Published: Improve Your Resume By Proving Your Writing Skills, Expertise and Marketability*, 37 Student Law 24(2), (2008), http://ssrn.com/abstract=1318388.

15. Mark E. Wojcik, *Introduction to Legal English: An Introduction to Legal Terminology, Reasoning, and Writing in Plain English* (3d ed., Intl. Law Inst. 2009).

CHAPTER SUMMARY

- Your legal communication classes are among the most important classes of your LL.M. year.

- It is critical that during your LL.M. year you develop strong analysis, research, and writing skills. Prospective employers will expect this.

- Take as many legal communication courses as possible. They can only help.

- Legal communication courses will help you in school (exams, exercises, theses) and after you graduate (briefs and court filings, contracts, bills to clients).

- Legal communication courses will help you in practice. They will help even if you choose not to practice law!

- Ask whether your LL.M. legal communication classes will be taught by professors with extensive professional training and experience in the field. LL.M. students deserve the best education on offer at their U.S. law school.

Chapter 18

Writing an LL.M. Thesis

CHAPTER HIGHLIGHTS

- Some schools *require* LL.M. theses; others *permit* LL.M. theses (optional); and others *prohibit* LL.M. theses.
- When you are choosing which school to attend, and which LL.M. track or concentration within that school, pay attention to the rules regarding theses.
- This chapter discusses theses generally, and offers some guidance on writing theses, and possibly publishing them in law journals in the U.S. or overseas.
- This chapter also lists a number of factors to consider when choosing a particular school or LL.M. track.

A. Introduction — Thesis Option Available Only at *Some* Schools

1. Possibilities for Writing an LL.M. Thesis

LL.M. programs in the U.S. generally have in place one of three possibilities regarding writing a thesis:

    a. **Mandatory Thesis.** Students are **required to write a thesis** and receive academic credit for it;

    b. **Optional Thesis.** Students are **permitted to write a thesis** and receive academic credit for it; or

    c. **Prohibited Thesis.** Students are **prohibited from writing a thesis** and *cannot* receive academic credit for it.

2. Different Schools, Different Tracks, Different Thesis Rules

A school may have one rule for one track or concentration, and a different rule for another track or concentration. For example, a school that offers an LL.M. in International Law, an LL.M. in Bankruptcy, and an LL.M. in American

Law may (a) **require** a thesis in the International Law track; (b) **permit** a thesis in the Bankruptcy track; and (c) **prohibit** a thesis in the American Law track.

When you are choosing schools — and more precisely, **when you are choosing an LL.M. track within an LL.M. program** — ensure that you understand the rules regarding theses.[1]

You may want to write a thesis to serve as the basis for your S.J.D. dissertation proposal or as the basis for a scholarly article you want to publish; to satisfy conditions for becoming a law teacher in your home country; or because you enjoy scholarly research and you would prefer to write a thesis rather than to take additional classroom classes. If you want to write a thesis and submit it for academic credit, you should ensure that your LL.M. program either *requires* or *permits* a thesis.

If you *do not* want to write a thesis, make sure that the LL.M. track you choose renders theses *optional* or *prohibits* theses for academic credit.[2] You will earn your academic credits through traditional classroom courses, or through experiential courses such as moot court, clinics, pro bono work, or internships.

This chapter describes generally how the term "thesis" is defined (or actually *not defined!*); the elements of theses required or permitted by LL.M. programs; and steps you might take in researching and writing your thesis.

B. What Is a "Thesis"?

There is no uniform definition of "thesis" in the LL.M. context at U.S. law schools. Indeed, not all law schools even refer to the major LL.M. paper as a "thesis," but may refer to it as a "substantial scholarly paper" or "major paper" or "LL.M. paper."

Nevertheless, various websites and other sources suggest that there is substantial agreement that the following characteristics define what I will refer to herein as a "thesis":

1. A thesis involves substantial legal research that culminates in a scholarly paper;
2. A thesis must involve a systematic and authoritative explanation of legal issue(s);

Schools Respond

---

1. "Theses" is the plural of "thesis."

2. If you choose a school that prohibits theses or renders theses optional, make sure that this is *not* because the school is a cash cow or diploma mill that is simply unwilling to commit resources to LL.M. research and writing activities (such as thesis courses, thesis faculty supervision, and other scholarly activities). Such LL.M. programs would disfavor theses *not* for pedagogical reasons, but due to profit motive — it may be less expensive for the school to have students take regularly scheduled classroom courses rather than for the school to create special research or writing opportunities for which the school may need to provide paid supervision and instruction. Students generally consider research and writing a thesis to be a tremendous, time-consuming undertaking, and if an LL.M. student is interested in doing as little work as possible to earn his or her LL.M. degree, he may choose an LL.M. program that offers an easier curriculum, without theses or similarly demanding requirements. **Ask the school why it does not permit or require a thesis. Be particularly wary if a school abolishes a longstanding LL.M. thesis requirement.**

3. A thesis must make a contribution to the understanding and analysis of its topic—a contribution to (and not just a reiteration or summary of) extant literature in the field;

4. A thesis must do significantly more than merely report, compile, or describe cases, statutes, treaties, legal theories, or other authors' work;

5. A thesis must be the original work of the student;

6. A thesis must demonstrate a thorough and scholarly command of the material it addresses;

7. A thesis can be doctrinal or quantitative or empirical;

8. A thesis can be multidisciplinary;

9. A thesis must be of publishable quality; and

10. A thesis need not be as long or in-depth as an S.J.D. dissertation (although it is unclear how much less is required for a thesis, or alternatively, how much more is needed for a dissertation).

C. Distinguish "Thesis" from Other Sorts of Papers an LL.M. Student Might Write

A thesis might be distinguished from another type of paper an LL.M. student might write based on length and the degree of research and analysis required. For example, LL.M. (and J.D.) students routinely write 25-page papers as part of regular lecture courses, and 35- to 50-page papers as part of regular seminar courses. Though many LL.M. programs require theses to be at least 50 pages, presumably, a 50-page thesis would be more in-depth and with more sophisticated analysis than a paper to fulfill a requirement of a regular law school lecture course.

The **Harvard** LL.M. program distinguishes among papers written by LL.M. students as follows:

> International students . . . must write either the 75- to 100-page LL.M. paper, the more extensive LL.M. thesis, or a paper of 25 or more pages that involves independent reflection, formulation of a sustained argument and, in many cases, outside research. Both types of papers may be written either independently or in conjunction with a seminar.

> *Source:* www.law.harvard.edu/academics/degrees/gradprogram/llm/ll.m.-degree-requirements.html.

D. LL.M. Supervision—Choosing a Thesis Topic, and Researching, Writing, and Submitting an LL.M. Thesis

Houston Professor Greg R. Vetter distributes a memorandum that advises LL.M. students seeking thesis topics and other students seeking topics for other

Schools Respond

types of writing projects.[3] He spells out steps students must follow if they want to approach him to supervise their written work. He notes that many resources are available for helping students arrive at viable topics, and directs students toward such resources. Among the sources he cites that are relied on by many other LL.M. thesis advisors and students around the U.S. is a book published by Professor Eugene Volokh, titled *Academic Legal Writing: Law Review Articles, Student Notes, Seminar Papers, and Getting on Law Review* (4th ed., Found. Press 2010). Professor Volokh discusses his book at www.volokh.com/writing.

Professor Vetter also provides his thesis supervisees with another document that describes substantive and procedural requirements for the thesis, and that explains his criteria for evaluating the thesis.[4]

E. Factors to Consider When Choosing a Thesis Track (Different Schools Have Different Thesis Rules)

The following section identifies the characteristics of the thesis component of LL.M. programs at different law schools around the U.S. Not all programs possess all of the characteristics. They do not need to in order to have an excellent thesis component to their LL.M. programs. You, as a student, must decide what level of instruction and guidance you need in producing your thesis, and

which school you believe can and will support your needs and help you write a thesis of the quality you desire. If you want to write a thesis that is barely enough to give you a passing grade, your choices are different from a student who wants to write a high-quality thesis she can publish in a prestigious law journal and use as the basis of an S.J.D. dissertation.

---

3. Greg R. Vetter, *Input for Students Selecting Journal Paper Topics and Planning to Discuss Journal Topics with Me*, www.law.uh.edu/faculty/gvetter/documents/StudentJournalPaperTopicSelection.Prof.Vetter1c.5.1.2005.pdf.

4. Greg R. Vetter, *Supervised Writing Requirement, Procedures, and Evaluation Criteria for Prof. Vetter*, www.law.uh.edu/faculty/gvetter/documents/Prof.Vetter.SupervisedWriting.RequirementsProceduresEvaluation_7.22.2005.pdf.

Schools Respond

F. Thesis Courses and Seminars, and Thesis Manual and Thesis Guidelines (including Formatting Guidelines)

1. Questions to Ask

a. Does the school have a Thesis Writing course in which you can receive instruction on thesis research and writing?

b. Does the school have an *LL.M. Thesis Manual* available to you before you enroll in a mandatory thesis track, or before you opt to write a thesis?

c. Does the *LL.M. Thesis Manual* provide adequate information to help you successfully research and write the thesis?

d. Does the *LL.M. Thesis Manual* provide clear guidelines about the form of the completed thesis, as well as the substance?

e. Are students writing theses required to participate in thesis seminars, workshops, roundtables, or other meetings where they may present their research and the status of their research, engage in discussion with participants, and receive feedback (particularly from thesis advisors and other faculty) — and if so, at what period intervals (weekly, monthly)?

f. Does the school provide adequate information and training on plagiarism?

g. What are the rules for being accepted into a thesis track? Can you apply directly to the thesis track when you submit your original application to the school? Must you gain acceptance to the school first, and then gain acceptance to a thesis track?

h. If you are enrolled in a non-thesis track but you decide you want to write a thesis, can you switch to a thesis track? Or can you write a thesis-quality paper for independent credit — and possibly publish it?

i. Once you are enrolled in a thesis track, can you change your mind and switch to a non-thesis writing track?

j. Will the school accept a quantitative-based analysis, using economic models?

k. Does the school provide thesis formatting guidelines and instruction?[5]

2. Thesis Faculty Advisor

a. Must you work with a faculty thesis advisor in developing the thesis topic, and throughout research and writing?

---

5. **Iowa** offers students substantial guidance on preparing theses and dissertations, posing this question: "Why format my thesis manually when there is a Thesis Template with built-in Styles that I can use?" (cs.its.uiowa.edu/sda/index-thesis.shtml#clinics). I agree. Why "re-create the wheel" (another expression common in the U.S.) when templates are available, particularly when the templates and instructions are almost as long as a thesis itself!

Schools Respond

b. Do you choose your faculty advisor alone? What assistance is given in helping you choose? How early in the year must you choose an advisor? What happens if the faculty advisor you want is on sabbatical?

c. Must you submit a thesis outline for approval by a faculty advisor or thesis committee?

d. Must you submit periodic progress reports on research and writing?

e. Will a faculty advisor review progress reports and thesis drafts and provide written and/or oral feedback?

f. Will your advisor be skilled, committed, ready, willing, and able to assist you in the thesis conception, research, and writing stages?

3. Thesis Committee

a. Does each LL.M. student have a Thesis Committee?

b. How is the Thesis Committee selected? Is it selected by the LL.M. Director or Associate Dean? Is it selected by the student?

c. What are the responsibilities of the Thesis Committee?

d. Will the Thesis Committee review and comment on drafts of your thesis?

e. Will you "defend" your thesis in front of the Thesis Committee?

f. Will the Thesis Committee critique your thesis?

g. Will the Thesis Committee grade your thesis?

4. Publishing Your Thesis

a. Will the school assist you in publishing your thesis in a U.S. law journal or elsewhere?

b. Will the school pay subscription fees for journal article submission services?

c. Does the school maintain bound copies of LL.M. theses in the law library?

d. Are links to LL.M. theses on the school's LL.M. website?

5. Staff Working With Thesis-Writing Students

a. Does the school have devoted LL.M. librarians to help guide your thesis research?

b. Does the school have ESL or other instructors to help you in thesis writing?

c. Are there trained linguists on staff in the LL.M. program?

6. Thesis Defense

a. Are you required to defend your thesis, allowed the option of defending your thesis, or prohibited from defending your thesis?

b. Will your defense be in front of the thesis committee? Will it be open to the public?

c. What happens if you "fail" your thesis defense?

d. Are you familiar with, and prepared to abide by, the thesis defense rules contained in the school's *LL.M. Thesis Guidelines*?

An LL.M. Thesis — A Typical Law School Set of Student and Faculty Advisor Responsibilities and Duties (adapted from various school websites)

Duties of a Student Researching and Writing a Thesis

1. Select a thesis advisor (if the student is not assigned an advisor).
2. Meet with the advisor.
3. Select a research area and topic (upon consultation with the thesis advisor).
4. Select a thesis committee (if school has such committees).
5. Research the topic preliminarily.
6. Submit a thesis outline to the thesis advisor, and discuss the outline with the advisor.
7. Thoroughly research the topic.
8. Produce thesis drafts and submit them to the thesis advisor.
9. Produce a completed thesis draft.
10. Be solely responsible for the form, style, clarity, and proper use of English.
11. Follow all guidelines contained in the school's *LL.M. Thesis Manual*.
12. Consult with the thesis advisor or the LL.M. administration on issues that arise.
13. Organize thesis binding and submission to the law school library for archiving.
14. Be conscientious and meet or beat all deadlines.

Duties of a Faculty Thesis Advisor

1. Discuss possible topics and research areas with the student.
2. Be available to meet with the student on thesis-related matters.
3. Help ensure that the student does not stray from a sound research and writing strategy.
4. Provide general direction to the student throughout the process.
5. Discuss issues of law and strategy with the student.
6. Monitor the student's progress.
7. Assess the soundness of the student's legal analysis.
8. Review the student's outline(s) and drafts.
9. Assess the merits of the thesis's arguments and legal analysis.
10. Constructively criticize the substance and structure of the thesis.
11. Generally review the grammar and syntax. Make broad comments, as needed.
12. Do not research, write, or heavily edit, which are wholly the student's responsibility.
13. Grade the thesis (unless the thesis committee performs the grading).

Schools Respond

7. Thesis Characteristics; Thesis Research and Writing Process; Thesis Grade

a. How many words or pages are required for your thesis?

b. How many thesis credit hours are awarded? Does the school offer a fixed number of credits for your thesis, or will it allow you to receive more credits for a lengthier or more in-depth thesis?

c. Must the student submit a "preemption check" or a "literature review" (with bibliography) to help establish that the topic is fresh?

d. Does the school require that theses be bound, with copies maintained in the school library's permanent collection?

e. Will the school provide current students copies of theses submitted by previous students and accepted by the school?

f. Do you receive a thesis grade, and if so, is the grade pass or fail, satisfactory or unsatisfactory, or a letter grade? Can you opt for no grading?[6]

g. Can you complete your thesis in your home country, rather than be forced to remain in the U.S. to finish it?

G. Selected Thesis and Scholarly Writing Resources

1. LexisNexis Directory of Law Reviews, www.lexisnexis.com/lawschool/prodev/lawreview/

2. Jurist Law Reviews, http://jurist.law.pitt.edu/lawreviews/

3. C. Steven Bradford, *As I Lay Writing: How to Write Law Review Articles for Fun and Profit*, 44 J. Legal Educ. 13 (1994).

4. Elizabeth Fajans & Mary R. Falk, *Fajans and Falk's Scholarly Writing for Law Students, Seminar Papers, Law Review Notes and Law Review Competition Papers* (3d ed., West 2005).

5. Austen L. Parrish & Dennis T. Yokoyama, *Effective Lawyering: A Checklist Approach to Legal Writing and Oral Argument* (Carolina Academic Press 2007).

6. Choosing a Topic for Your Journal Article, http://library.law.umn.edu/researchguides/choosingatopic.html

H. How to Submit Articles for Publication

If you want to publish your thesis in a law review or law journal, you might check the resources below. Ask your LL.M. office if it will pay any submission fee,

---

6. For example, **Wake Forest** permits student to "elect to have the thesis graded on a pass-fail basis" (http://law.wfu.edu/llm/academics/thesis/).

or at least part of it. (It doesn't hurt to ask!) The LL.M. office might at least pay for postage and envelopes if you post the materials manually rather than online.

1. Express online deliveries to law reviews, http://law.bepress.com/expresso/
2. *Getting Published in Law Reviews and Journals*, http://f.law.harvard.edu/gettingpublished
3. *Guide to Publishing Articles in Law Reviews and Journals*, www.ll.georgetown.edu/guides/Publishing.cfm
4. Law Journals: Submissions and Ranking, http://lawlib.wlu.edu/LJ/
5. Allen Rostron & Nancy Levit, *Information for Submitting Articles to Law Reviews & Journals*, Social Science Research Network, http://papers.ssrn.com/sol3/papers.cfm?abstract_id=1019029
6. *Writing for and Publishing in Law Reviews*, http://lib.law.washington.edu/ref/lawrev.html

---

CHAPTER SUMMARY

- If you want to write a thesis (as the basis for an S.J.D. proposal, or to publish as a law review article), make sure you choose a school that permits or requires theses.

- If you do not want to write a thesis, make sure you do not choose a school that requires a thesis.

- Find out the thesis rules before you apply to the school!

- Each school has different thesis rules. Schools require different numbers of pages, formats, and thesis committee composition. Check the *LL.M. Student Handbook* before you apply.

- Choose a school that publishes *LL.M. Thesis Guidelines*.

Schools Respond

Chapter 19

Student Organizations and Extracurricular Activities

CHAPTER HIGHLIGHTS

- International LL.M. students benefit greatly from joining student organizations and participating in their activities.
- Before you choose a school, look at the school's website to find out if it has major extracurricular organizations involved in areas that interest you.
- Student organizations are a great place to find friends with shared interests, and to make bonds that can last the year or a lifetime.
- If the school has no student organization that focuses on a subject area that interests you, take initiative and create such an organization. Chances are that other students will also be interested and will join.

A. Introduction

International LL.M. students can derive dramatic short-term and long-term benefits from joining law student organizations and participating in law school extracurricular activities during the LL.M. year, beginning as soon you reach campus, if not before.

This chapter does the following:

1. Defines "law student organization" and "extracurricular activity";
2. Explains why some LL.M. and first-year J.D. students tend not to join these groups and get involved in these activities right away, even though they are eligible and would benefit;
3. Mentions some of the short-term and long-term benefits of joining law student groups and participating in extracurricular activities;
4. Lists a selection of student organizations that exist at different law schools around the country, describes some of the extracurricular activities they sponsor, and tells you how you might get involved; and

5. Explains how and why you, as an LL.M. candidate, might create student organizations in areas where they do not yet exist at your school.

B. Law Student Organizations

Law student organizations are groups formed by law students, officially registered with and recognized by the law school. The organizations' purposes are varied, and include social, career, professional, skill-building, political, spiritual, service, sports, academic, or other purposes. A group's focus can be related to an area of law or law practice; a type of law organization; a political ideology or party; rights promotion of different groups or issues; law reform; a religion; minority groups; law related to racial or ethnic groups, or nationalities; sexuality, gender, or sexual orientation; a fraternity; or some other group or cause. Many of these groups have been in existence for many decades, and have national or international chapters with local chapters at different law schools around the U.S. Others exist only on a few campuses with no national affiliates, and are relatively new. In all cases, the law school must approve the creation and operation of the law student organization.

The organizations will have constitutions and bylaws that govern their membership, finances, and operation. Law schools may support the organizations by providing funding, office space, computer access, bulletin boards, and access to networks for advertising events.

C. Extracurricular Activities

1. What Are They?

Extracurricular activities are events that typically take place at or near the law school that are organized by, and sponsored by, law student organizations. Law schools support these extracurricular activities by providing event funding that might be used for food; drinks; music; flyers, posters, or other advertising; publications; travel (for students to attend related events in other cities or countries, or for visitors to come to the law school campus); or other expenses. Faculty, administration, and fellow students — and sometimes members of the outside community — participate in extracurricular activities sponsored by the law student groups.

2. More About Extracurricular Activities

Group activities tend to complement classroom education, promote physical and/or mental health, help students maintain balance in their lives during a period that could prove to be stressful, and assist students in achieving their personal and professional goals. Extracurricular activities sponsored by law student groups tend to be "win-win" situations.

3. Types of Activities

Activities can include moot courts, guest speakers, panel discussions, conference sponsorship (on-campus or off-campus), human rights and pro bono projects, fund-raisers for charity, sporting events, law firm and corporate in-house counsel visits for student networking, visits to judges' chambers, UN volunteer work, bake sales, concerts, talent shows, casino nights, newsletter publication, issues fairs, general lawyer networking events on campus, or job fairs. The list of activities is limited only by the imaginations and initiative of the different student groups!

D. LL.M. Students Getting Involved in Student Organizations and Extracurricular Activities

1. Reasons LL.M. Students (and First-Year J.D. Students) Often Do Not Join Student Groups Immediately or Participate in Extracurricular Activities

LL.M. students, like first-year J.D. students, are busy in the first weeks and months of the fall semester getting adjusted to life as students at a U.S. law school. That is a full-time job, and you might think you have no time to participate in anything besides classes and study groups. Hence, law student groups tend to be populated by second-year and third-year J.D. students, and not by first-year or LL.M. students.

First-year students will have at least two more years to get involved with student groups. But LL.M. students have only one year (two semesters). LL.M. students may want to join (or create) student organizations immediately upon arriving on campus.

2. The Process of Getting Involved

At the beginning of each semester, law student organizations tend to have "call out meetings" or "membership meetings" to which new, incoming students are invited to learn more about the respective organizations. Even though you will have many other challenges in your early weeks and months at school — classes, study, advisor meetings, adjusting to the culture and food, more study, and many other challenges — I encourage you to investigate joining one or more of the organizations whose subject matter appeals to you. It is a great way to meet other students with interests similar to your own, and to develop friendships — among J.D., LL.M., and other students. You might meet students who are taking the same courses you are taking, who have professional and personal goals similar to yours, or who may even have had the sort of internship or work experience that you are seeking. You can learn a great deal from other students. You are at the U.S. law school to participate and collaborate in activities with other students — not just to take courses and learn the material and legal skills the LL.M. program offers.

E. Benefits to LL.M. Students of Joining Student Groups and Participating in Extracurricular Activities

1. Meet Students Who Share an Interest

Because each group is based on a theme or purpose, if you are interested in one of the groups, you can be assured that other members of the group will share your interest in that subject area. It is an easy and great way to meet other students interested in subjects that interest you. You can make short-term connections with other students to participate in sports or other leisure activities, study, or even debate. You can meet students interested in working in the same areas of law as you (for example, public interest, human rights, tax, or criminal law), or who can serve as mentors to you during school (or whom you can mentor). You can form lifelong bonds with fellow students, based on shared interests and associations. If you are interested in an area that does not have a student group, you can start one, as LL.M. students did recently at one school where they formed the Master of Laws Association (MLA) (primarily to help resolve issues within the LL.M. program).

2. Faculty Advisor

Each student organization has a faculty advisor professor who offers advice to the group, may serve as a liaison between the group and the administration, and generally serves as a resource and sounding board for the group. A substantial benefit of participating in student organizations is that you will be able to work with the faculty advisor, cultivate a relationship with him or her, and perhaps get to feel comfortable enough to ask him or her for a recommendation letter later. The faculty advisor shares an interest in the subject matter and focus of the group, and this gives you a common ground on which to develop that relationship.

3. Form Lifelong Bonds

As suggested, extracurricular law school activities are excellent ways to form lifelong bonds between and among students, faculty, and staff. Gaps that might otherwise separate international LL.M. students and U.S. J.D. students are readily bridged or dissolved altogether through these vital, informative, and enjoyable mutual activities.

F. List of Student Organizations That Exist on Law School Campuses

Below are names of some of the many dozens of organizations active on law school campuses around the country. Organizations with similar purposes may have different names at different schools. For example, an organization focusing on sexual orientation issues may be known as the Gay and Lesbian Student Association at one school and "LAMBDA" or "OUTlaw" at another. One school may have a "Business Law Association" or "BLA" and another school may have a "Business Law Society" or "BLS." These business-focused groups tend to have a similar focus, even if they have different names, such as "Business Law Club" or "Business Law Federation." Do not get confused. Read the descriptions of the organizations on the law school's website.

Get involved!

Names of Selected Law Student Organizations

1	Advocates for Youth Justice
2	African Students Association
3	American Association for Justice
4	American Civil Liberties Union (ACLU)
5	American Constitution Society
6	American-Japanese Law Students Alliance
7	Amnesty International Student Chapter
8	Animal Law Society
9	Arab Law Student Association
10	Asian Law Student Association
11	Asian Pacific Law Student Association
12	Association of American Trial Lawyers
13	Black Law Students Association (BALSA)
14	Bridge or Chess Society
15	Business Law Association
16	Caribbean Law Students Association
17	Catholic Student Association
18	Central Asian Law Student Association
19	China Law Association
20	Christian Legal Society

Schools Respond

Schools Respond

21	Corporate Law Association
22	Criminal Law Association
23	Critical Race Scholars' Society
24	Dean's Student Advisory Board
25	Death Penalty Reform Society
26	Democratic Law Society
27	Disability Law Society
28	Diversity Coalition
29	East European Law Student Association
30	Elder Law Society
31	Entertainment Law Society
32	Environmental Law Society
33	Equal Justice Works
34	Federalist Society
35	Feminist Law Society
36	Gay and Lesbian Student Association
37	Habitat for Humanity
38	Health Law Society
39	Hispanic Law Society
40	Human Rights Students' Association
41	Immigration Law Society
42	Indian Law Association
43	Innocence Project
44	Intellectual Property Law Association
45	International Criminal Court Network
46	International Human Rights Law Society
47	International Law Society
48	Islamic Legal Forum
49	Japanese Law Society
50	Jewish Law Students Association
51	Korean Law Students Society
52	La Raza Law Student Association

53	Labor Law Coalition
54	Lambda Law Society
55	Latin American Law Student Society
56	Law Students for Israel
57	Law Students for Justice in Palestine
58	Law Students for Reproductive Justice
59	Middle Eastern Law Student Society
60	Military Law Society
61	Mock Trial Association
62	Moot Court Association
63	Muslim Law Students Association
64	National Lawyers Guild
65	Native American Law Student Association
66	Outlaw
67	Patent Law Society
68	Phi Alpha Delta
69	Phi Delta Phi
70	Pilipino American Law Society
71	Public Interest Law Fund
72	Republican Law Coalition
73	Society for Justice in Israel/Palestine
74	South Asian Law Students Association
75	Sports Law Society
76	Students Opposing Domestic Violence
77	United Nations Law Society
78	Veterans or Armed Forces Association
79	Volunteer Income Tax Assistance
80	Women's Law Society
81	Women of Color Collective
82	Workers' Rights Clinic

Schools Respond

CHAPTER SUMMARY

- All international LL.M. students should get involved in one or more extracurricular activities during their LL.M. year. The benefits are immense.

- Before choosing a school, ask if it has major extracurricular organizations involved in areas that interest you. Contact current members. Learn about their activities.

- If there is no student organization that focuses on issues of interest to you, start such an organization!

- Ask how much the school supports the various student organizations. Does the school provide funding for organization activities?

- Student organizations are a source of ready-made friends for international students, who share your interests. These groups are a great place to meet friends and to make bonds that can last the year or a lifetime.

Part V

Student Visas and Other Immigration-Related Documents

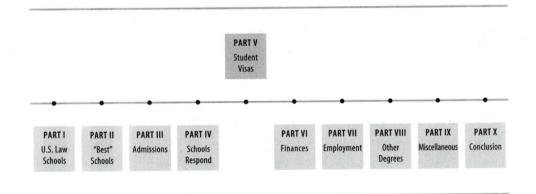

Chapter 20

U.S. Student Visa Hurdles

CHAPTER HIGHLIGHTS

- You will need a student visa to travel to the U.S. for your LL.M.
- You can apply to the U.S. embassy or consulate in your country to get your visa.
- You may apply for an F-1 visa if you (or your family or other private person) will be paying for your LL.M. ("self-funded").
- You may apply for a J-1 visa if you or the U.S. government or another agency working with the U.S. will be paying for your LL.M. ("sponsored").
- This chapter discusses other documents including the I-20, DS-2019, and I-94.
- You will have your visa interview at the U.S. embassy or consulate in your home country.
- Thousands of international students each year overcome visa hurdles to acquire a U.S. student visa and join an LL.M. program in the U.S. — and you can, too!

A. The Student Visa and Other Immigration-Related Documents

1. Your Student Visa, Generally

By now, ideally, you have been admitted to the LL.M. program in the U.S. that is "best" for you. You may now apply for a student visa — U.S. government authorization to seek permission to enter the U.S. to begin your program. This chapter will help you navigate this process.

You may have heard stories about international students getting bogged down in the U.S. visa quagmire, "failing" their visa interviews at the U.S. embassy or consulate, or getting delayed by immigration when their plane arrives in the U.S. Sometimes there are administrative hurdles. If you follow the important guidelines in this chapter, you will be in good shape to overcome most major hurdles.

2. Visa-Related Documents and Forms

a. *Your student visa.*   A U.S. embassy or consulate in your country will issue a student visa to you so that you may enter the U.S. to study.

b. *Your I-20 or DS-2019 student status eligibility certification form.*   Your law school will issue this form to you when it admits you. It will be form I-20 ("eye-20") if you will have F-1 visa status, or form DS-2019 if you will have J-1 visa status.

c. *Your I-94 ("eye-94") form — Arrival Departure Record.*   You will receive this form on the plane or when you land at the U.S. airport.

d. *Miscellaneous forms.*   As an example, you will need to fill out a form to allow you to get a **Social Security Card** if you plan to work in the U.S.

Student Visas

3. The SEVIS System

This chapter also introduces you to the **Student and Exchange Visitor Information System (SEVIS)**. SEVIS is an Internet-based system that maintains data on international students before and during their stay in the U.S. It is administered by the U.S. Immigration and Customs Enforcement (ICE) within the Department of Homeland Security (DHS).[1]

4. Your Student Visa

To be sure you understand everything you need to know about your student visa, consider first the following five important points:

First, a student visa is a piece of high-quality paper that a U.S. embassy or consulate in your home country pastes inside your passport. This visa is *permission for you to apply* to enter the U.S. It is *not automatic permission* to enter the U.S. When you arrive at a U.S. airport, immigration officials assess whether you may enter. Do not get nervous — now, in imagined anticipation, or at the moment you disembark the plane and wait in line with the other travelers! Immigration assesses *all* foreigners at the border, whether they are have business, tourist, student, or other visas. Even U.S. citizens have to be assessed for proper evidentiary documentation when entering the U.S.

Second, U.S. visa regulations can change at any time. Some people jest that U.S. visa regulations change *all* the time. Follow closely the most current visa guidelines found on the U.S. State Department and embassy or consulate websites, or from personal visits to U.S. embassies or consulates in your home country.[2] Visa counseling is available from EducationUSA Student Advising Centers, which are affiliated with the U.S. State Department, and which are housed in 450 offices in 200 countries and territories (www.educationusa.info/pages/students/visa.php; www.educationusa.info).

Third, ask your U.S. law school for help with visa issues. *There is no substitute for obtaining visa information directly from a U.S. government official.* But your school is expected to advise you on visa issues, help get your visa issued, and help you follow all government (and school) guidelines before and after you arrive in the U.S. Your U.S. school must provide you with LL.M. admission documents (I-20 or DS-2019). It may contact the U.S. embassy or consulate on your behalf if necessary, and answer your questions. For example, **Michigan State** provides that it "will work with the U.S. Department of Homeland Security to obtain visas for foreign attorneys studying in the LL.M. Program" (www.law.msu.edu/llm). **Washington University — St. Louis** notes that it "works closely with all of our admitted students to ensure timely and correct filings of visas"

---

1. www.ice.gov/sevis/index.htm. ICE is the largest DHS investigative arm.
2. www.travel.state.gov/visa/temp/types/types_1270.html; http://hevisaforms.state.gov; http://usembassy.state.gov.

and they urge applicants "to get your applications in early, and we promise to work on your visa documents early" (http://law.wustl.edu/llmint/index.aspx).

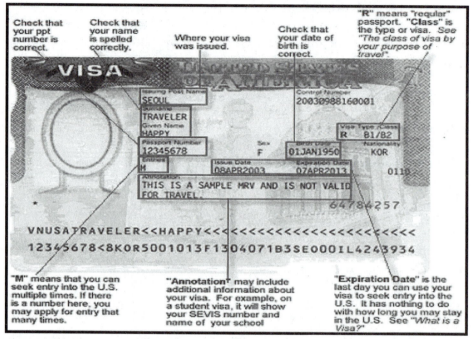

Source: http://travel.state.gov/visa/questions/what/what_4429.html

Fourth, complying with U.S. law means more than having a student visa in your passport. When in the U.S., you must register full time as a student to maintain your non-immigrant "visa status" (either "F-1 student status" or "J-1 exchange visitor status"). *Your legal non-immigrant status is not evidenced and legally satisfied only by your visa, but is evidenced and legally satisfied by the combination of your travel documents: Passport; I-20 or DS-2019 Form; and I-94.*

Fifth, acquiring a U.S. visa (or a visa for any country) is a privilege, not a right. Countries are sovereign and need not explain or justify decisions to permit foreigners to enter, to deny entry to foreigners, or to expel foreigners. Being admitted to a U.S. LL.M. program, even to a "prestigious" program at a famous law school, or being granted a large scholarship, is **no guarantee** that the U.S. will issue you a student visa. Just because you have a U.S. visa does not mean you are guaranteed to be able to keep it. *To help avoid visa denial or revocation, you must follow all government and university regulations.*

B. Types of Non-Immigrant Visas for International LL.M. Students — F-1 and J-1 Visas

U.S. visa officers seek to assess whether international LL.M. students plan to remain in the U.S. temporarily and leave after they complete their degree or after brief post-LL.M. employment. The U.S. issues students "non-immigrant" visas, ordinarily valid for the length of the degree program.

LL.M. students are normally issued one of two types of non-immigrant visas, either an F-1 "student visa" or a J-1 "exchange visa."[3]

1. *F-1 non-immigrant visa ("student visa").*   The F-1 is the most common visa issued to LL.M. students, and is granted when a student's funding comes substantially from personal or family (private) funds.

2. *J-1 non-immigrant visa ("exchange visa").*   The J-1 is granted to LL.M. students supported substantially by funding other than personal or family funds. This may include public funding from the U.S. government, the student's home government, or a foundation. Individuals sponsored by organizations such as Fulbright and Muskie are J-1 students/scholars. If your program involves an agreement between your government and the U.S., or between a U.S. school and a foreign institution or government, you may qualify for a J-1 visa.

C. Steps for Acquiring and Complying with Your F-1 or J-1 Visa

Acquiring your U.S. student visa is essentially the same for students from any country, but may be more challenging for students from certain countries due to political or diplomacy concerns. The student visa process is complex but by no means insurmountable. Students from *every* country in the world have been

---

Documents You Should Be Familiar With

VISA.   Either an F-1 or a J-1 for international LL.M. students. A visa is a piece of paper pasted in your passport used to seek entry to the U.S. at an air, land, or sea border crossing.

I-20.   Sent to you by the law school upon LL.M. admission. An I-20 (pronounced "eye 20") is used to apply for an F-1 visa at a U.S. embassy.

DS-2019.   Sent to you by the law school upon LL.M. admission. A DS-2019 is used to apply for a J-1 visa at a U.S. embassy.

I-94.   An I-94 (pronounced "eye 94") is a small white card stapled into your passport at a U.S. airport on arrival and collected during departure.

---

3. The J-1 is technically an "exchange visa," and the F-1 is a "student visa." Both are commonly referred to as "student visas." Most relevant visa regulations apply equally to LL.M. students under an F-1 or J-1 visa, although there are some differences.

granted U.S. student visas. Complying with U.S. visa regulations is achievable. Thousands of international students obtain and maintain their student status in the U.S. each year.

I have divided the student visa process into the following steps:

1. *Apply for admission to the LL.M. program(s) of your choice.*   You, as the prospective student, will have applied for admission to one or more LL.M. programs that you considered "best" for you, given your finances, background, needs, and aspirations. (See Chapter 7.)

2. *LL.M. program admits you!*   One or more U.S. law schools sends you an LL.M. admission letter and predeparture documentation. *Congratulations!* (See Chapter 14.)

3. *Welcome to SEVIS — I-20 form and DS-2019 form.*   The U.S. law schools that admit you will send you one of two types of SEVIS-generated documents:

   • *USCIS Form I-20, A-B/ID.*   Known as an I-20, its full official name is Certificate of Eligibility for Nonimmigrant (F-1) Student Status — for Academic and Language Students. The I-20 is sent to students who qualify for an F-1 visa; or

   • *USCIS Form DS-2019.*   Known as DS-2019, its full name is Certificate of Eligibility for Exchange Visitor Status. The DS-2019 is sent to students who qualify for a J-1 visa.

4. *You accept the school's LL.M. admission offer.*   Next, you must decide which law school's offer to accept, and let the school know that you intend to join their program. (See Chapter 14.) You then sign the I-20 or DS-2019 that the school sent you, preferably using blue ink. Be certain to use the I-20 or DS-2019 *for the school you plan to attend,*

Steps in Getting a Student Visa

1. Apply to LL.M. program
2. LL.M. program admits you!
3. Welcome to SEVIS (school sends you I-20 or DS-2019)
4. Accept school's admission offer
5. Pay SEVIS fee; apply for J-1 or F-1 visa
6. Student visa interview
7. Student visa fee
8. Student visa processing; visa issued
9. Travel to U.S. — Bon voyage!
10. Arrive in the U.S.
11. Arrive on campus
12. Comply with visa, take classes, graduate

because each form has a specific SEVIS ID number associated with that particular school. SEVIS ID numbers begin with the letter "N" and have 11 digits.

5. *Pay SEVIS I-901 fee and apply for visa.*   To apply for a visa you must pay a SEVIS fee to the U.S. government using Form I-901 (www.ice.gov/sevis/i901/faq1.htm).

   • Your I-20 or DS 2019, coupled with the I-901 fee, permit you to begin the visa-acquisition process at the U.S. embassy or consulate in your country. This does not guarantee that a visa will be issued for you.

   • You may pay the SEVIS fee online using certain credit or debit cards. The current fee is U.S. $200 for F-1 visas, U.S. $180 for most J-1 visas, and U.S. $35 for some subsidized J-1 visas (www.fmjfee.com).

   • Print a copy of your SEVIS receipt to take to the U.S. embassy or consulate for your visa interview.

   • If you do not have a credit card, check with a U.S. embassy or consulate for payment directions.

   • Be certain to check with EducationUSA Advisors, who are affiliated with the U.S. State Department. They may offer you an *Opportunity Grant* or *Gap Scholarship* to pay your SEVIS fees (or pay for such things as English lessons, document translations, and transportation). Currently students from 28 different countries qualify for these awards. Ask an EducationUSA Advisor. (See Chapter 24 and Appendix II.)

6. *Student visa interview.*   You must appear for a student visa interview at the U.S. embassy or consulate in your country. In some countries, you must make an online or telephonic visa interview appointment. (This is discussed further below.)

7. *Student visa fee.*   At your interview, depending on your country, you may be required to pay a visa fee. *The visa fee is separate from the SEVIS fee you paid earlier.* The *SEVIS fee* pays for the SEVIS system to keep track of international students and exchange visitors in the U.S. The *visa fee* pays for consular and other immigration services. Ask an EducationUSA Advisor if you qualify for an *Opportunity Grant* or *Gap Scholarship* to pay your visa fees. (See Chapter 24 and Appendix II.)

8. *Student visa processing and issuing.*   After your visa interview, the consular officer will tell you how long it will take to process and issue your visa. The State Department acknowledges that in the post-9/11 era "visa applications are subject to a greater degree of scrutiny than in the past." You can check the average visa issuance time in your country through the U.S. embassy or U.S. State Department website (http://travel.state.gov/visa/temp/wait/wait_4638.html). After consular

officials paste the student visa in your passport, you may make plans to travel to the U.S.

9. *Travel to the U.S.*   Bon voyage! With your visa, you may arrive in the U.S., usually no more than 30 days before the date your LL.M. program will commence for classes or for pre-semester orientation, English language or introduction to U.S. law classes, or other preliminary program matters. You may be able to arrive earlier if you acquire a visitor or other visa. *If you arrive earlier than 30 days on a tourist visa or with a visa waiver, you must inform U.S. Immigration when you arrive that you plan to start school soon under your F-1 or J-1 visa.* (See Chapter 21.)

10. *Arrive in the U.S.*   When you arrive at an airport in the U.S., you will pass through formalities with the U.S. Customs and Border Protection and U.S. Immigration. (See Chapter 21.)

11. *Arrive on your campus.*   Finally, you have arrived at your law school campus! You should report to your school's LL.M. office or the Office of International Affairs. That office will report your arrival to SEVIS, answer your outstanding questions, and sort out any other administrative issues.

12. *Comply with visa rules, take classes, graduate, and celebrate.*   It is critical that you stay "in visa status," which means that you must comply with your F-1 or J-1 visa restrictions and requirements while in school, after you graduate, while you work in practical training (OPT or AT), and until you return home. You should never fall "out of status," which could cause your visa to be revoked, and cause you to be deported to your home country, even before you finish your degree. To ensure long-term professional and personal success you must remain in bona fide student status while you are in the U.S.

D. The Student Visa Interview

1. The Interview, Generally

Your visa interview will ordinarily take place at the U.S. embassy or consulate in your country. There is no standard set of questions asked. Two students from the same country seeking visas to attend the same LL.M. program may be asked different questions. EducationUSA Educational Advising Centers are there to help you. They are a particularly good place to turn for advice on visa interviews. These centers often invite U.S. embassy consular officers (maybe the same ones who conduct student visa interviews) to conduct sessions about the student interview process.

Common Visa Categories

- F-1 — Academic students (granted to most LL.M. students)
- F-2 — Spouses and children of F-1
- F-3 — Canadian or Mexican academic commuter students
- J-1 — Exchange visitors (granted to some LL.M. students)
- J-2 — Spouses and children of J-1
- H-1B — Specialty workers (Post-LL.M. degree)
- H-4 — Dependents of H-1

2. What U.S. Consular Officers Consider When Deciding Whether to Issue a Visa

Most visa interviews are usually brief, perhaps only three to five minutes. U.S. consular officers quickly assess the items and documents critical to the decision making:

a. whether you are a bona fide admitted student who wants to travel to the U.S. for the study purposes stated in your visa application;

b. whether you have been admitted to a bona fide LL.M. program in the U.S. as a full-time student;

c. whether your background is appropriate for the LL.M. study plan;

d. whether you will likely succeed in the LL.M. program;

e. whether you are proficient in English;

f. whether you have "sufficient funds" for tuition and living expenses to sustain you for your study period (or otherwise demonstrate that you will not become a public charge or have to resort to unauthorized work). You need not have all the cash on hand at the time of the visa interview, but you must show it will be available when payment is due. F-1 students can show family funds, scholarships, loans, or corporate support. J-1 students can show funds from your sponsoring government, school, or other public institution;

g. whether you will likely obey U.S. laws and not pose a threat; and

h. whether you have sufficient "ties" to your home country—such as a residence, other assets, family or social ties, or a job that you do not intend to abandon.

Students' Responsibilities to Comply with U.S. Immigration Law

- U.S. visa regulations are subject to change — at any time.
- It is *your* responsibility to follow current U.S. immigration law.
- Your school should be willing and able to assist you, every step of the way.
- You can also contact the U.S. government directly. (www.ice.gov)
- Keep your eyes and ears open about changes to the law or university policy that may affect you as a student or graduate.

E. What to Take to the Student Visa Interview

1. *Signed and valid I-20 or DS-2019.*
2. *Valid passport.*   Typically it must be valid for at least six months when you enter the U.S.
3. *Financial documents to show you can pay for a full academic year of tuition and expenses in the U.S.*   The documents should be dated within three months. This proof of financial responsibility can be yours, your parents', or your sponsor's bank statements or tax documents showing sufficient funds.
4. *Official LL.M. admission letter from your law school.*
5. *Visa application (completed).*
6. *Visa application fee.*
7. *SEVIS payment receipt.*
8. *Documents to support your intent to return to your home country.*   This could be information regarding family ties, family property, employment in your country, or family businesses.
9. *Transcripts and diplomas from previous institutions attended.*
10. *For F-1 students:*   http://travel.state.gov/visa/temp/types/types_1268.html
11. *For J-1 scholars:*   http://travel.state.gov/visa/temp/types/types_1267.html

F. Tips for Students When They Appear for a Student Visa Interview

Circulating among U.S. international advisors is a list of "10 Points to Remember" when applying for a student visa. In this section I paraphrase and supplement the list (and cite several points of attribution, though it is not clear who contributed what to this list).[4]

1. Ties to Your Home

You must show that you want to return to your home country after you complete your LL.M., and show that you do not intend to try to immigrate to the U.S. During your interview, the consular officers will assess if your "ties" to your home country are strong enough that you would not want to leave your country permanently. The stronger the ties to your home country, the more likely your visa will be granted. Evidence of ties could be family, a home, or a job to return to. They may ask about your U.S. ties — whether you have family, close friends, or post-LL.M. job offers in the U.S. If you have strong U.S. ties, the consular officials may get suspicious about your intent to return to your home country post-LL.M. degree completion.

2. Questions About U.S. Law, the LL.M., Your School, and Your Post-Degree Plans.

The consular officer may ask about your law school, the LL.M. program, and degree requirements. He or she will want to know that you are qualified for the program and that you are legitimately going to enroll. Be prepared to discuss your post-LL.M. plans. It is okay to want to work temporarily in the U.S. post-LL.M. to gain law-related experience, but your primary purpose for being in the U.S. is to study law.

3. English Language: Speak for Yourself

You will be expected to speak English at your interview. If you lack confidence or think you may be nervous, have practice interviews with friends, family, professors, or advisors beforehand. The consular officer will interview you, not your parents, friends, or financial guarantors (who may remain in the waiting area in case there are any questions for them). Visit EducationUSA for advice and practice interviews.

Student Visas

---

4. Versions of this paraphrased list appear in many different publications online and in hard copy. *See, e.g.,* www.american.edu/ocl/isss/visa-interview-tips.cfm (noting that "[t]his list was compiled by NAFSA: Association of International Educators. NAFSA would like to credit Gerald A. Wunsch, Esq., 1997, then a member of the Consular Issues Working Group, and a former U.S. Consular Officer in Mexico, Suriname, and the Netherlands, and Martha Wailes of Indiana University for their contributions to this document. NAFSA also appreciates the input of the U.S. Department of State.").

4. Communicate Clearly, Concisely, Directly, and Honestly

U.S. consular officers are very busy, have large caseloads, and only have a brief period to interview you. Make their job easier by communicating clearly, concisely, directly, and honestly.

5. Supporting Documents

The consular officer will expect you to present your passport, I-20 or DS-2019 form, a financial support statement, and other materials (as discussed above). Organize your documents to make it easy for the consular officer.

6. Dress Appropriately

You need not dress formally. But you should be neat. You want to make a positive impression — that you are a legal professional prepared for a serious educational undertaking. Be sure to look the part.

7. Dependents

If you have dependents (e.g., a spouse or minor children under the age of 21) that will go with you to the U.S., the consular officer may ask if they will work, go to school, or neither. If they will remain in your home country, you should mention that, as it will help show your strong ties, i.e., your desire to return home to your family after you complete your degree.

8. Not All Countries Are Treated "Equally"

The U.S. government knows well that some students have remained in the U.S. after their allotted period of LL.M. study due to economic or political conditions in their home countries. If you come from such a country, you may face tougher questioning about your desire to return home postdegree. Be prepared for difficult questions. Do not take it personally. You must be able to show that you have reasons for returning to your home country that are stronger than any reasons for remaining in the U.S.

9. Be Respectful

The consular officer will seek to gather important information from you in a short period, perhaps three to five minutes, or shorter. Do not get upset, even if you think the official does not believe your answers. Answer truthfully, as best you can, even if you do not like the question, or if they ask for information you do not have. Try to be helpful.

10. Maintain a Positive Attitude

It will not help your case if you are rude, dismissive, or argumentative. If they ask you to appear for a follow-up interview or to bring additional information, do so. If in the end the consular officer denies your visa, respectfully ask for the reasons in writing. They may inform you of what you might do to correct any deficiencies when you reapply.

G. When Should You Apply for Your Student Visa?

Apply for your visa as soon as you can. The process can be time-consuming, depending on where you live, how many students from your country are seeking visas, and other factors. It could take three to four months or more. You can check online for waiting periods in your country. The U.S. usually will not issue a visa more than 120 days before your departure date for the U.S. (www.ice.gov/sevis/travel/faq_f.htm; www.educationusa.info/centers.php). If you enter on a tourist visa or on a visa waiver program, you will not be permitted to begin your LL.M. program without possible complications. (See Chapter 21.)

H. Working in the U.S. After Earning an LL.M. Degree

You have various options for acquiring permission to work in the U.S. after you complete your degree. Four possibilities are:

1. *Optional Practical Training (OPT).*   F-1 students are permitted to work in a law-related job for one year (12 months) after graduation. (See Chapter 27.)
2. *Academic Training (AT).*   J-1 students are permitted to work in a law-related job after graduation. (See Chapter 27.)
3. *H-1B specialty worker visa.*   The U.S. permits non-U.S. citizens (including LL.M. graduates) to work in the U.S. for up to six years if a U.S. company sponsors them and other conditions are satisfied. (See Chapter 27.)
4. *Labor certification.*   Employers may hire foreigners to work in the U.S. if the U.S. Department of Labor certifies that no qualified U.S. workers are able, willing, qualified, and available to accept a given job at the prevailing wage in the area of intended employment, and if the work will not adversely affect the wages and working conditions of similarly employed U.S. workers. (See Chapter 27.)

I. Legal Advice

Please remember that *LL.M. Roadmap does not offer legal advice,* but only provides information that may be useful to you. Administrators at your law school may also not provide legal advice, though administrators are in a very good position to assist on this topic. Your law school administrators can refer you to campus or outside immigration lawyers to handle matters that may arise with your visa. *Legal advice and advice about legal matters are not the same thing. Be careful that you rely on sound advice from legitimate sources, particularly regarding legal advice when you should consult a licensed lawyer.*

CHAPTER SUMMARY

- Do not let red tape and paperwork deter your student visa quest.
- Your U.S. school will assist you.
- You can consult EducationUSA in your home country.
- You will learn many new immigration terms — F-1, J-1, I-20, DS-2019, and I-94.
- Thousands of students get visas each year. You can do it, too!
- Honesty is the best policy when dealing with government officials.

Chapter 21

Visa and Immigration Issues After You Arrive in the U.S.

CHAPTER HIGHLIGHTS

- When you leave your country bound for the U.S., you will already be familiar with basic U.S. immigration law and policy pertaining to LL.M. students, particularly regarding the type of U.S. visa you will be on — either an F-1 student visa or a J-1 exchange visa.

- You will receive additional U.S. immigration documents when you are on the airplane, which you must complete and turn in when you arrive at the U.S. port of entry.

- This chapter discusses additional documents and some of the U.S. immigration responsibilities you will have when you are in the U.S.

- Your law school will help you comply with your immigration obligations, but, ultimately, the burden is on you to comply.

A. Your Airplane Journey to the U.S.

Before you board the plane in your home country, the airline will check your passport for the F-1 or J-1 student visa issued at the U.S. embassy or consulate. Either on the plane or when you arrive at your U.S. "point of entry" (the first U.S. airport at which your plane touches down), you will complete an **I-94 Arrival/ Departure record/card** (often called an "eye-94"). This chapter discusses the I-94 as well as other immigration documents you need to acquire and protect, and visa and immigration procedures you must follow to ensure personal and professional success.

B. Arrival at Your U.S. Point of Entry

1. You Have Arrived!

After your plane touches down in the U.S. you will proceed to a large arrival hall with several lines of people leading to different U.S. immigration officers, each at a computer station. One line is for U.S. citizens and legal permanent residents. Choose the other line, for non-citizens/temporary visitors. This second line may be further divided into two categories: (a) "USA Visit Visa"; and (b) NSEERS — National Security Entry & Exit Registration System. Ask an immigration officer if you need assistance.

If you are in either of the two non-citizens/temporary visitors lines, the immigration officer will ask for the I-94 card you filled out on the plane. The I-94 is a small white card that indicates nonimmigrant status category (F-1 student or J-1 exchange visitor) and contains an 11-digit "Admission Number" in the upper left corner, which you may need for work or social security purposes. You must surrender the I-94 when you depart the U.S., even for a short trip. You will get a new I-94 card each time you enter the U.S.

2. U.S. Immigration Officers at the Airport

You will have to go through a series of steps when speaking with the immigration officer. The immigration officer most likely will:

a. Ask to see your visa, and ask about your school, your financial sponsor, or other matters;

b. "Admit" you to the U.S. by notating your I-20 or DS-2019 form with "Duration of Stay" (D/S);

c. Electronically report your arrival to SEVIS;

d. Add information to your I-94, including how long you may stay in the U.S., and:[1]

 • Your category of nonimmigrant student visa (F-1 or J-1)

 • Your U.S. arrival date

 • The name of the city where you entered

 • The amount of time you may remain in the U.S.;

e. Staple your I-94 into your passport; and

f. Return your passport and I-94 to you.

---

1. If the immigration officer marks "D/S — Duration of Stay" on your I-94, then you may remain in the U.S. for as long as you maintain your student status; that is, as long as you remain enrolled full time, make normal academic progress, and your I-20 (F-1) or DS-2019 (J-1) form has not expired. In some situations the U.S. immigration officer may write a specific date on your I-94 card, by which time you must depart the U.S.

Student Visas

If you are in the NSEERS line, the Immigration Officer may stamp "NSEERS Registrant" on your I-94 card and indicate that you are subject to "Special Registration," which is a security program instituted after 9/11 for certain non-immigrants based on criteria such as nationality (www.ice.gov/nseers/). This process is uncommon, and in the spring of 2011 it was said to be suspended. It requires you to use designated cities when you leave the U.S. and follow other special procedures, which you should check before you make plans to depart the U.S. You may qualify for a "waiver" of Special Registration requirements.

Source: www.uscis.gov/portal/site/uscis/menuitem.eb1d4c2a3e5b9ac89243c6a7543f6d1a/?vgnextoid=cd831a48b9a2e210VgnVCM100000082ca60aRCRD&vgnextchannel=cd831a48b9a2e210VgnVCM100000082ca60aRCRD

3. Three Critical Points About the I-94 Card

a. Your I-94 is important documentary evidence that you entered the U.S. legally;

b. Your I-94 and I-20 or DS-2019 (*not your visa*) indicate the amount of time you are permitted to remain legally in the U.S.; and

c. Your I-94 coupled with your I-20 or DS-2019 (*not your visa stamp!*) are documentary evidence of your F-1 or J-1 status.

C. Visa Challenges at the U.S. Airport

Things to Bring to the U.S.

- Prescription drugs (with English translations of the prescriptions), glasses, contact lenses
- Travelers checks (replaceable if lost or stolen)
- Small cash bills for incidental expenses
- Clothes suitable for your climate (but you can buy more in the U.S.)
- Hard to get items
- Bilingual dictionaries not easy to find in the U.S.
- Small tokens from home to give as gifts (small!)
- Camera (though good digital cameras are affordable in the U.S.)
- Traditional clothes from home to wear on special occasions

Student Visas

> ### Things Not to Bring to the U.S.
>
> - Over $10,000 in cash or instruments (unless you declare it at U.S. Customs when you arrive)
> - Khat, captogen, or other drugs illegal in the U.S.
> - Electrical equipment (it may not match U.S. voltage)
> - Pirated software, books, videos
> - Vegetables, meat, or soft cheeses (unless on "cleared" list — but save time by leaving it at home)
> - Items available (and maybe cheaper) in the U.S.
> - Check www.customs.gov/xp/cgov/travel

1. Post 9/11

Crossing a U.S. border has changed since 9/11. Security is tighter. People are subject to closer scrutiny. Students from certain countries may be subject to even higher scrutiny. However, this should not deter you from coming to the U.S. for your LL.M.! The U.S. wants you to study here, and wants to make that as easy as possible. Nearly everyone benefits from international education programs.

If you arrive in the U.S. with your student visa and supporting documents, and you are challenged by U.S. officials at the airport, you should follow the advice given to you by your school. That may mean telephoning a special number the school gave you. If you omitted information on your visa application or if you are violating some other law (e.g., carrying illegal substances), then your school may not be in the best position to assist you.

In most cases, you will present your documents at the U.S. port of entry, be asked a few questions, be photographed, have your fingerprints taken (without ink),[2] have your documents processed and stamped, and then be permitted to go to your campus.

For more details about entering the U.S. with a student visa, visit www.customs.gov/linkhandler/cgov/travel/id_visa/study_exchange/student_visit_prog.ctt/student_visit_prog.doc

2. Secondary Inspections

You may be selected for "secondary inspection," where officials will ask you more detailed

---

2. The U.S. collects "biometrics" (such as fingerprints) on non-citizens who enter the U.S. These help establish and verify a person's identity. Biometrics can be checked against a watch list of known or suspected terrorists, criminals, and immigration violators; be checked against all fingerprints in government files to help prevent fraud using aliases; or help determine if the person presenting a passport or other document is the correct person. Some herald biometrics as accurate, reliable, convenient (non-invasive to acquire, and easy to store and retrieve), and difficult to forge (www.dhs.gov/files/programs/gc_1208531081211.shtm). Some believe biometrics invade privacy.

Do Not Be Alarmed When Your Plane Arrives in the U.S.

- All persons entering the U.S., *including U.S. citizens*, must pass through U.S. Customs & Border Protection (CBP).
- You may be asked many questions.
- You may be searched, fingerprinted (without ink), and photographed.
- You may be asked to undergo a "secondary inspection."
- Do not take it personally if they give you extra attention — or do not come across as particularly welcoming — at the airport!
- *Do not panic*. Practice patience.

questions and probe deeper into your documents, luggage, family, background, and other issues that may not seem relevant to letting you enter the U.S. for your LL.M. Remain calm and cooperate! You are not alone in seeking entry to the U.S. You are not alone in being asked to jump extra hurdles. On a typical day, Customs and Border Protection welcomes more than 1.1 million international travelers into the U.S. at land, air, and sea ports. Even U.S. citizens are sometimes subject to secondary inspections (including on occasion the author of *LL.M. Roadmap!*).

3. Handling Questions Arising at the Airport

If questions or problems arise at the U.S. airport or during your stay in the U.S., you may seek assistance from your country's embassy in Washington, D.C.,

Documents to Bring in Your Hand Luggage on the Plane (Do Not Check These Items in Your Luggage!)

- Passport (valid for at least 6 months)
- U.S. Visa (F-1 or J-1 pasted in your passport)
- I-20 or DS-2019 (SEVIS form; sent by school)
- SEVIS receipt
- Health records (e.g., immunizations)
- Evidence of financial support (as sent to school)
- LL.M. admission letter
- Correspondence with the school (brochures, letters they sent to you)
- Emergency contact information (e.g., LL.M. school advisor, your country's embassy or consulate in the U.S., family or friend you may have in U.S.)
- Instructions on how to get from airport to school
- Airline ticket
- Photos of family, friends, your country (to share with new classmates and friends)
- Any other materials you do not want to risk losing

Student Visas

or consulate in another U.S. city. They should help you on almost any matter, particularly if you are treated improperly by U.S. officials, or if you have visa issues, financial or health problems, or complaints against the school. Your country's consular officials are in the U.S. *to assist you,* as one of their citizens. Always have their names and contact details with you (along with contact details of your law school administrators) who should all be ready and willing to assist you if issues arise.

4. Customs Officers

After you pass through immigration, you will encounter U.S. Customs officials who want to determine if you are carrying contraband. They may stop you for screening. Again, this is routine.

D. Student Responsibilities After Receiving an F-1 or J-1 Visa Stamp and Arriving in the U.S.

Your visa imposes responsibilities for you as you enter the U.S. and while you are here. If you do not fulfill these duties, you will be "out of status," you may lose your visa, and you could be deported to your home country and barred from reentering the U.S. for many years. If your school learns you have violated your student visa terms, the school is obligated to record that violation on SEVIS, which could, again, result in delays in LL.M. completion, or your being deported and barred from reentering the U.S.

E. How Long Is Your Visa Valid? How Long Can You Stay in the U.S.?

Your visa will normally be valid for the expected duration of your LL.M. program. The face of your visa will indicate a visa expiration date (and visa issuance date). The time between visa issuance and expiration dates is called your **visa validity.** *The visa validity is the length of time you are permitted to travel to a port of entry in the U.S.*

If your visa will expire before you complete your degree, *do not panic! The amount of time you may remain in the U.S. is indicated on your I-94 card with Duration of Status "D/S" coding, and is separate from your visa.*

Your visa must be valid whenever you enter the U.S., but if your I-94 and I-20 or DS-2019 are valid (that is, you remain a bona fide international student), you may stay in the U.S. legally, even if your U.S. visa expires.

If your student status remains unchanged, your visa is expired, and you would like to leave the U.S. temporarily (e.g., for a short visit home), you

How to Avoid Getting Deported Before You Finish Your LL.M. Degree

1. Report to the International Office on your campus when you arrive.
2. Keep your passport up-to-date (at least 6 months validity at all times when in U.S.).
3. Ensure your I-20 or DS-2019 are current. Do not overstay the date on your I-94.
4. Get authorization before you work. Work only where, and the number of hours, permitted.
5. Alert your school before you depart the U.S., even for short trips.
6. Present your passport, student visa, and I-94 to your school for photocopying.
7. Follow all U.S. government and law school regulations.
8. Register for LL.M. classes at the school that issued your I-20 or DS-2019.
9. Stay enrolled as a full-time student while in the U.S., and attend classes regularly.
10. Do not get suspended or expelled, or academically dismissed.
11. Maintain the LL.M. program's required GPA.
12. Ask your school to extend your I-20 or DS-2019 if you need extra time to complete your degree.
13. Inform your school of changes in address, funding source, or other important information.
14. Give your school documents of your dependents (spouse, children under 21) for copying.

Student Visas

must have a valid visa to return to the U.S. **Student visas are not issued within the U.S.**, and you may only be able to acquire a **new** visa in your home country (or in a third country). *Be sure to keep your visa and passport expiration dates in mind, especially when planning international travel and reentry.*

F. Various Visa Issues

1. Visitor Visa and F-1 or J-1

Even if you have a tourist visa or are eligible to visit the U.S. with a visa waiver, you need a student visa to study for your LL.M. degree.

2. Visa Denial

If the U.S. embassy or consulate denies your visa, it should ordinarily tell you why and should provide the reasons in writing. You may apply again if you "cure" the defect (for example, if you did not bring the correct paperwork or if you did not show sufficient proof of financial responsibility).

Student Visas

3. U.S. Arrival More Than 30 Days Before Classes Begin

If you are a new F-1 or J-1 student you *may* be able to enter the U.S. *earlier* than 30 days before your LL.M. begins if you obtain a *visitor's visa* (B-1) annotated with a "prospective student notation." You must file Form I-539 (Application for Change of Nonimmigrant Status), and obtain approval for a change. **You cannot begin your LL.M. studies until your classification change is approved by U.S. Citizenship and Immigration Services (USCIS).**

4. Make Sure Your Passport Remains Valid

Your passport must ordinarily have at least six months validity whenever you seek entry at the U.S. port for study in the U.S. If your passport might expire before you finish your LL.M., you should acquire a new passport *before* you arrive in the U.S. If you are already in the U.S. you might seek passport revalidation through your government's embassy or consulate in the U.S.

5. Document Safekeeping

Keep your passport and visa documents in a safe place. Keep photocopies in *another* safe place, separate from originals. If your documents get lost, stolen, or damaged, *do not panic* — consult your law school officials immediately.

6. Falling Out of Status

If you fall out of status, go to your LL.M. administrator, who will report you to SEVIS and will try to help get you back in status so you can graduate. Penalties for falling out of status are severe. *So do not fall out of status!*

7. Delay in LL.M. Graduation for a Semester Because You Did Not Finish Your Coursework or Thesis

If you need more time, upon your request your school may extend your I-20 or DS-2019 for up to one year without government approval. These extensions *must* be processed *before* your original I-20 or DS-2019 expires. The school cannot extend an expired I-20 or DS-2019 form. Consult your LL.M. administrators, and if you hold a J-1 visa, also consult your sponsor. With an extended I-20 or DS-2019, your F-1 or J-1 responsibilities remain.

8. Immigration Status After LL.M. Degree Completion and Graduation

F-1 status remains until you complete your LL.M. When your program ends, your I-20 program ends. After you complete your studies, you have a 60-day grace period to depart the U.S., begin OPT, or change to another immigration status ("Change of Status"). "Completion of Studies" would ordinarily be the date listed on your I-20, or the day after grades for your final semester are due (which would be after the exam period, and after the time for turning in course

Differences between F-1 and J-1 Visa Benefits and Obligations

	F-1 Visa	**J-1 Visa**
Work during LL.M.?	Yes.	Yes. Need written approval from J-1 visa sponsor.
Qualify for "economic hardship" off-campus work?	Maybe. If requirements are satisfied.	Not likely. Because J-1 sponsor covers the student's expenses, the student would not likely qualify for "hardship" off-campus work.
Work in U.S. postdegree?	Yes. F-1 students can work for 12 months under Optional Practical Training (OPT).	Yes. J-1 students can work for up to 18 months under Academic Training (AT).
Dependents can join student?	Yes. F-2 dependents may enter U.S.	Yes. J-2 dependents may enter U.S.
Grace period to leave after degree?	F-1 student has 60 days. Can travel in U.S., prepare to depart.	J-1 student has 30 days postdegree. Can travel in U.S. or prepare to depart.
Student restrictions on returning to U.S. postdegree?	No.	Postdegree, may be required to return to home country for 2 years before returning to U.S.
Dependents can work?	No. F-2 dependents may not work.	Yes. J-2 dependents may apply for work authorization after arriving in U.S. May not use earnings for J-1's tuition, fees, or living expenses.
Dependents can study?	Yes. F-2 dependents may study full time or part time.	Yes. J-2 dependents may study full time or part time.
Must file U.S. tax forms?	F-1 students must file tax forms.	J-1 students must file tax forms.
Health insurance?	Usually required by the school.	Required.

Student Visas

assignments and papers). If you are on OPT, you still must comply with visa regulations. Please be certain to check current guidelines for J-1 (and F-1) visa-holders.

9. Can You Travel Outside the U.S. During Your Studies? Will It Affect Your OPT?

F-1 or J-1 students may leave the U.S. temporarily during their LL.M. Your school should endorse page 3 of your I-20 or page 1 of your DS-2019 with a "travel signature" to verify your good LL.M. program standing. When you return to the U.S. you must present your I-20 or DS-2019 with your school's travel signature and your passport.

Make sure your *visa* will be valid when you wish to return to the U.S. Sometimes visas are issued at the discretion of the U.S. visa officer for periods shorter than the I-20, and sometimes they are issued for only one entry to the U.S. (rather than for multiple entries). If your visa will be invalid when you seek to reenter the U.S., you will need a new student visa stamp, **which can be issued only at a U.S. embassy or consulate outside the U.S.** The U.S. visa officer in your home country is considered to be in the best position to determine whether you are a bona fide international student.

10. Multiple-Entry or Single-Entry Visa

Your student visa will indicate whether you may enter the U.S. one time, a fixed number of times, or unlimited times.

CHAPTER SUMMARY

- You will receive U.S. immigration documents before you depart your country and while on the plane to the U.S.

- You must learn relevant immigration rules, and follow them.

- Your school will help you comply with U.S. law and university policy.

- Thousands of international students arrive in the U.S. each year, and successfully comply with all immigration regulations. You can, too!

- Ask school officials any immigration-related question you have.

- Consult a licensed immigration attorney for issues that require legal advice.

Student Visas

Chapter 22

Working On-Campus and Off-Campus with Your Student Visa

Student Visas

CHAPTER HIGHLIGHTS

- As an F-1 or J-1 visa holder, you can work in the U.S. during your LL.M. study period under certain circumstances.
- During the academic year, most work is confined to the school campus (though in some circumstances an international student may work off-campus).
- Be certain that you understand the rules for employment authorization, and that you follow them.
- Penalties for violating student visa employment rules can be severe.

A. Student Employment: Five Options With Your Student Visa

International students in the U.S. may seek authorization to work part time during their LL.M. year. Some LL.M. students work to earn extra spending money. Others need money to help pay for living expenses, books, or tuition. Some work solely to gain U.S. work experience and do not need or require compensation.

This chapter outlines five options for international LL.M. students to be employed, pursuant to U.S. visa regulations, during your LL.M. program. Some options apply to both F-1 and J-1 visa holders. Other options apply only to F-1 students *or* J-1 exchange visitors.[1] These employment options are:

---

1. For further information, please consult your campus international office and the U.S. State Department website.

1. *On-campus part-time employment.* F-1 and J-1 students may work on-campus for up to 20 hours per week while school is in session, and up to 40 hours per week during school holiday periods, in jobs affiliated with the educational mission of the university. Students may be eligible for on-campus employment up to 30 days before their I-20 or DS-2019 start date. Eligibility for student on-campus employment ends the day students complete the LL.M. degree, even if their I-20 or DS-2109 remains valid for postcompletion practical training. (See Chapter 27.) J-1 students need permission from their sponsors to work.

2. *Optional Practical Training (OPT) for F-1 students.* This practical training applies for F-1 students only. OPT most often commences no later than 60 days after an F-1 student completes her LL.M., at which point she can work in a law-related area for up to 12 months, full time. Under some circumstances, F-1 students may commence their OPT *before* they graduate, and work part time while completing their degrees.

3. *Academic Training (AT) for J-1 students.* This practical training applies for J-1 students only. Under AT, LL.M. students may work in a law-related job, typically after they complete their LL.M., for up to 18 months (though usually for less than a year). J-1 students under some circumstances may commence AT before they graduate.

4. *Curricular Practical Training (CPT).* This practical training applies for F-1 students only. Under CPT, students may work full-time or part-time in a law-related job *during* their LL.M. The training must be an "integral part" of the curriculum required for the LL.M. degree, must be completed *for credit*, and as a general rule is available *only* after the student has been a part of the LL.M. program for at least nine months. Law internships could qualify for CPT.[2] For LL.M. students, a CPT placement does not usually affect eligibility for the one-year OPT permitted after graduation.

5. *Economic Hardship (EH).* This applies to F-1 and J-1 visa holders who experience unexpected extreme economic or financial hardship. If EH status is granted, the student is permitted to work off-campus. J-1 students would ordinarily not qualify because their U.S. government or other sponsors are expected to ensure that the student does not have extreme economic or financial hardship. F-1 students are typically self-financed, and may be more subject to financial hardship in cases such as currency devaluation or a sponsor's death. In all cases, it is difficult for a student to qualify for economic hardship because the standards are stringent, including a requirement that students show that earning compensation through on-campus employment would not be adequate.

---

2. **Golden Gate University**'s standard form and procedure for LL.M. and S.J.D. students wishing to participate in CPT can be found online (http://tinyurl.com/ggulawcpt).

B. On-Campus Employment with an F-1 or J-1 Visa

Both F-1 and J-1 students are permitted to work "on-campus" while studying for their LL.M. degrees. They may work for one or more jobs simultaneously, part time — up to 20 hours per week — during school terms, and up to 40 hours per week during holidays and other school breaks. Guidelines for on-campus employment (which can be found in U.S. Code of Federal Regulation at 8 CFR 214.2(f)(9)(i)) include:

1. *"On-Campus" position involving "student services."* F-1 or J-1 students must work "on campus," generally meaning "physically" on the campus. "Student services" work includes such positions as library staff, research assistant for professors,[3] bookstore clerk, food service, lab worker, tutor, or teaching assistant. It *would not* include construction work, for instance, even if it were done on the campus, because that *would not* involve student services. It *would* include on-campus work for a commercial business, like a bookstore or cafeteria, if that job provides student services.

2. *"Off-campus" position involving "student services."* A student may work physically off-campus if the job is "educationally affiliated" with your school. For example, you may work for a school-affiliated law clinic or office if it is off-campus, so long as the clinic or office is "educationally affiliated." If the company is not "educationally affiliated" — such as a food service company — you can work for the company on-campus, but not at an off-campus location.

3. *Impact on U.S. citizens.* The F-1 or J-1 student's work may not displace a U.S. citizen or lawful permanent resident.

4. *Process.* The student's prospective employer should give the student an employment letter. The law school's designated school official (DSO) will then give the student a certification letter stating the job title or description, start date, number of work hours, and supervisor's name and telephone number. The student will take these and his or her immigration documents to the local Social Security Administration Office to secure a Social Security card.

5. *Rule changes.* These regulations are subject to change. *Please check with your school for up-to-date regulations as soon as you decide you want to work.*

---

3. Law professors have funds available to hire LL.M. students as research assistants. Students *are not* obligated to serve as a professor's research assistant (RA) *as a volunteer* — without pay — no matter how valuable the experience may be for the students. If a professor asks you to work, you should acquire a Social Security number, and generally you should be paid. You are *not* entitled to pay, however, if you receive academic credit, pro bono credit, or another type of school-related credit for that work.

C. Off-Campus Work — Permitted Under Four Circumstances

Four situations exist in which F-1 and J-1 students may work off-campus during their LL.M. study period: (1) the work involves *student services*; (2) the student encounters *severe economic hardship* occurring subsequent to a student's enrollment; (3) the government declares *emergent circumstances*; or (4) the student commences *practical training (OPT, CPT or AT) pre-graduation.*

1. **"Off-campus" work involving "student services."** As described above, an LL.M. student may work off campus at an "educationally affiliated" position, including, for example, work for a school-affiliated legal aid clinic or office located off campus.

2. *Severe economic hardship.* If a student (usually F-1) experiences unexpected circumstances beyond the student's control that have created severe economic hardship, the student may work off-campus at a job unrelated to his LL.M. program. You *may* qualify for economic hardship permission to work off campus *if you satisfy one or more of the following criteria*:

   • You lose financial aid or on-campus employment (if it is not your fault); *or*

   • You have large increases in tuition or living costs; *or*

   • The relative value of currency you depend on to pay expenses substantially decreases; *or*

   • The financial conditions for your sources of financial support unexpectedly change; *or*

   • You have unexpectedly large medical bills not covered by insurance; *or*

   • You have other substantial, unexpected expenses.

   If you meet *one* of the criteria above, you must also meet *all* the following conditions:

   • You have been enrolled for at least one academic year; *and*

   • You are enrolled in a full course of study; *and*

   • You are in good academic standing; *and*

   • Working will not adversely impact your ability to attend school full-time and maintain good academic standing; *and*

   • You cannot get on-campus employment, or the pay from on-campus employment is insufficient to meet your financial needs.

   If you satisfy the above, your law school *may* recommend you for economic hardship and endorse your I-20 form for adjudication by a U.S. Citizenship and Immigration Services (USCIS) Service Center. You must file Form I-765 and pay a fee to USCIS within 30 days of the Form I-20 endorsement. If the application is approved, you will receive an Employment Authorization Document (EAD) work permit card, and can begin working off campus up to 20 hours per week during school periods, and up to 40 hours per week during summer and winter breaks. The approval will be valid for one year. If your need continues beyond that one-year period, you must reapply to USCIS for economic hardship. You can learn the status of your employment authorization application by checking https://egov.uscis.gov/cris/ Dashboard.do using your USCIS application receipt number. **If you engage in unauthorized employment, the law school may terminate your SEVIS record, and you will be "out of status" and subject to deportation and/or a bar from reentering the U.S. for three to ten years.**

3. *Emergent circumstances (also known as "special student relief")*. If a world event adversely impacts a group of non-immigrants (including students on F-1 or J-1 visas), the government may grant special relief by waiving certain restrictions for affected students. This could include, for example, if an earthquake or tsunami causes devastation in your home country and your family cannot support you as planned, and your country is included in an official U.S. government notice. In September 2010 the government granted special student relief to F-1 Haitian students who suffered severe economic hardship resulting from the January 2010 earthquake in Haiti. A similar example is the March 2011 earthquake and tsunami in Japan. Furthermore, on June 10, 2011, the U.S. announced special relief for certain F-1 Libyan students who suffered economic hardship as a direct result of the civil unrest in Libya since February 2011.

Emergent Circumstances — Japan
USCIS Reminds Japanese Nationals Impacted by Recent Disaster of Available Immigration Benefits (March 17, 2011)

WASHINGTON — In light of the recent earthquakes and tsunami in Japan, U.S. Citizenship and Immigration Services (USCIS) reminds Japanese nationals of certain U.S. immigration benefits available upon request.

USCIS understands that a natural disaster can affect an individual's ability to establish or maintain lawful immigration status. Temporary relief measures available to eligible nationals of Japan may include:

• The grant of an application for change or extension of nonimmigrant status for an individual currently in the United States, even when the request is filed after the authorized period of admission has expired. . . .
• Expedited adjudication and approval, where possible, of requests for off-campus employment authorization for F-1 students experiencing severe economic hardship [and] . . .
• Expedited employment authorization where appropriate."

Source: www.uscis.gov/portal/site/uscis/menuitem.5af9bb95919f35e66f614176543f6d1a/? vgnextoid=d219c337ab5ce210VgnVCM100000082ca60aRCRD&vgnextchannel= 68439c7755cb9010VgnVCM10000045f3d6a1RCRD

Student Visas

> ### U.S. Granted Emergent Circumstances ("Special Student Relief") to F-1 students from Haiti Affected by January 2010 Earthquake (ICE E-Mail of September 14, 2010)
>
> WASHINGTON, DC—[ICE] has announced special relief for certain F-1 Haitian students who have suffered severe economic hardship as a result of the January 12, 2010 earthquake in Haiti. This relief applies only to students who were lawfully present in the United States in F-1 status on January 12, 2010, and enrolled in an institution that is certified by U.S. Immigration and Customs Enforcement's (ICE) Student and Exchange Visitor Program.
>
> The suspension of certain regulatory requirements . . . allows eligible Haitian F-1 students to obtain employment authorization, work an increased number of hours during the school term, and, if necessary, reduce their course load while continuing to maintain their F-1 student status.

Source: www.ice.gov/news/library/factsheets/haitian-students.htm

4. *Pre-completion OPT or AT (on-campus or off-campus).* Generally, a student's OPT or AT period commences after the student's LL.M. program is finished. However, F-1 and J-1 students may apply to commence practical training *during* their academic program, rather than wait to begin until after they graduate. In these instances, the student is still limited to 20 hours per week, but she can perform law-related work off-campus. The amount of permissible practical training post-LL.M. is decreased based on a formula that takes into account the amount of time the student is engaged in precompletion training.

U.S. Work Authorization in Conjunction with a Student Visa and Poststudent Visa Stage

Chart items (a)–(e) are in conjunction with student visas. Chart items (f)–(g) are only available *after* graduation but *not* in conjunction with a student visa. (See Chapter 27.)

	Can Work *Before* Degree Completion?	Can Work *After* Completing Degree?	Can Work Off-Campus?	For F-1	For J-1
(a) On-Campus Part-Time Employment	Yes, 20 hours per week during classes; 40 hours per week during breaks.	Yes, but *not* as a student after LL.M. is complete.	N/A	Yes.	Yes.[1]

(continued on next page)

	Can Work *Before* Degree Completion?	Can Work *After* Completing Degree?	Can Work Off-Campus?	For F-1	For J-1
(b) Economic Hardship	Yes. May work off-campus if student experiences unexpected extreme financial hardship.	No. Must be current student.	Yes.	Yes.	Yes.[2]
(c) Curricular Practical Training (CPT)	Yes. If work is "integral part" of LL.M. degree program. For law-related work required to receive your degree.	No. Must be current student.	Yes.	Yes.	Yes.
(d) Academic Training (AT)	Yes, 20 hours per week during classes; 40 hours per week during breaks and after completing degree.	Yes. Up to 18 months post-LL.M.[3]	Yes.	N/A	Yes.
(e) Optional Practical Training (OPT)	Yes, 20 hours per week during classes; 40 hours per week during breaks and after completing degree.	Yes. Up to 12 months post-LL.M.[4]	Yes.	Yes.	N/A
(f) H-1 Visa	No. This visa is not for current students. A company in the U.S. may petition the U.S. for a non-citizen to work in the U.S.	Yes. For 3 years. May extend to 6 years.	Yes.	N/A	N/A
(g) Labor Certification	No. This visa is not for current students. Employers may hire foreigners for U.S. work if the U.S. Labor Department certifies that no qualified U.S. workers are able, willing, qualified, and available to	Yes.	Yes.	N/A	N/A

Student Visas

(continued on next page)

	Can Work *Before* Degree Completion?	Can Work *After* Completing Degree?	Can Work Off-Campus?	For F-1	For J-1
accept the job at the prevailing wage in the area of intended employment, and the work will not adversely affect the wages and working conditions of similarly employed U.S. workers.					

[1]J-1 students ordinarily would not qualify, because sponsors should be providing funds.
[2]J-1 students ordinarily would not qualify, because sponsors should be providing funds.
[3]Deduct from 18 months a period based on time you worked at AT before you graduated.
[4]Deduct from 12 months a period based on time you worked at OPT before you graduated.

D. Social Security Number for F-1 and J-1 Students

If an F-1 or J-1 student is authorized to work in the U.S., she or he may secure a Social Security number, which is an accounting mechanism used to report an individual's wages to the government and to determine a person's eligibility for Social Security benefits. Some students get a part-time job solely to establish eligibility for a Social Security number, even though a Social Security number is needed and used only for work purposes. If you want an "official government number" for other purposes, the Internal Revenue Service (IRS) may issue you an *Individual Taxpayer Identification Number (TIN)*.

E. Curricular Practical Training (CPT)

Homeland Security permits students on visas to gain practical law work experience, on-campus or off-campus, in a curricular practical training (CPT) program that is an "integral part of an established curriculum" (8 CFR 214.2(f)(10)(i)). CPT is defined as an "alternative work/study, internship, cooperative education, or any other type of required internship or practicum that is offered by sponsoring employers through cooperative agreements with the school." To qualify for CPT you must meet these criteria:

1. You work in an internship or practicum in your LL.M. degree program approved by your law school faculty or DSO;
2. The CPT work fulfills the requirements of an LL.M. course you enroll in;

3. You register for an LL.M. course or thesis, and your work benefits your course or thesis in a material and substantial way;

4. You have been a full-time student for at least one full academic year in the U.S. (unless your school makes use of the federal regulations exception permitting "immediate participation," which allows LL.M. students to qualify during their first semester, because the LL.M. program is typically only two semesters long); and

5. You have an employer's offer letter containing the employer's name and address, job title and description, the job's start and end dates, and the number of hours of work per week the work will entail.

CHAPTER SUMMARY

- LL.M. students who hold F-1 or J-1 visas may engage in law-related work.

- Students may work up to 20 hours per week during class periods, and up to 40 hours per week during school breaks.

- Make sure you understand the employment authorization rules, and follow them.

- The penalties for violating U.S. work regulations are severe. However, it is easy to comply with these simple rules!

Student Visas

Part VI

How Will I Pay for My U.S. Law Degree?

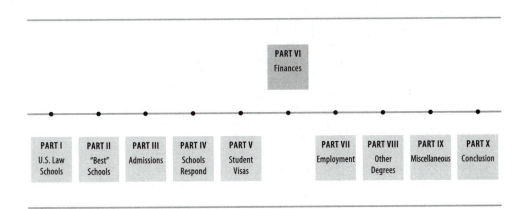

PART VI
Finances

PART I
U.S. Law
Schools

PART II
"Best"
Schools

PART III
Admissions

PART IV
Schools
Respond

PART V
Student
Visas

PART VII
Employment

PART VIII
Other
Degrees

PART IX
Miscellaneous

PART X
Conclusion

Chapter 23

LL.M. Degree Costs
Hidden Expenses, Cutting Costs, and Saving Money

CHAPTER HIGHLIGHTS

- Getting an LL.M. degree in the U.S. is not cheap.
- Although not all students can afford all the costs associated with an LL.M. degree, there are many ways to help secure funding.
- There are sometimes "hidden" costs associated with obtaining an LL.M. degree. The figures appearing on a school's website may not include all the costs.
- This chapter discusses hidden expenses, how to cut costs, and how to save money.

A. Introduction

1. LL.M. Finances

Law school in the U.S. is expensive. This is not a secret.[1] On the bright side, as *LL.M. Roadmap* discusses elsewhere, there are many ways to help cover international LL.M. student costs.[2] This chapter discusses LL.M. costs, divided into seven general categories:

(a) *LL.M. application costs* (pre-application and application costs)
(b) *Travel to and from the U.S.* (including visa fees)

---

1. The ABA Law School Division's Legal Education and Admissions to the Bar section recognizes that "[o]btaining a degree from an ABA-accredited law school is not cheap" (November 2009) (ABA, *The Value Proposition of Attending Law School*, www.abanet.org/lsd/legaled/value.pdf).
2. Paying for an LL.M. degree is discussed in Chapter 22 (working while enrolled); Chapter 24 (scholarships, grants, and fellowships); Chapter 25 (loans); Chapter 27 (practical training); and Chapter 28 (practicing law in the U.S.).

(c) *Tuition and school fees* (including books and laptops)

(d) *Living expenses in the U.S.*

(e) *U.S. employment costs* (during period of study and postdegree)

(f) *Costs of applying to S.J.D. or other law or non-law programs post-LL.M.*

(g) *Entertainment*

2. How to Survive By Cutting Costs and Saving Money

This chapter also examines and offers tips on cost-cutting and money-saving before you apply, while applying, while in school, and postdegree.

B. Seven Cost Categories

The seven categories of costs overlap, and are not rigid. Fortunately, not every applicant or student will face all the expenses at the levels described. Actual expenses differ based on where you live when you apply; to which schools you apply and to how many; the living costs in the U.S. city where your school is located; and other factors.

Not everyone can avail themselves of the cost-cutting methods mentioned below . . . you will not be able to ride a bike to class to save money in the middle of snowstorms in the Northeast or Midwest. But you certainly can and must plan well. Your ability to predict likely costs and savings depends in part on how transparently your school outlines expected costs when they publish cost of attendance figures, or whether they have excessive hidden costs that you may not discover, or think about, until you arrive on campus.

While family or other personal resources, scholarships, or grants may help make financial issues easier to handle, they will not change the actual costs. An LL.M. in the U.S. is expensive, irrespective of how you acquire the funds to pay for it.

1. Preapplication and Application Costs of Applying for an LL.M.

There are many direct and indirect expenses associated with applying to an LL.M. program. The actual application fee is only a small portion of the costs associated with the LL.M. preapplication and application process.

a. **Miscellaneous Preapplication Costs**
(1) Translating your transcript, diploma and other documents into English.
(2) Travel to, and use of, libraries for information.
(3) Acquiring a comprehensive, authoritative guide or handbook to LL.M. programs in the U.S. (such as *LL.M. Roadmap*).
(4) Costs to surf the Internet to gather LL.M. program information.
(5) Costs to use English language educational centers in your home country.
(6) Travel to and from the U.S. embassy or consulate for information.

b. **English Language Proficiency Tests (Preapplication)**
(1) Cambridge ILEC (£253 [British pounds]); IELTS (up to U.S. $185); PTE Academic (U.S. $170-250); TOEFL (U.S. $165-225);
(2) Courses or tutoring to prepare you for English language proficiency tests.
(3) If you live far from the test site, you might have to pay for transportation, hotel, and food.

c. **Application Fees**
(1) The average LL.M. application fee is about U.S. $50 (although one school charges U.S. $105!).
(2) Photocopying materials associated with the application (see above).

d. **Transmitting Application to the School**
(1) Speedy delivery can be expensive. Some schools permit online applications. (See the text box on this page for additional transmittal options.)

Transmitting Applications to the School — Options

1. **Online.** Submit applications online (though you still must send document originals later).
2. **Hand delivery.** Maybe a friend or family member can carry your application to the school.
3. **Law school representative.** Submit to law school representative who is visiting your city or country (law school representatives often travel to recruit, and for conferences).
4. **Post or speedy deliver.** Post documents. Make sure you can trace the shipment.
5. **Student's educational agent.** Submit application to an agent *working for the student*.
6. **School's educational agent.** Submit application to an agent *working for the school*.

e. Authenticating, Notarizing, or Certifying Applications Materials (See Chapter 13)

(1) Many LL.M. programs require you to submit application materials through a credential verification service that collects, authenticates, and processes transcripts, English language proficiency test scores, and other documents. These firms charge applicants a fee. (See Chapter 13.)

f. Educational Agent and LL.M. Consultant Fees (See Chapter 8)

(1) If you hire an educational agent or LL.M. consultant to help you in the LL.M. admission process, you will have to pay.

(2) Fees vary from country to country, and among different agents and consultants. Fees also vary based on the range of services provided on your behalf.

g. Costs Pending Scholarship Awards (See Chapter 24)

(1) Some scholarships are not awarded until an applicant is accepted into an LL.M. program. However, a highly qualified applicant may not have funds to pay costs associated with applying, such as application fees, English language proficiency test fees, or travel fare to the city where tests are offered. You can explain to scholarship grantors that you need funds to apply to LL.M. programs: ask if they can grant you a small amount for applications.

(2) Ask LL.M. programs to waive your application fee.

(3) Ask the EducationUSA Advisor at a U.S. embassy or consulate for an "Opportunity Grant" or "Gap Grant" to help you cover these expenses. (See Chapter 24 for other suggestions.)

h. Costs Associated with Recommendation Letters

(1) You may pay postage to send recommendation forms to your referees and referees' letters to the U.S.

2. Costs Associated with Visas and Travel to and from the U.S.

a. Passport

You will need to have a valid passport issued by your home government. If you already have a passport, you may need to acquire a new one if the current passport is set to expire soon. Generally, you would need at least six months validity remaining in your passport when you enter the U.S. to study. But it would probably be a good idea to renew or extend your passport before you apply for your U.S. visa, if possible, so you will not have to worry about renewing or extending it once you are in the U.S.

b. U.S. Visa Application Fee

The current U.S. visa "application" fee is U.S. $131. All students must pay an "application" fee even if there is no visa "issuance" fee.

c. U.S. Visa Issuance Fee

If a foreign government charges U.S. students a "visa issuance fee," the U.S. will charge students from that country a reciprocal visa issuance fee. This fee is in addition to the visa application fee, which all students must pay. These reciprocity fees can be U.S. $250 or higher. The U.S. government "reciprocity schedule" can be found at http://travel.state.gov/visa/fees/fees_3272.html.

d. Other Costs Associated with Getting a Student Visa

(1)   If your home city is far from the U.S. embassy or consulate, you will need to travel for your visa interview, and possibly spend the night away from home. This is particularly so if there is no U.S. embassy or consulate in your country and you need to travel to a third country to acquire your U.S. visa. If the consular officer requests additional information, you may need to return on a different day. You may incur costs for plane or train fare, hotel, and food. You may have to pay for the embassy or consulate to send your passport and visa back to you in your home city via post.

(2)   **SEVIS Fee**
   - You must pay a SEVIS fee before going to your visa interview.
   - SEVIS fees are currently U.S. $200 for an F-1 visa and U.S. $180 for a J-1 visa.
   - The SEVIS fee is in addition to the visa application or visa issuance fees.

(3)   **Postage.** It can be expensive to post your application materials to the school.

(4)   **Air Ticket.** Round-trip air tickets to the U.S. can be expensive.

3. Costs of Tuition and Mandatory School Fees

a. Tuition

At some schools all LL.M. students pay the same tuition rate, whether the student is a U.S. citizen or a foreign national, and regardless of whether the student is a "resident" of the state where the school is located. At some "state schools" ("public schools"), students who are "residents" of the state may pay a lower rate than students who are residents of other states or other countries. Generally, to be a "resident" for tuition purposes you must be a U.S. citizen, legal permanent resident, or be otherwise granted indefinite stay in the U.S. You do not become a "resident" simply because you live in the state to attend school.

b. Books

Book costs vary based on which courses you take, how many courses you take, and how many and what types of books the professor requires. Books are expensive generally, and the more books you have to buy the greater your book costs.

c. Special Course Fee

Such fees are not unknown. For example, **Houston** charges a "Legal Research & Writing Fee."

d. Other Fees

In addition to tuition, some schools charge athletic, library, technology, and other fees. Students frequently complain, particularly if they do not use the corresponding services. Why pay an athletic fee if they do not use the gym?

e. Health Insurance

Most schools require LL.M. students to have health insurance, which you may purchase through the school or independently.

f. Vaccinations

Virtually all international students are required to be inoculated against certain diseases and must produce a certificate to that effect either before they arrive on campus or soon after.

g. Laptops

(1) *Required laptops.* Virtually all law students (LL.M., J.D., S.J.D.) have laptops. Some schools, such as **Wake Forest**, require *all LL.M.* students to have laptops. Make sure any laptop you bring from your home country is based on U.S. English operating systems so that your U.S. school can support you on technology issues. **It is safest to acquire a laptop in the U.S.** Get laptop theft and damage insurance.

(2) *Laptop and other supplies.* Students need USB drives, pens, pencils, and paper. A small printer for your apartment may be useful.[3]

4. Living Expenses in the U.S.

a. Housing

At universities in many countries students can live in campus dormitories or student hostels. Many U.S. law schools have no such facilities available for international LL.M. students, who must live in private off-campus apartments. This can be expensive. The law school administration or housing office should help you find an apartment. Be aware that some landlords require renters to pay two or more months rent when they sign the lease. The landlord will most likely hold a portion of that payment as a "security deposit," to be used to cover the costs of any cleanup, damage repair, or other expenses at the end of the year when you are preparing to move out.

---

3. Schools may permit you to print or photocopy a certain number of pages using school printers. **Wake Forest** allots each LL.M. student 1,000 pages per semester.

b. Utilities

In addition to rent, you may have to pay for the gas (or other fuel), electricity, and water you use in the apartment, plus an optional Internet or cable connection. Utilities such as electricity can be expensive if your school is in a warm city (where you pay for electric air conditioning) or if you are in a cold city (where you pay for electric heat, or any other heating fuel, like oil or gas). Your best bet is to try to find a landlord who will include some, if not all, of these utilities.

c. Deposits for Utilities

Some utility companies will require you to pay a deposit before your utilities (e.g., gas, electricity, water) are turned on in your apartment. Often, a deposit is required when an individual has never had an open account with the utility company or has a limited or poor credit history in the U.S. The deposit will be used to pay for your last bill of the year, or will be put toward any outstanding bills after you vacate the apartment.

d. Transportation

You may use a bicycle, car, bus, train, or subway to get from your apartment to school and back, and to get around in your city. If you buy a car, you must also pay for insurance, registration, and license plates. You may also need to pay for a vehicle inspection and any applicable taxes, depending on the laws of the state where your school is located. Also, don't forget about gas and any maintenance costs, such as oil changes, and any parking permits required by your school or possibly the neighborhood in which you live. Some schools, such as **Pace** and **McGeorge**, offer free campus parking for LL.M. students.

e. Food

You need not eat at restaurants every night. (*This is expensive!*) But you must eat somewhere—at your apartment, using a campus meal plan, or at the homes of new-found friends.

f. State-Issued Identity Card

Each person in the U.S. must produce identification if a police officer requests it. A state-issued ID card or driver's license is adequate. Your school ID will likely be issued free of charge, but other IDs issued by the state will cost money.

g. Personal Expenses

You will purchase clothes, toiletries, and other items throughout the year. These items add up. You may need clothes for seasons you have not experienced before. If you are from the tropics, you may not own the wool sweaters, warm coat, scarves, and gloves needed if your law school is in the Northeast or Midwest.

Finances

h. Medical Expenses

You may have unexpected medical expenses. Set aside a prudent reserve for this possibility or other unexpected expenditures that may come up.

i. Telephone

Which LL.M. student does not have a handheld communication device?

j. Dependents

You may have expenses associated with a spouse, partner, or child who is with you in the U.S. Some such expenses are predictable. Many can be unexpected (health care expenses, and education expenses if the dependents enroll in a U.S. school).

5. Costs Associated with Postdegree Employment in the U.S.

a. Employment Authorization Document (EAD)

For Optional Practical Training (OPT) during or post-LL.M., you must pay an EAD application fee of U.S. $380. *If you lose your EAD card you will have to pay an additional U.S. $380* (www.uscis.gov/files/form/i-765.pdf). (See Chapter 27.)

b. Joining Professional Organizations

Membership fees might be charged for legal organizations you join to network as you seek employment opportunities.

c. Student Organization Fees

Student organizations often charge small membership fees (U.S. $10 or $20 per year).

d. Faxes

On occasion, you might have to pay a fax charge to send a resume, writing sample, or official document.

e. Postage

Some schools will pay postage for your application packages to prospective employers. This can get expensive if you send copies of law review articles and writing samples along with your resume and cover letter. You may need to send these materials by overnight delivery, which is more expensive than regular post.

f. CVs, Resumes, and Writing Samples

Your law school will likely provide you with a reasonable supply of plain, white photocopy paper free of charge, on which you could print your CV, cover letter, and other documents. If you want bond or other high-quality paper for your CV, you may have to pay for this on your own.

g. Color Printing

You might want to photocopy (in color) your transcripts, diplomas, newspaper articles about or by you, or other documents before you send them to prospective employers. Ask your school if they will pay.

h. LL.M. Job Fairs

These fairs are held throughout the U.S. You (or your school) may have to pay a fee to participate. You may have to travel to the city where the fair is, pay for a hotel, food, and local transportation. (See Chapter 26.)

i. Professional Attire

You cannot wear "regular" law school clothes to job interviews, job fairs, conferences, internships, or work. Many LL.M. students "update" their wardrobes in the U.S., and purchase new business attire.

6. Costs Associated with Applying for Other Non-LL.M. Degrees

(a) S.J.D. application fee
(b) J.D. application fee (and LSAT fee if the LSAT is not waived)
(c) Application fee for other degree programs
(d) GRE, GMAT, or other graduate program tests
(e) Postage (particularly if you are applying for a degree outside the U.S.)

7. Entertainment

a. Have Some Fun!

International LL.M. students should not spend all of their time studying! Have fun outside of the classroom and away from the law school. Life will be more balanced and enjoyable — and you will work better!

b. Local Fun

Many cities where LL.M. programs are located have many attractions. Enjoy!

c. Explore the U.S.

Visit other states and cities. The U.S. is a huge country with much to offer. From Maine to California, Florida to Hawaii — there is a lot to see and do!

d. Entertainment Expenses

Your entertainment expenses will depend on what you choose to do. But please include in your budget extra money for nonacademic fun!

C. How to Pay for These Costs

(1)   Family and personal savings.
(2)   Employers — corporations, government, university, law firms, NGOs.

(3) U.S. law school LL.M. "tuition discounts" (scholarships). (It is possible that no two LL.M. students will pay precisely the same amount of tuition because a school may offer "tuition discounts" in different amounts to all students. Schools may also offer "endowed scholarships.") (See Chapter 24.)

(4) Scholarships from government ministries, foundations, NGOs. (See Chapter 24.)

(5) On-campus employment while enrolled. (See Chapter 22.)[4]

(6) Off-campus employment while enrolled (if emergency). (See Chapter 22.)

(7) Loans. (See Chapter 25.)

(8) The EducationUSA Advisor at a U.S. embassy or consulate may provide you with an "Opportunity Grant" or "Gap Grant" to help pay your expenses. (See Chapter 24.)

(9) Remember that receiving an LL.M. is an investment in your future. This recognition may make it easier for you (and your family) to justify sacrifices you may make to join an LL.M. program in the U.S.

D. Tips on How to Save Money and Budget as an LL.M. Student

LL.M. students always look for ways to save money and to stretch their limited dollars. Some tips from students (and professors) from throughout the years include:

1. Create a Budget

(a) Include larger items (tuition, housing, food).
(b) Include smaller items (inexpensive entertainment).
(c) Include unexpected expenses (replacement iPod or running shoes).
(d) Allow a little extra cushion—just in case.
(e) And again, do not forget to treat yourself every once in a while!

2. Stick to Your Budget!

(a) If you stray, do not fret. Go back to the budget *immediately*.

---

4. The **University of Washington** LL.M. program notes that international LL.M. students are "automatically considered for tuition waivers and paid research positions" and "[s]tudents in exceptional financial need may submit a statement indicating this with their application."

3. Hand-Me-Downs

(a) **LL.M. office "inventory" or "warehouse."** When LL.M. students arrive from overseas, they need basic supplies for their apartments, such as linens, kitchen supplies, furniture, and other items they did not bring from home. At the end of each year, graduating LL.M. students want to dispose of the linens, kitchen supplies, furniture, and other items they no longer need. Some schools have a "warehouse" where outgoing students can donate their items to incoming LL.M. students, providing a great service to the next group of incoming students. Ask your school if it has such a warehouse. It can save money.

4. Books and Supplies

(a) *Buy used textbooks.* Law professors often announce early which textbooks you need for their classes. Check course webpages. You can purchase used textbooks from students who took the course previously, from campus and community bookstores, or online.

(b) *Books on library reserve.* Ask professors if they will put books on reserve (meaning that the book is held behind the law library's circulation desk, and students may borrow the book for a few hours at a time).

(c) *"Share" books with other students.* If your class only meets once or twice per week, you and classmates might "share" a textbook, with each student using the book at different times. Ask your professor first, because the professor may require students to each have a copy during each class session. You may need the book if the final exam is "open book" (meaning you can bring the book to the exam).

5. Food

(a) *Cook.* Buy groceries you can cook and eat in your dorm room or apartment. This is much cheaper than eating at restaurants or even campus cafeterias.

(b) *Bring your lunch.* A salad or sandwich you make at home saves money.

6. Housing and Furnishings

(a) *Live near campus and walk or bike.* If housing costs near school are reasonable, you might live nearby and walk or bike to school. Walking is good exercise. So is bicycling. You can sell your bike to another student or someone else at the end of the year.

(b) *Live far from campus and take public transportation.* If housing is expensive near school, you might live far away and use public transportation to get to school.

Finances

(c) *Purchase used furniture.* You may find high-quality used furniture at stores such as Goodwill or the Salvation Army.

(d) *Used furniture — from school.* Ask if your school has a "warehouse" where graduating LL.M. students donate household items that are given to the next year's incoming LL.M. students.

(e) *Roommates.* Share housing, which will cut household expenditures. But be careful, and selective, in choosing with whom you might live. You do not have to be friends — but try to find a no-drama, responsible person.

7. Student "Discounts" on Public Transportation

(a) Ride the free campus bus to school.

(b) Ride the city bus and take advantage of the student discount that some cities provide to students who have school IDs.

(c) Subways are not available in all cities, or to all areas within each city, but if you live on a subway route, chances are it will be cost effective for you to take the subway to and from school. Look for an apartment on a subway line, near a stop that connects with stops near the school. (It is possible to live further from school in an apartment that is nicer and cheaper than the more expensive ones near campus *and* be closer to school in terms of commuting time.)

(d) Walk! It is great exercise, and good for thinking — and it is excellent, economical time management because you can combine your daily commuting and exercise routines.

(e) Biking can be great exercise. Many campuses have bike racks where you can lock your bike, and shower facilities where you can clean up before class.

(f) Carpool. Share rides to school with other students, campus staff, professors, and others who live near you who work near your school. It is practical, and regular social contact is vital.

(g) Students may be able to buy weekly or monthly discount public transportation passes.

8. Phone

(a) You can choose from many U.S. companies with many calling plans at different costs. Learn about Skype or other free call services.

9. Entertainment

(a) *Cable television.* If you have a television in your apartment, *do not pay extra for cable!* (You will be too busy studying, right?)

(b) *Enjoy on-campus entertainment.* Campuses often have lectures, movies, plays, student language tables, cultural and arts events, and other events. Access all listings and take advantage.

(c) *Law school library.* You never need to buy books (except textbooks). Your library has plenty you can borrow. Many law school libraries also have movies (DVDs and maybe even VHS tapes), and not just courtroom dramas.

(d) *Public library.* Public libraries in most communities offer some free services.

(e) *Museums.* Museums often offer student discounts or free admission.

(f) *Sports.* Sporting events often offer student discounts.

10. Medical

(a) Check with the campus infirmary or health center if you need medical items, as they may provide some items as part of your health insurance.

11. Finances

(a) *Fee-free accounts.* Choose a bank that does not charge for checking accounts (current accounts). If there is a charge for writing checks, perhaps you can do free money transfers from your U.S. savings account without having to write checks.

(b) *Debit card.* Some banks will issue you a debit card, which can be used at retail establishments as though it were a credit card, except the funds are debited directly from your account immediately after the transaction. Be careful that you are not charged a fee to use your debit card in this fashion.

12. Professional and Trade Publications

(a) *Journals.* Journals of the *American Bar Association*, the *National Bar Association*, the *International Bar Association*, and other professional groups provide interesting insights, job leads, and career advice. Subscriptions may be expensive. Use your law school library's subscriptions to these and other publications, or view them online.

13. Coupons and Discount Cards

(a) *Coupons for city and online use.* Discount coupons are available for restaurants, dry cleaners, grocery stores, electronics dealers, textbooks, and many other products and services.

(b) *School ID discounts.* School IDs are often valid for discounts at drugstores, barbershops, restaurants, and other outlets located near the school. Some school IDs are valid for bargains on local bus or taxi transportation, AAA, eyeglasses, or even for big-ticket items such as automobiles or apartment rentals.

(c) *Discount stores.* Many stores sell most of their items at "discount prices" — for less money than at other retail stores. Some of these stores sell new items. Others sell slightly damaged goods, but still new. Yet others sell secondhand goods that have been donated, with proceeds going to charity. If you did not have a heavy winter coat to bring from Singapore or Riyadh to New York or Boston, you can buy one at Salvation Army or Goodwill and donate it back, or donate it to other incoming LL.M. students . . . after the snow stops.

(d) *AAA card or AARP card.* "Triple A" cards of the American Automobile Association (AAA) provide roadside assistance while you are a car passenger (even if you are not driving). It provides airline, hotel, and rental car discounts and **free travelers checks.** If you are 50 or older, you may get an AARP (Association of American Retired People) card that offers discounts. We have LL.M. students of many ages!

14. Miscellaneous

(a) *Treat yourself.* Every once in a while see a movie at a local cinema. Buy a new book or a new item of clothing. Spend an afternoon at an amusement park or golfing. Do something you enjoy. Relax.

(b) *Tuition tax deductions.* If possible, deduct tuition from home country taxes (check with a tax accountant or other professional about this).

(c) *Frequent flyer.* If you fly to the U.S. from your home country, join the airline's frequent flyer club where you accrue points good for free air travel.

15. Insurance — Acquire Inexpensive Insurance

(a) Ask your LL.M. office for help getting insurance for **your belongings** (laptop, camera, car, other expensive items), **your apartment or house** (which may cover instances of burglary, fire, or flood), and for your **mobile or cell phone.**

16. Employment

(a) *On-campus work.* F-1 and J-1 students may work up to 20 hours per week on campus. This will help you earn money, and help you to develop networking contacts that may help you get a post-LL.M. job. (See Chapters 22 and 26.)

(b) *Types of on-campus jobs.* You may work as a research assistant; library clerk; tutor; lab technician; security guard; residence hall monitor; non-law exam proctor; foreign language instructor; nursery attendant (for infants — or trees!); or an assistant in an administrator's office (in the career development, alumni, or admissions office).

(c) *Faxes.* Your school's LL.M. career office should let you send faxes during your job search. You could also convert documents to PDF and send them as e-mail attachments free of charge. PDF converters can be downloaded online for free.

(d) *Postage.* Some schools will pay the postage for your application packages when you send them to prospective employers.

(e) *CVs, resumes, and writing samples.* Your law school will likely provide you with a reasonable supply of plain, white photocopy paper free of charge on which you can print your CV, cover letter, and other documents.

(f) *Color printing.* Ask if your school will let you use a faculty or staff color printer.

17. Save Money by Obeying the Law and School Rules Regarding Work

(a) Do not work off campus without authorization.

(b) Do not work illegally ("under the table" or "off the books").

(c) If you violate these rules, you may be penalized, expelled from school, or deported from the U.S. back to your home country. You may forfeit your LL.M. degree, and receive no reimbursement for tuition or fees paid. Or violations could come back to haunt you later. In the long run, you will be better off — and save money — by obeying all laws.

CHAPTER SUMMARY

- There are many "hidden" costs that applicants do not readily think of.
- Hidden costs begin even before you submit an application.
- Application costs can be high, particularly if you apply to many schools.
- Visa, travel, and vaccinations are expensive.
- At school, you will have many mandatory expenses, including tuition, fees, and books.
- You will need money to eat, sleep, and travel to and from school.
- Think about how you can save money, to help make your LL.M. experience more affordable.

Finances

Chapter 24

Scholarships, Tuition Discounts, and Other Funding for International LL.M. Students

CHAPTER HIGHLIGHTS
• Many LL.M. applicants want to know how they can get assistance to help pay the high costs of an LL.M. degree.
• This chapter focuses on the sources and types of financial assistance most readily available to international students who want to receive an LL.M. in the U.S.
• Do not be afraid to contact a law school, a governmental body, or a private organization and ask for more information about financial assistance for which you may be eligible.

Finances

A. Introduction

1. Types of LL.M. Funding, Generally

Many prospective international LL.M. students desperately seek funding for their U.S. LL.M. degrees. Not everyone has sufficient personal savings or the benefit of adequate family assistance to pay the high cost of school in the U.S. The following three broad categories of financial assistance exist for international LL.M. students who need additional funds to help pay for their LL.M.

a. Law School Endowed Scholarships for International LL.M. Students

Some law schools are custodians of large sums of money that have been donated to the school for the purpose of providing scholarships to LL.M. students. These "endowed scholarships" are awarded to LL.M. students pursuant to selection guidelines set by the donor, and may be awarded irrespective of the rate, tuition, any tuition discount offered to the student, or the student's financial need.

b. Law School Tuition Discount Funding for International LL.M. Students

Many U.S. law schools offer LL.M. students "tuition discounts." For example, if the tuition is $30,000 per year, the school may inform you that you have received a scholarship of 50%, so you will only need to pay $15,000. Tuition discounts may be offered irrespective of financial need of a student, and can be used to entice students to enroll.

c. Non-Law School Funding for International LL.M. Students

Many non-law school scholarship sources exist that all prospective students should explore. Even if you think you might not qualify for a particular opportunity, study its details anyway. You may find that you are indeed eligible. And if not, you might develop further ideas about where you can look for additional funding sources. *And you can pass funding information to friends and others who might benefit.*

2. Chapter Highlights

This chapter discusses tuition discounts, scholarships, grants and fellowships provided by law schools, and by many other sources, including private foundations in the U.S. and abroad, membership organizations, intergovernmental organizations, and LL.M. students' home governments, employers or home universities. Appendix II lists 258 scholarship sources, websites, books, and other references to help guide LL.M. students to funding.

B. Law School Scholarships, Tuition Discounts, and Other Funding for LL.M. Students — General

1. "Scholarships," Generally

The terms "scholarship," "grant," and "fellowship" all refer to funding provided to an LL.M. student that the student *need not* repay.[1] I use the three terms interchangeably, and leave it to you to read the terms of the awards listed below and in Appendix II, determine your eligibility, and apply. What the award is called matters less than whether you are eligible to apply and receive the award.

Nevertheless, a distinction should be drawn between (a) a prestigious scholarship granted through an endowment (an "endowed scholarship") set up by a

---

1. An LL.M. student may have to repay a scholarship if they breach the scholarship terms, for example, by providing false information in the application, receiving unacceptable grades during the degree program, or withdrawing from the program before completing it.

school benefactor for the purpose of providing scholarships (cash payments) to LL.M. students; and (b) an ordinary tuition discount (or "tuition discount scholarship") a school grants an international student, which could range from about a $1,000 or $2,000 discount to a full, 100% discount (when the LL.M. student would pay zero tuition).

2. Endowed LL.M. Scholarships

For an endowed scholarship, a benefactor of the school donates a large sum of money to the school to support scholarships, the money is placed in an interest-bearing fund, and interest from the fund is used to award scholarships to LL.M. students who satisfy any condition(s) the benefactor placed. For example, if John Doe wants scholarships to be awarded to African students who are studying for an LL.M. in international human rights law, John Doe may donate $1,000,000 to a particular school and instruct the school to use interest from the money to pay scholarships to African LL.M. students studying international human rights law. The school will place the million dollars into an interest-bearing fund, and the interest would be used to award "John Doe Scholarships" to students who fit into that category. Such scholarships would tend to be competitive, based on academic and other achievements. Recipients of such endowed scholarships would proudly list the "John Doe Scholarship" on their resume or CV. Such scholarships would tend to have no bearing on the tuition the student pays, or on any tuition discount the school may offer.

3. Tuition Discount Scholarships (with or without Fancy Names to Try to Increase Enrollment)

Tuition discount scholarships generally result in less tuition revenue for the school, but they do not require the school to transfer money to the student (as an endowed scholarship may require transfer from the scholarship fund). Thus tuition discount scholarships cost the school *zero* in outlays. Some students list tuition discount scholarships on their resume, even if the "scholarship" was only $1,000 and the tuition was over $45,000, and even though the discount may have been awarded not based on merit or on a competition, but based on a desire of the school to increase enrollment.

For a list of 258 scholarship sources for international LL.M. students, see Appendix II.

A law school may attach fancy names to its tuition discounts to try to increase enrollment by attracting students who receive a "Millennium Scholarship" or a "Harriet Tubman Scholarship" or a "Christopher Columbus Scholarship" — when in fact those "scholarships" are nothing other than the exact same tuition discounts the school has been giving all along, and will continue to give. Attaching fancy names to tuition discounts could be a sign that the school is a *cash cow*, in that it is trying to attract people through financial mechanisms

Finances

(tuition discounts, attaching fancy-sounding names to tuition discounts, lowering tuition costs), rather than increasing enrollment by overhauling and improving its LL.M. program to make it more attractive academically.[2] For serious students, LL.M. programs must be about more than tuition discounts with fancy names. It must be about the quality of the program. If you are offered a scholarship, find out whether it is simply a tuition discount.

C. Factors Schools Consider in Offering LL.M. Tuition Discounts

Schools consider many factors when deciding whether to offer an applicant a tuition discount, how much to give, and any terms attached to the award. Funding is based on three basic categories: (1) applicant's merit (without regard to the applicant's financial need), (2) applicant's financial need, or (3) other factors.

1. Tuition Discount Based on Achievement or Merit

Schools may offer scholarships to students based on their outstanding academic, professional or other achievements. Schools are interested in attracting bright, talented, accomplished students, and try to make themselves more attractive by offering scholarships. Merit scholarships are extremely competitive.

2. Tuition Discount Based on Need

Schools offer scholarships to students who need financial assistance for tuition. Many students find it impossible to attend a U.S. law school without a scholarship or tuition discount. Schools should offer scholarships based on need only to students who meet ordinary academic requirements.

3. Tuition Discount Based on Other Factors (Including if the School Is a "Diploma Mill" or "Cash Cow")

If a school's new LL.M. program is not well known, it might offer significant tuition discounts to attract students who would not otherwise want to join

---

2. When you visit a computer shop or a restaurant, do you always purchase the least expensive items, or always buy the items that are "on offer" or "discounted"? What if the discounted computer doesn't possess the technical capabilities you need, and the restaurant has no food that meets your dietary needs? Do you buy the computer and eat at the restaurant anyway? I hope you will not choose an LL.M. program based primarily on price if that program will not offer you what you need to meet your academic, personal, and professional goals.

a new program. As the program matures, improves, and enjoys a positive reputation, large tuition discounts may decline. Good schools may offer tuition discounts to increase diversity — for example, to attract students from a particular country or region, in certain fields of study, or with certain career goals. Non-competitive schools with poor reputations may offer large tuition discounts to attract students whose credentials are insufficient for competitive schools. Some diploma mills and cash cow LL.M. programs may offer large tuition discounts to applicants to increase enrollment so more students pay tuition, as schools may profit more with a larger number of students paying partial tuition than a smaller number of students paying full tuition. If the school diverts LL.M. tuition away from LL.M. program resources (for example, to the J.D. program), the LL.M. program may suffer, and will not attract serious LL.M. students with strong qualifications, but may attract less serious students with weaker qualifications who will accept the LL.M. admission offer at the school offering the largest tuition discount, regardless of the school's academic prowess. More than one LL.M. student or graduate has confided that the primary reason they chose a particular school was either because they had not been admitted at any other school, or because the school they chose offered the largest tuition discount.

D. Why Did a Law School Lower Its LL.M. Tuition Rate?

At most U.S. law schools, tuition rates will either remain the same from year to year, or they will increase. It is unusual for tuition rates to fall. However, on occasion an LL.M. program may *lower* its tuition rate.

If you find a school that lowered its tuition, you might ask yourself several questions before you decide to enroll:

- Was the law school being greedy when it set its initial, higher LL.M. tuition rates? Was the school unrealistic in thinking that students would pay the higher rate?
- Was the law school out of touch with the marketplace when it set the higher LL.M. tuition rates in earlier years, or is it out of touch with the marketplace now, with the new, lower LL.M. tuition rates?
- When the school lowered its LL.M. tuition rate, did it also lower the level of services it provides to LL.M. students?
- Did the LL.M. students who were enrolled the previous year (when the tuition was higher) receive greater services than you will receive with lower LL.M. tuition? Did they receive fewer services the year before?
  - If the *services will be equal*, why was the tuition higher before? *Ask.*
  - If the *services were lower before*, how can the school afford to provide greater services this year with less revenue? *Ask.*

- If the *services were greater before*, do you want to attend a school that is reducing its benefits and services, even if the LL.M. tuition is lower?
- Is the law school and its LL.M. program a cash cow? Is the school seeking to maximize its profits from the LL.M. program, minimize its expenses, and divert LL.M. tuition revenue to the J.D. or other programs?

The bottom line is that you would be better off attending a school that can compete with other schools based on the quality of the education you can receive there, rather than a school that competes primarily based on the cost of tuition. Schools should strive to increase offerings to LL.M. students, not slash them. All schools do, and must, charge tuition. All law schools have expenses. And, as mentioned, law schools are entitled to make a "profit" if they choose, as legal education is indeed run like a business, to a large degree. But, law schools should provide the services they promise. And, you should be just as concerned about a school that competes by lowering its tuition, as you might be concerned about a school that does somewhat the opposite — charges students a very high tuition, recognizing that some students will equate cost with quality. And yes, it is not uncommon for LL.M. administrators to argue that if their tuition is not high enough, applicants and students will think that the school's quality is low!

E. Other Scholarship and Tuition Discount Tips

Continue to pursue scholarships and tuition discounts even after you arrive at your law school. Visit the Dean of Student Affairs, the Associate Dean, and other law school faculty and staff. Ask whether there are any new funding opportunities.

You might also ask whether any endowed scholarships (*not* tuition discounts) that are normally given to J.D.s could be given to you as an LL.M. student. Some administrators take for granted that such scholarships are limited to J.D. students. However, you (or administrators) should read any given scholarship's creation documents carefully to determine if they can be used for LL.M. students as well. Persist.

F. Scholarship Scams

As you surf the web seeking scholarship sources, you may encounter advertisements that promise to send you lists of guaranteed scholarship sources *if you send them a certain amount of cash*. If you see notices like this, *beware*. Many scholarship scams exist on the web.

The U.S. Federal Trade Commission (FTC) offers advice on evaluating Internet scholarship websites and how to avoid scholarship scams. The

FTC notes: "Need Money for College? Doesn't everybody? Unfortunately, in their efforts to pay the bills, many students and their families are falling prey to scholarship scams" (www.ftc.gov/bcp/edu/microsites/scholarship/index.shtml). A private website that warns against scams is www.finaid.org/scholarships/scams.phtml.

As a general rule, you should never have to pay money to apply for a legitimate scholarship, grant, or fellowship. There may be fees associated with commercial loans, but not with scholarships, grants, or fellowships offered through foundations, charities, schools, or governments.

G. Other Creative Funding Directly from Law Schools

As mentioned, many law schools offer LL.M. students tuition discounts. Some schools publicize these opportunities widely on their websites and elsewhere. Others do not advertise them at all. Rest assured, however, that U.S. law schools *should not* be offended if you request a scholarship, in whole or in part. Do not be bashful. *It does not hurt to ask.* If you don't believe this bit of assurance and you think asking for a large scholarship might hurt your chances of the school admitting you, you can wait until *after* the school admits you to ask.

If you want to work in public service or for a human rights or humanitarian organization after you graduate, you may be able to convince a U.S. law school to waive your tuition if you agree to work in a public service post-LL.M., particularly if you choose a specific public service or human rights group, perhaps in your home country. If the first administrator you ask says "No," ask faculty members, your academic advisors, or others at the law school. A "no" can turn into a "yes," particularly if you can make a compelling case, and the law school realizes that by acquiescing and adapting to this possibility, it (and you) can and will further human rights.

Remember, many law schools will offer international LL.M. students a discount *if the student asks.*

Finances

Scholarship Tips

1. Keep checking for scholarships even *after* you arrive at school for classes. Sometimes new scholarships develop.
2. Ask everyone you know about scholarships!
   - Employers
   - Home universities
   - U.S. government
   - Private foundations in the U.S. and abroad

H. Negotiating a Scholarship — School "A" Scholarship Offer as Leverage for School "B" Scholarship

If you receive an endowed scholarship or tuition discount from School A, you can inform School B, and ask School B if it will match A's offer. School B *might* offer you a larger award. You have nothing to lose by asking! School B will not rescind its firm offer of aid or admission if you ask it to match a higher award offer.

I. Categories of Scholarship Listings in Appendix II

Appendix II lists 258 scholarship sources in the following categories:

(1) Scholarships and grants for women only
(2) Scholarships for persons with disabilities
(3) U.S. Government sources for LL.M. funding
(4) Intergovernmental organization funding sources
(5) Private websites containing scholarship, grant, and loan information
(6) Foundations and membership organizations
(7) Nationality-based scholarships and grants — regional awards — listed by region
(8) Nationality-based scholarships and grants — listed by country
(9) Books and other resources

J. Reminder . . . Do Not Forget to Ask for an Endowed Scholarship *and* a Tuition Discount Scholarship!

At some point in the application or admission process, you should consider requesting a tuition discount or a scholarship. Some applicants request such awards even if they (or their parents) can afford to pay for their LL.M. without it. Some schools will provide awards based on merit, without regard to an applicant's need. A funding request is *not* likely to have any negative repercussions. So why not ask for a scholarship or tuition discount, either in your application, *or* after the school admits you, but before you accept the admission offer?

When you request funding, be certain to ask to be considered for any endowed scholarships for which you might qualify *and* for a regular tuition discount scholarship. You have *nothing* to lose by asking for both, particularly after you have been admitted to the school.

CHAPTER SUMMARY

- You must persevere in searching for scholarship and grant opportunities; find out the requirements, and apply.
- Check. Double check. The eligibility rules may change in your favor! Requirements change.
- Do not hesitate to contact an organization and ask for more information.
- Even if you think you will not qualify, why not apply anyway?
- Be sure to check the scholarship and related information in Appendix II.

Finances

Chapter 25

Avoiding U.S.-Based Student Loans

CHAPTER HIGHLIGHTS

- Based on financial information you included in your LL.M. and U.S. visa applications, the school and the U.S. government expect that you will not need to take out a student loan.
- Circumstances may arise in which you believe you need to borrow money.
- Taking out a U.S.-based student loan in the U.S. should be a last resort.
- If you get a student loan, carefully examine the terms *before signing*.

A. Loans for International LL.M. Students, Generally

After international students arrive in the U.S. to begin their LL.M. programs, it is **almost impossible** to get loans from, or guaranteed by, the U.S. government; **difficult but not impossible** to get loans from a U.S. bank; and **difficult** to get loans directly from most LL.M. schools. It is advisable that you have all your financial matters sorted out before you arrive, because it will not be easy to get loans in the U.S., for various reasons.

First, the U.S. government ordinarily restricts government educational loans to U.S. citizens or permanent residents.

Second, private banks in the U.S. consider international students to be high risks for default, because after they finish their degrees the students may leave the U.S. and not return, making it difficult for the banks to get repaid. U.S. banks will loan to international students if the student finds a U.S. citizen or permanent resident to co-sign the loan, rendering the co-signer responsible for repaying the loan if the student defaults.

Third, when you apply for your student visa, you must demonstrate to the U.S. consular officials that you possess sufficient scholarship, family, or other funds to cover tuition, travel, and living expenses for the length of your LL.M. program. So, in theory, you will not need to borrow funds once you arrive.

Sometimes an LL.M. student in the U.S. encounters financial difficulties, and feels a need to try to borrow money. Some of those financial difficulties may be wholly unexpected, although others may be entirely predictable. This chapter discusses unforeseen and foreseen financial difficulties, options to raise money when funds are exhausted, and cautions against private borrowing.

B. Unforeseen and Foreseen Circumstances That Cause Financial Difficulties

At times LL.M. students in the U.S. face unforeseen situations beyond their control that require funds in addition to those listed in their visa applications, which convinced U.S. consular officials that the students could finance their degrees themselves. Financial difficulties might be caused by improper budget planning; unanticipated housing or school fee increases; unexpectedly high textbook prices; or nonapproval of loans from the home country.

The student's sponsor, who promised to pay the student's fees, may unexpectedly become unable or unwilling to continue support. The sponsor could have faced his own financial difficulties, or could have changed his mind for other reasons. Sponsoring employers or the student's family may withdraw funding due to business collapse; divorce or family illness; crop failure; or a marked decrease in the local currency caused by the decline of a country's economy due to acts of God or man such as drought or floods, earthquakes, or nuclear or financial meltdowns.

However, some students have predictable, foreseen, or at least foreseeable, financial difficulties. They knew before they left their country that the funds listed for student visa purposes would not be available to support them in the U.S. The visa application might include bank statements of a "sponsor" who has no intention whatsoever of providing the money for the student to use in the U.S., but intended to use the documentary evidence of the money for visa purposes only. Consular officials are aware of this phenomenon — or attempts at outright deception, which amount to fraud — and thus they examine financial documents carefully. Such deception is morally wrong and illegal, and harmful, in particular to the students, who find themselves in the U.S. with insufficient funds, and maybe a dark legal or ethical cloud hovering over their U.S. experience and LL.M. study endeavor.

Irrespective of how a student ends up with insufficient funds, the question becomes what can be done — how to get funds needed for tuition, housing, and/ or food?

The first answer is a note of caution: **Do not put yourself in dire financial straits,** hoping or vaguely thinking that you will figure it out — or that someone will figure it out for you — when the time comes.

Still, problems arise — and must be resolved. Students can work on campus (with school permission, and a U.S. Social Security card), up to 20 hours per week during school, usually at no more than $10 per hour. That may not be enough.

I have known LL.M. students to collect donations from faculty and students for LL.M. classmates who needed money. I have heard of bake sales and other creative ways to raise money on campus, and of assistance from churches and community groups. I have known faculty members to loan money to LL.M. students. I have known LL.M. students to take out student loans co-signed by a U.S. citizen or permanent resident.[1]

Ideally, if an international LL.M. student experiences serious financial difficulties, a law school would increase the student's LL.M. endowed scholarship, waive part of the student's tuition or fees (or increase the waiver), or grant the student a small loan. These would seem to be easy solutions; however, I am aware of a law school that refused to assist a second-semester international LL.M. student who was short $800 on a tuition bill that was many times greater than that small amount.

C. Emergency Loans Directly from Law Schools

Some LL.M. programs have funds set aside to provide loans to LL.M. students who encounter financial difficulty after they begin classes. For example, **Georgetown** offers *Short-Term Emergency Loans* for LL.M. students for up to U.S. $1,500 per semester throughout the student's LL.M. program. The loans are interest-free for a month, and then accrue 1.75 percent interest compounded monthly. (p. 15 of Handbook)[2]

---

1. Matters can be worse at four-year medical schools. For example, I heard of a first-year medical student from a developing country who recently learned that his sponsors were unable to continue paying his first-year tuition, and that he would be forced to withdraw and return home without a degree. His classmates collected and donated over $60,000 for his first-year tuition. They also raised tuition for his three subsequent years, and started a foundation to fund students at other U.S. medical schools. The university the student attended no longer accepts international students, with a rule that "International applicants must have a permanent resident visa to be eligible for" admission (http://admissions.medicine.iu.edu/admissions-frequently-asked-questions). Unfortunately, this policy is calculated to limit the number of international medical school students and graduates who would have been able to take their training back to help in their home countries, and has a dramatically negative impact on the developing world.

2. **Brigham Young** provides: "If you have a cosigner (a person who will officially sign your loan papers and be legally responsible to pay back the loan money if you do not), you may apply for and likely receive a Law School Woolley Loan. A total of $6,000 (U.S. dollars) per year is available to law students from this fund" (p. 11 of brochure).

Will your U.S. law school support LL.M. students who develop financial or other difficulties during their studies? This is a question that may not be answered until, or if, a crisis arises in the middle of a term and you no longer have access to the funds originally set aside to cover your LL.M. expenses. If family, friends, or others are not able to contribute, and you cannot get a private loan, then you would have to ask the school for assistance. Will your school assist you if you have a financial emergency? Unfortunately, I have observed instances in which a school refused to assist students who were in desperate need due to no apparent fault of their own.

D. Should International LL.M. Students Take Out Private Commercial Loans in the U.S.?

I would not ordinarily recommend that international students take private loans in the U.S. The interest rates may be high, other terms may be strict, and the students may have difficulty repaying the loans after they graduate and return to their home countries. And then problems arise for co-signers, who have the burden and legal obligation of repayment if the international students fail to repay the loans.

LL.M. graduates may not be able to repay the loans from earnings during their one-year OPT, as they will have living expenses then and their salaries may not be high. However, if a graduate obtains an H-1B work visa allowing him to work in the U.S. for a longer period, he may be able to repay the loan.

Private loans should not be considered an ordinary option — if considered at all. At best, they should be an extraordinary, last option. Students should first exhaust all other avenues and options, such as scholarships, grants, financial assistance from sources in their home countries, and emergency assistance from their U.S. law school before they explore the possibility of private loans with U.S. co-signers. The student might also consider postponing her study, working to earn additional money, and returning to complete her LL.M. after a year or two when she may have sufficient time to get her finances in order.

E. Cautions

International LL.M. students should be aware that even if you can meet the stringent qualifying tests for a private loan in the U.S., you should take caution. Closely examine the repayment terms, interest rates, and other terms. Take care to protect your own creditworthiness and reputation, and that of your U.S. citizen or permanent resident co-signatories, who must repay the loan if you cannot. You should contact the LL.M. Office, the Office of International Affairs, and even an on-campus or off-campus lawyer, to review any proposed loan agreement — **before you sign.**

Furthermore, you might consider these questions:

(1) Is your proposed lender reputable? You can check the *Better Business Bureau* where your school is and where your lender is located.

(2) Check with your LL.M. office and Office of International Affairs. Does the school have "preferred lenders"? Is the lender you are considering a "preferred lender" of your school? Does your school have a relationship with the lender?

(3) Have other international LL.M. students from your school used this lender? Have any LL.M. graduates used the lender? Did they have good experiences? Ask your LL.M. administration to connect you with others who used the lender.

(4) Will the lender "own" your loan for the loan's duration, or might the lender sell your loan to another company?

(5) When will you have to start repaying the loan? Will you be ready and able to start making payments on that date? Where will you get the repayment money?

(6) What is the loan's interest rate? How is the interest calculated? Do you pay interest while you are in school, or only after you graduate?

(7) Will the interest that accrued during your time in school be added onto the loan after you graduate (so you will be paying interest on interest)? Or will the interest accrual begin after you graduate, when you begin the scheduled repayments?

F. Do Not Break the Law!

Do not — *under any circumstance* — work and earn money without specific legal authorization and a Social Security card. Please check the rules that govern your F-1 or J-1 visa, and check the rules for hardship or other provisions that may permit an exception or exemption from the normal work regulations. If you break the law and work off-campus or work more than 20 hours on-campus during the school term (or more than 40 hours during breaks), you will be subject to penalties, including possible deportation. Your LL.M. advisors and the campus International Affairs personnel are obligated to inform the government, through SEVIS, of immigration violations of students. Please do not violate your visa terms or breach any other U.S. law or school regulation. Penalties can be harsh for international students.

Finances

CHAPTER SUMMARY

- It is difficult for international students to get loans once they arrive in the U.S.

- The U.S. government, banks, and law schools themselves are not good sources for such loans.

- You are advised to have all financial matters arranged before you arrive in the U.S.

- If unforeseen financial difficulties arise, consult your LL.M. program administrators. Ask them about options, including deferred tuition payments, endowed scholarships, tuition discounts, waiver of certain fees, or low- or no-interest law school loans.

- If you borrow money, be certain you understand the repayment requirements.

Getting a Job or Achieving Other Career Goals Post-LL.M.

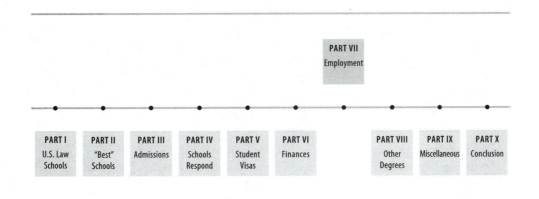

						PART VII				
						Employment				

PART I	PART II	PART III	PART IV	PART V	PART VI		PART VIII	PART IX	PART X
U.S. Law Schools	"Best" Schools	Admissions	Schools Respond	Student Visas	Finances		Other Degrees	Miscellaneous	Conclusion

Employment

Chapter 26

Eighty-Eight Strategies for Achieving Your Career Goals

CHAPTER HIGHLIGHTS

- All international LL.M. students and graduates have career aspirations. This chapter describes 88 strategies you can use to help you reach those goals, with your U.S. law school assisting you.

- LL.M. programs are obligated to help LL.M. students and graduates reach their career goals. Be certain to choose a program that has a solid track record of effectively assisting LL.M. students and graduates in this regard.

- Your school will help you reach your goals through "career counseling," which law school personnel provide at the school's LL.M. career services office. The LL.M. "career counselors" or "career coaches" should be trained to assist international LL.M. students who may aspire to work in the U.S., their home country, or a third country—in a wide range of positions at many types of institutions.

- Your career coach should be able to assist you whether you want to practice law at a U.S. or overseas law firm, or work for a multinational corporation, a bank, a law faculty (as a law teacher), a governmental body, a prosecutor's office, a court (as a judicial law clerk or as a judge), a human rights law organization, or an intergovernmental organization like the United Nations. You may want a "non-traditional" job that does not directly involve law or the practice of law.

- Your career coach will assist. But you have responsibilities too. Your school cannot help you effectively unless you do your part. Attend classes, study, perform well academically, join student organizations, get to know professors (who can write recommendations for you), and get involved generally.

- Actively participate in the process of achieving your career goals. Start early, even before you arrive on campus. Take initiative. Be proactive. Persevere.

- Work with your LL.M. career coach to develop a career plan. Follow that career plan. You will have a greater chance of achieving your career goals.

Employment

A. Range of Career Possibilities for LL.M. Graduates

1. Career Goals

Each international LL.M. student has career objectives. You may want to return to your home country to the job you left behind, or take a new job at home or in a third country. You may want to work in the U.S. long-term, or for a year under optional practical training (OPT) or academic training (AT) (Chapter 24), to earn an S.J.D. (Chapter 29), or take a non-legal job. Your post-LL.M. degree career ambitions may be among those earlier discussed in the context of reasons for international students to do an LL.M. in the U.S. (Chapter 2). As your LL.M. year progresses, you may discover that you are uncertain of what you want to do post-LL.M., or you may change your mind about your desired career path.

In all cases, you will want to do everything possible to help you reach whatever you ultimately choose as personal and career goals. *LL.M. Roadmap* offers guidance. But you must make proper decisions along the way, including choosing a school that has a career office with trained personnel who are willing and able to help you — as an international LL.M. student — reach your goals.

2. LL.M. Program and Student Obligations

LL.M. programs, principally through their career and placement offices,[1] are obligated to assist you in achieving your professional and career goals. The career office at your school should go the extra mile to help ensure that you and your classmates are provided with training, tutoring, exposure, and general assistance to help prepare and present you to the career marketplace. The career office should help make you as attractive as possible — professionally! — to help you meet the challenges of fulfilling your aspirations, whatever they may be.

You — the LL.M. student — also have obligations in this process. You must devote all necessary effort to studying, keeping up with your classes, and performing well academically. If you do not perform well, and do not live up to your part of the bargain, it may not be easy for the career office to do its part in assisting you. You must make yourself as attractive as possible for the career marketplace, and avoid anything that will detract from your presentation. You must also take personal responsibility for your career search, recognizing that the career office will not conduct your search for you.

You must actively participate in the process of achieving your career goals. You should start early (even before you arrive on campus), and be proactive, flexible, creative, perseverant, and strategic.

Reaching career goals is not always easy, particularly given the state of the global economy in recent years, and with the extra hurdles placed before

---

1. Different law school LL.M. programs have different names for this office, including "Office of Professional Development," "Career Office," or "Career Counseling Services."

international students in U.S. LL.M. programs. But reaching reasonable goals is not impossible. Indeed, reaching reasonable goals *is your goal!*

B. Career Development and Assistance Resources

This chapter highlights career development and assistance mechanisms and tools that should be available for LL.M. students at your U.S. law school. If you learn that the school you are considering attending does not have effective career development and assistance plans and resources in place for LL.M. students, *you might do well to consider choosing a school that does aggressively help LL.M. students reach their career goals.*

C. Eighty-Eight Strategies to Reach Your Post-LL.M. Career and Personal Goals

Below are 88 tips and suggestions about seeking temporary or permanent employment, either in the field of law or in an alternative field. As you read through the list, I encourage you to keep an open mind about the wide range of possible employment opportunities for you in the U.S., in your home country, or in a third country. You might work for one of many types of organizations, such as a corporation (in-house counsel), a government (judge, lawyer, mediator), a law firm (corporate, criminal, trade law), or a public interest or intergovernmental organization (such as the UN or EU). You might "hang out a shingle" (work for yourself!). You might teach at a law faculty, or at an undergraduate institution. You might decide that you do not want to work in the field of law after all.

Irrespective of what sort of work you want to do, or where, I hope you will find some of the following tips, suggestions, and strategies useful.

D. Identify Who and What Can Help You

1. Identify Your Allies (People Who Can Assist You!)

(a) Career office staff
(b) Career coach
(c) Law school professors
(d) Law school Dean, Associate Dean, or Assistant Dean
(e) Law school administrators (including J.D. admission officers)
(f) LL.M. administrators (including LL.M. admission officers)
(g) LL.M. classmates
(h) J.D. classmates
(i) Classmates in student organizations
(j) LL.M. alumni (in the U.S., in your home country, and in other countries)
(k) J.D. alumni (in the U.S., in your home country, and in other countries)
(l) University alumni (in the U.S., in your home country, and in other countries)
(m) Professors, administrators, and students from other university departments
(n) Lawyers, judges, and others you meet while networking
(o) Directors of study abroad or other international programs at your law school (even if they involve countries other than your own)
(p) Employment agents or "headhunters" in the U.S. and in your home country
(q) Law school roommates, neighbors, and friends
(r) People you meet casually, perhaps at activities you enjoy
(s) Outsourcing company representatives in the U.S. and overseas
(t) Educational agents and LL.M. admission consultants (who may have contacts)

2. Acquire Career Advancement Tools

(a) U.S. resume and CV formatted in a U.S. style
(b) Cover letter
(c) Briefcase (with a legal pad and pens)
(d) Cell phone, laptop, tablet, and other equipment to stay connected

Employment

(e) E-mail address (professional, i.e., do not use your fun, partying nickname)

(f) Appropriate interview attire

(g) Interview skills

(h) Etiquette at business meals. Yes, some employers actually do pay attention to which knife, spoon, or fork you use at a business lunch — Use the outside fork first, for salad; the bigger fork set closer to the plate is for the main course! And yes, law school career offices are expected to conduct training sessions for international LL.M. students on the topic of business dining.

(i) Business cards with your school's logo

3. Identify Entities and Things That Can Assist You

(a) LL.M. career office

(b) J.D. career office

(c) University career office (also career offices of other departments of fields that interest you, such as Business, Public Health, Political Science)

(d) Graduate or undergraduate departments generally — criminal justice, foreign languages, pre-law (for volunteer or paid work)

(e) Law student organizations (see also Chapter 19)

(f) Undergraduate student organizations (and also at other graduate schools)

(g) LL.M., law school, and university alumni offices

(h) Your country's embassy (Washington, D.C.) or consulate (other U.S. cities)

(i) Your country's UN mission in New York City

(j) Local and international bar associations

(k) Athletic facilities (swimming pools, golf and tennis clubs, running clubs)

(l) Law school, university, local libraries (great research tools)

(m) Lawyer databases, such as Lexis, Martindale Hubbell, and Westlaw

(n) LL.M. job fairs (sponsored by law schools, law firms, nonprofits)

(o) Internet searches (using search engines such as Google)

4. Identify and Exploit *Internal* Resources Within Yourself

(a) Recognize that international LL.M. graduates face high hurdles in trying to land OPT and AT jobs, and even more difficulties in finding H-1B jobs (See Chapter 27)

(b) Exercise determination and perseverance

(c) Gain a positive attitude. This will help in all your personal contacts (e-mail, phone, paper correspondence, face-to-face) while networking, corresponding with employers, and interviewing for jobs

(d) Self-assess
- *Inventory* your strengths and weaknesses, pluses and minuses
- *Understand* your strengths and weaknesses, pluses and minuses

Employment

> • *Accept* your strengths and weaknesses, pluses and minuses
> • *Exploit* your strengths and weaknesses, pluses and minuses

(e) Understand what expectations are reasonable

(f) Develop "a tough skin" to protect you from the many disappointments and rejections you are sure to face on the path to reaching your career and personal goals

5. Develop a Timeline

Vermont's Career Manual[2] notes that LL.M. students generally do not have as much time for job hunting as J.D. students, who tend to be at the law school for three years versus only one year for an LL.M. student. **Vermont** strongly suggests "that LL.M.'s begin networking and researching potential employers immediately upon their arrival at [the U.S. school]. In addition, LL.M.'s should schedule an appointment with a career counselor in early September to develop an effective job search strategy." I would go one step further and suggest you begin networking even before you arrive on campus!

6. Learn About Different Types of Jobs That May Be Available

Vermont's *Career Manual* outlines different scenarios in which international LL.M. students and graduates may seek employment, and notes differences between U.S. and foreign-educated LL.M. opportunities, and between graduating LL.M. and J.D. students (including limitations based on visa status), as follows (paraphrased and elaborated upon)[3]:

(a) *Large law firms.* LL.M. graduates tend to compete against experienced attorneys for positions, and not against fresh J.D. graduates. Some of these firms have "foreign lawyer programs" that hire LL.M. graduates for up to a year, either at the firm's U.S. or overseas office.

(b) *Small and midsized law firms.* Many of these firms do not have regular LL.M. hiring programs, but they hire if the firm has a particular need for an LL.M. graduate with certain backgrounds, skills, or potential.

(c) *Federal government jobs.* Most agencies hire lawyers; but most federal jobs only hire U.S. citizens.

---

2. *Career Development: A Manual for J.D., Joint Degree and LL.M. Students* (www.vermontlaw.edu/Documents/career%20services/Career%20Development%20Manual.JD.Feb10.pdf).

3. Your law school's LL.M. career office should be able to direct you to online lists of large, medium, and small law firms in the city and state where your law school is located, in other major cities in the U.S., and outside the U.S. Your LL.M. career office should be able to provide you information about firms with special programs for foreign lawyers, and information about those firms' hiring partners. They should be able to provide information about federal, state, and local government jobs, judicial clerkships, and a range of non-traditional or non-legal jobs. In short, your law school's LL.M. career office should be able to help you no matter where your career ambitions lie. But, keep in mind that you must do your share of the work as well!

(d) *State and local government jobs.* Non-U.S. citizens may work in many state and local government positions.

(e) *Judicial clerkships.* Non-U.S. citizens may work for many state judges as clerks, but ordinarily not for federal judges.

E. Strategies *Before* You Arrive on Campus

7. Networking *Before* You Enroll

Networking begins when you decide to apply to an LL.M. program, if not before.

There is no universally recognized definition of "networking," but I would generally define networking in the context of career development as "reaching out to and interacting with people informally for the purpose of furthering your career ambitions." Before applying to any U.S. law school, you might network with LL.M. graduates, prospective employers, officials at different law schools, and others who may advise on which educational choice might best help you reach your career goals. They may advise enrolling in an LL.M. program in Europe or Australia rather than in the U.S. If you choose the U.S., they may recommend specific schools based on what they learned while in the U.S., or what they learned postdegree. Before you apply, and certainly before you accept an offer to attend, you can contact the career office at your law school, as well as professors, staff, and current and prospective students. This may help you choose the best law school for yourself, and may help land you a part-time job during your LL.M. year, an internship, an OPT or AT position in the U.S. for the year post-LL.M., or a permanent job in the U.S. or elsewhere.

It is never too early to begin networking. Make contacts in the legal profession. Maintain those contacts throughout your legal education and beyond.

8. Learn What Career Resources Are Available at the Law School for LL.M. Students

A good LL.M. program will have dedicated personnel to help LL.M. students reach their career objectives. These personnel may work out of an office called the "Career Office," "Professional Development Office," or "Placement Office."

Find out — before you apply *and* before you enroll — what career resources the law school has. Do they have any (or many of) the resources discussed in this chapter? Most law schools devote ample attention to the career needs of J.D. students, but some do not provide adequate (or any) career assistance to LL.M. students. J.D. programs are significantly larger than LL.M. programs, and J.D. job placement assistance is highly scrutinized by different unofficial ranking systems and in law school accreditation and review processes — thus schools may devote more time and energy to J.D. employment. Good LL.M. programs

Employment

devote exceptional assistance to LL.M. students, some of whom will face more — and certainly different — challenges than J.D. students will have to face.

9. Learn If Your LL.M. Career Office Has Successfully Facilitated the Placement of LL.M. Students and Graduates

Good LL.M. programs keep statistics of the employment status and careers of its graduates, and information about current students who are employed part time. Your school should be able to easily tell you what percentage of graduates return to former jobs in their home countries, seek and acquire new jobs in the U.S. or elsewhere, enter another degree program, defer completing their LL.M. programs, or are currently seeking employment but are unable to find a job. Ask the LL.M. career office. *If the school does not maintain such statistics, or is unwilling to give them to you, then maybe you should choose another school.*

10. Contact Your School's Career Office *Before You Arrive*

Each LL.M. student should have an LL.M. program staff person assigned as that student's "career coach." You should be able to consult your career coach for guidance in assessing realistic career goals for you, in developing a job search strategy, and in implementing that strategy. Before you arrive, find out if the LL.M. school has career coaches (or someone serving that function). If the school does not, consider other schools. Contact your career coach *before* you arrive. Ask how to get an internship during your first semester, which courses to take to prepare and qualify for the New York bar, or other matters of interest to you and your career.

11. Before You Arrive on Campus, Look for Paid Part-Time Work

When class is in session, F-1 and J-1 students may work on campus for up to 20 hours per week and for up to 40 hours per week during breaks. If you want to work, contact your LL.M. office (or career coach) before school begins. They can tell you how to access your school's career website with password-protected listings.

LL.M. students qualify for many campus jobs but positions may be taken by J.D. students who were in town during the summer and applied early. You might work as a research assistant for a law professor, teacher assistant or instructor in the language department, law library clerk, computer room assistant, or undergraduate tutor (e.g., political science, criminal justice, or in a field in which you have expertise). If you register with the career office, or at least let them know your background and interests, they can keep you in mind as opportunities cross their desk.

If you wait until you arrive on campus, the good jobs may be taken.

Benefits of Campus Jobs *First*, they pay. *Second*, if you do well at your campus job, your supervisor might write you a good recommendation letter when you pursue your post-LL.M. job or higher degree. A job as a law professor's research assistant can be particularly good, as the professor will not only be in a position to recommend you, but also the professor may have good career ideas for you to pursue, or contacts at law firms, the UN, private corporations, or governmental departments.

12. Before You Arrive on Campus, Look for Part-Time Volunteer Work

On-campus volunteer work (meaning work without monetary pay) can be just as beneficial to you, or more beneficial to you, than paid on-campus work. Your volunteer supervisors might write you a great recommendation letter, and you might meet other contacts and develop good, life-long friends.

Volunteering for on-campus work is recommended *if you do not need the extra money* or *if you cannot accept the money* (for example, if your scholarship will not permit you to earn extra money). But professors usually have funds to pay research assistants — so you do not need to volunteer for them. *Get paid!*

You may be able to receive law school pro bono or independent credit for your part-time work. **Ask your LL.M. academic advisor if you can receive academic credit or pro bono credit for your volunteer work.**

13. On-Campus Graduate Admissions Office and International Affairs Office

In addition to contacting your career coach, you might contact the University's Graduate Admissions Office or its Office for International Affairs. Ask if they are hiring or if they know of any openings outside of the law school. These offices often hire international students from different departments, including law. They might hire you.

When you applied to the school and applied for your visa, you would have indicated that you had adequate funding to cover your expenses while you were in the U.S. When the school issued your I-20, it believed you had enough money to live, and that you would not need to work. When you apply for your campus job, it would seem incongruous if you indicated that you were "desperate" for money. However, earning a little extra spending money, gaining U.S. work experience to list on your resume, and possibly earning a supervisor's recommendation letter are excellent reasons to apply for an on-campus job, irrespective of any other financial questions.

Employment

F. Strategies *As Soon As* You Arrive on Campus

14. On-Campus Networking

If you did not begin networking before you arrived on campus, it is not too late. But start as soon as possible! Your campus has many networking sources available to you. Keep your eyes and ears open, and keep a smile on your face.

15. Register With Your Law School's Career Office

The school may require you to register with the career office. Register *as soon as possible*. You want to get notified about any upcoming LL.M. (or J.D.) job fairs, employer interview opportunities, networking events, resume building sessions, mock interviews, seminars, business meal etiquette "training" sessions, or other helpful activities. These sessions can be held as early as the first month of school. You do not want to miss any of these events!

16. Develop a Career Strategy and Work With Your Career Coach

Getting a good job after you earn your LL.M. degree may be like training to win an Olympic gold medal — you need spirited coaching — someone to tell you what you are doing right, what you are doing wrong, and what you should be doing that you are not doing. This is your career coach.

Your career coach should be a cheerleader, providing inspiration when the going gets tough. Use your career coach. It is their job to usher you through to the finish line — the career opportunity of your dreams (or at least a career opportunity that you can live with, and build on). Not every LL.M. student will win his or her first choice job. But LL.M. students should not be disadvantaged because the school did not provide them with a career coach. Meet your career coach early, and as often as necessary.

17. After You Map Out Your Job Search Strategy, Follow It!

Once you and your career coach have developed a career strategy, implement it. Stick to it and persevere.

18. Convert Your Overseas Resume to a U.S. Resume

Convert your resume (and cover letter) to a U.S. format. Ask your career office to review it and offer advice. Your *LL.M. Student Handbook* should offer conversion suggestions, and should provide samples.

19. Acquire Business Cards With Your School's Logo

Start looking for a job early—even before you arrive on campus.

Your career coach should inform you how to order business cards. Your cards should have your name, the name of your LL.M. degree program (e.g., "Jane Doe, Student, LL.M. in Tax" or "Jane Doe, Candidate, LL.M. in International Human Rights Law"), your law school's name and logo, your local contact information, and possibly permanent home country contact information if you plan to return home postdegree. You may list your school e-mail address, but note that it may expire several months after you graduate. You might choose to list a "permanent" e-mail address, perhaps one offered through your school's alumni association, or through Yahoo!, Hotmail, or Gmail. Make certain your e-mail address sounds "professional," and is not silly or fun. Skip e-mail addresses such as "eyegraduated@yahoo.com," or "work4food@hotmail.com." Using your name—for example, "MaryDoe@yahoo.com"—is more professional.

Carry your business cards with you always, but use them only in accordance with your LL.M. program's usage guidelines, which, like **San Diego**'s, may include not using your cards to represent yourself as an agent of the school. You may give cards to friends, family, classmates, and, more important, lawyers, judges, and other professionals with whom you network. *You never know who will use your business card, when, or how.*

20. Create a Chart to Track Your Job Search

Searching for a job *is* a full-time job. You will need to take many steps over a long period of time. Keep track of your job-seeking efforts.

It is easy to keep track using a log or chart you create in Microsoft Excel, Microsoft Word, or Word Perfect. The chart should list job search strategies, contacts, and communications with dates and follow-up details. Do not waste effort by recontacting people who were not helpful. Do not overlook or misplace promising contact information. Keep precise, detailed, accurate, and organized information.

21. Monitor the Official Job Placement Process at Your School and Participate in *All* Job Placement Activities

After you register, you will likely receive e-mail messages notifying you of procedures for on-campus interviews, resume building seminars, networking events with local lawyers, and other opportunities. *Monitor those e-mail messages!* In the first weeks of school, you may be bombarded with e-mail messages. Read them. Do not overlook important ones! Follow guidelines. Do not miss deadlines. Participate in *all* career office activities, whether sponsored by the J.D. career

Employment

office or the LL.M. career office, even if you feel you do not need them. You might pick up tips, or make unexpected connections with a lawyer, professor, or student not in your field.

22. Use Resources in Your School's LL.M. Career Office

Your school's career office should have a library of books, magazines, articles, pamphlets, brochures, and other materials with information about the marketplace for legal services, and types of law practices and specializations. The LL.M. career office should also have substantial information about how to go about finding a job, and information about alumni and other friends of the LL.M. and J.D. programs who may be willing to assist you.

G. Strategies Throughout Your LL.M. Period

23. Develop An Excellent "Writing Sample"

Employers may require you to submit a "writing sample," which would demonstrate your ability to communicate in written English generally and your ability to communicate in "legal English." Writing samples also demonstrate your legal acumen — your knowledge of the law, your ability to distill controlling principles of law, and your ability to apply the law to the facts and arrive at reasonable conclusions.

Your writing sample could be a Legal Writing class exercise, a seminar paper, your thesis (or draft thesis), an independent research paper, or a pro bono paper. It could be a memorandum you wrote in conjunction with an internship or part-time work with a law firm, judge, or corporation — but in these instances you must secure approval from your work supervisor before using it as a writing sample, and you may need to redact confidential information.

Make sure your writing sample is error-free, with no typographical, spelling, grammar, citation, or other mistakes. Date it and indicate the circumstances under which it was written (e.g., whether it was a memorandum for a class or for a client). If you send it via e-mail attachment, it should be in a PDF file so that it retains its formatting. You should paginate it in "page x of y" format so the reader will know how many pages there are, in case pages at the end of the document accidentally drop off. (By the way, you should paginate *all* documents using "page x of y" format!) It should probably be no more than ten pages. If your document is longer, you can submit an excerpt.

24. Hone Legal Skills Before and During Your Job Search

You can prepare for a traditional or nontraditional job in many ways. You should endeavor to continue to hone your legal skills at all times, beginning as

Employment

early as possible, even before you arrive in the U.S., and certainly during your academic year. Your legal skills are honed through coursework. Legal research and writing skills can be gained through pro bono work, research assistance work (even as a volunteer), assisting at conferences, doing internships or externships (with or without academic credit), and working with student organizations.

25. Read Law-Related National, International, and Local Newspapers, Journals, Newsletters, and Other Periodicals

Read as many law-related periodicals as you can. These newspapers, journals, and newsletters will help keep you informed about current events in law, which may help when you are interviewing or networking. They may contain job listings. They may contain information about new firms opening in town, law firms merging (or splitting up), in-house counsel offices reorganizing, or lawyers resigning from government — all of which could lead to a job for you. The people you read about in publications may be your future interviewers, employers, or colleagues.

Some important national periodicals of note would include the *American Lawyer*, the *Student ABA*, the *ABA Journal*, and the *National Law Journal*. Different cities and regions have their localized journals — for example, the *New York Law Journal*. You can read these periodicals in hard copy in your library, or on the Internet. Some services (*Lexis*, *Westlaw*, *New York Times*, *Google*, *USA Today*) will send you news articles about specific legal topics of interest to you. Lawyers read periodicals that focus on their region or their specialized area of law. You should, too.

26. Read Law Blogs

Keep abreast of what is going on in the areas of law that interest you. But keep in mind that blogs can be addictive. And they may contain inaccurate information, at times deliberately.

27. Consult With Your "Career Coach"

From time to time during your LL.M. year (and after), contact your career coach. Discuss your goals and your achievements. Assess and reassess. Finding a job involves determination and perseverance.

28. Search for and Attend Special Events

Search for and attend programming and/or special events offered by your school's career office. You never know at which event you might casually meet your next employer!

29. Search for Nontraditional Jobs

When you begin your LL.M., you might think you want to do a particular type of legal work for a particular type of institution. Maybe you initially wanted to work for a Wall Street law firm, the UN, or a government law department. During your LL.M. year, you may discover that you might be interested in creative opportunities. Check the *Non-Traditional Careers Report*, which suggests how you might use your LL.M. outside of traditional law practice. Your law school should subscribe to this report.

30. Build Your Resume

Engage in professional activities and list them on your resume.

(a) *Write and publish articles* (on-campus and off-campus).
(b) *Participate in extracurricular student activities.*
(c) *Become an officer of a law student or campus-wide organization.*
(d) *Tutor undergraduates or law students in your native language.*
(e) *Give presentations about events in your home country or region* (particularly if topical issues are being covered in U.S. news).

31. Publish

Publish in your field of law to help you develop a positive reputation among academics and practitioners in your field. You could publish a law review or law journal note, short pieces for law magazines, bar journals, or essays for blogs. You can co-author pieces with students, practicing lawyers, or maybe even a professor. Prospective employers in all fields look for evidence of a candidate's interest in that field. Publications in an area demonstrate such evidence. Professor Mark Wojcik of **John Marshall-Chicago** notes that "There is no shortage of publications that are looking for your contributions" (*Getting Published: Improve Your Resume By Proving Your Writing Skills, Expertise and Marketability,* Student Lawyer, Vol. 37, No. 2, 2008, http://ssrn.com/abstract=1318388).

32. Participate in Prestigious Student Activities, as Well as Student Organizations and Extracurricular Activities

Work on a law review or journal, moot court, in client counseling, or other activities that involve students competing in the academic context. Join the law student newspaper. Prospective employers value these activities.

Join a law school legal fraternity, an "Inn of Court," or a student organization or other extracurricular group that focuses on areas that interest you. Participate in their activities. These are great networking opportunities. If your school permits only J.D. students to participate in some of these activities, ask the LL.M. administration why. Does the school have legitimate grounds for discriminating against LL.M. students? Do you have a justifiable complaint? (See Chapter 19.)

33. Join Global Student Organizations in the U.S. and Overseas

Be certain to join student organizations with global reach, which will help you connect with international students in the U.S.; international students outside the U.S.; and lawyers, judges, professors, and other legal professionals from around the globe. Student organizations with global reach include the International Law Students Association (ILSA); the Council for American Students in International Negotiations (CASIN); and (overseas) the European Law Students Association (ELSA).

(a) *International Law Students Association (ILSA)* (www.ilsa.org). ILSA is a nonprofit association of students and lawyers dedicated to the promotion of international law. Student members study, research, and network in the international legal arena. ILSA organizes three conferences each year and publishes international law books and other academic resources. ILSA coordinates chapters at law schools across the country, and globally administers the Philip C. Jessup International Law Moot Court Competition, which is the largest moot court competition in the world, with thousands of law student participants from over 500 schools in over 80 countries. U.S. schools with international students in LL.M. programs, particularly if the schools have emphases in international law areas, *should have* active ILSA chapters, and those schools *should* actively participate in Jessup. (In the interest of full disclosure, the author is a former member of the ILSA Board of Directors, and is donating his profits from this edition of *LL.M. Roadmap* to the Association.)

(b) *Council for American Students in International Negotiations (CASIN)* (www.americanstudents.us). CASIN is an educational nonprofit, non-governmental organization that organizes student delegations to meetings of various UN bodies, the Assembly of States Parties of the ICC, the Pan-American Health Organization, and the Biennial Meeting of States on Small Arms. CASIN publishes student-edited scholarly journals and provides young persons unprecedented access to the international policymaking process. (The author has served as Member and Chair of the CASIN Advisory Board.)

(c) *The European Law Students Association (ELSA)* (www.elsa.org). ELSA is an international, independent, nonpolitical, nonprofit organization run by and for law students and recent graduates. It was founded in 1981 by five law students (from Austria, Hungary, Poland, and West Germany), and is now the world's largest independent law students association. ELSA is represented at 200 law faculties in 42 countries across Europe with over 30,000 student and young lawyer members. ELSA offers traineeship programs, publications, a WTO moot court competition, and significant professional networking opportunities. (The author recognizes the depth and breadth of ELSA's work over the years.)

Employment

34. Keep Your Career Tools in Good Working Order

The first strategy lists tools you need for career development. Make sure you keep those tools polished and sharpened so that they continue to serve you well. Update your resume. Do practice interviews, playing the roles of both interviewee and interviewer. Discover what it is like to be an employer conducting an interview! You might be surprised that it is not as easy as you had imagined.

H. On-Campus Strategies

35. Join Law Student Study Groups

This is a great way to meet smart, dedicated students who are determined to succeed. It is particularly helpful to meet students who work part time at law firms, or who entered law school after being in the workforce for some years. They have experience. And connections. It would also help to study with people interested in the same areas of law that interest you. The more students who know you, the greater the chances for you to learn of job career prospects. For instance, students might pass on to you interesting opportunities they learn about. (See Chapter 19.)

36. Meet and Strategize with J.D. Students

It is great to get to know J.D. students. Most have English as their native language. They can help you retool your resume, cover letters, and writing samples (though they should not do any writing for you). They can also share job tips and help you network. You can do practice interviews with them. And, perhaps best of all, J.D. students — like LL.M. students — can become your life-long friends!

37. Develop Ties Between Your Law Faculty in Your Home Country and Your U.S. Law School

U.S. law schools routinely seek formal and informal ties with foreign law schools. You may liaise between administrators and professors of your law faculty in your home country and those of your new U.S. school. Your schools might engage in faculty or student exchanges or might co-sponsor conferences. You can become well known among your U.S. law school's staff, which would help when you need a recommendation letter, or could lead to an employment opportunity by word of mouth or otherwise through the web of connectedness.

38. Develop Ties With Your Law Professors

A law professor's job has three principal components: (a) *Research and writing* (publishing articles and books); (b) *Teaching* (instructing students in the classroom, overseeing internships and clinics, and engaging in other non-classroom activities); and **(c)** *Service* (serving on law school committees, providing pro bono services to the community, and engaging in domestic and international human rights activities).

Professors are expected, as part of their responsibilities, to interact with students inside and outside the classroom, to hold office hours or otherwise be available to answer student questions, to write letters of recommendation for students, and to mentor students. Professors involved with LL.M. programs are particularly expected to be available for international and other students enrolled in those programs. Get to know your professors, and they will get to know you.

39. Find On-Campus Employment

Law school administrators and staff are great sources for identifying opportunities for you and helping you make connections. Here are a few on-campus job possibilities:

(a) *Research assistant for a professor* (obvious good networking contacts)

(b) *Library* (meet faculty who conduct research in the library)

(c) *Tutor* (great experience that will stand out on your resume)

(d) *Clerical work* (you never know what you might learn while working in the law school's alumni, development, or career office!)

(e) *Restaurant* (law professors, visiting judges and lawyers, and other notable people have to eat — develop contacts as you serve tables)

(f) *Law school cafeteria* (may be even better than a restaurant, because you will meet hundreds of students and some professors each day)

(g) *Lab technician* (meet people in other fields)

(h) *Security guard* (meet many people who come and go)

(i) *Residence hall monitor* (meet students, their friends, and parents)

(j) *Exam proctor in a non-law department* (develop relationships with assistant deans and other administrators)

(k) *Foreign language instructor* (you can develop life-long friendships with other students who have an interest in your language and culture)

(l) *On-campus nursery (for infants or trees!)* (You can network anywhere!)

(m) *Assistant in administrator's office* (career, development, alumni, or admissions office; obvious networking opportunities)

40. Talk With Professors, Administrators, and Staff

Law school administrators and staff are great sources for career tips. Get to know as many as possible, particularly those who have interests similar to yours, those who have lived and worked abroad (especially in your region), or those who are just nice people.

41. Attend Presentations, Lectures, Roundtables, Fairs, Conferences, and Sporting Events

You can learn a great deal and make great contacts at academic conferences, and at other academic functions such as receptions and dinners. People you meet may be able to offer career guidance, directly or indirectly. For instance, by meeting legal professionals from all walks of life, you might get an idea of career avenues you *do not* want to explore.

Following are a few tips:

(a) *Always carry your business cards* to lectures, conferences, and fairs. Distribute them to people you meet. Business cards help people remember who you are, and they give people your contact details, which they can use if they want to contact you later, or pass to others who may help you find work.

(b) *Read a person's business card immediately* after he or she hands it to you *before* you place the card in your pocket or purse. This small sign acknowledges the person and his or her position, and helps cement the person's name and position in your mind. It is respectful.

(c) *Wear your nametag on the right side of your chest.* When you encounter people and shake their right hand with your right hand, it is easier for their eyes to drop to the right side of your chest and read your nametag.

(d) *Be on time!* Do not arrive late. You can miss a lot. However, as they say in the U.S., it is better to arrive late than never.

42. Attend Receptions and Dinners, and Use Proper Etiquette

Different cultures have different norms regarding consuming food and drink during business lunches, dinners, and receptions. Your law school should sponsor a "Business Etiquette" seminar for LL.M. students, sharing "unwritten rules" of interaction at such events. If your school does not offer such a seminar, *request that they provide instruction in some form.* Eating and drinking at a business function *is not* the same as eating and drinking with LL.M. classmates on a Friday night after a long week of classes! You will be expected to abide by certain unwritten rules.

Following are a few tips to consider if you attend a U.S. business function.

(a) *Never* arrive at a reception, cocktail party, or lunch or dinner *very* hungry. Eat something beforehand. This will help ensure you are not overly focused on food. Your mouth will be empty so you can network with other attendees. If you are starving, you will not be able to concentrate if a law firm partner or judge engages you in discussion. *Focus on the people and conversation, not the food.*

(b) *Avoid* ordering food at a restaurant that is sloppy to eat or that requires using your hands, such as spaghetti or corn on the cob.

(c) *Use* your knife to cut food that needs it. It is safer and easier — and more polite, or genteel — than using the side of your fork.

(d) *Place* business cards face up near your plate if you are at a sit-down dinner or lunch and others at the table hand you business cards. This will help you remember their names during the meal.

(e) *Turn* your empty unused wine glass upside down and a passing waiter should remove it from your place setting. Do the same for a coffee cup if you do not want coffee.

(f) *Avoid* alcohol at business functions.

(g) *Keep* a glass filled with a drink (e.g., water, juice) in your hand at receptions. This will keep the waiters from interrupting your conversation asking you if you want a refill, and it may help you feel less nervous. Remember to drink enough liquid beforehand so you will not be thirsty.

43. Read the Law School's and LL.M. Program's Website Updates

Law school websites always contain information about current events, upcoming activities, and new developments, particularly as they relate to prospective and current students, and to graduates. Read the website updates, which at the better programs will appear on a daily basis.

Some LL.M. programs do not update the LL.M. website daily. Still, try to keep up to date with developments, especially regarding news of LL.M. graduates who may pass the bar exam in a state where you might want to practice, join a firm that interests you, or take a job in a city or country where you might want to work. They may be able to assist you in your job search — now, soon, or later — or offer you other career advice.

44. Make News That Your Law School and LL.M. Program Can Put on the Website Updates

Inform the law school if you publish an article, participate in a law conference, give a presentation, help organize a law school event, or volunteer for a community activity. Those and similar activities are "news" items that the school or the LL.M. program will want to place on its website. It would be easiest if you write up a short "news item" and send it to your LL.M. administrators, who can place it on the website. It is always great if you can include one or two photographs. Law schools like to demonstrate to current students, prospective students, and graduates that LL.M. students can have great academic and outside experiences during their LL.M. year. (Be certain to send in news items even after you graduate!)

45. Give Presentations About Your Country

Volunteer to give presentations in international or comparative law classes, undergraduate international politics classes, or other classes in your areas of expertise (even if you are not enrolled in these classes). This is good experience, adds another line to your resume, could lead to connections, and may lead to a professor's letter of recommendation.

46. Participate in Law School and University Extracurricular Activities

This is a great way to meet fellow students, professors, graduates, and members of the community interested in particular activities. (See Chapter 19.)

47. Teach Your Language to Students at the Law School.

This is a great experience in itself, and can lead to more work experience (for your resume), connections, and possible professors' letters of recommendations.

48. Post a Notice on the Student Bulletin Board. Why Not?

I have never seen an LL.M. student post a note on a school bulletin board saying "**LL.M. Student Looking for a Job.**" *Why not try it?* Students post their resumes on virtual social media sites all the time, why not on the actual physical wall of a law school hallway — maybe in the cafeteria, library, or computer lab? Maybe a fellow student who sees the ad will contact you and tell you about a job opening. However, be sure not to post your physical address or other personal information. An e-mail address is good enough.

49. School Event Invitation List

Your school's career office will host receptions, outings, or other events with alumni and prospective employers. Sometimes they invite a few selected J.D. or LL.M. students to attend. Give your name and contact details to the career office so that you might be on any "special list" when they invite students. The more familiar the career office becomes with you, the greater the chance that they may remember you and select you for one thing and another.

I. Volunteer

50. Volunteer as Much as Possible, On-Campus and Off-Campus

You would be amazed at the contacts you can develop and the practical experience you can gain while volunteering, on-campus or off-campus. You meet people, and they meet you, which makes it easier for them to recommend you to prospective employers and others who may assist. You may learn about the legal community (if you volunteer at a local bar association), about substantive law (if you volunteer at a law conference or seminar), or about some other activity (if you volunteer with a fund-raising road race, silent auction, or gala dinner).

Possible volunteer activities that may prove professionally useful might include:

(a) Volunteer to make nametags for a law school conference. You will learn names of lawyers and their employers (law firms, corporations, government offices, nongovernmental organizations, legal services and other), which will come in handy when you are looking for a job.

(b) Volunteer to hand out documents, take tickets at the door, or troubleshoot at law functions. You will meet lawyers, judges, law professors, and students.

(c) Volunteer to work at the reception desk of a bar meeting for lawyers in your community. You will meet lawyers, judges, law professors, and others from your community. When you apply for jobs, your cover letter can mention that you met the lawyer or judge at the conference.

(d) Volunteer to work in the law school's career office. (The benefits of working in the career office are obvious!)

51. Volunteer to Assist Your Law School LL.M. Office With Recruitment and Other Outreach Projects

By the time you enroll at a U.S. law school, you will be an expert on a wide range of issues that future prospective LL.M. students would be interested in hearing about. LL.M. recruitment offices receive inquiries from applicants about many of these issues, and current LL.M. students are uniquely qualified to reply. Tell your LL.M. office you will answer questions prospective students might have about your school, the application process, your experiences as a student thus far, your insights about the F-1 or J-1 visa process, and other issues. You will develop a relationship with students who may join the program the following semester or year, and help develop your relationships with LL.M. administrators. The LL.M. office may even hire you as an assistant, and pay you!

52. Volunteer at Your Local Courthouse

You could volunteer to interpret for local court proceedings, particularly for poor defendants who may not speak English. Judges, lawyers, and the client will be grateful. You will get a taste of the U.S. judicial system, and may make networking contacts for a future paid job or internship with a judge or law firm.

J. Employment Agencies, Headhunters, Paralegal Work, Part-Time or Contract Work, EducationUSA, and Legal Outsourcing Firms

53. Employment Agencies or Headhunters

Thousands of legal employment agencies or headhunting firms exist in the U.S. and overseas. They may be retained by corporations, governments, or intergovernmental organizations to identify prospective lawyers to fill jobs for which LL.M. graduates qualify. Identify and register with such firms. Get on their radar for when jobs open up. You can send an unsolicited cover letter and resume and ask to be placed in their database. They may contact you if an appropriate opening comes to their attention. Such companies may know of job openings long before the general public finds out, and before advertisements appear in traditional outlets.

54. Paralegal Work

If you practiced law in your home country, you might object to working as a paralegal in the U.S. However, it may be difficult to get a job as a lawyer in the U.S. with your LL.M. alone (or even if you have a J.D.). Though you may be able to practice based on your foreign credentials, or if you pass a U.S. bar, you still may not find a job as a lawyer. Being a paralegal has its benefits. You will gain access to a law office, which you may be able to convince to hire you as a lawyer later. You will gain law experience, which will bolster your resume. You will have a job, which many lawyers do not have. And you will earn money, though not as much as a lawyer. Finally, unbelievably, it is sometimes difficult to distinguish between work assigned to paralegals and work assigned to junior lawyers at some firms.

55. Part-Time or Contract Law Work (For Licensed or Unlicensed Law Graduates)

Law firms or other types of firms with legal work will hire "contract law agencies" that maintain a roster of law graduates (including licensed and unlicensed), who the agencies recommend to law firms or other companies that have legal needs but do not need or want to hire a full-time, permanent law graduate. These law agencies retain "contract lawyers," but are sent to the law firms as "temporary contract lawyers." These agencies may also send unlicensed law graduates to perform law-related work that does not require a law license. Contract work pays less than a full-time job, and provides no health or other benefits. But it provides an opportunity for you to gain experience at firms that may eventually hire you. Get in the door, make yourself useful, show your worth — make yourself indispensable!

56. Educational Agents or LL.M. Admission Consultants

Educational agents or LL.M. admission consultants would normally work with persons seeking to get admitted to U.S. LL.M. programs. However, agents and consultants will also have contacts with current LL.M. students with whom they worked, and with LL.M. graduates. If you are a current LL.M. student or an LL.M. graduate, you might contact agents or consultants, even if you did not work with them to gain admission, because those agents and consultants may be happy to share with you information about their clients who received their LL.M. degrees and are in the workforce. Those graduates may be good contacts for you as you seek employment. (See Chapter 8.)

57. Legal Outsourcing Firms in Your Home Country or in Another Country

U.S. law firms and corporations are increasingly "outsourcing" legal work to lawyers overseas who provide legal services for a fraction of the cost of a U.S. lawyer working in the U.S.[4] Since the 1990s, local lawyers in India, the Philippines, Sri Lanka, and other countries have provided many millions of dollars of legal services for U.S. entities.[5] Many lawyers who provide these services do not have U.S. law degrees, nor have they ever touched U.S. soil. But more are receiving U.S. LL.M. degrees, studying in a traditional residential program, an online program, or a program involving mixed modes of instruction.

If U.S. firms are outsourcing from your country or a country in which you are licensed to practice, contact the U.S. firms and their overseas counterparts. If a firm works in a legal area that interests you, contact them before you begin your

Employment

---

4. You may qualify to work in a country that provides outsourcing services even if you are not a citizen of that country. (See Chapter 2.) For example, you need not be an Indian citizen to work in India outsourcing legal services to the U.S. or the U.K. *See* Heather Timmons, *Outsourcing to India Draws Western Lawyers*, New York Times, www.nytimes.com/2010/08/05/business/global/05legal.html?_r=3&adxnnl=1&adxnnlx=1290355330-LlRU9MEHjcbWKpnzKkhYKA&pagewanted=print (4 August 2010) (also noting that the "number of legal outsourcing companies in India has mushroomed to more than 140 at the end of 2009, from 40 in 2005").

5. *See id.* ("Revenue at India's legal outsourcing firms is expected to grow to $440 million this year, up 38 percent from 2008, and should surpass $1 billion by 2014.")

LL.M. and tell them you will gear your LL.M. studies to that area, and that you want to work for them when you graduate.

K. Join Bar Associations

International students and graduates may join local, state, national, or international bar associations, or bar associations catering to different substantive areas of law or backgrounds of lawyers. Bar associations, which tend to be voluntary groups, have "committees" or "interest groups" in various substantive areas. Join bar associations and their committees or interest groups. I do not know of a bar association that excludes LL.M. students as members or associate members. Student membership fees are generally small. At bar associations, you will meet many lawyers and legal professionals with whom you can network. You can receive their publications in hard copy or electronically. You can attend workshops, conferences, career fairs, and other functions, and participate in substantive research and pro bono projects undertaken by these groups. Some bar associations have special events for LL.M. students.[6] Contact information for many bar associations around the world is available at www.hg.org/bar.html. Several bar associations are listed below.

58. American Bar Association (ABA)

The ABA is dedicated to all sectors of the legal profession. Its 400,000 members include lawyers, law professors, law students, and judges. It invites students to "become part of the most prestigious legal organization in the U.S.," to stay apprised of developments in law and the legal community, and to access "career advice and other important benefits to help you launch your career." The ABA hosts conferences, roundtables, and other events in which international LL.M. students can participate and learn about U.S. law and legal employment opportunities (www.abanet.org).

59. State Bar Associations

Join bar associations of the state where you want to work, whether your school is in that state or not. Contact information is available at www.hg.org/bar.html.

---

6. For example, in October 2010 the New York City Bar Council on International Affairs held a panel discussion entitled "Program and Reception for LLM Candidates," at which panelists spoke about their careers in international practice, effective contact-making and networking, and how joining the New York City Bar and participating on its committees may help one's career. Official participants included Samuel W. Seymour (President, New York City Bar); Mark R. Shulman, (Pace Law School graduate programs); Michael H. Byowitz (Wachtell, Lipton, Rosen & Katz); Lucy Martinez (Freshfields Bruckhaus Deringer US LLP); and Hon. Delissa A. Ridgway (Judge, U.S. Court of International Trade) (http://www.abcny.org/EventsCalendar/show_event.php?eventid=1464).

60. Minority Bar Associations

If you are a member of, or have an interest in working with, or on behalf of, particular minority groups, join related law associations. These include the *Hispanic National Bar Association* (www.hnba.com), the *National Bar Association* (www.nationalbar.org) (African-American lawyers, judges, and students), the *National Asian Pacific American Bar Association* (NAPABA) (www.napaba.org), and many more.

61. Specialty Bar Associations (Based on Practice Area)

Specialty bar associations include the *American Intellectual Property Bar Association* (www.aipla.org) and the *International Criminal Law Network* (www.icln.net). There are many specialty bar associations!

62. International Bar Association

The International Bar Association (IBA) was established in 1947, and is the world's leading organization of international legal practitioners, bar associations, and law societies. Its members include over 40,000 individual lawyers, and 197 bar associations and law societies around the globe. It covers all practice areas and professional interests, and has many publications, conferences, networking, and career-development opportunities. The IBA Human Rights Institute (IBAHRI) works to promote, protect, and enforce human rights under a just rule of law, and to preserve the judiciary's and the legal profession's independence globally (www.ibanet.org).

63. National LGBT Bar Association

The National LGBT Bar Association is a national association of lawyers, judges, and other legal professionals and law students that promotes justice in and through the legal profession for the lesbian, gay, bisexual, and transgender community in all its diversity. The National LGBT Bar Foundation is a nonprofit organization that supports the LGBT Bar, encouraging charitable, scientific, and legal educational purposes (www.lgbtbar.org).

64. Other International or Global Bar Associations

A comprehensive guide to bar associations around the world can be found at www.hg.org/bar.html and includes:

(a) North American bar associations
(b) Latin American and Caribbean bar associations
(c) European bar associations
(d) Asian-Pacific bar associations
(e) African/Middle Eastern bar associations

L. Other Off-Campus Strategies

65. Use Career Resources at Other Law Schools — *Reciprocity*

Many law schools arrange with other schools to permit students from one school to access career materials at the other school. For example, if your school is in Tennessee and you want to work in California, your school may have reciprocity with a school in California. When you visit California, you could present your Tennessee school I.D. card and be admitted to the California school's career office.

66. Recruiting, Career, or Job Fairs

Job fairs (also known as "recruiting fairs" or "recruiting programs" or "career fairs" or "career programs") fall into five main categories: (a) *Geographic* (recruiting students from schools in a certain region, or from around the U.S. to work within a certain region); (b) *Diversity* (recruiting students from traditionally underrepresented groups, such as racial, ethnic, or sexual minorities); (c) *Public interest* (recruiting to work in the nonprofit sector); (d) *Specialized* (recruiting for work in specific disciplines such as intellectual property or energy law); or (e) *Foreign lawyer* (recruiting international LL.M. students to work for law firms or companies in the U.S. or overseas).

Depending on your career objectives, one or more of these types of job fairs may interest you. Your law school's LL.M. career office will have information about major job fairs around the country, and about other job fairs in the region where your school is located. Some of the job fairs may be hosted in the city where your school is, or perhaps even at your school. Some will charge students a fee to participate, and some may charge a school to permit students from that school to participate. Some schools may subsidize student participation. *Ask!*

Reciprocity Agreements with Career Offices at Other Law Schools

If you go to school in *one state* and want to find work in *another state*, make sure your school has *reciprocity agreements* with law school career offices in the state where you want to work. This will make it easier for you to find a law job in a different region of the U.S. from where your law school is located. Also, if you use career offices at different law schools, you necessarily increase the exposure you have to employment prospects and opportunities.

Some of the job fairs — particularly some of the job fairs for foreign lawyers — are "invitation only," in that only LL.M. students enrolled in particular schools may participate. In those cases, certain law schools decide that they want to host a job fair for students from those schools, and they choose dates and a venue. The schools invite law firms, corporations, government offices, and other employers to interview LL.M. students *from those schools that organized the job fair*. If you are not enrolled in the LL.M. program at one of the organizing law schools, you are not permitted to interview at those particular job fairs.

Job fairs around the U.S. typically consist of one or more of the following activities: formal interviews, networking tables, career-oriented seminars or presentations, informational events, and/or social activities. If there is a job fair near you — even if it targets J.D. students or focuses on a type of job you do not think you want — you should plan to attend or try to participate in some of the activities. You can use them as practice for job fairs that target you and interest you. And, of course, you can use them as networking opportunities.

More information about some of these opportunities can be found at *www.LLMRoadMap.com*.

67. Law School, LL.M., and University Alumni

Alumni are almost always happy to hear from prospective and current LL.M. students and other graduates. They are generally eager to help you make contacts and secure the employment or other professional opportunity you seek.

68. Law School Alumni Association in the U.S., in Your Home Country, and in Other Countries

Register with your law school's alumni association. It may sponsor events that could help you. Alumni have special interests in helping graduates find jobs. Alumni may participate in law school career office mock interviews to help current students develop interviewing skills (while exposing them to different career paths). *Do not wait until you graduate to join your alumni association.*

69. University Alumni Association in the U.S., in Your Home Country, and in Other Countries

If your law school is part of a larger university, join the university's alumni association in addition to other alumni associations available to you (such as the Law School or LL.M. Alumni Associations).

Employment

70. LL.M. Alumni Association in the U.S., in Your Home Country, and in Other Countries

Some law school LL.M. programs have large classes, have operated for many years, and have thousands of alumni. Other schools have only a few LL.M. students each year, have operated for only a few years, and have few alumni. The larger, older programs will likely have separate LL.M. alumni associations; smaller, younger programs may not. In any case, there should be an alumni association for the Law School itself (J.D. and LL.M.), and possibly a University alumni association. As an LL.M. student and LL.M. graduate, you are eligible to join these organizations, which I encourage you to do.

71. Attend Alumni Events *Even If You Are Not a Graduate!*

If you are a prospective student or applicant and you learn that a school that interests you is holding an Alumni Association event in your country, contact the school and ask if you can attend. The answer will probably be "yes"—you can attend at least part of the event and meet some alumni. Furthermore, if you hold an LL.M. from U.S. school *A*, and you learn that U.S. school *B* is hosting an alumni event in your home country, ask if you can attend. You will broaden your network, and possibly meet new clients or a new employer.

72. Your Country's Ambassador to the U.S. (Washington, D.C.), UN Ambassador (New York City), or Consular Officials (in Other U.S. Cities)

The embassies and consulates from your country in Washington, D.C. and in other U.S. cities will often have an educational attaché responsible for assisting students from your country interested in studying in the U.S., and students from your country already studying in the U.S. Contact your embassy or consulate in the U.S., let them know that you are here, and ask how they can assist you. *Also ask how you can help them!* Foreign governments help their students who may encounter educational, financial, health, legal, or other issues while in the U.S. They can also connect you with LL.M. students from your country enrolled at other U.S. schools, and with citizens of your country who work in law and related areas. Your embassy and consulates may invite you to National Day celebrations, receptions, or conferences, or visits with your homeland's dignitaries who travel to the U.S. You can develop very valuable ties through your country's embassy in Washington or consulates in other U.S. cities.

73. The Ministry of Education of Your Home Country (and Your Ministry of Justice, Ministry of Foreign Affairs, and Other Ministries)

Most governments have an official ministry dedicated to education, and that ministry will assist students who seek to go to the U.S. to study in LL.M. and other degree programs. They will provide information for you about U.S. LL.M. programs, scholarships, and other matters and issues, and will provide you with information about contacting U.S. government officials for visa and other purposes. They may also point you toward prospective employers. You might acquire helpful information, and maybe a job (or job leads), from your country's Ministry of Justice (if your LL.M. focused on criminal law or international humanitarian law), Ministry of Foreign Affairs (if your LL.M. focused on any international law topic), or Ministry of Human Rights (if your LL.M. focused on international human rights law or civil rights law). *Do not underestimate the ability of and willingness of government ministries to assist you.*

74. Law Professors, Academic Advisors, Law Faculty Administrators from Your Home Country University

Stay in touch with law professors from your home law faculty, and your former academic advisors and law faculty administrators. They will likely be in contact with other LL.M. students and graduates from your home school and from your country, and may be able to put you in contact with some of these people, who can be very valuable resources to you.

75. Lectures or Other Events Attended by Legal Professionals

You should attend every lecture, roundtable, or other event you can where lawyers or law professors or community leaders are present. Introduce yourself. Tell people if you want to remain in the U.S. Pass out business cards. Follow up for coffee or lunch. Stay in touch.

76. Community, Social, Civic, Religious Institutions, or Activities

People meet other people in many different places. You might meet any number of helpful, interesting people in any of these environments. Keep an open mind. Carry your business cards with you—and distribute them.

M. Web Activity and Libraries

77. Websites

Websites are an invaluable source for information about jobs. Many law school LL.M. program websites will provide links to job search resources.

78. ABA-SIL Human Rights Committee Job Board

A comprehensive job board consisting of web pages for potential employment opportunities from dozens of international human rights NGOs. The job board was developed by ABA member Ellen J. Tabachnick and can be accessed at www.abanet.org/dch/committee.cfm?com=IC950000.

79. Check Your "Electronic Profile"

Prospective employers are increasingly conducting electronic searches before hiring applicants, as part of the interview or background check. Check your "electronic profile" to ensure that you have no text or image postings that might adversely affect a decision to hire you. Prospective employers routinely check Facebook, Twitter, personal and group blog sites, and personal and group websites.

Some students choose a "nickname" when creating a social website, rather than their full name. There is nothing dishonest about using a nickname that makes it less likely to trace postings to you. After all, if you have a social website, your intention is that it is for your friends, and friends of friends, and not necessarily for your next boss.

Purge your professional electronic profile of the following:

(a) Postings containing racy language
(b) Photos and other content you think would embarrass you
(c) Anything you would not want a prospective employer to see
(d) Anything that might give the wrong impression of you, your abilities, your character, or your competence
(e) Postings that are more appropriate for family and friends than for employers

80. Set Up Your Own Website or Blog

Many if not most LL.M. students have a social-networking presence, on Facebook, MySpace, or another site. You could also develop your own website or blog to share or discuss law-related material, perhaps about your area of specialized law or the law of your country. This might attract readers or subscribers who may become your new employers, or who may lead you to a new employer. Your blog might target students, lawyers, judges, law librarians, and others who you think might be able to help you make an appropriate professional connection.

81. Job Search Books

Your career office and law school library should have a wide selection of job search books. I need not list dozens of these because you should be able to find them at your law school. However, I mention one such guide that has over 1,300 pages on job searching in the legal field — *Guerilla Tactics for Getting the Legal Job of Your Dreams . . . Regardless of Your Grades, Your School or Your Work Experience*, written by Kimm Alayne Walton, J.D. (2d ed., Thompson/West 2008).

82. Martindale Hubbell

Martindale Hubbell provides comprehensive listings of lawyers and law graduates from all U.S. law schools and from many non-U.S. law schools. You may use www.martindale.com to locate alumni from your school, lawyers and law firms that work in the geographic region from which you hail, or lawyers who live and work where you want to be employed. You can gain valuable information about the educational backgrounds of lawyers, their areas of practice, their work histories, and other information that might help you as you network. You can isolate lawyers by state, law school, practice area, and other categories. You can also search for information about law firms or companies where lawyers or legal professionals work (www.martindale. com/Find-Lawyers-and-Law-Firms.aspx).

The website also houses the Martindale-Hubbell Career Center, the goal of which is "to help attorneys, paralegals, law school students and legal professionals develop their careers and find legal jobs in law firms, corporations and other employers of legal talent" (www.martindale.com/Careers/Careers. aspx). It has a "Legal Job Board Network" where employers may post job listings with Martindale-Hubbell and over 20 other law websites. You can join the Martindale-Hubbell network (http://community.martindale.com/ SignIn.aspx).

83. Lexis and Westlaw

These companies maintain directories of law firms, lawyers, in-house counsel, specializations in major countries around the world, lawyers and law firms that work in the geographic region from which you hail, or who live and work where you want to be employed (www.lexis.com; www.westlaw.com).

84. National Association for Law Placement's (NALP) Directory

The NALP has an online legal directory that provides information about job opportunities across the U.S (www.nalpdirectory.com).

Employment

N. The Search Within: Internal Strategies and Realizations

85. Recognize That Job-Hunting Can Be a Full-Time Job

Respect it, like you would respect any other job. It is like training for a marathon, with months of dedicated effort.

86. Use Your Lawyering Skills!

You have learned how to think like a lawyer. By now, you have developed a plan to help you reach your career goals. You will take proactive measures to ensure that you maximize your skill sets and marketability. You will take advantage of opportunities to develop your skills through clinical and practical skills courses, externships, part-time employment, and research. And you will apply your legal skills to the job search process. You are on your way!

87. Use Action Verbs to Enhance Your Resume. Enhance Your Life and Career Experience!

Use strong action verbs on your resume to describe your experiences. More important, while in your LL.M. program, you should strive to undertake experiential and other opportunities (internships, externships, live-client clinics, and pro bono activities) that are reflective of these strong action verbs. These are presumably the types of experiences you want to have in your legal career post-LL.M. Lists of these words appear in career materials on various law school and other websites, but most often in the context of words to use on your resume. You can also find additional information on *www.LLMRoadMap.com.*

88. Remain Optimistic and Be Proactive in Your Search

Work hard. Never give up. Persevere. Smile. Keep a positive attitude. Prevail.

CHAPTER SUMMARY

- Each international LL.M. student has personal and professional goals.
- Use school resources to help you reach your goals.
- Your school promised to provide you career resources, offer you advice, help with your resume, provide career counseling, and answer your questions.
- Even if you have a job, you can still benefit from the school's career counseling.
- You must do your part, or your school cannot easily help you. You must attend classes, study, perform well, get to know your professors, join student organizations, and get involved in those activities. Flourish!

Employment

Chapter 27

Work in the U.S. During and After Your LL.M. Program
OPT, CPT, AT, and Other Work

CHAPTER HIGHLIGHTS

- F-1 visa and J-1 visa students may work in the U.S. during and after they complete their LL.M. degree. U.S. law governs the type and location of permissible work, the maximum number of work hours, and allowable time frames for the work. The rules differ for F-1 versus J-1 students.

- Students are obligated to ensure that they comply with the government guidelines. However, your LL.M. program is expected to provide you with ample guidance.

- F-1 visa students may remain in the U.S. post-LL.M. to work for up to 12 months in a program called "Optional Practical Training" (OPT).

- J-1 visa students can work for up to 18 months in a program called "Academic Training" (AT).

- With both OPT and AT, students may begin their work period before they complete their degree.

- F-1 students may also work in "Curricular Practical Training" (CPT), but only while they are enrolled in their LL.M. program.

- Your law school will assist you if, after you arrive, you decide that you would like to work. You may work as a volunteer or for pay.

- The OPT and AT rules may change, so check the relevant U.S. government websites for any updates. Also, ask your LL.M. administrators.

A. Work in the U.S. for F-1 and J-1 LL.M. Students

No matter what U.S. law degree program you are enrolled in, or what U.S. law degree you hold, if you are not a U.S. citizen you must satisfy U.S. visa regulations before you can work legally in the U.S. Students who hold F-1 and J-1 visas

Employment

may work: (a) part time when classes are in session; (b) full time during school breaks and holidays; and (c) for a defined, fixed period of time after they complete their studies. F-1 and J-1 employment rules differ.

This chapter discusses two U.S. government schemes that **permit F-1 students** to engage in law-related work: Optional Practical Training (OPT) and Curricular Practical Training (CPT). The chapter also discusses Academic Training (AT), which **permits J-1 students** to do law-related work.

Finally, the chapter briefly mentions the H-1B (Specialty Worker Visa) and labor certification that **permit LL.M. graduates** to work in the U.S. for longer periods — after they receive their LL.M. degrees.

B. Introduction to OPT For F-1 Students

Optional Practical Training (OPT) permits F-1 students (LL.M., S.J.D., or J.D.) to gain practical experience by working in paid or unpaid jobs directly related to law. Under OPT, F-1 students may work for up to 12 months either before they complete their degrees (precompletion OPT) or after they complete their degrees (postcompletion OPT).

OPT can be *any* law-related job in the U.S. for which the student is qualified and is hired. It can be on-campus (e.g., teaching or researching), or off-campus (e.g., at a law firm, corporation, nonprofit organization, intergovernmental organization, or human rights group; or as a judge's clerk, or possibly some other state or federal government position). Your OPT application must be recommended by your school and approved by the government.

OPT-Related Immigration Forms You Should Be Familiar With

- **I-538 Form** — Certification by campus designated school official (student immigration advisor). Used to process program extension, off-campus employment permission, CPT, and OPT.
- **I-765 Form (Application for Employment Authorization Document (EAD))** — F-1 students use this form to request OPT, off-campus employment under the sponsorship of a qualifying international organization, or off-campus employment due to severe economic hardship.
- **Employment Authorization Document (EAD)** — A laminated work permit card with a photo. Issued after OPT has been granted. Indicates length of OPT period authorized.

Source: www.ice.gov/SEVIS/STUDENTS/OPT.HTM

C. OPT Categories After a Student Has Been Enrolled for Two Semesters, Nine Months, or One Academic Year

(a) *Precompletion part-time OPT* (when school is in session and training does not exceed 20 hours a week)

(b) *Precompletion part-time or full-time OPT* (during vacation or school breaks)

(c) *Postcompletion full-time OPT* (after you complete all course requirements for the degree except for a thesis or dissertation)

(d) *Postcompletion full-time OPT* (after you complete your program of study)

D. Eligibility for OPT

(1) To qualify for OPT, a student must ordinarily have held lawful full-time F-1 status for one academic year (defined as two complete semesters or approximately nine months).[1]

(2) The job must be directly related to your field of study—namely, law (but it can be in any area of law, not necessarily an area in which you might have specialized).

(3) Before you complete your LL.M. degree, your OPT work may only be part time while school is in session, but may be full time during designated breaks.

(4) If you work precompletion OPT, the period of that part-time OPT is deducted from the 12 month maximum at half the full-time rate. For example, if you work 3 months (or 12 weeks) pre-completion OPT, 1 1/2 months (6 weeks) will be deducted from your postcompletion OPT allowance.

(5) No specific job offer is required to apply for OPT.

(6) You may only begin OPT work after you receive your official approval Employment Authorization Document (EAD) work permit from USCIS.

(7) You must submit your OPT application before you complete your LL.M., and you must finish OPT no later than 14 months (12 months OPT plus 2 months or 60-day grace period) after you complete your LL.M.

---

1. Most LL.M. students complete their degree after two semesters (fall and spring), and thus would ordinarily not be eligible for part-time precompletion OPT, because for part-time OPT, the student must have been enrolled for two entire semesters. Part-time LL.M. precompletion OPT would ordinarily be used by F-1 students who take longer than two semesters to complete their LL.M. degrees.

Permitted Post-LL.M. OPT Employment

The following types of employment are permitted on your post-LL.M. law-related OPT:

- **Paid Employment** — You may work full-time (40 hours per week) or part-time (up to 20 hours) during Post-LL.M. OPT.
- **Multiple Employers** — You may work for more than one employer on Post-LL.M. OPT.
- **Work for Hire** — You need not be a "regular" employee. You may work on a contract basis.
- **Self-Employed** — You may work for yourself if you start your own business. You may practice law if you are licensed.
- **Work Through an Employment Agency** — You must work an average of 20 hours per week.
- **Volunteer Employment** — You may do volunteer work an average of 20 hours per week *if the job is always a volunteer, unpaid job*. You *may not* volunteer for a job that is normally paid. Unpaid internships count as qualified employment.

(8) You may submit your OPT application up to 90 days before you are enrolled for 1 full academic year (or 90 days before the program's end-date indicated on the I-20 form). So if you begin a two-semester LL.M. that runs from August-May, you may apply for OPT 90 days before the May end-date. Thus you can apply for OPT as early as February or March.

(9) Your school must recommend you — the F-1 student — for OPT.

E. OPT Application Packet Checklist[2]

(1) Completed USCIS Form I-765 (EAD application) (www.uscis.gov/files/form/i-765.pdf)

(2) Two passport-style photos ($2'' \times 2''$)

(3) U.S. $380 check or money order, made out to "Department of Homeland Security"

(4) Photocopy of passport data page and F-1 visa stamp in passport

(5) Photocopy of front and back of the I-94 arrival/departure card (that was stapled into your passport by customs officials at the airport when you arrived)

---

2. Be certain to check current OPT regulations, which can be found on the U.S. government website.

(6)   USCIS I-538 Form Certification by designated school official (DSO)

(7)   Photocopy of I-20 that has been designated by the DSO for OPT and all prior I-20s

(8)   Academic advisor's recommendation form

(9)   Mail your application to USCIS Service Center via U.S. Postal Service "Certified Mail Return Receipt Requested" (Your school's LL.M. program should assist you with this process.)

(10)   You must apply before you complete your LL.M. course of study

(11)   You must complete OPT within 14 months after you complete your LL.M.

F. Obligations of the Law School, LL.M. Students, and USCIS

1. Law School's Obligations

- Recommend the student for OPT and update the student's SEVIS record if the law school supports a student's OPT.
- Maintain student's SEVIS record for the 12-month authorized training.
- Indicate in SEVIS if employment is full time or part time, and include start date and end date.
- Print the employment page of the student's SEVIS Form I-20, and sign and date the form to indicate that OPT has been recommended.

2. Law Student's Obligations

- File OPT application materials with USCIS for an *Employment Authorization Document (EAD)* work permit, using Form I-765, with a $380 fee and the SEVIS Form I-20 employment page indicating that the school has recommended OPT.
- Follow all SEVIS reporting requirements as an F-1 student.
- Report any change of name or address, interruption of employment, or transfer to another institution. The school that recommended OPT must then update the student's record to reflect changes during OPT.
- If the student transfers to another school or begins another academic program, OPT is automatically voided.

3. USCIS Government Obligations

- Adjudicate the Form I-765 in a timely fashion (average USCIS processing was about six weeks during 2010 at most USCIS service centers).
- Issue an EAD work permit card on the basis of the law school's recommendation, unless the student is found otherwise ineligible (for example, a late application that arrived after LL.M. graduation).
- Notify the student of the decision; and if the application is denied, tell the reason(s) for the denial. (The applicant *may not* appeal the decision.)

Employment

G. OPT Basics — Frequently Asked Questions (FAQ)

1. Can You Leave and Return to the U.S. Before and During OPT?

Yes. Check the current rules. Be sure to have the following:

- Valid passport (should have at least six months validity remaining)
- Valid F-1 visa stamp pasted in your passport
- Form I-20, declaring that your school has authorized you for travel (before you leave, you can send your I-20 to your law school for travel signature)
- Valid EAD card (work permit)
- Letter from employer verifying employment status, or, if you are not employed, proof that you are actively seeking employment in the U.S. or returning to the U.S. to commence OPT

2. Do You Get Extra OPT If You Earn More Than One Degree in the U.S.?

An F-1 student may receive 12 months of OPT for each higher degree completed. If you complete an LL.M. *and* an S.J.D. you may receive 24 months OPT. You may not accumulate or "bank" OPT time and take both years at the same time after the second, higher level degree. The first OPT must be used within 14 months from the date the first degree is completed.

3. What If You Do Not Have a Job Offer When Applying for OPT?

It is *not required* that you have a job offer to be eligible for OPT. But you must be employed *during* the OPT period. Paid or unpaid law-related work counts as qualified employment.

4. Are You Eligible for OPT While Writing Your Dissertation or Thesis?

Candidates who successfully complete all course requirements but are still working on a dissertation or thesis are eligible for full-time OPT before conferment of the degree.

5. May You Work in the U.S. After You Finish Your OPT?

- Law schools will provide advice and assistance regarding which forms need to be filed, and when
- Current guidelines can be found at www.uscis.gov/portal/site/uscis
- See Section J below.

H. Curricular Practical Training (CPT) for F-1 Students

F-1 students may work *off-campus* in a CPT program that is an "integral part of an established curriculum." CPT is defined as "alternative work/study, internship, cooperative education, or any other type of required internship or practicum that is offered by sponsoring employers through cooperative agreements with the school."

For example, **Golden Gate's** U.S. Legal Studies LL.M. program requires an internship, and F-1 students enrolled in it may do CPT. The school endorses the CPT during the same semester or term as the internship period. The student may receive academic credit for the internship.

I. Academic Training (AT) for J-1 Students

1. General AT Information

Academic training (AT) permits J-1 students to engage in temporary employment directly related to your field — law.

Academic training permits you to gain practical experience and legal training under the supervision of a U.S. employer. Under AT, you may work for up to 18 months, or for the duration of your degree (which is typically 9 months for LL.M. students), either before you complete your degree (precompletion AT), or after you complete you degree (postcompletion AT). The period of time in AT cannot exceed the time in full-time study. Because this gets tricky in the context of LL.M. degrees that require only two semesters of full-time study, J-1 students interested in AT should inquire early, even before they enroll in the LL.M. program.

Academic training can be *any* law-related job in the U.S. (for which you are qualified and hired, and which is integral and critical to your program of study). AT can be on-campus (e.g., teaching or researching), or off-campus (at a law firm, corporation, nonprofit organization, intergovernmental organization, human rights group; or a judge's clerkship, and possibly some other state and federal government positions). Your AT application must be approved by your J-1 sponsor and approved by your law school (typically your academic advisor and responsible officer).

2. Academic Training Categories

(a) *Precompletion part-time AT* (when the school is in session and "training" does not exceed 20 hours a week)

(b) *Precompletion part-time or full-time AT* (during vacation time or breaks)

(c) *Postcompletion full-time AT* (after you complete all course requirements for the degree, excluding a thesis or dissertation)

(d) *Postcompletion full-time AT* (after you complete your program of study; though the AT status must be authorized before you complete your program of study, and before your DS-2019 expires)

3. General AT Requirements Summary

(a) Your primary purpose in the U.S. must be to study law (which is the case for LL.M. students).

(b) You must be in good academic standing at your law school.

(c) Your AT job must be directly related to law.

(d) During AT you must maintain bona fide J-1 status in the U.S.

(e) You must maintain health insurance coverage outlined per your DS-2019 and required by U.S. federal regulation.

(f) You must file for AT with your J-1 sponsor before you complete your LL.M. degree. Your J-1 sponsor must approve your application.

(g) Your work must be a critical or integral part of your program of study.

(h) Your AT period may not exceed the program time. For example, if you enroll in a nine-month LL.M. program you are eligible for up to nine months of AT *only*.

(i) For every month you work at least part time, even during the academic year, one month is deducted from the amount of time you have in AT. Thus, if a J-1 student works part-time AT in April and May and completes his program in June, then he would have seven months left for AT, because two months were used for part-time employment.

4. Travel Outside the U.S. During AT

If you hold a J-1 visa and you plan to travel outside the U.S. during your AT period, when you return you must have:

(a) Your sponsor authorization letter

(b) Your DS-2019 (signed for reentry)

(c) Your valid J-1 visa

(d) Your valid passport

(e) A letter from your employer (noting that you are returning to work)

(f) If you need a new J-1 visa to reenter the U.S., *take caution*. It may be difficult to acquire it unless you return to your home country. Even then there is no guarantee. Check with your school *before* you depart the U.S. if you think there is a chance your U.S. student visa may expire before you will likely try to return. J-1 visas cannot be issued in the U.S.

J. Temporary Employment in the U.S. — H-1B Visa (Unrelated to OPT, AT, or CPT)

The U.S. permits applications on behalf of non-U.S. citizens for H-1B visas that will permit them to work in the U.S. for up to six years. If an LL.M. graduate finds a company in the U.S. to hire her, the company could petition the government for an H-1B visa on behalf of that graduate. Each year the government sets a numerical limit on the number of H-1B visas it issues; when that number is reached, no additional H-1B visas are issued until the following October.[3]

The U.S. may grant an initial H-1B visa for up to three years, then extend it for a maximum of six years. If you want to stay longer than six years, you may apply for permanent residency (a "green card") while your H-1B visa is still valid.

K. "Permanent" Employment in the U.S. — Labor Certification

LL.M. graduates might seek "permanent" employment in the U.S. under the "labor certification" scheme. Employers may hire foreigners to work in the U.S. if the Department of Labor certifies that no qualified U.S. workers are able, willing, qualified, and available to accept the job in question at the prevailing wage in the area of intended employment, and that the work will not adversely affect the wages and working conditions of similarly employed U.S. workers.

To qualify for U.S. Labor Certification, the employer must petition the government and demonstrate the following eligibility requirements:

(1) The employer must hire the foreign worker as a full-time employee.
(2) The position must be a bona fide job opening available to U.S. workers.
(3) The employer cannot tailor job requirements to the foreign worker's qualifications, but must adhere to what is customarily required for the occupation in the U.S.
(4) The employer must document that the job opportunity has been and is being described without unduly restrictive job requirements, unless adequately documented as arising from business necessity.
(5) The employer must pay at least the prevailing wage for the occupation in the area of intended employment (www.foreignlaborcert.doleta.gov/perm.cfm).

L. Do Not Violate U.S. Immigration Law or Labor Law

An international LL.M. student or graduate should work in the U.S. only if authorized, and only to the extent authorized by U.S. immigration law. If you perform unauthorized work, you may be subject to harsh penalties, including fines or deportation.

---

3. A problem arises if an F-1 student on OPT is waiting for his H-1B visa to be issued, but while he is waiting his OPT/F-1 status is set to expire. The F-1 student would have a gap in U.S. work authorization, and/or ability to remain in the U.S., between the end of the OPT authorization and the beginning of H-1B working visa status. In 2008, the U.S. issued a "Cap Gap" regulation to automatically extend work authorization and bona fide status for F-1 OPT students who are awaiting their H-1B visas to begin with the October 1 U.S. government fiscal year (FY).

CHAPTER SUMMARY

- F-1 students can work in OPT or CPT.

- J-1 students may work in AT.

- OPT, CPT, and AT rules are strict. Be certain you understand them and comply with them. Your school will assist you. However, it is your responsibility to comply with U.S. federal regulations and law school policy.

- Your school's career office should help you find OPT, CPT, and AT work. Before you enroll, ask your school what assistance it is willing and able to provide. Ask whether current and former LL.M. students have found OPT, CPT, or AT jobs. If the answers are not satisfactory, you may want to consider choosing another U.S. law school.

- Employment rules may change. Check U.S. government websites for updates. Ask your law school.

Employment

Bar Exams and Practicing Law in the U.S. Post-LL.M.

CHAPTER HIGHLIGHTS

- LL.M. students and LL.M. graduates have no automatic right to practice law in the U.S.
- Foreign-educated lawyers who are licensed overseas have no automatic right to practice law in the U.S.
- Typically, you must become a member of a U.S. state's bar — that is, you must acquire a law license in that state — to practice law in that state.
- This chapter examines bar admission rules in the U.S., with a focus on the New York bar (one of several U.S. states that permits foreign lawyers to sit for its bar exam).
- Because bar admission rules are subject to change, you are strongly encouraged to learn the current rules, by consulting the bars of the states that interest you.

A. Introduction

1. Generally

You need a law license issued by the bar licensing agency in a U.S. state to practice law in the U.S.[1] When you are granted a law license, you are "admitted to" and become a member of the state's "bar" and can practice law in that state. The most common way to become a member of a bar is to pass a state's "bar exam." Each state decides what it tests on its bar exam, who can sit for it, and its general bar admission requirements. No one — including U.S. citizens or non-

---

1. "State" includes U.S. territories and special jurisdictions that regulate the practice of law locally, including Guam, the Northern Mariana Islands, Puerto Rico, the U.S. Virgin Islands, and Washington, D.C.

citizens — has an automatic right to sit for a bar exam or to practice law in the U.S.

2. Chapter Highlights

This chapter covers:

(a) Law practice in the U.S. — practice settings
(b) State bar admission authorities ("Law Boards")
(c) Foreign lawyers practicing law in the U.S.
(d) Newly modified New York bar exam regulations (and a proposed ABA model rule on admitting foreign-educated lawyers to U.S. bars)[2]
(e) The New York Bar exam itself
(f) How to prepare for a bar exam

B. The Many Possible Settings of Law Practice in the U.S.

Lawyers admitted to a U.S. bar may work in many subject areas in many types of institutions around the country.[3] **Vermont Law School** summarizes law practice "settings" in a publication titled *Career Development: A Manual for J.D., Joint Degree and LL.M. Students,* which they post online. Below are **Vermont**'s categories — maintained but paraphrased, with built-on descriptions.

1. Law Firms

Law firms tend to be for-profit businesses, owned by partners, with associate lawyers as employees. Firms may have as few as one lawyer (sole practitioner) or many hundreds of lawyers. Some firms provide a wide range of legal services in many substantive areas of law, while some specialize in client type, service, or substantive areas of law. Law firms exist in every U.S. state.

Employment

---

2. Bar admission rules in all U.S. states are always subject to change. For example, New York bar admission rules for foreign-educated lawyers were changed effective May 18, 2011. Furthermore, the ABA has circulated for discussion a proposed model rule on admission of foreign-trained lawyers to U.S. bars. The New York and ABA provisions are discussed in this chapter.

3. The U.S. Bureau of Labor Statistics (BLS) notes that in 2008 lawyers "held about 759,200 jobs," that 26 percent were self-employed as law firm partners or in solo practice, and most salaried lawyers worked in government (mostly local); law firms or other corporations; or nonprofit organizations. Federal government lawyers worked in many agencies, but primarily in the Departments of Justice, Treasury, and Defense. Non-government lawyers worked as in-house counsel for public utilities, banks, insurance companies, real-estate agencies, manufacturing firms, other business firms, and nonprofit organizations. Some had part-time independent practices. Others worked part time as lawyers. The BLS lawyer employment estimate excludes lawyers who work as law school professors and administrators. (www.bls.gov/oco/ocos053.htm)

2. Government

Lawyers work for federal, state, and local governments. Foreign lawyers are prohibited from working for certain governmental offices, but many offices welcome U.S. and foreign lawyers.

a. Federal

Vermont notes that the "federal government is the largest legal employer in the world," and that most "agencies, departments, commissions, and boards hire attorneys, including law students during the summer and academic year."

b. State and Local

Many lawyer positions exist at state, county, and city levels. Typically, the Attorney General's Office is the primary state employer of lawyers, but lawyers work in other departments, including health and family services, commerce and trade, environment, education, and employment. They are also county and city attorneys, district attorneys, and public defenders.

3. The Judiciary

Attorneys serve as judges, magistrates, law clerks, referees, mediators, prosecutors, staff attorneys, and bailiffs. LL.M. students may work as law clerks or participate in Judicial Observation Programs like the one started at the **University of Minnesota School of Law**. *Judicial law clerks* help judges research, write, run their chambers, and work with litigants.

4. Congress and State Legislatures

At both the state and federal levels, lawyers work for individual elected legislators, for committees, or for a legislative body itself. Legislatures are law-making bodies, and lawyers advise on drafting and interpreting legislation, and other law-related tasks. Legislators are involved in policy making in many areas including foreign relations, international trade, national security, tax, and labor issues.

5. Executive Branch

Lawyers work for the U.S. president, state governors, and many federal and state executive agencies.

6. Public Interest

Lawyers in this area work for poor people who cannot afford legal assistance, for individuals and groups struggling for human rights, as advocates on civil

Employment

and political issues, and on issues that generally touch on social concerns, particularly for indigent clients. Public interest lawyers help level the playing field, by helping clients who would otherwise go unrepresented. **Vermont** points out that public interest lawyers work in a wide variety of areas, including immigration, environment, employment, housing, civil rights, consumer rights, education, and child abuse. Public interest practice settings generally fall into two categories:

a. Public Interest Organizations

These organizations include civil rights groups, legal services corporations, legal aid societies, public defender offices, childrens' rights centers, prisoners' rights centers, and disability law centers.

b. Private Law Practitioners

These practitioners include law firms that have regular paid clients (perhaps on issues related to human rights, immigration, or public health), but that perform some amount of *pro bono* work (with no fees, for the good of the public).

7. Corporations

Corporations hire lawyers to work as "in-house counsel" who handle corporate legal matters, and they often retain outside counsel for external business projects.

8. Academia

In the U.S., most law professors, law deans, and law school academic administrators are trained as lawyers, though holding a law degree or being licensed to practice is not required. LL.M. students may use their LL.M. period to research, write, and publish scholarly works to prepare them for careers as an academic. In many other countries, law teachers are required to hold either an LL.M. degree, *or* an S.J.D. or PhD in law.

9. Nontraditional or Alternative

Many law graduates do not practice law. They may work in many industries and positions, some of which are not directly related to law, but require lawyerly skills. LL.M. graduates can work in corporate management, at accounting firms, as a lobbyist or politician, or in a university or law school nonteaching position. They may work as administrators of LL.M. programs, as educational agents (helping law schools recruit international LL.M. students), or educational consultants (helping international students get admitted to LL.M. programs). Keep your eyes peeled — and keep an open mind!

C. Bar Admission Authorities of Each State Set Admission Rules

To find out if you are eligible to sit for the Bar Examination in *any* particular state, visit www.ncbex.org.

Everyone who seeks a license to practice law in the U.S. must apply to the bar admission authorities of the state in which the license is sought. *LL.M. Roadmap* refers generally to these authorities as the "Board of Law Examiners" (or "Law Board"). The Law Board is associated with the state's highest court and determines eligibility and admission requirements for that state. The Law Boards of all U.S. jurisdictions are listed at the National Conference of Bar Examiners (NCBEX) website.[4]

Most Law Boards require U.S.-trained law graduates to possess a J.D. "from a law school that meets acceptable established educational standards." Law Boards in the U.S. rely on the ABA's assessment of law school J.D. programs, and thus a J.D. degree from an ABA-approved law school meets the requirements in every jurisdiction in the United States. The ABA is considering a proposed model rule that would permit LL.M. programs in the U.S. to be certified so that international LL.M. graduates of "ABA-certified" LL.M. programs might also be eligible to sit for U.S. bars.[5]

D. Foreign Lawyers Practicing in the U.S.

A person with foreign law training and/or law practice may be admitted to practice law in the U.S. under several circumstances, pursuant to rules of each

---

4. www.ncbex.org/bar-admissions/offices. The NCBEX is a not-for-profit company founded in 1931. Its mission is:

> to work with other institutions to develop, maintain, and apply reasonable and uniform standards of education and character for eligibility for admission to the practice of law; and to assist bar admission authorities by providing standardized examinations of uniform and high quality for the testing of applicants for admission to the practice of law, disseminating relevant information concerning admission standards and practices, conducting educational programs for the members and staffs of such authorities, and providing other services such as character and fitness investigations and research.

5. In spring 2011, the ABA circulated for discussion the "Proposed Model Rule on Admission of Foreign Educated Lawyers" ("ABA proposed model rule") "to aid state courts and bar examiners in identifying LL.M. programs that meet specific criteria designed to prepare graduates of foreign law schools to take the bar examination and to practice law" in the U.S. ABA, Section of Legal Education and Admissions to the Bar, *Report and Proposed Model Rule on Admission of Foreign Educated Lawyers*. (www.americanbar.org/content/dam/aba/administrative/legal_education_and_admissions_to_the_bar/council_reports_and_resolutions/20110420_model_rule_and_criteria_foreign_lawyers.authcheckdam.pdf). (The ABA report also contains the Proposed Criteria for ABA Certification of an LL.M. Degree for the Practice of Law in the United States ("ABA Proposed Criteria for LL.M. Certification")). The ABA noted that the "primary goal is to provide a Model Rule for those state courts that have not adopted requirements governing the admission of foreign lawyers." As of summer 2011, the ABA Model Rule has not yet been adopted by the ABA Council. *See also* Karen Sloan, ABA Proposes Big Changes for LL.M.s (*The National Law Journal*; May 24, 2011) (www.law.com/jsp/article.jsp?id=1202494952850&ABA_Proposes_Big_Changes_for_LLMs&slreturn=1&hbxlogin=1).

state's Law Board. As mentioned, each state has its own bar eligibility guidelines for J.D. and/or LL.M. graduates, the ABA proposed model rule for LL.M. eligibility has not come into effect, and there is no uniformity in the J.D. or LL.M. eligibility across the various states. It is suggested that you consult Chapter X of the annually published *Comprehensive Guide to Bar Admission Requirements* that provides details of which persons with which U.S. and non-U.S. law education and practice experience are eligible to become members of the bar of U.S. states.[6] You should also check the websites of the Law Boards in the state where you want to practice, and examine closely the rules in the state, determine whether you meet that state's eligibility requirements, and then follow the rules and procedures in applying to that state's Law Board. This section of the chapter describes *generally* eligibility criteria considered by *some* states that admit foreigners to practice based on the following:

1. **Taking a U.S. Bar Exam (If You Have a Foreign Law Degree or Foreign Law License — Even Without an LL.M.)**

Some states will permit you to sit for their bar exam based on your possessing a law degree or law license from another country, typically a common law country. In these cases, you do not need an LL.M. degree to sit for that bar exam.

2. **Taking a U.S. Bar Exam, Coupled With Your Earning a U.S. LL.M. Degree**

This is the route most commonly taken by foreign lawyers from civil/continental law countries (and some common law countries) who want to sit for a U.S. bar. They come to the U.S., enroll in and complete an LL.M. program, then sit for the bar exam of one of the states that permits this. Many foreign graduates of U.S. LL.M. programs take the New York bar, which as mentioned, is subject to new eligibility rules. (See paragraph E below.) The California bar is also a popular choice. If the ABA proposed model rule takes effect, U.S. LL.M. programs may apply for "ABA certification," and international LL.M. graduates of ABA-approved LL.M. programs could sit for the bar in states that adopt the model rule, which could possibly trigger an increase in foreign-educated graduates of U.S. LL.M. programs taking U.S. bar exams in more states. State Law Boards may rely on the ABA certification of the LL.M. just as they rely on ABA accreditation of the JD — as an indication that law graduates possess the training and education necessary for bar admission.

---

6. The *Comprehensive Guide to Bar Admission Requirements 2011* (www.ncbex.org/comprehensive-guide-to-bar-admissions) is published by the NCBEX and the ABA Section of Legal Education and Admissions to the Bar (www.ncbex.org/fileadmin/mediafiles/downloads/Comp_Guide/2011_CompGuide.pdf). J.D. graduates from ABA-approved J.D. programs may sit for the bar of *any* state in the U.S.. For bar admission flexibility, international students may decide to earn a J.D. in lieu of, or after completing, the LL.M.

3. "Waiving In" From One State's Bar to the Bar of Another State

If you are a member of one state's bar, you might be able to join the bar of another state without taking that second state's bar exam. A typical rule is that you must be a member in good standing in the first U.S. state's bar for five years before you are able to waive into the second state. Some states (such as Hawaii, Arizona, and Florida) do not permit waiving in, even for U.S.-trained lawyers.

4. Gaining "Foreign Legal Consultant" Status (*Without* a U.S. LL.M. and *Without* Sitting for a U.S. Bar Exam)

A person with a non-U.S. law license may qualify as a "foreign legal consultant" in some states.[7] She may advise on foreign law (and may not advise on U.S. or state law), with or without a U.S. LL.M. degree, and is not considered full members of that state's bar.

E. New York Bar Admission for Foreign-Educated Lawyers — New Rules

New York's modified bar eligibility rules for foreign-trained lawyers came into effect on May 18, 2011.[8] If you are interested in taking the New York bar, it is highly advisable that you visit their website (www.nybarexam.org) for current, detailed information on taking (and passing) the exam.

This section of the chapter briefly describes the process for foreigners who want to take the New York bar exam.[9] First, you must prove that you are eligible to take the exam. **Second,** you must register for the exam. Note that thousands of foreign-trained lawyers prove their eligibility and take the exam each year. And many pass!

---

7. Fewer than 100 foreign law consultants were granted authorization to practice in the U.S. in each of the years 2005-2009. In 2009, 85 foreign legal consultants became authorized in these states: Arizona (5); California (10); Delaware (2); District of Columbia (13); Florida (29); Illinois (2); Massachusetts (1); New York (10); Ohio (1); Texas (11); and Utah (1).

8. The bar admission rules for those who study law outside the U.S. are contained in *Rules of the Court of Appeals for the Admission of Attorneys and Counselors at Law*, Rule 520.6. This rule is titled "Study of law in foreign country; required legal education." *Id.* For a summary of New York bar exam requirements for foreign lawyers *see* www.nybarexam.org (under the link "Foreign Legal Education") or *see* www.nybarexam.org/Foreign/ForeignLegalEducation.htm.

9. The new rules that took effect on May 18, 2011 outline which provisions (old or new rules) apply to LL.M. candidates who had already commenced their LL.M. study as of that date, or those who will be commencing their study before another specified date. In short, the new rules apply fully to LL.M. students who commence their study in the U.S. "in the 2012-2013 academic year." It is imperative that you check the website to learn whether the old rules or the new rules will apply to you. It is not inconceivable that if you commence LL.M. study in the 2012 Spring or Summer, you might wish to argue that the *old*, more lenient rules apply to you, since the "2012-2013 academic year" would not commence until fall (August/September) 2012. Good luck!

Employment

1. Proving That You Are Eligible to Sit for the New York Bar[10]

New York bar admission rules permit you to sit for the New York bar exam if you can provide "satisfactory proof of the legal education required by" Rule 520.6. This rule contains seemingly complex criteria, with multiple, variable prongs, some of which you must satisfy based on your background studying or practicing law. But, it is not *that* complicated.

Because the majority of international LL.M. students who wish to sit for the New York bar exam will face Rule 520.6(b)(1) hurdles, I will focus on that provision, which permits some foreign-educated law graduates under some circumstances to sit for the New York bar exam based in part on their education.[11]

Rule 520.6(b)(1) has four primary eligibility requirements that you must satisfy:

(1) *Qualifying degree.* You must show that you "fulfilled the educational requirement for admission to the practice of law in a country other than the" U.S. Your qualifying degree *must* be a law degree. (Rule 520.6(b)(1))

(2) *Accreditation.* Your qualifying law degree must have been earned at one or more law schools "recognized by the competent accrediting agency of the government of the foreign country". (Rule 520.6(b)(1))

(3) *Durational equivalence.* Your period of law study must have been "at least substantially equivalent in duration to that required" in a full-time or part-time program at an ABA-approved law school in the U.S. (Rule 520.6(b)(1))

(4) *Substantial equivalence.* The jurisprudence of the country where you studied must be based on the principles of English Common Law and the program and course of law study "were the substantial equivalent of the legal education provided by an approved law school in the" U.S. (Rule 520.6(b)(1)(i))

Good news first: If you satisfy all four of the above-mentioned prongs, great. You may be eligible to sit for the New York bar *without* pursuing an LL.M. degree in the U.S.

Not so good news: Many of you will fall short, usually in either the third or fourth prong, or both. For example, if your overseas law study was not long enough, you would have a "durational deficiency" under the third prong. If your degree was not in English Common Law, you would have a "substantive deficiency" under the fourth prong. If you have *both* a durational deficiency

Employment

---

10. *See* www.nybarexam.org (under the link "Foreign Legal Education") for a summary of New York bar requirements for foreign lawyers.

11. I will not discuss New York bar requirements for overseas-trained lawyers who seek to sit in New York based on admission to practice law in a country whose jurisprudence is based on English Common Law, or admission overseas based on law school and/or law office study. That information can be found in Rule 520.6(b)(2).

(overseas law study too short) *and a* substantive deficiency (overseas study *not* in English Common Law), then you *cannot* sit for the New York bar exam under Rule 520.6(b)(1).[12]

More good news: If you have *either* a durational deficiency *or* a substantive deficiency, you may be permitted to "cure" that one deficiency. The rules do not permit you to cure *both* deficiencies, only one. The way you can cure that one deficiency is to graduate from an LL.M. program in the U.S., pursuant to the amended Rule 520.6, that became effective on May 18, 2011, as discussed below.

2. Documents and Forms

If you are relying on Rule 520.6 to demonstrate your eligibility to sit for the New York bar exam, you must complete an online *Foreign Evaluation Form* before applying to sit, whether your overseas training was in English Common Law or otherwise.[13] After you submit your evaluation form, you must submit the following documents:[14]

(a) **Official Transcript(s).** From *every* law school attended (with dates of attendance and degree, courses passed, degrees awarded).

(b) **Degree Certificate(s).** Evidencing completion of all relevant degrees.

(c) **Proof that you fulfilled the educational requirements for admission to the practice of law in the foreign country:**[15]
   - If you *are admitted* to practice law in a foreign country, attach a copy of your admission certificate; or
   - If you are *not admitted* to practice law in a foreign country, submit proof of the educational requirements for admission to practice law in your country and proof that you fulfilled these requirements.

(d) **Accreditation.** Statement from the accrediting agency of your foreign government that it recognizes as qualified and approved the law school you attended during the *entirety* of your attendance.

(e) **English translation.** English translations must be prepared by "an official translator" (and not translated by yourself).

Employment

---

12. You may still be able to sit for the New York bar under Rule 520.6(b)(2). Though it is unlikely that a person who fails the durational and substantive equivalency prongs of Rule 520.6(b)(1) might qualify under Rule 520.6(b)(2), you should explore all options.

13. More than one LL.M. program director has suggested that international LL.M. students interested in sitting for the New York bar exam complete their Online Foreign Evaluation Form as soon as they get admitted to a U.S. LL.M. program (www.nybarexam.org/Docs/eval_form.pdf).

14. When you travel to the U.S. to begin your LL.M., bring your original transcripts and bar admission certificates from your home country, as they may be hard to acquire later. It is better if they are in envelopes sealed by the issuing schools or agencies. Please read the rules regarding documentation coming directly from the issuing institutions or government agencies, the need for original or certified copies, the unacceptability of certain faxed or photocopied documents, and other requirements. Furthermore, documents submitted become the property of the Law Board and they will not return them to you.

15. You *do not* have to be a member of your country's bar to qualify to sit for the New York bar exam.

3. Law Board Evaluation of Your Submission — Timing.

The Law Board will not review your evaluation form until it receives all your documents, and will render its decision on your evaluation ten to twelve weeks later. The Law Board notes that applicants relying on Rule 520.6(b) "are *strongly* encouraged to request an evaluation of their foreign educational credentials and anticipated course of American law study *at least one year in advance* of their application to sit for the bar examination."[16]

4. Law Board Replies to Your Submission

The Law Board will write back and inform you that either:

a. You are eligible to take the New York bar without any further educational requirements. (This would be for people with qualified and approved English Common Law training for the requisite duration); or

b. Based on a review of your submitted documents, you are not eligible, but you can become eligible if you "cure" one of the "deficiencies" by graduating from an LL.M. program (as discussed below in the section of this chapter that focuses on curing deficiencies).

   i. If you are from a common law country, but the period of study for your degree was shorter than required, you would have a "durational deficiency." You can "cure" this deficiency with an LL.M. degree earned in the U.S. if your LL.M. satisfies the new rules.

   ii. If you are from a civil law country, you will be deemed to have a "substantive deficiency," because your degree is not a common law degree. You can "cure" this deficiency with an LL.M. earned in the U.S. if your LL.M. satisfies the new rules.

   iii. If your education period was shorter than required under the durational requirement (durational deficiency), and you are from a civil law country (substantive deficiency), then you cannot cure, because you have two deficiencies.

5. Curing a Durational or Substantive Deficiency — Graduating from a U.S. LL.M. Program

If it is determined that you may cure a durational or substantive deficiency by supplementing your education to be eligible to sit for the New York bar exam,

---

16. www.nybarexam.org/Foreign/ForeignLegalEducation.htm (emphasis in the original). It gives the following example: If you want to sit for a July exam, you should submit your evaluation request "at least one year prior to the commencement of the April filing period for that July exam." Thus, you are encouraged to submit your request 15 months in advance of the July test date.

you must complete an LL.M. degree as follows (pursuant to the new rules effective May 18, 2011), and submit proof of such to the Law Board:[17]

a. **LL.M. degree.** You must commence your LL.M. program during or after the 2012-2013 academic year. Your LL.M. transcript must be submitted to prove that you completed the LL.M. degree.

b. **Number of credit hours — minimum.** You must earn at least 24 semester credit hours (or its equivalent if your school is not on a semester basis).

c. **Coursework.** All 24 credits, unless as otherwise permitted by the rule, shall be in "classroom courses" in "substantive and procedural law and professional skills."

d. **Specific courses required.** The LL.M. program you complete must contain the following:

   i. a minimum of two semester hours of credit in the history, goals, instruction, value, rules and responsibilities of the U.S. legal profession and its members;

   ii. a minimum of two semester hours of credit in legal research, writing and analysis (which may not be satisfied by a research and writing requirement in a substantive law course);

   iii. a minimum of two semester hours of credit in American legal studies, the American legal system or a similar course designed to introduce students to distinctive aspects and/or fundamental principles of U.S. law. This may be satisfied by a course in U.S. constitutional law or U.S. or state civil procedure; and

   iv. a minimum of six semester hours of credit in subjects tested on the New York State bar exam.

e. **Correspondence courses.** No credit shall be permitted for correspondence courses, online courses, courses offered on DVD or other media, or other distance learning courses.

f. **Instruction time.** The school must require a minimum of 700 minutes of instruction time (exclusive of exam time) for the granting of each semester credit hour.

Employment

---

17. For the rules related to LL.M. study commencing before or after the 2012-2013 academic year, see www.nybarexam.org/Foreign/ForeignLegalEducation.htm. As a point of comparison, the ABA proposed model rule, like the modified New York rule, enhances curriculum content and credit-hour quantity requirements. *See generally* ABA, Section of Legal Education and Admissions to the Bar, Report, Proposed Model Rule on Admission of Foreign Educated Lawyers, and Proposed Criteria for ABA Certification of an LL.M. Degree for the Practice of Law in the United States. (www.americanbar.org/content/dam/aba/administrative/legal_education_and_admissions_to_the_bar/council_reports_and_resolutions/20110420_model_rule_and_criteria_foreign_lawyers.authcheckdam.pdf). The ABA would require 26 credit hours (with at least 18 credit hours in courses taught by full-time or emeritus faculty, and not adjunct faculty); and courses on U.S. constitutional law, civil procedure of state and federal courts, the history of the U.S. legal system, professional responsibility, and legal writing. *Id. at 6* (ABA Proposed Criteria for LL.M. Certification). Significantly, U.S. law schools would be required to "publicly disclose on its website the first-time bar passage rates by state of its most recent class of graduates of an LL.M. program specifically designed to comply with this rule." *Id. at 7.*

g. **Length of degree program**. The LL.M. program must be no fewer than two semesters of at least 13 calendar weeks (or the equivalent), exclusive of reading period, examinations, and breaks.

h. **Clinical courses**. A maximum of four semester credit hours is permissible for certain clinical courses, per the guidelines in amended 520.6(b)(vii)(a).

i. **Other courses related to legal training**. With some restrictions, a maximum of six semester credit hours is permissible if taught by certain non-law school faculty, or by faculty of schools with which the law school has a joint degree program.

j. **Summer study**. The LL.M. program *shall not* be completed exclusively during summer semesters. A maximum of four semester credit hours may be earned during summer courses.

k. **Time to complete LL.M.** The LL.M. degree must be completed "within 24 months of matriculation."

l. **Location of instruction**. "[A]ll coursework for the program shall be completed at the campus of an approved law school in the [U.S.], except as otherwise expressly permitted by subdivision (b)(3)(vii)."[18]

6. The Two-Day New York Bar Exam Itself

For a complete description of the New York bar exam and the testing process, for sample questions, and for other information about the exam, please refer to www.nybarexam.org/TheBar/TheBar.htm. The twice-yearly New York bar exam is administered on the last Tuesday and Wednesday of each February and July, and on each day it consists of morning and afternoon sessions.

(a) *Day 1 (Tuesday)*. Five essay questions, 50 multiple-choice questions (developed by the New York Law Board), and a Multistate Performance Test (MPT) (developed by the National Conference of Bar Examiners). These questions relate to New York law.

(b) *Day 2 (Wednesday)*. Multistate Bar Exam (MBE). Two hundred multiple-choice questions on contracts, torts, constitutional law, criminal law, evidence, and real property. These questions relate to general principles of law in the U.S., and not specifically to New York law.

7. Multistate Professional Responsibility Exam (MPRE)

(a) In addition to taking the New York Bar exam, before you can get admitted to the bar you also must take and pass an ethics test, known as the Multistate Professional Responsibility Exam (MPRE).

---

18. Rule 520(b)(3)(vii) permits the LL.M. program to include a maximum of four semester hours of clinical courses, and a maximum of six semester hours of courses taught by certain non-law faculty including faculty at schools with which the law school offers a joint degree. Please refer to the complete rule for details.

(b) You may take the MPRE *before* or *after* you take the New York bar. The MPRE has 60 multiple-choice questions that focus on legal profession ethics. The test is offered three times per year, in March, August, and November. Many students take the exam in the spring of their LL.M. year.

8. "Bar Review Courses" versus "Bar Courses"

a. Bar Review Courses

Many J.D. and LL.M. graduates who sit for bar exams take "bar review" courses, which private companies conduct during the months immediately preceding bar exams. They are specifically geared toward teaching students the substantive law they need to know to pass the bar, and teaching test-taking techniques and strategies. Some courses specifically target foreign LL.M. students. Bar review courses are expensive. Some post-LL.M. employers may pay for your bar review course. A list of bar review courses can be found at http://stu.findlaw.com/thebar/barreview.html.

b. Bar Courses

These courses are taught as part of any J.D. law school curriculum. They are in subject matters that tend to be tested on any state's bar exam, hence the name "bar course." These courses may include criminal law, constitutional law, evidence, corporations, and a variety of other courses. Because many J.D. students want to take these courses, they may be oversubscribed. Does your school give priority to J.D. students to enroll in these courses? Will your school permit LL.M. students to take these courses?

Disclaimer and Note of Caution

The National Conference of Bar Examiners (NCBE) published the *2011 Comprehensive Guide to Bar Admission Requirements* (www.abanet.org/legaled/baradmissions/bar.html), which offers information about bar admission in each U.S. state. Bar admission requirements change periodically. You *must* check with the Board of Law Examiners of the state where you wish to sit for the bar or practice.

Employment

CHAPTER SUMMARY

- No one, including a U.S. citizen, has an automatic right to practice law in the U.S.

- Ordinarily you must pass a state's bar exam and become a member of the state's bar in order to practice law in that state.

- Consult the Board of Bar Examiners of states that interest you for their current bar admission information. Various U.S. states permit foreign-trained lawyers to sit for their bar exams.

- Bar admission rules of all states are subject to change.

- The ABA Proposed Model Rule on Admission of Foreign Educated Lawyers has not taken effect.

- The rules for foreign-educated lawyers to sit for the New York Bar exam were amended, with new rules taking effect May 18, 2011.

Employment

Part VIII

Other U.S. Law Degrees

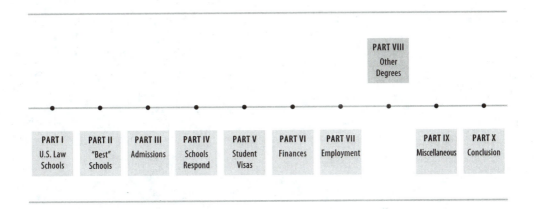

PART VIII
Other
Degrees

PART I
U.S. Law
Schools

PART II
"Best"
Schools

PART III
Admissions

PART IV
Schools
Respond

PART V
Student
Visas

PART VI
Finances

PART VII
Employment

PART IX
Miscellaneous

PART X
Conclusion

Other Degrees

Chapter 29

S.J.D. (or J.S.D.) Degree

CHAPTER HIGHLIGHTS

- The Doctor of Juridical Science (S.J.D. or J.S.D.) degree is the terminal degree in law—the highest degree in law offered in the U.S.
- The S.J.D. is not required for a person to hold any position in the U.S., academic or otherwise.
- The S.J.D. or its equivalent is required in some non-U.S. jurisdictions for persons seeking high-ranking academic positions, including Professor or Dean.
- Admission to U.S. S.J.D. programs in the U.S. is highly competitive.

A. Introduction

The Doctor of Juridical Science (S.J.D. or J.S.D.) degree is the terminal law degree offered at U.S. law schools.[1] Most S.J.D. students at U.S. schools are foreign lawyers who received their first law degrees outside the U.S.[2] They seek an S.J.D. for two principal reasons, both related to career aspirations in teaching law. **First,** S.J.D. students seek a credential to qualify them to teach at a law faculty in their home country. Many overseas law faculties require professors to hold S.J.D. or equivalent degrees (such as the Ph.D. in law). **Second,** they seek a U.S. law school credential to help their chances of teaching at a U.S. law school, or of teaching law-related subjects at a U.S. college or university. If you want to practice law for a U.S. firm or corporation, an LL.M. or J.D. from a U.S. school may be more appropriate than an S.J.D.

Other Degrees

---

1. The Ph.D. in law is more commonly offered outside the U.S. rather than at U.S. law schools, and is also a terminal degree, meaning that it is the highest degree available in its field.

2. As mentioned elsewhere in *LL.M. Roadmap*, the overwhelming majority of U.S. law graduates earn a J.D. degree, and do not pursue an LL.M., S.J.D., or any other law degree. A J.D. is sufficient for law practice, law teaching, judicial positions, and virtually all other types of law jobs in the U.S.

In the U.S., a J.D. is a graduate degree.[3] All J.D. students in the U.S. already have an undergraduate degree. As mentioned, a J.D. is a sufficient academic credential to become a law professor, and most U.S. law professors do not hold an S.J.D. nor an LL.M. Increasingly, U.S. law professors, along with their J.D. degrees, also hold Ph.D. degrees in areas such as economics, sociology, or engineering; but such additional degrees are not required. Though the J.D. and S.J.D. are not equivalent degrees, S.J.D. graduates compete against J.D. graduates from the U.S. for coveted positions as law professors at U.S. law schools.

Entry into S.J.D. programs in the U.S. is extremely competitive. Of the schools that offer this degree, many accept only one or two students per year.[4] It is not uncommon for some programs to accept *zero* S.J.D. students in any given year.

The S.J.D. by definition is a general law degree, even though a student's research, coursework, and dissertation *must* focus on a specific legal area.[5]

B. S.J.D. Admission Requirements

The overarching requirement for S.J.D. program admission is an applicant's distinguished academic record that demonstrates his or her ability to produce a scholarly dissertation of publishable quality. The dissertation must represent an original contribution to legal literature with long-term value.

The application process varies significantly from school to school, and academic requirements similarly vary.

C. The Application and the Application Process

Each school has its own S.J.D. application procedure, of which there are many variations. I list below several existing models. Each applicant must study the rules of each school and follow them carefully. No two processes appear to be the same.

(1) *Model #1 — Streamlined application process.* The applicant submits the following simultaneously: (a) S.J.D. application; (b) dissertation proposal; and (c) statement confirming that a faculty member from the school has agreed to supervise the dissertation if the applicant is

---

3. In many other countries, law is an undergraduate subject and students earn a B.A. or LL.B. in law. (See Chapter 5.) For a discussion of J.D. programs, see Chapter 30.

4. For example, UCLA accepts a maximum of two S.J.D. students per year.

5. This is not so for LL.M. degrees. Chapter 4 discusses "general" LL.M. degrees (with students taking courses in many legal areas) and "specialized" LL.M. degrees (with students taking many courses in a particular legal area). (See also Appendix I.)

Other Degrees

accepted. Then the S.J.D. committee reviews the application and decides whether to admit the applicant into the S.J.D. program.[6]

(2) *Model #2 — Two-part application process.* The applicant submits an S.J.D. application. The committee reviews the application and decides whether to let the applicant proceed to the next step, which is for the applicant to seek a dissertation advisor. The applicant then contacts school faculty members seeking to identify and secure the agreement of a dissertation advisor from the faculty. After a faculty member agrees to serve as a dissertation advisor, the school decides whether to admit the applicant.

(3) *Model #3 — Invitation to apply.* The S.J.D. program website lists preliminary questions it invites an applicant to answer. The S.J.D. committee reviews the applicant's answers and then decides whether to invite the student to submit an S.J.D. application. Only then would an applicant submit an application. The committee would review the application and decide whether to admit the applicant.

D. Component Parts of the S.J.D. Application

1. Evidence of Exceptional Promise as a Legal Scholar

The applicant must demonstrate high potential for completing a scholarly dissertation that constitutes a substantial, original, long-term contribution to legal literature and knowledge.

Components of an S.J.D. Application
1. Evidence of promise as a legal scholar
2. First law degree (J.D. or LL.B. or BA in law)
3. Second law degree (LL.M. or other masters)
4. Writing sample
5. Dissertation proposal
6. Dissertation advisor
7. Recommendation letters
8. English language proficiency proof
9. Financial resources proof
10. Personal statements
11. Transcripts and other credentials
12. Curriculum vitae
13. Application fee

---

6. A variation of Model #1 is when a school permits the applicant to submit a single application for a combined LL.M./S.J.D. program. After the student completes the LL.M. program, the school decides whether the student may commence the S.J.D. After completing the LL.M., the student may still apply to an S.J.D. program at another school.

S.J.D. programs do not require the LSAT or GRE.

2. First Law Degree

All schools require *at a minimum* either a J.D. from the U.S. or an LL.B. or B.A. from another country.

3. Second Law Degree

All schools require an LL.M. or similar master level degree such as a Juris Master (J.M.), Master of Jurisprudence (J.M.), or Master of Comparative Law (M.C.L.). Some U.S. schools accept only those S.J.D. applicants who have received their LL.M. from that school,[7] while other schools strongly prefer their own LL.M. graduates. Some schools are more open about accepting students who obtained their LL.M. degrees from other schools, though they may require or strongly prefer that the LL.M. be from a U.S. school.[8] If you are considering doing an S.J.D. after your LL.M., check S.J.D. admission guidelines *before* you begin your LL.M. to learn if your LL.M. would be acceptable to the S.J.D. program you want to join.

4. Writing Sample

Some schools require a writing sample as evidence of an applicant's scholarly potential. A substantial published or draft research paper, article, or monograph may be acceptable. It is advisable to select an LL.M. program in which you can write an LL.M. thesis that you can use as the basis for an S.J.D. application. Your submission should be written in, or translated into, English.

5. Dissertation Proposal

Each school's dissertation proposal requirements differ.

Other Degrees

---

7. Wisconsin's S.J.D. is "designed for people . . . *who have earned the University of Wisconsin Law School's LL.M. degree.*" **Cornell** notes "In general, J.S.D. students will be considered for the program only after initial candidacy for the LL.M. degree at Cornell Law School" (www.lawschool.cornell.edu/international/degrees.cfm).

8. Some argue that it is unreasonable for U.S. schools to require an S.J.D. applicant to hold a master's degree from a U.S. school. Some non-U.S. schools have very high standards, even higher than some U.S. schools. Others argue that this requirement is reasonable, considering differences between the legal systems of the U.S. and other countries. If you hold a master's degree from a non-U.S. school, ask the U.S. school if they will accept it.

American University Dissertation Proposal Requirements

"Applicants must submit a dissertation proposal *using the following five headings*. A dissertation proposal lacking these five subparts will not be considered. The proposal must be 10-15 pages long, double spaced, with Times New Roman 12 point font, and 1 inch margins on all sides. . . .

1. The topic of the proposed dissertation
2. A preliminary literature review, including:
   • Discussion of the existing literature on the subject and overview of what other scholars have already addressed; and
   • Explanation of how the applicant's dissertation will differ from, and add to, the existing literature.
3. A clear statement of the proposed hypothesis to be explored in the dissertation:
   • Identification of a dissertation statement to be developed in the course of research and writing. The statement should not simply say you want to investigate a topic, study an area, or summarize a field. Rather, the dissertation statement requires a developed perspective that takes a particular approach or analyzes a specific theme in the desired topic of study.
4. A statement of the methodology to be followed in developing the dissertation. Consider the following:
   • What is the plan of research?
   • What bodies of writing will be consulted?
   • Are empirical studies necessary? If so, explain.
   • Will the dissertation be primarily theoretical in nature?
   • Will the study to be comparative in perspective?
   • Will the study be policy-oriented?
   • In short, what kind of investigations will the candidate undertake to research the chosen topic and develop the dissertation?
5. Faculty advisor
   • If the applicant has secured [a law school] professor to serve as a faculty advisor, he or she should identify the faculty advisor in the proposal. Securing a faculty advisor is not a required component of the application."

Source: www.wcl.american.edu/sjd/sjdadmissions.cfm#dissertation

Other Degrees

6. Dissertation Advisor

All S.J.D. programs require students to have an S.J.D. dissertation advisor, who would ordinarily be a law professor at the school. The advisor oversees the students' academic work and ushers them through the S.J.D. program. Some schools require applicants to secure a commitment from a faculty member *before* applying to the S.J.D. program. Some require applicants to search the faculty roster and identify prospective advisors, but caution applicants *not to contact* the faculty members directly. Some schools wait until the student's first S.J.D.

semester and then ask the student to submit names of professors with whom the student wishes to work.

7. Recommendation Letters

The recommendation letters required by S.J.D. program admission committees are similar to recommendation letters needed to get admitted to an LL.M. program. (See Chapter 11.) But S.J.D. recommendation letters should be certain to focus on the applicant's potential for completing a scholarly dissertation that constitutes a substantial, publishable, original, long-term contribution to legal literature and knowledge. Even if an S.J.D. program does not expressly require a letter from your LL.M. thesis advisor, *strive to provide such a letter*. Your LL.M. thesis advisor should be in an excellent position to comment on your ability to produce a high-quality S.J.D. dissertation: hopefully you will have made a favorable impression on your thesis advisor, who will readily write you a strong letter.

8. Proof of English Language Proficiency

S.J.D. English language proficiency requirements are similar to those for LL.M. programs. (See Chapter 12.) However, the successful completion of an LL.M. program in the U.S. is sufficient evidence of English language proficiency. If you hold an LL.M. from a U.S. school, you will *not* need to take a new Cambridge ILEC, IELTS, PTE Academic, or TOEFL exam.

9. Proof of Financial Resources

You must demonstrate your ability to pay tuition, fees, and living expenses (including health insurance). If you do not, the S.J.D. program will not admit you, and the U.S. government will not issue you a student visa. The discussions in Chapters 13, 20, and 23 about financial resources for an LL.M. are relevant to the S.J.D. as well, though S.J.D. tuition should be less than LL.M. tuition.

10. Personal Statement or Statement of Purpose

These requirements vary among schools. You might be requested to comment on:

- Why you are seeking an S.J.D. degree.
- How the S.J.D. will advance your professional objectives.
- The specific position, if any, you seek after you complete your degree.
- How your LL.M. degree and thesis helped prepare you for the S.J.D.
- Why you wish to write a dissertation.

Some schools may be quite specific. For example, **Tulane** requires a "[s]tatement describing how your LL.M. studies have furthered your understanding of

Other Degrees

law and legal processes and assisted you in attaining your intellectual and career objectives."

11. Transcripts, Diplomas, and Bar Certificates — Verified and Authenticated

Schools require you to submit many documents demonstrating your achievements. You can easily obtain your U.S. LL.M. transcripts and U.S. bar admission records. It may be more difficult to obtain similar documents from your home country. When you come to the U.S. for your LL.M., you might bring extra sets of original transcripts, diplomas, or bar certificates in case you need them to apply to an S.J.D. program. Bring them in an envelope sealed by the school or issuing authority, if possible. (See Chapter 13.)

12. Curriculum Vitae

A school's website will inform you if it requires a CV.

13. Application Fee

This fee varies among S.J.D. programs.

E. S.J.D. Degree Requirements

1. Coursework

All S.J.D. programs are substantially research-based (not course-based), though it is common for S.J.D. students to enroll in some courses during their program. Some S.J.D. programs require a certain amount of coursework, while other programs permit coursework but discourage it.

a. S.J.D. Programs That Require Coursework

Virginia, UCLA, NYU, Golden Gate, and **Georgetown** require S.J.D. students to complete a certain number of courses or seminars. At **Golden Gate,** S.J.D. students must earn a minimum of eight credits, which is the equivalent of about two or three courses.

NYU notes that because "foundation in legal theory is the first step in writing a successful dissertation," S.J.D. students must register for two theoretical seminars that consider aspects of legal theory. UCLA requires S.J.D. students to take two semesters of classes of a minimum of ten credits (equivalent to three to four classes) of courses related to the student's research.

b. S.J.D. Programs That Permit Coursework but Discourage It

At **Wisconsin** "No course work is required; in fact, degree candidates are actively discouraged from enrolling in courses. Applicants should already have a sufficient education in the field of research to pursue a serious scholarly project."

NYU (which uses the term "J.S.D.") requires some coursework specific to J.S.D. students and discourages enrollment in non-J.S.D. courses:

> JSD students . . . are permitted to enroll in courses outside of the JSD program and are permitted to request permission to audit Law School courses or seminars. However, given that the requirements of the JSD program alone are quite demanding, it is expected that a majority of a JSD [student's] time is spent on program requirements and the research and development.

2. Auditing Courses

S.J.D. students may be permitted to audit J.D. or LL.M. courses — to sit in on lectures in areas of interest to them, without having to take the course's exam. Usually, the S.J.D. student is not required to pay tuition to audit courses.

3. Other S.J.D. Requirements

Some schools require S.J.D. students to participate in workshops or colloquia, join academic roundtable discussions, give informal presentations, or engage in other scholarly endeavors. For example, second-year **NYU** S.J.D. students must participate in a series of research workshops that permit students to interact with faculty and experts from around the world. Each week, the group discusses recent scholarship by authorities in the field, who present their work to the group.

4. Study Plan Approval

In all S.J.D. programs, either a dissertation committee, the faculty advisor, or an administrator, must approve the S.J.D. students' study plans. Students must propose a plan to complete their dissertation and other S.J.D. requirements.

5. Dissertation

The dissertation would typically be a book or series of related articles suitable for publication and constituting substantial contribution to knowledge in its field. The standard is about 300 pages — 80,000 and 100,000 words including footnotes, but excluding bibliography, front pages, table of contents, and annexes or appendices.

6. Dissertation Advisor

Each S.J.D. student has a dissertation advisor who helps you refine your dissertation topic, reviews research plans and draft outlines, and guides your academic work throughout the S.J.D. process. The dissertation advisor is the primary contact that you have with the law school.

Many S.J.D. programs require applicants to secure a faculty member's commitment to serve as dissertation advisor *before* the school considers an application or admits applicants. Serving as a dissertation advisor is a major commitment for a professor, because of the nature of the S.J.D. as a research degree. The advisor will likely read multiple drafts of the dissertation, meet with the student regularly, and be available to serve as a kind of liaison between the student and the school. Some schools accept only one or two S.J.D. applicants each year, because many professors are not readily willing to take on S.J.D. advising responsibilities, which are additional to professors' regular teaching, research, and other work obligations. It can be difficult to secure an S.J.D. advisor. One way to secure an advisor is if a professor in your home country knows U.S. law professors and is willing to contact them and advertise your wonderful and promising academic skills.

7. Dissertation Committee

A dissertation committee usually has three or four members, and comprises a chair (typically the dissertation advisor), one or more law faculty members, and perhaps a professor from another university department.

Some schools create the dissertation committee upon the student's admission. Others create it only after the student completes a certain residency period, performs well in required courses, or develops an acceptable research plan.

Some committees review the dissertation at different stages before it is complete, while other committees review the "final" dissertation submitted by the student; engage the student in a discussion or an "oral exam" (see below) on the dissertation's topic; determine whether the student must revise the dissertation; approve or disapprove the dissertation; and finally make a recommendation as to whether the S.J.D. degree should be conferred.

8. S.J.D. Residency

All S.J.D. programs appear to require students to fulfill a "residency requirement," meaning that they should conduct at least part of their work at the school. The amount of required time "in residence" varies from approximately two semesters (e.g., **Golden Gate**, **UCLA**) to three years (e.g., **NYU**). Required residency would not ordinarily include summer (June-August), but rather only the fall and spring semesters, in addition to any residency time spent obtaining the LL.M. degree. After the residency requirement is satisfied, the S.J.D. student is free to conclude the research and write the dissertation in another city or country.

9. S.J.D. Oral Exam

Some S.J.D. programs require students to pass one or more formal "oral exams."[9] A **first oral examination** (which may be called a "qualifying exam") may focus on the dissertation proposal. At **Harvard**, the first oral examination occurs after 12-18 months of research, and involves a "rigorous two-hour exercise that tests student's mastery of his or her fields of study and provides guidance for proceeding" to the dissertation phase. The **second oral exam** may focus on the dissertation itself.

10. Time Limit for Completion of the Degree

Most programs require students to complete their degree within two to five years.

11. Finances — Tuition; Financial Aid; and Scholarships

S.J.D. tuition varies among schools and among program components. Most schools require S.J.D. students to be "in residence" for certain periods and are assessed "in residence" tuition, which may be higher than the tuition when not "in residence." For example, the student may be physically at the school for one or two years "in residence," conducting research, auditing courses, and meeting with advisors and committee members. During a third or fourth year, the student may conduct research in their home country or elsewhere, and not be "in residence" on their school's campus. The school may charge higher tuition rates for the first and second years when the student is on campus than it charges for the third and fourth years when the student is away.

Not many schools provide direct financial assistance to S.J.D. students. Schools may permit S.J.D. students to work, but you should be aware of, and abide by, your visa limitations.

12. Becoming a Law Professor in the U.S.

This is difficult, even for J.D. graduates. Each year thousands of U.S. lawyers with stellar credentials compete for a few hundred teaching positions. It is even more difficult for foreign lawyers. However, foreign scholars with significant scholarly publications and an S.J.D. degree from a U.S. school may acquire

---

9. **SMU** provides: "It is within the discretion of a S.J.D. candidate's Supervisory Committee to require [an oral exam] at which the S.J.D. candidate will be asked 'to defend' orally his/her dissertation in the presence of the members of the Supervisory Committee."

Other Degrees

such coveted positions. Some have even become deans of U.S. law schools, e.g., Makau W. Mutua (**Buffalo**) and Symeon C. Symeonides (**Willamette**), or associate deans, e.g., James Thuo Gathii (**Albany)** and Penelope Penny Andrews (**CUNY**).

The Association of American Law Schools (AALS) facilitates entry-level law professor hiring. The central event is the annual AALS Faculty Recruitment Conference, at which U.S. law schools interview hundreds of candidates to determine who to invite for full-day on-campus interviews (www.aals.org). Resources about law professor hiring include *Breaking into the Academy: The 2002–2004 Michigan Journal of Race and Law Guide for Aspiring Law Professors*, 7 Mich. J. Race & L. 457 (2002). A recent book on the topic is *Becoming a Law Professor: A Candidate's Guide* (ABA 2010) by Brannon P. Denning, Marcia L. McCormick, and Jeffrey M. Lipshaw.

Some law schools may help their S.J.D. students prepare for law teaching by, for example, conducting training programs on the law teaching market, helping S.J.D. students publish law articles or publish their dissertations, or permitting S.J.D. students to teach U.S. law school courses or seminars to give them experience that will be valuable when they apply for teaching jobs. If you want to teach law in the U.S., or elsewhere, choose an S.J.D. program at a law school that has a proven track record of preparing S.J.D. candidates for law teaching, and a proven track record of S.J.D. graduates acquiring law teaching positions.

CHAPTER SUMMARY

- The S.J.D. (or J.S.D.) is the terminal law degree in the U.S., and is thus the highest law degree offered there.

- The S.J.D. is not required to become a U.S. law professor.

- The J.D. is sufficient to sit for a U.S. bar, to teach, or to become a judge.

- Most S.J.D. candidates at U.S. schools are international students.

- S.J.D. admission is competitive. Many schools accept only one or two students per year.

- To help prepare you for an S.J.D., be certain to write an LL.M. thesis, which can be the basis of your S.J.D. dissertation proposal.

- Some schools accept only S.J.D. candidates who have an LL.M. from the same school.

- If you want to teach, choose an S.J.D. program that will help you get hired.

Chapter 30

J.D. Degree

CHAPTER HIGHLIGHTS

- The Juris Doctor (J.D.) degree is the first available law degree in the U.S.
- Law is not offered in the U.S. as an undergraduate degree at any university or college.
- The overwhelming majority of J.D. students in the U.S. receive their undergraduate degrees from U.S. universities or colleges.
- Increasingly, international students are seeking entry into U.S. J.D. programs.
- International students in the U.S. may join a J.D. program before they join an LL.M. program, while they are enrolled as an LL.M. student, or after they graduate from an LL.M. program.
- J.D. programs are competitive to enter for U.S. students, and perhaps even more competitive for international students.
- Generally, it is easier for international students to enter a J.D. program *during* their LL.M. year or *after* they receive their LL.M. degree, rather than try to enter before they enter an LL.M. program.
- J.D. programs in the U.S. may waive LSAT scores for LL.M. students or LL.M. graduates. International students who seek to join J.D. programs may avoid the LSAT requirement by joining a U.S. LL.M. program first.

A. J.D.: The First Professional U.S. Law Degree

U.S. schools do not offer undergraduate law degrees. The first available U.S. law degree is the J.D. (Juris Doctor or Juris Doctorate), which is considered a graduate professional degree.[1] U.S. students who seek to enter a J.D. program ordinarily must have received a four-year undergraduate B.A. or B.S. degree. The J.D. degree is typically earned in three years.

---

1. Schematics in Chapter 5 outline the principal law degrees U.S. law schools offer and depict "typical" degree progressions for U.S. and overseas-trained law graduates.

Other Degrees

447

Most J.D. students at U.S. law schools receive their undergraduate degrees at U.S. colleges and universities. In recent years, increasingly more J.D. candidates have earned their undergraduate degrees overseas.

As suggested in Chapter 5, international students typically enroll for a J.D. at one of three stages of their educational careers.

First, they may enroll for a three-year J.D. after they complete an LL.B. or B.A. or other undergraduate degree outside the U.S. After they complete the J.D., they may decide to study for an LL.M. degree in the U.S., and possibly pursue an S.J.D. afterward.

Second, they may enroll in a J.D. program after they complete an LL.M., in which case they may qualify to complete the J.D. in two years, rather than in three. After their J.D., they would be able to proceed to an S.J.D., based on their having completed the LL.M. An international student requires an LL.M. to enter an S.J.D. program, but does not need a J.D. to enter an S.J.D. program.

Third, they may enroll in a joint J.D./LL.M. degree program, which can be earned at some schools in approximately three years, instead of the four years it would take to earn the two degrees separately.

With few exceptions, all students entering J.D. programs must satisfy essentially the same requirements, whether the applicants received their undergraduate degrees in the U.S. or overseas.

B. J.D. Program Entry Requirements

Generally, J.D. program applicants must take the Law School Admissions Test (LSAT) and receive an acceptable score.[2] An exception is that some schools *do not* require the LSAT if you enroll in the J.D. *during* or *after* your LL.M. year. These schools waive the LSAT for international LL.M. students who may be admitted to the J.D. program with "advanced standing." In these cases, some or all LL.M. credits will or may count toward the J.D. degree.

To enter a J.D. program, in addition to taking the LSAT, an applicant must also obtain an undergraduate degree with solid marks or grades, submit letters of recommendation, present a well-written application, pay an application fee, and satisfy other demands made by schools' admission committees.

Applicants who received their prior degree outside the U.S. may be required to submit evidence of the their English language competence, which usually

---

2. Some schools require international LL.M. students or graduates to take the LSAT before joining the J.D. program, but they may admit you even if your score is very low. Other schools hold all J.D. applicants to the same high LSAT standards whether they are international or domestic applicants, or whether or not they are currently enrolled in or have completed an LL.M. Some schools waive the LSAT requirement for international LL.M. students or graduates. It is significantly easier for international students to enter U.S. LL.M. programs than it is for them to enter J.D. programs. An international LL.M. student may "slip in the back door" of some J.D. programs through the LSAT waiver and other loosened admission standards.

takes the form of high-enough scores on English language tests such as the Cambridge ILEC, IELTS, PTE Academic, or TOEFL; or evidence that they received a degree in which the language of study was English. (See Chapter 12.) Applicants can take the LSAT, English language proficiency tests, and other tests in many locations around the world.

Students considering a J.D. program are not required to major in a particular field of undergraduate study. Many U.S. applicants have studied history, political science, philosophy, English, international relations, business, geography, psychology, economics, or sociology. Students may also hold degrees in engineering, computer science, mathematics, or any number of other disciplines.

Regardless of the undergraduate degree — whether it is an LL.B. from overseas, or a B.A. or B.S. from a U.S. university — law schools expect the undergraduate course of study to have been sufficiently demanding and structured to demonstrate that the student has a high likelihood of success in a graduate law degree program. Law schools want applicants to have demonstrated that they are able to engage in skills required in the practice and study of law — to think critically, to read and comprehend large amounts of information, to conduct legal research, to communicate effectively orally and in writing, and to resolve complex legal problems using logical reasoning.

C. J.D. Structure

The J.D. is a general law degree that focuses more on teaching students how to think like lawyers than it focuses on teaching students how to practice law. Law school is not a vocational school where a student enrolls to learn a trade. Many U.S. law schools offer legal aid clinics and other experiential courses where students gain practical experience working with real-life clients with real-life legal problems. These are important training aspects of the legal education. But every U.S. law school has more traditional classroom, theory-oriented courses than they have experiential courses or programs.

1. First Year

Students typically complete the J.D. in three years (or four years, or more, in a part-time program). The first year consists of five or six (or more) classes that all first-year students are required to take during each of the first two semesters. These courses are standard at law schools across the U.S., and include civil procedure, criminal law, contracts, torts, constitutional law, and property. First-year students often also take legal writing, research, and analysis, where they have the opportunity to write memoranda and other legal documents. They may get appellate experience by participating in "moot appellate court" exercises, where they prepare written court submissions and argue cases before "moot judges," who could be law professors, judges from the community, or practicing lawyers. First-year students may also engage in mock trials, where they select mock juries, examine and cross-examine mock witnesses, and make opening and closing arguments to the jury.

2. Second and Third Years

In the second and third years of the J.D. program, students are given considerable flexibility in choosing their courses. A law school may offer 100-150 (or more) different upper-level courses (depending on the size of the student body and size of the faculty). During their final two years of law school, most students would ordinarily be able to take no more than 20 to 25 of those courses.

3. Specialized Courses; Certificates

Depending on how many upper-level courses are offered, and in what specific areas, students may be able to specialize in particular areas of law, such as corporate law, finance, tax, health, environmental, international human rights, or criminal law. At some schools, students who specialize may be awarded with "certificates" in that particular area of law. Schools may place specialization notations on the diplomas and transcripts of students who concentrate or specialize in particular areas.

4. General Courses

Some students with varied interests choose to take a wide variety of classes across several fields of law. They may choose an eclectic curriculum because they believe that this may render them more attractive in the job market. Of course, as suggested above, some students may concentrate because of their own interests, or because they definitely want to work in a particular discipline and want to gain as much exposure as possible in that area. To satisfy student interests or desires for expertise, some law schools permit J.D. students to earn academic credit for courses taken in non-law departments at the university, or permit J.D. students to earn joint degrees with other departments.

Despite the wide variety of courses offered, many students select from a relatively small number of courses that the school "recommends" for most law students who want to prepare to sit for the bar and to prepare to enter law practice. Schools generally seek to teach students how to think like lawyers, and do not necessarily or specifically teach students how to pass a bar exam. Indeed, in the months after graduating from law school, many J.D. graduates take bar review courses, offered by private corporations, that are geared toward preparing for the bar exam. (See Chapter 28.)

D. Other Activities for J.D. Students (See also Chapter 19)

1. Law Journals

Upper-level J.D. students may get involved with student-run law reviews and journals. Students compete for highly coveted, prestigious spots on the editorial boards of law reviews, and then work hard at fulfilling and excelling in these positions. Some schools offer students academic credit for work on law reviews or other publications in which students edit articles submitted by outside authors, research and write notes and comments, and generally gain solid publication experience.

2. Clinics

Upper-level J.D. students may receive academic credit for practical experience working in law clinics on behalf of live clients with real legal issues. Supervised by professors, students represent clients involved in a broad range of legal matters.

3. Internships (Externships)

Internships at courts, companies, or other organizations provide upper-level students with further opportunities to gain practical legal experience for academic credit outside the classroom setting.

4. Study Abroad

J.D. students study abroad (outside the U.S.) in programs sponsored by their own schools, or sponsored by another ABA-accredited law school.

5. Extracurricular Activities and Student Organizations

All U.S. law schools permit and encourage students to form and join groups devoted to areas of law and practice of interest to them. Such groups may focus on areas of law (International Law Societies, Environmental Law Societies); race or ethnicity (Hispanic Law Societies, Black Law Students Association, Asian-Pacific Law Society); politics (Democratic or Republican Law Societies); sexual orientation (Gay, Lesbian, Bisexual or Transgendered Societies); human rights and humanitarian issues (Human Rights Law Associations); religion-focused groups (Jewish, Muslim, Christian Law Societies); and student leadership or governance (Student Bar Association, Master of Laws Association). (A more comprehensive list of student organizations is found in Chapter 19.)

E. The J.D. Experience (See also Chapter 16)

The J.D. program is often depicted in the media as a competitive and stressful, if not distressing, experience. It is demanding, but need not be maddening. Chapter 16 discusses the educational process from the perspective of LL.M.

students (and professors) — but that chapter is also very relevant to the J.D. experience. Indeed, all law schools with LL.M. programs have significantly more J.D. students than LL.M. students. At most schools the J.D. and LL.M. students sit side-by-side in the same classes with the same professors and class assignments, and the J.D. and LL.M. students also take the same exams. J.D. students have three years of this experience, whereas LL.M. students have only one. There are *many* other differences aside from length of time studying for the respective degrees, but altogether it is fair to say that J.D. and LL.M. students have similar academic experiences.

F. A Cross-Section of First-Year Mandatory Courses

As mentioned, the first-year curriculum is generally fixed at law schools across the country. In seeking to provide a standardized platform on which students can build in their second and third years of study, law schools typically require first-year law students to take most, if not all, of the following introductory law courses (listed below in alphabetical order):[3]

(1) *Civil procedure*   deals with rules related to the process of non-criminal law suits in U.S. state and federal courts;

(2) *Constitutional law*   deals with identifying and applying rules contained in the U.S. and state constitutions;

(3) *Contracts*   focuses on law related to binding oral and written agreements between and among individuals and entities;

(4) *Criminal law*   deals with wrongs committed for which the law provides penal sanctions;

(5) *Criminal procedure*   deals with rights of suspects and defendants (and the government) during investigations, trials, and appeals of penal matters;

(6) *Legal analysis, research, writing, and communication*   assists in developing legal research, oral and written communication, as well as legal advocacy skills; and

(7) *Property*   covers law related to individual and group ownership of buildings, land, and personal items.

G. J.D. Electives (See also Chapter 16)

Many second- and third-year J.D. students, before completing their degrees, take courses in administrative law, civil litigation, commercial law, corporations, evidence, family law, professional responsibility, taxation, and wills and trusts. These courses are generally considered to be "basic" to a law degree program, and are tested on many state bar exams. Every law school supplements this basic

---

3. Increasingly schools are requiring first-year students to take a course in international law, given the relationship between globalization and the practice of law in the U.S. and around the world.

curriculum with additional courses, such as international law, environmental law, conflict of laws, labor law, jurisprudence, civil and human rights — which may not be tested on U.S. bar exams.

H. American Bar Association Accredited J.D. Programs

If a law school's J.D. program in the U.S. meets stringent requirements, the ABA accredits the J.D. program (but will not accredit the school itself). Many J.D. programs in the U.S. *have not* earned ABA accreditation, and J.D. graduates from those schools are not automatically eligible to sit for the bar exam of all U.S. states. The ABA does not accredit LL.M., S.J.D., or any degree program other than the J.D. However, the ABA has considered whether to certify certain U.S. LL.M. programs. (See Chapters 6 and 28.)

I. Transferring to a J.D. Program from an LL.M. Program, and Joint J.D./LL.M. Programs

1. Easy Transfer to the J.D. Program at Some Schools

Some schools permit easy transfer from the LL.M. to the J.D. program, even granting credit in the J.D. program for courses taken as an LL.M. student. Some schools expressly *prohibit* LL.M. students to transfer to the J.D. program. Below are some illustrative examples of programs that permit transfer.

Hawai'i provides that "In rare cases, we allow exceptional LL.M. students to transfer into our J.D. program upon graduating from the LL.M. Program. This is a case-by-case determination based upon the candidate's academic performance during the year."

Miami permits international LL.M. students to transfer to the J.D. program, which they may then complete in approximately two years, rather than three. And, further, it advertises that the "transfer between both programs is made seamless and is open to any LL.M. student who compiles a strong record in the LL.M. coursework and fulfills the minimum law school requirements" (www.law.miami.edu/iglp/us_transnational_law/).

Hastings permits LL.M. candidates to apply to transfer to their J.D. program, and if they are accepted they can transfer 24 credits to count toward the J.D. However, they would *not* receive the LL.M. degree and would be required to complete two additional years of study and all the requirements to receive the J.D. degree, essentially putting them in the same position as if they had begun as J.D. students.

2. Bonuses and Hazards of Easy Transfer to the J.D. Program

A law school gains significant bonuses if it permits LL.M. students or LL.M. graduates to transfer to the J.D. program. A transferring LL.M. student will take several semesters of additional courses at the school and will pay corresponding tuition, generating substantial revenues for the school. If the school does not require the international student to take the LSAT, the school will not need to report a possibly low score to the ABA or elsewhere, possibly creating a false impression about the average LSAT scores of students.

Hazards mostly fall on LL.M. students who transfer to a J.D. program. Many law schools artificially inflate the grades of LL.M. students, who then develop a warped view of how they compete academically with J.D. students. If LL.M. and J.D. students in the same course are graded using different curves, the LL.M. student may receive a higher grade (for example, a "B" for the same level of work for which a J.D. student in the same course receives a "C"). The LL.M. student who earned the "B" may believe she is a stronger student than the J.D. student who received the "C" when in fact the curve distorted the comparison. That LL.M. student might enroll in the J.D. program (perhaps as a transfer student *without taking the LSAT or earning a high LSAT score*), take a course with the same J.D. student, and find that what she thought was "B" work is actually "C" work or worse, as compared to the work of the J.D. student. In the worst cases, when students with average or below average LL.M. grades enter a J.D. program, they may end up on academic probation or possibly dismissed from the program. Some law schools permit LL.M. students or graduates to enter J.D. programs without full regard as to how poorly that student might perform in the J.D. program. This could be a sign of a cash cow. (See Chapter 6.)

CHAPTER SUMMARY

- The Juris Doctor (J.D.) degree is the initial U.S. law degree.
- There is not a U.S. undergraduate professional law degree. The J.D. is a graduate-level degree.
- Most J.D. students receive their undergraduate degrees in the U.S.
- More international students are now seeking J.D. degrees.
- Most U.S. law schools require applicants to submit an LSAT score as part of your J.D. application. If you do not want to submit an LSAT score, you may enter an LL.M. program and try to transfer to a J.D. program. Some schools do not require LL.M. students or graduates to submit LSAT scores when applying for admission or transfer to a J.D. program.
- International students can earn a J.D. before or after an LL.M., or you can earn a joint J.D.-LL.M.
- If you complete your LL.M. first, some of your LL.M. credits may count toward the J.D. You may also transfer some of your LL.M. credits to a J.D. program if you transfer before you complete your LL.M.

Other Degrees

Chapter 31

Other U.S. Degree and Non-Degree Law Opportunities

CHAPTER HIGHLIGHTS

- A variety of other U.S. law degrees exist aside from the J.D., LL.M., and S.J.D.
- This chapter describes some of these other degrees, as well as non-degree opportunities for foreign lawyers or students who want to come to the U.S.
- Some of these other law degrees are post-J.D. (similar to the LL.M. and S.J.D.), while others are geared toward non-lawyers who do not possess J.D. degrees.
- Many exchange programs and visitor programs exist where foreign lawyers and law students can study, research, or even teach at U.S. law schools without matriculating in a degree program.

A. Introduction

1. General

As discussed in Chapters 5 and 30, the J.D. is the first professional law degree offered in the U.S., and is available to B.A. or B.S. degree-holders from U.S. universities, and also to students who hold LL.B., B.A., or similar degrees from outside the U.S. The LL.M. is a post-J.D. graduate law degree, and is the principal subject of *LL.M. Roadmap*. The S.J.D. is the principal terminal post-J.D. law degree offered at U.S. law schools — meaning it is the last and highest-level law degree offered at U.S. law schools. (See Chapters 29 and 30.) All the law schools discussed in *LL.M. Roadmap* offer J.D. and LL.M. degrees, a few offer S.J.D. degrees, and few offer one of several other post-J.D. law degrees.[1]

---

1. Other post-JD law degrees, not discussed in *LL.M. Roadmap*, include the Master of Comparative Law (M.C.L.) and the Doctor of Comparative Law (D.C.L.).

Other Degrees

Some overseas law graduates are unwilling or unable to matriculate for a law degree in the U.S., but want to come to the U.S. to have a U.S. law experience in a law school setting. Some foreign non-lawyers want to earn law degrees in the U.S., or possibly enjoy a U.S. non-degree law experience.

2. Chapter Highlights

This chapter explores:

a. Non-degree law opportunities in the U.S. **for foreign lawyers and law graduates**; and
b. Law-related degrees in the U.S. **for non-lawyers.**

B. Non-Degree Law Opportunities in the U.S. for Foreign Lawyers and Law Graduates

Many opportunities exist for foreign lawyers and legal professionals to travel to the U.S. for limited periods for academic and other experiences in law without matriculating in a degree program, without sitting for a bar exam, and without practicing law. Examples of some of these types of opportunities are embedded into the following discussion of the four major issues foreign lawyers consider in choosing such opportunities: (a) U.S. institutional sponsorship; (b) "status" within the U.S. host institution; (c) funding; and (d) visitor entitlements and obligations.

1. U.S. Law School as the Host or Sponsor Institution

Many U.S. law schools formally host for short periods foreign lawyers who join the schools to research, teach, collaborate with faculty on projects, or otherwise become involved in the academic life of the host school. These schools may have application materials for these opportunities on their websites, perhaps under a link for "Visiting Professionals" or "Non-Degree Visitors." If you want to spend time at a U.S. law school but the school does not have a formal visitor program, you can write to the dean, associate or vice dean, or LL.M. program administrators indicating who you are, your background, and the nature of the visit you seek. You can even write to professors at the institutions who work in your areas of interest and expertise. Be certain to tell them the approximate amount of time you would hope to be in residence.

You might also contact persons who have been foreign visitors at U.S. law schools and ask them for advice about the application process and other details of their experience. You might look at the bios of foreign professors at foreign law schools and identify ones who have visited U.S. law schools. For example, the **Peking University Law School** website reveals that faculty members have been Visiting Professors, Visiting Fellows, or Visiting Scholars at numerous law schools including **Berkeley, Columbia, Georgetown, Harvard, Northeastern, Michigan, Minnesota, NYU,** and **Yale.** Furthermore, you might check to see which U.S. faculty members at U.S. law schools have been Visiting Fellows or Scholars at overseas law faculties. Those professors may be more inclined to host you in the U.S.

2. Funding a Short-Term Law Experience in the U.S.

Some U.S. law schools will pay for some or all of a visitor's expenses, or you might fund your own experience. Other possible funders are the U.S. government (e.g., through a Fulbright grant); your home government (e.g., Ministries of Education, Foreign Affairs, or Justice); your employer (e.g., law firm, UN, multinational or domestic corporation, or educational institution); or a private foundation (e.g., Soros). Appendix II lists some of the scholarship and grant funders that fund international LL.M. students and also fund foreign law professionals to come to the U.S. for short-term law experiences. Even if a funder from Appendix II states that it will only fund students who matriculate in an LL.M. program, you could still inquire about funding for a short-term visit. It is possible that the funder may not be able to identify suitable LL.M. candidates to fund in a given year, and may be willing to fund a non-degree candidate — you.

If your overseas law firm or law faculty is willing to host U.S. law students or U.S. law faculty members, you may be able to organize an "exchange." The visitors from the U.S. will not need to pay for using facilities at your law firm or law faculty. Reciprocally, when you spend time at the law firm or law faculty in the U.S., you will not need to pay for facility use.

3. Faculty Versus Student Status

At some U.S. law schools the terms "Visiting Scholar" and "Visiting Fellow" might both refer to students or student-level visitors in residence from abroad. At other U.S. schools, one or both of those terms might refer to faculty-level visitors. You might not expect to be considered at faculty rank if you are a recent graduate from an overseas LL.B. or B.A. program, but if you are a seasoned lawyer in your home country, or a judge or other government official, you might be more appropriately afforded faculty rank at the U.S. law school. These issues matter if you are interested in prestige and ego. Also, they are of interest because at some schools you may be afforded certain privileges with one status but not the other: for example, use of a faculty lounge or parking garage,

Other Degrees

or permission to sit in on faculty meetings. Your status will also help determine your obligations and role as a visitor.

Before you agree to join a U.S. law school at a particular "rank" or with a particular "title," ask who else has held that rank or title. This is not because you want to be a snob. This is to help ensure that you are accorded a rank or title that is commensurate with your education, experience, and accomplishments.

4. Entitlements as a Visitor

Your host institution in the U.S. may provide you with an office (or at least workspace), library and recreational facility access, a telephone or access to a telephone, a computer and technical support, and access to a fax machine and other office equipment. You may be permitted to send letters using the host organization stationery, to use business cards with the host organization logo, to have an e-mail address from your host institution, and to be listed on the organization's website and in its personnel directories as a visitor. You may even be offered an opportunity to audit classes, a stipend, living accommodations, and other privileges that might otherwise be afforded only to alumni. Schools with formal visitor programs may have significantly more experience negotiating these entitlements than schools with occasional, ad hoc visitors.

In all cases, if you feel you need something additional to further your goals as a visitor, you might ask the relevant administrators at the host organization. U.S. law schools and their students benefit greatly from the on-campus presence of foreign law visitors, and you may be surprised at the extent to which those schools are willing to meet your needs. Find out. See what you can secure. Once on campus and settled into your position, be certain to satisfy all obligations you undertake.

5. Obligations as a Visitor

Your obligations as a visitor are determined in great part by your status (student or faculty), and further depend on the specific arrangement you make with the host institution. As a visitor, you might obligate yourself to participate in and be present at conferences, colloquia, and workshops sponsored by the host law school. You might agree to teach a course, either individually or collaboratively with host institutional faculty; you might guest lecture in campus classes, or present public lectures. You may agree to write an article, or series of articles or essays, to be published in a host organization journal. You may also agree to pay expenses related to postage, long distance telephone, photocopying, or miscellaneous other costs of consumables associated with your visit. The school may even charge a general fixed "administrative fee" or "bench fee" for the privilege you have of being a visitor and for the benefits you receive.

Other Degrees

C. Law-Related Degrees in the U.S. for Non-Lawyers[2]

1. General

Several U.S. law schools offer law-related degrees for U.S. and non-U.S. students who do not hold prior degrees in law. These would ordinarily be nonprofessional degrees that, even if offered at an ABA-accredited school, would not render degree-holders eligible to sit for a U.S. state bar. For some of these degrees, you may be required to take the Graduate Record Exam (GRE), and possibly an English Language proficiency test such as the Cambridge ILEC, IELTS, PTE Academic, or the TOEFL. (See Chapter 12.) Check the websites of schools that offer these degrees for full admission requirements.

2. Several Law-Related Degrees for Non-Lawyers

A few of the law-related degrees in the U.S. for non-lawyers that exist are as follows:

(a) Master of science in legal studies (M.S.L.S.)

This degree would tend to be for graduate students or postdoctoral fellows who have no legal training. It would focus on legal reasoning, analysis, and general legal theory.

(b) Master of science in legal administration (M.S.L.A.)

This degree would help prepare a graduate for work as an administrator of a law firm, court, or other legal institution.

(c) Master of juridical studies (J.M.) or master of jurisprudence (M.J.)

This degree is similar to an LL.M., but designed for persons who have no legal training, but whose careers in other fields would benefit from formal exposure to the law.

(d) Criminal justice master and Ph.D. degrees

If you do not hold an LL.M. or B.A., you could still earn a higher degree that focuses on criminal law and the criminal justice system.

2. Recall that some U.S. law schools *do not* require LL.M. students to hold a prior law degree. Some U.S. LL.M. programs will admit students who are admitted to practice in their home countries without earning a law degree. But, more relevant to this chapter, a few U.S. law schools will admit as LL.M. students people with overseas educational credentials who do not possess a law degree *and* are not admitted to practice law overseas.

Other Degrees

CHAPTER SUMMARY

- Lawyers, judges, or professors from overseas may spend time in a U.S. legal environment without entering an LL.M. or other degree program.

- Non-degree opportunities in the U.S. may be perfect for you.

- Law-related degrees and non-degree opportunities in the U.S. exist for persons who do not hold law degrees.

- Many sources of information exist for law-related opportunities in the U.S. Find them.

- Come to the U.S. for a law-related experience, whether or not you have law training in your home country.

Part IX

Legalities, Lifestyles, and Leisure in the U.S.

What International Students Need To Know

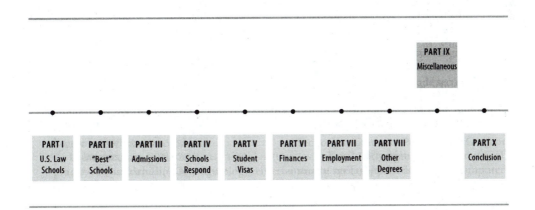

PART I U.S. Law Schools	**PART II** "Best" Schools	**PART III** Admissions	**PART IV** Schools Respond	**PART V** Student Visas	**PART VI** Finances	**PART VII** Employment	**PART VIII** Other Degrees		**PART X** Conclusion

PART IX Miscellaneous

Miscellaneous

Chapter 32

International Students Obeying U.S. Law
Safety, Security, and Health in the U.S.

CHAPTER HIGHLIGHTS
• Everyone in the U.S., whether foreign or not, must obey U.S. law—even if you do not know that a particular law exists.
• As a non-U.S. citizen coming to the U.S., you may not be familiar with all the laws you will be expected to know, and expected to obey.
• This chapter highlights some of the laws that may not be so obvious to someone who is not from the U.S.
• Your *LL.M. Student Handbook* may mention some of these laws also.

A. Introduction

1. Welcome to the U.S.!

Your LL.M. year may mark your first trip to the U.S., and it may be the first time that you will be in the U.S. for an extended period. For some students it will be the first time you have lived outside your home country. Many of you will know, based on watching television or movies, or reading books and newspapers, that life and laws in the U.S. may be quite different than what you are used to. And some will find that life in the U.S. is quite similar to life in your home country.

When in the U.S., you are required to comply with U.S. law, which may be substantially different from the law of your home country. Pay careful attention to safety, health, and security issues, as you encounter situations that may be new to you. Thousands of international students come to the U.S. each year, and they all have briefings about how to prepare for a healthy, happy, and productive degree program here. Overwhelmingly, these international students have wonderful experiences in the U.S. You, too, can have a great experience studying for your LL.M. in the U.S.

2. Chapter Highlights

This chapter covers law, safety, security, and health issues you may encounter in the U.S. Ignorance of the law is no excuse. (Especially for a law student!) You must obey *all* laws, even if you are not aware of those laws. Discussed in this chapter are the following:

   a. Specific laws you will be required to abide by in the U.S.
   b. Safety, security, health, and assistance issues.
   c. How to identify or create a network to assist if emergencies arise.
   d. What an international LL.M. student should do if he or she is arrested or detained in the U.S. (*Vienna Convention on Consular Relations*).
   e. How to get legal advice from a licensed lawyer.

B. Everyone Must Abide by U.S. National, State, and Local Law — Even Students (and *Especially* Law Students)

Each person in the U.S. — citizen, permanent resident, and F-1 or J-1 student — is expected to know the law of the U.S. and to obey that law. You are expected to know and follow the law of the state where you live, the law of your city or town, and the rules of the school and campus. *Everyone* is subject to fines and/or other penalties if they violate the law or breach school rules — *even if they did not know that the laws or rules existed.*

The U.S. has laws that some other countries do not have. State law varies from state to state, as does the law of cities and towns. Rules of each school also differ.

International students can run afoul of these mandates because they are not familiar with them. A good example is the law related to motor vehicle seat belts (or safety belts). Some states require motor vehicle passengers to wear seat belts. Some states may have no such laws or may not enforce them. You are expected to comply with the seat belt laws that exist in each state, even if you are just passing through on a road trip.

Sometimes Americans violate the law. For example, they may drive over the speed limit, smoke in no-smoking areas, or jaywalk. That does not mean that you, as an international student, should do the same. The ramifications for international students may be greater. *A U.S. student will not have a visa revoked or be deported. International students on F-1 or J-1 visas could be subject to such harsh consequences.* Be careful!

> If you break a law in the U.S., you could lose your F-1 or J-1 student visa status. You may be requested voluntarily to return to your home country, or you could be deported — without receiving your LL.M. degree and without receiving a refund for money spent in tuition and fees. *Be careful!*

This chapter identifies some laws and rules you should know and follow. Review *all* of the materials that your school gives to you about laws before you arrive in the U.S., as you enter the U.S. and pass through Immigration and Customs, and during your stay here.

C. Some Laws That You Should Become Familiar With (and Obey!)

1. Ignorance of the Law — No Excuse

The first "law" you should know is an old English maxim, "Ignorance of the law is no excuse." Police, campus administrators, and immigration officials presume that each person subject to U.S. law *knows* the law. You are not excused simply because you did not know the law existed. Take the seat belt law example again: In most cities the driver and front seat passengers in cars must wear a seat belt. You may be fined if caught without your belt. Ignorance of the seat belt law is no excuse. You are expected to know that law, and comply with it!

2. Customs Laws (See Chapters 20 and 21)

Every person entering the U.S., whether foreigners or U.S. citizens, must comply with U.S. customs laws that prohibit people from bringing certain items into the U.S.

a. It is a crime to carry into the U.S. more than $10,000 in cash or instruments unless you declare it at Customs. (It is safer to transfer money through a bank account.)

b. Khat (leaves of the *Catha edulis* shrub) is illegal. Do not bring it in or use it even if it is used in your home country!

c. You are prohibited from importing pornography into the U.S.

3. Alcohol Consumption

All states restrict the sale and consumption of alcoholic beverages. In all states, persons over the age of 21 may purchase and consume alcohol. Follow local regulations. Law school campuses may restrict on-campus consumption. Be mindful if you are with students who are below the drinking age in your state. It is unlawful to purchase alcohol for them or to share alcoholic drinks with them.

4. Motor Vehicles

Each state has motor vehicle laws that govern vehicle operation, licensing, and safety inspection of cars, trucks, motor bikes, buses, and vans.

Miscellaneous

a. **Seat belt.** Seat belt rules may apply even in taxis. Buckle up!

b. **Helmets.** In some cities, you must wear a helmet when you are riding a motorcycle *or* bicycle.

c. **Driver's license.** You must have a valid driver's license to drive in the U.S. In some states, for limited periods, you may be able to use an international driver's license or a license from your home country. Check with the Department of Motor Vehicles in your state before you drive a motor vehicle (or motorcycle).

d. **Traffic rules.** If you drive, please obey all traffic rules.

e. **Drive on the "right" side.** If you come from a country that drives on the left, you might find it difficult to switch to driving on the right. But if you are going to drive, you have to do it! Thousands of people make the switch. You can too. **Be careful when you are walking or riding a bicycle — look both ways! — because your instincts may be geared toward the left rather than the right traffic.**

f. **Vehicle-related insurance.** Owners of vehicles in the U.S. are required to have a minimum level of liability insurance for their automobiles. If you are involved in an accident, this insurance will help pay the costs. Note that there are two primary types of automobile insurance:
   • *Liability insurance.*   This covers the *other driver* if *you cause* an accident.
   • *Collision insurance.*   This covers *your* expenses if you have an accident.

g. **Vehicle registration.** Any car you purchase *must* be registered in your state.

h. **Drunk driving. If you drink alcohol, do not operate a motor vehicle.** Do not even ride a bicycle. It is dangerous. You can get arrested and be in great trouble. You can even be arrested for *walking while intoxicated*. Most states have very strict laws against driving under the influence, and they enforce them to protect the public. You should choose to either (a) drink; *or* (b) drive. Do not risk your life or the lives of others.

i. **Children riding in cars.** Each U.S. state has rules regarding safety of children when traveling in motor vehicles. **Generally, children of up to about 8 years of age and/or a height of 57 inches must be transported in a child safety seat or booster seat that meets federal safety standards.** Check with state authorities if you will have a child in your car. **Small children are prohibited from riding in the front seat of any vehicle at any time — it is not safe.**

j. **Vehicle documents.** When driving you should have your license, car registration, and proof of insurance with you in your car. Many people leave a copy of their car registration and proof of insurance in their car at all times.

5. Tobacco/Smoking Bans

Many localities ban tobacco smoking inside public transportation stations and vehicles, inside government buildings, and in other public places, such as restaurants, bars, and retail outlets. Fines can be stiff. **Obey "no smoking" signs!**

6. Pets

Some states require certain pets to have licenses and to receive vaccinations. Different jurisdictions have different animal laws.

7. Bank Accounts

If you do not have a Social Security number, ask a bank for a "Form W-8," which you can use for banking purposes.

8. Individual Taxpayer Identification Number (ITIN)

If you need an ITIN for tax purposes, you can file for the ITIN at tax preparation time.

9. U.S. Tax Rules and Regulations

International students must file U.S. tax returns. Check with your LL.M. office or with an authorized tax consultant.

10. Carrying Identification

Carry identification with you at all times. A driver's license or school ID may be fine. Keep your original passport and other important documents in a safe place — rather than carry them around with you — and use copies of them unless you must have the originals for a particular purpose.

11. Visa Requirements

You are expected to know all the restrictions and requirements associated with your visa and concomitant permission to remain in the U.S., and you should comply with them. Violating those terms can result in stiff penalties and fines.

12. Jaywalking

Cross streets at pedestrian crosswalks, typically at intersections. These are often indicated by white stripes across the dark pavement ("zebra crossings"). You could be fined for "jaywalking" (crossing outside of a pedestrian crosswalk).

> Ignorance of the law excuses no man; not that all men know the law, but because 'tis an excuse every man will plead, and no man can tell how to confute him.
> —John Selden, a British jurist (1584–1654)

Miscellaneous

13. Jogging in the Streets

It is perfectly legal in many cities to jog on the streets. But take caution, and follow some simple rules.

a. Run on the sidewalk as much as possible, and not in the street itself.
b. Generally, run *facing* the traffic (and not with traffic at your back). You will be able to see oncoming traffic and more easily avoid harm.
c. If you run at dusk or dawn, wear reflective clothing (perhaps a belt or vest) so drivers can see you more easily.
d. Abide by traffic rules (such as crossing at pedestrian crosswalks and respecting traffic lights).
e. Do not listen to loud music on headphones (you may not hear vehicles or a person screaming, *"Watch out!"*).
f. Carry a photo ID, a credit card, and a small amount of cash (in case you get injured or you need to take a bus or taxi home).

14. Safety of Children

a. **Leaving children unattended.** In the U.S. it is unlawful to leave unattended children nine years old or under (whether on the street, at home, or in a car). You can be arrested for "child endangerment" or "child abandonment." Officials may place the children in "Child Protective Custody" until they determine it is safe to return them to you. You must arrange for someone to care for any child if you or another responsible adult cannot stay with the child.
b. **Corporal and other punishments — and treatment of children.** Different jurisdictions have different laws regarding child abuse, which includes physical, mental, emotional, and psychological abuse. Be certain that you understand these laws and abide by them.
c. **Children riding in cars.** As mentioned, special rules protect children riding in motor vehicles. **You must abide by these child safety rules.**

15. Immunizations: Vaccinations

States and schools may require you to be immunized against certain diseases, including measles, mumps, rubella, pertussis, polio, meningitis, or diphtheria. Some of these diseases require one shot; others, such as the MMR vaccine (mumps, measles, rubella), require two shots. *When you get admitted to a school, ask immediately about vaccinations so you can plan.* **Some schools will not let you enroll without vaccination proof.** Some schools recognize religious exemptions. For more information about vaccinations, visit the U.S. Center for Disease Control at www.cdc.gov/vaccines.

16. Discrimination

Broad federal and state law protect citizens and non-citizens against discrimination in many areas, including sex, race, creed (religion or absence of religion), color, ethnic origin, disability, sexual orientation (status or sexual conduct, except for different treatment in matters of family relations, including marriage, divorce, and adoption), nationality (except in matters such as access to federal student loans and visa requirements, which apply to non-citizens), gender, and similar characteristics. If you believe that you have been unlawfully discriminated against, or believe that someone else has been a victim or discriminated against, contact LL.M. administrators, your advisor, or a campus official.

> If a U.S. LL.M. student breaks the law, he may be expelled from school. But *he will not be deported.* If an international LL.M. student on an F-1 and J-1 visa breaks the law, *he may be expelled and deported* back to his home country.
> A small offense for a U.S. student can be a *major* offense for an overseas student.

17. Sexual Harassment

Sexual harassment violates federal, state, and local law, and the policies of every U.S. school. All students, male and female, should be aware of, and comply with, sexual harassment laws. Any victim or witness should take appropriate recourse. Males or females can be perpetrators or victims, and it can involve same- or opposite-sex activity, irrespective of gender, gender identity, or sexual orientation. It can involve student/student or subordinate/superior relationships. Unwelcome sexual advances, requests for sexual favors, and other verbal or physical conduct of a sexual nature constitute sexual harassment when:

a. submission to such conduct is made either explicitly or implicitly a term or condition of an individual's employment or academic advancement;
b. submission to or rejection of such conduct by an individual is used as the basis of employment or academic decisions affecting such individual; or
c. such conduct has the purpose or effect of unreasonably interfering with an individual's work or academic performance, or of creating an intimidating, hostile, or offensive working or learning environment.

18. Identity Theft

Sometimes a thief will learn your identity card numbers (e.g., passport number, Social Security number, student ID number) and use them to open credit card accounts and purchase items or engage in other transactions. Learn what you must do in your state to protect yourself from legal harms if your "identity" is stolen. **Safeguard your identity card numbers.**

Miscellaneous

19. Safeguard Your Credit Cards and Credit Card Numbers.

Thieves with your credit or debit cards in hand can charge large sums at stores and restaurants. Thieves with your card numbers can charge large sums online. Contact your credit card company the moment you realize your card is missing, and certainly the moment you learn that an unauthorized charge has been made or attempted. Ask your card companies about your obligations and rights.

D. Safety, Security, Health, and Assistance Issues

20. Know What to Do If You Need Emergency Assistance

Your law school will provide you more specific information, but reach out for assistance as follows:

a. *Fire and crime*   (city or campus police, fire department, telephone operator)
b. *Health care emergency*   (doctor, pharmacy, hospital, clinic, ambulance, police, fire department)
c. *Alcohol or drug problems*   (Alcoholics Anonymous, Narcotics Anonymous, physician, counselor, advisor)
d. *Stress, anxiety, adjustment, or related issues*   (physician, counselor, advisor)
e. *Suicidal thoughts*   (counselor, physician, city or campus police, telephone operator, clinic, advisor, hospital, Suicide Hotline)
f. *Domestic violence*   (city or campus police)

Of course the associate dean of your LL.M. program should be available 24 hours, 7 days per week to handle emergencies, and LL.M. students should be able to rely on him or her should emergencies arise. Be certain to choose an LL.M. program in which your associate dean (LL.M. Dean) lives in the same city or geographical area where your school is, and who will be present on campus when you are enrolled.

E. Identify or Create a Network to Help Ensure Your Safety and Security — Physical, Mental, Emotional Health and Well-Being

With advanced technology and social networking, and with an increased emphasis on safety, security, and well-being, students are more connected than ever with friends, family, and even professors. In the U.S., it is extremely common for students to contact their professors by e-mail, computer course communication system, or sometimes even by phone. Students in the U.S.

today are fully networked, and are expected to use their network for safety, security, health, and other concerns.

Below are 13 phone numbers you should have on speed dial[1] in your cell phone:

1. *Campus emergency services number.* Each campus has a phone number for campus police, fire, ambulance, or other emergency. Learn that number. Put it on speed dial. If you cannot find the number, dial "911" or "0". You might also find "Emergency Call Boxes" located on different parts of campus — on poles on sidewalks, on walls of parking garages, and other places. Use these call boxes for emergencies. (And not for an "emergency" midnight pizza order!)

2. *City or town emergency services number.* The town or city in which you live will have phone numbers for local police, fire, ambulance, or other emergency services. If you cannot find the number, dial "911" or "0."

3. *The academic head of your LL.M. program.* This person may have the title of "Associate Dean," "Vice-Dean," "Faculty Director," or some similar title. Contact that person if you have a serious health or other issue, particularly if it could affect your academic situation. Again, be certain that you choose to attend a law school at which the Associate Dean is vested (or invested) in the LL.M. program and its students. This person should live close to the school and should be physically present on campus during your LL.M. period, and should not be on sabbatical, on leave, or serving as a visiting professor at another law school. You need a "present" Associate Dean, not an "absent" one.

4. *The administrative director of your LL.M. program.* This person may have the title of "Assistant Dean," "Director," or a similar title. This person may not be a member of the faculty, but would certainly be a member — and an important one — of the law school staff or administration. He or she would handle the day-to-day, administrative, non-academic aspects of the LL.M. program.

5. *Law school or university health center (for physical or mental conditions).* At most law schools, LL.M. students are required to carry health insurance. Use it! If you are ill, contact the law school or university health center. You can make an appointment, or just stop in for a visit. Have the phone number ready for when you need it. Some students feel they do not have time to get minor physical illnesses checked, or they underestimate the seriousness of mental health issues. LL.M. students (like J.D. students, law school faculty and staff, and others) can experience stress, anxiety, and other issues. If you experience these,

---

1. If emergencies arise, you should phone the person rather than send a text message if possible. A person may be more likely to hear the phone ring than to check for text messages. Also, text messages are more indirect than calls, and are inherently more passive, or casual, implying less importance or urgency than a direct call.

Miscellaneous

you can get appropriate attention at your law school or university health center. U.S. students, faculty, staff, and many others seek counseling when needed. You should, too.

6. *Students in your courses.*   You will not be friends with every student in every course you take. You do not have to be. But you should develop relationships with at least one or two people in each of your courses. If you miss a class, they can tell you the assignments. They can help you if you do not understand some of the course material. You might study with them before exam time. These classroom acquaintances could turn into good friends.

7. *Faculty academic advisor.*   Your academic advisor should ordinarily be a member of the law faculty. You should have this person's contact details handy in case issues arise related to your academic program. You will most likely communicate via e-mail or in person, and reserve phone calls for emergencies. Your faculty academic advisor can counsel on which courses you should take, how your courses fit in with your career goals, progress in your classes, and academic and other difficulties. *Try to alert the faculty academic advisor before issues arise, if possible.*

8. *Friends.*   Of course your friends will be on speed dial. This is important. You need to have balance in your life, and friends can be a lifeline for you, to help you deal with challenges of life in a U.S. law school. With technological convenience, you can certainly reach out to friends and family from your home country, and friends and family all over the world. In every single class of LL.M. students I have known — dating from the 1980s to today — I have witnessed extremely strong bonds develop among LL.M. classmates — with the bonds based on the trials and satisfactions they share as LL.M. students, on a day-to-day, semester-to-semester basis as they proceed through their LL.M. year. *Do not underestimate how you will be positively impacted by those in your LL.M. class in the U.S., and how you will positively impact your classmates.*

9. *ICE number — In Case of Emergency number.*   "ICE" is an acronym for "In Case of Emergency." Under the name "ICE," you might list the phone number of a friend or family member to contact in an emergency. Emergency responders who recover cell phones will look to see if there is an "ICE" entry to notify about the emergency. (Note that "ICE," coincidentally, is also the acronym for Immigration and Customs Enforcement. In an emergency, responders will look for the "In Case of Emergency" friend or family member you listed in your phone, not the other U.S. government ICE!)

10. *Spiritual leader.*   If you enjoy a religious or spiritual tradition, you might have on speed dial a religious or spiritual leader you might want to phone if you have troubles, or if you just want to hear a friendly, calming, and reassuring voice.

11. *Landlord.*   Your landlord may be a private corporation, an individual person, or maybe the university itself. Keep your landlord's phone

number handy. If problems arise at your home, you can quickly request assistance from your landlord.

12. *Your favorite pizza delivery company.* Virtually all law students I have ever met enjoy a disproportionate amount of pizza during school. Pizza is a U.S. law school tradition! Multiple pizza delivery companies are located near *every* law school campus. They offer students discounts, quick service, and a filling meal. Be careful — the calories in a pizza may be more than you bargained for!

13. *Consular official from your embassy.* Your country may have an embassy in Washington, D.C., and consular offices in other U.S. cities. They should assist if you have immigration, legal, or serious problems with your LL.M. program. (See the discussion of the Vienna Convention on Consular Relations below.)

F. Vienna Convention on Consular Relations (24 April 1963, 21 U.S.T. 77)

1. The Vienna Convention on Consular Relations ("Vienna Convention") is a multilateral treaty that codifies law related to consular officials who represent their countries in a foreign country.

2. The Vienna Convention protects international students who are arrested or otherwise detained by any federal, state, or local government officials *anywhere* in the U.S., at anytime — even if your student visa has expired or you are otherwise out of academic or legal status. The U.S. is party to and bound by the Vienna Convention, and the U.S. is fully obligated to

---

Vienna Convention on Consular Relations — General Rules

If you are an international student in the U.S. and your country is a party to the Vienna Convention, the following rights apply:

- Consular officers from your country shall be free to visit you and communicate with you (in writing and orally).
- U.S. officials should inform your country's consular officials that you have been detained.
- The U.S. officials should inform you of your rights.
- Your country's consular officials have the right to correspond with you and arrange for your legal representation.
- You have the right to refuse visits, communication, and assistance from your country's consular officials.
- Rules may differ slightly depending on terms your country agreed to in becoming a party to the Vienna Convention. *Check with your embassy or consulate in the U.S. for accurate details.*

Miscellaneous

comply with all the Vienna Convention rules related to international students who are arrested or otherwise detained in the U.S.

3. Per the *Vienna Convention*, if an international student is detained by U.S. authorities, the U.S. must inform consular officials from that student's home country. U.S. officials should inform the detained student that the student can consult with his country's consular officials who are generally at the embassy in Washington, D.C., or a consulate in another U.S. city.

4. For example, if a Brazilian LL.M. student is detained anywhere in the U.S., the U.S. government is required to inform Brazilian consular officials (ordinarily at the Brazilian embassy or consulate). The Brazilian government will have the opportunity to meet with the student, to check on the student's health and well-being, and to provide for legal counsel if necessary. The consul could also arrange for medical attention or contact with the student's family.

5. If you are detained in the U.S., you may request authorities to inform your country's consulate or embassy. Occasionally students are detained by immigration authorities while entering the U.S., or by police on routine matters in the city where they live. Your consulate or embassy has *the right* to meet with you, provide you with legal assistance, or otherwise help you.

G. No Substitute for Legal Advice

LL.M. Roadmap does not provide legal advice! For immigration, criminal matters, tax, and other legal issues, you may need to consult an attorney licensed in your state. The administrators at your U.S. law school or your university *might not be licensed to practice law or to give you legal advice.* You may ask your LL.M. program director for contact details of licensed attorneys who can provide legal advice.

CHAPTER SUMMARY

- When you are in the U.S., you must obey U.S. law.

- Everyone subject to U.S. law is expected to know the law of the U.S. (whether you in fact know the law or not).

- There is more to U.S. law than you find in movies, TV shows, or books.

- The law discussed in this chapter is but a small part of what you must know.

- Check your *LL.M. Student Handbook,* your *LL.M. Orientation Manual,* and other LL.M. program office materials for more information.

- Be certain to ask your LL.M. program administrators any questions you have about U.S. law — before you inadvertently breach it.

- When you arrive in the U.S., register with the embassy or consulate from your country. Consular officials can assist you if you need it while you are in the U.S.

Part X

Conclusion

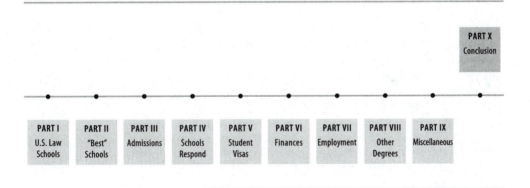

Chapter 33

Conclusion

CHAPTER HIGHLIGHTS

- *LL.M. Roadmap* has sought to walk you through deciding whether to pursue an advanced law degree (in particular, the LL.M.), and if so, whether to choose the U.S. or another country. Then, it offers guidance on choosing a school, applying, getting accepted, preparing to arrive, arriving, succeeding in school, graduating, and pursuing your professional and personal goals post-LL.M.

- *LL.M. Roadmap* might be likened to an encyclopedia. Not many people read an encyclopedia front to back. If they pick one up at all, they might flip through it, land on an interesting and useful section, and enjoy it.

- *LL.M. Roadmap* is like any other comprehensive source book. If you need clarification on a specific point, please flip to the Index, find the pages on which *LL.M. Roadmap* covers the subject, turn to the relevant section, and get answers to your questions.

- You may decide not to pursue an LL.M. You may decide to earn your LL.M. in another country. You may decide to come to the U.S. for an LL.M., or a J.D. You may change your mind later, and choose one of the options you rejected earlier.

- I hope that *LL.M. Roadmap* will help you make the "best" decision for you, whatever that may be. Good luck on this journey!

A. Introduction

LL.M. Roadmap has demonstrated that LL.M. programs offered by U.S. law schools come in many varieties. They have different goals and resources, different types of students from different countries, professors with expertise in different areas, and students and graduates with different accomplishments and aspirations.

Different stakeholders involved in the LL.M. marketplace have different ideas about what makes an LL.M. program "good." They debate issues such as what promises schools make to students and graduates; whether schools fulfill their promises to students and graduates; whether students entering LL.M. programs have reasonable expectations; and whether LL.M. programs adequately prepare graduates for the globalized legal marketplace.

Law firms, corporations, governments, the UN, nonprofit groups, and other organizations that hire LL.M. graduates want assurance that these students have received high-quality legal training in U.S. law or whichever specialized area of law they studied. Graduates want to feel secure knowing that the law school devoted maximum resources to their LL.M. education, helping to ensure that the graduates are fully equipped for career challenges that lie ahead. Governments and foundations that sponsor lucrative LL.M. scholarships want to be confident that their funds were well spent. Clients and constituents of LL.M. graduates want to know that their LL.M. lawyers are as highly trained in law, ethics, and leadership as possible, and will provide high-quality service.

LL.M. graduates work for corporations who need legal services to survive. They work for the UN as it seeks to promote peace and security around the globe. They work for human rights groups, helping eradicate gross human rights violations and other unspeakable abuses. They teach at law faculties in many countries, helping make the world smaller and more interconnected by sharing insights gained from U.S. law professors, law school administrators, and LL.M. classmates from around the world. LL.M. graduates from U.S. law schools carry the rule of law to their home countries, and wherever in the world they choose. The reach of LL.M. graduates is boundless!

B. A Picture of the "Ideal" U.S. LL.M. Program

LL.M. Roadmap paints a picture of the ideal U.S. LL.M. program, one through which LL.M. graduates become empowered to serve in their chosen fields of law, in whichever type of organization they choose, in whatever city, town, or country they end up.

An ideal LL.M. program has high-quality professors and staff devoted to servicing the needs of high-quality LL.M. students. It is fully resourced, with funding in part from the high LL.M. tuition revenues. It makes implicit and express promises to students and graduates and fulfills those promises, and even goes above and beyond. In an ideal LL.M. program, LL.M. student expectations are reasonable, crafted in part based on comprehensive and truthful advertising by the schools about what the school is willing and able to offer students, as well as what the school has chosen not to offer. There is no "bait and switch" in an ideal LL.M. program, and no hint of "cash cow" or "diploma mill" status. The ideal LL.M. program provides the best services that tuition dollars can buy.

C. LL.M. Roadmap — Tool to Learn about the "Ideal LL.M. Program"; LL.M. Administrator, Professor, Student, and Graduate Contributions

LL.M. Roadmap is the sort of guide that you would likely not pick up and read cover to cover in one sitting. It is more like an encyclopedia, a resource you can turn to whenever you seek guidance on a particular phase or aspect of the LL.M. process. You might read and reread different chapters at different times, depending on what topic interests you at that juncture — choosing schools to apply to, deciding how to prepare once admitted, applying for a U.S. student visa or scholarship, taking and passing the New York bar, or getting a new job in the U.S. post-LL.M.

Many LL.M. program administrators, professors, students, graduates, and other stakeholders contributed to *LL.M. Roadmap*. If *you* have comments, questions, or other feedback, please let us know at *www.LLMRoadmap.com* or *LLMRoadmap@yahoo.com*. We may include your thoughts in the next edition or post them on the website!

Much of *LL.M. Roadmap* is written for persons seeking to join an LL.M. program, who are currently enrolled or who have graduated. *LL.M. Roadmap* has walked you through deciding whether to pursue an LL.M., and if so, whether to choose the U.S. or another country; and how to choose a U.S. school, apply, get accepted, succeed in school, graduate, and pursue your professional and personal goals post-LL.M.

LL.M. Roadmap is also useful for anyone or any group interested in graduate legal education generally, including law firms, corporation counsel offices, public interest law groups, and other legal practitioners in the U.S. and overseas; foreign government education and scholarship ministries and embassies in the U.S.; U.S. State Department EducationUSA Advisors; U.S. Congress; U.S. law school professors, librarians, administrators, and other staff; academic advisors and law teachers at universities and law faculties; and education agents and consultants.

LL.M. Roadmap will be of interest to parents and families of foreign lawyers who may play a role in deciding whether you should come to the U.S. for an LL.M. degree. Friends concerned about your career will also be interested in *LL.M. Roadmap*.

Finally, *LL.M. Roadmap* is particularly geared toward you, the overseas-trained law graduate who is considering or is already embarked on the life-changing strategy of coming to the U.S. to study for your LL.M.

Congratulations on making it this far! And good luck as you continue on your journey!

CHAPTER SUMMARY

- *LL.M. Roadmap* has sought to walk you through major decisions regarding pursuing an advanced law degree in the U.S.

- Though *LL.M. Roadmap* seeks to address concerns of the many stakeholders in U.S. graduate legal education, *LL.M. Roadmap* has been particularly focused on you, the international student who may embark on a life-changing adventure of a year studying for an LL.M. degree at a U.S. law school.

- I hope you find *LL.M. Roadmap* and *www.LLMRoadMap.com* to be useful sources to address major questions you have.

- Whether or not you decide to pursue an LL.M., or which country or school you choose for yourself, I am hopeful that you will make whatever decision you truly feel is the "best" decision for you.

- Good luck! And, please let us know of your successes — please write to us at *LLMRoadMap@yahoo.com*!

Part XI

End Material

Appendix I

Specializations Offered at One or More U.S. Law School LL.M. Programs[1]

A. Specializations Listed on U.S. Law School Websites (Or Otherwise Advertised)

1. Administrative Law (Public Policy; Government Law)
2. Admiralty Law (Maritime Law; Coastal Law; Ocean Law)
3. Advanced Legal Studies (General LL.M.; As Approved)
4. Agriculture Law (Food Law)
5. American Business Law (Business Law; International Business Law; International Economic Law; International Trade Law; Trade Regulation)
6. American Law for Foreign Lawyers (Foreign Scholars Program; U.S. Law for Foreign Lawyers; U.S. Legal Studies)
7. As Approved (Advanced Legal Studies; General LL.M.)
8. Asian and Comparative Law (Comparative Law; Comparative Legal Thought)
9. Asylum Law (Immigration Law)
10. Banking Law
11. Bankruptcy Law
12. Biotechnology Law (Genetics Law; Genomics Law)
13. Business Law (American Business Law; Global Business; International Business Law; International Economic Law; International Trade Law; Trade Regulation)
14. Child Law (Family Law; Juvenile Law)
15. Civil Rights Law (Human Rights Law; International Human Rights Law)
16. Climate Change (Environmental Law; International Environmental Law; Oil & Gas Law; Natural Resources Law; Sustainable Development Law)
17. Coastal Law (Admiralty Law; Maritime Law; Ocean Law)
18. Communications Law (Telecommunications Law)
19. Comparative Law (Comparative Legal Thought; Asian and Comparative Law; International Law)

---

1. Descriptions of LL.M. specializations in this Appendix include paraphrases of program promotional materials from different LL.M. programs. Different schools describe similar specializations differently, and assign different names to similar specializations. Please assess the specializations based on their descriptions, and not based solely on their names. The descriptions may reveal that the subject matter of the specialization is different than what the name might suggest at first glance. The specializations are cross-referenced to related specializations. *Please* check law school LL.M. program websites for current offerings and descriptions.

20. Comparative Legal Thought (Comparative Law; Asian and Comparative Law; International Law)
21. Corporate Finance Law (Corporate Law; Finance & Financial Services Law)
22. Corporate Law (Corporate Finance Law; Finance & Financial Services Law)
23. Criminal Law (Prosecutorial Science; International Criminal Law)
24. Democratic Governance Law (Rule of Law)
25. Development Law (Environmental Law; International Development Law; Land Development Law; Sustainable Development Law)
26. Dispute Resolution
27. Economics (Law and)
28. Education Law
29. Elder Law
30. Employee Benefits (Employment Law; Labor Law)
31. Employment Law (Employee Benefits; Labor Law)
32. Energy Law (Development Law; Environmental Law; Environmental Sustainability; Land Development Law; Natural Resources Law; Oil & Gas Law; Sustainable Development Law)
33. Entertainment (Media Law)
34. Entrepreneurship (Law and)
35. Environmental Law (Climate Change; Development Law; Environmental Sustainability; International Environmental Law; Land Development Law; Natural Resources Law; Oil & Gas Law; Sustainable Development Law)
36. Environmental Sustainability (Climate Change; Development Law; Environmental Law; International Environmental Law; Land Development Law; Natural Resources Law; Oil & Gas Law; Sustainable Development Law)
37. Estate Planning
38. Experiential Law Teaching (Teaching, Experiential Law)
39. Family Law (Child Law; Juvenile Law)
40. Finance & Financial Services Law (Corporate Finance Law; Corporate Law)

41. Food Law (Agricultural Law)
42. Foreign Relations Law of U.S. (Comparative Law; International Law; International Legal Studies)
43. Foreign Scholars Program (Advanced Legal Studies; American Law for Foreign Lawyers; As Approved; General LL.M.; U.S. Law for Foreign Lawyers; U.S. Legal Studies)
44. General LL.M. (Advanced Legal Studies; As Approved)
45. Genetics Law (Biotechnology Law; Genomics Law)
46. Genomics Law (Biotechnology Law; Genetics Law)
47. Global Business Law (American Business Law; Business Law; International Business Law; International Economic Law; International Trade Law; Trade Regulation)
48. Government Law (Administrative Law; Public Policy)
49. Health Care Law (Health Law)
50. Health Law (Health Care Law)
51. Human Rights Law (Civil Rights Law; International Human Rights Law)
52. Immigration Law (Asylum Law)
53. Indian Law (Indigenous Law; Tribal Policy, Law & Government)
54. Indigenous Law (Civil Rights Law; Human Rights Law; Indian Law; International Human Rights Law; Tribal Policy, Law & Government)
55. Information Technology Law
56. Insurance Law
57. Intellectual Property Law (IP Law)
58. Inter-American Law (Latin American Law)
59. International Business Law (American Business Law; Business Law; Global Law; International Economic Law; International Trade Law; Trade Regulation)
60. International Criminal Law (Criminal Law; Prosecutorial Science)
61. International Economic Law (American Business Law; Business Law; Global Law; International Business Law; International Economic Law; International Trade; Trade Regulation)

62. International Environmental Law (Climate Change; Environmental Law; Natural Resources Law; Sustainable Development Law)
63. International Human Rights Law (Civil Rights Law; Human Rights Law; Indigenous Law; Indian Law; International Law; Tribal Policy, Law & Government)
64. International Law (Comparative Law; International Human Rights Law; International Legal Studies; U.S. Foreign Relations Law)
65. International Legal Studies (Comparative Law; International Law; U.S. Foreign Relations Law)
66. International Tax Law (Tax Law)
67. International Trade Law (American Business Law; Business Law; Global Business Law; International Business Law; International Economic Law; Trade Regulation)
68. IP Law (Intellectual Property Law)
69. Judicial Process (Juridical Studies)
70. Juridical Studies (Judicial Process)
71. Jurisprudence (Legal Theory)
72. Juvenile Law (Child Law; Family Law)
73. Labor Law (Employee Benefits; Employment Law)
74. Land Development Law (Development Law; Environmental Law; Oil & Gas Law; Natural Resources Law)
75. Latin American Studies (Inter-American Law)
76. Legal Theory (Jurisprudence)
77. Litigation (Trial Advocacy)
78. Maritime Law (Admiralty Law; Ocean Law; Coastal Law)
79. Media Law (Entertainment Law)
80. Military Justice System (Military Law)
81. Military Law (Military Justice System)
82. National Security Law
83. Natural Resources Law (Climate Change; Energy Law; Environmental Law; International Environmental Law; Land Development Law; Oil and Gas Law; Sustainable Development Law)
84. Ocean Law (Admiralty Law; Coastal Law; Maritime Law)

85. Oil & Gas Law (Energy Law; Environmental Law; Natural Resources Law; Sustainable Development Law)
86. Prosecutorial Science (Criminal Law; International Criminal Law)
87. Public Policy (Administrative Law; Government Law)
88. Real Estate Law
89. Religion (Law and)
90. Research
91. Rule of Law (Democratic Governance)
92. Science/Technology (Law and)
93. Securities & Financial Regulation
94. Space Law
95. Sports Law
96. Sustainable Development Law (Climate Change; Development Law; Environmental Law; International Environmental Law; Land Development Law; Natural Resources Law; Oil and Gas Law)
97. Tax Law (International Tax Law)
98. Teaching, Experiential Law
99. Technology/Science (Law and)
100. Telecommunications Law (Communications Law)
101. Trade Regulation (American Business Law; Business Law; Global Business Law; International Business Law; International Economic Law; International Trade Law)
102. Trial Advocacy (Litigation)
103. Tribal Policy, Law & Government (Indian Law; Indigenous Law)
104. U.S. Foreign Relations Law (Comparative Law; International Law; International Legal Studies)
105. U.S. Law for Foreign Lawyers (American Law for Foreign Lawyers; Foreign Scholars Program; U.S. Legal Studies)
106. U.S. Legal Studies (American Law for Foreign Lawyers; Foreign Scholars Program U.S.; Law for Foreign Lawyers)
107. Urban Affairs Law (Urban Studies Law)
108. Urban Studies Law (Urban Affairs Law)

B. LL.M. Specializations Defined

1. Administrative Law (*see* Government Law).
2. Admiralty Law (Coastal Law; Maritime Law; *see also* Ocean Law). Admiralty law involves business and commercial aspects of oceans, seas, lakes, rivers, bays, ports, harbors, and other navigable bodies of waters and vessels that travel on them. Issues include port and harbor access; sea worker and salvage rights; injury to persons and property and death involving navigable waters; shipping lanes; ships navigating waters; shipping contracts; maritime liens; navigation accidents; and the relationship among ships, ship owners, crews, flag states, and ship registration. The law of the sea is relevant, as is maritime law of national jurisdictions. Lawyers with this degree work for law firms, governments, shipping or manufacturing companies, and the United Nations or other intergovernmental organizations.
3. Advanced Legal Studies (*see* General LL.M.).
4. Agricultural Law (Food Law). Agricultural law (or "Ag Law") deals with plants, seeds, waters, fertilizers, pesticides, food, land tenure systems, and farming rights and labor. It can deal with food and agriculture issues related to marketing and finance, biotechnology, international trade, tax planning, soil and water conservation, land use, food safety, federal farm programs, environmental sustainability, and global warming. It explores concerns of the growers, processors, retailers and consumers. Food law deals with food safety and labeling and animal welfare. Graduates may work for the United Nations (e.g., UN Development Fund, World Food Program); government agencies (of many countries); law firms; or multinational corporations that produce food (plant or animal), fertilizer, or other products.
5. American Business Law (*see* Business Law; *see also* International Business Law).
6. American Law for Foreign Lawyers (Foreign Scholars Program; U.S. Law for Foreign Lawyers; U.S. Legal Studies; *see also* General LL.M.). This "general" LL.M. law degree covers wide-ranging U.S. law subjects ordinarily covered in a J.D. degree, and helps prepare LL.M. students for a U.S. bar exam, for U.S. law practice, or to work with U.S. clients in the students' home countries or with foreign clients doing business in the U.S. In general LL.M. programs, students are integrated into the J.D. student body and sit in classrooms alongside J.D. students. They select from a wide range of courses in many areas. LL.M. students may gain deep insights into a specific area of U.S. law by taking a series of courses in that area, for example, corporate law, health law, tax law, or any other U.S. law area.
7. As Approved (*see* General LL.M.).
8. Asian and Comparative Law (*see* Comparative Law). Asian and comparative law focuses on theory and practice of law related to Asia. This degree compares law and legal systems between Asia and other regions and between Asian countries and countries of other regions. It may interest students concerned with national, regional, or multijurisdictional commercial and non-commercial issues. Areas of inquiry could include international governance, institution building, regulation, commercial transactions and sustainability.
9. Asylum Law (*see* Immigration Law).
10. Banking Law. Banking law covers laws that regulate domestic and international banks and other financial institutions, including law governing structure and strategies of these entities; structure and operation of capital markets; and regulation of accounts, deposits, and loans. Holders of this degree may work for many types of entities, including government regulatory bodies, law firms, corporations, commercial banks, the World Bank, or the International Monetary Fund (IMF).
11. Bankruptcy Law. Bankruptcy law relates to proceedings when businesses are unable to repay business debts when due or where the value of the business is less than the debts owed,

and a court orders action such as restructuring of the debt of the business. Individuals may file with a court for voluntary bankruptcy if they are unable to pay their debts.

12. **Biotechnology Law (Genetics Law; Genomics Law).** Biotechnology involves altering the genetic composition of organisms to create products. Genomics is a branch of genetics that studies organisms in terms of their genomes (their full DNA sequences). Biotechnology, genomics, and genetics issues recur in many legal practice areas, including intellectual property, health, constitutional, employment, criminal, agricultural, and international human rights. These areas highlight legal, ethical, and policy concerns, including national and international permission to further biotechnology, genomic and genetic production, and national and international prohibitions. Graduates may work for government regulatory agencies, pharmaceutical or other multinational corporations, law firms, NGOs (including human rights groups), or intergovernmental organizations (including the United Nations).

13. **Business Law (American Business Law; Global Business Law; International Business Law; International Economic Law; International Trade Law).** Business law deals with domestic and international business and business practice. It may involve business formation (e.g., sole proprietorships, partnerships, limited-liability entities, corporations), the nature of businesses (e.g., not-for-profit, for-profit, quasi-governmental), business operations and regulation (e.g., domestic, transnational, or global regulation and regulation compliance), or business extinction (e.g., bankruptcy, dissolution). This LL.M. may explore law and economics, corporate finance law, international human rights law, consumer law, international trade law, environmental law, domestic and international tax law, antitrust law, and domestic and international labor law. It may deal with practical matters such as drafting and filing articles of incorporation, obtaining necessary permits or privileges to operate, and negotiating with domestic or international regulatory bodies. It may have courses in corporations, tax, commercial transactions, business organizations, corporate finance, contracts, antitrust, and bankruptcy.

14. **Child Law** (*see* **Family Law**).

15. **Civil Rights Law** (*see also* **International Human Rights Law**). Civil rights law protects individuals and groups from deprivation of liberties and freedoms to which they are entitled under domestic and international law. Civil rights protections are broad, and include, for example, the right to vote; non-discrimination in health care and education; and freedom from discrimination based on or race, ethnicity, sex, religion, status as a veteran, family status, physical or mental disability, creed, sexual orientation, or other similar status. Civil rights law works in tandem with all other areas of law, and all other areas of law must be consistent with civil rights law. Civil rights law must be followed when implementing employment law, housing law, family law, sports law, education law, voting law, and other types of law. The government, private individuals, corporations, partnerships, and all other entities must comply with civil rights law. Graduates may work for public interest law firms, governments, or international organizations. Some consider civil rights law to be international human rights law operating on the domestic front.

16. **Climate Change** (*see* **Environmental Law**).

17. **Coastal Law** (*see* **Admiralty Law**).

18. **Communication Law (Telecommunications Law).** Communication law concerns U.S. Federal Communications Commission (FCC) regulation of radio and TV broadcasting and other telecommunications, electronic mass media, and wireless and digital communications and services. Courses may include international law, cyber law, intellectual property law, international human rights law, and telecommunications law. It may also explore copyright law, network security, privacy, cybercrime, copyright enforcement, free expression, the communications industry, and gathering and disseminating of news. Topics within these courses may include libel, privacy invasion, censorship, punishing obscenity and indecency,

restricting reporting of matters affecting national security and foreign relations, reporter access to persons and places, privileges for news persons not to divulge confidential sources and information, free press/fair trial issues, judicial secrecy, "fair use" of copyrighted materials, and the internet.

19. **Comparative Law (Comparative Legal Thought;** *see also* **Asian and Comparative Law;** *see also* **International Law).** Comparative law introduces students to law and practice of one jurisdiction, then comparatively explores law and practice of one or more other jurisdictions. Graduates in this area will be well-poised to represent foreign clients in the U.S. or U.S. clients in other countries. Students might specialize in one or more substantive law areas to complement their general comparative law education.

20. **Comparative Legal Thought** (*see also* **Comparative Law**)

21. **Corporate Finance Law** (*see* **Corporate Law;** *see also* **Finance & Financial Services Law).** Corporate finance law concerns law regarding the creating and functioning of financial markets and regulations, securities law, financial services law, and related areas on domestic and international fronts. It covers black-letter law regarding corporate financing and underlying policies. Deals with regulating corporations and corporate actors related to financing, and includes courses in commodity futures markets, mutual fund industry, banks and insurance companies, financial accounting and reporting, corporate governance, financial derivatives, securities litigation, mergers and acquisitions, venture capital, and technology transactions and project finance.

22. **Corporate Law** (*see* **Corporate Finance Law;** *see also* **Finance & Financial Services Law).** Corporate law deals with domestic and international regulations of the creation, operation, modification, and dissolution of corporations that fall into many categories, including domestic or multinational, large or small, for-profit or nonprofit, or manufacturing or service corporations. Graduates may work on mergers and acquisitions or joint ventures, in transactions between and among entities, or other matters.

Securities law involves the regulation of public and private financing of corporations and corporate transactions, and includes matters such as complying with Securities and Exchange Commission (SEC) regulations. It also involves financial investments in stocks, bonds, and debentures issued by corporations and governments.

Corporate lawyers may be involved in transactional or litigation matters, or be involved in regulatory work. They may work for law firms, corporations, or governments.

23. **Criminal Law (Prosecutorial Science; International Criminal Law).** *Criminal law* deals with crimes, which are behaviors that states deem to violate societal norms and for which the state imposes a criminal penalty. Criminal law practice is divided between prosecution (investigating, prosecuting, and trying persons suspected of and charged with crimes) and defense (representing persons suspected of, accused of or convicted of crimes). Prosecutors represent government or societal interests, which include the victims' interests.

Criminal procedure deals with law related to identifying persons suspected of perpetrating crimes, investigating them, arresting them, trying them, convicting them upon a finding of guilt, acquitting them upon a finding of not guilty, imposing sentences upon those found guilty, and facilitating appeals on verdicts and sentences.

This LL.M. could focus on domestic and international crimes and also on investigations, arrests, arraignments, bail hearings, pleadings, plea agreements, charges, trials, defenses to criminal charges, sentencing, parole, convictions, appeals, and other post-conviction remedies. It could highlight U.S. Constitutional protections in the criminal process (e.g., right to a fair trial, right to counsel, right to a speedy trial, Miranda rights). It could include an international or comparative law focus, and could highlight international or transnational criminal law and procedure, and cover topics such as the International Criminal Court. It could deal with the relationship between domestic law and international criminal law, and could explore civil rights and international human rights law violations.

24. **Democratic Governance and Rule of Law.** This LL.M. deals with law reform in transitional societies moving toward democracy.

25. **Development Law** (*see* **Environmental Law**).

26. **Dispute Resolution.** Dispute resolution covers disputes resolved within a judicial structure (e.g., trials before courts and tribunals) or extra-judicially (e.g., negotiation, arbitration, mediation). It may survey domestic or transnational disputes involving many types of decision makers. It may cover the relationship between trial systems and alternative dispute resolution processes, and may contain clinical or other experiential teaching methods to offer students hands-on experience working within public and private dispute resolution structures.

27. **Economic Law (Law & Economics).** The discipline of law and economics ("economic analysis of law") views law through the lens of economics and applies principles, theories, and methods of economics to issues that arise in legal contexts. It uses economics to evaluate how law is understood and impacts society and societal choices. It discerns which legal results are economically efficient, and thus desirable. Economics helps determine which laws are made, how laws are interpreted, and how law is applied to facts to resolve legal problems.

28. **Education Law.** Education law deals with regulating public and private schools of all types at all levels. Many areas of education are subject to governmental regulations, including school accreditation, teacher credentialing, education standards, school safety for students and staff, unions and other collective bargaining arrangements for teachers, teacher employment contracts and other related issues, teacher hiring and firing, student and teacher conduct and discipline, relationship between church and state, gifted children and children with special needs in compulsory educational schemes, curricula design and implementation, student organizations and extracurricular activities, school sports, discrimination, student rights, liability for injuries, immunities, and tenure. Education lawyers may work with local or national governmental regulatory agencies, teachers' unions, law firms, or nongovernmental organizations focusing on religious or secular issues and schools.

29. **Elder Law.** Elder law deals with issues related to a specific type of client—senior citizens. Elderly people may have legal needs in the areas of Medicare and Medicaid entitlements and benefits, Social Security, other retirement issues, and age discrimination in housing or employment. Elders may also have needs related to long-term care, duties of families, rehabilitation programs, conservatorship and guardianship, incapacity, protective services, managed health care matters, fraud, and nursing home abuse. Legal issues include dispute resolution, administrative proceedings, and medical information privacy.

Although elder law overlaps with many other areas of law, in elder law the client is always a senior citizen. An elder law practice might involve estate planning for senior citizens, taxation, wills and trust, access to housing and food, employment discrimination, disability, mental and physical health care planning, governmental regulation, and civil and human rights. These areas of law are relevant to younger populations, but they have different relevance and applicability to senior citizens. These issues are particularly important as elders are living longer and have increasing legal needs. Practitioners must know about the aging process (just as juvenile law practitioners must know about childhood development, transitioning to adulthood, and related matters).

30. **Employee Benefits** (*see also* **Employment Law**). Employee benefits deals with employee rights (and obligations) and with reciprocal employer obligations (and rights). It concerns employee retirement plans, and issues such as rights related to insurance (e.g., life, health, disability), holiday/vacation rules, employee stock ownership plans (e.g., options, deferred compensation, bonuses), employee loyalty, and employee work obligations. It is related to other law areas such as tax, labor and employment, and civil rights law. This LL.M. also deals

with how employee benefits plans are created, administered, maintained, modified, or taxed. Degree holders may work for law firms, regulatory bodies, unions, or corporations.

31. **Employment Law** (*see also* **Employee Benefits**). Employment law deals with law governing the operation of workplaces and the rights and obligations of those involved in the workforce, including employers, workers, and unions. It deals with the relationship between a company (management) and its employees (labor), including types of employment arrangements (employment at will, employment contracts, tenure). It deals with how labor and management communicate, set and abide by work policies, and resolve issues through collective bargaining, particularly regarding wages, work hours, and working conditions.

   It also deals with employee obligations, including the duties to comply with company policy, not to steal or be insubordinate, and not to deprive the company of an honest day's work. Legal issues may relate to employment terms and conditions, wage and salary, employee benefits, affirmative action, disclosure and privacy issues, vacation and leave policies, dispute resolution procedures, and safety and health issues.

   Other issues include employment contracts, workplace injuries, hazardous work conditions, equal pay for equal work, right to form unions, termination or suspension, workplace discipline, workplace privacy, wages and the payment of wages, pensions, non-citizen workers, permission of non-citizens to work, drug testing, unemployment benefits, whistle-blowing, and wrongful termination.

   Employment law overlaps with civil rights and human rights law. Rights include freedom from unlawful workplace discrimination based on age, race, religion, sex, color, family status, disability, creed, sexual orientation, or other similar status. They include rights to be free from sexual harassment, hostile work environments, retaliation and whistle-blowing, wrongful termination of employment, employee discipline, and occupational safety hazards.

   Employment or labor lawyers may work for corporations as "in-house counsel" (monitoring compliance with employment laws and regulations), government labor departments (regulating labor, enforcing labor laws, negotiating labor treaties), labor unions, law firms (representing workers, corporations, or unions), nongovernmental organizations (advocating for fair labor standards, abolition of sweatshops, enforcement of child labor laws), and international organizations (e.g., the International Labor Organization — ILO).

32. **Energy Law (Oil & Gas Law; Environmental Law; Natural Resources Law).** Energy law deals with energy production, transportation, and use. Energy law may also deal with the interrelationship between energy development law and environmental protection law. Areas of law could include local, national, and international law related to the environment and to land and resource usage. Topical issues in this arena include the commercial oil production in Ghana (begun in December 2010), the oil spill in the Gulf of Mexico (spring 2010), and the nuclear power issues following the earthquake and tsunami in Japan (2011).

33. **Entertainment Law (Media Law).** Entertainment lawyers work in a wide variety of legal areas related to the arts generally, which would include publishing, television, radio, music, theatre, cinemas and motion pictures, performers and actors, the recording industry, and newspapers and magazines. Entertainment lawyers routinely work on matters related to intellectual property, labor and employment, securities, personal services contracts, contract breaches, arbitration or other dispute resolution, and litigation. Entertainment lawyers negotiate entertainment contracts for clients, mediate disputes, or litigate or arbitrate. They may work for law firms or in-house for production companies, movie studios, entertainment conglomerates, major publishing houses, or trade unions. Clients may include actors, entertainers, media stars, musicians, media distribution networks, production companies, film studios, TV and radio stations, filmmakers, and authors.

34. **Entrepreneurship (Law and).** This subject area explores historical and current perspectives on law and entrepreneurship; introduces students to business, legal, institutional, and strategic considerations applicable to entrepreneurs; fosters understanding of public policy and legal frameworks that promote innovation; offers students substantive knowledge and lawyering skills needed to represent entrepreneurs; and explores students' own entrepreneurship potential. Courses may include finance, intellectual property, and venture capital.

35. **Environmental Law (Climate Change; Environmental Sustainability; International Environmental Law; Oil & Gas Law; Natural Resources Law; Sustainable Development Law).** Environmental law focuses on protecting the environment (the ecosystem) against harmful public and private actions. It deals with regulating and conserving land, water, air, and fauna and flora, and pays particular attention to endangered species. This subject area also concerns natural resource sustainability (leaving natural resources for subsequent generations), water and air pollution, ozone depletion, global warming (climate change), conserving forests and mountains, regulation of industrial waste, and land use. Environmental law can involve domestic or international regulation.

    Environmental lawyers work for private companies (complying with government regulations, conducting environmental impact studies that assess impact of business operations on the environment, complying with international human rights law), government agencies (enacting environmental protection legislation; enforcing legislation through civil or administrative channels; prosecuting environmental crimes; negotiating environmental treaties on behalf of countries), and nongovernmental organizations (advocating domestically for healthy, sustainable environmental practices and enforcement of regulations; challenging harmful governmental regulations and harmful practices; advocating in the international arena (e.g., at the December 2009 Copenhagen Conference)). Practitioners deal with issues such as climate change and the Gulf of Mexico oil disaster of 2010.

36. **Environmental Sustainability** (*see* Environmental Law).

37. **Estate Planning.** An LL.M. in estate planning deals with rules related to transfer of a person's assets after the person dies. Students learn law related to income and wealth transfer, wills, trusts, estate law, charitable giving, fiduciary responsibilities in administering estates, and ethics. Students may also gain experience devising and drafting estate plans. Students may take courses in estate planning and probate, wealth transfer taxes, trusts and estates, corporate and partnership tax, taxation for blended families, marital taxation, tax aspects of charitable giving, multinational estate planning, and estate and gift tax.

38. **Experiential Law Teaching** (*see* Teaching, Experiential Law).

39. **Family Law (Child Law;** *see also* **Juvenile Law).** Family law deals with legal relationships between individuals who are related to each other through blood, marriage or similar bond, such persons including spouses, domestic partners, children, parents, guardians, and wards. Family lawyers work with issues such as creating families (e.g., marriage, adoption, civil unions) or dissolving them (e.g., divorce). They deal with issues when involved individuals are not related by blood or marriage, but might be in loving, committed relationships such as same-sex couples in domestic partnership or civil unions.

    This LL.M. may deal with prenuptial arrangements, domestic or international adoption, international child abduction by a parent, spousal support, paternity, divorce or legal separation, marital property, parental rights, and child custody. It may deal with family violence, abuse and neglect. It could also deal with tax law, contracts law, real estate law, partnership law, and child psychology and treatment options.

    Family law overlaps with other law areas, including elder law (caring for parents living in the home, elder abuse), juvenile law (parental obligations to send children to school, juvenile delinquency, truancy, runaway children), criminal law (child abuse or neglect, domestic violence), and civil rights law and international human rights law (freedom from discrimination because of sexual orientation or race).

An LL.M. in family law would be useful for lawyers who want to remain in the U.S. and practice in the areas of matrimonial relations, family relations, and other related issues. It may also be useful for foreign lawyers working in their home countries who represent individuals who have family members (e.g., parents, siblings) in the U.S. and unification of the family is being sought (e.g., individuals who are engaged in child custodial battles where one parent is in one country with a child and the other parent is in the other country). Thus, you may practice in transnational or international family law.

40. **Finance & Financial Services Law** (*see also* **Corporate Finance Law; Corporate Law**). Finance and financial services law deals with law, business and regulation of the global financial services industry. It introduces students to global financial institutions and their business and regulatory policy concerns, as well as structuring and negotiating related agreements. It could deal with government or private financing practices and procedures, securities and taxation, and also with services related to loans, account services, deposits, and investments.

41. **Food Law** (*see* **Agricultural Law**).

42. **Foreign Relations Law of U.S.** (*see* **International Law**).

43. **Foreign Scholars Program** (*see also* **American Law for Foreign Lawyers; General LL.M.**).

44. **General LL.M.** (**Advanced Legal Studies; As Approved; Foreign Scholars Program**). In a general LL.M., a student designs her own curriculum by choosing courses that interest her or that further her personal or professional goals. You can choose from a wide range of courses in many areas of law. You can take lecture, seminar, or experiential courses, or focus on intensive research and writing. You could take numerous courses in a particular legal area, in effect "specializing" in that area (but without a specialization listed on your transcript or diploma).

45. **Genetics Law** (*see* **Biotechnology Law**).

46. **Genomics Law** (*see* **Biotechnology Law**).

47. **Global Business Law** (*see* **Business Law; International Business Law**)

48. **Government Law** (**Administrative Law; Public Policy**). Covers how law regulates public and private aspects of society. Deals with constitutional, statutory, administrative and other regulatory law, and with federal, state, local, and international law.

   It could focus on political theories and regulatory policies that affect policymaking and enforcement in domestic and foreign jurisdictions. It could explore the relationship between governments and their actions and individuals and entities.

49. **Health Care Law** (*see* **Health Law**)

50. **Health Law** (**Health Care Law**). Health law deals with wide-ranging rules and regulations concerning health care delivery, public health policy and practice, and enforcing regulations. Topics include bioethics, health care devices, the practice of medicine, malpractice, insurance, and drugs. Health law involves health care regulation, investigation, and prosecution. Individuals and entities subject to such regulation include doctors (e.g., dentists, surgeons, general practitioners, and chiropractors), health care facilities (e.g., hospitals, and hospices), and nurses. Legal issues may include professional licensing, institution accreditation, certification and registration requirements, unfair trade practices, and governmental and private health insurance plans.

   Graduates may work for health product manufacturers (e.g., drugs, medical devices), unions, nonprofit nongovernmental advocacy organizations, hospitals, private medical practitioners, domestic governments, intergovernmental organizations, or law firms representing any of the above. Graduates may represent hospitals, medical personnel, patients, governments, insurance companies, pharmaceutical companies, HMOs — health management organizations, or other individuals and entities.

51. **Human Rights Law** (*see* **Civil Rights Law; International Human Rights Law**).

52. **Immigration Law** (**Asylum Law**). Governments dictate which non-citizens are permitted to enter their country, how long they can stay, and the types of activities they may engage in.

Immigration and asylum lawyers work on these issues, and may help corporations bring in foreign workers, or private individuals who want to enter or remain in the U.S. to work, study or live. They may assist international students in the U.S. who decide they want to stay postdegree and work, persons who are in the U.S. unlawfully and want to remain, or persons who seek asylum because they have a well-founded fear of persecution if they return to their home country. Immigration lawyers may work for the government, for private corporations, for schools, or for law firms. Many immigration lawyers work for public interest law firms or for similar legal services centers for poor clients.

53. **Indian Law** (*see* Indigenous Law; *see also* Tribal Policy, Law & Government).

54. **Indigenous Law** (Civil Rights Law; Human Rights Law; Indian Law; International Human Rights Law; Tribal Policy, Law & Government). Indigenous law governs rights and obligations of indigenous peoples vis-à-vis domestic governments and the international community. Graduates may help formulate domestic and international laws and policies to resolve conflicts between indigenous peoples and governments, domestically and internationally. A degree in this field might cover many issues, including the law of tribal or other indigenous groups, domestic laws of countries regarding indigenous peoples, and applicable international law (e.g., international human rights law treaties and customary international law norms). Topics might include discrimination based on race or religion, minority rights, indigenous peoples and the environment, and cultural protection.

55. **Information Technology Law** (IT Law). Information technology law concerns digital information and its impact on our increasingly technologically advanced society. It deals with domestic and international law and practice regarding the creation and flow of IT, commercial applications (e.g., e-commerce), criminal law (e.g., cybercrime), and Internet law. It would highlight public policy tensions, for example, by fostering information flow while protecting privacy, and protecting business investments and creativity through intellectual property protections while facilitating widespread inexpensive dissemination of technology and information. It necessarily raises issues of intellectual property law, computer law, Internet or cyberspace law, privacy law, entertainment law, mass communication law, international human rights law, and other areas of domestic and international law.

56. **Insurance Law.** Insurance law deals with risk and responsibility, and business and policy decisions related thereto, from the perspectives of insurance companies, insurance industry regulators, and insurance product consumers, in the domestic and international arenas. The area could deal with insurance law as relates to state and national insurance regulators, health care providers and other related organizations, corporate insurance sellers and brokers, corporate and individual insurance purchasers, and insurance in the nonprofit arena.

57. **Intellectual Property Law** (IP Law). Intellectual property law deals with nontangible rights that an author, artist, or inventor has over his creations. IP grants authors and inventors monopolies over owning or using copyrights, patents, trademarks, and trade secrets. IP law deals with inventions, ideas, brands and logos, counterfeiting, and piracy. Issues include application for IP protection, registration and licensing requirements, misuse, misappropriation, infringement and fraudulent procurement, anticompetitive activity, ownership, licensing, and transfer rights.

    IP lawyers may work on transactional matters as well as in litigation, in a wide range of practice areas, including biotechnology, entertainment, sports, pharmaceuticals, computer and related technology, the Internet, and the arts (including book and magazine publishing and music). IP law relates to international human rights and international trade law.

58. **Inter-American Law** (Latin-American Law). Inter-American law explores legal rules and institutions in the Americas, including North, South, and Central America and the Caribbean. It is useful for LL.M. graduates wanting to serve clients, sit on tribunals, or otherwise be engaged in matters spanning the legal systems of countries in the region.

59. **International Business Law (American Business Law; Business Law; Global Business Law; International Economic Law; International Trade Law).** *International Business Law* deals with legal, policy, and institutional issues that arise in cross-border commercial transactions in the global environment. It covers domestic and international rules, regulations and legal approaches to dealing with commercial transactions that span more than one country.

   International Trade Law is the mixture of domestic law and international law that applies to goods and services transactions that cross national boundaries. It includes rules and customs for handling trade involving countries, private individuals, and/or companies across borders.

   International Business and Trade Law concerns relationships among laws of different countries, and international law, involving trans-border transactions, including commercial transactions involving goods and services. Topics may include agency agreements, international contracts and administrations, regulations of exports and imports, technology transfers, regional transactions, intellectual property, product liability, illicit trade (such as human trafficking, drug trafficking, money laundering) and legal organizations. Multilateral instruments play an important role in this field, including the Convention for the International Sales of Goods, the GATT-WTO instruments, and instruments dealing with dispute resolution and international human rights law.

60. **International Criminal Law** (*see* Criminal Law).

61. **International Economic Law** (*see* Business Law; International Business Law).

62. **International Environmental Law** (*see* Environmental Law).

63. **International Human Rights Law (*see* Civil Rights Law; Human Rights Law; Indigenous Law; International Law; Tribal Policy, Law and Government).** International human rights law focuses on domestic and international laws that afford each person a wide range of rights, including civil, political, economic, social, cultural, and other rights. International human rights law is the system of domestic and international law, policies, practices, and institutions in place to ensure that those rights are fully afforded to everyone. International human rights law protects individuals irrespective of where in the world they may be, irrespective of their nationality, and irrespective of who or where the alleged rights violation perpetrators are.

   Because of its breadth and scope, this field touches on many fields in the international arena, including general public international law, international criminal law, international humanitarian law, international intellectual property law, and international trade law. It also touches on domestic law, for example in the areas of criminal law and criminal procedure (e.g., rights of suspects and the accused), civil rights law, and constitutional law (e.g., constitutional protections related to privacy, life, and liberty).

64. **International Law (International Legal Studies; International & Comparative Law; Foreign Relations Law of the U.S.; *see* International Business Law).** An LL.M. in international law (or in "public international law") would focus on the law that governs relations between and among states, intergovernmental bodies, individuals, and other actors in the international arena. International law is the body of laws, rules, or principles that are based on custom, treaties, or legislation and that control or affect the duties and rights of sovereign nations in relation to each other, and between and among other international law actors. An LL.M. degree in international law would offer training in basic and advanced public international law courses, but would also offer a wide variety of courses in subject matters that are considered to be subsets of public international law, such as international environmental law, international intellectual property law, international trade law, international criminal law, international humanitarian law, and international human rights law. International law LL.M. graduates might work for intergovernmental organizations (such as the United Nations, the European Union, the World Trade Organization, or the ASEAN), for national governments (in ministries or departments), for

corporations (particularly multinational corporations), law firms, and NGOs (for example, in human rights or humanitarian law). Or, they might have private practices representing individuals with matters before domestic or international fora.

An international law LL.M. could delve into private international law (as well as public international law) and deal with, among other things, conflict of law issues presented when disputes arise between companies doing business transnationally.

65. **International Legal Studies** (*see* **International Law**).
66. **International Tax Law** (*see* **Tax Law**). International tax law provides in-depth exposure to U.S. and international tax law and policy. Courses include individual income tax, corporate tax, partnership tax, international tax, income tax treaties, financial instrument taxation, or business transaction taxation. It would deal with tax planning (U.S. or global), and would look at U.S. statutes, public international law, and bilateral and multilateral tax treaties. It would deal with many domestic and international issues related to taxing individuals and entities.
67. **International Trade Law** (*see* **Business Law**; *see also* **International Business Law**).
68. **IP Law** (*see* **Intellectual Property Law**).
69. **Judicial Process (Juridical Studies)**. Judicial process deals with the U.S. judicial system, and explores its establishment, operation, and effectiveness. Although such a degree program would tend to focus on U.S. law and theory and deal primarily with the federal, state, and local judiciaries, it could also explore international tribunals.
70. **Juridical Studies** (*see* **Judicial Process**).
71. **Jurisprudence** (*see* **Legal Theory**).
72. **Juvenile Law (Child Law**; *see also* **Family Law**). Juvenile law deals with children not eligible to be prosecuted as adults but are subject to proceedings in the "juvenile justice system." Special substantive and procedural rules are applied when children are criminal suspects and defendants. A child may be sent to a juvenile detention center, released on probation, forced to pay restitution, or ordered to undergo counseling or other treatment. The principal goal of the juvenile justice system is to rehabilitate the child. Graduates may work with local prosecution or defense attorneys, NGOs, intergovernmental organizations, or other organizations that work on rights of the child and related issues. Issues may include a child's rights to liberty, food, health, education, and shelter, along with the rights to be free from child prostitution, child pornography, child trafficking, and child soldiering.
73. **Labor Law** (*see* **Employee Benefits**; *see also* **Employment Law**).
74. **Land Development Law** (*see* **Environmental Law**).
75. **Latin American Law** (*see* **Inter-American Law**).
76. **Legal Theory (Jurisprudence)**. Legal theory deals with scholarly reflection on a range of domestic and international law issues. It examines different approaches to and perspectives on law and philosophy, and examines historical origins and underpinnings of different streams of legal reasoning. It explores legal theory as expounded upon in institutions, including the judiciary and the academy. It draws on multidisciplinary sources and theories, including philosophy, economics, sociology, psychology, anthropology, history, and politics. Critical race theory, GLBT theory (gay, lesbian, bisexual, transgendered), and feminist theory could be explored.
77. **Litigation (Trial Advocacy)**. In a litigation program, students gain practical, hands-on experience in pretrial practice and trying civil and criminal cases in different court systems. Students are exposed to alternative dispute resolution mechanisms such as negotiation, settlement, mediation, and international dispute resolution. Students may work with real clients with real legal issues, or in mock or simulated proceedings. Students may work on civil law suits (including contract or real estate disputes, constitutional law issues, administrative agency issues, and torts) or criminal cases (up to and including death penalty cases).

78. Maritime Law (*see* Admiralty Law).

79. Media Law (*see* Entertainment Law).

80. Military Justice System (*see* Military Law).

81. **Military Law (Military Justice System).** U.S. military law governs members of the U.S. armed forces, whether or not they are physically in the U.S. Sources of U.S. military law include the U.S. Constitution, federal statutes, Executive Orders (issued by the U.S. President) and common law. The principal statutory law is the Uniform Code of Military Justice (UCMJ), which deals with the courts martial—discipline, trial, and punishment of members of the armed forces suspected of breaching U.S. military law.

82. **National Security Law.** National security law deals with law related to protecting the U.S. against terrorism and other threats. Issues relate to gathering intelligence, engaging in diplomacy and other strategies to protect the U.S., and capturing and prosecuting those who unlawfully threaten the U.S. The U.S. Constitution and federal statutes would be studied, including topics such as separation of constitutional powers, war powers, and intelligence activities. National security law is closely linked to international human rights law, international humanitarian law, and international criminal law, and may deal with issues such as torture, prolonged detention without charge or trial, using force in international relations, the "war against terrorism," and domestic and international venues for resolving disputes (e.g., domestic civil courts, military courts-martial, international criminal tribunals).

83. Natural Resources Law (*see* Environmental Law; *see also* Energy Law).

84. **Ocean Law (*see also* Admiralty Law).** Ocean law deals with regulating and managing natural resources and protecting the environment of coastal and marine ecosystems. It also deals with conflicts between public and private uses of coastal zones, and domestic and international conflicts regarding coastal zones and oceans. Topics may include delimitation of marine boundaries and jurisdiction, regimes to protect marine habitats and critical ecosystems, fisheries and marine mammal conservation regimes, and issues related to marine and coastal waters. The topics covered may also include coastal management, beach access and public trust, the law of the sea, ocean dumping, admiralty, marine law, and maritime commercial law. Relevant international instruments include the United Nations Convention on the Law of the Sea, and instruments related to international environmental law, international trade law (GATT and the WTO), and international human rights law.

85. Oil and Gas Law (*see* Energy Law; Environmental Law).

86. **Prosecutorial Science (*see* Criminal Law).** Prosecutorial science deals with local, state, national, and international theories and practice of prosecutions in criminal courts and tribunals. It may cover domestic and international criminal law and procedure, international human rights law, and international humanitarian law.

87. Public Policy (*see* Government Law).

88. **Real Estate Law.** Real estate law deals with ownership and use of real property (land and structures on the land). Graduates in this subject area deal with issues related to possession, use, sale, and other real property transfer, and payment of property tax. Real estate lawyers may help negotiate contracts for the purchase and sale of real estate, or work on issues of land zoning regulations.

89. **Religion (Law and).** An LL.M. in this area has a cross-cultural, interdisciplinary, and comparative focus. Sources of law may include U.S. law (e.g., Constitution, and federal and state statutory law), international law (e.g., international human rights law), and Canon law. Issues might include religious freedom, privacy, freedom of expression, cultural relativism, and violations of domestic civil rights or international human rights law.

90. **Research.** This area involves researching specific areas of domestic or international law, and writing a thesis or other scholarly law work.

91. Rule of Law (*see* Democratic Governance and Rule of Law).

92. Science and Law (*see* Technology).

93. Securities and Financial Regulation (*see* Corporate Finance Law; Corporate Law).

94. Space Law. Space law governs activities in outer space, and relates to ownership, transport, and accidents in outer space. Outer space begins about 39 miles (62 kilometers) above the earth, which is the lowest point above sea level at which it is possible to orbit the earth. Issues include where space begins (boundary between Earth's atmosphere and outer space), sovereignty claims of matter in space, the use of outer space for military purposes, commercial space launch regulation, monitoring launches exploration; liability for damage by objects in or from space; jurisdiction over space vehicles; and moon "ownership"; and sale of lunar real estate. Relevant law includes the Outer Space Treaty and the Moon Agreement of 1979. Space lawyers may advise on commercial space projects (including space tourism), negotiate space contracts, or advise on celestial regulation or on launching and insurance. The law of common spaces (of which space law is a part) also covers areas such as the law of Antarctica and the law of the sea.

95. Sports Law. Sports law deals with regulating amateur, professional, and Olympic sports. Sports law issues are wide ranging, and relate to, for example, antitrust and labor law. They work with sports organizations (such as the international Olympics Committee), leagues and teams, and individual athletes.

96. Sustainable Development Law (*see* Environmental Law). Sustainable development law deals with global development policies and legal systems that implement them. It offers interdisciplinary training in law, public policy, economics, political science, international studies, sociology, public health, and environmental studies. Graduates may work for government ministries (e.g., U.S. Agency for International Development — USAID), the World Bank, the United Nations, NGOs, or in the private sector.

97. Tax Law (*see* International Tax). A tax law LL.M. helps prepare graduates to teach, to enter a high-level tax practice for a law firm (with U.S. or foreign clients), or to work as an in-house lawyer for a U.S. or foreign corporation.

98. Teaching (Experiential Law Teaching). A teaching degree would help aspiring law teachers enhance their teaching ability. Geared toward non-U.S. junior faculty, the degree would focus on adapting American-style experiential learning approaches to your own academic context. It would also help provide aspiring professors with tools needed to introduce experiential learning into future classes, in addition to helping improve their talents at teaching lawyering skills.

99. Technology/Science (Law and) (*see also* Information Technology Law and Intellectual Property Law). Technology/science law deals with law, policy, and practice related to e-commerce, jurisdiction, and dispute resolution in cyberspace, biotechnology, and health science. Other topics could include intellectual property law or information technology issues.

100. Telecommunications Law (*see* Communication Law).

101. Trade Regulation (American Business Law; Business Law; Global Business Law; International Economic Law; International Trade Law; *see* International Business Law). Trade regulation deals with economic regulation. It combines the competition policy, intellectual property, and private international topics of law. Students may take courses on U.S. antitrust law, comparative competition law, European Union law, government regulation, antitrust law, economics, copyright, patents, trademarks, international trade, and the WTO.

102. Trial Advocacy (*see* Litigation).

103. Tribal Policy, Law and Government (Indian Law; Indigenous Law). Tribal policy focuses on tribal law and federal Indian law, and explores the nature of tribal government, law, and policy development within the domestic federal structure.

104. U.S. Foreign Relations Law (*see* International Law).

105. U.S. Law for Foreign Lawyers (*see* American Law for Foreign Lawyers).
106. U.S. Legal Studies (*see* American Law for Foreign Lawyers).
107. Urban Affairs Law (*see* Urban Studies Law).
108. Urban Studies Law (Urban Affairs Law). Urban studies law covers planning and governance of cities or metropolitan areas. It deals with public policy, public services, and financial matters related to cities. Relevant legal areas include environmental and natural resource law, real estate development, alternative methods of dispute resolution, civil rights, and construction law.

Appendix II

Scholarships, Grants, and Fellowship Sources for International LL.M. Students

The scholarship, grant, and fellowship information below complements information provided in Chapter 24. The information below is divided into the following categories:

A. Scholarships and Grants for Women Only
B. Scholarships for Persons With Disabilities
C. U.S. Government Sources for LL.M. funding
D. Intergovernmental Organization Funding Sources
E. Private Websites Containing Scholarship, Grant, and Loan Information
F. Foundations and Membership Organizations
G. Nationality-Based Scholarships and Grants — Regional Awards — Listed by Region
H. Nationality-Based Scholarships and Grants — Listed by Country
I. Books and Other Resources

For all the opportunities listed, you are encouraged to read carefully all the eligibility and selection guidelines, and not simply the name of the particular listing. Sometimes names of awards may be misleading, and you may find that you are eligible to participate.

Also, please note that some of the awards could easily have been listed in two or more different categories. For example, an award for LL.M. women students from Australia could be listed in category A (Scholarships and Grants for Women Only) as well as in category H (Nationality-Based Scholarships and Grants — Listed by Country).

Furthermore, there is no separate category for racial or ethnic minorities or other groups, although some of the awards listed below may apply specifically to these students.

A. Scholarships and Grants For Women Only[1]

1. **American Association of University Women (AAUW).** Awards $18,000 each for women from various countries for LL.M. study in the United States for one year. Renewable on a case-by-case basis for a second year. The women commit to returning to their home country for leadership roles. Since 2004, the AAUW has awarded over 20 scholarships for LL.M. and

---

1. Several scholarships or grants for women only are listed in section G of this Appendix.

S.J.D. study and approximately 30 scholarships for J.D. study, all in the United States. (www.aauw.org/learn/fellows_directory/international.cfm)

2. **College Women's Association of Japan — Scholarship for the Visually Impaired to Study Abroad (SVI-SA).** Provides 2 million yen to visually impaired Japanese citizens or permanent residents for study abroad. (cwaj.org)

3. **Graduate Women Queensland (GWQ, formerly AFUWQ), Fellowship Fund Incorporated.** As part of the International Federation of University Women (IFUW), it offers "Commemorative Fellowships" awarded for a maximum of one year. Eligible recipients include graduates of Queensland universities studying anywhere, or any woman studying at an accredited institution in Queensland. (www.fellowshipsfund.com.au/main-menu/fellowships-and-scholarships/general-information; www.fellowshipsfund.com.au)

4. **International Federation of University Women.** Provides LL.M. grants and S.J.D. fellowships for women. Open to members of IFUW's national federations and associations and IFUW Independent Members. Fellowships for 8,000 to 10,000 Swiss francs. Grants for 3,000 to 6,000 Swiss francs. IFUW Recognition Awards for 1,000 Swiss francs. (www.ifuw.org/fellowships/international.shtml)

5. **Margaret McNamara Memorial Fund (MMMF).** Fund goals and target audience are as follows: "To support the education of women from developing countries who are committed to improving the lives of women and children in a developing country. For students from developing countries who are currently studying in the United States or Canada, the MMMF awards annually grants of approximately $12,000 each." (mmmf@worldbank.org; www.mmmf-grants.org/grants-us.html)

6. **Patsy Takemoto Mink Education Foundation for Low-Income Women and Children.** Provides $2,000 for single mothers with low incomes enrolled in graduate school. (www.patsyminkfoundation.org/edsupport.html)

7. **P.E.O. International Peace Scholarship.** Established to provide scholarships for international women pursuing graduate study in the United States and Canada. Maximum award is $10,000. (www.peointernational.org)

8. **Yvonne A. M. Smith Scholarship.** For women in master's or doctoral studies. (www.fortunemanning.co.nz/Publications/Yvonne+A+M+Smith+Charitable+Trust.html)

B. Scholarships for Persons With Disabilities

9. **Alexander Graham Bell Association for the Deaf and Hard of Hearing.** For students with hearing loss, pre-and post-lingual. (http://nc.agbell.org/netcommunity/page.aspx?pid=486)

10. **American Council of the Blind.** Lists financial assistance opportunities, including scholarships and grants, for blind and visually impaired students. (www.acb.org/resources/finaid-scholarships.html)

11. **College Women's Association of Japan — Scholarship for the Visually Impaired to Study Abroad (SVI-SA).** Provides 2 million yen to visually impaired Japanese citizens or permanent residents for study abroad. (cwaj.org)

12. **Disability Scholarships U.S.** Scholarships for persons with chronic illnesses. (www.disabilityscholarships.us)

13. **Disabled World.** Lists many scholarships for students with disabilities. (www.disabled-world.com/disability/education/scholarships)

14. **Mobility U.S.A.** Contains significant information useful for persons with disabilities seeking to study in the U.S., including information regarding scholarships, grants, and fellowships. See also National Clearinghouse on Disability and Exchange. (www.miusa.org)

15. **National Clearinghouse on Disability and Exchange (NCDE).** Lists numerous financial assistance opportunities. Whereas persons with disabilities would be eligible for all the listed

opportunities, persons without disabilities are eligible for only some of them. See also Mobility U.S.A. (www.miusa.org/ncde/financialaid/scholarshipsearch; www.miusa.org/ncde/financialaid/scholarshiplist)

16. **Proyecto Vision.** Provides information for scholarships and other funding sources for persons with disabilities. (www.proyectovision.net/english/resources/scholarshipsearch.html)

C. U.S. Government Sources for LL.M. Funding

17. **Amideast.** Seeks to improve understanding between the United States and the Middle East/North Africa by providing scholarship programs and exchange opportunities. Amideast is affiliated with EducationUSA and the U.S. Department of State. (www.amideast.org; www.educationusa.info)

18. **EducationUSA Opportunity Grants — for overseas students seeking U.S. degrees.** Grants pay for test and test preparation fees (including English language proficiency tests such as TOEFL), transportation for in-country testing, LL.M. application fees (includes courier fees), U.S. visa and visa application fees (including transport to U.S. Embassy) and SEVIS fees, postage, transcript translations and certifications, international phone-fax-internet to communicate with schools, transportation to/from U.S., advanced English lessons, books, a one-time settling-in allowance and a possible top-up toward tuition.[2] Opportunity Grants may not exceed $10,000 USD. EducationUSA Opportunity Grants are competitive, and are available for LL.M. student applicants in these countries (www.educationusa.info):

   - *Asia*:   Bangladesh, Burma, Cambodia, Indonesia, Kazakhstan, Kyrgyz Republic, Laos, Malaysia, Mongolia, Nepal, Philippines, Sri Lanka, Tajikistan, Turkmenistan, Uzbekistan
   - *Europe*:   Belarus, Russian Federation, Turkey, Ukraine
   - *Middle East & North Africa*:   Algeria, Bahrain, Egypt, Jordan, Lebanon, Morocco, Oman, Syria, Tunisia, Yemen
   - *Sub-Saharan Africa*:   Ghana, Madagascar, Malawi, Nigeria, South Africa, Uganda, Zimbabwe
   - *Latin America & Brazil*:   Bolivia, Brazil, Colombia, Costa Rica, Ecuador, El Salvador, Guatemala, Honduras, Nicaragua, Panama, Paraguay, Peru, Venezuela

19. **Federal Student Aid Application.** Used by many schools to determine need-based aid. (www.fafsa.ed.gov)

20. **Fulbright Foreign Student Program.** Administered by U.S. State Department. Provides scholarships to study in the U.S. for students, scholars, and teachers. Fulbright offers over 1,800 grants to non-U.S. students for U.S. study annually. International LL.M. applicants should apply to their home country Fulbright Commission or U.S. Embassy. (foreign.fulbrightonline.org; www.cies.org; www.educationusa.info)

21. **Institute of International Education (IIE).** An extensive database of scholarships, fellowships, and grants organized and maintained by the Institute of International Education. Funding sources organized by subject area (for example, law), by state, region or program name. Although IIE is a nonprofit nongovernmental organization, it is listed in this category because of ties with governmental international education efforts. (www.iie.org; www.fundingusstudy.org)

---

2. Opportunity Grants are funded by the Bureau of Educational and Cultural Affairs within the U.S. Department of State. They support "underserved students of modest means" by covering up-front costs of applying to U.S. law schools.

22. **International Research and Exchanges Board (IREX).** Information on exchange study programs with Commonwealth of Independent States (CIS) countries, other newly independent states, and others. (www.irex.org)

23. **Muskie Fellowships — Muskie Graduate Fellowship Program.** Sponsored by U.S. State Department and administered by IREX for one-year non-degree, one-year degree, or two-year degree study in the U.S. for students from *Armenia, Azerbaijan, Belarus, Georgia, Kazakhstan, Kyrgyzstan, Moldova, Russian Federation, Tajikistan, Turkmenistan, Ukraine, and Uzbekistan.* (www.irex.org/programs/muskie/index.asp)

24. **State Department Educational Advising Centers.** Scholarship and fellowship information for U.S. study. (www.educationusa.info/students.php)

25. **Students.Gov.** U.S. government site designed to help students and their families with information about university study in the United States, scholarships, and grants. (www.students.gov/STUGOVWebApp/Public?topicID=15&operation=topic)

26. **U.S. Department of State — Bureau of Educational and Cultural Affairs (ECA).** Fosters relations between countries through educational exchange. (exchanges.state.gov)

D. Intergovernmental Organization Funding Sources

27. **Leo S. Rowe Pan American Fund.** Available to students in Organization of American States (OAS) member countries. Grants interest-free student loans up to $15,000 for LL.M. students who return to their home country. Applicants are accepted and reviewed year round. (www.oas.org/rowe)

28. **Organization of American States (OAS).** Fellowships for citizens of OAS member countries. (www.educoas.org/portal)

E. Private Websites Containing Scholarship, Grant, and Loan Information

29. **EduPass.** Information for international students interested in U.S. study, including financial aid information. Free registration. (www.edupass.org)

30. **Fastweb.** Scholarship search that matches selected criteria with regular updates. Free registration. (www.fastweb.com)

31. **FinAid.** Matches your profile with available scholarships. Provides financial calculators and information on loans, savings, and aid. (www.finaid.org)

32. **Foreignborn.com.** Financial aid guide for international students. (www.foreignborn.com/study_in_us/8-paying4school.htm)

33. **Funding U.S. Study Online.** An extensive database of scholarships, fellowships, and grants organized and maintained by the Institute of International Education (IIE). Includes all types of funding programs, for all levels of postsecondary study, across all law and other academic areas. (www.fundingusstudy.org)

34. **Global Alliance for Justice Education (GAJE).** Organization promoting global cooperation in justice education. (www.gaje.org)

35. **GradSchools.com.** Database and links to LL.M. programs and graduate school financial aid. (www.gradschools.com)

36. **GRAPES Database.** Database containing information on over 500 private and publicly funded awards, fellowships, and internships. (www.gdnet.ucla.edu/grpinst.htm)

37. **Institute of International Education (IIE).** An extensive database of scholarships, fellowships, and grants organized and maintained by the IIE. Funding sources organized by subject area (law), state, region, or program name. Although IIE is a nonprofit nongovernmental organization, it is listed in this category because of ties with governmental international education efforts. (www.iie.org; www.fundingusstudy.org)

38. **International Education Financial Aid (IEFA).** Provides grant, scholarship, and loan information for students wishing to study overseas. (www.iefa.org)
39. **InternationalScholarships.com.** Searchable financial aid database for international students. (www.internationalscholarships.com)
40. **InternationalStudent.com.** Funding information for international students. (www.internationalstudent.com/international-financial-aid)
41. **Law School Admissions Council.** Website for prospective LL.M. and J.D. students discussing many aspects of law school, including financing. (www.lsac.org/jd/finance/financial-aid-overview.asp)
42. **LLM-Guide.com.** A guide including links to information useful for LL.M. applicants and students. (www.llm-guide.com/funding-your-llm)
43. **LL.M. Insider.** Listing of LL.M. scholarship resources. (www.llminsider.com/BeforeTheLLM/LLM-Scholarships-Fellowships-Grants-Loans)
44. **LL.M. Roadmap.** Official website for this book, containing links to LL.M. funding resources. (www.LLMRoadMap.com)
45. **LL.M. Study.** A guide containing links useful for LL.M. applicants and students. (llmstudy.com)
46. **Peterson's U.S. College Search for International Students.** Searchable scholarship database. (www.petersons.com/college-search/scholarships.aspx)
47. **Scholarships.com.** Website that matches your needs with scholarships. (www.scholarships.com)
48. **Social Science Research Council.** Fellowships and grants. (www.ssrc.org/fellowships)
49. **Studentawards.com.** Search scholarships and grants. Free registration. (www.studentawards.com)
50. **CollegeNET.** Search scholarships either by keyword or profile. Free registration. (www.collegenet.com/mach25/app)

F. Foundations and Membership Organizations

51. **Adell & Hancock Fund Scholarship.** Awards up to $2,500 in supplemental support to international students. Applicant must be enrolled at a U.S. institution in the "Rocky Mountain region." (www.rockymountainiie.org/scholarships)
52. **American Society of International Law (ASIL).** Arthur C. Helton Fellowship Program "micro-grants" for students in the human rights subject area. (www.asil.org/helton-fellowship.cfm)
53. **American-Scandinavian Foundation (ASF).** Provides over $500,000 each year to Scandinavians for up to one year of study in the U.S. Awards vary in number and size. (www.amscan.org/study_in_america_details.html)
54. **Association of American Law Schools (AALS).** Network of legal education professionals with the goal of improving legal education. (www.aals.org)
55. **Equal Justice Works.** Organization that supports debt relief for public service and postgraduate fellowships. (www.equaljusticeworks.org)
56. **Foundation Center.** Large database of U.S. foundations, assistance programs, and financial resources. Specifically lists scholarships for non-U.S. students, and has an interactive e-learning tutorial to help locate scholarships. (www.foundationcenter.org)
57. **Foundation Grants to Individuals Online.** Over 7,000 grant programs. Paid monthly subscription. (gtionline.foundationcenter.org)
58. **Golden Key International Honor Society Scholarships & Awards.** Each year, over $1,000,000 USD in scholarships and awards offered to members from different regions. (www.goldenkey.org/GKIHS/MemberBenefits/ScholarshipsandAwards/ScholarshipandAwardListing)
59. **Harry S. Truman Good Neighbor Award Foundation Scholarships.** Offers six (6) scholarships yearly of $2,500 to U.S. and international students for study at particular U.S. universities. (www.trumanaward.org/web/scholarships.html)

60. **Institute for Humane Studies.** Offers Humane Studies Fellowships ranging from $2,000-15,000 (USD). (www.theihs.org/humane-studies-fellowships)

61. **Institute of International Education (IIE).** Administers programs helping international students study abroad. Online search engine at www.fundingusstudy.org. (www.iie.org)

62. **NAFSA: Association of International Educators.** Lists scholarships and grants. (www.nafsa.org/students.sec; www.nafsa.org/about.sec/institutional_grants)

63. **Open Society Foundations.** Offers scholarship programs that focus on numerous geographic areas, including the United States. (www.soros.org/grants)

64. **Point Foundation — The National LGBT Scholarship Fund.** For lesbian, gay, bisexual, or transgendered students. Average award is $13,600 USD. (www.pointfoundation.org)

65. **Top Study Links.** Lists LL.M. scholarships offered at different U.S. law schools. (www.topstudylinks.com/scholarships.aspx?tag=Law/LLM&tid=80)

G. Nationality-Based Scholarships and Grants — Regional Awards — Listed by Region

66. **Africa — Advance Africa.** Lists scholarships for African students to join LL.M. programs in the United States and elsewhere. (www.advance-africa.com/LLM-Scholarships.html)

67. **Africa — Sub-Sahara. Richard A. Horovitz Fund.** Applicants must be citizens of a Sub-Saharan African country and enrolled in a graduate program at an accredited U.S. university. The award ranges from $10,000-17,000 for one year and may be used for thesis research, tuition, living costs, etc. Renewable for a second year based on academic performance and need. (www.iie.org/en/Programs/Richard-A-Horovitz-Fund-for-Professional-Development)

68. **Asia — Asia Foundation.** Operates exchange programs and lists several grant and fellowship programs. (asiafoundation.org)

69. **Asia — Open Society Institute Scholarships.** Funds students, scholars, and professionals from South Asia, Indonesia, and Burma (Myanmar) for academic programs outside their home countries. (www.soros.org/grants)

70. **Central America and the Caribbean. — LASPAU: Academic and Professional Programs for the Americas.** LASPAU manages scholarship and educational programs such as the Fulbright Academic Exchange Program (U.S. State Department), the Becas Caldas program of COLCIENCIAS (Colombia), and the Academic Scholarship Programs of the Organization of American States (OAS). (www.laspau.harvard.edu/programs)

71. **Eastern Europe — Muskie Graduate Fellowship Program.** (See Muskie, above.)

72. **Europe — Open Society Institute Scholarships.** Funds students, scholars, and professionals from Eastern Europe, the former Soviet Union, Mongolia, the Middle East, South Asia, Indonesia, and Burma (Myanmar) for academic programs outside their home countries. (www.soros.org/grants)

73. **Global — International Student Exchange Program (ISEP).** (www.isep.org)

74. **Middle East — Amideast.** Seeks to improve understanding between U.S. and the Middle East/North Africa by providing scholarship programs and exchange opportunities. Amideast is affiliated with EducationUSA and the U.S. Department of State. (www.amideast.org; www.educationusa.info)

75. **Middle East — Open Society Institute Scholarships.** Funds students, scholars, and professionals from the Middle East for academic programs outside their home countries. (www.soros.org/grants)

76. **North Africa — Amideast.** Seeks to improve understanding between U.S. and the Middle East/North Africa by providing scholarship programs and exchange opportunities. Amideast is affiliated with EducationUSA and the U.S. Department of State. (www.amideast.org; www.educationusa.info)

77. Scandinavia — American-Scandinavian Foundation (ASF). Provides over $500,000 each year to Scandinavians for up to one year of study in the U.S. Awards vary in number and size. (www.amscan.org/study_in_america_details.html)

H. Nationality-Based Scholarships and Grants — Listed by Country

78. Algeria — EducationUSA Opportunity Grants. (See EducationUSA, Section C above.)
79. Argentina — Barsa Scholarship Program. For Fulbright students from select South and Central American countries. Supports cost of living, tuition, and fees. (www.iie.org/en/Programs/Barsa-Scholarships-Program)
80. Armenia — Armenian Bar Association's Scholarship Program. Supports students of Armenian descent for study in the U.S., Armenia, or elsewhere. (www.armenianbar.org/content/scholarship)
81. Armenia — Armenian Educational Foundation. Supports students of Armenian descent. (www.aefweb.org)
82. Armenia — Armenian General Benevolent Union. Provides scholarship and fellowship programs for graduate and post-graduate students of Armenian descent enrolled overseas. (www.agbu.org)
83. Armenia — Armenian International Women's Association (AIWA). Provides scholarships to full-time female graduate students of Armenian descent studying in the U.S. (www.aiwa-net.org/scholarshipinfo.html)
84. Armenia — Armenian Professional Society Scholarships. For graduate students in the U.S. Selection is based on financial need, scholastic achievements, faculty recommendations, and involvement in the Armenian Community. (www.apsla.org/APS_Website/scholarships.html)
85. Armenia — Armenian Relief Society of Eastern USA. Provides graduate scholarships to students of Armenian descent. In awarding scholarships, the committees evaluate applicants' merit, financial need, and Armenian community involvement. (www.arseast-us.com/programs/scholarships.html)
86. Armenia — Armenian Scholarship Foundation. Grants scholarships to graduate Armenian students in the U.S. and non-Armenians significantly involved in the U.S. Armenian community. (www.armenianscholarships.org)
87. Armenia — Fulbright. (See Fulbright, Section C above.) (armenia.usembassy.gov/fulbright_program.html)
88. Armenia — Fund for Armenian Relief. Supports students from underprivileged families throughout Armenia. Recipients must work in Armenia for five years after graduation. (www.farusa.org/Gulamerian.html)
89. Armenia — John M. Azarian Memorial Armenian Youth Scholarship Fund. For students of Armenian descent who demonstrate compelling financial need, academic achievement and Armenian church-related activities. (www.azariangroup.com/scholarship.html)
90. Armenia — Junior Faculty Development Program. Provides university instructors with training in the fields of Humanities and Social Sciences at U.S. host universities. (americancouncils.am)
91. Armenia — Luys Foundation. Provides financial support, mentoring and other services to Armenian students attending the world's leading universities. (luys.am)
92. Armenia — Muskie Graduate Fellowship Program. (See Muskie, Section C above.)
93. Armenia — Rotary Foundation Ambassadorial Scholarships. Provides funding for study abroad for one year. (www.rotary.am)
94. Australia — Endeavour Awards. Offered by Australian government for overseas study, research, and professional development abroad. (www.deewr.gov.au/International/EndeavourAwards/Pages/Home.aspx)

95. Australia — Graduate Women of Queensland (GWQ, formerly AFUWQ), Fellowship Fund Incorporated. See Graduate Women Queensland, above. (www.fellowshipsfund.com.au)

96. Austria — Austrian Database for Scholarships and Research Grants (Österreichische Datenbank für Stipendien und Forschungsförderung). Database for grants and scholarships, principally for Austrians and other German speakers. (www.grants.at)

97. Azerbaijan — Azerbaijani Government Scholarship Program. (www.edu.gov.az)

98. Azerbaijan — Muskie Graduate Fellowship. (See Muskie, Section C above.)

99. Azerbaijan — The State Oil Company of Azerbaijan Republic Scholarship Program (SOCAR). Full funding for Azerbaijani students interested in oil and gas industry careers. (www.socar.az/12-snews-view-en.html)

100. Bahrain — EducationUSA Opportunity Grants. (See EducationUSA, Section C above.)

101. Bangladesh — EducationUSA Opportunity Grants. (See EducationUSA, Section C above.)

102. Belarus — EducationUSA Opportunity Grants. (See EducationUSA, Section C above.)

103. Belarus — Muskie Graduate Fellowship. (See Muskie, Section C above.)

104. Belgium — Fulbright. Grants may include tuition, travel, and stipend. This site contains videos of Belgians who hold U.S. LL.M. degrees. (www.fulbright.be) (See Fulbright, Section C above.)

105. Belgium — Foundation Fernand Lazard. Grants and interest-free loans to citizens of European Union who have earned a degree in Belgium. (www.redweb.be/lazard/fr.htm)

106. Belgium — Fonds Wetenschappelijk Onderzoek — Vlaanderen (Research Foundation Flanders (FWO)). Fellowships and grants. Helpful for students interested in attending conferences and conducting research. (www.fwo.be/Predoctorale-mandaten.aspx)

107. Bolivia — EducationUSA Opportunity Grants. (See EducationUSA, Section C above.)

108. Brazil — Barsa Scholarship Program. (See Argentina — Barsa Scholarship Program, above.)

109. Brazil — Coordination of Improvement of Higher Education Personnel (CAPES). Government website — scholarships. (capes.gov.br)

110. Brazil — Conselho Nacional de Desenvolvimento Cientifico & Tecnologico (CNPQ). (www.cnpq.br)

111. Brazil — EducationUSA Opportunity Grant. (See EducationUSA, Section C above.)

112. Brazil — Fulbright Program for Foreign Students. (See Fulbright, Section C above.)

113. Brazil — Fundação Estudar — Brazilian Scholarship Program. Scholarships for Brazilians studying in the United States, and career development and networking opportunities during and post-LL.M. (www.estudar.org.br)

114. Burma — CETANA Scholarship Program. Generally co-sponsored with other organizations, includes tuition, room and board, travel, and associated expenses. Applicants must currently reside in Myanmar/Burma, have no political affiliation, and pledge to return for a minimum of three years after completion of degree. (www.cetana.org)

115. Burma — EducationUSA Opportunity Grant. (See EducationUSA, Section C above.)

116. Cambodia — EducationUSA Opportunity Grant. (See EducationUSA, Section C above.)

117. Canada — Canadian Federation of University Women (CFUW) Dr. Margaret McWilliams Pre-Doctoral Fellowship. Awards $11,000 to a woman in doctoral program abroad. (www.cfuw.org/ourawards_51.html)

118. Canada — Canadian Federation of University Women (CFUW) Dr. Alice E. Wilson Awards. Awards $5,000 to mature students returning to graduate studies in any field. (www.cfuw.org/ourawards_51.html)

119. Canada — Mackenzie King Scholarships. For graduates of Canadian universities for graduate study. Recently valued at $11,000. For more information, please contact your home university's website. (www.mkingscholarships.ca)

120. Canada — The P.E.O. Scholar Awards Program. For U.S. and Canadian women pursuing a doctoral degree or postdoctoral research. Must be nominated by a local P.E.O. chapter and be a U.S. or Canadian citizen. (www.peointernational.org/peo-projectsphilanthropies)

121. **Chile — Barsa Scholarship Program.** For Fulbright students from select South and Central American countries. (See Argentina — Barsa Scholarship Program, above; see also Fulbright, Section C above.)
122. **Chile — Becase Chile.** Chile Ministry of Education opportunities. (See also Chile — Comision Nacional de Investigation Cientifica & Technologica, below.) (www.becaschile.cl)
123. **Chile — Comision Nacional de Investigation Cientifica & Technologica (CONICYT).** Chile Ministry of Education opportunities. (See also Chile — Becase, above.) (www.conicyt.cl)
124. **Chile — Fulbright Program for Foreign Students.** (See Fulbright, Section C above.)
125. **China — Fulbright Program for Foreign Students.** (See Fulbright, Section C above.)
126. **Colombia — EducationUSA Opportunity Grant.** (See EducationUSA, Section C above.)
127. **Colombia — Colciencias.** (www.colciencias.gov.co)
128. **Colombia — Barsa Scholarship Program.** (See Argentina — Barsa Scholarship Program, above.)
129. **Colombia — COLFUTURO.** Scholarship loan program for graduate study abroad. (www.colfuturo.org/index.php?page=5&site=1&idFile=7103&id=7103&owner=0)
130. **Colombia — EducationUSA Opportunity Grants.** (See EducationUSA, Section C above.)
131. **Costa Rica — Barsa Scholarship Program.** For Fulbright students from select South and Central American countries. (See Argentina — Barsa Scholarship Program, above.)
132. **Costa Rica — EducationUSA Opportunity Grants.** (See EducationUSA, Section C above.)
133. **Costa Rica — Ministry of Foreign Affairs (Ministerio de Relaciones Exteriores y Culto).** Scholarship search engine. (www.rree.go.cr)
134. **Democratic Republic of Congo — Fulbright Program for Foreign Students.** (See Fulbright, Section C above.)
135. **Denmark — American-Scandinavian Foundation (ASF).** Provides over $500,000 in funding to Scandinavians for U.S. study each year. (www.amscan.org)
136. **Denmark-America & Fulbright Foundation.** Grants for graduate studies and research. (www.wemakeithappen.dk)
137. **Ecuador — EducationUSA Opportunity Grants.** (See EducationUSA, Section C above.)
138. **Ecuador — Barsa Scholarship Program.** (See Argentina — Barsa Scholarship Program, above.)
139. **Egypt — EducationUSA Opportunity Grants.** (See EducationUSA, Section C above.)
140. **Egypt — Fulbright Program for Foreign Students.** (See Fulbright, Section C above.)
141. **El Salvador — EducationUSA Opportunity Grants.** (See EducationUSA, Section C above.)
142. **Finland — American-Scandinavian Foundation (ASF); Scholarship Foundation of the League of Finnish-American Societies.** Provides over $500,000 in funding to Scandinavians for U.S. study each year. (www.amscan.org/study_in_america_details.html)
143. **France — Marcel Bleustein-Blanchet Foundation.** Funding for French students abroad in all fields. (www.fondationvocation.org)
144. **France — Bourses des Conseils Généraux.** Need-based grants or loans. (www.europub-health.org/us/bourse/11/French%20students/#bourse39)
145. **France — Égide — Ministry of Foreign Affairs.** Grants for Master's Degree. (www.egide.asso.fr)
146. **France — Fondation de France.** Scholarships. (www.fdf.org/jsp/site/Portal.jsp)
147. **Georgia, Republic of — Muskie Graduate Fellowship.** (See Muskie, Section C above.)
148. **Germany — DAAD — German Academic Exchange Service (Deutscher Akademischer Austauschdienst).** Graduate scholarships for one year with monthly stipend. (www.daad.org/?p=gradstudy)
149. **Germany — Bucerius Law Programme.** Qualifying LL.M. programs must include a research project. (www.studienstiftung.de/bucerius-jura.html)
150. **Germany — E-Fellows.** Learn about LL.M. funding at LL.M. Fair. (www.e-fellows.net/show/detail.php/12489)
151. **Germany — ERP Scholarship.** $25,000 per year for master's study in the United States after graduating from a German university. (www.studienstiftung.de/erp.html)

152. **Germany — Fulbright.** (See Fulbright, Section C above.) (www.fulbright.de)
153. **Germany — German-American Lawyers' Association (GALA-DAJV).** Scholarships, grants, and links to information about U.S. LL.M. programs. (www.dajv.de)
154. **Germany — JurStart and University of Muenster.** Learn about LL.M. funding at LL.M. Fair. (www.jurstart.de/node/19)
155. **Germany — Studienstiftung des deutschen volkes.** (www.studienstiftung.de)
156. **Ghana — EducationUSA Opportunity Grant.** (See EducationUSA, Section C above.)
157. **Ghana — Fulbright Program for Foreign Students.** (See Fulbright, Section C above.)
158. **Guatemala — Barsa Scholarship Program.** (See Argentina — Barsa Scholarship Program above.)
159. **Guatemala — EducationUSA Opportunity Grants.** (See EducationUSA, Section C above.)
160. **Guatemala — Fulbright Program for Foreign Students.** (See Fulbright, Section C above.)
161. **Honduras — Barsa Scholarship Program.** (See Argentina — Barsa Scholarship Program, above.)
162. **Honduras — EducationUSA Opportunity Grants.** (See EducationUSA, Section C above.)
163. **Iceland — American-Scandinavian Foundation (ASF); Iceland American Society.** Provides over $500,000 in funding to Scandinavians for U.S. study each year. (www.amscan.org/study_in_america_details.html)
164. **India — Fulbright Program for Foreign Students** (See Fulbright, Section C above.)
165. **India — Inlaks Foundation.** Scholarships for LL.M. students to permit them to develop their special skills and talents. (www.inlaksfoundation.org)
166. **India — J.N. Tata Endowment for the Higher Education of Indians.** Principally awards "loan scholarships." Scholars may also qualify for a gift. (www.dorabjitatatrust.org/about/endowment.aspx)
167. **Indonesia — EducationUSA Opportunity Grant.** (See EducationUSA, Section C above.)
168. **Indonesia — Fulbright Program for Foreign Students.** (See Fulbright, Section C above.)
169. **Israel — Fulbright.** (See Fulbright, above.) (www.fulbright.org.il)
170. **Iraq — Fulbright.** (See Fulbright, Section C above.) (http://iraq.usembassy.gov)
171. **Iraq — Government of Iraq Ministry of Higher Education and Scientific Research (GOI MoHESR) Programs.** This Iraqi governmental body hopes to award 1,000 scholarships to Iraqi students for Master's and Ph.D. studies this coming academic year and wants to increase that number in later years. Students are obligated to repay the scholarship money if they fail to complete the program or fail to return to Iraq. In 2009, scholarships were awarded for Master's and Ph.D. studies to the top student in each program in each public university; in 2010, scholarships were awarded to the top three students in each program. Students obtain their own placement at a university, but U.S. and Western European universities are preferred. Funding covers tuition and fees, salary and family allowances (50% of salary for spouse), books, travel expenses, conferences, and health insurance. (www.moheiraq.org)).
172. **Iraq — Higher Committee for Education Development in Iraq (HCED).** Started in 2009 with funding from the Iraqi Prime Minister's Office. HCED plans to award thousands of scholarships to Iraqi students for master's and doctorate studies. Students must repay the scholarship if they do not complete the program or do not return to Iraq. HCED must find a suitable job in Iraq for the student within one year of completing the degree and returning from the U.S. Master's applicants must be under 30 years of age; Ph.D. applicants must be under 35. Full scholarship for up to one year of intensive English language study. Scholarship includes tuition, fees, books, and travel to the United States. Students receive a monthly stipend of $1,750, plus 50% of that amount for a spouse, and health insurance. All receive J1 or J2 visas. (www.hcediraq.org)
173. **Iraq — Human Capacity Development Program (HCDP) (or "Human Capacity Development Scholarship Program") — Kurdistan Regional Government (KRG).** Started in 2010 with $100 million from the KRG. Administered by the KRG Ministry of Higher Education

and Scientific Research (KRG MoHE) in northern Iraq (Iraqi Kurdistan Region). The KRG MoHE plans to award thousands of scholarships in the coming years for master's and doctorate studies outside Iraq. Master's applicants must be under 30 years of age; Ph.D. applicants must be under 40. Full scholarship for 6 to 9 months of intensive English language study in the United States (up to $10,000). Scholarship includes tuition, fees, books, and travel to the U.S. Students receive a monthly stipend of $1,800, plus 50% of that amount for a spouse, and health insurance. Most students receive J1 visas. (www.mhe-krg.org)

174. **Iraq — Iraq Scholars & Leaders Program (ISLP).** For Iraqi citizens residing in Iraq for U.S. degrees. Administered by Institute of International Education (IIE). IIE works with U.S. law schools to obtain placement for selected candidates. Candidates may *not* contact U.S. universities during placement process. (www.iie.org/en/Programs/ISLP)

175. **Italy — Italian Student Loan Fund (Fondo Per Studenti Italiana).** Financial assistance to Italian college graduates for a Master's or Ph.D. in the U.S. (www.fondostudentiitaliani.it)

176. **Japan — College Women's Association of Japan (CWAJ) — Graduate Scholarship for Japanese Women to Study Abroad.** Provides 3 million yen to Japanese women citizens or permanent residents residing in Japan for study abroad. (cwaj.org)

177. **Japan — College Women's Association of Japan — Scholarship for the Visually Impaired to Study Abroad (SVI-SA).** Provides 2 million yen to visually impaired Japanese citizens or permanent residents for study abroad. (cwaj.org)

178. **Japan — Fulbright.** (See Fulbright, Section C above.) (www.fulbright.jp)

179. **Japan — Joint Japan/World Bank Graduate Scholarship Program (JJ/WBGSP).** Students from World Bank member countries may study in fields related to economic development. Funds LL.M. focusing on human rights, environment, or good governance. (go.worldbank.org/6KLLM2C0Q0)

180. **Jordan — EducationUSA Opportunity Grant.** (See EducationUSA, Section C above.)

181. **Kazakhstan — Kazakhstan Bolashak Presidential Scholarship.** For more information, contact the American Councils for International Education, Kazakhstan's Center for International Programs, or Kazakhstan's Ministry of Science and Education. Covers tuition, fees, stipend, books, transportation, and health insurance.

182. **Kazakhstan — EducationUSA Opportunity Grant.** (See EducationUSA, Section C above.)

183. **Kazakhstan — Muskie Graduate Fellowship.** (See Muskie, Section C above.)

184. **Kenya — Fulbright Program for Foreign Students.** (See Fulbright, Section C above.)

185. **Korea — NAFSA: Association of International Educators / KSAAP: Korean Student Assistance Awards Program.** Provides $1,000-5,000 in matching funds for Korean students nominated by and supported by their universities. (www.nyu.edu/pages/gsas/files/nafsa) (See Fulbright, Section C above.)

186. **Kurdistan — Iraqi Kurdistan Region — Iraq — Human Capacity Development Program (HCDP) (or "Human Capacity Development Scholarship Program") — Kurdistan Regional Government (KRG).** Started in 2010 with $100 million from the KRG. Administered by the KRG Ministry of Higher Education and Scientific Research (KRG MoHE) in northern Iraq (Iraqi Kurdistan Region). The KRG MoHE plans to award thousands of scholarships in the coming years for master's and doctorate studies outside Iraq. Master's applicants must be under 30 years of age; Ph.D. applicants must be under 40. Full scholarship for 6 to 9 months of intensive English language study in the United States (up to $10,000). Scholarship includes tuition, fees, books, and travel to the United States. Students receive a monthly stipend of $1,800, plus 50% of that amount for a spouse, and health insurance. Most students receive J1 visas. (www.mhe-krg.org)

187. **Kuwait — Practical Training Award.** For practical training postdegree in the United States, but award cannot be combined with Master's study. (www.kuwaitculture.com)

188. **Kyrgyz Republic — EducationUSA Opportunity Grant.** (See EducationUSA, Section C above.)

189. Kyrgyz Republic — Muskie Graduate Fellowship. (See Muskie, Section C above.)
190. Laos — EducationUSA Opportunity Grant. (See EducationUSA, Section C above.)
191. Lebanon — EducationUSA Opportunity Grant. (See EducationUSA Section C above.)
192. Madagascar — EducationUSA Opportunity Grant. (See EducationUSA, Section C above.)
193. Malaysia — EducationUSA Opportunity Grant. (See EducationUSA, Section C above.)
194. Malaysia — Malaysian-American Commission on Educational Exchange (MACEE). Fulbright grants for Master's or Ph.D. (See Fulbright, Section C above.) (www.malaysia-scholarship.com/Fulbright_Malaysian_Graduate_Study_and_Research_Scholarship.html)
195. Malaysia — MARA Scholarship Programs Must be Bumiputra, Malaysian citizen. (www.malaysia-scholarship.com/mara.html)
196. Malawi — EducationUSA Opportunity Grant. (See EducationUSA, Section C above.)
197. Mexico — Barsa Scholarship Program. (See Argentina — Barsa Scholarship Program, above.)
198. Mexico — Consejo Nacional de Ciencia and Tecnologia. (www.conacyt.gob.mx)
199. Mexico — Fulbright Program for Foreign Students. (See Fulbright, Section C above.)
200. Middle Eastern Countries — Amideast. For students from Iraq, Jordan, Kuwait, Lebanon, Oman, Qatar, Syria, UAE, West Bank–Gaza, Yemen. (www.amideast.org)
201. Moldova — Muskie Graduate Fellowship. (See Muskie, Section C above.)
202. Mongolia — EducationUSA Opportunity Grant. (See EducationUSA, Section C above.)
203. Morocco — EducationUSA Opportunity Grant. (See EducationUSA, Section C above.)
204. Mozambique — Fulbright Program for Foreign Students. (See Fulbright, Section C above.)
205. Myanmar — CETANA Scholarship Program. Generally co-sponsored with other organizations, includes tuition, room and board, travel, and associated expenses. Applicants must currently reside in Myanmar/Burma, have no political affiliation, and pledge to return for a minimum of three years after completion of degree. (www.cetana.org)
206. Myanmar — EducationUSA Opportunity Grant. (See EducationUSA, Section C above.)
207. Nepal — EducationUSA Opportunity Grant. (See EducationUSA, Section C above.)
208. New Zealand — Ethel Benjamin Scholarship. Honors centenary of Ethel Benjamin's admission as the first woman barrister and solicitor. (www.lawfoundation.org.nz)
209. New Zealand — William Georgetti Scholarship. Scholarships usually for study in New Zealand, but awards have been made to students attending U.S. schools in fields "important to the social, cultural or economic development of New Zealand." (www.universitiesnz.ac.nz/scholarships/williamgeorgetti)
210. New Zealand — Yvonne A. M. Smith Scholarship. For women in Master's or Doctoral studies. (www.fortunemanning.co.nz/Publications/Yvonne+A+M+Smith+Charitable+Trust.html).
211. Nicaragua — Barsa Scholarship Program. (See Argentina — Barsa Scholarship Program, above.)
212. Nicaragua — EducationUSA Opportunity Grant. (See EducationUSA, Section C above.)
213. Nigeria — EducationUSA Opportunity Grant. (See EducationUSA, Section C above.)
214. Nigeria — Fulbright Program for Foreign Students (See Fulbright, Section C above.)
215. North African Countries — Amideast. For students from Egypt, Morocco, and Tunisia. (www.amideast.org)
216. Norway — American-Scandinavian Foundation (ASF). Over $500,000 to Scandinavians for U.S. study each year. (www.amscan.org/study_in_america_details.html)
217. Norway — Norwegian State Education Fund. Government loan and grant fund for Norwegians studying in the US. (www.lanekassen.no)
218. Oman, Sultanate of — Ministry of Higher Education (MOHE). Distinguishes between scholarships and grants, noting that a "scholarship is provided by the Ministry, while a grant is offered by an outside country or by an outside organisation within the framework of cultural and academic cooperation agreements, or through a separate arrangement." The MOHE advertises grants through the Higher Education Admissions Center (HEAC) and supervises and follows up with students abroad. (www.mohe.gov.om/english/tabid/214/Default.aspx; www.heac.gov.om)

219. **Oman, Sultanate of — Higher Education Admission Center.** Provides information about Omani government scholarships and grants for study in the U.S., including information on how to apply. (www.heac.gov.om; www.mohe.gov.om/english/tabid/214/Default.aspx)

220. **Palestine — The Palestinian Rule of Law Fellowship Program (PROL).** Funds LL.M. study at U.S. law schools. Fellows must be normally resident in the Gaza Strip or West Bank, including East Jerusalem. (www.soros.org/initiatives/scholarship/focus_areas/prol)

221. **Palestine — Fulbright Program for Foreign Students.** (See Fulbright, Section C above.)

222. **Panama — Barsa Scholarship Program.** (See Argentina — Barsa Scholarship Program, above.)

223. **Panama — EducationUSA Opportunity Grant.** (See EducationUSA, Section C above.)

224. **Paraguay — EducationUSA Opportunity Grant.** (See EducationUSA, Section C above.)

225. **Peru — Barsa Scholarship Program.** (See Argentina — Barsa Scholarship Program, above.)

226. **Peru — EducationUSA Opportunity Grant.** (See EducationUSA, Section C above.)

227. **Peru — Fulbright Program for Foreign Students.** (See Fulbright, Section C above.)

228. **Philippines — EducationUSA Opportunity Grant.** (See EducationUSA, Section C above.)

229. **Philippines — Fulbright Program for Foreign Students.** (See Fulbright, Section C above.)

230. **Poland — Kosciuszko Foundation.** Polish citizens living in Poland. Covers travel, housing, and insurance, but not tuition (in the United States). (www.thekf.org/kf/scholarships/exchange-us)

231. **Qatar — The Qatar Hamad bin Khalifa Al Thani scholarship.** For Qatar citizens. Tenable at U.S. law schools on a list of approved schools. (www.english.education.gov.qa/section/sec/hei/sco)

232. **Qatar — The Qatar Tamim bin Hamad scholarship.** The requirements are similar to those for the Qatar Hamad bin Khalifa Al Thani scholarship, but the amounts awarded through the Tamin bin Hamad are lower. (www.english.education.gov.qa/section/sec/hei/sco)

233. **Russian Federation — EducationUSA Opportunity Grant.** (See EducationUSA, Section C above.)

234. **Russian Federation — Fulbright Program for Foreign Students.** (See Fulbright, Section C above.)

235. **Russian Federation — Muskie Graduate Fellowship.** (See Muskie, Section C above.)

236. **Russian Federation — Tatarstan Higher Education Fellowship Program.** Administered by American Councils for International Education. Covers tuition, fees, books, and monthly stipend. (www.americancouncils.org/program/3e/THEF)

237. **Saudi Arabia — King Abdullah Scholarships.** Fully funds citizens of Saudi Arabia for an LL.M. at U.S. schools that appear on the Saudi Arabian Ministry of Higher Education's list of approved schools. (www.mohe.gov.sa)

238. **Senegal — Fulbright Program for Foreign Students.** (See Fulbright, Section C above.)

239. **Singapore — Fulbright Program for Foreign Students.** (See Fulbright, Section C above.) (singapore.usembassy.gov/fulbright_program.html)

240. **South Africa — EducationUSA Opportunity Grant.** (See EducationUSA, Section C above.)

241. **South Africa — Fulbright Program for Foreign Students.** (See Fulbright, Section C above.)

242. **Sri Lanka — EducationUSA Opportunity Grant.** (See EducationUSA, Section C above.)

243. **Swaziland — Fulbright Program for Foreign Students.** (See Fulbright, Section C above.)

244. **Sweden — American-Scandinavian Foundation (ASF).** Provides over $500,000 in funding to Scandinavians for U.S. study each year. (www.amscan.org/study_in_america_details.html)

245. **Swedish National Agency for Higher Education.** Grants and loans. (www.csn.se)

246. **Syria — EducationUSA Opportunity Grant.** (See EducationUSA, Section C above.)

247. **Tajikistan — EducationUSA Opportunity Grant.** (See EducationUSA, Section C above.)

248. **Tajikistan — Muskie Graduate Fellowship.** (See Muskie, Section C above.)

249. **Tanzania — Fulbright Program for Foreign Students.** (See Fulbright, Section C above.)

250. Thailand — Ministry of Foreign Affairs Scholarship. (www.mfa.go.th/web/2630.php)
251. Thailand — Fulbright Program for Foreign Students. (See Fulbright, Section C above.)
252. Thailand — Royal Thai Scholars Program (and other Thai scholarship programs). Royal Thai Embassy, Washington, D.C. (www.ts47.org/download/TSProgramDescription.pdf)
253. Tibet Fund — Tibetan Scholarship Program. Funded by U.S. State Department. For 2-year Master's program in the United States in International Law. (www.tibetfund.org/tsp_english.pdf)
254. Tunisia — EducationUSA Opportunity Grant. (See EducationUSA, Section C above.)
255. Turkey — EducationUSA Opportunity Grant. (See EducationUSA, Section C above.)
256. Turkmenistan — EducationUSA Opportunity Grant. (See EducationUSA, Section C above.)
257. Turkmenistan — Muskie Graduate Fellowship. (See Muskie, Section C above.)
258. Uganda — EducationUSA Opportunity Grant. (See EducationUSA, Section C above.)
259. Uganda — Fulbright Program for Foreign Students. (See Fulbright, Section C above.)
260. Ukraine — EducationUSA Opportunity Grant. (See EducationUSA, Section C above.)
261. Ukraine — Muskie Graduate Fellowship. (See Muskie, Section C above.)
262. Ukraine — World Wide Studies. Provides grants up to $50,000 USD for LL.M. tuition, fees, books, and health insurance. (worldwidestudies.org/en)
263. United Arab Emirates (UAE) — Ministry of Higher Education. Provides full scholarships for UAE students to join LL.M., S.J.D., and other law programs in the United States. (www.uae-embassy.org/uae-nationals/students/scholarship-programs/ministry-higher-education-mohe)
264. United Kingdom — BUNAC Best Scholarship. $5,000-10,000 for a UK passport holder whose tertiary education was in the UK. (www.bunac.org/uk/awards)
265. Uruguay — Barsa Scholarship Program. (See Argentina — Barsa Scholarship Program, above.)
266. Uzbekistan — EducationUSA Opportunity Grant. (See EducationUSA, Section C above.)
267. Uzbekistan — Muskie Graduate Fellowship Program. (See Muskie, Section C above.)
268. Venezuela — Barsa Scholarship Program. (See Argentina — Barsa Scholarship Program, above.)
269. Venezuela — EducationUSA Opportunity Grants. (See EducationUSA, Section C above.)
270. Vietnam — Fulbright Program for Foreign Students. (See Fulbright, Section C above.)
271. Vietnam — Vietnam Government — "3-2-1" (Three-Two-One) Scholarship Program. For Vietnamese students to study in countries such as the United States. (www.moet.gov.vn/?page=1.3)
272. West Bank — Open Society Institute Palestinian Rule of Law Program Fellowships for the LL.M. Tenable at selected U.S. law schools & Central European University (CEU) in Budapest. (www.amideast.org)
273. West Bank — Open Society Institute Palestinian Rule of Law Program Short-Term Faculty Visit Fellowship. Useful for a West Bank/Gaza lawyer in the United States for a short term.
274. Yemen — EducationUSA Opportunity Grant. (See EducationUSA, Section C above.)
275. Zimbabwe — EducationUSA Opportunity Grant. (See EducationUSA, Section C above.)

I. Books and Other Resources

276. The A's and B's of Academic Scholarships. (Anna Leider, Octameron Associates, 26th ed. 2007)
277. Annual Register of Grant Support: A Directory of Funding Sources 2010. (Marquis Professional Publications, 2009)

278. **Chronicle Financial Aid Guide.** (www.chronicleguidance.com) (2009–2010 ed.)

279. **Directory of Research Grants 2010.** (Oryx Press, 2009)

280. **Directory of Financial Aid for Women, 2009-2011.** (Gail Schlachter and R. David Weber, Reference Service Press, 2009)

281. **Foundation Grants to Individuals.** (The Foundation Center, New York, NY, published annually). Profiles over 7,000 foundation programs making grants to individuals for education, arts and culture, general welfare, and more. (www.gtionline.fdncenter.org)

282. **Funding for U.S. Study: A Guide for International Students and Professionals, 2011 Edition.** (Institute of International Education, New York, NY). Provides information on more than 500 grants, fellowships, scholarships, internships, and other sources of financial assistance for international students pursuing educational objectives in the United States. (www.iiebooks.org)

283. **Grants Register: The Complete Guide to Postgraduate Funding Worldwide.** (Palgrave Macmillan, Ltd., published annually). Lists scholarships, fellowships, and awards for graduate study from regional, national, and international sources. (us.macmillan.com/ thegrantsregister2010)

284. **LLM Guide Website.** Provides information about LL.M. scholarships at schools in different countries. Applicants may search for scholarship opportunities. (www.llm-guide.com/ scholarships; www.llm-guide.com/search/q/scholarship)

285. **LL.M. Roadmap, Chapter 24.** Please do not forget to review information contained in Chapter 24. Furthermore, you should explore very carefully *all* the entries in this Appendix. Do not ignore a listing simply because you believe you do not qualify for a particular scholarship, grant, or fellowship cited. The website you think does not apply to you may lead you to websites of scholarships for which you may be eligible. For example, some websites in Section B above — Scholarships for Persons with Disabilities — also list scholarships for persons *without* disabilities.

286. **LL.M. Roadmap Website.** Official website for this book, containing links to LL.M. funding resources. (www.llmroadmap.com)

287. **Study Abroad: Etudes a l'etranger. Estudios en el extranjero.** (U.N. Educational, Scientific and Cultural Organization (UNESCO), Paris, France, 2009). Financial aid offered by international organizations, governments, foundations, universities, and other institutions in 150 countries. Updated every 2 years.

288. **Websites of U.S. Law School LL.M. Programs.** Many U.S. law schools offer LL.M. student scholarships, grants, or fellowships. Schools may advertise these opportunities on their websites, and may describe the application process. Some schools automatically consider all applicants or admitted students for these opportunities, whereas other schools will consider you only if you submit a separate application. *Be certain to read carefully the websites of all schools that interest you to learn about any special financial arrangements they may make. Also be certain to ask those schools whether any scholarships or other financial awards may be available that the school does not advertise.* After you enroll at the school and arrive on campus, you may inquire again about funding. New, creative funding apportunities may arise at any time.

Appendix III

Endorsements of LL.M. Roadmap[1]

I regret that *LL.M. Roadmap* was not available when I was Director of Admissions of *Harvard's* LL.M. program. I would have recommended it to every recruit and admitted student who passed through *Harvard's* doors. I recommend *LL.M. Roadmap* now to anyone, anywhere in the world, thinking about undertaking the LL.M. It's a fabulously helpful text!

> — *Athena Mutua (LL.M. Harvard)*
> *Director of Admissions and Financial Aid,*
> *LL.M. Program of the Harvard Law School (former)*
> *Professor of Law, University of Buffalo School of Law*

LL.M. Roadmap will greatly assist students in China and neighboring East Asian countries like Japan and South Korea who want to study law in the U.S. Each year more students from Renmin Law School and other area schools are getting admitted to top U.S. law schools for their LL.M. and J.D. degrees, and they frequently inquire about legal education in the U.S. I will recommend that students read *LL.M. Roadmap before* they apply to a U.S. law school, and to pay attention to the book *during* their LL.M. year. This comprehensive book will help *after* they receive their LL.M. degree, because *LL.M. Roadmap* offers guidance on taking a U.S. bar exam, working in the U.S., and helping with careers after the LL.M. graduates return home to China, Japan, South Korea, and other countries in the Region.

> — *Ding Xiangshun (PhD in Law, Renmin University of China Law School,*
> *Beijing; LL.M., Indiana University School of Law)*
> *Assistant Dean for Foreign Affairs & Associate Professor of Law,*
> *Renmin University of China Law School, Beijing*
> *Director, Comparative Law Program, Renmin University of China*
> *Law School, Beijing. Visiting Professor & Fellow, Waseda University*
> *Faculty of Law & Meiji University Faculty of Law, Japan*

---

1. Many legal professionals have spoken highly about *LL.M. Roadmap*, and about how the book may serve very important purposes within global legal education, within transnational business, and even within the quest to promote international peace, security, and human rights. This Appendix collects some of these comments in written form. Additional comments can be found at www.LLMRoadmap.com. You are welcome to submit your own comments, to supplement the comments made by professors, deans and

This book will prove an invaluable resource for students thinking of studying law in the U.S.

— Bruce Carolan (LL.M., University College, Dublin)
Head, Department of Law, Dublin Institute of Technology, Dublin, Ireland

LL.M. Roadmap is a comprehensive guide, and perhaps the only one readily available, for Japanese and other Asian students who are contemplating pursuing this advanced legal degree in the United States. I have recruited U.S.-admitted Japanese lawyers and other Japanese legal and compliance professionals from this key pool of talent for many years. Practicing lawyers, law school graduates and members of Japanese corporate legal departments have long recognized the potential value to their legal and business careers of intensive exposure to the U.S. legal system, immersion in an English-language legal learning and living environment, and possible admission to a U.S. state bar. This guide, reflecting Professor Edwards' many years of experience working with LL.M. students and lawyers from around the world, should be required reading in their due diligence on how to plan for and make the most of the LL.M. opportunity.

— Laurence W. Bates (B.A. Yale; J.D. Harvard)
General Counsel, GE Japan
Director, Government Affairs and Policy, GE Asia Pacific

Unlike many other international students, my first law degree in the U.S. was a J.D., which I followed with an LL.M. My law school experiences in the U.S. were fantastic, but it would have been great to have had a comprehensive resource at my fingertips to help me align my academic and career aspirations with offerings at different U.S. law schools. *LL.M. Roadmap* provides comprehensive, valuable insights, whether you are choosing an LL.M. or a J.D. program. The book helpfully guides on how to distinguish among different law schools and programs, and how to decide which school is "best" for you. Each student wants their final decision about schools to be the right decision, and *LL.M. Roadmap* will help you make the right choice. LL.M. programs in the U.S. come in all shapes and sizes, and if you carefully consider the hundreds of criteria that Professor Edwards identifies and discusses in *LL.M. Roadmap,* you can make more informed, better choices that will help you as you apply, get accepted, secure your U.S. student

---

associate deans, other law program administrators, law practitioners, former judges, and LL.M. and S.J.D. graduates. Thus far, the written comments do not include feedback from current LL.M. or S.J.D. international students, though many current LL.M. students reviewed drafts of the *LL.M. Roadmap* manuscript at all stages of its production. Indeed, *LL.M. Roadmap* as published draws very heavily on substantive feedback received from many current graduate law students from many corners of the globe. We look forward to current students' written comments appearing on the *LL.M. Roadmap* website and in future editions of *LL.M. Roadmap.*

visa, organize funding, undertake intense study, graduate and embark on your career path.

> — *Luz Estella Nagle (J.D., College of William & Mary; LL.M., M.A.,*
> *UCLA; LL.D., Universidad Pontificia Bolivariana)*
> *Professor of Law, Stetson University College of Law*
> *Judge (Former), Medellín, Colombia*

LL.M. Roadmap is a clear, concise, and complete guidebook for anyone thinking about doing a graduate law degree in the U.S. It provides detailed step-by-step advice on every aspect of the process: programs, application, financing, visas, studying, graduating, careers and beyond. Professor Edwards seems to have thought of everything and shares his experience fully.

> — *M. C. Mirow (J.D. Cornell; Ph.D., Cambridge; Ph.D. Leiden)*
> *Associate Dean of International & Graduate Studies & Professor of Law*
> *Florida International University College of Law, Miami*

Lawyers around the world face difficult decisions when choosing the LL.M. program best-suited to their needs. The *LL.M. Roadmap* is an important tool for any prospective LL.M. student to have when making the tough choice about which law school is most appropriate. The criteria, the discussion, and the insight provided in this book will give international lawyers a better understanding of options and opportunities to them in the U.S., and will motivate law schools to reflect critically on the LL.M. programs they offer.

> — *Meredith McQuaid, Associate Vice President, and Dean,*
> *Global Programs and Strategy Alliance, University of Minnesota*
> *President, Chair of Board of Directors, NAFSA: Association*
> *of International Educators (2011-13)*

Bravo. The book is brilliant and long-overdue. This is going to be a great book that students around the world will read.

> — *Mark Wojcik (LL.M., New York University)*
> *Professor of Law, The John Marshall Law School, Chicago, Illinois*
> *University of Lucerne Faculty of Law, Lucerne, Switzerland*
> *Permanent Guest Professor of Comparative Law and Anglo-American Law*

LL.M. Roadmap is a truly remarkable tool for anyone — anywhere in the world - planning to pursue post-JD legal studies in the United States. As one who has traveled this path, I can think of no better resource. Professor Edwards has produced the important manual for all potential international LL.M. students in the United States. *LL.M. Roadmap* fills a gaping hole.

> — *Makau Mutua (LL.M. Harvard; S.J.D. Harvard; LL.B.*
> *and LL.M. University of Dar-es-Salaam)*

Dean & SUNY Distinguished Professor of Law
Floyd H. & Hilda L. Hurst Faculty Scholar
University of Buffalo School of Law,
The Associate Director, Harvard Human Rights Program (former)

I read [*LL.M. Roadmap*]. I loved it. Drawing on the experiences, successes, and mistakes of generations of LL.M. students – and his own experiences running an LL.M. program – Professor Edwards has demystified the process of choosing and getting admitted to a great American LL.M. program. This is how *I* would conduct my own LL.M. search.

— Michael Peil, Associate Dean for International Programs
Washington University School of Law, St. Louis, Missouri
Executive Director, International Law Students Association (ILSA) (former)

I have worked in human rights and access to justice for over 20 years, much while living in Asia. Global South students earning U.S. LL.M. degrees gain a premier educational experience, with unparalleled benefits, including development of critical knowledge, skills and jurisprudential values. They gain access to global connective networks that help in their human rights and humanitarian work upon graduation. *LL.M. Roadmap* is an important resource to help international students learn which U.S. LL.M. programs are more interested in receiving tuition dollars than they are in helping LL.M. students and graduates achieve their goals, which can include returning to make a positive difference in their home countries.

— Bruce A. Lasky (J.D., University of Florida; LL.M., Central European University)
Founder, Bridges Across Borders Southeast Asia (BABSEA)
Director, BABSEA Community Legal Education Initiative (BABSEA CLE)
Adjunct Professor of Law, Chiang Mai University, Chiang Mai, Thailand
Adjunct Professor of Law, Universiti Teknologi MARA, Selangor Darul Ehsan, Malaysia
Visiting Senior Lecturer, University of Malaya, Kuala Lumpur, Malaysia

LL.M. Roadmap informs U.S. law school deans, professors, and administrators what international LL.M. students should reasonably expect from their U.S. law school experiences. *LL.M. Roadmap* will empower students with information needed to maximize their U.S. law school experience, and empower U.S. law schools with tools to provide high-quality student services. Congratulations to Professor Edwards for this indispensable resources book that can be used by all stakeholders in U.S. graduate legal education.

— María Pabón López (J.D., University of Pennsylvania; B.A., Princeton)
Dean & Judge Adrian G. Duplantier Distinguished Professor of Law
Loyola University New Orleans College of Law

Glossary[1]

1-L. A first-year law student in a 3-year J.D. program at a U.S. law school.

2-L. A second-year law student in a 3-year J.D. program at a U.S. law school.

3-L. A third-year law student in a 3-year J.D. program at a U.S. law school.

4-L. A student in a 3-year J.D. program at a U.S. law school who has not completed the program after 3 years. A 4-L may be enrolled in a joint-degree program or be enrolled part-time and plan to complete the program in 4 years rather than 3.

A

AARP. An organization that provides discounts and other services for persons in the U.S. 50 years of age or over, including LL.M. students or dependents. Formerly the "American Association for Retired People."

ABA (American Bar Association). A professional organization of U.S. lawyers that "accredits" U.S. J.D. programs. The ABA has accredited 200 J.D. programs in the U.S. All LL.M. programs for international students described in *LL.M. Roadmap* that are offered at U.S. law schools are at schools that also offer ABA-accredited J.D. programs. The ABA does not accredit LL.M. degree programs or any law degree programs outside the U.S.

Academic Advisor/Adviser. Ordinarily a law faculty member who assists an LL.M. student to plan his or her course of study, select his or her classes, and help him or her achieve educational objectives. Each international LL.M. student should be assigned to a specific law faculty member Academic Advisor who meets with the student; discovers the student's background, interests, and career objectives; and advises the student on how best to achieve those objectives.

Academic Calendar. Often posted on a law school's website, this calendar identifies starting and ending dates of classes each semester, exam periods, holidays and other breaks, and other significant information related to the academic year. It might highlight critical information specific to LL.M. students, such as LL.M. orientation dates and English language placement testing dates.

Academic Standing. A status requiring an LL.M. student to maintain a certain GPA, attend and participate in classes, turn in assignments, sit for exams, and satisfy all other school requirements.

Academic Training (AT). A U.S. government program that permits J-1 students to supplement their LL.M. classroom experience with a law-related job, on or off campus, possibly commencing before graduation or up to 18 months after graduation.

Academic Year. Typically the 9-month period from August-September to April-May when LL.M. classes are held. Some schools divide

---

1. Sources include:

- Common Data Set of U.S. Higher Education Terminology
- Glossary of Immigration Terms, Immigration Equality
- Glossary of U.S. Educational Terminology, World Educational Services, NY.
- Glossary of Visa Terms, State Department
- ICE website: http://www.ice.gov/sevis/sevisii/overview.htm; http://www.ice.gov/sevis/i901/faq10.htm
- If You Want to Study in the U.S. (Book 2): Graduate and Professional Study & Research, U.S. State Department
- One-L Dictionary, Harvard Law School
- U.S. State Department website: travel.state.gov/visa/frvi/glossary/glossary_1363.html
- Websites of various U.S. law schools

their academic year into semesters (2 terms), trimesters (3 terms), or quarters (4 terms). Some schools also offer LL.M. classes during the summer (May-August).

Accommodation. A law school's attempt to ensure that students with special needs, including disabilities, have a fair opportunity to access school facilities, take exams, and participate in school activities. Accommodations could include extra time to take exams for non-native English speakers, improvised exam-taking conditions for students with visual or hearing challenges, or a modified classroom infrastructure to allow access to wheelchairs or other mechanisms required by students.

Accreditation. The process by which the ABA determines whether a J.D. program satisfies rigorous standards in teaching, research, and service. Currently the ABA has accredited 200 J.D. programs. The ABA does not accredit LL.M. programs, but reviews an LL.M. program only to determine if it would have an adverse impact on the law school's ability to comply with the ABA's requirements for the school's J.D. program. According to the ABA Council, if "no adverse impact is indicated, the ABA acquiesces in the law school's decision to offer the [LL.M.] program and degree. Acquiescence in [an LL.M.] program does not constitute ABA approval or endorsement of such a program." Thus, no LL.M. program in the U.S. is ABA-accredited.

Add/Drop. Period during the first few weeks of a term when students may modify their course schedules by increasing or decreasing the number of courses they are enrolled in for the term.

Adjunct Professor. A nonpermanent, nontenured, part-time member of a law faculty hired on an ad hoc basis to teach one or more courses. On business cards, stationery, and e-mail signature lines they are referred to as "Jane Doe, Adjunct Professor of Law," and may be addressed as "Adjunct Professor Jane Doe." An adjunct professor would ordinarily be paid a small fraction of full-time faculty salary, whereas visiting professors would routinely receive a salary at a rate similar to that of a full-time faculty member. (*See* Visiting Professor; Professor of Law.)

Adjustment of Status (or Adjust Status) (AOS). Change of a visa from a nonimmigrant status (temporary) to immigrant status (permanent). For example, a person may change from a work visa holder (temporary) to a permanent resident (permanent). This is not the same as a "change of status." (*See* Change of Status.)

Admission (Academic). An LL.M. program's process in evaluating applicants and selecting to whom it will offer a seat in the incoming LL.M. class. (*See also* Admission (Immigration).)

Admission (Immigration). Each time you arrive at a U.S. port of entry, irrespective of your type of visa, you must be "admitted" to the U.S. A visa permits you to board a plane, but immigration officials still must grant you entry or admit you upon arrival. (*See also* Admission (Academic).)

Admission Committee (LL.M.). Typically a collection of faculty members and/or others who decide which applicants to admit to the school as LL.M. students.

Advanced Standing. Granted to a newly admitted LL.M. or J.D. student when the program permits the student to transfer credits earned at another school or in another program of the same school, reducing the number of credits the student must earn in the LL.M. or J.D. program. (*See* Transfer Credit.)

Affidavit of Support. A document in which a person or entity promises to support a student financially in the U.S.

Agent (or Educational Agent). An individual or entity that earns money by facilitating matches between prospective students and LL.M. programs, with the goal of prospective students enrolling at U.S. law schools to study for the LL.M. degree. Educational agents may work for schools seeking to recruit LL.M. students ("school agent"), for prospective LL.M. students seeking LL.M. program admission ("student agent"), or both schools and prospective students ("dual agent" or "double agent").

Alien. For immigration purposes, a person who is not a U.S. citizen or permanent resident.

Alumni Association. An association of graduates (alumni) or, more broadly, of former students. Law schools have alumni associations for law graduates (J.D., LL.M., and S.J.D.) and should have separate, specific alumni associations for LL.M. graduates. If a law school is part of a university system, the university should have an alumni associate which J.D., LL.M., and S.J.D. students may join, along with joining the law school associations. These organizations are valuable, and LL.M. graduates (and current students) are encouraged to join all for which they qualify.

American Automobile Association (AAA). An organization that provides roadside assistance to drivers and occupants of motor vehicles, and other services such as travel, hotel, and restaurant discounts, and free travelers' checks. Excellent for LL.M. students who drive in the U.S. or who ride as passengers in cars driven by others.

American Bar Association. (*See* ABA.)

Application Deadline. The last date on which an LL.M. program states that it will accept an application for admission for the upcoming year. Some schools accept applications after their stated application deadline.

Application Fee. Money an LL.M. program charges to process a prospective student's admission application. This fee varies widely across LL.M. programs; some charge no fee.

Appointment Package. Envelope containing documents you must complete before you visit the U.S. Embassy or Consulate in your home country to apply for your student visa.

Arrival-Departure Card (or Form I-94). When you arrive at your U.S. port of entry, a U.S. Immigration official will staple a small white card (Form I-94) in your passport. The I-94 indicates your entry date, the length of time you may remain in the U.S., and your student classification. You should retain the I-94 in your passport until you leave the U.S., at which point you surrender the I-94. A new I-94 is issued each time you enter or re-enter the U.S.

Assistant Dean. Typically a nonfaculty staff member who handles an LL.M. program's administrative functions. Generally responsible for day-to-day LL.M. program planning and organizing under the supervision of a Dean or Associate Dean. Assists LL.M. students with various administrative matters. (*See* Dean; Associate Dean.)

Assistant Professor of Law. An entry-level rank for law professors, who may be promoted to Associate Professor of Law and then to Professor of Law. On business cards, stationery, and e-mail signature lines they are referred to as "Jane Doe, Assistant Professor of Law" and may be addressed as "Assistant Professor Jane Doe." (*See* Associate Professor of Law; Professor of Law.)

Associate Dean. Typically a law professor with administrative responsibilities in addition to his or her regular faculty teaching responsibilities. A school may have Associate Deans with administrative and academic responsibility for LL.M. and S.J.D. programs. (*See* Dean; Assistant Dean.)

Associate Professor of Law. Mid-level rank for law professors who enter as Assistant Professor of Law, who are promoted to Associate Professor of Law and then to Professor of Law. On business cards, stationery, and e-mail signature lines they are referred to as "Jane Doe, Associate Professor of Law" or may be addressed as "Associate Professor Jane Doe." (*See* Assistant Professor of Law; Professor of Law.)

Association of American Law Schools (AALS). The AALS is a nonprofit educational association of law schools representing over 10,000 law faculty members in the U.S. The purpose of the Association is "the improvement of the legal profession through legal education." If you want to become a law professor, you should check the AALS website for information about the law professor hiring process in the U.S. (www.aals.org).

AT. *See* Academic Training.

Audit. Taking a course without receiving a grade or credit for it. Some schools permit LL.M. and S.J.D. students to audit courses for a small or no fee. Auditing is useful if you want to learn a particular subject area, do not need or want academic credit for the course, do not want to pay the full tuition for the course, and do not want to take an exam or write a paper for the course.

Authentication/Verification. Some schools require that applicants submit documents only after the documents are officially verified or affirmed as original and legitimate. The applicant would request an outside official or company to "attest" to or to "affirm" the authenticity of the original transcripts, diplomas, certificates, or other documents.

Authorized Stay. When you enter the U.S., an Immigration official will stamp your I-94 indicating the date by which you must leave the U.S. This would typically be a date specifically marking the expected length of your LL.M. program, or a "D/S" (duration of stay), which means you may stay so long as you remain in good student status.

Award Letter. Sent to you by a school if it grants you a tuition discount, endowed scholarship, or other form of financial assistance. It is valid only at the sending school and only for the duration and under the conditions identified therein.

B

B1/B2 Visa. Nonimmigrant visas valid for tourism or business, not for study.

B.A. Bachelor of Arts undergraduate degrees. (*See* Bachelor Degree.)

B.S. Bachelor of Science undergraduate degrees. (*See* Bachelor Degree.)

Bachelor Degree (or Undergraduate Degree) (B.A. or B.S.). Awarded in the U.S. after completing four years of higher education. J.D. programs in the U.S. require applicants to possess at least a bachelor degree, typically a B.S. or B.A.

Bachelor of Laws (LL.B.). The first professional law degree in many English-speaking countries. The LL.B. may be a three-, four-, or five-year undergraduate degree. Most U.S. law schools require foreign lawyers to hold an LL.B. or higher to enter an LL.M. program. The LL.B. is no longer awarded at U.S. schools.

Bar. Refers to the group of people admitted to practice law in a particular U.S. jurisdiction and are accordingly "members of the bar." "Bar" may also refer to a "bar examination" of a specific U.S. jurisdiction.

Bar Association. An organization of legal professionals that promotes lawyering generally, or with regard to a specific subject area, type of legal practice, geographic region, ethnic or other background or status of the professionals, or other criteria. Examples include the International Bar Association, the Hispanic Bar Association, the Patent Bar Association, the National Bar Association (for African American and other lawyers of color), the LGBT Bar Association (related to lesbian, gay, bisexual and transgendered people and issues), and the California State Bar Association.

Bar Course. A regular law school class on a topic that is routinely covered on bar exams.

Bar Exam (Bar Examination). Each U.S. state administers this type of test to those seeking to practice law in that state. The test varies among states, though they generally contain essay questions focusing on the laws of the particular state and multiple-choice questions focusing on federal law.

Bar Review Course. Usually given by private companies to recent law graduates, these classes are specifically geared toward teaching students the substantive law they need to know to pass the bar, and teaching them test-taking strategies and techniques.

Biometrics. Fingerprints, iris scans, facial recognition, and other biologically unique information used for purposes such as verifying a person's identity.

Bursar. Law school or university official to whom students tender tuition and student fees. If you fail to pay your "Bursar Bill" (tuition and fees), you may be suspended from school or prevented from enrolling in classes.

C

Cambridge ILEC. *See* International Legal English Certificate.

Candidate Referral Service (CRS). Program operated by the Law School Admissions Council (LSAC) in which prospective LL.M. students submit biographical and other information, LSAC disseminates that information to different U.S. LL.M. programs, and those LL.M. programs may decide that they wish to recruit those students who may not have otherwise applied to those particular schools (www.lsac.org/ LLM/Choose/LLM-crs.asp).

Career Office. An office within the law school that provides career counseling to LL.M. students and helps them achieve their professional objectives. It also helps LL.M. students fine-tune their career aspirations, facilitates LL.M. job interviews, and helps LL.M. students and graduates find jobs in the U.S. and elsewhere.

Carrel. A desk or study area for individual students, usually in the law library. Carrels may be reserved for specific LL.M. students or open for whichever student arrives first.

Casebook. A text used in law classes. Usually contains judicial decisions, legal principles, statutes, law journal articles, and other material related to the course's subject matter.

Cash Cow. An LL.M. program that generates revenues from LL.M. tuition and fees, and diverts that revenue away from the LL.M. program, leaving the LL.M. program lacking resources needed to meet LL.M. students' reasonable needs and expectations. The mentality of a school that creates or runs an LL.M. program to raise money to support the school's non-LL.M. programs.

CASIN. *See* Council for American Students in International Negotiations.

Catalog (or Course Catalog). Lists school's degree programs, requirements, curriculum, courses, extracurricular activities, teaching staff, and administration members.

Change of Status. When a foreign visa-holder in the U.S. asks to shift from one nonimmigrant status (such as tourist) to another nonimmigrant status (such as student). This is not the same as an "adjustment of status." (*See* Adjustment of Status.)

Cheating. A type of conduct prohibited by educational institutions to ensure that students perform their academic tasks without unfair advantages over their colleagues. In law schools, such conduct (e.g., plagiarism) and its consequences are usually explained in an honor code.

Citizen (U.S.). A person born in the U.S. regardless of parents' immigration status is a U.S. citizen. A person may also become a U.S. citizen through the process of "naturalization."

Citizenship and Immigration Services or CIS (USCIS). U.S. Department of Homeland Security division that handles applications for visas, legal permanent residence, employment authorization, and naturalization.

Clinical Professor. *See* Professor of Law.

Class (Class Session). *See* Course.

Class Participation. A law student's contribution to classes or class sessions, for example by joining in classroom discussions, taking in-class exams, or giving presentations during class sessions.

Class Rank. LL.M. students may be assigned an order that correlates with how their grades compare with LL.M. classmates' grades. A person "first" in the class would have a grade point average (GPA) higher than the GPA of all other classmates. Class rank may be listed numerically (e.g., number 10 of 100), or by percentage (e.g., top 10%).

Clerkship (or Judicial Clerkship; Law Firm Clerkship). Prestigious employment where a law graduate assists a judge, often in researching and drafting legal opinions. Some people refer to a student's part-time student law firm work as a "law firm clerkship." If the law firm work is during the summer, it would be a "summer clerkship" and the student may be referred to as a "summer associate" or "summer clerk" of the firm.

Clinic. Academic, credit-bearing experiential law school program offering law students practical legal experience by permitting them to handle real cases with real clients. Clinics may be general or may focus on cases in a particular area such as international human rights law, immigration, housing, disability, criminal law, or environmental law.

College or University. An institution of higher education that offers undergraduate four-year bachelor of arts (B.A.) or bachelor of science (B.S.) degrees.

Commencement (or Graduation). A ceremony held at the end of an LL.M. academic year, usually in May or June, marking completion of the degree program.

Concentration (or Track or Specialization). A substantive area of law in which an LL.M. student is permitted to gain fine-tuned, in-depth knowledge in a specific area of law. (*See* Specialized LL.M. Program; General LL.M. Program.)

Conditional Admission. An LL.M. program's promise to admit a particular student if she fulfills one or more conditions. An LL.M. program may decide that an applicant satisfies most of an LL.M. program's admission requirements but falls short in an area, such as English language proficiency scores. So, for example, the program may issue the LL.M. applicant documents that permit her to travel to the U.S. to study English, and promises her that it will admit her to the LL.M. program *only if* she satisfies the condition of raising her English language test scores to a certain level in a certain amount of time. She will only be able to enroll in the LL.M. program and take LL.M. classes *if* she raises her English language test scores as stipulated in the condition. If she does not raise her scores, she will not be permitted to enroll in the LL.M. program.

Consulate. A U.S. Embassy suboffice operated by the U.S. State Department in a foreign country. U.S. Consulates, along with U.S. Embassies, issue student visas. "Consulate" also refers to a suboffice of a foreign Embassy in the U.S. responsible for nationals of that country who are students in the U.S. The Embassy of your country will be in Washington, while a Consulate of your country may be in New York, Chicago, or another U.S. city.

Continuing Student. A student who has not completed or terminated his or her LL.M. program and has maintained visa status.

Cost of Attendance (COA). The amount a school predicts it will cost for a student to enroll in and complete an LL.M. program. The COA includes tuition, fees, housing, food, insurance, books, and miscellaneous expenses. Law schools should publish accurate, comprehensive and transparent COA figures.

Council for American Students in International Negotiations (CASIN). An educational nonprofit, nongovernmental organization that organizes student delegations to meetings of various United Nations bodies, the Assembly of States Parties of the International Criminal Court (ICC), the Pan-American Health Organization, and the Biennial Meeting of States on Small Arms.

Counsel (or Counselor or Counselor at Law or Attorney). A person who is licensed to practice law in a state of the U.S. People may become eligible to receive a law license if they pass the bar exam of a state, or if the state waives the bar exam for them. In some U.S. states, a person may sit for the bar exam even if his or her law degree was received outside the U.S., and in some instances even if he or she does do not hold a law degree at all.

Counseling Service (or Mental Health Counseling). Services that assist LL.M. students (and others) with stress, adjustment, and other similar issues that may arise during the LL.M. year. Unfortunately, many students who need counseling services are afraid to or ashamed to seek these valuable services. *There is no shame in seeking any sort of counseling, including mental health counseling, while you are an LL.M. student or after you graduate! Many U.S. law students and graduates do seek such assistance.*

Course. An LL.M. program requires students to earn approximately 20 to 30 credit hours, in units of instruction called "courses." Courses are then segmented into "classes" or "class sessions." Each course would last for 13-16 weeks, may be valued at 2-3 credit hours, and may involve 2-3 hours of class sessions per week (corresponding to the number of credit hours, at the ratio of approximately 1 hour of class session for each credit hour). A "class" or "class session" would typically be one classroom segment of a course. So, if a student is taking a 3-credit hour torts course, they may have 3 torts classes a week, and each torts class would last 1 hour for a total of 3 hours of torts class instruction per week. It may get a little confusing because *many* people (including students, professors, and staff) at times use the terms "course" and "class" interchangeably. For example, someone may ask you how many *classes* you have this semester when what they really want to know is how many *courses* or how many *credit hours* you have. Don't worry; you will know how to answer such questions by the context in which the questions are asked. If you have any doubt, simply ask them something like, "Do you want to know how many credit hours I am enrolled in for the semester?"

Course-Based. A type of LL.M. program that requires a student to earn most or all of his or her academic credits by taking traditional classroom courses. Compare this to research-based LL.M. programs. (*See* Research-Based.)

Course Load. The number of credit hours a student takes in a given semester.

CPT. *See* Curricular Practical Training.

Credits or Credit Hours. A unit of measure that roughly corresponds to the number of hours per week the course meets. Thus, a 3-credit hour course would typically meet for approximately 3 hours each week, usually spread over two or more days. Each LL.M. course taken is assigned a particular number of credits or credit hours, and a student must accumulate a specified number of credit hours to earn his or her LL.M. degree. Courses are typically assigned from 1 to 4 credits, with an average of 3 credits per course. An LL.M. degree generally requires 22 to 30 credits to graduate, and LL.M. students generally take from 8 to 10 courses during their LL.M. year. A student who enrolls in or takes 12 credit hours a semester will likely be in the classroom for about 12 hours per week during the semester. (*See* Course.)

Cross-registration. Permits LL.M. students to sign up for courses in non-law departments within a University system without being admitted to the other department.

Curriculum. Courses and other formal learning experiences associated with an LL.M. degree program.

Curriculum Vitae (or Resume). Lists a person's educational, work, professional and certain personal details. Submitted to prospective employers when applying for jobs, or to schools when applying for admission. *Be certain to convert your overseas CV or resume to U.S. format if you are seeking employment in the U.S. or with a U.S. company overseas.*

Curricular Practical Training (CPT). A U.S. government program that permits F-1 students to supplement their LL.M. classroom experience with a law-related job, on- or off-campus, during their LL.M. year. The training must be an "integral part" of the curriculum required for the LL.M. degree, must be completed for credit, and as a general rule is available only after the student has been a part of the LL.M. program for at least 9 months.

Customs and Border Protection (CBP). Division of U.S. Homeland Security responsible for protecting U.S. borders.

D

Dean. The highest authority at the law school, responsible for all aspects of the law school's operation. If an LL.M. student has a problem that is not resolved by the LL.M. Director, Assistant Dean or Associate Dean, the LL.M. student should approach the Dean, who should be able to resolve the issue. (*See* Assistant Dean; Associate Dean.)

Dean's List. A list of students in a law school degree program who earn a grade point average at or above a designated high level during a semester, and are thus on an "honor roll" for that period.

Debit Card. A card usually issued by a bank that permits the holder to use the card to purchase goods or services with funds that transfer instantly from the holder's bank account. It is not a credit card that involves borrowing from a creditor.

Deferred Admission. When a school permits an admitted applicant to postpone his or her matriculation to a later semester or academic year.

Degree. Awarded upon a student's completion of a degree program. Also the diploma issued upon graduating from a degree program, such as an LL.M. program. (*See* Diploma.)

Department of Homeland Security. U.S. government department with the following three parts responsible for immigration policy, procedures, implementation and enforcement: (a) U.S. Citizenship and Immigration Services (USCIS); (b) Customs and Border Protection (CBP); and (c) Immigration and Customs Enforcement (ICE).

Deposit. Partial tuition an admitted student pays a school to reserve a seat.

Derivative Status. F-2 or J-2 visa status for a spouse or minor child who gains a visa to travel to the U.S. with an LL.M. student on an F-1 or J-1 visa.

Designated School Official (DSO). At schools authorized to receive international students one or more DSOs are chosen as official representatives to the U.S. government and are responsible for the school's compliance with USCIS rules regarding international students and applicants.

Diploma. A certificate evidencing that the recipient has earned a degree. A graduate from an LL.M. program will receive an LL.M. diploma. If the LL.M. degree was earned in a specialized area, the name of the specialized area should appear on the face of the diploma. (*See* Degree.)

Diploma Mill. An LL.M. program that has low admission standards and bestows LL.M. degrees at a high price but of little worth.

Dissertation. An in-depth, scholarly research paper written in partial fulfillment of S.J.D. or other terminal degree requirements.

Distance Learning. Delivery of course content via Internet, satellite, correspondence, videotape, or other methods not involving on-site/on-campus classes.

Dormitory. Student housing located on campus.

Driver's License. State-issued permit authorizing the holder to operate a motorized vehicle or cycle on roads. Each state regulates whether and how long you may drive in that state with a non-U.S. driver's license.

Drop/Add. *See* Add/Drop.

Drop-out. A person who has withdrawn from all classes entirely, often with no intention to return to school.

D/S. *See* Duration of Status.

DS-2019. A U.S. government form that the U.S. law school sends to a person they admit into their LL.M. program when the person's LL.M. course will be funded by a U.S. government or similar scholarship. The person presents the DS-2019 to the U.S. Embassy when applying for a J-1 visa to enter the U.S. to enroll in the LL.M. program. (Compare the I-20 form issued for an F-1 visa.)

Dual Degree. Program in which a student earns two degrees at the same time, often in less time than it would take to complete the two degrees separately.

Duration of Status or D/S. At a point-of-entry into the U.S., an Immigration official writes on the student's I-94 form the amount of time the student is permitted to remain in the U.S. A notation of "duration of status" or "D/S" indicates that the student may remain in the U.S. as long as he or she maintains student status pursuant to his or her visa. (*See* I-94.)

E

Economic Hardship (EH). This applies to F-1 and J-1 visa holders who experience unexpected extreme economic or financial hardship. If EH status is granted, the ordinary student employment restrictions are lifted, and, for example, the student may be permitted to work off-campus during the school year.

Educational Agent. *See* Agent.

EducationUSA. A network of over 450 advising centers in 200 countries and territories supported by the U.S. State Department's Bureau of Educational and Cultural Affairs. Its Advisors provide advice to millions of foreign individuals overseas about education in the U.S. (www.educationusa.info).

Electives. Courses that are not required but that students may choose freely.

ELSA. *See* European Law Students Association.

Employment Authorization Document (EAD). U.S. government card that reflects permission for foreign LL.M. students and graduates to work legally in the U.S. on Optional Practical Training Program (OPT—for F-1 students) or in Academic Training (AT—for J-1 students).

English Language Competency. The ability to communicate effectively in English. Proof of this may be required when applying to LL.M. programs and can be shown through Cambridge ILEC, IELTS, PTE Academic, TOEFL, or similar testing results.

English as a Second Language (ESL) Course. Classes designed to teach English to students whose mother tongue is not English.

Enroll. To matriculate or join a degree program.

Enrollment. The total number of students registered in a degree program.

ETS (Educational Testing Service). A U.S.-based nonprofit organization widely known for producing standardized exams such as the TOEFL.

European Law Students Association (ELSA). An international, independent, nonpolitical, nonprofit organization run by and for law students and recent graduates. Founded in 1981, it is the world's largest independent law students association, represented at 200 law faculties in 42 countries across Europe with over 30,000 student and young lawyer members. ELSA offers traineeship programs, publications, and a WTO moot court competition (www.elsa.org).

Examinations (Exams). Tests administered in law schools to assess competence and learning in subject areas. Some law school exams may be multiple-choice, and others may be essay-based. A law school course may have only one exam at the end of the semester that covers all material from throughout the term.

Executive LL.M. Program. These programs may require the same number of academic credits as a traditional, residential program, but the classes may be spread out over more than 9-10 months, or squeezed into concentrated, shorter periods. These programs tend to enroll mid-career professional students with well-established jobs.

Experiential Learning. Formal learning outside the classroom. Students learn by doing, and they may engage in real lawyering.

Externship. *See* Internship.

Extracurricular Activities. Group activities organized by students (LL.M., S.J.D., or J.D.), faculty, and staff, that complement classroom education, promote physical and/or mental health, help students maintain balance in their lives during a period that could be stressful, and help students achieve their personal and professional goals.

F

F-1 Visa. The most common visa under which LL.M. students enter the U.S. to study. Issued to "self-funded" students whose LL.M. expenses are paid by themselves or family or other private resources. Compare J-1 visa students whose expenses are paid by the U.S. government or another sponsor.

F-2 Visa. A visa issued to a spouse or minor child dependent of an F-1 visa holder. The F-2 visa is valid so long as the F-1 visa holder remains in the U.S. lawfully.

Faculty. Law school staff hired to teach, though faculty members may also have LL.M. or other administrative responsibilities.

Fees. An amount law schools require LL.M. students to pay, in addition to tuition. Fees could be for sports facility use, photocopying, technology services, or other services.

Fellowship. Financial assistance a school gives to a student that may be based on merit, need or other factors such as desire to attract a particular type of student or a student from a particular country. A fellowship may also be used as a general tuition discount for LL.M. students, to attract additional LL.M. students and to increase the size of the LL.M. class. The student need not repay the fellowship amount. (*See* Grant; Scholarship; Tuition Discount.)

Final Exam. A test administered at the end of a semester or academic year that usually covers all material covered during the particular course. U.S. law school course grades are frequently based on the grades students receive on their final exam.

Financial Aid. Funding intended to help students pay educational expenses including tuition and fees, room and board, and books and supplies, for education at a university. Financial aid might include endowed scholarships, tuition discounts, fellowships, or loans.

Financial Standing. Status of a student paying tuition and fees when they are due. A student must maintain this status when enrolled in an LL.M. program.

Firm Admission. When a law school admits an LL.M. applicant unconditionally, that is, the school does not require the prospective student to fulfill any special requirements before the student enrolls in the LL.M. program. This is unlike a conditional admission, in which the applicant must satisfy certain requirements before enrolling. (*See* Conditional Admission.)

Flunk. To receive a nonpassing grade on an exam or assignment, or for a course. Students do not receive academic credit for courses they flunk (or fail).

Full-Time Student. To be full-time, F-1 and J-1 students must generally be enrolled for at least 8 credit hours per term but may drop below 8 hours during their final semester or in certain circumstances.

G

GATT. The General Agreement on Tariffs and Trade (GATT). A 1947 multilateral treaty that regulates trade among over 150 countries. Its preamble notes that its purposes include the "substantial reduction of tariffs and other trade barriers and the elimination of preferences, on a reciprocal and mutually advantageous basis." A subsequent GATT agreement in 1994 created the World Trade Organization (WTO) which implements GATT, provides a forum for negotiating and discussing trade barrier issues, and provides for a mechanism for resolving trade disputes.

General LL.M. Program. An LL.M. program offering students a wide range of courses in many different areas of law, with no area of specialization or concentration noted on the diploma or transcript. (Compare with Specialized LL.M. Program.)

Grade (or Mark). The evaluative score a professor assigns to a student's work during or at the end of a course. Professors typically express grades or marks as a letter (e.g., A, B, C, D, or F), as a percentage, or as a number of points earned.

Grade Point Average (GPA). The sum of the raw grades or marks earned divided by the number of academic credit hours a student takes during a particular period. Grade point averages may be calculated per semester, calculated cumulatively over the course of a student's time in school, or calculated for select semesters or other periods. A GPA may also be calculated for specialized courses, or for any other subset of courses taken.

Grading Curve. A statistical method of assigning grades designed to yield a predetermined distribution of grades among the students in a class. Some law schools require that professors use this grading method.

Graduate Management Admission Test (GMAT). U.S. business schools commonly use this test as one of multiple selection criteria for admitting students into graduate business programs. A student seeking admission to a joint J.D./LL.M. program might be required to take the GMAT, but a student entering only the LL.M. would not be required to take it.

Graduate Programs. In the U.S. all law programs are "graduate programs," which follow U.S. "undergraduate programs." There are no U.S. undergraduate degrees in law, only graduate degrees. Students must complete an undergraduate program before joining a J.D. program, which is the first available law degree program in the U.S.

Graduation. *See* Commencement.

Grant. Financial assistance a school gives to a student that may be based on merit, need or other factors such as desire to attract a particular type of student or a student from a particular country. A grant may also be used as a general tuition discount for LL.M. students to attract additional LL.M. students and to increase the size of the LL.M. class. Grants may be used for tuition or other expenses associated with the LL.M. degree. The student need not repay the grant amount. (*See* Fellowship; Scholarship; Tuition Discount.)

GRE (Graduate Record Examination). A standardized test that many U.S. graduate schools require for admission. LL.M. programs in the U.S. do not require applicants to take a GRE, though it may be required for a joint degree involving a combined non-LL.M. degree and an LL.M. degree.

Green Card. A wallet-sized card issued by the U.S. government showing that the person is a lawful permanent resident (immigrant) in the U.S. A permanent resident may acquire citizenship. Note that the green card is not a visa.

H

H-1B. A U.S. government visa category for workers who possess skills in certain categories and who are permitted to enter and remain in the U.S. for fixed periods when no U.S. citizen is available for the position.

Headhunter. An employment agency retained by and paid a "headhunter fee" by a company, law firm, law faculty, or other entity to find legal professionals to become employees of the company, law firm, law faculty, or other entity.

Health Services. Physical and mental primary and preventive health services provided to LL.M. students, often included in LL.M. fees and tuition paid to the law school.

High School. Usually the final 3-4 years (grades 9-12) in the U.S. secondary school system. In the U.S., a high school diploma is usually required for entry into an undergraduate B.A. or B.S. university degree program. In the U.S., a B.A. or B.S. is required for entry into a J.D. program.

Higher Education. U.S. post-high school education, including undergraduate and graduate degrees at universities or colleges.

Hold (or Put on Hold). When an LL.M. admission committee defers consideration of an application, without deciding to admit, reject, or waitlist the application. Putting an application "on hold" is not a definitive negative or positive reply.

Homework. Assignments that professors give to students to complete outside the classroom.

Honor Code. A law school's ethics rules that students must follow or be subject to discipline. Rules typically deal with submitting another's work as one's own, cheating on exams, engaging in unpermitted collaboration, giving unpermitted or receiving unpermitted assistance on an examination or paper, plagiarizing, or being involved in criminal behavior or general dishonesty.

Honors. Awards bestowed at graduation recognizing a student's academic achievement. Terms such as summa cum laude, magna cum laude, cum laude, highest honors, high honors, and honors are used to indicate honors.

I

I-20. (Pronounced "eye-20"). A government document that your LL.M. school will send you when it admits you if your LL.M. expenses will be paid by you or family. A student needs an I-20 when applying for an F-1 student visa. (Compare the DS-2019 form issued for a J-1 visa.)

I-94. (Pronounced "eye-94") The small white card placed in your passport when you arrive in the U.S. It indicates how long you are authorized to stay in the U.S., either with a specific date you must leave, or with a notation such as D/S (duration of status) meaning you may stay so long as you remain in student status. (*See* Duration of Status.)

IELTS. *See* International English Language Testing System.

ILSA. *See* International Law Students Association.

Immigrant. A foreign national who has been granted permission to remain in the U.S. permanently, that is a "legal permanent resident" or "green card holder." This is distinguished from a "non-immigrant" who comes to the U.S. on a temporary visa, such as a non-immigrant student visa.

Immigrant Visa. Permission the U.S. grants to persons to allow them to live in the U.S. indefinitely and permanently.

Immigration and Customs Enforcement (ICE). The U.S. Department of Homeland Security's enforcement branch.

In Case of Emergency (ICE) Number. A phone number of a friend or family member you might list in your mobile phone, under the name "ICE," for emergency responders to dial to notify in case you have an emergency and are unable to communicate.

Incomplete. If a student does not finish all course work before a term ends, the professor may assign the grade of "incomplete" and assign a letter or numerical grade when the work is completed. An "incomplete" may be issued if the student cannot do the work due to illness or other complications.

Independent Study/Supervised Study/Guided Research. A nonclassroom research, writing, or practical project supervised by a professor.

In-House Counsel. A lawyer who works in the legal department of a corporation, rather than working for a law firm.

In-Status. If an individual holds an F-1 or J-1 visa and complies with all the F-1 or J-1 regulations, he or she will be deemed "in status." If the visa-holder does not comply, he or she is "out-of-status" and subject to penalties, including deportation. (*See* Legal Standing; Out-of-Status.)

International English Language Testing System (IELTS). An exam that measures English-language proficiency. It contains four sections — listening, reading, writing, and speaking. Some LL.M. programs accept IELTS in lieu of Cambridge ILEC, PTE Academic, or TOEFL.

International Law Students Association (ILSA). A nonprofit association of students and lawyers dedicated to the promotion of international law. It sponsors academic conferences, publications, and the Philip C. Jessup International Law Moot Court Competition. Chapters exist at most U.S. law schools (www.ilsa.org).

International Legal English Certificate (Cambridge ILEC). An exam that measures English-language proficiency. This test consists of four separate papers testing reading, writing, listening, and speaking. Some LL.M. programs accept Cambridge ILEC in lieu of IELTS, PTE Academic, or TOEFL.

International Student. A student whose earlier law training was received outside the U.S.

International Student Advisor. Person designated by an educational institution to assist and advise its international students on visa, immigration, and other related topics.

Internship (or Externship). Experiential, supervised professional academic experiences, outside the classroom, where students gain practical skills.

J

J-1 Visa. A nonimmigrant visa for persons entering the U.S. as "exchange visitors" sponsored by a government or private sponsor in an organized program. LL.M. students who receive Fulbright or similar scholarships to pay for their study use J-1 visas. Compare F-1 visa students who pay their LL.M. expenses using family or other private resources. (*See* F-1 Visa.)

J-2 Visa. A nonimmigrant visa issued to a spouse or minor child dependent of a J-1 visa holder. It is valid so long as the J-1 visa holder remains in the U.S. lawfully.

J.D. Juris Doctor (or Juris Doctorate or Doctor of Jurisprudence). The first professional law degree in the U.S. Formerly known as the LL.B.

Joint Degree or Dual Degree. Two or more degrees received at the same time, where partial requirements for one degree count toward the other degree, such that it takes less time and fewer credits to earn the joint degree than it would take to earn the two degrees separately. Examples include LL.M.-MBA, J.D.-LLM.

Judge Advocate General (JAG). A lawyer commissioned in the U.S. military system.

Judicial Observation Courses. Offered in some LL.M. programs, where international LL.M. students receive academic credit for working with federal judges, observing appellate and trial proceedings, and memorializing and recording observations in journals or portfolios.

L

Labor Certification. Process through which foreign citizens gain permission to work in the U.S. for an extended period. Employers request the Labor Department to certify the need for the foreigner.

Labor, Department of. A U.S. cabinet level department that issues rules regarding which foreign citizens may work in the U.S. and under what conditions.

Lawful Permanent Resident (LPR). A person who expressed intent to remain indefinitely or permanently in the U.S. and was issued permission accordingly. An LPR is given a wallet-sized Permanent Resident Card (widely known as a *green card*). An LPR may be called a "permanent resident alien" or a "legal permanent resident alien" (LPRA).

Law School Admissions Council (LSAC). A private, U.S.-based company that administers the Law School Admissions Test (LSAT). Over 200 public and private law schools from Canada, Australia, and the U.S. are LSAC members. LSAC provides various services, including the Candidate Referral Service (CRS) in which LL.M. students enroll with LSAC and U.S. law schools are able to recruit those students. It also offers the LL.M. Credential Assembly Service — LLM CAS — that provides transcript/credential evaluation, letter of recommendation collection, and electronic application services through which students' materials are collected and disseminated to U.S. law schools (www.LSAC.com).

Law School Admissions Test (LSAT). Most J.D. programs in the U.S. and Canada require applicants to take this standardized exam. Postgraduate law programs, such as the LL.M., do not ordinarily require the LSAT. Some U.S. law schools waive the LSAT for current LL.M. students or LL.M. graduates who want to join the J.D. program.

Lecture. Instruction method in which the professor stands before the class and delivers speeches or otherwise engages in essentially one-way communication vis-à-vis the students. Other instruction methods include the Socratic Method in which professors pose probing questions to students whose answers lead to more probing questions, or general discussion in which professors and students engage in free-flowing, directed conversation.

Legal Communication. Law courses that help students improve their analytical and problem-solving skills, and allow them to think more critically and improve their legal argumentation and counter-argumentation skills. These courses involve one or more of the following: Legal Analysis, Legal Research, and Legal Writing.

Legal Education Reform Index (LERI). An index to gauge whether legal education in selected transition countries reflects internationally established principles. It uses 22 factors to analyze legal education-related laws and practices in select countries, and is drawn from legal education standards developed by many entities, including the United Nations.

Legal Standing. A student must maintain this status while enrolled in an LL.M. program. This refers to maintaining legal immigration status, including compliance with law school and university rules and regulations. Committing certain crimes can affect a student's legal standing.

Lexis. A law database offering services and information, such as legal research, alumni contacts, and information on law firms. (Compare Westlaw.)

Library Reserve. A repository in the law library for professors to deposit books for the exclusive use of students enrolled in particular classes. A professor may "put on library reserve" supplementary reading material that students can access when they visit the library's reserve room.

LL.M. *See* Master of Laws (LL.M.) Degree.

M

Machine Readable Passport (MRP). Contains a data page with biographic information stored on it to meet international specifications.

Machine Readable Visa (MRV). Affixed to a passport and contains biometric information about the passport holder, type of visa, and visa terms.

Maintain Status. To comply with visa and duration of stay requirements.

Martindale Hubbell. This website provides comprehensive listings of lawyers and law graduates from all U.S. law schools and from many non-U.S. law schools.

Master of Laws (LL.M.) Degree. A graduate level law degree following a J.D. (for U.S. students) or following an LL.B. or similar entry law degree for most non-U.S., international students. Students enrolled in an LL.M. program at a U.S. law school typically complete the LL.M. degree in one academic year, which is usually two semesters totaling about 9–10 months.

Master of Laws Association (MLA). At different schools, the association of students with interests in the LL.M. program may have a different name.

Master's Degree. After receiving an undergraduate bachelor degree, students may pursue a higher degree (Master's) in a one- or two-year program.

Matriculated. A student who enrolls in a degree program is said to have matriculated.

MBE. *See* Multistate Bar Examination.

Mental Health Counseling. *See* Counseling Service.

Moot Court. Simulated courtroom exercises in which law students play the roles of prosecutors, defense counsel, witnesses, appellate lawyers, and judges. Most U.S. law schools sponsor student participation in local, national, and international moot competitions.

MPRE. *See* Multistate Professional Responsibility Examination.

Multiple Choice Examination. An objective test in which a question is posed, several possible answers are listed, and students must select the one or more correct answers.

Multiple Entry Visa. A visa that permits double or multiple entries into the country with the same visa.

Multistate Bar Examination (MBE). A portion of the bar examination consisting of 200 multiple-choice questions on contracts, torts, constitutional law, criminal law, evidence, and real property. These questions relate to general principles of law in the U.S.

Multistate Professional Responsibility Examination (MPRE). All U.S. states incorporate the MPRE into their bar examination. The 100-question, multiple-choice test relates to the model code of professional responsibility, which deals with ethics and integrity in the legal profession.

N

NAFSA. The preeminent global professional organization for persons who work in the international education arena. It has about 10,000 members, and is the world's largest nonprofit professional association dedicated to international education. The acronym "NAFSA" originally stood for "National Association of Foreign Student Advisors." The name of the organization is now "NAFSA: Association of International Educators," and is commonly referred to simply as "NAFSA" (www.nafsa.org).

NALP. *See* National Association for Legal Career Professionals.

National Association for Legal Career Professionals (NALP). A nonprofit educational organization established in 1971 to assist participants in the legal employment process, namely law schools, legal employers, law students, and law graduates.

National Conference of Bar Examiners (NCBE). A not-for-profit organization that helps develop, maintain, and apply standards of education and character for law practice eligibility and admission. It provides bar admission authorities with exams that test bar applicants, disseminates information about admission standards and practices, conducts educational programs, and provides character and fitness investigations.

National Security Entry-Exit Registration System (NSEERS). Security program instituted by U.S. government post-9/11 for certain nonimmigrants based on criteria such as nationality. Requires registrants to exit the U.S. only from designated cities and follow other procedures. Nonimmigrants may qualify for "waivers" of special registration.

Naturalization. The process by which a non-U.S. citizen acquires U.S. citizenship at some point after birth.

Nonimmigrant Visa. Issued for temporary U.S. visits for specific purposes, including to work, to be a tourist, or to study for an LL.M. degree at a U.S. law school.

NSEERS. *See* National Security Entry-Exit Registration System.

O

Office of International Affairs (OIA). Each law school or university will have an office of international affairs or office with a similar name to look after the interests of its international students and international programs.

On-Campus Day Care. Facility on a law school or university campus that is licensed to care for children of faculty, staff, and students.

Open-Book Examination. A law school test during which students are permitted to access and use materials from notes, casebooks, and other materials approved by the professor. Open-book examinations vary in the type and amount of material usable during the exam.

OPT. *See* Optional Practical Training.

Optional Practical Training (OPT). Government program permitting F-1 students to take temporary jobs in the U.S., directly related to law, for up to 12 months post-LLM. An LL.M. student may engage in pre-completion OPT after being enrolled for a full academic year but before receiving an LL.M. degree, and may work parttime while school is in session and full time during school breaks.

Orientation. In the first days of an LL.M. academic year, the school holds a program to introduce LL.M. students to the school, faculty, staff, facilities, and the LL.M. program as a whole. This orientation may be jointly held with J.D. and LL.M. students, but have special sessions exclusively for new LL.M. students. Orientations should be comprehensive.

Outlines. Notes a student compiles during the semester to summarize course material and to use to study for exams.

Out-of-Status. If an individual holds an F-1 or J-1 U.S. visa and does not comply with all the F-1 or J-1 regulations, he or she will be deemed "out of status" and may face arrest, fines, and possible deportation back to his or her home country. If a student complies with regulations, the student is "in status." (*See* In-status; Legal Standing.)

Outsourcing. The concept of U.S. law firms and corporations hiring lawyers outside the U.S. who can perform legal work, typically for a lower fee.

Overstay. If an individual does not depart the U.S. on or before the date indicated on the Arrival/Departure (I-94) card, he or she will have "overstayed," and be subject to arrest, fine, deportation, and denial of future entry into the U.S.

P

Part-Time Student. Student in a degree program who is enrolled for fewer academic credits than required to be a full-time student. For F-1 and J-1 students, 8 credit hours per semester is generally considered full-time.

Pass/Fail. A system of law school grading in which professors assign a "P" (pass) if the student satisfactorily completes the course requirements and an "F" (fail) if the student does not meet the course work requirements.

Permanent Resident (U.S. Permanent Resident). A person who immigrated legally and has a Permanent Resident Card (green card). (*See* Lawful Permanent Resident.)

Personal Admission Interview. These interviews provide an opportunity for admissions personnel to get to know prospective students beyond the written application. These are normally not required for LL.M. program applicants.

Personal Statement. A focused essay about a prospective LL.M. student's career or research goals, experiences, interests, or other information. A personal statement or similar writing is usually required as part of the LL.M. application process. Different schools have different personal statement requirements.

Plagiarism. When a student copies the work of another person and improperly seeks to pass off that work as his or her own.

Port of Entry. This is the airport, seaport, or land border crossing point where students touch down for the first time at the U.S. frontier when they arrive to begin their LL.M. study. At this port of entry the student requests that Immigration Officers permit him or her to enter the U.S.

Prerequisite. A foundational law school course that LL.M. students are required to take before enrolling in a higher level, more advanced, or related course. For example, a student may be required to take a course titled "Introduction to Public International Law" before being permitted to take advanced international law courses.

Private Institution. A law school or university that is not supported directly by government funding.

Pro Bono Publico (or Pro Bono). A Latin term meaning "for the good of the public." It refers to law school or other law-related legal services or activities performed without charge, usually for clients who are unable to afford or otherwise have access to paid lawyers. Some law schools require students to do pro bono work, while other schools grant special pro bono credit or certificates or special notations on diplomas.

Probation. Status of an LL.M. student whose academic work is unsatisfactory. A student must improve his or her grades or be dismissed from the program.

Professor (or Law Professor). The generic name assigned to U.S. law teachers who are members of a law faculty who are at the rank of Assistant Professor of Law, Associate Professor of Law, or Professor of Law. Their rank is based on their level of experience, the structure of their faculty, and whether they are tenured.

Professor of Law. The title assigned to a full-time, tenured law professor in the U.S. who has achieved the highest rank of professor at a U.S. law school. On business cards, stationery, and e-mail signature lines they are referred to as "Jane Doe, Professor of Law" or "Professor of Law Jane Doe." Other titles available in the professor "ranks" include Assistant Professor of Law and Associate Professor of Law. Some schools have parallel professorial titles in the "clinical ranks," where full-time professors may have one of the following titles: "Clinical Assistant Professor of Law"; "Clinical Associate Professor of Law"; and "Clinical Professor of Law." Compare ranks and titles of temporary professors, including Adjunct Professors and Visiting Professors. When you arrive at your law school, *ask* about the appropriate manner of addressing faculty and staff. (*See* Assistant Professor of Law; Associate Professor of Law; *see also* Adjunct Professor and Visiting Professor.)

PTE Academic. An exam that measures English-language proficiency and tests four areas: listening, reading, speaking, and writing. Some LL.M. programs accept PTE Academic in lieu of Cambridge ILEC, IELTS, or TOEFL.

Public Charge. A person who relies on the state or federal government for daily sustenance (food, water, shelter, etc.). The U.S. will not permit a person to enter the U.S. if it believes the person will become a public charge.

Public Institution. A law school or university supported directly by government funding.

Public Interest. This refers to the general societal welfare, or to the common welfare of members of society. Public interest lawyers work with underrepresented persons, help ensure equal access to the legal system for all, and promote human and civil rights.

Put on Hold. *See* Hold.

Q

Quiz. A test administered to students that is typically shorter and less formal than an examination. Whereas law school examinations are typically held at the end of the semester, quizzes are often given in the middle of the semester, and are at times administered without giving students prior notice ("pop quizzes").

R

Recommendation Letter. Letter written by a referee to support an applicant for admission to a school, for a job, or for other purposes. These letters are written by people with personal knowledge of the applicant and comment on his or her abilities, accomplishments, and suitability for the degree or position.

Referee. A person who an LL.M. applicant or graduate solicits to write a letter of recommendation for admission to an academic program (like the LL.M.), for a job, or for other purposes.

Registrar. Law school official who facilitates the enrolling of students in the law school, registers them for courses, maintains course records and their grades or marks, and issues transcripts.

Registration. The process where an LL.M. student consults with his or her law professor academic advisor, chooses courses in which to enroll for the next term, and then requests the Registrar to register him or her for the courses.

Reputation. The level of regard with which an LL.M. program is viewed. Programs with a favorable or positive "reputation" are viewed with high regard, and programs with an unfavorable or negative reputation are viewed with low regard.

Required Courses. Classes that LL.M. students are mandated to take. These could be general courses, legal writing courses, or courses related to an LL.M. specialization. (Compare Electives).

Research Assistant (RA). A student who is hired by a faculty or staff member to assist in research, writing, or other academic work. Law professors may hire F-1 and J-1 LL.M. students as Research Assistants.

Research-Based. This type of LL.M. program requires you to earn a substantial number of credits researching and writing a thesis. Compare course-based LL.M. programs. (*See* Course-Based.)

Residency Requirement. The minimum amount of time an educational institution requires a student to be enrolled in and physically present for a course of study. LL.M. programs in the U.S. typically have a residency requirement of 2 semesters, meaning that students must be enrolled for that period and physically on campus for classes or other obligations for that period.

Resume. *See* Curriculum Vitae.

Revocation of a Visa. The U.S. government cancellation of a visa, making it no longer valid for U.S. travel.

Rolling Admissions (or Rolling Basis). An admissions process where schools decide to admit or not admit each application as that particular application is complete.

S

S.J.D. (J.S.D.). Doctor of Jurisprudential Science. Equivalent to a Ph.D. in Law. Typically sought in the U.S. by international students who have completed an LL.M. in the U.S.

Sabbatical. Leave with pay granted to a law professor every 7 years to permit them uninterrupted time to focus on research, publications, or other creative activity. Professors will typically not be available on the law school campus during their sabbatical.

Scholarship. Financial assistance a school gives to a student that may be based on merit, need or other factors such as desire to attract a particular type of student or students from a particular country. A scholarship may be also be used as a general tuition discount for LL.M. students, to attract additional LL.M. students, and to increase the size of the LL.M. class. The student need not repay the scholarship amount. U.S. LL.M. programs may award "endowed scholarships" that are unrelated to tuition and fees, that the student recipients may use as they wish. Programs may also award "tuition discounts," which schools refer to as scholarships. At times, entities outside the law school may award "scholarships" for students to join specific LL.M. programs or an LL.M. program of the student's choice. (*See* Fellowship; Grant; Tuition Discount.)

School Ranking. The hierarchical ordering or rating of schools in comparison to each other, based on performance or some other rating system. There are no official ranking systems for U.S. law schools or LL.M. programs.

Semester. Period of time in which the academic year is divided. U.S. law schools generally have two semesters per year, each containing 13–16 weeks.

Seminar. A small, nonlecture course that instructs through teachers leading group discussions, students making in-class presentations, and students researching and writing papers related to a specialized area of law.

Single Entry Visa. A visa that is valid for a person to enter a country, and canceled as soon as the holder leaves that country.

Social Security Number. Assigned by the U.S. Social Security Administration to individuals so a portion of their wages can be paid into the Social Security system. An international LL.M. student who wants to work in the U.S. should obtain a number by applying to and getting approved by the U.S. Citizenship and Immigration Services.

Socratic Method. Teaching technique used in most U.S. law schools in which professors engage in a questioning dialogue with students. LL.M. and J.D. students will typically sit side-by-side with each other in classes in which instructors employ the Socratic Method.

Specialized LL.M. Program. An LL.M. program focusing on a particular area of law, with the area of legal "specialization" or "concentration" typically noted on the diploma or transcript. (*See* Concentration; compare with General LL.M. Program.)

Staff. A law school's nonacademic, nonfaculty employees, including nonfaculty assistant deans, associate deans, or directors. They provide administrative and clerical support for faculty and administrators.

Student Advisor. Staff member who advises LL.M. students on nonacademic topics. A Student Advisor would advise on issues such as visas, housing, interviewing for jobs, bursar relations, and physical and mental health services.

Student & Exchange Visitor Information System 1 (SEVIS 1). A U.S. government Internet-based system that monitors and maintains data on F-1 and J-1 students before and during their stay in the U.S. SEVIS also maintains information about U.S. schools, exchange visitor program sponsors, and associated officials. SEVIS is administered by the U.S. Bureau of Immigration and Customs Enforcement (ICE) within the Department of Homeland Security (DHS).

Student & Exchange Visitor Information System II (SEVIS II). A modernized, updated version of SEVIS I.

Student Bar Association (SBA). A law school student organization that has quasi-governing powers over the student body. Members are typically elected by J.D., LL.M., and other law students. International LL.M. students should be permitted to play an active role in law school governance and should be permitted to participate in the SBA.

Student Visa. A piece of high-quality paper that a U.S. Embassy or Consulate in a prospective LL.M. student's home country pastes inside your passport. This visa is permission to travel to the U.S. border, that is, it will allow you to board the plane in your country to fly to the U.S. When you arrive at a U.S. airport, you will show your visa and other documents to authorities, who will then admit you to the U.S. Students are usually granted F-1 or J-1 visas to study at a law school in the U.S.

Study Abroad Program. U.S. law schools often offer these programs, which typically give U.S. students the opportunity to pursue educational opportunities outside the U.S. International LL.M. students may be able to pursue study abroad programs but should be aware of complications arising from their U.S. visa status if they leave the U.S. to take law school classes.

Study Group. Two or more students who join together to prepare for law school examinations. LL.M. students are advised to join study groups with J.D. students who have more experience taking law school exams.

Summer Associate. A law student who during a summer break from school works for a law firm, a corporation's law department, a government agency, or other entity. (*See* Clerkship.)

Summer Session. A semester or term occurring between the fall and spring, typically May–August, in which students may be permitted to earn academic course credit.

Syllabus. A list of topics, reading and writing assignments, and other substantive work that a professor assigns for a course during a semester. Professors may post the course syllabus online at the beginning of the semester, and may update the syllabus during the semester.

T

Take-Home Examination. A law school test students are permitted to complete outside the classroom.

Taxpayer Identification Number (TIN). A number issued by the Social Security Administration (SSA) to international students not eligible for a Social Security number.

Test of English as a Foreign Language (TOEFL). A test meant to assess English proficiency for LL.M. applicants whose native language is not English. Some LL.M. programs accept TOEFL in lieu of Cambridge ILEC, IELTS or PTE Academic.

Thesis. An in-depth scholarly research paper prepared by a student in partial fulfillment of an LL.M. degree. (Compare Dissertation)

Thesis Defense. An LL.M. student's opportunity to appear before a committee that poses questions the student is required to answer about the student's in-depth scholarly research paper prepared in partial fulfillment of the student's graduate law degree.

TOEFL. *See* Test of English as a Foreign Language.

Track. *See* Concentration; Specialized LL.M.

Transcript. Document listing a student's courses, grades, degrees conferred, and dates.

Transfer Credit. Credit earned in one degree program but awarded to count toward another degree program. For example, a J.D. student may be awarded transfer credit for courses he earned in an LL.M. program or in another J.D. program. An LL.M. student at one school may earn transfer credits for coursework taken as a visiting student in another school's LL.M. program (*See* Advanced Standing.)

Tuition. The amount of money a law school charges LL.M. students for teaching the students and providing other academic, career, and related services. Tuition may be charged per semester, credit hour or course, or as a flat fee for the LL.M. program.

Tuition Discount (or Tuition Remission or Tuition Waiver). When a school permits a student to pay less tuition than the full price. The remission can be full (in which case the student will pay zero tuition) or partial (in which case the student pays only part of the tuition). Many U.S. LL.M. programs refer to tuition discounts as "scholarships." (*See* Fellowship; Grant; Scholarship.)

U

Undergraduate. An "undergraduate degree program" is a bachelor degree program, such as a bachelor in arts (B.A.) or a bachelor in science (B.S.) program. A student enrolled in a bachelor program is called an "undergraduate" student.

Unlawful Presence. When a non-U.S. national is in the U.S. without U.S. governmental authorization. A person would be unlawfully present if he or she enters the U.S. without a valid visa, if he or she remains in the U.S. after a valid visa has expired, or if he or she is a student who is "out of status."

U.S. Citizen and Immigration Services (USCIS). *See* Citizen and Immigration Services.

V

Verification. *See* Authentication.

Visa. A government's permission to citizens of other countries to travel to a U.S. port of entry to enter the U.S. for the purpose for which the visa was granted. An international student coming to the U.S. must receive a visa, usually an F-1 or J-1 visa.

Visa Expiration Date. A student visa is only valid, and usable, until the expiration date that is indicated on the face of the visa.

Visa Interview. Before the U.S. issues a student visa, the individual must appear before a U.S. Department of State official at a U.S. Embassy or Consulate, usually in his or her home country, and answer questions posed by a U.S. official. If the individual satisfies the conditions to study in the U.S., the official will grant a "student visa" (usually F-1 or J-1), which is pasted into his or her passport.

Visa Validity. The time between the date of the issuance of a visa and the date it expires. A visa becomes invalid when it expires.

Visiting Fellow. A person invited by an academic institution to conduct research, teach or give occasional lectures. The person may be a professor at another institution, a government official, a student, or an expert in a particular field.

Visiting Professor. A person retained by a host university (or law school) to teach on a temporary basis. The person may be a full-time professor at another law school who teaches a course to fill a temporary need at the host school. A visiting professor may also be a well-known expert in a field of law, a high-ranking government or U.N. official, or another person with stellar credentials. A visiting professor would ordinarily be paid a salary at a rate similar to the rate paid to full-time faculty, whereas an adjunct professor would ordinarily be paid a small fraction of full-time faculty salary. A person who is visiting as a professor might be a Visiting Assistant Professor of Law, Visiting Associate Professor of Law, or Visiting Professor of Law. (*See* Adjunct Professor; Professor of Law.)

Visiting Scholar. A person who affiliates with a law school, usually for research or similar purposes, without matriculating in a degree program.

Visiting Student. If you are enrolled in an LL.M. program at one law school, you may wish to take courses offered by another LL.M. program at a different law school. The other law school may permit you to be a "visiting student," and to enroll in one or more courses, and to earn "transfer credits" that your home school may count toward your LL.M. degree. Your LL.M. degree will be awarded by your home school, not by the school at which you visited. (*See* Transfer Credit; Advanced Standing.)

Voluntary Departure. A non-U.S. citizen who breaches visa regulations may be permitted to agree to leave the U.S. voluntarily rather than be deported.

W

Waitlist. A list of LL.M. applicants that the school has decided to admit only if a fully admitted candidate fails to enroll or a space in the entering class otherwise becomes available. Schools typically offer admission to more students than the ideal size of the LL.M. class, anticipating that some admitted students will not enroll. For example, a school may offer 100 admission letters to fill 75 LL.M. seats, anticipating that 25 applicants will reject the admission offer, leaving a class of 75. If you are on the waitlist, the school will wait to determine how many people have rejected the school's offer before deciding if you will be offered a seat. If 75 admitted students accept, then you will not be offered a seat. The school will admit students off the waitlist, if necessary, until the class size reaches 75.

Waiver of Ineligibility. Certain foreign citizens are ineligible for visas to enter the U.S. because of medical, criminal, security, or other reasons. The U.S. may "waive" this ineligibility and permit an individual to join an LL.M. program.

Westlaw. A law database offering services and information, such as legal research, alumni contacts, and information on law firms. (Compare Lexis.)

World Trade Organization. *See* GATT.

Index